THEGREENGUIDE
California

Palm trees in Palm Springs, California © katgal/iStockphoto

MICHELIN

| General Manager | Cynthia Clayton Ochterbeck |

THEGREENGUIDE **CALIFORNIA**

Editor	Jonathan P. Gilbert, Rachel Mills
Principal Writer	Anne-Marie Scott
Production Manager	Natasha G. George
Cartography	Peter Wrenn
Photo Editor	Yoshimi Kanazawa
Photo Researcher	Claudia Tate
Proofreader	Jenni Hairsine
Interior Design	Chris Bell
Cover Design	Chris Bell, Christelle Le Déan
Layout	John Higginbottom
Cover Layout	Michelin Apa Publications Ltd.

Contact Us	The Green Guide
	Michelin Maps and Guides
	One Parkway South
	Greenville, SC 29615, USA
	www.michelintravel.com
	Michelin Maps and Guides
	Hannay House
	39 Clarendon Road
	Watford, Herts WD17 1JA, UK
	℘01923 205240
	www.ViaMichelin.com
	travelpubsales@uk.michelin.com

Special Sales	For information regarding bulk sales, customized editions and premium sales, please contact our Customer Service Departments:
	USA 1-800-432-6277
	UK 01923 205240
	Canada 1-800-361-8236

Note to the reader Addresses, phone numbers, opening hours and prices published in this guide are accurate at the time of press. We welcome corrections and suggestions that may assist us in preparing the next edition. While every effort is made to ensure that all information printed in this guide is correct and up-to-date, Michelin Apa Publications Ltd. accepts no liability for any direct, indirect or consequential losses howsoever caused so far as such can be excluded by law.

PLANNING YOUR TRIP

The blue-tabbed PLANNING YOUR TRIP section gives you **ideas for your trip** and **practical information** to help you organize it. You'll find tours, practical information, a host of outdoor activities, a calendar of events, information on shopping, sightseeing, kids' activities and more.

INTRODUCTION

The orange-tabbed INTRODUCTION section explores California's **Nature** and geology. The **History** section spans from prehistoric California to Arnold Schwarzenegger. The **Art and Culture** section covers architecture, art, literature and music, while **California Today** delves into the modern region.

DISCOVERING

The green-tabbed DISCOVERING section features Principal Sights by region, featuring the most interesting local **Sights**, **Walking Tours**, nearby **Excursions**, and detailed **Driving Tours**. Admission prices shown are normally for a single adult.

ADDRESSES

We've selected the best hotels, restaurants, cafes, shops, nightlife and entertainment to fit all budgets. See the Legend on the cover flap for an explanation of the price categories. See the back of the guide for an index of hotels and restaurants.

Sidebars

Throughout the guide you will find blue, orange and green-colored text boxes with lively anecdotes, detailed history and background information.

😊 A Bit of Advice 😊

Green advice boxes found in this guide contain practical tips and handy information relevant to the sight in the Discovering section.

STAR RATINGS★★★

Michelin has given star ratings for more than 100 years. If you're pressed for time, we recommend you visit the ★★★ or ★★ sights first:

★★★	**Highly recommended**
★★	**Recommended**
★	**Interesting**

MAPS

- 😊 Regional Driving Tours map, Places to Stay map and Sights map.
- 😊 Region maps.
- 😊 Maps for major cities and villages.
- 😊 Local tour maps.

All maps in this guide are oriented north, unless otherwise indicated by a directional arrow. The term "Local Map" refers to a map within the chapter or Tourism Region. A complete list of the maps found in the guide appears at the back of this book.

PLANNING YOUR TRIP

INTRODUCTION TO CALIFORNIA

© California Travel & Tourism Commission

CONTENTS

DISCOVERING CALIFORNIA

© Photodisc

Welcome to California

Thanks to the film and television industries, California can seem a familiar place to first-time visitors. Its sun-baked beaches, city streets, picturesque villages and desert canyons have appeared as settings for countless movies and TV shows. But beyond the familiar backdrops, an endlessly fascinating variety of sights, attractions and experiences invites exploration and enjoyment in the Golden State's many regions.

CENTRAL COAST (p76–105)

The beautiful and historic cities of Santa Barbara and Monterey bookend the Central Coast region between San Francisco and Los Angeles. Highway 1, one of the nation's most spectacular byways, traces the stunning Big Sur landscape along the lip of the continent, offering dramatic vistas at every turn and passing awe-inspiring Hearst Castle enroute. Historic missions dot the inland foothills of the Coast Ranges, quiet reminders of California's Spanish Colonial past.

CENTRAL VALLEY (p106–114)

The long, fertile valley in the very heart of California is an agricultural powerhouse of huge farms producing an enormous variety of fruits, vegetables, nuts, grains, livestock and dairy products. Farming communities, university towns and the state capital Sacramento are all graced with pretty neighborhoods, historic downtowns and nuggets of California's past; most enjoy a traditional atmosphere that feels worlds away from the trendsetting urban centers along the coast.

DESERTS (p115–127)

Vast, sparsely vegetated and ruggedly beautiful, California's Deserts region occupies the state's southeastern corner. The irrigated golf courses, parks and lawns of sophisticated Palm Springs and its suburbs glisten jewel-like in the surrounding desert terrain, but elsewhere towns and service centers are few and far between. In this region, man-made sights play second fiddle to the lordly mountain ranges, stunning rockscapes, high plateaus and contorted canyons preserved in Death Valley and Joshua Tree National Parks.

GOLD COUNTRY (p128–137)

Cradled in the scenic foothills between the Central Valley and the Sierra Nevada, the Gold Country is studded with traces of the 1849 Gold Rush. Nevada City, Marshall Gold Discovery State Historic Park and Columbia State Historic Park, along with smaller towns and communities along Highway 49, proudly preserve the frontier feel of the mid-19C.

INLAND EMPIRE (p138–141)

A haven for outdoor enthusiasts, the Inland Empire boasts glorious mountain resorts and scenic lakes that provide abundant recreation opportunities all within a short drive east from Los Angeles. In cities like Redlands and Riverside you'll find charming Victorian neighborhoods that were home to prosperous leaders of the citrus industry.

LOS ANGELES AREA (p142–199)

The enormous metropolitan region of Los Angeles boasts sights and attractions known around the globe. You'll find world-class art museums, trendsetting shopping districts, ground-breaking architecture and popular theme parks competing for your attention with iconic sights like Hollywood, Sunset Boulevard and the renowned beach communities of Santa Monica, Malibu and lively Venice Beach.

NORTH COAST (p200–216)

A region of fog-draped redwood forests, vertical cliffs plunging steeply into the roiling Pacific and reminders of California's logging industry, the northwestern corner of the state is appealing in its remoteness. The area immediately north of San Francisco offers a gentler landscape of pretty coastal villages, charming state parks and thriving vineyards and wineries.

ORANGE COUNTY (p217–232)

Tucked between Los Angeles and San Diego, affluent Orange County is perhaps best known as the home of the Disneyland Resort. The heavily developed inland suburbs intersect with attractive beach cities overlooking the Pacific; Huntington Beach in particular is renowned as a surfer's paradise, with the best waves on the West Coast.

SAN DIEGO COUNTY (p233–263)

An incredible variety of landscapes is located within the boundaries of California's largest county, occupying the southwestern corner of the state. Scenic beach towns like Encinitas, Carlsbad and Oceanside; rugged mountains and the arid deserts of Anza-Borrego Desert State Park; and the museums and historic sights of cosmopolitan La Jolla and San Diego all play their role in attracting travelers here. The county also boasts two of the finest zoos in the nation: the San Diego Zoo and the San Diego Wild Animal Park.

SAN FRANCISCO AREA (p264–318)

San Francisco's architecture, cuisine, culture, history, and above all, its glorious setting on a hilly finger of land between ocean and bay make this one of America's most visited cities. Sights like the Golden Gate Bridge, Chinatown, Alcatraz and Fisherman's Wharf are favorites, along with the iconic cable cars that trundle up and down the steep hillsides.

SHASTA-CASCADE (p319–326)

This remote area in northeastern California bears the marks of thermal activity beneath the earth's surface. Two volcanoes—Mount Shasta and Lassen Peak—tower over the surrounding landscapes, and Lava Beds National Monument preserves a fascinating, if bleak, volcanic terrain. Lake Shasta, near the city of Redding, is very popular with houseboaters.

SIERRA NEVADA (p327–351)

The stunning peaks of the Sierra Nevada mountain range punctuate one of California's most scenic areas. This region is home to sparkling Lake Tahoe; the giant trees of Sequoia and Kings Canyon National Parks; and the stunning rock formations, woodlands and waterfalls of Yosemite National Park, jewel of America's park system.

WINE COUNTRY (p352–369)

Acre upon rolling acre of vineyards in the Napa Valley, Sonoma Valley and Russian River Regions just north of San Francisco produce grapes worthy of being transformed into some of the most acclaimed wines in the US. Boutique and family-run wineries rub shoulders with some of the industry's heavy hitters like Mondavi, Beringer, Simi, Chandon and Sebastiani, to name a few.

Bixby Creek Bridge, Big Sur, Central Coast
©Brent Reeves/Fotolia.com.

Michelin Driving Tours

REGIONAL DRIVES

The routes described below are plotted on the map on the following pages.

NORTHERN CALIFORNIA

From San Francisco, the route traverses the vineyard-cloaked spine of the Napa Valley, then heads through the upper Central Valley. North of bustling Redding, the route penetrates the glorious mountainscapes of the Shasta-Cascade region, then detours to the remote expanse of the Modoc Plateau, home to Lava Beds National Monument. From there the drive skirts Lassen Volcanic National Park enroute to popular Lake Tahoe astride the California/Nevada border, then crosses the Gold Country to Sacramento, through the East Bay, to San Francisco.

GOLD COUNTRY/SIERRA NEVADA

Starting in the capital city Sacramento, this tour traverses the length of the scenic and historic Gold Country, rife with sights related to the 1849 Gold Rush. From there the drive threads Yosemite National Park, taking in some of the finest scenery in the US. At Mono Lake the tour heads south through desolate Owens Valley past spectacular Sierra Nevada mountains and the stunning desertscapes of Death Valley National Park before crossing the southern Central Valley enroute to Los Angeles.

COASTAL CALIFORNIA

This drive skirts California's stupendously scenic coastline from San Diego near the Mexican border all the way to Cresent City near the Oregon state line, passing enroute through Los Angeles and San Francisco and past every one of California's historic missions. For much of the way the tour follows Highway 1—the renowned Pacific Coast Highway—but alternate routes and detours offer the option of visiting those missions located away from the coast.

CALIFORNIA DESERTS

California's awe-inspiring desert parks are the focus of this scenic route, which heads west from San Diego to Anza-Borrego Desert State Park near the inland Salton Sea. From there the drive goes through the resort city of Palm Springs before jogging east to Joshua Tree National Park, paradise for hikers and rock climbers. After traversing a series of small desert towns, the route fringes the barren

Distance Chart
(distances given in miles; to estimate kilometers, multiply by 1.6)

	Los Angeles	San Diego	San Francisco
Chicago	2048	2093	2173
Denver	1031	1095	1255
Dallas	1399	1348	1752
New York	2795	2803	2930
Seattle	1134	1258	810

Example: San Diego – South Lake Tahoe = 542 mi

	Barstow	Death Valley NP (Furnace Creek)	Eureka	Fresno	Las Vegas, NV	Los Angeles	Palm Springs	Redding	Sacramento	San Diego	San Francisco	San Jose	San Luis Obispo	Santa Barbara	South Lake Tahoe
Death Valley NP (Furnace Creek)	166														
Eureka	696	703													
Fresno	241	408	462												
Las Vegas, NV	122	213	797	395											
Los Angeles	123	206	664	221	286										
Palm Springs	562	306	788	334	276	103									
Redding	412	566	154	331	640	545	658								
Sacramento	403	435	294	167	567	385	484	161							
San Diego	174	407	776	342	332	123	135	675	507						
San Francisco	419	505	274	181	568	395	504	233	87	539					
San Jose	382	491	324	153	524	351	460	252	118	474	46				
San Luis Obispo	257	352	507	137	414	204	306	440	301	321	229	183			
Santa Barbara	203	366	606	249	354	96	199	536	395	222	328	283	99		
South Lake Tahoe	395	346	388	267	466	456	435	249	107	542	192	197	382	490	
Yosemite Natl. Park	330	310	473	86	435	311	414	341	171	432	189	184	223	329	133

expanse of the Mojave National Preserve before heading north into Death Valley National Park, land of climatic extremes and breathtaking desert vistas. From there the drive threads the southern Owens Valley as it heads to Los Angeles.

LOCAL DRIVES

Big Sur – Drive this spectacular coastline of redwoods and rolling seas from Point Lobos to Hearst Castle.

Gold Country (Northern) – This drive unearths the history of the Gold Rush.

Gold Country (Southern) – This region has a greater share of historic towns than its northerly neighbor. Highlights include Calaveras Big Trees and Columbia state parks.

Lake Tahoe – 6,229ft high and enshrouded by the snowy sierra Nevada, Lake Tahoe is home to casinos, glitz and outdoor sports in equal measure.

Mendocino-Sonoma Coast – Follow Highway 1 on the rim of California's North Coast past sleepy seaside towns.

Skier on a slope at Lake Tahoe

Owens Valley – An arid slice carved out between the Sierra Nevada, Mojave Desert and the Great Basin.

Redwood Empire – Remote, rugged spires of redwood stand astride US 101, which winds to highlights like the Avenue of the Giants and Patrick's Point.

Yosemite – Alpine lakes, meadows and towering mountains from the valley to Tioga Road and the south.

When and Where to Go

With the diversity of California's geographic regions comes a dramatic variation in climatic conditions. Although coastal areas are subject to relatively little seasonal temperature change, late **spring** and **summer** bring fog to the coastline. In the San Francisco Bay area, the weather can change suddenly throughout the day from warm and sunny to foggy and chilly. Like much of the coast, the Pacific Coast Highway (Highway 1) is crowded with visitors during summer. Temperatures tend to increase with distance from the coast. Inland areas of the Los Angeles basin are hot and hazy in summer and early fall. Tourism peaks during spring and summer holidays; television show tapings, studio tours and other Hollywood sights are quite crowded at this time. Late spring and early fall are the best times to visit the Wine Country (harvest season is Sept–Oct) and southern areas of the North Coast. The northernmost reaches of California's coast are prone to fog, rain and chill, especially during late fall and winter, so visit the redwoods during the warmer months. **Fall** brings colorful aspens, crisp temperatures and fewer visitors to northern California. While **winter** sports season at Mt. Shasta runs from November to March, the season begins as early as late October in the High Sierras and may extend through mid-April. Winter temperatures are cold in the northern areas and higher elevations, where snow closes backcountry roads sometimes for months at a time. Spring and fall are good times to visit high desert areas. Wildflowers bloom gloriously in March and April. Desert summers are searing; many resorts in Palm Springs drastically lower their prices. Avoid the deserts in summer.

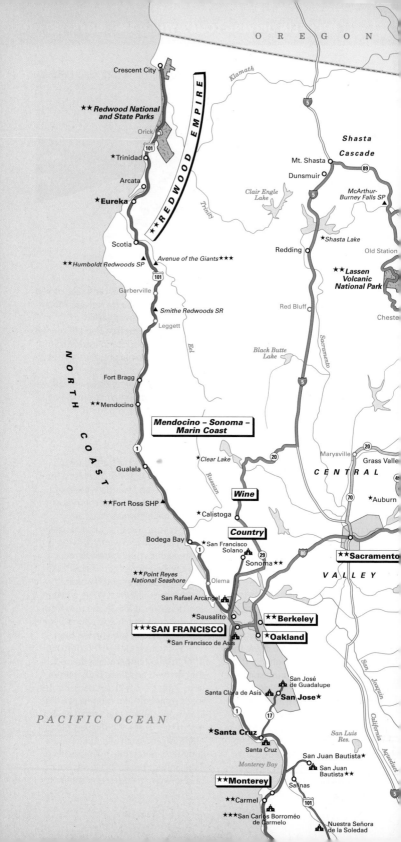

OREGON

Crescent City

★★ *Redwood National and State Parks*

REDWOOD EMPIRE

Orick

101

★ Trinidad

Arcata

★ Eureka

Scotia

Avenue of the Giants ★★★

101

★★ *Humboldt Redwoods SP*

Garberville

▲ *Smithe Redwoods SR*

Leggett

Fort Bragg

★★ Mendocino

Mendocino – Sonoma – Marin Coast

1

Gualala

★★ Fort Ross SHP

Bodega Bay

San Francisco Solano

1

★★ *Point Reyes National Seashore*

Olema

San Rafael Arcangel

★ Sausalito

★★★ SAN FRANCISCO

★ San Francisco de Asís

Klamath

Trinity

Clair Engle Lake

Shasta Cascade

Mt. Shasta

Dunsmuir

5

89

McArthur-Burney Falls SP ▲

Redding

★ *Shasta Lake*

Old Station

5

★★ *Lassen Volcanic National Park*

Red Bluff

Cheste

Black Butte Lake

Sacramento

Eel

Russian

★ *Clear Lake*

20

Wine

★ Calistoga

Country

29

Sonoma ★★

Marysville

70

20

C E N T R A L

Grass Valle

4

★ Auburn

80

★★ Sacramento

V A L L E Y

★★ **Berkeley**

★ **Oakland**

N O R T H   C O A S T

P A C I F I C   O C E A N

San José de Guadalupe

Santa Clara de Asís

San José ★

17

★ **Santa Cruz**

Santa Cruz

Monterey Bay

San Juan Bautista ★

San Juan Bautista ★★

Salinas

★★ Monterey

★★ Carmel

★★★ San Carlos Borroméo de Carmelo

San Luis Res.

San Joaquin

California Aqueduct

101

5

Nuestra Señora de la Soledad

Regional Driving Tours

NORTHERN CALIFORNIA

━━━ **Northern California:** 1,020 miles
14 days – Round trip from San Francisco

━━━ **Gold Country/Sierra Nevada:** 650 miles
11 days – Sacramento to Los Angeles

┗━┓ **Coastal California:** 875 miles
22 days – San Diego to Crescent City
(additional 330 miles/3 days with side trips
to missions)

o   Town described in this guide *(see Index)*

★★**Monterey** City or region with local map in guide

```
0          50 mi
├─────────┤
0          75 km
```

★★ **Lava Beds
National
Monument**

*Goose
Lake*

*Upper Alkali
Lake*

(139)

Alturas

*Middle Alkali
Lake*

(299) Adin

Eagle Lake

Valley Quail
(California State Bird)

*Lake
Almanor*

Honey Lake

Quincy

(89)

N E V A D A

evada City ★★

★Truckee

American   Tahoe City

*Lahontan
Res.*

★★**LAKE TAHOE**

(50)   South Lake Tahoe

Placerville

GOLD

San Andreas

COUNTRY

★ Mono Lake

(49)

(120)   Lee Vining

Merced   (140)

**★★★YOSEMITE
NATIONAL PARK**

Mariposa

Owens

★ **Mammoth Region**

Bishop

San   Joaquin

**Kings Canyon
National Park**

(395)

Kings

O
w
e
n
s

V
a
l
l
e
y

*Giant Sequoia
National Monument*

Independence

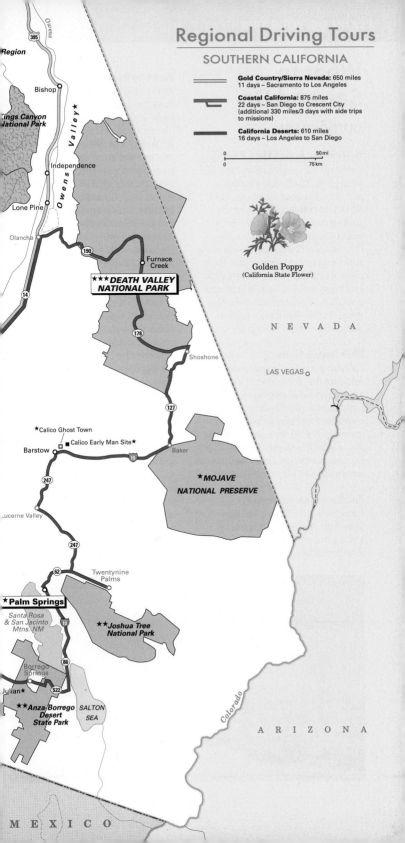

Regional Driving Tours
SOUTHERN CALIFORNIA

Gold Country/Sierra Nevada: 650 miles
11 days – Sacramento to Los Angeles

Coastal California: 875 miles
22 days – San Diego to Crescent City
(additional 330 miles/3 days with side trips
to missions)

California Deserts: 610 miles
16 days – Los Angeles to San Diego

0   50mi
0   75km

Golden Poppy
(California State Flower)

NEVADA

LAS VEGAS

★395
Bishop
Region
Kings Canyon
National Park
Independence
Owens Valley
Lone Pine
Olancha
190
★★★ DEATH VALLEY
NATIONAL PARK
Furnace
Creek
14
178
Shoshone
127
★Calico Ghost Town
Calico Early Man Site★
Barstow
15
Baker
247
★MOJAVE
NATIONAL PRESERVE
Lucerne Valley
247
62
Twentynine
Palms
★Palm Springs
Santa Rosa
& San Jacinto
Mtns. NM
10
★★Joshua Tree
National Park
86
Borrego
Springs
Julian★
S22
★★Anza-Borrego
Desert
State Park
SALTON
SEA
Colorado
ARIZONA

MEXICO

What to See and Do

OUTDOOR FUN

NATIONAL AND STATE PARKS

California has seven national and 265 state parks, all offering a variety of activities. Entrance fees range from $4 to $20; entrance to some state parks is free. The busiest season is from Memorial Day through Labor Day, although central and south coast parks may be busy year-round. Most parks have information centers with trail maps and informative literature on park facilities and activities. Park rangers often lead nature hikes or excursions to sights within the parks.

Park Regulations

Gathering downed wood, or cutting wood for fires is prohibited; campfires are limited to fire pits; hunting is prohibited in most parks; all pets must be leashed and may be prohibited; current proof of rabies vaccine is usually required; an additional fee per pet may be charged; all plants and animals within the parks are protected.

Food storage guidelines

Hang food 12ft off the ground and 10ft away from tree trunk, or in storage lockers. Improper storage of food is a violation of law and subject to a fine.

Parks by Region

Parks in the **Central Coast** region make the most of the dramatic meeting of land and sea; both Channel Islands NP (&p85) and Pfeiffer Big Sur SP (&p82) offer some of the loveliest coastal hikes in the nation. Stunning scenery and extreme conditions are the hallmarks of Death Valley and Joshua Tree national parks in the **Deserts**. When in the **Gold Country**, visit Calaveras Big Trees SP (&p137) for camping and hiking among giant sequoia trees. Both Mt. San Jacinto SP in the **Inland Empire** and Santa Monica Mountains SRA in the **Greater Los Angeles Area** offer cool mountain hikes.

California's rugged **North Coast** harbors a wealth of parks that preserve and protect ancient coast redwood trees. Popular Muir Woods NM (&p204) and the assemblage of protected areas known as Redwood National and State Parks (&p215) book-end the region with glorious trails through the unspoiled wilderness. More stunning trails link coastal overlooks at Patrick's Point SP (&p215) and Mendocino Hedlands SP (&p209); you can spot whales from here, and also from Point Reyes National Seashore (&p204).

In **Orange County**, Crystal Cove SP (&p231) protects a beach-fringed swath of undeveloped coastline. Farther south, **San Diego County**

Mojave Desert, Joshua Tree National Park

© Steve Geer/iStockphoto

Desert Safety

When traveling through the desert areas of California, particularly in summer, it is essential that certain precautions be taken. Before traveling through remote areas or hiking on remote trails, notify someone of your destination and your planned return time.

For Your Vehicle
Always stay on marked roads; most unpaved roads are suitable for four-wheel drive vehicles only. Since service stations tend to be far apart, be sure to fill the gas tank if it is less than half full, and carry plenty of radiator water. If the vehicle is running hot, turn off the air conditioning. If it overheats, pull to the side of the road, turn on the heater and slowly pour water over the radiator core (do not stop the engine). Refill the radiator after the engine has cooled. In the event of a breakdown, do not leave the vehicle to seek help; instead, stay with your vehicle and wait for passing traffic.

For You
Temperatures in July and August can reach over 120°F. It is imperative that visitors carry plenty of water and drink it at least once an hour. Do not lie or sit in the direct sunlight. Always wear loose-fitting clothes (preferably long-sleeved), a broad-brimmed hat and sunglasses.

Heat exhaustion is caused by over-exertion in high temperatures. Symptoms include cool, clammy skin, dizziness or headache and nausea. If experiencing any of these symptoms, rest in the shade and drink plenty of fluids. Symptoms of **heat stroke** include hot, dry skin; victim may become delirious. If experiencing any of these symptoms, try to lower the body temperature with cold compresses (do not use analgesics) and seek medical assistance.

Abandoned mines are common in desert areas, and all are potentially dangerous. Never enter tunnels without a flashlight. Watch for loose rock, and do not touch support timbers. Be watchful for sudden storms that can produce flash floods.

parks bridge the coastal and desert landscapes; Anza-Borrego Desert SP (🐾p235) offers diverse camping and hiking opportunities plus historic sites. In the **San Francisco Bay Area**, the Golden Gate National Recreation Area (🐾p303) encompasses a wealth of diverse historical and recreational protected areas with hiking, camping, swimming and other activities. Trails and sites in Lassen Volcanic NP (🐾p320) and Lava Beds NM (🐾p323) in the remote Shasta-Cascade region explore this unique volcanic landscape. The High Sierras region harbors national treasures like Yosemite NP (🐾p343), with its stunning glacier-carved canon and Sequoia & Kings Canyon National Parks (🐾pp340, 342), preserving great stands of awe-inspiring giant sequoia trees. Parks in the **Wine Country** offer a variety of land

scapes from vineyard vistas, forested mountains and even ancient redwoods at Armstrong Redwoods SP (🐾p365). For complete listings and detailed information on recreational opportunities, contact the **National Park Service** (www.nps.gov) and **California State Parks** (www.parks.ca.gov).

😊 A Bit of Advice 😊

In most natural areas of California, tampering with plants or wildlife is prohibited by law. Avoid direct contact with any wildlife; an animal that does not shy away from humans may be sick. Most active from early April through mid-December, bears will approach campsites and cars, especially if they smell food.

BEACHES

California is renowned for its beaches, but the stereotypical image of a broad stretch of sand where swimmers and sunworshipers frolic in the waves or bake in the rays is actually common only to areas south of Santa Barbara. California beaches come in a variety of forms; some sandy and sunny but others covered with pebbles, strewn with agates or framed by giant rocks and backdropped by sheer cliffs. Beachcombing, birdwatching, hiking, camping, scuba diving and surfing are all popular pursuits in addition to swimming and sunbathing, depending on the location. Surf and scuba shops in beach towns can offer equipment rentals as well as recommendations.

Beaches by Region

San Diego County beaches are wonderful for swimming. Surfers can take their pick of locations around La Jolla or Coronado; a reef break at Windansea Beach makes for consistently strong waves, but the gentle swells at Carlsbad State Beach are perfect for beginners. Beaches near Encinitas tend to be flat and sandy; Moonlight State Beach is packed with amenities. Just north of San Diego, Ocean Beach and Mission Bay offer sun and sand a short drive from the city.

Sunworshipers flock to the broad, sandy beaches in **Orange County**; Huntington State Beach is especially good for swimming and sunbathing. Surfing is very popular at Doheny and San Clemente State Beaches. Scuba divers head for Crystal Cove and Corona del Mar Beaches; and birdwatching is best at Bolsa Chica State Beach.

In the **Greater Los Angeles Area**, surfers gather at Zuma Beach, while scuba enthusiasts have a wealth of choices, among them Cabrillo and Leo Carillo beaches. Swimming and sunbathing reign along the coast south of LA; try Manhattan, or Rendondo State Beaches. The famous boardwalk at Venice Beach is an added attraction.

California's **Central Coast** offers swimming, surfing and scuba, in addition to scenic views. Try Pismo State Beach for swimming, hiking, clamdigging, or fishing from the pier. Just west of Santa Barbara, Gaviota, Refugio and El Capitan state beaches offer gentle, warm water and a southern exposure. Farther north in the heart of Big Sur, Pfeiffer Beach boasts glorious scenery.

The **San Francisco Bay Area** waters are too cold for swimming without a wetsuit, but dramatic landforms make for stunning beauty. Pescadero State Beach is great for tidepooling and birdwatching, and Santa Cruz Beach boasts an old-time boardwalk. Along the **North Coast**, the Sonoma Coast State Beaches are popular for beachcombing and sunbathing and Point Reyes National Seashore offers whalewatching. Spectacular scenery and beachcombing are the draw at Crescent and Enderts beaches.

For detailed information on state beaches, check the **California State Parks** website (*www.parks.ca.gov*).

😊 A Bit of Advice 😊

Cold water borne by the California current makes ocean swimming uncomfortable north of Point Conception, near Santa Barbara. Waters along the California coast can be deceptively tranquil and large waves can appear suddenly, even on the calmest days. Riptides (strong, narrow, seaward flows) also often develop in the waters off the coast of California. If caught in a riptide, swim parallel to the shoreline until out of the current. Children should be supervised at all times; children and adults alike should never swim alone.

Exercise caution when near the water's edge. Be watchful of the incoming tide when exploring beaches and tide pools. Avoid sea urchins, which may be venomous; stinging jellyfish; and watch out for stingrays, which often bury themselves in shallow water. Obtain medical treatment immediately if stung by any of these sea creatures.

WATERSPORTS

Boating

California offers many opportunities for freshwater and ocean boating. Most oceanside communities have boat rental agencies, many of which offer sightseeing cruises. Agencies on larger lakes also rent sailboats and powerboats. "The Delta," where the San Joaquin and Sacramento rivers flow into the San Francisco Bay, is a popular **houseboating** area, as is Shasta Lake; boats can be rented through local agencies. In addition to state law, many cities and counties have special laws restricting speed or activities. For more information, contact the **California Dept. of Boating and Waterways**, *(2000 Evergreen St. Suite 100, Sacramento CA 95815, ℘888-326-2822; www.dbw.ca.gov).*

Fishing

California's coastal waters, inland lakes, rivers, the Sacramento Delta and San Francisco Bay offer limitless opportunities for sportfishers angling both freshwater and saltwater fish. Deep-sea fishing excursions are also popular *(see Hunting and Fishing).*

Kayaking and Rafting

The American, Tuolumne, Merced, Kern, Klamath, and Kings rivers, among others, draw whitewater enthusiasts, particularly in late spring when snowmelt whips rapids into a frenzy. Contact local tourism offices for information on private outfitters, who generally provide permits, insurance, equipment, guides and shuttle service.

Surfing and Windsurfing

California's beaches are famous for long sea swells that surfers dream of *(see Beaches)*. Surf shops in coastal cities (often just steps from the beach) rent surf boards, sails, wetsuits and other gear, and many also offer surfing lessons.

RECREATION

Golf

California claims more than 600 public and private courses. The Monterey Peninsula courses feature white sands, stately forests and steep cliffs overlooking the Pacific. The Palm Springs area, known for its desert resorts, offers more than 100 courses. Contact local tourism offices for the location of public links.

Hiking and Biking

Many trail systems lace the state, and national and state parks also boast opportunities for hiking and biking. The **John Muir Trail** *(211mi)* extends from Mt. Whitney to Yosemite National Park; the **Pacific Crest Trail** joins the Canadian and Mexican borders, with 1,615mi in California *(wilderness permits required; contact the National Forest Service or national or state park*

Surfer on the San Diego Coast

Joanne DiBona/San Diego CVB

Hiking

offices for maps and information). In addition, some 231mi of former railroad tracks throughout California have been converted into paved and dirt paths for bikers and pedestrians. For maps and information, contact **Rails-to-Trails Conservancy**, 235 Montgomery St. Ste. 769, San Francisco, CA, 94104. ℘415-814-1100. www.railstotrails.org. For information on biking and hiking trails, and on local mountain biking regulations, contact local tourism offices.

When hiking in the backcountry, stay on marked trails. Taking shortcuts is dangerous and causes erosion.

☺ A Bit of Advice ☺

Altitude sickness is caused by overexertion at high elevations (above 9,000ft). If planning to hike or camp, you should allow 1–4 days to acclimatize to the reduced oxygen level and lowered atmospheric pressure. Symptoms of altitude sickness include headache, nausea, dizziness, and general weakness. If you experience any of these symptoms, rest and eat high-energy foods such as raisins, trail mix or granola bars. If symptoms become more severe, descend to a lower altitude; if symptoms persist beyond 2–5 days, you should seek medical advice.

If hiking alone, notify someone of your destination and planned return time. Bicycles are prohibited on most unpaved trails. Riders should stay on paved paths and roads (on public roads, stay to the right and ride in single file). Bicyclists are encouraged to wear helmets and other protective gear. Hikers and bicyclists should be well equipped with detailed maps and appropriate gear, and alert to current weather conditions, particularly at higher elevations.

Hunting and Fishing

Licenses are required to hunt and fish in the state of California. Two-day non-resident fishing licenses are available in fishing supply stores. Non-resident hunting licenses tend to be considerably more expensive than resident licenses. Most fish are in season year-round, whereas most game can be hunted only seasonally. **Deep-sea fishing** excursions depart along the coast from cities with major ports; contact local tourism offices for information. Rifles and shotguns may be brought into the state for hunting or sporting purposes.

For regulations on transporting game out of the state, contact:
- **California Department of Fish & Game**,
  1416 9th St.. Sacramento CA 95814.
  ℘916-445-0411. www.dfg.ca.gov.

Horseback Riding

California's coastal, mountain, desert and forest landscapes make for lovely trail rides. Stables offering horse rental, gear and lessons can be found throughout the state. For a complete vacation experience, consider an all-inclusive week at a dude ranch (☞p37), where meals, trail rides, lessons and other activities are part of the package.

SNOW SKIING

For information on **ski conditions**, access www.californiasnow.com or www.skireport.com/california. Most ski area communities offer accommodations including B&Bs, alpine lodges and major hotel chains. Some feature discount packages for stays of three or more days, which can include lift tickets, equipment rental, meals and transportation to the slopes.

Downhill Skiing

The primary **downhill** ski area in California is the High Sierras region, particularly around Lake Tahoe, although smaller resorts can be found in the Shasta-Cascade region and San Bernadino Mountains. Resorts generally offer food service, equipment rental and lessons. Prices for lift tickets range from $39–$85/day (reduced rates for kids).

Alpine Meadows – *2600 Alpine Meadows Rd., Tahoe City, CA 96145. ☎530-583-4232. www.skialpine.com.* The largest resort in Lake Tahoe with more than 100 trails, Alpine also boasts several terrain areas for snowboarding, including a special kids' area.

Mammoth Mountain – *1 Minaret Rd., Mammoth Lakes, CA 95546. ☎760-934-2571. www.mammothmountain.com.* With annual snowfall of 400in this high-elevation resort boasts a 6-month-plus ski season on 150 trails. Snowboarders can take their pick from seven terrain parks.

Heavenly – *3860 Saddle Rd., So. Lake Tahoe, CA 96150. ☎530-544-6263. www.skiheavenly.com.* Gorgeous Lake Tahoe views extend from the runs (91

of them) at this south lake resort. It's very popular with snowboarders.

- ◆ **M. Shasta Ski Park**
  104 Siskiyou Ave.
  Mt. Shasta, CA 96067
  ☎530-926-8610
  www.skipark.com

- ◆ **Bear Mountain**
  800 Summit Blvd.
  Big Bear Lake, CA 92315
  ☎909-866-5766
  www.bearmountain.com

- ◆ **Sugar Bowl**
  629 Sugar Bowl Rd.
  Norden, CA 95724
  ☎530-426-9000
  www.sugarbowl.com

Cross-Country Resorts

Almost all of California's **cross-country skiing** resorts are in the High Sierras region. Most resorts offer equipment rentals, food service and warming huts along the trails; others function as full-service getaways with gourmet dining, comfortable accommodations and shopping options. Trail pass prices range from $18–$30 per day, depending on the season, with no charge for under-tens. Night skiing is available at some resorts.

In higher elevations, public trails run throughout the state and national park systems, most offering few amenities.

Royal Gorge – *9411 Hillside Dr., Soda Springs, CA 95728. ☎800-500-3871. www.royalgorge.com.* One of California's largest, this Lake Tahoe-area resort boasts 100 trails in varying degrees of difficulty, along with a full-service day lodge. Two lodges provide comfortable trailside accommodation.

Tahoe Donner – *15275 Alder Creek Rd., Truckee, CA 96161. ☎530-587-9484. www.tahoedonner.com.* Nestled high in the Sierras near Donner State Park, this popular resort features two wilderness trails and three snowshoeing trails in addition to 47 groomed cross-country trails. A day lodge

Whale-watching near San Diego

provides food, ski rentals, lessons and other amenities.

Bear Valley – *1 Bear Valley Rd., Bear Valley, CA 95223. ℘209-753-2834. www.bearvalleyxc.com.* Situated at 7,000ft, Bear Valley boasts a long ski season on its 35 groomed trails. There's a day lodge offering rentals and lessons, along with several lodging options and a sledding area.

- ◆ **North Star at Tahoe**
  100 Northstar Drive
  Truckee, CA 96161
  ℘800-466-6784
  www.northstarattahoe.com

- ◆ **Kirkwood**
  Hwy. 88 at Carson Pass
  Kirkwood, CA 95646
  ℘209-258-6000
  www.kirkwood.com

- ◆ **Squaw Creek**
  1960 Squaw Valley Rd.
  Olympic Valley, CA 94146
  ℘530-583-6985
  www.squaw.com

- ◆ **Montecito Sequoia Lodge**
  63410 Generals Hwy.
  King's Canyon Nat'l Park, CA 93633
  ℘800-227-9900
  www.mslodge.com

Nature Tours

A variety of nature-related activities, from horse-pack trips to ecotours, can be found throughout the state; contact the California Tourism Office for further information. Guided specialty tours of California, offering in-depth exploration of flora and fauna can be arranged through **Sierra Club Outings** *(85 Second St., 2nd floor, San Francisco, CA 94105; ℘415-977-5500; www.sierraclub.org/outings; outings restricted to members; $25–$150/year membership fee).*

For rock climbing excursions, contact **Vertical Adventures**, *(PO Box 7548, Newport Beach, CA 92658; ℘949-854-6250 or 800-514-8785; www.verticaladventures.com).*

Whale, Seal and Sea Lion Watching

Whales can be seen along the California coast year-round as they migrate to and from the northern Pacific Ocean to Baja California. Gray whales migrate from December through May; prime locations for sightings include Mendocino Headlands State Park, Point Reyes National Seashore, Carmel, Santa Barbara, San Pedro, Palos Verdes Peninsula and Cabrillo National Monument. Humpback and blue whales arrive in June and leave in December to feed in northern waters; prime locations for sightings include Point Reyes National Seashore and

Davenport Bluffs *(near Santa Cruz)*. Many state beaches also offer whale-watching programs.

For up-to-date information, call the Oceanic Society's whale-watching hotline: *415-474-3385*.

California sea lions, harbor seals and elephant seals can be found along the coastline year-round; prime locations for sightings include Cliff House, Año Nuevo State Reserve, the 17-Mile Drive and Cabrillo National Monument.

Whale-Watching Cruises

Here's a selection of cruises offering whale-watching opportunities;

Oceanic Society Expeditions: *Fort Mason Qrts. 35, San Francisco, CA 94123, 800-326-7491 (US only) or 415-441-1106. www.oceanic-society.org.* Cruises depart from Half Moon Bay and San Francisco late Dec–Apr; 3hrs or 6hrs 30min, $45/$85. Humpback whales and blue whale sightings Jun–Nov

weekends, 8hrs, $95; 2-week advance reservations required.

Davey's Locker – *400 Main St., Balboa CA 92661 949-673-1434. www.daveyslocker.com.* Cruises depart from Balboa late Dec–Mar; 2hrs 30min; reservations suggested; $30.

Sea Landing – *301 W. Cabrillo Blvd., Santa Barbara, CA 93101, 805-963-3564. www.sealanding.net.* Cruises to the Channel Islands late Dec–Feb; half-day whale watching cruises $94.

Natural Habitat Adventures – *2945 Center Green Ct., Ste. C, Boulder Ca 80301 800-543-8917 (North America) or 303-449-3711. www.nathab.com.* six-day tours of San Ignacio Whale Camp depart from Loreto *(Feb only)*; $2,495 per person double occupancy.

Spectator Sports

It's always a good idea to plan ahead if you'd like to see one of California's professional sports teams play a

PROFESSIONAL TEAM SPORTS			
Sport/Team	Season	Venue	✆ Information
⑪ BASEBALL	Apr–Oct		
Los Angeles Angels		Angel Stadium (Anaheim)	714-940-2054
Los Angeles Dodgers		Dodger Stadium	866-363-4377
Oakland Athletics		Oakland Coliseum	510-638-4900
San Diego Padres		PETCO Park	619-795-5000
San Francisco Giants		AT&T Park	415-972-2000
🏀 BASKETBALL	Oct–Apr		
Golden State Warriors		Oracle Arena	510-986-2200
Los Angeles Clippers		STAPLES Center	213-742-7500
Los Angeles Lakers		STAPLES Center	213-742-7400
Sacramento Kings		ARCO Arena	916-928-0000
🏈 FOOTBALL	Sept–Dec		
Oakland Raiders		Oakland Coliseum	510-864-5000
San Diego Chargers		QUALCOMM Stadium	619-280-2121
San Francisco 49ers		Candlestick Park	415-656-4900
🏒 HOCKEY	Oct–Apr		
Los Angeles Kings		STAPLES Center	213-742-7100
Mighty Ducks of Anaheim		Honda Center	714-704-2500
San Jose Sharks		HP Pavilion	408-287-7070

Baseball game in AT&T Park

home game. Tickets can generally be acquired through Ticketmaster (☏800-745-3000; www.ticketmaster.com) or the team's website. Advance tickets may cost slightly less than same-day tickets purchased at the venue. Bear in mind that games tend to sell out later in the season if a team is playing particularly well. It's always a good idea to arrive well in advance of the start; negotiating security checkpoints can take up to an hour at some venues. Public transportation is usually an efficient way to get to the stadium or arena; plan extra time to park if you arrive by car.

Baseball – The Major League Baseball regular season runs from April to September, with post-season playoffs and the World Series held in October. Tickets at home stadiums cost from $200 for field-level center or dugout seats to $18 high in the upper left- or right-field decks. Some teams have special theme days with giveaways for those in attendance; check team websites for information. Games usually last 3–3.5 hrs.

Basketball – The National Basketball Association regular season runs from October to April, with playoffs and championships in May. Courtside seats can cost as much as $3,000, but most seats are much less, with top-tier seats going for as little as $25. Games usually last a little more than 2 hours without overtime.

Football – The National Football League season begins in late August, winding up with playoffs and the

Superbowl Championship in late January. Home games for some football teams sell out to season ticket holders, but you can still acquire unused tickets through waitlists (check the team's website) or resellers like StubHub (www.stubhub.com). Prices range from $600 seats on the 50-yard line to around $100 for upper-level seats in the endzone. Games usually last around three hours.

Hockey – The National Hockey League season lasts from October to April. It's best to acquire single-game tickets through Ticketmaster; expect to pay $25–$175 for regular-season games.

ENTERTAINMENT

From opera to striptease shows, California's entertainment scene runs the gamut. There's plenty of high-brow culture to be found at such venues as L.A.'s **Music Center** (☏p162) and **Walt Disney Concert Hall** (☏p162) or San Francisco's **War Memorial and Performing Arts Center** (☏p285), where orchestras of world renown give seasonal performances. San Diego's **Old Globe Theatre**, the **La Jolla Playhouse** and the **Pasadena Playhouse** are a few of the many theaters thriving throughout the state. Classical and modern ballet and opera and light opera are performed year after year in the major cities. Resident dance companies include the **San Jose Ballet**, the **Sacramento Ballet**, the **San Diego Ballet** and San Francisco's **African Music and Dance Ensemble**. Outdoor performances are held in the summer at, among other places, L.A.'s **Hollywood Bowl** (♿ *p181*) and San Diego's **Starlight Bowl** (♿ *for details, consult the Practical Information sections in Discovering California*). California also has its share of comedy clubs, cinemas, video arcades, and even vaudeville shows such as the **Fabulous Palm Springs Follies**, in Palm Springs. Jazz, blues, rock and soul music, performed live or supplied by DJs with their own cult follow-ings, make for a lively after-hours scene at various city nightclubs and dance clubs. Seek them out in San Francisco's Broadway, North Beach and Union Square areas; in West L.A. around the UCLA campus; and in San Diego's Gaslamp Quarter, among other areas. Casinos can be found in Rancho Mirage, in the Coachella Valley and in Reno, Nevada, near Lake Tahoe, among other places.

👫 ACTIVITIES FOR CHILDREN

California has something to offer every family from Disneyland to its expansive coast. In this guide, sights of particular interest to children are indicated with a KIDS symbol (👫). Some attractions may offer discount fees for children. California is rich in attractions and activities for children: most local zoos, science museums, natural history museums and art museums have ongoing programs that cater to kids. Often these facilities include a discovery center where children can participate in hands-on learning activities. Local, state and national parks offer educational programs for youngsters. Natural areas such as the beaches, forests, mountains and even the deserts provide opportunities for children to familiarize themselves with a variety of animals and plants.

SHOPPING

The California shopping experience is as broad as the state. From outlet malls to multilevel shopping centers anchored with major department stores, from tacky commercial strips to exclusive neighborhood enclaves, the Golden State offers a variety of retail outlets.

OPENING HOURS

Most retail stores and large shopping centers operate 10am–9pm weekdays, and on Sundays from 1pm–6pm. Bookstores (especially those with coffeeshops) stay open later. Farmers' markets usually operate 7am–noon/2pm, or in the evenings 4pm–7pm.

WHAT TO BUY

California has shopping options to suit all tastes and budgets. **Beachwear** (bikinis, tankinis and exotic swimsuits) and resort fashions can especially be found in the coastal cities of Southern California. **Surf shops** are profuse in Ocean Beach, Mission Beach and Pacific Beach between San Diego and La Jolla.

The roster of **designer boutiques** on Beverly Hills' Rodeo Drive includes Valentino, Dior, Chanel, Gucci, Harry Winston and Armani. Gucci, Cartier, Macy's and Saks Fifth Avenue reside at San Francisco's Union Square. More affordable off-the-rack, retro and vintage duds fill the shops along L.A.'s Melrose Avenue and in San Francisco's Mission District.

For fine art, **art galleries** are clustered in Laguna Beach along Highway 1, Santa Monica's Bergamot Station, Los Angeles' Melrose Avenue, the Design District of Solana Beach and San Diego's Spanish Village Art Center in Balboa Park, among other places.

Look for books at national chain stores and independent **bookshops** such as Warwick's in La Jolla, famed City Lights in San Francisco, Bluestocking Books in San Diego's Hillcrest neigh-borhood and for rare and used tomes, Arundel Books in Los Angeles. Foodstuffs and kitchen gadgets come in all flavors and sizes in the state, especially in the towns of the Wine Country. Purchase olive oil or an exotic-flavored marinade to take home. At a wine tasting, buy a bottle or two of California wine.

The **Chinatowns** of San Francisco and Los Angeles explode with jewelry, bamboo, ceramics, teas, exotic foods and tchotchkes galore.

BOOKS
REFERENCE

A Natural History of California.
Allan A. Schoenherr. (1995).
For amateur naturalists and nature lovers, this book answers questions on the state's geology, flora and fauna.

California: 88 Great Vacations and Easy Outings. Lou Bignami. (1997).
Particularly useful for residents and weekend travelers, this guide ferrets out lesser known places.

California Wine Country.
Peter Fish and Sara Schneider. (2007).
This new *Sunset* magazine field guide zeroes in on the state's popular wine regions, including Baja California.

FICTION

Two Years Before the Mast.
Richard Henry Dana. (1840; 1986).
Seafaring classic of Dana's service on ship bound from Boston to California's coast during the cow-hide trade.

Of Mice and Men. John Steinbeck. (1937). Literary classic set in Salinas Valley tells of the rural life of farm laborers and their dreams gone wrong. The play deal with the unpredictability of life and its ultimate vulnerability to tragedy.

Cannery Row. John Steinbeck. (1945).
Classic tale of down-on-their-luck characters at Monterey's sardine canneries. "Doc Ricketts" and his lab are here too.

The Joy Luck Club. Amy Tan. (1989).
Set in San Francisco, this story traces the immigrant experience and the tensions of Chinese mothers and their Americanized daughters.

FILMS

Sunset Boulevard (1950).
Fearing loss of fame, an aging starlet of the silent-film era employs a destitute screenwriter to help her make a comeback.

East of Eden (1954).
In this adaptation of Steinbeck's classic set in the Salinas Valley, a youth searches for love and acceptance.

The Way We Were (1973).
Love story of opposites attracted in college, but subsequent marriage and life in Hollywood during McCarthy-era blacklists can't keep them together.

Chinatown (1974).
Private-eye unearths family scandals and shady dealings in the city's water supply among the wealthy and influential of Los Angeles.

Big Lebowski (1997).
"They call Los Angeles the City of Angels" begins the story of a California slacker who gets mixed up in a kidnapping caper.

Sideways (2004)
Two almost middle-aged men try to "come of age" in this trip through the Wine Country.

King of California (2007).
Released from a mental institution, a father gets acquainted with his 16-year-old daughter as they search suburbia for elusive buried treasure.

Milk (2008).
San Francisco's first openly gay councilman finds his voice and rises to power on a civil rights agenda, but is subsequently assassinated.

Calendar of Events

Listed below is a selection of California's most popular annual events; some dates may vary each year. For detailed information, contact the California Office of Tourism ☎800-862-2543 *(North America only)* or 916-444-4429. www.visitcalifornia.com.

SPRING

MID-MAR

Return of the Swallows *San Juan Capistrano; www.missionsjc.com/swallowsfest.html*

APR

Northern California Cherry Blossom Festival *San Francisco; www.nccbf.org*

Toyota Grand Prix *Long Beach; www.gplb.com*

EARLY APR–LATE MAY

Renaissance Pleasure Faire *Irwindale; www.renfair.com*

LATE APR

Cowboy Poetry & Music Festival *Santa Clarita; www.cowboyfestival.org*

Asparagus Festival *Stockton; www.asparagusfest.com*

Fiesta Broadway *Los Angeles; www.hprala.org*

Fisherman's Festival *Bodega Bay; www.bodegabay.com*

Newport-Ensenada Yacht Race *Newport Beach; www.nosa.org*

LATE APR–EARLY MAY

Ramona Pageant *Hemet; www.ramonabowl.com*

San Francisco International Film Festival *San Francisco; www.sfiff.org*

MAY

Venice Art Walk *Venice; www.venicefamilyclinic.org*

EARLY MAY

Cinco de Mayo *Los Angeles and other cities*

MID-MAY

ING Bay to Breakers Foot Race *San Francisco; http://ingbaytobreakers.com*

California Strawberry Festival *Oxnard; www.strawberry-fest.org*

Calaveras Co. Fair & Jumping Frog Jubilee *Angels Camp; www.frogtown.org*

Luther Burbank Rose Parade & Festival *Santa Rosa; www.roseparadefestival.com*

LATE MAY

Carnaval San Francisco *San Francisco; www.carnavalsf.com*

Sacramento Jazz Jubilee *Sacramento; www.sacjazz.com*

Cross-Country Kinetic Sculpture Race *Arcata-Ferndale; www.kineticsculpture.org*

EARLY JUN

Auction Napa Valley *St. Helena; www.napavintners.com/anv*

Ojai Music Festival *Ojai; www.ojaifestival.org*

Concours d'Elegance *Huntington Beach; www.hbconcours.org*

MID-JUN

Playboy Jazz Festival *Hollywood; www.playboyjazz.com*

SUMMER

LATE JUN

LGBT Pride Celebration *San Francisco; www.sfpride.org*

Monterey Bay Blues Festival *Monterey; www.montereyblues.com*

LATE JUN–JUL

Robert Mondavi Summer Music Festival *Napa Valley; www.robertmondaviwinery.com*

JUL

Carmel Bach Festival *Carmel; www.bachfestival.org*

JUL 4

Fourth of July Waterfront Festival *San Francisco*

JUL–AUG

Festival of Arts & Pageant of the Masters *Laguna Beach; www.foapom.com*

Rose Bowl Independence Day Show *Pasadena; www.rosebowlstadium.com*

MID-JUL

Cable Car Bell-Ringing Contest *SF; www.cablecarmuseum.org*

27

California Rodeo
Salinas; www.carodeo.com
Lotus Festival *Los Angeles;*
www.lotusfestival.org
LATE JUL
Gilroy Garlic Festival *Gilroy;*
www.gilroygarlicfestival.com
LATE JUL–AUG
Shakespeare Festival
Lake Tahoe;
www.laketahoeshakespeare.com
AUG
Shakespeare Santa Cruz
Santa Cruz; www.shakespeare
santacruz.org
EARLY AUG
Steinbeck Festival *Salinas;*
www.steinbeck.org/festival.html
Old Spanish Days Fiesta
Santa Barbara;
www.oldspanishdays-fiesta.org
MID-AUG
Nisei Week Japanese Festival
Los Angeles; www.niseiweek.org
MID-AUG–EARLY SEPT
California State Fair *Sacramento;*
www.bigfun.org/fair
EARLY SEPT
Sonoma Wine Country Weekend
Sonoma Valley; www.sonomawine
countryweekend.com
Sausalito Art Festival *Sausalito;*
www.sausalitoartfestival.org
Jazz on the River
Guerneville; www.omegaevents.
com/jazzontheriver

FALL
MID-SEPT
Danish Days
Solvang;
www.solvangusa.com
Mexican Independence Day
Los Angeles
Monterey Jazz Festival
Monterey;
www.montereyjazzfestival.org
LATE SEPT
San Francisco Blues Festival
San Francisco; www.sfblues.com
Valley of the Moon Vintage Festival
Sonoma; www.sonomavinfest.org
Cabrillo Festival *San Diego;*
www.cabrillofestival.org

OCT
Art & Pumpkin Festival *Half Moon*
Bay; www.miramarevents.com/
pumpkinfest
LATE OCT
San Francisco Halloween Festival
San Francisco;
www.halloweeninthecastro.com
NOV
Dia de los Muertos Festival
Los Angeles; www.olvera-street.com

WINTER
DEC
Christmas in the Adobes
Monterey;
www.monterey.org/events
Las Posadas *Los Angeles;*
www.olvera-street.com
Christmas Boat Parades
Harbor cities
JAN 1
Tournament of Roses Parade &
Rose Bowl Game
Pasadena;
www.tournamentofroses.com
EARLY JAN
Palm Springs International
Film Festival
Palm Springs; www.psfilmfest.org
Doo Dah Parade
Pasadena;
www.pasadenadoodahparade.info
FEB
AT&T Pebble Beach National
Pro-Am Golf Tournament
Pebble Beach;
www.attpbgolf.com
MID-FEB
Chinese New Year
Parades and Festivals
San Francisco and Los Angeles
Riverside County Fair &
National Date Festival
Indio; www.datefest.org
LATE FEB–EARLY MAR
Academy Awards *Los Angeles*
www.oscars.com
EARLY MAR
North Lake Tahoe
Snow Festival
Tahoe City;
www.tahoesnowfestival.com

Know Before You Go

USEFUL WEBSITES
www.visitcalifornia.com
Official site of the California Travel &
Tourism Commission (👆see *Tourism
Offices below*).
www.california.gov
Official site of the state government,
with links to specific services and
branches.
www.californiahistory.net
Official site of the California Historical
Society, with an illustrated timeline of
events.
www.california.com
Travel and relocation, home services,
national parks, directories, and more.
www.latimes.com
Daily coverage of California's local and
state news in the *Los Angeles Times*.
www.sfgate.com
Local and state news in the *San
Francisco Chronicle*.

TOURISM OFFICES
The following tourism offices provide
information and brochures on points
of interest, seasonal events and
accommodations, as well as road and
city maps.

- **California Office of Tourism**
  PO Box 1499
  Sacramento CA 95812
  ℘916-444-4429; ℘877-225-4377
  www.visitcalifornia.com

- **Central Coast**
  **Monterey County Convention
  & Visitors Bureau**
  PO Box 1770
  Monterey CA 93942
  ℘877-221-1010
  www.seemonterey.com
  **Morro Bay
  Chamber of Commerce**
  845 Embarcadero Rd., Ste. D
  Morro Bay CA 93442
  ℘805-772-4467; ℘800-231-0592
  www.morrobay.org

**Santa Barbara Conference
& Visitors Bureau**
1601 Anacapa St.
Santa Barbara CA 93101
℘805-966-9222; ℘800-676-1266
www.santabarbaraca.com

- **Central Valley**
  **Fresno Convention
  & Visitors Bureau**
  848 M St., 3rd Floor
  Fresno CA 93721
  ℘559-445-8300; ℘800-788-0836
  www.fresnocvb.org
  **Sacramento Convention
  & Visitors Bureau**
  1608 I St. Sacramento CA 95814
  ℘916-808-7777; ℘800-292-2334
  www.sacramentocvb.org
  **Stockton Conference
  & Visitors Bureau**
  445 W. Weber Ave., Ste. 220
  Stockton CA 95203
  ℘209-547-2770; ℘877-778-6258
  www.visitstockton.org

- **Deserts**
  **Barstow Area
  Chamber of Commerce**
  PO Box 698, Barstow CA 92311
  ℘760-256-8617
  www.barstowchamber.com
  **Mojave Desert
  Information Center**
  43779 15th St. W.
  Lancaster CA 93534
  ℘661-942-0662
  www.parks.ca.gov
  Palm Springs Visitor Center
  2901 North Palm Canyon Dr.
  Palm Springs CA 92262
  ℘760-778-8418; ℘800-347-7746
  www.palm-springs.org

- **Gold Country**
  Calaveras Visitors Bureau
  PO Box 637, Angels Camp
  CA 95222.
  ℘209-736-0049; ℘800-225-3764
  www.calgold.org
  **El Dorado County
  Visitors Authority**
  542 Main St.
  Placerville CA 95667

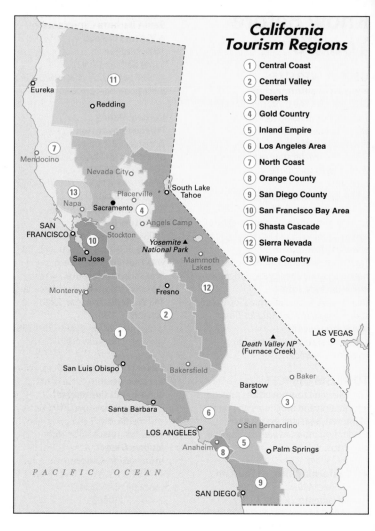

California Tourism Regions

1. Central Coast
2. Central Valley
3. Deserts
4. Gold Country
5. Inland Empire
6. Los Angeles Area
7. North Coast
8. Orange County
9. San Diego County
10. San Francisco Bay Area
11. Shasta Cascade
12. Sierra Nevada
13. Wine Country

☎530-621-5885; ☎800-457-6279
www.visit-eldorado.com
Mariposa County
Visitors Bureau
PO Box 967, Mariposa CA 95338
☎209-742-4567; ☎866-425-3366
www.homeofyosemite.com

❖ **Inland Empire**
California Welcome Center –
San Bernardino
1955 Hunts Lane, Ste. 102
San Bernardino CA 92408
☎909-891-1874
www.cwcinlandempire.com

❖ **Los Angeles Area**
Los Angeles Convention
& Visitors Bureau
333 S. Hope St., 18th Floor
Los Angeles CA 90017
☎213-624-7300; ☎800-228-2452
www.lacvb.com

❖ **North Coast**
Mendocino County Alliance
525 S. Main St., Ste. E
Ukiah CA 95482
☎707-462-7417; ☎866-466-3636
www.gomendo.com

**Humboldt County Convention
& Visitors Bureau**
1034 2nd St.
Eureka CA 95501
☎800-346-3482
www.redwoodvisitor.org

◆ **Orange County**
**Anaheim Area Visitor &
Convention Bureau**
800 W. Katella Ave.
Anaheim CA 92802
☎714-765-8888
www.anaheimoc.org or
www.visitorangecounty.net

◆ **San Diego County**
**San Diego Convention
& Visitors Bureau**
2215 India St.
San Diego CA 92101
☎619-232-3101
www.sandiego.org

◆ **San Francisco Area**
**San Francisco Visitor
Information Center**
900 Market St.
San Francisco CA 94102
☎415-391-2000
www.onlyinsanfrancisco.com
**San Jose Convention
& Visitors Bureau**
408 Almaden Blvd.
San Jose CA 95110
☎408-295-9600; ☎800-726-5673
www.sanjose.org
**Marin Convention
& Visitors Bureau**
1 Mitchell Blvd. Suite B
San Rafael, CA 94903
☎415-925-2060; ☎866-925-2060
www.visitmarin.org

◆ **Shasta-Cascade**
**Shasta Cascade
Wonderland Assn.**
1699 Hwy. 273, Anderson
CA 96007
☎530-365-7500; ☎800-474-2782
www.shastacascade.org

◆ **Sierra NevadaWine Country**
Lake Tahoe Visitors Authority
PO Box 5878.
Stateline, NV 89449
☎530-544-5050
www.visitinglaketahoe.com
**Mammoth Lakes
Visitors Bureau**
PO Box 48, Mammoth Lakes
CA 93546
☎760-934-2712; ☎888-466-2666
www.visitmammoth.com

◆ **Wine Country**
**Napa Valley Visitor
Information Center**
1310 Napa Town Center
Napa, CA 94559
☎707-226-5813
www.legendarynapavalley.com
Sonoma Valley Visitors Bureau
453 First St. E., Sonoma, CA 95476
☎707-996-1090
www.sonomavalley.com

INTERNATIONAL VISITORS
In addition to the tourism offices, visitors from outside the US may obtain information from the nearest US embassy or consulate in their country of residence *(below)*. For a complete list of American consulates and embassies abroad, visit the US State Department Bureau of Consular Affairs listing on the Internet at http://travel.state.gov.

◆ **Australia**
553 St. Kilda Rd.
Melbourne, VIC 3004
☎03–9526–5900
http://melbourne.usconsulate.gov

◆ **Canada**
490 Sussex Drive
Ottawa, ON K1N 1G8
☎613-688-5335
http://ottawa.usembassy.gov

◆ **New Zealand**
P.O. Box 1190
Wellington, New Zealand
☎04-462–6000
http://newzealand.usembassy.gov

◆ **United Kingdom**
24 Grosvenor Square
London, W1A 1AE
☎ 20-7499-9000
http://london.usembassy.gov

ENTRY REQUIREMENTS

Citizens of countries participating in the **Visa Waiver Program** (VWP) must apply for authorization online through the Electronic System of Travel Authorization *(www.cbp.gov)* and present a machine-readable passport to enter the US for general business or tourist purposes for a maximum of 90 days; otherwise a US nonimmigrant visa is required. For a list of countries participating in the VWP, contact the US consulate in your country of residence or check the official Visa Services website *(http://travel.state.gov)*. Citizens of nonparticipating countries must have a nonimmigrant visa.

US citizens arriving from countries participating in the **Western Hemisphere Travel Initiative** (Canada, Mexico, Bermuda and the Caribbean nations) must present a passport if traveling by air; a passport, passport card or other WHTI-compliant document if traveling by land or sea. Children age 16 and under entering from WHTI countries by land or sea must present proof of citizenship. Naturalized Canadian citizens should also carry their citizenship papers. Inoculations are generally not required.

CUSTOMS REGULATIONS

All articles brought into the US must be declared at the time of entry. **Exempt** from customs regulations: personal effects; one liter (33.8 fl oz) of alcoholic beverages per traveler over age 21; either 200 cigarettes, 50 cigars or 2 kilograms of smoking tobacco; and gifts that do not exceed $100 in value.

Prohibited items include plant material; firearms and ammunition; meat or poultry products. For other prohibited items, exemptions and information, contact the US embassy or consulate before departing, or the US Customs Service (☎ *877-227-5511; www.cbp.gov*).

Plant Material: All plant material entering the state of California must be declared and inspected for diseases at agricultural inspection stations located at state borders.

HEALTHCARE

The US does not have a national health program. Before departing, visitors from abroad should check with their health-care insurance to determine if it covers doctor's visits, medication and hospitalization in the US. Prescription drugs should be properly identified and accompanied by a copy of the prescription.

DRIVING IN THE US

Visitors bearing valid driver's licenses issued by their country of residence are not required to obtain an International Driver's License to drive in the US. Drivers must carry a vehicle registration and/or a rental-car contract and proof of automobile insurance at all times. Rental cars in the US are usually equipped with automatic transmission, and rental rates tend to be less expensive than overseas.

Gasoline is sold by the gallon *(1 US gallon = 3.8 liters)* and is cheaper than in most other countries. Self-service gas stations do not do repairs, but may sell standard maintenance items.

Road regulations in the US require that vehicles be driven on the right side of the road. Distances are posted in miles *(1 mile = 1.6 kilometers)*. Travelers are advised to heed posted speed limit signs.

ACCESSIBILITY

Many of the sights described in this guide are accessible to people with special needs. Sights marked by a ♿ symbol offer access for wheelchairs. However, it is advisable to check beforehand by telephone. Federal law requires that businesses (including hotels and restaurants) provide access for the disabled, devices for the hearing impaired, and designated parking spaces. Many public buses are equipped with wheelchair lifts;

many hotels have rooms designed for visitors with special needs. For details, contact the following organizations:

- **Disability Rights Education and Defense Fund**
  2212 Sixth St., Berkeley CA 94710
  ✆510-644-2555
  www.dredf.org
- **Los Angeles County Commission on Disabilities**
  500 West Temple St.
  Los Angeles, CA 90012
  ✆213-974-1311
  www.laccod.org
- **Accessible San Diego**
  ✆858-279-0704
  www.accessandiego.com
- **Society for Accessible Travel and Hospitality (SATH)**
  347 Fifth Ave., Suite 605,
  New York NY 10016
  ✆212-447-7284
  www.sath.org

NATIONAL PARKS

All **national parks** have rest-rooms and other facilities for the disabled (such as wheelchair-accessible nature trails or tour buses). Free or discounted passes for disabled visitors are available from state and national parks. Requests for federal and state discounts must include a copy of your ID card; a vehicle registration card with disabled person's license number; SSI or SSA letter; or a doctor's certification. The permanently disabled are eligible for the America the Beautiful pass at no charge, which entitles the carrier to free admission to all national parks and a 50 percent discount on user fees (campsites, boat launches). The pass is available at any national park entrance fee area with proper proof of disability.

For details contact the **National Park Service**, *(Office of Public Affairs, 1849 C St. NW, Washington DC 20240; ✆202-208-6843; www.nps.gov).*

STATE PARKS

California **state parks** offer the Disabled Discount Card *($3.50)* entitling the holder to a 50 percent discount on campsites and day-use fees at most state-operated facilities; visit in person a district office or the Park Pass Sales Office, 3930 Seaport Blvd., West Sacramento, California. Inquiries concerning the accessibility of a particular state park should be directed to the Human Rights Office, California State Parks *(PO Box 942896, Sacramento, CA 94296-0001 ✆916-653-8148. www.parks.ca.gov).*

Passengers who need assistance with **train** or **bus** travel should give advance notice to Amtrak *(✆800-872-7245 or 800-523-6590/TDD; www.amtrak.com)* or Greyhound *(✆800-231-2222, US only; or 800-345-3109/TDD; www.greyhound.com).* Reserve hand-controlled **rental cars** well in advance.

Getting There Getting Around

BY PLANE

Most international flights arrive at Los Angeles International Airport (LAX), San Francisco International Airport (SFO) and San Diego International Airport (SAN). Domestic flights arrive at these and other airports throughout the state, including Monterey (MRY), Oakland (OAK), Orange County (SNA) and Sacramento (SMF). Smaller regional airports are usually accessible through commuter carriers.

BY TRAIN

With access to more than 200 communities in California, the Amtrak rail network offers a relaxing alternative for the traveler with time to spare. Advance reservations are recommended. First-class, coach, sleeping accommodations and dome cars with glass ceilings that allow a panoramic view are available; fares are comparable to air travel. Travelers from

Canada should inquire with their local travel agents about Amtrak/VIARail connections. **USA Rail Pass** (*not available to US or Canadian citizens or legal residents*) offers unlimited travel within Amtrak designated regions at discounted rates; 15- and 30-day passes are available. A **California Rail Pass** allows seven days of travel over a 21-day period. Schedule and route information: ℘800-872-7245 *(North America only)*; www.amtrak.com.

BY BUS

Greyhound, the largest bus company in the US, offers access to most communities in California and at a leisurely pace. Overall, bus fares are lower than other forms of commercial transportation. **Discovery Pass** allows unlimited travel for 7, 15, 30 or 60 days within the US and Canada. Advance reservations suggested. Information for disabled riders is listed in the *Accessibility* section. For schedules and route information: ℘800-231-2222 *(US only)*; www.greyhound.com. Greyhound, Trailways *(www.trailways.com)* and a few local **bus** lines offer service between cities within the state as well; check the Yellow Pages.

BY BOAT

Eleven major cruise ship lines dock at the vast World Cruise Center terminal located south of Los Angeles in San Pedro *(www.portoflosangeles.org)*. The Cruise Ship Terminal at the Port of San Diego also maintains a busy schedule of departures. Fisherman's Wharf is an active landing point for local ferries between San Francisco and other Bay Area destinations. Ferries to Catalina Island depart from Long Beach, San Pedro, Dana Point and Marina del Rey.

BY PUBLIC TRANSPORTATION

California is a place for drivers. Given its vast area, the state has a remarkable network of roads and highways. Only major cities such as San Francisco and Los Angeles have underground **rapid-transit systems**. San Diego offers broad coverage with its **bus**, **trolley** and **commuter rail** lines, which service major attractions, the beaches and Tijuana, Mexico. Oceanside, Carlsbad, Escondido, La Jolla and other towns are serviced by North County Transit District buses and trains *(www.gonctd.com)*. Santa Barbara has an in-town trolley, and Monterey-Salinas and even Yosemite have free shuttles to points of interest. But a car is needed to visit the deserts and remote places like the redwood forests, Lake Tahoe or the Shasta-Cascade region. ℘*See the Practical Information sections in this guide for details on local public transportation.*

BY TAXI AND BUS

Most moderately large and all major cities have **taxi** service. ℘*See the* **Discovering California** *section*. The Yellow Pages in the local telephone directory should list taxi companies for smaller towns and villages.

BY CAR

For information on **road conditions** call ℘800-427-7623 *(CA only)*. The California Highway Patrol maintains a website with driving tips: www.chp.ca.gov. California has an extensive system of major roads. I-5 is the major north-south interstate highway from Oregon south to San Diego County. I-10, I-40 and I-15 enter Southern California from the east; I-80 enters Northern California from Reno, Nevada.

℘Be cautious when driving on unpaved roads in desert and mountain areas. In the winter months tire chains may be required to navigate roads at higher elevations.

Visitors driving long distances or through remote areas should pack an **emergency car kit** with first-aid supplies, bottled water, nonperishable food, blanket, flashlight, tools and matches. If traveling in snowy conditions, pack an ice scraper for car windows and sand or burlap for traction if your car becomes stuck in the snow.

RENTAL CARS

Most large rental companies have offices at major airports as well as downtown locations. A major credit card and valid driver's license are required for rental (some agencies also require proof of insurance). Payment of an additional drop-off charge may be required if a vehicle is returned to a different location from where it was rented.

If you plan to drive to **Mexico**, check in advance if the rental company allows its vehicles to be driven there.

- **Alamo** ℘800-462-5266
- **Avis** ℘800-331-1212
- **Budget** ℘800-527-0700
- **Dollar** ℘800-800-4000
- **Enterprise** ℘800-261-7331
- **Hertz** ℘800-654-3131
- **National** ℘800-227-7368
- **Thrifty** ℘800-847-4389

(toll-free numbers may be US calls only)

ROAD REGULATIONS

Speed limits on major freeways throughout the state of California range from 55mph–70mph. Within cities, speed limits are generally 35mph, and average 25–30mph in residential areas. The use of **seat belts** is mandatory for all persons in the car; child safety seats are required for children under 6 years or weighing less than 60 pounds *(available at most rental car agencies; reserve in advance)*. The law requires motorists in both directions to bring their vehicles to a full stop when the flashing red lights on a **school bus** are activated. Unless otherwise posted, it is permissible to turn right at a red traffic light after coming to a complete stop.

ROUTE PLANNING

Automobile associations and motorists' clubs typically offer route planning advice to their members, with reciprocal privileges for members of affiliated organizations in other countries. Online map sites can also provide driving directions. Many rentalcar companies offer GPS devices for an additional fee.

DOCUMENTS

A driver's license is required to operate a motor vehicle in the US. For international visitors, a drivers' license issued in the home country is valid for one year in the US. Some carrental companies require international visitors to have an International Driving Permit obtained in their home country. When operating a vehicle, always keep your driver's license, proof of insurance and car registration (ownership and licensing documents) available.

INSURANCE

California law requires drivers to carry a minimum of $35,000 liability coverage while operating a car in the state. Visitors from outside the US should check with their auto insurance provider to see if their policy covers them while driving outside their home country. Rental-car companies offer collision and comprehensive policies as well as liability insurance; some credit-card companies also offer coverage when rental-car fees are charged to the card. For information contact the California Department of Insurance *(℘800-927-3457; www.insurance.ca.gov)*.

IN CASE OF ACCIDENT

If you are involved in an accident resulting in personal or property damage, you must notify the local police and remain at the scene until dismissed. If blocking traffic, vehicles should be moved as soon as possible. Automobile associations such as the **American Automobile Association (AAA)** (℘800-463-8646), **Mobil Auto Club** (℘800-621-5581) and **Shell Motorist Club** (℘800-355-7263) provide their members with emergency road service. Members of AAA-affiliated automobile clubs overseas benefit from reciprocal services:

- **Canadian Automobile Association (CAA)**
  ℘613 247 0117

Where to Stay and Eat

WHERE TO STAY

Selected hotels are described in the Address Books within the *Discovering California* section.

USEFUL WEBSITES

http://california. accommodationsusa.com
Hotel and motel information organized by region and property type.
www.californiahotels.com
Hotel listings organized by city, with online reservation system.
www.quikbook.com.
National listing directory and online reservation service with many options in larger cities and towns.

California offers accommodations to suit every taste and pocketbook, from luxury hotels, which are usually located in major cities, to **motels** found in clusters on the edge of town, or where two or more highways intersect. **Bed-and-breakfast inns** are often situated in residential areas of cities and towns. Many **resorts** are located throughout the state.
Local tourist offices *(telephone numbers are listed under entry headings in the main section of this guide)* provide detailed accommodation information. Advance reservations are recommended. Always advise reservations clerks if you may be arriving late; rooms, even though reserved, may not be held after 6pm. Off-season rates are usually reduced.

HOTELS / MOTELS

Major hotel chains with locations throughout California include:
- **Best Western** ✆800-780-7234
- **Clarion, Comfort & Quality (Choice Hotels)** ✆877-424-6423
- **Days Inn** ✆800-329-7466
- **Embassy Suites** ✆800-362-2779
- **Hilton Hotels** ✆800-445-8667
- **Holiday Inn** ✆800-315-2621
- **Hyatt** ✆888-591-1234
- **Marriott** ✆888-236-2427
- **Motel 6** ✆800-466-8356
- **Radisson** ✆888-201-1718
- **Ramada Inn** ✆800-272-6232
- **Sheraton** ✆800-325-3535
- **Travelodge** ✆800-578-7878
- **Westin** ✆800-937-8461

(toll-free numbers may not be accessible outside of North America)

Accommodations range from luxury hotels *($200–$400 and up/day)* to moderate hotels *($100–$200/day)* to budget motels *($700–$100/day)*. Rates vary with season and location; rates tend to be higher in cities and in coastal and resort areas. Many hotels and motels offer packages and weekend specials. Typical amenities include television, computer hookups, and smoking/non-smoking rooms. The more elegant hotels also offer gourmet restaurants, in-room stereos and flat-screen TVs, swimming pools, valet service and exercise/spa facilities.

BED AND BREAKFASTS

The California Bed & Breakfast Inns Directory is available by mail or via internet from the California Association of Bed & Breakfast Inns, 414 29th St., Sacramento, CA 95816-3211, ✆800-373-9251, **www.cabbi.com**. Another helpful resource is Bed and Breakfast Explorer, offering direct links to B&B websites throughout the US. **www.bbexplorer.com.**

Most B&Bs are privately owned and located in historic structures or private homes *($105–$600/day)*. Amenities include complimentary breakfast ranging from continental fare to a gourmet repast; some offer afternoon tea, wine and cheese, and the use of sitting rooms or garden areas where hosts and guests mingle. Most establishments are small, offering fewer than 10 rooms, and some require a minimum stay. Private baths are not always available, and individual rooms may not be equipped with phones. Smoking indoors may not be allowed. Be sure to book reservations well in advance, especially during tourist and holiday seasons; rates may vary seasonally.

CAMPING

National and state park listings below.

Campsites are located in national parks, state parks, national forests and private campgrounds. Types of campsites range from those equipped with full utility hookups to rustic backcountry sites *($7–$30/day)*. Advance reservations are recommended, especially during summer and holidays; some campgrounds do not accept reservations year-round.

Wilderness camping is available on most public lands. A Wilderness Permit *(usually free)* is generally required, and advance reservations are suggested (required for popular parks like Yosemite). Topographic maps of most wilderness areas are available. Contact desired location or the addresses below for further information.

Campground Information

For information about **California State Parks**, contact:
Dept. of Parks and Recreation P.O. Box 942896, Sacramento CA 94296, www.parks.ca.gov; or California State Park Information Line, ✆916-653-6995.

Campsite Reservations

For state park camping reservations contact **ReserveAmerica**, Inc., 2897 Kilgore Rd, Rancho Cordova, CA 95670, ✆800-444-7275, www.reserve america.com. For all US national park reservations (both camping and other recreation), contact the park you are visiting or the **National Recreation Reservation Service** (✆*877-444-6777; www.recreation.gov*). Camping reservations for groups of six or fewer can be made (1 day to 6 months in advance; 5 months in advance for Yosemite National Park) for national parks, forests and other federally managed recreation lands.

The *RV & Camping Guide* gives facility information about **private camp-**

grounds and is available via mail or internet from California Travel Parks Association, PO Box 5648, Auburn CA 95604, ✆888-782-9287, www.camp-california.com.

HOSTELS

Hostels offer simple, budget accommodations averaging $16-$30/night. Amenities include community living room, showers, laundry facilities, full-service kitchen and dining room, and dormitory-style rooms (some hostels offer family-style accommodations. Blankets and pillows are provided, but guests are required to bring their own linens; some hostels offer bed linens and towels for rent. Advance reservations are suggested during peak travel times. There are 21 certified American Youth Hostels in California. To acquire a membership card or for information, write to **Hostelling International-American Youth Hostels**, 8401 Colesville Rd., Ste. 600, Silver Spring MD 20910 ✆301-495-1240, www.hiayh.org.

GUEST RANCHES

Primarily located in the mountain regions, guest ranches offer such amenities as meals, equipment, guided pack rides and horsemanship instruction. Rates average $1200–$1600/week. The following California ranches are affiliated with the Dude Ranchers' Association:

- ◆ **Coffee Creek Ranch**
  4310 Coffee Creek Rd., Trinity Center, CA 96091, ✆800-624-4480; ✆530-266-3343; www.coffeecreekranch.com.

- ◆ **Greenhorn Creek Guest Ranch**
  2116 Greenhorn Ranch Rd, Quincy CA 95971, ✆800-334-6939; www.greenhornranch.com.

- ◆ **Hunewill Guest Ranch**
  Box 368, Bridgeport CA 93517, ✆760-932-7710 (summer & fall); ✆775-465-2201 (off-season); www.hunewillranch.com.

RESORTS AND SPAS

Located throughout the state, resorts offer a variety of programs, from fitness, beauty and wellness to weight or stress management. Amenities may include mud baths and thermal treatments, massage, exercise programs and nutritional counseling as well as tennis, golf, hiking and skiing. Facilities range from rustic cabins to luxury suites *($200–$700/day)*; meals are usually included and packages for multi-day stays including selected amenities may be available.

WHERE TO EAT

Selected restaurants are described in the Address Books within the Discovering California section.

Dining in California is an adventure in global tastes, served up in eateries from Mexican cantinas, family-run Italian trattorias and Parisian-style bistros to Japanese tea houses and neighborhood brew pubs. Given the Golden State's broad immigrant population, you'll find restaurants serving Indian, Polynesian, Australian, Chinese, Algerian, Latin American, Greek and other international food.

Seafood plays a starring role on local menus, especially along the coast. From **dockside shacks** to the high-end dining rooms of oceanside resorts, the catch of the day may well have been hauled in that morning, although much of California's seafood no longer comes from local waters. California orchards, farms and fields produce a huge variety of **vegetables and fruits**. At restaurants, cafes and takeout counters, at farm markets and festivals across the state, patrons can enjoy the freshest imaginable produce and learn how to prepare it at home. **Outdoor dining** is hugely popular here, particularly in the south. Celebrity chefs helm the kitchens at posh restaurants and upscale dining rooms throughout the state; Los Angeles, San Francisco and the Wine Country are culinary hotspots.

For restaurants like these you'll need to reserve several weeks in advance. In large cities, expect to pay for valet parking.

In the Wine Country, gourmet **picnic** lunches are the thing. In Napa and Sonoma valleys, gourmet shops can provide visitors with a fully-stocked (utensils included) basket of gourmet treats like meats, cheeses, artisan breads and desserts, complete with local wines, of course.

While it hasn't quite become the state beverage, wine is certainly a key product in California's economy. Freshly squeezed orange juice is a California staple, and teas, especially herbal teas, are preferred over caffeinated coffee by a growing number of Californians. California is also known for its excellent microbreweries, which can be sampled in bars throughout the state.

USEFUL WEBSITES

www.opentable.com
Online restaurant reservation site with restaurant profiles, reviews and search features.

www.dinnerbroker.com
National reservation site covers large cities in California.

The Michelin Guide (Red Cover)

For a comprehensive selection of hotel and restaurant listings in San Francisco take along the red-cover **Michelin Guide San Francisco Bay Area and Wine Country**. For Los Angeles, try the red-cover **Michelin Guide Los Angeles**. Inside these annually published Michelin guides, you'll find a wide range of listings, from modest guesthouses to luxurious grand hotels and from family-run trattorias to the finest of haute cuisine. Selections are classified according to the standard of their amenities and their inclusion is based on regular on-the-spot visits.

Basic Information

BUSINESS HOURS
Most businesses operate Monday to Friday 9–10am to 5.30pm; some retail stores may stay open until 9pm. **Shopping centers** Monday to Saturday 9.30–10am to 8pm–9pm, Sunday 11am to 6pm. **Banks** Monday to Thursday 10am to 3pm, Friday 10am to 5pm; some close later on Friday. Some banks in larger cities may open on Saturday morning.

COMMUNICATIONS
Instructions for using **public telephones** are listed on or near the phone. Some public telephones accept credit cards, and all will accept **long-distance** calling cards. For long-distance calls in the US and Canada, dial 1+area code+number. To place an **international call**, dial 011+country code+number. To place a reverse-charge call (person receiving call pays charges), dial 0+area code+number and tell the operator you are calling "collect". Telephone numbers that start with **1-800, 1-888, 1-877** and **1-866** are toll-free *(no charge)* and may not be accessible outside of North America. Most hotels add a surcharge for calls. Visitors using **mobile phones** compatible with GSM networks can avoid roaming charges by purchase a prepaid local SIM card for use in their phones. SIM cards are available at online and at service-provider outlets; you can buy vouchers to add minutes to your account at most newsstands and convenience stores. Another option for mobile calling is a pay-as-you-go phone, available from many local service-provider outlets. You can send or receive a telegram or money via **Western Union** (𝄞800-325-6000; www.westernunion.com).

ELECTRICITY
Electrical current in the US is 120 volts AC, 60 Hz. Foreign-made appliances may need voltage transformers and North American flat-blade adapter plugs (available at specialty travel and electronics stores and airports).

EMERGENCIES
In all major US cities, **dial 911** to call the police, ambulance, or fire department. Emergencies may also be reported by dialing 0 for the operator.

EARTHQUAKE PRECAUTIONS
Although severe earthquakes are infrequent, they are also unpredictable, making earthquake preparedness a fact of life in California. If you are **outside** when an earthquake occurs, stay clear of trees, buildings and power lines. If you are in a **vehicle**, pull to the side of the road and stop. Do not park on or under bridges; sit on the floor of the vehicle if possible. If you are in a **building**, stand inside a doorway or sit under a sturdy table; stay away from windows and outside walls. Be alert for aftershocks.

LIQUOR LAW
The legal minimum age for purchase and consumption of alcoholic beverages is 21; proof of age is normally required. Legal hours of sale: 6am–2am.

MAIL/POST
First-class postage rates within the US: letter 42¢ (1oz), postcard 27¢. Overseas: letter 94¢ (1oz), postcard 94¢. Letters and small packages can be mailed from most hotels. Stamps and packing material can be purchased at post offices, grocery stores and businesses offering postal and express shipping services. Most post offices are open Monday–Friday 9am–5pm; some are open Saturday 9am–noon.

MONEY
BANKS
Most banks are members of the network of Automatic Teller Machines (ATMs), allowing visitors from around the world to withdraw cash using bank

PUBLIC HOLIDAYS

Most banks and government offices are closed on the following legal holidays (*many retail stores and restaurants remain open on these days*):

New Year's Day	January 1
Martin Luther King Jr. Day*	3rd Monday in January
Presidents' Day	3rd Monday in February
Memorial Day*	Last Monday in May
Independence Day*	July 4
Labor Day*	1st Monday in September
Columbus Day*	2nd Monday in October
Veterans Day*	November 11
Thanksgiving Day	4th Thursday in November
Christmas Day	December 25

cards and major credit cards. ATMs can usually be found in banks, airports, grocery stores and shopping malls. To inquire about ATM service, locations and transaction fees, contact your local bank, Cirrus (☎800-424-7787) or Plus System (☎800-843-7587).

CREDIT CARDS AND TRAVELER'S CHECKS

Most banks will cash traveler's checks and process cash advances on major credit cards with proper identification. **Traveler's checks** are accepted at most stores, restaurants and hotels. To report a lost or stolen **credit card**: American Express, ☎800-528-4800; Diners Club, ☎800-234-6377; MasterCard/Eurocard, ☎800-622-7747 or the issuing bank; Visa/Carte Bleue, ☎800-847-2911.

CURRENCY AND EXCHANGE

The official currency in the USA is the **dollar**, with commonly circulated bills in denominations of $1, $5, $10, $20, $50 and $100. The American dollar is divided into 100 **cents**. A penny = 1 cent; a nickel = 5 cents; a dime = 10 cents; a quarter = 25 cents.

For a fee, the main offices of most national banks will exchange foreign currency. Los Angeles and San Francisco International Airports have currency exchange offices in the international arrival halls. **Travelex** (☎800-287-7362 www.travelex.com) operates numerous exchange offices throughout California.

TAXES

Prices displayed or quoted in the US generally do not include the sales tax. Sales tax (avoidable if the seller will ship the purchased items to another country) is added at time of purchase and is not reimbursable.

California sales tax is 8.25%, but most metro areas add an additional sales tax of .25%–1.25%. Motel taxes vary by locality, but the average is 10%.

SMOKING

California law prohibits smoking in enclosed places, including bars and restaurants.

TIPPING

In the US it is customary to give a tip (a small gift of money) for services received from food servers, porters, hotel maids and taxi drivers.

It is customary in restaurants to tip the server 15–20% of the check. At hotels, porters should be tipped $1 per suitcase, and hotel maids $1 per night of stay. Taxi drivers are usually tipped 15% of the fare.

TIME ZONE

California is on Pacific Standard Time (PST), 3hrs behind Eastern Standard Time (EST) and 8hrs behind Greenwich Mean Time. Daylight Saving Time (*clocks advanced 1hr*) is in effect for most of the US from the second Sunday in March until the first Sunday in November.

CONVERSION TABLES

Weights and Measures

EU	USA	UK	
1 kilogram (kg)	**2.2 pounds (lb)**	**2.2 pounds**	*To convert*
6.35 kilograms	14 pounds	1 stone (st)	*kilograms*
0.45 kilograms	16 ounces (oz)	16 ounces	*to pounds,*
1 metric ton (tn)	**1.1 tons**	**1.1 tons**	*multiply by 2.2*
1 litre (l)	**2.11 pints (pt)**	**1.76 pints**	*To convert litres*
3.79 litres	1 gallon (gal)	0.83 gallon	*to gallons, multiply*
4.55 litres	1.20 gallon	1 gallon	*by 0.26 (US)*
			or 0.22 (UK)
1 hectare (ha)	**2.47 acres**	**2.47 acres**	*To convert*
1 sq. kilometre	**0.38 sq. miles**	**0.38 sq. miles**	*hectares to*
(km²)	**(sq.mi.)**		*acres, multiply*
			by 2.4
1 centimetre (cm)	**0.39 inches (in)**	**0.39 inches**	*To convert metres*
1 metre (m)	**3.28 feet (ft) or 39.37 inches**		*to feet, multiply*
	or 1.09 yards (yd)		*by 3.28; for*
1 kilometre (km)	**0.62 miles (mi)**	**0.62 miles**	*kilometres to miles,*
			multiply by 0.6

Clothing

Women	EU	USA	UK
	35	4	2½
	36	5	3½
	37	6	4½
Shoes	38	7	5½
	39	8	6½
	40	9	7½
	41	10	8½
	36	6	8
	38	8	10
Dresses	40	10	12
& suits	42	12	14
	44	14	16
	46	16	18
	36	06	30
	38	08	32
Blouses &	40	10	34
sweaters	42	12	36
	44	14	38
	46	16	40

Men	EU	USA	UK
	40	7½	7
	41	8½	8
	42	9½	9
Shoes	43	10½	10
	44	11½	11
	45	12½	12
	46	13½	13
	46	36	36
	48	38	38
Suits	50	40	40
	52	42	42
	54	44	44
	56	46	48
	37	14½	14½
	38	15	15
Shirts	39	15½	15½
	40	15¾	15¾
	41	16	16
	42	16½	16½

Sizes often vary depending on the designer. These equivalents are given for guidance only.

Speed

KPH	10	30	50	70	80	90	100	110	120	130
MPH	6	19	31	43	50	56	62	68	75	81

Temperature

Celsius (°C)	0°	5°	10°	15°	20°	25°	30°	40°	60°	80°	100°
Fahrenheit (°F)	32°	41°	50°	59°	68°	77°	86°	104°	140°	176°	212°

To convert Celsius into Fahrenheit, multiply °C by 9, divide by 5, and add 32.
To convert Fahrenheit into Celsius, subtract 32 from °F, multiply by 5, and divide by 9.
NB: Conversion factors on this page are approximate.

Agua Caliente Indian Canyons, Palm Springs
© California Travel & Tourism Commission

INTRODUCTION TO CALIFORNIA

California Today

For many decades, growth was the operative word for the Golden State: a growing economy, increased tourism, a higher population (at least three million more since the 2000 census). Accompanying that growth, though, are thorny issues such as air pollution, illegal immigration and crime, which all vie for attention in a complicated and dynamic political scene. The economic downturn of 2008 and 2009 has brought enormous financial challenges to the state, forcing government leaders at all levels to grapple with reduced budgets and bringing political differences to the fore. At one time a bastion of conservatism, the state has shifted decidedly to the liberal left, despite having a Republican governor at the helm. California's progressive and forward-thinking nature has historically provided the foundation for its political, cultural and economic diversity.

POPULATION

If the US as a whole is a great melting pot, California resembles nothing so much as an enormous stew in which people of vastly diverse ethnic, racial and cultural backgrounds live side by side, retaining their distinctive characters. The state's 37 million inhabitants come from a wide variety of backgrounds, with non-Hispanic Caucasians making up about 43 percent of the population, Asians around 12 percent and African Americans about 6 percent; more than 35 percent of Californians are Latinos of various national origins.

This diversity is not consistent statewide. A much higher percentage of Latinos live in Southern California, for example, reflecting that region's closer ties to Mexico and Central America; larger Asian enclaves may be found to the north, particularly in the San Francisco Bay Area. Throughout the state there are tight-knit communities that steadfastly maintain the lifestyles of different lands, from the Laotian population of Fresno, to the Basques of Bakersfield, to San Francisco's world-renowned Chinatown. The great metropolitan centers of Los Angeles, San Francisco and San Diego possess a wide ethnic diversity, attracting steady streams of hopeful immigrants from across the nation and around the world, while smaller towns and rural areas can seem almost Midwestern in their homogeneity.

Californians have always been drawn by the state's reputation as a land of opportunity, a place to wipe one's slate clean and start anew. Inaccessible and distant, the territory attracted a slow trickle of Easterners during the early years of the Great Westward Migration in the early 19C. That trickle grew to a flood following the Gold Rush; after gold fever died down, the transcontinental railroad completed in 1869 continued to channel a steady stream of settlers seeking new lives in a beneficent climate amid magnificent scenery. Land booms, agriculture, the aircraft and defense industries, Hollywood, the Silicon Valley electronics boom: many and seemingly endless opportunities have drawn people to California, and that draw remains strong.

RELIGION

Though colonized in the 18C by Roman Catholic friars with a mission to convert Native Americans, California soon became a land of pronounced religious diversity brought on by the influx of settlers who carried their religious practices and establishments with them. Today more Catholics reside here than in any other state, but there are also large numbers of Protestants and Jews, and a burgeoning Muslim population as well. Organizations representing every major school of Buddhism thrive here, and the state has more Mormon temples than any state outside Utah.

OPPOSITES AND EXTREMES

Personal freedom is prized in California, and the resulting diversity can dazzle or disorient newcomers first confronted by bikini-clad in-line skaters on Venice Beach's Oceanfront Walk or Gay Pride paraders on the streets of San Francisco. And visitors who assume that freedom translates solely as liberalism should bear in mind that California is the birthplace not only of the Free Speech Movement but also of Orange County's ultra-right-wing John Birch Society.

Diversity in California takes many forms. Though the state's fabled reputation seems merely myth amid the crushing poverty of South Central Los Angeles or in the simple, rural communities of the Central Valley, the legend nonetheless springs fully to life along the state's many beaches, in the chic boutiques of Beverly Hills, on the ski slopes surrounding Lake Tahoe, and in the vineyards and tasting rooms of the Wine Country. Politically, culturally and socially, California is a land—and Californians a people—of opposites and extremes, at once steadfastly resisting and irresistibly inviting definition.

LIFESTYLE

With relatively easy access to some of the finest beaches, mountains, forests and desert scenery in the US, Californians enjoy a lifestyle strongly influenced by the outdoors. Many areas of the state are blessed with year-round fine weather, boosting residents' tendency to get outdoors and play. Innovations in the industries based here puts Californians at the forefront of new trends in technology, fashion and fine dining as well.

ECONOMY

The great diversity of economic activity in California was established early in the state's history, when isolation from the rest of the country made importing goods expensive and encouraged local enterprise in every field. Today bolstered by abundant natural resources and a diversified industrial base, the economy of California alone ranked eighth largest among the world's major industrial nations in 2007. The nation's most populous state was the top-ranking in the country with a Gross State Product, totalling $1.8 trillion.

COMPUTER INDUSTRY

The burgeoning of California's electronics industry over the past 50 years began with federal spending during the Cold War and has continued, supported by increasing demand for personal computers, integrated circuits and other products of advancing technology. California's major research institutions, among them the California Institute of Technology in Pasadena and Stanford University in Palo Alto, became seedbeds for small, innovative electronics concerns that were the hearts of early semiconductor and computer companies. Today Silicon Valley, formerly an orchard district northwest of San Jose, is a world-renowned center for research and development in computers and electronics.

ENTERTAINMENT

Formerly a quiet suburb of Los Angeles, Hollywood became the nation's leading center for motion picture production in the 1920s, when major film studios moved here from Chicago and New York. When the advent of television eroded movie ticket sales in the 1950s, the industry responded by making fewer but bigger films, by producing features for television and eventually by merging with television, recording and publishing companies to form giant media/entertainment conglomerates. Today, well over half of US feature films are produced in California. The business still thrives despite the diaspora of modern media.

TOURISM

338 million domestic travelers visited California in 2008 for business and pleasure, making it the leading US travel destination. Drawn by the state's appealing climate, natural features and multitude of tourist attractions, visitors spent $97.6 billion, benefiting a wide range of industries and services. During 2008, travel spending in California directly supported 924,000 jobs with earnings of $30.6 billion. Travel spending generated the greatest number of jobs in arts, entertainment and recreation, food service and accommodations.

AGRICULTURE

California is the nation's leading farm state, with more than 200 commercially grown crops and the highest US market value of its agricultural products in 2007. In 2007, it exported more fruits, vegetables, tree nuts and dairy products than any other state. Productivity benefits from irrigation on a grand scale, a benign climate that creates a year-round growing season in some areas, and a tendency toward mechanization and specialization that imparts an industrial intensity to the growing of crops. Nearly all of the nation's almonds, artichokes, dates, figs, kiwifruit, olives and pistachios are grown here, in addition to most of the apricots, broccoli, Brussels sprouts, garlic, grapes, lettuce, nectarines, plums, strawberries and walnuts. The vast Central Valley is California's principal farming area; others include the Salinas Valley and the Imperial and Coachella valleys in the southeastern corner of the state. The grape-growing districts in the Wine Country are the most famous of many small, highly productive fruit and vegetable districts in Coast Range valleys, and cattle ranching remains important in the unirrigated hills and plateaus of the state.

MANUFACTURING

Glamour industries like entertainment and tourism may obscure the fact that California is one of the nation's leading manufacturing states. Prior to the 1869 completion of the transcontinental railroad, the state's geographic isolation was a stimulus to manufacturers, who sought to produce equipment and other goods more cheaply than they could be shipped around Cape Horn. Mining equipment began to be produced in San Francisco in the 1850s, followed by farm machinery in Stockton; canning and other forms of food processing became important in the early 20C. Automobile assembly, airplane manufacturing and shipbuilding increased through the 1930s and boomed during World War II. California's apparel industry began in San Francisco in 1850 with the manufacture of heavy denim trousers for miners by Levi Strauss; today San Francisco and Los Angeles are outranked only by New York City in apparel manufacturing, and Los Angeles is a major center for fashion design. Other important manufactured products are chemical and petroleum products, plastics, paper, machinery of all kinds and home furnishings.

NATURAL RESOURCES

California is second only to Oregon in the nation's lumber production. **Logging** and **lumbering** dominate the economies of towns located amid the northern Coast Ranges and the Cascade Range. Redwood, Douglas fir, ponderosa pine and sugar pine are among the commercially important trees. However, deforestation has become an acute problem, and the viability of the logging industry has in recent years been challenged by conservation groups dedicated to protecting remaining old-growth redwood forests along the North Coast. Federal, state and county forest protection measures, including the creation of 18 national forests and of Redwood National and State Parks, have slowed logging activity and produced the expected economic consequences.

With more than 1,000mi of coastline, California is a leading state in **commercial fishing**; mackerel, salmon, squid, tuna, anchovies and sole are among the important ocean species. Crab, mussels, oysters and clams are also prevalent, and in recent years, sea urchins for export to Japan have become a significant catch along the northern coast. Los Angeles is by far the largest fishing port; other centers include Crescent City and the area around Ventura.

Though greatly diminished from its supreme importance during the Gold Rush, **mining** remains a significant contributor to California's economy. The state accounts for almost all of the nation's production of evaporite minerals such as borax and trona (sodium carbonate), and important iron ore and tungsten deposits have been exploited in the Mojave Desert. Commercially important oil fields near Bakersfield, Coalinga and Los Angeles were tapped

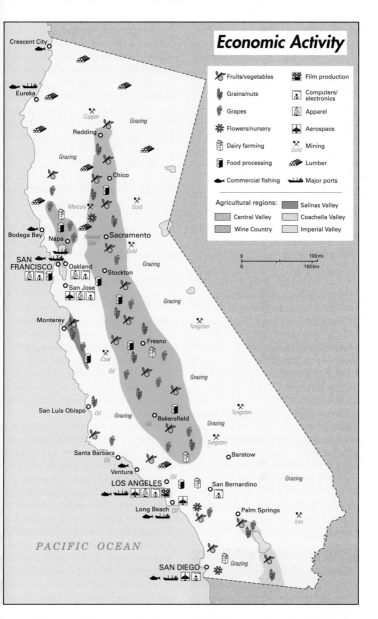

Economic Activity

Fruits/vegetables
Grains/nuts
Grapes
Flowers/nursery
Dairy farming
Food processing
Commercial fishing

Film production
Computers/electronics
Apparel
Aerospace
Mining
Lumber
Major ports

Agricultural regions:
Central Valley
Wine Country
Salinas Valley
Coachella Valley
Imperial Valley

0   100mi
0   150km

Crescent City
Eureka
Copper
Grazing
Redding
Grazing
Chico
Mercury   *Gold*
Bodega Bay
Napa   *Natural Gas*   Sacramento   *Gold*
SAN FRANCISCO   Oakland   Stockton
San Jose
Grazing
Monterey
Grazing
Fresno
Coal
Oil
Grazing
San Luis Obispo   *Oil*   *Grazing*   Bakersfield
Oil   *Grazing*   *Tungsten*
Santa Barbara   *Oil*   *Tungsten*
Ventura   *Oil*
LOS ANGELES   San Bernardino   *Grazing*
Long Beach   *Oil*   Palm Springs
Barstow
Iron
PACIFIC OCEAN
SAN DIEGO   *Grazing*

around the turn of the 19C, and rocker arms can still be seen pumping away offshore near Long Beach and other coastal areas.

SERVICES

As befits the nation's most populous state, the service sector is the stronghold of California's economy. About a third of the state's nonfarm jobs are in such industries as health care, finance, government, administration, business, education, and personal and professional services. In addition, **real estate** and **construction** have grown with the state's intermittent population surges. To some extent, growth in this sector has been based on nothing more than the anticipation of further growth, fueling a speculative real-estate market that keeps housing costs high compared with the rest of the country.

FOOD AND WINE

Distinguished California food essayist **M.F.K. Fisher** (1908-92) described her native state's approach to eating as "an agreeable tolerance of all that is good," summing up the regional cuisine's dedication to freshness and quality and its acceptance of myriad ethnic traditions. Without traveling more than a few miles in most cities or good-sized towns, California residents and visitors can readily sample cuisines from around the world, from pad thai to Tandoori dishes to Southern California favorites like fish tacos and abalone steak. The state's Mexican, Italian, Chinese, Japanese and Thai restaurants show particular distinction.

CALIFORNIA CUISINE

As a direct result of such global influences, so-called California cuisine combines a potpourri of American, French, Asian and Latino culinary styles. **Alice Waters**, founder of the acclaimed **Chez Panisse** restaurant in Berkeley, is generally acknowledged to be the cuisine's founder, and **Michael McCarty** further popularized it in Southern California at his **Michael's** restaurant in the Los Angeles coastal community of Santa Monica. The appellation appears today on hundreds if not thousands of menus throughout the state.

Fisherman's Wharf sign

Brigitta L. House/MICHELIN

California cuisine is distinguished by a reliance on outstanding local ingredients, including seafood from the Pacific; vegetables, fruits and poultry from the San Joaquin Valley and other regions; and countless items from small, specialist producers of gourmet quality ingredients—ranging from fresh goat cheese to organically raised lamb, from rare species of banana to bite-size baby vegetables.

Foods such as these stock not only grocery stores and restaurant kitchens, but also farmers' markets at locations throughout the state. Food-loving visitors may behold, taste, or purchase exotic seasonal delights such as juicy white peaches, sweet fresh apricots, fragrant herbs, young garlic and many varieties of tomatoes. Much of this produce is organically grown. Shoppers will also find fresh eggs, locally produced cheeses, and nuts from Central Valley. The organic movement and sustainable agriculture took their cue from California: chefs, who began cultivating associations with local farmers to bring not only hormone- and antibiotic-free and thus more flavorful, lamb, chicken and beef to the table.

Such foods are generally prepared quickly and simply, their presentation on the plate as beautiful as a still-life painting. Main-course meats and seafood are most likely to be grilled over the hot coals of a barbecue, a method well suited to the state's outdoor lifestyle. In recent years, many chefs have opted to cook over mesquite wood, which yields a searing and fragrant heat, or over other scented woods. Salads, often meals in themselves, display an extravagance of locally grown produce, sometimes garnished with meat, poultry, or seafood; they are also often graced with California **avocado**, an ingredient so common that it once enjoyed the nickname "Indian butter." Avocado also appears frequently in sandwiches and may be mashed with lemon or lime juice and chilies to make the popular Mexican dip guacamole.

Much of California's seafood no longer comes from local waters, but an enormous variety is flown or trucked in daily. Diners can select from a wide array—sea bass from Chile, salmon and oysters from Washington state, mussels from New Zealand, halibut from Canada—all absolutely fresh thanks to modern shipping techniques. From November through April, Dungeness crab appears on menus and in fish markets; this famed San Francisco treat is best consumed with sourdough bread and a glass of crisp white wine.

San Francisco's renowned **sourdough bread** remains a beloved local treasure. True devotees swear it cannot be produced anywhere but in the city. Dating from the 19C gold-mining days, the recipe for this tangy loaf calls for a yeast-like starter, no sugar, and microbes that apparently float only in San Francisco air.

Desserts in this health-conscious state tend to be light but flavorful offerings such as fresh fruit salads or sorbets; the state's chefs also take pride in creating riches to tempt the most unrepentant sweet tooth or chocolate addiction.

WORLD-CLASS WINES

As fresh-tasting and flavorful as its native foods and regional cuisine, California's own wines are a natural companion to any meal eaten in the state. Today some of North America's finest wines come from the Golden State. In recent decades, these wines have won the state's wine industry worldwide acclaim for their quality.

Along with fertile earth, wine grapes need a long growing season of hot days and cool nights, which several regions in California provide. While Napa and Sonoma counties, together known as the Wine Country, are the premier winemaking region, they are far from the only producers of California wines. Excellent vintages also come from Mendocino County, northwest of the Wine Country; the Livermore Valley east of San Francisco; the Monterey area; the upper Salinas Valley near Paso Robles; the Santa Ynez Valley inland from Santa Barbara; and the Temecula Valley in Riverside County, north of San Diego.

Oak barrels used for ageing wine
© Brent A. Miller/www.winecountry.com

California's current wine production is based primarily on the legacy of French immigrant Jean-Louise Vigne, who established a large vineyard near Los Angeles in the 1830s. Descendants of *Vitis vinifera* cuttings introduced in the 19C still thrive. The strains have been tested and adapted over subsequent generations, with tremendous strides in the science of agriculture and vinification made in this century by the Department of Viticulture and Enology at the University of California, Davis.

Best adapted to California growing conditions is the Cabernet Sauvignon, a small, blue-black grape from the Médoc district of France's Bordeaux region that produces a rich, full red wine. The Burgundy region's Pinot Noir grape is used primarily in the making of California sparkling wine. Other red wine grapes from Europe include Cabernet Franc, Petite Sirah, Napa Gamay (derived from France's Gamay Beaujolais) and Zinfandel, which is now grown chiefly in California.

Some of California's finest white wines are made from Chardonnay, the premier white grape of France's Chablis and Burgundy regions. Chardonnay produces a richly flavored, fruity, dry wine, further characterized by the taste of the oak barrels in which it is often aged. Sauvignon Blanc, often used in the making of French Sauternes and Pouilly-Fumé, a crisp, dry and refreshing character, and grows well in cooler areas. Pinot Blanc, of the same family as Burgundy's Pinot Noir, is an important ingredient in many sparkling wines. Other white European varieties include flowery, aromatic Riesling and Chenin Blanc.

History

The history of California is a tale of discovery and its consequences: the Spanish "discovered," then populated the land, marginalizing the native peoples. The Mexicans fought Spain for independence; the Americans fought the Mexicans for possession of the soil. The discovery of gold was a momentous event in the growth of California, as was the discovery of black gold. The discovery of California's climate and scenic beauty by Easterners seeking locales for film production changed the face of the state forever. Its status as the most populous in the Union attests to the Golden State's enduring allure as El Dorado, the place where fame, fortune, health and longevity may be found.

PREHISTORIC AND NATIVE CALIFORNIANS

At least 7,000 years ago, the area of North America that now includes California was first populated by descendants of the peoples who crossed the Bering land bridge from Asia between 20,000 and 15,000 BC. By the time Europeans first visited the Pacific Coast in the mid-16C, a Native American population estimated as high as 310,000 was divided into almost 500 self-governing tribes speaking more than 300 dialects of some 80 mutually unintelligible tongues. Chief among the tribal groups were the **Pomo** in the coastal lands near present-day Mendocino; the **Maidu** in the volcanic regions near Lassen Peak; the **Miwok** in the Sierra Nevada and its western foothills; the **Paiute**, east of the Sierra Nevada; the **Salinan** along the Central Coast around Monterey; the **Chumash** in what are now the areas of Santa Barbara and Ventura; the **Gabrieleño** in the Los Angeles area; and the **Cahuilla**, inland from present-day San Diego.

Occupying a landscape whose generally scant rainfall made agriculture difficult, tribal peoples supported themselves by hunting and fishing, and by gathering readily available foodstuffs such as acorns and manzanita berries. Complex barter networks enabled coastal, valley and foothill bands to trade these dried foods, as well as shells, beads and bear skins, for such Great Basin sundries as obsidian, mineral paints, salt, pine nuts and dried brine flies, a delicacy from Mono Lake. Tied to the natural world and its seasons, the tribes were largely migratory, establishing thousands of small and large villages statewide, especially in coastal areas.

Simple though their lives were, the Native Californians developed sophisticated cultures and social orders. They practiced complex religions based on nature and its phenomena, and the men of the tribe cured themselves of physical and spiritual ailments in airtight sweat lodges. In many parts of the state, tribes set fires to control the growth of grasses, promoting more abundant yields of wild crops. Basketry reached a fine art, providing vessels for food gathering and storage. Some coastal tribes fashioned seaworthy plank boats. Strings of shell beads provided a common currency by which foods could be exchanged among tribes in times of need.

SPANISH CALIFORNIA

Following the late 15C voyages of Christopher Columbus to the Caribbean, much of the New World fell under the flag of Spain. Having glimpsed the Pacific Ocean from Panama in 1513, and having conquered Mexico in 1521, the conquistadores were eager to push north and west.

In 1535 Spanish general **Hernán Cortés** (1485–1547) explored the narrow sea known today as the Gulf of California, stepping ashore near the present-day site of La Paz, Mexico. Thinking that the peninsula on which he landed (later to become the Mexican state of Baja California) was actually an island, he named it "California" after an imaginary island described in the 1510 novel *Las Sergas de Esplandián (The Adventures of Esplandián)* by Garcí Ordóñez de Montalvo.

Seeking the fabled **Strait of Anian**, a deepwater link between the Atlantic and Pacific, the Spanish Crown dispatched Portuguese explorer **Juan Rodríguez Cabrillo** to sail northward along the Pacific Coast in June 1542. During a seven-month voyage in which he became the first European explorer of **Alta California** ("upper" California north of Baja), Cabrillo landed in present-day San Diego; on Catalina Island and the Channel Islands; at the future sites of San Pedro and Santa Monica; and as far north as the northern Sonoma coast, failing en route to notice the entrance to San Francisco Bay.

For more than 40 years after Cabrillo's journey, Spain neglected its claims to California, providing entrée for English privateer **Francis Drake** to land his ship, the *Golden Hind*, at Point Reyes in 1579. England never took possession of the area Drake claimed as Nova Albion (New England), but his landing aroused Spain to protect the territory, sending Pedro Unamuno in 1587 and Sebastián Rodríguez in 1595 to sail along the shore in search of an anchorage and supply port for Spanish galleons. In 1602 **Sebastián Vizcaíno** dropped anchor in Monterey Bay; his inaccurate description of the cove indirectly inspired the first European sighting of San Francisco Bay by members of the Sacred Expedition 167 years later.

THE MISSION CHAIN

In 1697 Jesuit priests established in Baja California the first of a chain of Catholic missions that would set a pattern for Spain's eventual colonization of all of California. Each mission typically consisted of a church, residences for its priests, schools and dormitories for its Indian converts (neophytes), and thousands of acres of surrounding farmland. As it grew and became established, each mission was intended to be secularized as a *pueblo*, or town, for neophytes and Spanish colonists.

With the Jesuits fallen from favor and the Spanish government alarmed by the appearance of Russian settlements along the northern Pacific Coast in Alaska—in 1812, the Russians actually established a colony at Fort Ross, which

persisted into the 1830s—the Crown in 1767 turned to the Franciscan order to extend Spanish control northward into Alta California. Appointed head of the new missions was **Padre Junípero Serra** (1713–84). A diminutive 54-year-old priest, Serra, was born, educated and ordained on the Spanish island of Majorca, where he taught philosophy for 15 years at the Lullian University. He began his missionary work in Mexico in 1749, gaining a well-deserved reputation as a worker whose intensity, asceticism and tirelessness were made all the more dramatic by the fact that he was lame for the last 35 years of his life.

In 1769, the **Sacred Expedition** left Baja California with two land columns and three supply ships destined for San Diego. The long, difficult overland journey was made more arduous when one of the supply ships was lost at sea and the other two were late in arriving. About half of the 300 priests, soldiers and settlers died en route and, faced with starvation, the expedition nearly turned back. But the second column, headed by Serra and **Gaspar de Portolá** (1723–86), who was eventually named Spanish governor of Alta California, finally founded the territory's first mission at San Diego in July 1769. Over the next 54 years, 20 more missions would be established in a chain stretching from San Diego north to Sonoma. Located a day's travel apart, the outposts were linked by a trail known as **El Camino Réal**, "the Royal Highway," a route largely traced today by US Highway 101.

Neophytes living within the mission compounds were schooled in the Spanish language and the Catholic faith; the padres also taught them such trades as farming, brickmaking, blacksmithing, weaving, spinning, tanning and winemaking. But life was far from idyllic in the missions. Supplies and equipment from Mexico sometimes arrived late or fell scarce. Earthquakes leveled adobe brick buildings. Indians died from such European diseases as measles, chicken pox, diphtheria, pneumonia, tuberculosis and syphilis; others suffered physical

Missions

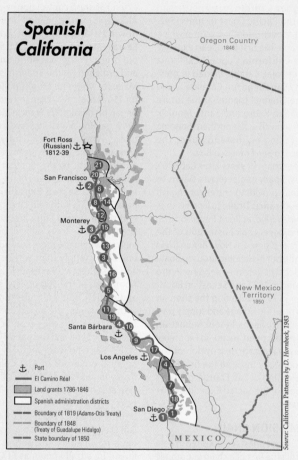

Spanish California

Oregon Country
1846

Fort Ross
(Russian) ⚓ ☆
1812-39

San Francisco ⚓

Monterey ⚓

New Mexico
Territory
1850

Santa Bárbara ⚓

Los Angeles ⚓

San Diego ⚓

⚓ Port
— El Camino Réal
▨ Land grants 1786-1846
▢ Spanish administration districts
-- Boundary of 1819 (Adams-Otis Treaty)
-- Boundary of 1848
(Treaty of Guadalupe Hidalgo)
-- State boundary of 1850

MEXICO

Source: California Patterns by D. Hornbeck, 1983

① **San Diego de Alcalá** (1769-1834)
② **San Carlos Borromeo de Carmelo** (1770-1834)
③ **San Antonio de Padua** (1771-1845)
④ **San Gabriel Arcángel** (1771-1846)
⑤ **San Luís Obispo de Tolosa** (1772-1835)
⑥ **San Juan Capistrano** (1775-1845)
⑦ **San Francisco de Asís** (1776-1834)
⑧ **Santa Clara de Asís** (1777-1836)
⑨ **San Buenaventura** (1782-1836)
⑩ **Santa Bárbara** (1786-1834)
⑪ **La Purísima Concepción** (1787-1834)
⑫ **Santa Cruz** (1791-1834)
⑬ **Nuestra Señora Dolorosísima de la Soledad** (1791-1835)

⑭ **San José** (1797-1834)
⑮ **San Juan Bautista** (1797-1835)
⑯ **San Miguel Arcángel** (1797-1846)
⑰ **San Fernando Rey de España** (1797-1834)
⑱ **San Luís Rey de Francia** (1798-1834)
⑲ **Santa Inés** (1804-1834)
⑳ **San Rafael Arcángel** (1817-1834)
㉑ **San Francisco Solano** (1823-1834)

PRESIDIOS
① San Diego (1769)
② San Francisco (1770)
③ Monterey (1770)
④ Santa Bárbara (1782)

or sexual abuse at the hands of settlers. Revolts broke out among neophytes; unconverted Indians outside mission lands frequently harassed those who lived within. At San Diego, Santa Barbara, Monterey and San Francisco, military garrisons known as **presidios** were built to safeguard the Spanish holdings against both foreign and Native American attacks.

Though conversion of Indians began slowly, by 1833 some 88,000 neophytes had been baptized and 31,000 lived within mission landholdings. In 1834, still grappling with the political and economic turmoil following its independence from Spain 13 years earlier, the Mexican congress voted to secularize the missions of Alta California. The state's governor at the time, **José Figueroa** (1792–1835), himself partly of Native American descent, issued proclamations of secularization that would prevent land-grabbing of mission property, but his orders were not strictly followed.

In 1845–46 his successor as governor, **Pío Pico** (1801–94), sold off 15 of the missions to private buyers, and all mission property eventually passed into private ownership. Mission buildings were used for a wide range of secular and profane purposes, and many fell into disrepair. Not until 1862 did some of the chapels and grounds revert to religious use, when President Abraham Lincoln signed executive orders returning them to the Catholic Church. Since the beginning of the 20C, many of the missions have been restored as legacies of California's Spanish past, their chapels in use today as local parish churches.

MEXICAN PERIOD

Bridling against rule from distant Spain, colonists of New Spain (Mexico) broke out in revolt against their mother country in 1810, finally gaining independence in 1821. The new republic adopted a laissez-faire attitude toward Alta California, appointing a succession of governors who promoted the colonization of the territory by granting huge parcels of land to loyal subjects and ambitious foreigners. These land grants formed the basis of vast cattle ranches, or *ranchos*. Some grants were bought up by wealthy families to form holdings of 300,000 acres or more; the Pico family of Southern California controlled more than half a million acres.

Out of these vast and lonely pastures came the cattle hides—"California bank notes"—and tallow that lured Yankee clipper ships from New York and Boston around Cape Horn on trading expeditions such as that described by Richard Henry Dana in *Two Years Before the Mast* (1840). The merchant ships in turn brought manufactured goods for California's growing population and carried back East tales of a gracious, hospitable way of life: leisurely roundups, exciting rodeos and weeklong fiestas centered on the sprawling adobe ranch houses. The romantic era of the California *ranchos* lasted only briefly during the 1830s and 1840s, but their style endures in the architecture of some areas of modern California and in the names of such great landholding families as Pico, Estudillo, Alvarado, Vallejo, Castro and Sepúlveda, which grace towns and thoroughfares from San Diego to Sonoma County.

AMERICANIZATION

Much of California's growth during the final years of Mexican rule came from immigration by US citizens seeking land grants. During the same period, California attracted adventurous and enterprising explorers and settlers. A party led by Jedediah Smith (1799–1831) crossed the Mojave Desert in 1826; the following year, the members of the group became the first white men to cross the Sierra Nevada. In 1827 James Ohio Pattie followed a desert route into California along the Gila River. In 1833–34, some 60 trappers led by Joseph Walker blazed what was later called the **Oregon Trail**—the preferred immigrant trail to the state and one of several passages that collectively became known as the **California Trail**.

The Sierra Nevada proved a perilous crossing throughout the 1840s, however, despite some well-advertised suc cesses by transcontinental wagon trains like the **Bidwell-Bartleson Party** from Missouri in 1841. The perils inherent in such journeys were tragically dramatized by the Donner Party, a group of 87 men, women and children who were trapped by heavy snows in the eastern Sierra during the fierce winter of 1846–47. Not until the 1850s were primitive roads developed for wheeled vehicles across the Sierra Nevada.

Mexican fears grew that the US might annex California, and American immigration was banned in 1845. The government was threatened by surveys across the Sierra conducted by **John C. Frémont** (1813–90), a US Army topographical engineer sometimes guided by legendary scout **Kit Carson** (1809–68). In March 1846, the armed foreigners were ordered from California, and Frémont defiantly raised the US flag on Gabilan Peak (above Mission San Juan Bautista) before retreating to Oregon.

Three months later, after the **Mexican War** broke out in Texas between the US and Mexico, Americans hoisted above the Mexican barracks in Sonoma a flag displaying a brown bear and a lone star; in what became known as the **Bear Flag** Revolt, Frémont announced an independent California Republic. Within weeks, John D. Sloat captured the California capital at Monterey, declaring the territory a US possession. War with Mexico in California ended in January 1847, and the **Treaty of Guadalupe Hidalgo** ceded California and other Mexican possessions in the Southwest to the US in February 1848. In September 1849, 48 elected delegates met at Monterey to draft and adopt a state constitution, and US President Millard Fillmore formally granted California statehood on September 9, 1850.

THE GOLD RUSH AND THE GREAT MIGRATION

A few weeks before the formal peace with Mexico, flecks of gold were discovered in the tailrace at John Sutter's lumber mill on the American River in the Sierra foothills. News of the discovery drew international attention, and by the following year (1849), fortune hunters—known ever since as "Forty-Niners"—began to pour by land and sea into California from the eastern US, Europe, Australia, Asia and South America. Along with thousands of would-be miners came more tradesmen, moneylenders, innkeepers, teamsters, preachers, gamblers, prostitutes and criminals.

Following statehood, the opportunities inherent in California's vast expanses drew settlers other than those seeking quick fortunes in the mines. In 1850 alone, an estimated 45,000 people migrated along the California Trail. The state's Caucasian population, estimated at 15,000 in 1848, had grown to almost 100,000 in 1850.

After the surface gold that drew so many people to the state was depleted, thousands of fortune hunters returned home or moved on to other opportunities. California's diverse and growing population raised cattle, farmed, mined and built booming commercial cities, including San Francisco, Sacramento and Stockton. By 1860 the state population exceeded 380,000, and there were 10 times as many cattle as in 1848. Wheat became the major crop of the Sacramento and San Joaquin Valleys, and California's year-round production of nearly every kind of nontropical fruit and vegetable began in the coastal valleys and the Los Angeles Basin.

The discovery of the vast **Comstock Lode** of silver near Virginia City, Nevada, in 1859 gave further impetus to California's growth. Yielding about $400 million in two decades, it pumped capital into the industrial development of the region and created a powerful San Francisco-based financial elite of mine owners, entrepreneurs and bankers, including the "Bonanza Firm" mine-owning quartet of John W. Mackay, James Fair, James C. Flood and William S. O'Brien; Bank of California founders William C. Ralston, William Sharon and Darius Ogden Mills; Adolph Sutro, who would become mayor and largest property owner in San Francisco; and mining magnate George Hearst, father of news mogul William Randolph Hearst.

THE RAILROADS

Despite its growth, prosperity and state-hood, California's links to the US east of the Mississippi remained tenuous and arduous. There were four-horse over-land coaches, ox-drawn wagons, sea routes around Cape Horn, steamships with land connections across Nicaragua or Panama, the short-lived Pony Express mail service, and finally, in 1861, the establishment of the transcontinental telegraph.

The Civil War (1861–65), during which a steady flow of California gold and Comstock silver was essential to the Union campaign, increased national demand for a transcontinental rail-road. In 1857 railroad construction engineer **Theodore D. Judah** (1826–63) developed and published his plan for building a railroad through Dutch Flat and Donner Pass in the Sierra Nevada. Financiers Collis P. Huntington, Mark Hopkins, Leland Stanford and Charles Crocker, whose subsequent wealth and power brought them the popular nickname "the **Big Four**," signed on to Judah's plan and in 1861 established the Central Pacific Railroad Co.

With the US Congress granting land for 20 miles in either direction of the route and providing generous subsidies as high as $48,000 per mile for track laid in steep terrain, the **Central Pacific Rail-road** began its eastward construction from Sacramento on January 8, 1863. As many as 15,000 Chinese laborers laid track in a frantic race to meet the west-ward-bound **Union Pacific Railroad**, eventually joining tracks at Promontory, Utah, on May 10, 1869, for the driving of the final Golden Spike linking East and West. Other railroads, built in the decades that followed, included the Southern Pacific Railroad and the Santa Fe Railroad; they linked San Francisco and Los Angeles to the rest of the US via Arizona, New Mexico and Colorado.

THE CLOSE OF THE 19C

While fostering growth, the railroads flooded California with comparatively cheaper industrialized goods from the eastern states, driving many Cali-fornia factories into bankruptcy and their workers into unemployment. A nationwide depression and antiforeign attitudes fostered acts of mob violence against Chinese immigrants in the 1870s, as well as federal **Chinese Exclusion Acts**. Racial tensions also found tragic outlet in 1872-73 in the US Army's crush-ing of an uprising by the Modoc tribe. California continued to lure immigrants, sometimes trapping them in boom-and-bust land speculation cycles, as in Southern California in the 1880s. The 1875 depression led to the failure of many banks. Despite another panic in 1893, California faced the 20C with its economic output more than double that of a decade earlier.

20TH CENTURY

In 1900, California had a population of nearly 1.5 million people. In the decades that followed, the state grew almost twice as quickly as the rest of the nation, achieving a 1920 population of more than 3.4 million and reaching almost 10.6 million in 1950.

Much of this growth was fueled by bur-geoning industries, predominantly in Southern California. Improvements in agricultural techniques during the 1890s and the advent of cooperative marketing through the founding of the California Fruit Growers Exchange (1905) boosted citrus growing. Oil drilling spread across Los Angeles and neighboring counties, with production rising from 4.3 million barrels in 1900 to 105.7 million in 1920. Before World War I, the movie industry found clement weather and a diversity of natural backdrops in and around the L.A. suburb of Hollywood, transforming it into the movie capital of the world.

Two world wars boosted the aircraft and shipbuilding industries, fed the econo-mies of towns near military bases, and swelled the population with servicemen and women who remained in Califor-nia after demobilizing. The population leaped from 6.9 million in 1940 to 15.6 million in 1960; by 1980 it had risen to 23.6 million, and to 29.9 million in 1990. By the year 2000, the state's population numbered nearly 34 million.

CONTEMPORARY CALIFORNIA

Such phenomenal growth has dramatically impacted many aspects of the state's 20C history. Water supplies, for example, have been sorely stressed. Although the greatest percentage of the population and the most extensive agricultural activity are concentrated in Southern California, approximately 75 percent of the state's water flows from streams in the north. Schemes to divert water, such as the Central Valley and Owens Valley projects and the State Water Project, have remained heated political issues throughout the century.

Spurred by a constant influx of new citizens, the state has become a hotbed for political action and change. In 1911 statewide political reforms gave Californians the right to exercise the **initiative**, whereby a petition signed by 8 percent of voters could place a proposed statute, ordinance or constitutional amendment on the ballot; the **referendum**, by which government measures could be put to a popular vote; and the **recall**, through which voters could remove an elected official from office.

The passage of a gasoline tax in 1923 raised funds to build a state highway system, literally paving the way for Californians' love affair with the automobile. In the fall of 1964, the **Free Speech Movement** on the campus of UC Berkeley gave students a voice in political and social causes nationwide. In unprecedented protests, students insisted that the university lift a ban on on-campus political activities. From the early 1960s until his death, **Cesar Chavez** (1927-93) organized and fought for the rights of farmworkers in California's agricultural regions. In June 1978, the Jarvis-Gann initiative, passed as **Proposition 13**, expressed the electorate's desire to curb state taxation of individuals.

Beginning in the 1970s, California's population growth began to taper somewhat. Some surveys indicated that more people were leaving the state than settling here. Yet since the 2000 census, the state's population has risen from 33.8 million to 37 million.

THE NEW MILLENNIUM

Like much of the rest of the US and the world, the state grapples with economic, social and environmental plagues at the start of the 21C. The recessions of the early 1990s and 2008, and federal spending cuts hurt California's defense industry, contributing to unemployment and a severe economic downturn. Pollution fouls the air, lakes, rivers and coastal waters; acid rain threatens the Central Valley and the Sierra Nevada; and offshore oil spills, such as that which occurred in the Santa Barbara Channel in 1969, occasionally blacken the coastline. Rioting in Los Angeles and its suburbs, following the first verdicts in the 1992 Rodney King civil-rights trial, placed severe social inequities into sharp relief. Immigration remains a sensitive topic as boat people arrive from Asia and Latinos stream across the Mexican border.

Nature can also be unpredictable. Statewide drought has led to strict water rationing in some areas, yet torrential rains and massive snowfalls have caused devastating floods in the North Coast, Central Valley and other isolated regions, including Yosemite Valley in 1997. Wildfires have devastate many areas, populated and not, and serious earthquakes such as those at Loma Prieta near San Francisco (October 1989) and the Los Angeles suburb of Northridge (January 1994) leave residents dreading the long-predicted "Big One" along the San Andreas Fault.

Responses to such challenges include the 1960 formation of the Motor Vehicle Pollution Control Board, charged with monitoring carbon-monoxide emissions from automobiles; work by such environmentalist organizations as the Sierra Club, TreePeople and Save the Whales; and development of new construction techniques and building codes designed to increase resistance to fire and earthquakes. Decades-long discussions about partitioning the state into two or three separate (and more easily governable) bodies continue into the 21C, the lack of resolution perhaps acknowledging the fact that there can only ever be one California.

TIME LINE

1542 **Juan Rodríguez Cabrillo**, a Portuguese explorer in the service of Spain, enters San Diego Bay.

1564 Manila galleons begin landing in Alta California en route to and from the Philippines.

1579 Explorer **Francis Drake** anchors near Point Reyes to repair his ship and claims Alta California for England.

1602 **Sebastián Vizcaíno**, a Spanish explorer, anchors in Monterey Bay.

1769 The Sacred Expedition, led by **Padre Junípero Serra** and **Gaspar de Portolá**, sets out from Mexico to establish the mission chain in Alta California. San Diego de Alcalá, the first of California's 21 missions, is founded.

1774 Juan Bautista de Anza forges the **Anza Trail**, an overland route from Sonora, Mexico, to the San Gabriel Arcángel Mission.

1776 Founding of San Francisco.

1781 Los Angeles is founded by a group of settlers led by Felipe de Neve, the Spanish governor of California.

1812 **Fort Ross** is established on the North Coast, marking the southernmost Russian presence in North America.

1819 **Adams-Onís Treaty** establishes northern boundary of Alta California along the 42nd parallel.

1821 **Mexican independence** from Spain is achieved.

1822 Spain cedes California to Mexico.

1826 American trapper **Jedediah Smith** travels overland from the eastern US to California.

1833-34 **Secularization** of the mission chain is decreed by the Mexican government.

1839 Swiss immigrant **John Sutter** establishes New Helvetia and builds Sutter's Fort in present-day Sacramento.

1841 **The Bidwell-Bartleson Party**, organized to blaze a trail across the Rocky Mountains, arrives in California, opening the way for settlers in the Great Westward Migration.

1846 Declaration of the **Mexican War**. American settlers stage the **Bear Flag Revolt** in Sonoma. One month later, Commodore John Sloat claims Alta California for the US.

1847 Capt. José María Flores and Gov. Pío Pico surrender to American forces in the **Cahuenga Capitulation**, completing US conquest of California. One of California's first newspapers, the *California Star*, is published in San Francisco by Sam Brannan.

1848 James Marshall discovers gold in the tailrace of John Sutter's sawmill at Coloma, sparking the California **Gold Rush** of 1849. **Treaty of Guadalupe Hidalgo** is signed, concluding the Mexican War.

19C firehouse, Main Street, Nevada City

Dave Carter/ Nevada City Chamber of Commerce

1849 California's Constitutional Convention meets in Monterey; the constitution is ratified by popular vote on November 13.

1850 California enters the Union as the 31st state.

1854 State capital is transferred from Benicia to Sacramento.

1859 The **Comstock Lode** silver deposits are discovered in neighboring Nevada; the resultant wealth fuels commerce and manufacturing in San Francisco and Los Angeles.

1861 Establishment of the first **transcontinental telegraph**.

1868 The College of California in Oakland is taken over by the state, chartered and renamed the **University of California**. The campus is moved to Berkeley in 1873.

1869 The Central Pacific and Union Pacific railroads are joined at Promontory, Utah, creating the first **transcontinental railroad**.

1872-73 Modoc War arises from conflict between Modoc natives and American settlers.

1878 Navel orange trees from Brazil thrive in the area around Riverside, giving birth to California's citrus industry.

1880–82 Chinese Exclusion Acts are passed by the federal government to restrict immigration of Asians to the US (act repealed in 1943).

1890 **Yosemite National Park** and **Sequoia National Park** are created by congressional act.

1891 **Stanford University** is established in Palo Alto.

1905 Produce wholesaler A.P. Giannini, an Italian immigrant, founds the Bank of Italy, later called the Bank of America, in San Francisco.

1906 **Great Earthquake and Fire** devastate San Francisco; the earthquake is estimated at 8.3 on the Richter scale.

1911 The current California state flag is adopted by the state legislature.

1913 **Los Angeles Aqueduct** brings water from Owens Valley to Los Angeles.
Hollywood's first feature film, *The Squaw Man*, is shot in a barn at the corner of Selma and Vine streets.

1915 **Panama-Pacific International Exposition** in San Francisco celebrates the city's recovery from the 1906 earthquake. **Panama-California International Exposition** opens in San Diego.

1927 Hollywood's first successful talkie is released: *The Jazz Singer,* starring Al Jolson, ends the era of silent films.

1932 **Summer Olympic Games** are held in Los Angeles.

1935 **Central Valley Project** is completed, bringing water from the Sacramento and San Joaquin rivers to irrigate the Central Valley.

1936-37 The **San Francisco-Oakland Bay Bridge** and the **Golden Gate Bridge** open in San Francisco.

1941 US enters **World War II.** California's aviation industry booms.

1942 President Franklin D. Roosevelt signs Executive Order 9066, stipulating internment of Japanese Americans.

1947 The "Hollywood Ten," a group of prominent personalities in the film industry, are blacklisted for their refusal to testify before the House Un-American Activities Committee.

1955 Great fanfare heralds the opening of **Disneyland**, situated in the orange groves of rural Anaheim.

1958 Major league baseball: the Brooklyn Dodgers relocate to L.A., and the New York Giants move to San Francisco.

1961 **The Beach Boys**, heartthrob singers of the "California sound," are formed. Their hit singles, including *Surfin' USA*, spread the California Dream across the US.

1964 Free Speech Movement sit-ins at the University of California, Berkeley, lead to mass arrests of student protesters.

1965 **Watts Riots** rage through an African-American enclave in suburban Los Angeles in response to the repeal of the Rumford Fair Housing Act forbidding racial discrimination.

1967 San Francisco's Haight-Ashbury district welcomes hippies to the "Summer of Love."

1968 **Robert F. Kennedy** is assassinated in Los Angeles.

1969 **Richard Nixon**, a native of Yorba Linda and former US senator (1950–52), takes office as the 37th US President.

late 1960s California surpasses New York as the nation's most populous state, with nearly 20 million inhabitants.

1978 San Francisco mayor and gay-rights sympathizer **George Moscone** and openly gay city supervisor **Harvey Milk** are assassinated by disgruntled city supervisor Dan White.

1980 **Ronald Reagan**, former movie star and governor of California (1966-75), is elected 40th US President.

1984 **Summer Olympic Games** are held in Los Angeles.

1989 Loma Prieta earthquake, measuring 7.1 on the Richter scale, strikes south of the San Francisco Bay Area.

1992 **Riots** occur in South Central Los Angeles, sparked by the verdict of the Rodney King civil rights trial.

1993 **Dianne Feinstein** and **Barbara Boxer** join the US Senate; California is the first state to have two women senators simultaneously in office.

1994 **Northridge earthquake**, measuring 6.8 on the Richter scale, strikes the San Fernando Valley north of L.A.
Congress passes the **Desert Protection Act**, creating Death Valley National Park, Joshua Tree National Park and Mojave National Preserve.

1998 Controversial state law bans smoking from all public areas, including bars and restaurants.

2000 The census reveals the state's population as 33,871,648.

2001 California experiences state-wide rolling blackouts in a severe energy crisis.

2002 The Anaheim Angels beat the San Francisco Giants to win the World Series.

2003 Known for his starring role in the *Terminator* films, Republican **Arnold Schwarzenegger** is elected governor in a recall election that defeats Democratic incumbent Gray Davis.

2004 Two mobile robots created in Cal Tech's Jet Propulsion Lab successfully land on Mars.

2005 The state applies for exemption from federal Clean Air Act to more aggressively regulate pollutants.

2006 Getty Villa Museum reopens after a nine-year renovation.

2007 California Congresswoman **Nancy Pelosi** becomes the first woman elected to serve as Speaker of the US House of Representatives.

2008 Three **California condor** chicks hatch in the wild; the largest bird in America, the condor is nearly extinct.

2008–2009 Worsening economic conditions in late 2008 left California State with a **budget crisis**. A referendum on compensatory measures was not approved in Feb 2009, while disagreement in the State legislature later left it issuing IOUs to meet its short-term financial commitment.

Art and Culture

California's legendary light, land-scape and climate, along with influ-ences of indigenous and immigrant cultures, have contributed to unique and vital developments in visual art, giving rise to the state's growing reputation as an international art and culture capital.

THE ARTS

NATIVE AND HISPANIC ART

Diverse and distinct Native American cultures flourished in California for more than 7,000 years prior to the arrival of Europeans. Pictographs by early cultures remain at Lava Beds National Monument and Chumash Painted Cave near Santa Barbara, while featherwork regalia and elaborately patterned basketry flour-ished throughout California.

Spanish Colonial arts were introduced into the region by the padres of the mission chain established after 1769. The wall and ceiling murals of churches at San Juan Bautista Mission and San Miguel Arcángel Mission reveal a min-gling of indigenous motifs and sym-bolism with Neoclassical and Spanish Colonial aesthetic traditions.

The blend is also evident in paintings, silverwork, church implements, textiles and furnishings of the period.

19TH-CENTURY INFLUENCES

The influx of people and wealth that ensued in the wake of the Gold Rush set the stage for the presence of imported art in California. The vast fortunes of railroad magnates and other "bonanza kings" gave rise to important private collections (including the Huntington Art Collections in San Marino, and the Crocker Art Museum, in Sacramento). Likewise, this wealth introduced art from Europe and the eastern US, enabling Impressionism, eclecticism and genre painting to influence art in the state.

Mid- to late-19C artists, including painter Albert Bierstadt and photog-rapher Carleton Watkins, were inspired by the state's magnificent vistas to cre-ate heroic landscapes that gave many people living in the East their first look at the wonders of California. A growing public interest in art was fueled during the last quarter of the century by the founding of the California School of Fine Arts (today known as the San Francisco Art Institute), the Fine Arts Museums of San Francisco and the Southwest Museum (now the Southwest Museum of the American Indian).

Valley of the Yosemite by Albert Bierstadt

© Burstein Collection/Corbis

EARLY 20TH CENTURY

Early in the century, art colonies were formed in Carmel, La Jolla, Laguna Beach and other picturesque coastal communities. California Impressionists and painters of the **Plein-air movement** (including Franz Bischoff), and later Oakland's Society of Six, created sparkling landscapes inspired by the region's unique light and natural features.

With the growth of Los Angeles in the early 20C and the burgeoning of the entertainment industry, Southern California art embraced a more modern and abstract profile, perhaps most notably in the work of Stanton Macdonald-Wright, who adapted Cubist forms to create a style that he dubbed Synchromist. Noted primitive and modern art collector Walter Arensberg was at the center of a growing art community that included ceramist Beatrice Wood. During the 1930s, abstraction, surrealism and social realism characterized the works of painters and muralists. Mexican painter **Diego Rivera** completed several murals in San Francisco, while José Orozco and David Siqueiros each painted murals in Los Angeles. These works inspired the realism of the Works Progress Administration murals as well as the murals of California's contemporary barrios and urban communities.

During the early part of the century, California's dramatic natural landscapes attracted such sharp-focus photographers as Edward Weston and Ansel Adams, the latter particularly noted for his transcendent portrayals of Yosemite National Park. Other photographers, among them Dorothea Lange and Imogen Cunningham, documented California's inhabitants.

POST-WORLD WAR II

As the mid-20C approached, San Francisco Art Institute visiting faculty members Clyfford Still and Mark Rothko inspired an explosion of abstract painting by their students, including Sam Francis and Robert Motherwell. In response, such painters as Elmer Bischoff, Richard Diebenkorn and David

Diego Rivera completing a mural in San Francisco, California Stock Exchange Club rooms

© Bettmann/Corbis

Park created a painterly representational movement known as **Bay Area Figurative**. The impact of the popular culture inspired 1960s Pop artists and photorealists (Ed Ruscha, Wayne Thiebaud, Robert Bechtle), followed by a wave of conceptualism (Bruce Nauman, William T. Wiley).

In Southern California during the postwar period, several art museums, including the Los Angeles County Museum of Art, expanded significantly. Los Angeles painters explored hard-edged abstraction (John McLaughlin, Lorser Feitelson), influencing a "finish fetish" focus on surface and light evident in the perceptualist works of Robert Irwin and James Turrel. An influential art scene developed in the 1950s around the Ferus Gallery, launching the careers of Edward Kienholz and Ed Moses. Subsequent decades brought several new museums and galleries to the Los Angeles area, including the J. Paul Getty Museum and the Museum of Contemporary Art, making that city an important international art center. Such noted resident artists as David Hockney, Jonathan Borofsky and Guillermo Gómez-Peña helped focus art-world attention on Southern California.

California's contemporary art scene is defined by its pluralism and eclecticism. Multicultural arts centers, such as

San Francisco's Yerba Buena Gardens, and spaces for large installations have appeared in the last several years. Performance artists such as Chris Burden continue to expand current conceptions of art, and innovative work can be seen at venues throughout the state.

PERFORMING ARTS

The state continues to be a recognized source of popular music, a trend which began in the 1960s with the hit songs of such groups as the Beach Boys, the Mamas and the Papas, and the Grateful Dead. Los Angeles is a capital of the recording industry nationwide, drawing hopefuls determined to make it big in any number of music genres from rock, jazz, pop and especially hip-hop. Classical music enjoys an avid following statewide, satisfied primarily by the regular performance schedules of high-caliber orchestras in Los Angeles and San Francisco; other orchestras thrive in the smaller cities. The Los Angeles Opera, the San Francisco Opera and the San Diego Opera mount major performance seasons, and the San Francisco Ballet maintains a resident dance company. Drawn by a creative, sunny environment as well as by Hollywood's siren song, many actors and writers practice their art and craft on California's stages, creating a thriving theater scene. Nationally recognized repertory programs of classics and original works are presented in San Francisco, Los Angeles, Pasadena, Berkeley, La Jolla and San Diego.

ARCHITECTURE

A benign, largely Mediterranean climate, abundant natural building materials, waves of immigrants and recurring collisions between romance and reality have all shaped the architectural mosaic.

NATIVE AND SPANISH ARCHITECTURE

Little architectural evidence remains of the peoples who occupied California prior to the arrival of the Spanish. The first of many imported building traditions arrived as the Spanish padres, soldiers and settlers, bent on colonizing

Alta California, erected forts (presidios), farming communities (pueblos) and religious edifices (missions). Though Padre Junípero Serra established nine missions prior to his death in 1784, it was a successor, Padre Fermín Lasuén, who developed the California mission style.

Based on Spanish and, more specifically, Mexican monastery prototypes, the California mission complex generally took the form of a large, rectangular garden courtyard surrounded by a narrow, adobe-walled church and arcaded structures containing padres' living quarters (*conventos*), barracks, workshops, infirmary, and dormitories for unmarried Indian women and young children. The church typically occupied the northeast corner of the courtyard. Its signature element became its bell tower or *campanario*, a simple, high front wall with arched openings for bells. Outbuildings included more workshops and neophyte dwellings.

For their primary building material, the Franciscans turned to adobe, a plentiful local black clay. Adobe bricks were made by filling molds with a mixture of mud and straw, which was then sun-dried. Walls were several feet thick and narrowed toward the top. Overhanging tile roofs and lime plastering kept the bricks from deteriorating in wet weather.

Inspiration for the details of design and ornamentation came from many sources, including antiquity (Santa Bárbara Mission) and the Baroque and Moorish architecture of Spain (San Carlos Borromeo de Carmelo Mission). The missions' arcaded walkways and bell towers reappeared in many Mission Revival buildings of the late 19C and early 20C.

19TH CENTURY

California's Mexican settlers typically built rectangular, one-story, adobe-walled structures with floors of packed earth and flat roofs covered in tar (*brea*). Houses of the wealthy, such as the Casa de Estudillo in San Diego and the Casa de la Guerra in Santa Barbara, opened to a courtyard along a covered porch or *corredor*.

Anglo architectural influences first appeared during the 1830s with the two-story, veranda-wrapped Larkin House in Monterey, which combined adobe and redwood frame construction with glazed, double-hung windows and fireplaces. The house's wrap-around balconies and shingled hip roof characterize the **Monterey Colonial** style.

The Gold Rush of 1849 caused an abrupt shift from Hispanic to American architecture. Settlers arriving in the aftermath of the Great Westward Migration built wood-frame houses with materials and embellishments shipped from abroad or from the eastern US, including chimney bricks, mantelpieces and Gothic Revival-style ornamentation. Other pioneers shipped entire houses of prefabricated sheet metal or wood from faraway places like Boston, London and Canton.

As the century progressed into the Victorian era, wooden, balloon-frame construction for residences came into vogue, reaching a climax in distinctive rows of houses built from the 1870s to 1890s in San Francisco and other cities of Northern California, where redwood lumber was readily available. Known popularly as Victorians, such houses displayed a hodgepodge of loosely defined

and overlapping architectural styles and resulted from rapidly evolving industrial processes, tastes and merchandising techniques. Pattern-book and millwork catalog publishers added to the rich stylistic soup preferred by an increasingly fashion-conscious middle class.

Victorians were built in a range of styles. The **Italianate** style, prevalent through the 1870s, employed flat-front or bay-windowed designs with relatively simple Classical details like keystones. Such houses were essentially wooden versions of the brick or brownstone row houses popular in eastern cities.

A more skeletal, "sticklike" ornamental emphasis, considered a variant of the American Stick style, appeared in the 1880s. In its time it was known by various names, including **Eastlake** after English author and furniture designer Charles Eastlake. Hallmarks were increasing verticality and rectangularity, and a new vocabulary of machined, wood-strip ornament that is often indistinguishable from furniture treatments. The so-called **Queen Anne** style produced some of California's most picturesque Victorian houses during the 1880s and 1890s, including the Carson Mansion in Eureka. Irregular plans and elevations, varied surface patterns, towers and

MICHELIN

Carson Mansion

63

turrets, high chimneys, bulging bays, recessed balconies and gables of all sizes abounded.

20TH CENTURY

Beaux-Arts Classicism came into vogue in California, as in the rest of the country, after it was popularized at the Chicago Fair of 1893, and reached its apogee in the San Francisco Civic Center. With the arrival of steel-frame construction, downtown commercial buildings—still clad in brick or stone for fireproofing—rose to 10 stories or more. Hinting at technological possibilities to come were two precedent-shattering designs: the glass-roofed atrium of George Wyman's 1893 Bradbury Building in Los Angeles, and the glass "curtain wall" facade of Willis Polk's 1917 Hallidie Building in San Francisco.

By the turn of the 19C, the high ideals of the international Arts and Crafts movement had migrated west and begun to blossom in the work of such local architects as Charles and Henry Greene and Bernard Maybeck. The Greenes' Japan-influenced emphasis on meticulous craftsmanship, structural expression, and the wedding of house and garden produced the landmark Gamble House in Pasadena and spawned California's first architectural export: the **bungalow**. Countless variations of the California bungalow—a one-story wood or

George Wyman's 1893 Bradbury Building in Los Angeles

© Tim Street-Porter/Beateworks/Corbis

stucco-sheathed house with a pergola or porch opening to a garden—were built from pattern books across the country during the first two decades of the century. A more radical, sculptural approach to house design arrived during the late 1910s, when Southern California's halcyon environment inspired preeminent US architect **Frank Lloyd Wright** to create some of his most inventive designs, including the Hollyhock House in Los Angeles.

The early 1920s saw the rise of the **Spanish Colonial Revival** style, stimulated by enthusiastic public response to the unabashedly romantic, stage-set buildings of San Diego's 1915 Panama-California Exposition. There, New York architect Bertram Goodhue took his inspiration directly from the elaborately ornamented, domed, tiled and stucco-walled Spanish Colonial architecture of Mexico. After a severe earthquake in 1923, Santa Barbara embraced the fashion by rebuilding its major institutional structures along Spanish Colonial Revival lines.

Throughout the US in the late 1920s, an increasingly industrialized society set architects searching for ways to express modernity without historical reference. **art deco** or **Moderne**, with its elegant lines, shiny surfaces and highly stylized ornamentation, was eagerly adopted by the automobile and movie-industry culture of Southern California as a fitting expression of its glamorous image. Early art deco ornament generally followed cubistic or zigzag patterns, as in the 1929 Bullocks Wilshire department store and Claude Beelman's 1930 Eastern Columbia Building in Los Angeles, while later structures borrowed the concept of streamlining from automobile and airplane design.

Other approaches eliminated applied ornament, allowing the structure to express its function. This philosophy formed the basis for the **International Style**, which first appeared in California in the primarily residential work of such architects as Richard Neutra, who emigrated from Vienna in the 1920s, and Rudolf Schindler.

Taking the idea of architectural packaging to its logical conclusion were the many idiosyncratic vernacular roadside eateries that took the form of such unlikely objects as a zeppelin or a hat, the most renowned example being the Brown Derby restaurant in Los Angeles (now demolished). Vernacular structures formed the basis of a type of architecture dubbed California Crazy; a recent incarnation is the binocular-shaped Chiat-Day-Mojo building (1991, **Frank Gehry**) in Venice.

POST-WORLD WAR II

California construction boomed prodigiously after the war, as aviation and other industries expanded and the incoming population reached a flood tide. The state functioned as a laboratory for experimentation in residential architecture, especially around Los Angeles and the San Francisco Bay Area, where architects perfected the modern, flowing, open-plan house. The subdivision ranch house, popularized by Los Angeles designer-developer Cliff May, became synonymous with California during the 1950s and early 1960s, and was rapidly adopted throughout the US. Descended from the California bungalow, the often sprawling ranch house was long and low, with a two-car garage, and combined modern built-in appliances with a vague hint of Spanish California romance.

Eastern Columbia Building

MICHELIN

Worlds apart aesthetically, but sharing a common ancestry in California barn architecture, is the shed-roofed condominium complex at Sea Ranch, designed in 1965 by Charles Moore and his associates. Sea Ranch's particular quality of blending with its surroundings spawned a new style that was adopted for beach and resort construction throughout the US.

RECENT TRENDS

The downtowns of Los Angeles, San Diego and San Francisco have been remade several times since the 1950s, sprouting ever-taller buildings in a wide variety of styles, from corporate

View of San Diego's contemporary skyline

Joanne DiBona/San Diego CVB

International Style through Postmodern and beyond. Renowned Los Angeles-based architect **Frank Gehry** expresses California's experimental nature in his work both at home and abroad, using ordinary materials like plywood or chain-link fencing in innovative and often sculptural ways; his most recent work is the **Disney Concert Hall** in Los Angeles. World-renowned architects who have left their marks on the state include Louis Kahn (La Jolla's Salk Institute; Michael Graves (the Napa Valley's Clos Pegase winery, and Burbank's Disney Studios headquarters); Cesar Pelli (Los Angeles' Pacific Design Center); and Philip Johnson (San Francisco's 101 California Street).

An international team of architects led by Fumihiko Maki designed San Francisco's new art and park complex at Yerba Buena Gardens; Mario Botta designed the San Francisco Museum of Modern Art, which opened at Yerba Buena in 1995; and Richard Meier's acclaimed Getty Center complex opened on a Los Angeles hilltop in December 1997. More recently, Renzo Piano is continuing his work on the expansion of the Los Angeles County Museum of Art, and recently completed his groundbreaking new building for the California Academy of Sciences in San Francisco. Cesar Pelli completed the Red Building (2009) for the Pacific Design Center.

LITERATURE

No Native California tribes practiced writing, but many passed rich legacies of oral myths down through the generations, to be recorded by 19C and 20C historians and anthropologists—notably Alfred L. Kroeber, author of the *Handbook of the Indians of California* (1925). Vivid impressions of the Native Americans and their lands may also be found in diaries kept by 18C explorers, among them Padre Juan Crespí's journal of the Sacred Expedition of 1769 and Padre Francisco Garcés' memoir of a trek through the Mojave Desert and Tehachapi Mountains in 1776.

English-language accounts of travel and life in Hispanic California form the state's earliest indigenous literature; *Two Years Before the Mast* (1840) by Richard Henry Dana (1815–82) described life at sea along the California coast. The Gold Rush fueled an increase in publishing, spurring the rapid growth of the state's first two newspapers: *The Californian*, launched in 1846, and *The California Star*, first published in 1848 by Sam Brannan. Several literary journals appeared at the same time, including the Golden Era (1852), which published early works by Bret Harte (1836–1902), **Mark Twain** (1835–1910) and poets Joaquin Miller (1837–1913) and Charles Warren Stoddard (1843–1909). These and other writers gained national and international reputations describing the rough-and-ready life of mid- to late-19C California. In short stories such as "The Luck of Roaring Camp" and "The Outcasts of Poker Flat," Harte sharply etched a larger-than-life picture of Gold Rush country in readers' minds. Twain, who sojourned in San Francisco and the Gold Country in the early 1860s, published sketches of the region in the *Overland Monthly* and included vivid descriptions of the state in his books *Roughing It* and *Innocents Abroad*, as well as in his famous yarn, "The Celebrated Jumping Frog of Calaveras County."

Others who memorably chronicled the state were San Francisco journalist and short-story writer Ambrose Bierce (1842–1914), naturalist **John Muir** (1838–1914) and Scottish writer **Robert Louis Stevenson** (1850–94), who lived briefly in the Napa Valley. In Southern California, Helen Hunt Jackson (1830-85) wrote the phenomenally popular *Ramona* (1884), romanticizing life in the mission era.

20TH CENTURY

The social consciousness that pervaded early-20C American literature found voice in many California writers, including novelist Frank Norris (1870–1902) and poet Edwin Markham (1852–1940). Oakland native **Jack London** (1876–1916) wrote more than two dozen highly personal adventure novels espousing his socialist ideals. Pasadena-based novelist **Upton Sinclair** (1878-1968) campaigned against social inequities in some 90 published works; in 1934 he ran for California governor on the Democratic ticket but was defeated.

Through the 1920s Dashiell Hammett made San Francisco his home; the fog-cloaked slopes of Nob Hill provided a noir backdrop for the nighttime rambling of Sam Spade, Hammett's hard-boiled detective hero of *The Maltese Falcon*.

Novelist and short-story writer **John Steinbeck** (1902–68), who in 1962 became California's only winner of the Nobel Prize for Literature, wrote compassionately of the working people of the Central Valley and Monterey in such works as *Tortilla Flat* (1935), *Of Mice and Men* (1937), *The Grapes of Wrath* (1939) and *Cannery Row* (1945). The dark side of Hollywood's dream factories was probed by screenwriter Nathanael West (1903–40) in his apocalyptic novel *The Day of the Locust* (1939), while Raymond Chandler (1888–1959) departed from traditional detective fiction with four novels featuring hard-boiled L.A. private eye Philip Marlowe.

Fresno-born **William Saroyan** (1908–81) bestowed everyday life and ordinary people with magical beauty in his many novels, short stories and plays. Poet Robinson Jeffers (1887–1962) celebrated Carmel and its surroundings, underscoring mankind's insignificance within nature's greater scheme. Prolific novelist and historian Wallace Stegner (1909–93), who taught at Stanford University, evoked the power of the American West, winning a Pulitzer Prize for *Angle of Repose* (1971).

Disaffection with American society following World War II found expression among a group of San Francisco writers and other artists self-described as the "Beat Generation." They possessed, in the words of novelist **Jack Kerouac** (1922–69), "an inner knowledge … a kind of 'beatness.'" It was the 1957 publication of Kerouac's *On the Road*, typed as one very long paragraph in 20 days of April 1951, that catapulted him and his Beat cohorts to fame. According to poet and City Lights Bookstore founder Lawrence Ferlinghetti (b. 1919), "The emergence of the Beat Generation made North beach *the* literary center of San Francisco—and it nurtured a new vision that would spread far beyond its bounds." Poet Allen Ginsberg (1926–97), one of that vision's most articulate proponents, gave birth to the San Francisco poetry renaissance in 1955 when he read his poem *Howl* (first published by City Lights) to a standing-room-only audience.

In 1960 and 1961 Ken Kesey wrote *One Flew Over the Cuckoo's Nest*, his best-selling novel about a mental institution, from his home in Palo Alto. Journalist Tom Wolfe vividly captured the psychedelic counterculture in his 1969 book *The Electric Kool-Aid Acid Test*. In the 1970s Armistead Maupin followed the lives of young drifters in his long-running *San Francisco Chronicle* column, later published as the book *Tales of the City*. Before he died of AIDs in 1994, *Chronicle* journalist Randy Shilts (*And the Band Played On*) gained renown writing about gay liberation and the AIDS epidemic.

Today, a new generation of writers is producing work that runs the gamut of subjects and styles, from bestselling novels by Maxine Hong Kingston (b. 1940) and Amy Tan (b. 1952) that forge epic ties between California and Asia, to quirky tales of life in Los Angeles by San Fernando Valley-based novelist T. Coraghessan Boyle (b. 1948). They extend from emotionally charged poetry and prose by African-American writers Alice Walker (b. 1944) and Wanda Coleman (b. 1946) to the innovative, nationally acclaimed verse of Fresno-born Chicano poet Gary Soto (b. 1952). Novelist Anne Lamott, who lives in Marin County, has generated a legion of fans with her hilarious and heartfelt nonfiction books about recovery and redemption, and Anna Deveare Smith blurs the boundaries between journalism, literature and theater with her documentary-style stage presentations. Newer California writers find voice in serious and experimental literary magazines and journals, including the Bay Area's *Zoetrope: All-Story*, *Threepenny Review* and *Zyzzyva*.

Nature

The third-largest state in the US (163,707sq mi), California is bounded naturally by the Pacific Ocean on the west and the Colorado River on the southeast. The northern boundary with Oregon, the eastern with Nevada and the southern with Mexico are surveyors' straight lines. California stretches 850mi from its southeast to northwest corners, and the distance from the coast to its land borders averages 200mi. At 14,494ft, Mount Whitney, near Lone Pine, is the highest point in the contiguous 48 states, while the lowest point in the Western Hemisphere (282ft below sea level) is found at Badwater in Death Valley National Park.

GEOLOGIC FOUNDATIONS

The western US was formed, and is today greatly affected, by the collision of two plates—giant solidified sections of the earth's crust that move about atop the molten material of the earth's mantle. About 400 million years ago, the eastern edge of the Pacific plate, which extends nearly to Asia, slipped beneath the North American plate's western edge in a process known as subduction. As the Pacific plate continued to slide eastward under the overriding edge of the North American plate, sections of the earth's crust along the contact zone were compressed and crumpled, creating mountain ranges; smaller, outlying land masses, or **terranes**, coalesced with the North American plate. This accretion of crust fragments over tens of millions of years has added some 500mi of new land to western North America; California is the most unstable of these accreted terranes. Over the past 25 million years, the Pacific plate has begun to rotate counterclockwise and has shifted direction.

Today it is heading generally northwest, while the North American plate continues to move steadily west.

EARTHQUAKES

California's area of greatest tectonic instability is the **San Andreas rift** zone, running from the Imperial Valley in southeastern California to Cape Mendocino on the North Coast. The **San Andreas Fault**, as well as California's

The Richter Scale

In the 1940s, Charles Richter, a seismologist at the California Institute of Technology, devised a scale to measure the amount of energy released by an earthquake. Each whole-number increase on the scale represents a 10-fold increase in the amount of ground vibration.

Some of California's 20C Earthquakes	Year	Scale
San Francisco (San Francisco Bay Area)	1906	8.3
Lompoc (Central Coast)	1925	7.5
Imperial Valley (Colorado Desert)	1940	7.1
Kern County (Central Valley)	1952	7.7
Eureka (North Coast)	1980	7.0
Whittier Narrows (Greater Los Angeles)	1987	6.8
Loma Prieta (San Francisco Bay Area)	1989	7.1
Petrolia/Ferndale (North Coast)	1992	7.1
Yucca Valley (Mojave Desert)	1992	7.6
Northridge (Greater Los Angeles Area)	1994	6.8

other fault systems, is created by the motion of the Pacific and North American plates as they slide past each other at an average speed of 2in per year. Movements along faults can occur frequently, but sometimes the slide is impeded by rigid materials such as granite, and pressure increases as the plates strain to move. When the obstruction gives way, the pent-up pressure is released in an **earthquake**.

VOLCANOES

The volcanic region of northern California—marked by lava beds, hot springs, geysers, fumaroles and volcanic cones—results from the heat and pressure at the earth's center. Pressure is created by the subducted edge of the Pacific plate as it is pushed deeper toward the earth's superheated core, where it melts and expands. This molten material is then forced upward, sometimes exploding through the crust. The openings and the cones of material that build up around them, are known as **volcanoes**.

Volcanic cones of several types exist in California. Composite volcanoes (such as Mt. Shasta) result from repeated eruptions of thick lava from the same vent over thousands of years. The cone is thus composed of many layers of lava, cinders and ash. Composite volcanoes tend to erupt violently and grow precipitously upward. Shield volcanoes form when more fluid types of lava erupt smoothly from a vent, flowing long distances over the surface and creating a relatively flat cone such as that of Mt. Harkness in Lassen Volcanic National Park.

Cinder-cone volcanoes form as lava spews upward, solidifying and shattering into fragments that rain down to build a cone of cinders around the vent. Schonchin Butte, in Lava Beds National Monument, is an example of a cinder cone.

REGIONAL LANDSCAPES

California's rough-and-tumble geologic history has resulted in a remarkable diversity of landscapes within the state, from lushly forested, fog-draped slopes to shade-forsaken deserts.

THE COAST RANGES

With most peaks and ridge tops between 2,000ft and 5,000ft, this rugged belt of mountains is between 50mi and 75mi wide, and extends some 500mi from the Oregon border to Santa Barbara County. The Coast Ranges began to uplift about 25 million years ago as the edge of the North American plate crumpled and folded with the pressure of the Pacific plate. Rising abruptly from the sea in many places, these mountains hug the coastline and roll inland over folded ridges and fertile valleys that tend—like the coast itself—to adhere to an axis running northwest and southeast. The region owes its geomorphic composition to the fact that it consists of different accreted land masses.

The Coast Ranges are bisected by **San Francisco Bay**, the only sea-level break through the mountains between the Central Valley and the Pacific Ocean. The rivers draining the western slope of the Sierra Nevada and the flat plains of the Central Valley join and pass to the sea through this break. When the immobilization of vast amounts of water in continental glaciation lowered the sea level by some 300ft (the prevailing situation as recently as 15,000 years ago), what is now the bay was a typical elongated Coast Range valley. As the glaciers melted, the sea rose and drowned this valley, creating one of the world's great natural harbors. San Francisco Bay today covers some 496sq mi.

THE CENTRAL VALLEY

Between the Sierra Nevada on the east and the Coast Ranges on the west, tectonic plate movements have made a great trough in the earth's crust. Much of this space has been filled with sediment washed down from the surrounding mountains, creating an area of immensely fertile flat land about 440mi long and averaging 50mi wide. The northern and southern portions of this great, elongated grassland bear the names of the rivers that drain them: the **Sacramento Valley** in the north and the **San Joaquin Valley** in the south. The two rivers meet just inland from San

Francisco Bay to form the **Delta**, under natural conditions a tidal marsh but now engineered into a maze of agricultural islands resembling Dutch polders. With some 7 million acres under irrigation, the Central Valley is today considered among the most productive and varied agricultural regions in the world.

THE CASCADE RANGE AND THE MODOC PLATEAU

California's Cascade mountains (among them Mt. Lassen and Mt. Shasta) form the southern end of the Cascade Range, a line of volcanoes that extends through the Pacific Northwest into British Columbia. The Cascades were created about 5 million years ago by volcanic activity that shows no sign of abating. Mt. Shasta is a geologic twin of Washington's Mt. St. Helens, which erupted violently in 1980. Inland from Mt. Lassen and Mt. Shasta, in the far northeastern corner of California, lies the Modoc Plateau, a relatively flat region created by great outpourings of lava that continued until as recently as 30,000 years ago. The lava beds of the Modoc Plateau are punctuated by cinder cones that are no more than 1,000 years old.

THE SIERRA NEVADA

Roughly paralleling the Central Valley along its eastern border, the majestic Sierra Nevada (Spanish for "snowy range") is one of the highest mountain ranges in the contiguous 48 states. The mountains comprise an enormous block of granite that began to uplift about 10 million years ago and today tilts gently to the west. Eroding forces of rivers and glaciers have etched deep canyons into the western slope, creating the stunningly beautiful formations in Yosemite National Park and Sequoia and Kings Canyon National Parks.

The range breaks off steeply to the east, and the 10,000ft vertical sweep from the Owens Valley floor to the Sierra crest near Mt. Whitney may be the highest escarpment in the contiguous US. The Sierra crest bifurcates into an eastern and western summit ridge in two areas: in the south, where it is divided by the canyon of the Kern River; and in the middle, where a deep basin has filled with water to form Lake Tahoe. The southern portion of the range, between Tioga Pass and Walker Pass, is called the **High Sierra**.

Within this broad alpine fastness stands Mt. Whitney, several small glaciers and perpetual snowfields, sheltered in north-facing recesses and protected, shadowed clefts.

THE TRANSVERSE RANGES

The south end of the Coast Ranges merges with this east-west line of mountains that began to uplift 25 million years ago, although most rapidly through the last 3 million years. Although composed of granite like the Sierra Nevada, the Transverse Ranges reveal fewer signs of

California's desert in bloom

glaciation and erosion, owing to their location farther south.

The ranges lie along fault lines that extend from the San Andreas Fault system. Individual ranges include the Santa Ynez Mountains, which create a backdrop for Santa Barbara; the Santa Monica Mountains, bordering the basin of Los Angeles; the San Gabriel Mountains; and the San Bernardino Mountains, whose snowy peaks loom over Los Angeles. The Transverse Ranges continue out to sea to form the Channel Islands.

THE PENINSULAR RANGES

Actually the Coast Ranges of the far south, these mountains are the northern end of the range that forms the backbone of Mexico's narrow Baja California peninsula. Dominating the coastal landscape of San Diego, Orange and Riverside counties are the Santa Ana, San Jacinto and Santa Rosa mountains; several peaks, including Mt. San Jacinto, top 10,000ft. Granite outcrops and boulder fields are characteristic features.

On the west side of the Peninsular and Transverse ranges and in the angle between them lies a broad area of coastal plain that continues inland as far as the southern deserts. These coastal lowlands (which include the Los Angeles Basin) enjoy a dry, sunny climate tempered by ocean winds. Today they are occupied by vast metropolitan regions, including Los Angeles, San Diego and the cities of the Inland Empire.

THE DESERTS

The Sierra Nevada, along with the Cascade, Transverse and Peninsular ranges, forms an effective barrier to atmospheric moisture carried by prevailing westerly winds from the Pacific Ocean. The areas lying in this **rain shadow** receive less than 10in of precipitation per year, and are thus defined as desert.

Three types of desert exist in California, their differences stemming largely from variations in elevation. Ranging along the state's eastern border and encompassing the Modoc Plateau is the California portion of the **Great Basin Desert**, a vast area of interior drainage

that comprises most of Nevada and portions of neighboring states. The Great Basin is semi-arid bushland rather than true desert, but Death Valley, which sinks to 282ft below sea level in places, is the hottest and driest desert in the US. Mountain ranges here, among them the Panamint and Amargosa ranges fringing Death Valley National Park, contain some of California's loftiest summits, including Telescope Peak (11,049ft) and White Mountain Peak (14,246ft).

To the south, occupying most of San Bernardino County and portions of adjoining counties, is the **Mojave Desert**, nicknamed the "high desert" because its elevation averages 3,500ft, with broad areas above 4,000ft. The Mojave receives between 10in and 15in of rain a year, and temperatures are relatively cool, resulting in less evaporation and more plant life.

Southernmost of the three deserts, situated in the eastern portions of Riverside and San Diego counties and all of Imperial County, is the **Colorado Desert**. Also called the "low desert," it ranges from 2,000ft elevation to below sea level around the Salton Sea. The Colorado Desert generally receives less than 5in of rain per year and is subject to blistering summer temperatures.

CLIMATE

Coastal regions of southern and central California enjoy a Mediterranean climate, generally characterized by warm, dry summers and cool winters. Rainfall tends to be heaviest between November and April; the northern coastal mountains receive as much as 100in a year, while the driest areas around Death Valley typically receive less than 2in a year. Summer rain is rare along the coast and in the Central Valley, where persistently high atmospheric pressure suppresses convection and the formation of rain clouds, and diverts moist westerly winds far to the north. In winter, the incidence of high pressure moves south and allows moisture-laden westerlies to blow through. In regions above 2,000ft, most precipitation falls as snow.

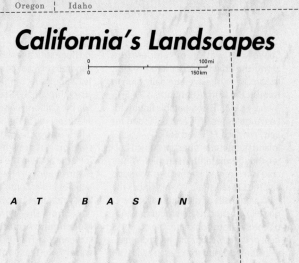

California's Landscapes

Oregon | Idaho

0 — 100mi
0 — 150km

G R E A T   B A S I N

Excelsior Mtns.

Mono Lake

White Mtns.

White Mtn Peak
△14246

Owens Valley

Inyo Mtns.

Panamint Mtns.

Death Valley

Amargosa Range

Mt. Whitney
14494△

N E V A D A

Telescope Peak
11049△

-282
Badwater

Kern

Spring Mtns.

LAS VEGAS ○

Nevada

Utah
Arizona

Lake
Mead

M O J A V E   D E S E R T

San Gabriel Mtns.

RANGES

Santa Monica Mtns.

Bullion Mtns.

San Bernardino Mtns.

Colorado River
Aqueduct

Santa Barbara

Aqueduct

apa

Los Angeles
Basin

○ Los Angeles

OS ANGELES

PENINSULAR

Santa Ana Mtns.

San Jacinto Mtns.

Coachella
Valley

Colorado
Desert

COLORADO

Santa Catalina

Santa Rosa Mtns.

Laguna Mtns.

Salton
Sea

Chocolate Mtns.

San Clemente

RANGES

SAN DIEGO ○

Imperial
Valley

M E X I C O

Seasonal variation of temperature along the coast is remarkably slight. In San Diego, the average daily high in August, the warmest month, is 77°F; in January it is 65°F. Comparable figures for Los Angeles are 76°F and 63°F; and for San Francisco 71°F and 56°F.

Inland the summers become much hotter, though winters remain mild. Winter cold is restrained by the Sierra Nevada and the Cascade Range, which block the cold air masses of the continental interior, allowing the relatively balmy winds off the Pacific to dominate. The potential heat of the dry, clear summer is dramatically tamed along the coast by the cold **California current** flowing south just offshore. This current, the eastern portion of a great clockwise swirl in the northern half of the Pacific Ocean, brings cold water down from Alaska.

WATER RESOURCES

About 75 percent of the state's precipitation falls north of Sacramento, while 75 percent of the demand for water comes from south of the capital city. To compensate, California has developed massive water storage and transportation systems that move about 60 percent of its water from the sources to the areas of demand. This has made possible the phenomenal growth of metropolitan Southern California and the massive irrigation system that transformed the Central Valley from a vast grassland into one of the nation's most productive agricultural regions. In recent years, water has become the subject of dispute among urban, agricultural and environmental interest groups.

Major urban water systems began in 1913 with the opening of the **Los Angeles Aqueduct**, built to that city from the east side of the Sierra Nevada in Owens Valley, 240mi away. The **Colorado River Aqueduct**, opened in 1941, carries water from Lake Havasu, on the state's southeastern border, to the San Diego area.

Coordinated control of the entire Sierra Nevada/Central Valley river system began in the 1930s with the federally funded **Central Valley Project**, including huge structures like Shasta Dam, and hundreds of miles of irrigation canals. In 1972 Southern California began to get water through the **State Water Project** (via the California Aqueduct) from Oroville Reservoir in the Sacramento Valley, 440mi away. Created in the 1960s, the state project provides irrigation water for large areas in the Central Valley and pumps water over the Tehachapi Mountains for urban Southern California. Oakland and other East Bay cities received water from the Sierra Nevada via the **Mokelumne Aqueduct** beginning in 1929, and San Francisco began to receive water from Yosemite National Park through the **Hetch Hetchy Aqueduct** in 1934.

FLORA AND FAUNA

California's natural vegetation reflects the climatic diversity that results from the variety of elevations as well as from the presence of the Pacific Ocean.

The lower western slopes of the northern Coast Ranges are the realm of the coast redwood. Other conifers here include Douglas fir and ponderosa pine. In the southern Coast Ranges and Bay Area, coniferous forests give way to chaparral—dense thickets of bushy, 6ft-high plants that enter a state of fire-prone dormancy during the summer, but grow back quickly after fires from a subsurface burl on the root system. Chaparral occupies a great area in the drier southern Coast Ranges as well as the Transverse and Peninsular ranges.

Running the length of the Sierra Nevada at elevations between 2,500ft and 7,000ft is a large belt of conifers—great forests of ponderosa pine, sugar pine, Douglas fir and incense cedar. Scattered groves of giant sequoias occur in the southern half of the range. The lower western slopes of the Sierra Nevada are covered with chaparral and scattered oak woodlands, which give way to conifers and alpine vegetation at higher elevations.

The margins of the Central Valley at the foot of both the Sierra Nevada and the Coast Ranges are characterized by open oak woodland.

Plants in both high and low deserts are adapted to the permanent drought conditions of these regions. Most common is the creosote bush, a ground-covering shrub that, like the Joshua tree, extends its roots deeply into the earth to secure adequate water. The **ocotillo**, denizen of the low desert, sheds its leaves during dry periods but flowers as soon as there is adequate rain. The **cholla** cactus stores water whenever it is available and protects itself from thirsty animals with its fuzzy-looking but painfully sharp spines.

Animal life in California has been greatly affected by the enormous increase in human population during the past two centuries. Some species are extinct; others are endangered. Some, driven to the verge of extinction, have staged remarkable comebacks thanks to conservation organizations.

Grizzly bears, which survive only on the state flag, once roamed all of California except the desert; the last one was shot in 1922. Black bears, smaller and less fierce, are still common in mountainous areas. The **bighorn sheep** declined because of grazing competition and transference of diseases from domestic sheep; the small remaining population lives in desert mountain areas. Varieties of **deer** are once again numerous. **Tule elk** have been successfully reestablished in some areas, such as Point Reyes National Seashore. The larger **Roosevelt elk** now thrive in the redwood parks. **Pronghorn antelope** have recovered in the thinly populated backcountry of the Modoc Plateau.

Bald Eagle at Chula Vista Nature Center
Joanne DiBona/San Diego CVB

The **California condor**, a vulture with a 9ft wingspan, came close to extinction. Today their numbers are growing, thanks to breeding programs. Greatly reduced in number are the many species of Central Velly native **waterfowl**.

The state's rich population of marine mammals includes **gray whales**, which can be seen from many points along the coast as they migrate to and from their winter quarters in Baja California. Permanent residents along the coast include winsome **sea otters** and aggressive **sea lions.**

Cholla
MICHELIN

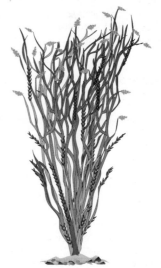
Ocotillo
MICHELIN

Alamo Square, San Francisco
© Photodisc

CENTRAL COAST

Once economically dependent on farming and fishing, the Central Coast now balances a vital agricultural economy with a robust tourist industry. Spectacular natural beauty, Spanish roots, vibrant literary and artistic traditions, and a blending of cultural sophistication with casual friendliness all contribute to its great popularity.

Highlights

1 A glass of wine on the terrace at **Nepenthe** (p82)

2 Playful otters and giant octupus at **Monterey Bay Aquarium** (p94)

3 The thrill of spotting humpback or blue whales during a **Channel Islands** boat trip (p85)

4 Over-the-top beauty of the Neptune Pool, **Hearst Castle** (p83, 87)

5 Hot or cool, a set at the Monterey Jazz Festival in **Monterey** (p90)

The Landscape – The rugged mountains of this coastline are scored with countless valleys, many of them quite fertile. Largest is the 100mi-long Salinas Valley; smaller ones include coastal plains at Monterey Bay and San Luis Obispo. These valleys, once rich in game, served as centers for Costanoan, Esselen and Salinan tribes, and later for Spanish, Mexican and American settlers.

Settlement – The Spanish found secure anchorage in Monterey Bay after sailing along the long, forbidding Big Sur coastline. Monterey, established in 1770, became colonial capital of Alta California and the hub of the chain of Spanish missions that stretched from San Luis Obispo north through the Salinas Valley to San Juan Bautista. Although thriving towns took root around most of these missions, others—particularly San Antonio de Padua and Nuestra Señora de la Soledad—to this day occupy sites in remote, undeveloped surroundings.

Evolution – After California was seized by the US at Monterey in 1846, the centers of economic and political power in California quickly shifted away from the Central Coast to booming hubs of population to the south and north. Farming and the fishing and canning industries along Monterey Bay were vividly pictured by Salinas-born novelist John Steinbeck, while other writers and artists found peace and inspiration in quaint Carmel or the stunning wilderness of Big Sur. The colorful communities, enchanting scenery and offbeat ambience that fired the imaginations of Henry Miller, George Sterling, Henry Weston and Robinson Jeffers, as well as Jack Kerouac and Richard Brautigan, today draw travelers from around the world.

Neptune Pool at Hearst Castle

ADDRESSES

⟐STAY

The properties listed below were selected for their ambience, location and/or value for money. Prices reflect average cost for a standard double room (two people) in high season (not including any applicable city or state taxes). Room prices may be considerably lower in off-season, and many hotels offer discounted weekend rates. ꙮSee the Index for a complete listing of accommodations described in the guide.

⊜	less than $100
⊜⊜	$100–$175
⊜⊜⊜	$175–$250
⊜⊜⊜⊜	$250–$350
⊜⊜⊜⊜⊜	over $350

⊜⊜⊜⊜⊜**The Lodge at Pebble Beach** – *1700 17-Mile Drive, Pebble Beach. ☎831-647-7500 or 800-654-9300. www. pebblebeach.com. 161 rooms.* A golf nirvana, Pebble Beach draws enthusiasts from around the world to its fairways and stunning scenery. **The Lodge** boasts sophisticated rooms with private decks or patios and brick fireplaces. Aside from the world-renowned links, guests here have access to the resort's private beach and tennis club, and full-service spa and salon. Five on-site restaurants include **Club XIX** (⊜⊜⊜⊜), known for its fine contemporary cuisine, and the casual **Tap Room** (⊜⊜⊜), which serves grilled steaks and chops, and hand-crafted beers.

⊜⊜⊜⊜⊜**Post Ranch Inn** – *Hwy. 1, Big Sur, 30mi south of Carmel. ☎831-667-2200 or 800-527-2200. www.postranch-inn.com. 40 rooms.* Exquisite views of the Pacific Ocean at Pfeiffer Point extend from the inn's steel-roofed redwood cottages, perched atop an 1,100ft-high cliff. Lodgings range from ocean houses with 180-degree views of Big Sur to tree houses nestled in greenery 9ft off the ground. All quarters have fireplaces, pull-out massage tables, spa tubs, private decks, and refrigerators stocked with complimentary snacks and beverages. Guests may recline under skylights on the denim bedspreads, or walk the 98-acre ranch through oak and madrone forest. The **Sierra Mar** restaurant (⊜⊜⊜) serves fine California cuisine along with dramatic coastal views.

⊜⊜⊜⊜**Hotel Oceana Santa Barbara** – *202 W. Cabrillo Blvd., Santa Barbara. ☎805-965-4577 or 800-965-9776. www.hoteloceanasantabarbara.com. 122 rooms.* "Beach-house chic" best describes the decor of guest rooms that wrap around garden courts at this beachside boutique hotel. Rooms are swathed in vibrantly colored ginghams and come equipped with such amenities as Egyptian cotton linens, duvets and CD players. Take a dip in one of two heated pools, soak up some rays on the hotel's sunterraces, or enjoy a cocktail in the lush courtyard.

⊜⊜⊜**La Playa Hotel** – *El Camino Real & 8th Ave., Carmel. ☎831-624-6476 or 800-582-8900. www.laplayahotel.com. 75 rooms, 5 cottages.* Bougainvillea and jasmine spill down the terraces of this imposing property, built as a Mediterranean-style villa two blocks from the beach in 1904. Handsome wood furnishings, colorful fabrics and bright decor maintain the ambience. The cottages offer more amenities, such as fireplaces, kitchens and patios or terraces.

⊜⊜⊜**Spindrift Inn** – *652 Cannery Row, Monterey. ☎831-646-8900 or 800-841-1879. www.spindriftinn.com. 45 rooms.* This small beachside hotel on Cannery Row was born in 1927 as the Ocean View Hotel, a favorite watering hole of sardine packers; it was rebuilt in the 1970s. Luxurious touches such as goose-down feather beds and marble baths highlight the guest rooms. Ask for a room with a corner window overlooking Monterey Bay.

⊜⊜**Madonna Inn** – *US-101 & Madonna Rd., San Luis Obispo. ☎805-543-3000 or 800-543-9666. www.madonnainn.com. 110 rooms.* Built by owners Alex and Phyllis Madonna in 1958, this Central Coast landmark is not a place you soon forget. "Overdone" most aptly describes the eclectic decor. Common areas, including the Gold Rush Steak House and the Silver Bar, are awash in "Madonna pink." Guests choose from among individually themed rooms: the Jungle Rock room is done in animal prints with rock walls and a waterfall shower; the Love Nest fosters romance with its pink walls and carpeting—and even a pink winding staircase leading to a rooftop cupola.

The Upham – *1404 De la Vina St., Santa Barbara. ☎805-962-0058 or 800-727-0876. www.uphamhotel.com. 50 rooms and cottages.* A charming Victorian hotel, the Upham was built in 1871 of redwood timbers with a broad wraparound porch. Hotel rooms are furnished in antiques and period pieces. Arranged around verdant landscaped gardens, seven restored cottages have porches and gas fireplaces. **Louie's** ( ), the on-site fine-dining restaurant, serves acclaimed California cuisine. Shops, restaurants and museums lie within easy walking distance.

¶/ EAT

The venues listed below were selected for their ambience, location and/or value for money. Rates indicate the average cost of an appetizer, an entrée and dessert for one person (not including tax, gratuity or beverages). Most restaurants are open daily—except where noted—and accept major credit cards. Call for information regarding reservations and opening hours. See the Index for a complete listing of eateries described in the text.

⊖	under $25
⊖⊜	$25–$50
⊖⊜⊜	$50–$75
⊖⊜⊜⊜	over $75

Nepenthe – *Hwy. 1, Big Sur, 31mi south of Carmel. ☎831-667-2345. www.nepenthebigsur.com.* **American**. Greek mythology describes "nepenthe" as a potion used to obliterate pain and sorrow. Indeed, the spectacular views from Nepenthe's terraces 800ft above the Pacific inspire pure joy. Built of redwood and adobe in the late 1940s, the restaurant offers a basic menu of chicken, steaks and seafood.

Grasing's Coastal Cuisine – *Sixth and Mission Sts., Carmel. ☎831-624-6562. www.grasings.com.* **Contemporary**. Bright yellow walls and high ceilings create a sunny, airy ambience at this excellent

Carmel restaurant, where fresh local ingredients are imaginatively married to delicious effect. Braised and grilled meats and delicately seared seafood dishes stand out. Try the tasty "paella" of seafood and sausage with orzo instead of rice.

Corkscrew Café – *55 W. Carmel Valley Rd., Carmel. ☎831-659-8888. www.corkscrewcafe.com. Dinner Fri & Sat only.* **American**. A popular place for lunch, this eatery entices customers with dishes that incorporate fresh produce and herbs from the restaurant's large on-site garden. Locally caught fish like trout as well as hormone-free meats are on the menu. Savor your meal in the rustic dining room or on the plant-filled outdoor patio. Before you leave, be sure to see the cafe's collection of vintage corkscrews.

The Fish Hopper – *700 Cannery Rd., Monterey. ☎831-372-8543. www.fishhopper.com.* **Seafood**. Overlooking seal rocks from the end of a pier beside the Monterey Aquarium, this eatery offers wonderful views from every table. Decor is nautical, of course; the menu features seafood, pasta and steaks, with an oyster bar and outside dining.

Passionfish – *701 Lighthouse Ave., Pacific Grove. ☎831-655-3111. www.passionfish.net. Dinner only.* **Seafood**. Sustainability and seasonality are what it's all about at this unpretentious Pacific Grove spot. The menu changes daily but the seafood dishes are uniformly raveworthy, and might include grilled prawns, seared striped bass with tomato butter, or oysters in citrus vinaigrette. There's a reasonably priced wine list too. Save room for the tempting array of desserts.

La Super-Rica Taqueria – *622 N. Milpas St., Santa Barbara. ☎805-963-4940. Lunch only.* **Mexican**. Julia Child heaped praise upon this old Santa Barbara institution, an erstwhile favorite of Ronald Reagan's White House press corps. Traditional Mexican food—with freshly made corn tortillas—is served in this diner painted in turquoise and white.

Big Sur★★★

Isolated redwood canyons, green meadows and sheer grantic ridges plunging into the frothy sea define this dramatic coastline at the western edge of the continent. Big Sur's history, mystique and spectacular scenery make it one of California's most popular tourist destinations.

A BIT OF HISTORY

Esselen Indians had occupied this wilderness for 1,800 years when the Spanish arrived in the 1770s and christened the raw land south of their Carmel Mission El País Grande del Sur ("the big country to the south"). The first Yankee homesteaders trickled into the area in the mid-1800s to establish cattle ranches, mine limestone from the Santa Lucia Mountains and log the coastal forests. By the turn of the 19C, Big Sur bustled with commercial activity, but local natural resources soon petered out.

In 1919 workers began blasting the **Cabrillo Highway** out of the western slopes that plummet into the ocean from heights topping 5,000ft. Previously, the only access to Big Sur was via an old wagon trail winding behind the hills. Completion of the highway in 1937 opened the area to visitors, and to hippies who flocked here in the 1960s.

Today, resorts and parks employ many Big Sur residents. Ranchers occupy the isolated canyons of the Big Sur hills, and artists, poets, writers and photographers continue to seek their muses in the coast's haunting beauty.

🚗 DRIVING TOUR

118mi

The terrain is rugged south of Carmel, and accessible beaches north of San Simeon are few. Occasionally you'll spot whales passing by off the coast as they make their annual migrations. Temperatures are mild year-round, but warmest in early fall. Rain falls between November and April, and fog frequently shrouds the shoreline.

- ⏱ **Michelin Map:** 585: A 9 and local map below.
- ▷ **Location:** The area known as Big Sur extends roughly 90mi along California's coastal Highway 1, from just south of Carmel to San Simeon. The rounded Santa Lucia Mountains backdrop the highway. The village of Big Sur has lodgings, restaurants and a gas station; otherwise, amenities are scarce from Big Sur to San Simeon.
- 🚫 **Don't Miss:** The view of the coast from Bixby Creek Bridge.

▷ *Leave Carmel by the Pacific Coast Highway (Hwy. 1) south.*

Point Lobos State Natural Reserve★★

3.5mi. Entrance off Hwy. 1. Sea Lion Point, Bird Island and Whalers Cove areas can be reached by car; the rest of the reserve is accessible by hiking trails. 🕐*Open Apr–Sept daily 9am–7pm; information station 9am–5pm; rest of the year daily 9am–5pm.* ⬤*$10/car.* 🅿 ℰ*831-624-4909. www.parks.ca.gov.*

Highlights of this 1,250-acre park include **Whalers Cove**, **Sea Lion Point Trail** *(.6mi round-trip)*, **Bird Island Trail** *(.8mi round-trip)*, **Cypress Grove Trail** *(.75mi loop)* to the park's highest point, and tiny **China Cove★**.

▷ *Continue south on Hwy. 1.*

You'll find outstanding trails and an accessible **beach** at **Garrapata State Park** *(10.8mi from Carmel)*, although rough waters make swimming inadvisable. The 714ft-long **Bixby Creek Bridge** *(3.5mi from Garrapata State Park)* affords stunning **views★★** south along the coastline from the overlook on its north side.

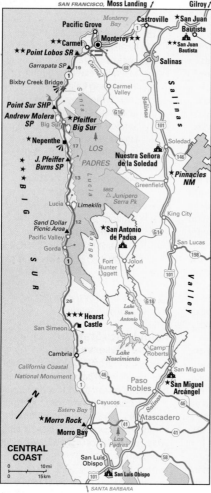

CENTRAL
COAST

0   10mi
0   15km

Point Sur State Historic Park

5mi from Bixby Creek Bridge. Light station open by guided tour (3hr) only, Apr–Oct Sat 10am & 2pm, Sun 10am, Wed 1pm, Thu 10am (Jul & Aug only); Nov–Mar weekends 10am, Wed 1pm. *Closed in bad weather.* $10. ℗ ☏831-625-4419. www.parks.ca.gov. Perched 272ft above the surf on a volcanic rock connected to the mainland by a sandbar, Point Sur Light Station was built in 1889. Visitors can tour the original stone lighthouse and the keeper's houses and workshops. A modern aero-beacon still guides ships along the central California coast.

Andrew Molera State Park

2.9mi. Entrance on right. *Open year-round daily 8am–dusk.* $10/vehicle. ⚠✕℗♿ ☏831-667-2315. www.parks.ca.gov. This largely undeveloped, 4,800-acre state park occupies part of the former Rancho El Sur. From the parking area, the easy **Headlands Trail** *(2.8mi round-trip)* traverses lush meadows and passes an 1861 redwood cabin before ascending to Molera Point, where a view extends over Molera Beach.

Pfeiffer Big Sur State Park★

4.4mi. Entrance on left. Open year-round daily 8am–dusk. $10/vehicle. ⚠✕♿℗ ☏831-667-2315. www.parks.ca.gov. Some 1,000 acres of redwoods, conifers and oak trees fringe the banks of the Big Sur River in this popular park. The **Pfeiffer Falls Trail** *(1mi round-trip)* ascends through redwood groves to **Pfeiffer Falls★**. The **Valley View Trail** climbs higher still, through oak woodland to a plateau, where a **view**★ extends to the ocean.

Pfeiffer Beach★★

1.1mi. From Hwy. 1, turn right on narrow Sycamore Canyon Rd. (look for "Narrow Road" sign); 2mi to parking lot. Open year-round daily dawn–dusk. $5/vehicle. ℗ ☏831-667-2315. Wave-eroded sea stacks sit just off the shore of this secluded bay, where Sycamore Creek flows into the ocean.

Nepenthe★

2mi. Open year-round daily 11.30am–10pm. Closed after 5pm Thanksgiving Day & after 5pm Dec 25. ✕♿℗ ☏831-667-2345. www.nepenthe bigsur.com. Named for a mythical potion to relieve pain and sorrow, this lovely restaurant offers sweeping **views**★★★ from its cliffside terraces 800ft above the ocean.

The rustic redwood **Henry Miller Memorial Library** *(entrance on the left, .3mi past Nepenthe)* houses memorabilia owned by the novelist (1891–1980), who lived in Big Sur for 18 years *(open year round Wed–Mon 11am–6pm;* 🅿 ✆*831-667-2574; www.henrymiller.org).*

Julia Pfeiffer Burns State Park

7.7mi. 🕐*Open year-round daily 8am–dusk.* 👜*$10/vehicle.* ♿🅿 ✆*831-667-2315. www.parks.ca.gov.*
From the parking lot alongside McWay Creek, **Waterfall Trail** *(0.5mi round-trip)* leads along the bluffs, where there's a **view**★ of the creek plunging 80ft to join the jade waters of the Pacific.

South of Julia Pfeiffer Burns State Park, the road rides the edge of the continent for 35 awe-inspiring if desolate miles, passing the tiny enclaves of Lucia, Pacific Valley and Gorda.

From such spots as **Limekiln State Park** *(15mi from Julia Pfeiffer Burns State Park)* and the **Sand Dollar Picnic Area** *(7mi from Limekiln),* views abound of granite slopes falling into the turquoise ocean. As it approaches San Simeon, the highway straightens, and rocky cliffs yield to rolling pastureland.

Hearst Castle★★★
51mi. 🕐*See Entry Heading.*

The languid beach town of **Cambria** *(9mi)* served in the 19C as a key shipping port for the local mining industry.

Carmel★★

One of California's most picturesque villages is Carmel-by-the-Sea (as it is officially named). A charming square mile of carefully tended houses under a canopy of pine, oak and cypress, Carmel has long attracted artists, writers, celebrities and tourists.

A BIT OF HISTORY
The village was originally planned in the 1880s as a seaside resort for Catholics. By the turn of the 19C that venture had failed, and Frank Devendorf, a young real-estate speculator from San Jose, had begun planning a community that would preserve the pristine beauty of the natural setting and attract "people of aesthetic taste."

In 1905, aspiring poet George Sterling settled in Carmel and enticed fellow writers and artists to the area. Soon the quaint village developed a reputation as a bohemian retreat, with Sterling hosting abalone parties for literary figures Jack London, Mary Austin and Upton Sinclair. Among celebrated residents of Carmel in later decades were photographers Edward Weston and Ansel

- ▶ **Population:** 4,084.
- **Michelin Map:** 585 A9 and local map below.
- **Info:** San Carlos between 5th & 6th Aves. ✆831-624-2522. www.carmelcalifornia.org.
- **Location:** The village lies at the western base of the Monterey Peninsula and just south of Pebble Beach.
- **Don't Miss:** Carmel's mission.

Adams, writer Lincoln Steffens and poet Robinson Jeffers.

Carmel's charming cottages and village ambience are protected by a strict 1929 zoning ordinance concerning commercial development. Upscale boutiques, galleries, inns and restaurants are concentrated in the commercial area *(Ocean, 6th & 7th Aves. between Junipero Ave. & Monte Verde St.).*

Scenic Road winds south along the beachfront for 1.5mi, ending at Carmel River State Beach *(accessible off Ocean Ave.; one-way southbound for first 0.7mi).*

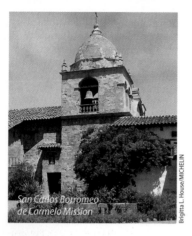

San Carlos Borroméo
de Carmelo Mission

Brigitta L. House/MICHELIN

SIGHTS

San Carlos Borroméo de Carmelo Mission★★★

3080 Rio Rd. at Lasuen Dr. ◷*Open year-round Mon–Sat 9.30am–5pm, Sun 10.30am–5pm.* ◷*Closed Easter Sun & Mon, Thanksgiving Day, Dec 24–26.* ◉*$5.* ♿ 🅿 ✆*831-624-1271. www.carmelmission.org.*

Headquarters of the California mission chain during its expansive early years, the Carmel mission was founded by Padre Junípero Serra, whose remains are interred here. The old chapel (now designated a basilica) and rebuilt mission grounds continue to serve as an active parish church and school.

In 1771, when Padre Serra decided to move the mission out of the presidio at Monterey, he chose this site near the Carmel River. The current stone church was completed in 1797, replacing an adobe chapel built in 1782.

The mission began a slow decline in 1803 when the headquarters was transferred elsewhere. In 1931 a 50-year preservation effort restored the complex.

Visit – Built of rough-hewn sandstone, the facade is offset by two asymmetrical, Moorish-style bell towers and a star window. The interior is supported by catenary arches that slope upward more steeply than a traditional barrel vault. Below the elaborate **reredos** lies the grave of Padre Serra. The mission's original stone baptismal font remains in the baptistry.

Historical artifacts and liturgical art are displayed throughout the church and in several small mission museums.

Carmel City Beach★★

ⓘ*Heavy surf; swimming not recommended.*

This wide sweep of white sand is pounded by the breakers of Carmel Bay. Sea otters may be spotted and gray whales seen during the migratory season (*Dec–Apr*).

Tor House★★

26304 Ocean View Ave., 1.2mi south of Ocean Ave. ⛵ *Visit by guided tour (1hr) only, year-round Fri & Sat on the hour 10am–3pm.* ◷*Closed Jan 1, Dec 25.* ◉*$7. Reservations required.* ✆*831-624-1813. www.torhouse.org.*

This stone complex was built on the "tor," or rock promontory, by poet Robinson Jeffers, whose writing was inspired by the raw beauty of the Pacific coast. of Carmel Point. Jeffers built the whimsical **Hawk Tower** himself; it contains his desk and chair.

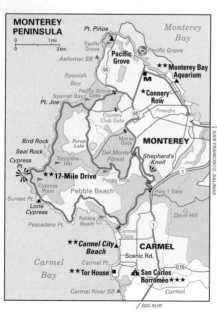

SAN FRANCISCO, SALINAS

Channel Islands National Park ★

- **Michelin Map:** 585 A, B 10.
- **Info:** Ventura Marina *(see overleaf).* ℘805-658-5730. www.nps.gov/chis.

Encompassing the northernmost five of the eight Channel Islands that extend along the coast between Santa Barbara and San Diego, this unique national park nurtures rich plant, animal and marine life, including many species not found on the mainland. With public access tightly controlled, the largely unspoiled Islands offer an experience of coastal life as it might have existed throughout the southern part of the state several centuries ago.

A BIT OF HISTORY

Topography – The islands are actually the tops of submerged mountains. The northern four are a westward extension of the Santa Monica Mountains, which, as part of the Transverse Ranges, rotated counterclockwise into their present positions by the movements of the Pacific Ocean and the North American plates along the San Andreas Fault.

Early Inhabitants – The islands' current names were fixed in 1793 by English Capt. George Vancouver, but the first European to visit and document them was Juan Rodríguez Cabrillo in 1542. (An injury he incurred the following year while landing on San Miguel or Santa Rosa led to his death; he is believed to be buried on one of the islands.) Fur traders in the late 18C and 19C threatened the abundant populations of otters, seals and sea lions, and relocated the Chumash and Gabrieleño Indians—who had lived on the islands for some 6,000 years—to mainland missions. Sheep and cattle ranches were established by the mid-19C and thrived into the 20C, particularly on Santa Rosa.

Creation of the Park – In 1938 Anacapa and Santa Barbara Islands were declared the Channel Islands National Monument, and in 1980 the five islands and 1mi of ocean around each were declared a national park. (A portion of Santa Cruz remains under private ownership.) Six-mile bands around each island are designated national marine sanctuaries.

VISIT

For access to the islands, see Practical Information p. 86.

Anacapa

△Lying just 14mi off the coast of Ventura, Anacapa Island comprises three sparsely vegetated islets. Endangered brown pelicans breed on its inaccessible western reaches, and the entire island is home to western gulls, black oyster-catchers and cormorants. A ranger station and lighthouse are located on relatively flat East Anacapa; off its coast stands water-eroded Arch Rock.

Santa Cruz

The largest of the Channel Islands offers a diverse landscape of wooded mountain slopes and beach-fringed cliffs. Santa Cruz's deep central valley indicates that it was formed of two separate land masses now joined. **Painted Cave★**, the state's largest sea cave, inhabited by sea lions, is accessible by boat on the island's

Island Fox, Santa Cruz, Channel Islands National Park

© NHPA/Photoshot.

PRACTICAL INFORMATION
Area Code: 805
GETTING THERE: From Ventura Marina, **Island Packers** (1691 Spinnaker Dr., Ste. 105 B, Ventura CA 93001; ℘642-1393; www.islandpackers.com) provides access to all five islands and runs whale-watching trips in season. From Santa Barbara Harbor, **Truth Aquatics** (301 W. Cabrillo Blvd.; ℘962-1127; www.truthaquatics.com) caters especially to divers and hikers, **Condor Cruises** (301 W. Cabrillo Blvd.; ℘882-0088; www.condorcruises.com) to whale watchers, and the **Santa Barbara Sailing Center** (133 Harbor Way; ℘962-2826 or 800-350-9090; www.sbsail.com) to yachtsmen and women. Advance reservations are recommended for all boat crossings. Closest Greyhound **bus** station: 291 E. Thompson Blvd., Ventura; ℘800-231-2222. Amtrak **train**/bus service from Los Angeles to Ventura Station (Harbor Blvd. & Figueroa St.; ℘800-872-7245). **Air** service is available to Santa Rosa Island for day or overnight visits: **Channel Islands Aviation** (305 Durley Ave., Camarillo CA 93010; ℘987-1301; www.flycia.com).
VISITOR INFORMATION: The park is open daily year-round. **Channel Islands National Park Headquarters & Robert J. Lagomarsino Visitor Center** (year-round daily 8.30am–5pm; Thanksgiving Day & Dec 25; ℘658-5730; www.nps.gov/chis), at Ventura Marina, can provide maps as well as information on boating, camping, hiking, tours and the flora and fauna of the islands. Mailing address: Superintendent, Channel Islands National Park, 1901 Spinnaker Dr., Ventura CA 93001. **Weather** on the islands can vary year-round from windy and cold to hot and humid; it is wise to be prepared for both. Facilities on the islands include campsites, pit toilets and picnic tables. Each visitor should bring an extra pair of shoes (waves can be high during on- and off-loading), one gallon of drinking water per day and food. All trash must be packed out.

RECREATION: *There are no services or concessionaires on the islands.* A favorite activity is **hiking**, though a park ranger must lead hikes on certain rugged trails. Rustic **camping** is available year-round on all islands by permit only ($15; up to 5 months in advance; ℘877-444-6777 or online at www.recreation.gov). Campers must provide their own equipment and water. Because of unpredictable weather, landings cannot be guaranteed; it's a good idea to pack an additional day's rations in case your return boat is delayed. **Water sports** include swimming, snorkeling, scuba diving and kayaking; equipment rentals, guided tours and classes may be arranged through local shops, outfitters and Truth Aquatics (above). A good time to visit is **whale-watching** season. Condor Cruises offers gray whale watching tours in spring (mid Feb–Apr, 2hrs30min, $48) and winter (Dec–early Feb, 4hrs30min, $94); humpback and blue whale watching available in summer (May–Nov, 4hrs30min, $94).

northwestern shore. Diverse animal species live on Santa Cruz, including island foxes, spotted skunks, sheep, feral pigs, mice and bats.

Santa Rosa
Reached by a sometimes-rough ocean crossing, the second-largest island (approx 53,000 acres) boasts sandy beaches and an inland terrain of grassy rolling hills with oaks and Torrey pines. Animal life includes more than 195 bird species. The island's low profile is broken by a central mountain range, 1,589ft at its highest.

San Miguel
The windswept, relatively flat westernmost island harbors a caliche forest, the calcium-carbonate castings of ancient trees. Point Bennett, on the island's western tip, is the only place in the world where six different species of seals and sea lions breed in large numbers.

Santa Barbara
The smallest island, 33mi south of Anacapa, is a breeding ground for sea lions and elephant seals, and offers excellent bird-watching.

Hearst Castle★★★

Overlooking the Pacific Ocean from high atop a crest of the Santa Lucia Mountains, this expansive 127-acre estate and the opulent mansion crowning it embody the flamboyant image of publishing magnate **William Randolph Hearst** (1863–1951). Formally known as **Hearst San Simeon State Historic Monument**, the eclectically designed and lavishly embellished castle contains a world-class collection of Mediterranean art and antiques.

A BIT OF HISTORY

The Man – The son of mining magnate George Hearst and his wife Phoebe Apperson Hearst (who fostered in her child an appreciation for art and culture), William Randolph Hearst began his journalism career with Joseph Pulitzer's sensational newspaper, the *New York World*. A year later, in 1887, the budding journalist convinced his father to put him at the helm of *The San Francisco Examiner*, which the elder Hearst had acquired in 1880. Thus began a media empire that eventually included 26 newspapers, 16 magazines, 11 radio stations, five news services and a movie company. In 1902 Hearst successfully ran for a seat in the US House of Representatives and served two consecutive terms.

The Estate – As a boy Hearst loved camping at his father's San Simeon ranch. When Hearst inherited the San Simeon lands in 1919, he hired San Francisco architect **Julia Morgan** to design a "bungalow" on the site. Over the next 28 years, the project snowballed from a modest residence to a palatial estate. With Hearst's collaboration, Morgan drafted plans for the imposing main house, called **Casa Grande**, and three guest houses, all inspired by the southern Mediterranean Revival style. From Casa Grande's twin Spanish Colonial towers, with their arabesque grillwork and Belgian carillon bells, to the Etruscan colonnades that complement the

Greco-Roman temple facade of the Neptune Pool, the design emerged as a mélange of elements drawn from different architectural traditions.

Michelin Map: 585 A9; also see Big Sur.

Info: ☎805-927-6811 (visitor center); ☎805-927-2020 (recorded information), 800-444-4445 (reservations). www.hearstcastle.org.

Location: The castle is located on the California coast near the seaside village of San Simeon at the southern end of Big Sur, 47mi north of San Luis Obispo and 98mi south of Monterey via Highway 1. The estate is situated well off the highway, and is accessible by a road that leads to the visitor center.

Parking: Park in the visitor center lot; buses drive visitors up the hill to the castle. The bus ride takes 10min.

Timing: To visit the castle, you must take a tour. There are 4 day tours and one in the evening. If this is your first visit, we recommend Tour 1, the least strenuous and most comprehensive. It includes the 40min film on the castle's construction, shown in the visitor center. Be sure to reserve your tour in advance, especially in summer.

Hearst and Kane

The title character of Orson Welles' 1941 masterpiece **Citizen Kane** was loosely modeled on William Randolph Hearst. Hearst unsuccessfully attempted to suppress the film prior to its release.

Secluded San Simeon served as a playground for Hearst, his mistress Marion Davies (a starlet he met in 1915) and a host of Hollywood glitterati. In 1957, six years after the millionaire's death, the Hearst Corporation deeded the 127-acre estate to the State of California; the family still owns the working ranch land surrounding the castle.

The Collection – Hearst's zeal for collecting art was born during an 18-month trip to Europe with his mother when he was 10 years old. During the 1920s, Hearst amassed enough treasures to fill six warehouses. Highlights of the castle's collection include silver, furnishings, **16C tapestries**, Florentine Renaissance terracotta sculpture and a superb group of ancient **Greek vases** that line the shelves of Hearst's 5,000-volume library.

VISIT

Visit by guided tour (1hr 45min) only, year-round daily 8.20am–3.20pm (last tour). Closed Jan 1, Thanksgiving Day & Dec 25. Tours 1–4 $20, Tour 5 $30. Reservations strongly suggested. 800-444-4445. 805-927-2020 (recorded information). www.hearstcastle.org.

At the castle, guides lead groups through buildings and grounds; visitors may not roam the site or linger during

Hearst Castle
© California Travel & Tourism Commission

or after tours. All tours entail walking at least 0.5mi and climbing 150-400 steps. Included on all tours are Hearst's two spectacular swimming pools: the outdoor **Neptune Pool**★, with its graceful Classical design, and indoor **Roman Pool**★ lined with gold-inlaid Venetian glass tiles.

Tour 1 – *150 stairs. Recommended for first-time visitors.* Hearst Castle's most spectacular features are revealed on this tour, including the Assembly Room, Refectory, Morning Room, Billiard Room, Theater and the 18-room Casa del Sol guest cottage. Lined with choir stalls from a 14C Spanish cathedral, the **Refectory** contains a remarkable display of antique silver. A rare example of a Flemish *mille fleurs* tapestry (c.1500) hangs in the **Billiard Room**. This tour ticket includes a screening of the excellent film *Hearst Castle: Building the Dream* in the visitor center.

Tour 2 – *377 stairs.* Doge's Suite, Cloisters (including the **Della Robbia Room**), **Library**, pantry, cavernous kitchen and Hearst's private Gothic suite and study.

Tour 3 – *316 stairs.* Completed during Hearst's final years at the castle, the three floors of bedroom suites serve as a showcase for antique Spanish ceilings and priceless Oriental carpets. The 10-room Casa del Monte guest cottage and a short (*8min*) film about the estate's construction are also featured.

Tour 4 – *Apr–Oct only. 306 stairs.* On the grounds and gardens tour, visitors will discover the **Hidden Terrace**, a spidery network of stairs that was concealed by construction in the 1930s. Also here are Hearst's wine cellar, the Neptune Pool dressing rooms and the 18-room Casa del Mar, largest of three guest cottages.

Tour 5 – *377 stairs. Call for tour schedule & availability.* Beginning at sunset, the evening tour imparts a feel for the carefree social life at the estate during its heyday in the 1930s. Docents in period dress, posing as guests and staff, animate the rooms and gardens, allowing visitors to imagine they have stumbled into one of Hearst's legendary parties.

La Purísima Mission★★

Cradled in a tranquil valley just outside the town of Lompoc, La Purísima is considered among the best-restored of California's missions. Today the authentically re-created buildings and pastoral setting★ are preserved as a state historic park.

- **Michelin Map:** 585 A 10.
- **Location:** The mission lies just east of Lompoc and some 50mi northwest of Santa Barbara. The 1,920-acre site encompasses 20mi of hiking and equestrian trails, a rare chaparral plant community and the restored mission structures.
- **Timing:** Allow at least an hour for your visit.

A BIT OF HISTORY

Officially named Mission la Purísima Concepción de María Santísima ("Mission of the Immaculate Conception of the Most Holy Mary"), the 11th mission was first located in the foothills near present-day Lompoc in 1787. In the early 19C violent earthquakes struck the mission, which had been inadvertently built over a fault line. Prolonged rains that followed the tremors demolished the church and other structures. The mission was rebuilt 3mi to the northeast.

The second site of La Purísima lay in a wide plain of the Santa Ynez River Valley, with fertile soil, ample water supply and access to El Camino Réal. By 1883 secularization and a succession of owners reduced the complex to one building. The Civilian Conservation Corps began restoring the mission in 1934, reviving construction methods used by the original builders. Seven years later, La Purísima was opened to the public as a state historic park.

VISIT

53mi northwest of Santa Barbara; from Santa Barbara take US-101 north; continue north on Hwy. 1, 19mi to intersection with Rte. 246. Turn right 1.8mi, then left on Mission Gate Rd. to park entrance. 2295 Purisima Rd. Open year-round daily 9am–5pm. Guided tours available daily (1hr 30min) 1pm. Closed Jan 1, Thanksgiving Day, Dec 25. $4/vehicle. 805-733-3713. www.lapurisimamission.org.

Main Complex

Designed without a formal facade, the long, narrow **church** (1818) was built with its main entrance on the sidewall to provide easy access to travelers on El Camino Réal.

Next to the church, the **shops and quarters building** housed soldiers and contained workshops for weaving, candle-making, leather-working and carpentry operations. Rooms in this building have been furnished with period pieces to reflect their original appearance.

The mission's largest structure, the 318ft-long **residence building**★, which

La Purísima

MICHELIN

served as the padres' quarters, incorporated 4ft-thick adobe walls and wide, square pillars topped with fluted corbels. A stone buttress at the south end further shored up the structure, which also housed a library, office, wine cellar, guest quarters and the simple chapel.

Grounds

Plants raised for both food and medicinal purposes are cultivated in the restored **mission garden**★. The central fountain and two laundry basins once formed part of the site's elaborate water system. Other buildings on the grounds include a blacksmith shop, spring house, barracks for neophytes and a women's dormitory.

ADDITIONAL SIGHT
Lompoc
3mi west via Rte. 246.
This former Chumash village, now a thriving town, is known today as one of the world's largest producers of flower seeds. In summer, a kaleidoscope of blossoms festoons fields in the area.
Glimpse the town's ancient history in the **Lompoc Museum** *(200 S. H St.)*, which houses an impressive collection of Chumash artifacts (◔*open year-round Tue–Fri 1pm–5pm, weekends 1pm–4pm;* ◔*closed major holidays;* ✆*$1;* ✆*805-736-3888).*

Monterey★★

At the southern end of Monterey Bay, 115mi south of San Francisco, California's longtime Spanish-Mexican capital retains its historic adobe charm, while celebrating its 20C fishing and cannery heritage.

A BIT OF HISTORY

Ohlone Indians had lived in this area for more than 1,000 years before the Spanish expedition under Juan Rodríguez Cabrillo sighted the bay from the sea in 1542. In 1602 Sebastián Vizcaíno rediscovered the area, and named the bay after his patron, the Count of Monte Rey. In 1770 Gaspar de Portolá arrived here to establish the first presidio in Alta California. With him was Padre Junípero Serra, charged with founding Catholic missions along the coast.
In 1775 Spain declared Monterey the capital of Alta and Baja California. After Mexican independence in 1821, Monterey remained the provincial capital, and a center of the hide and tallow trade. Increasing US interest in California culminated on July 7, 1846, when Commodore John Sloat landed in Monterey with 225 soldiers and proclaimed California part of the US. After the peaceful takeover, Monterey's fortunes turned.

▶ **Population:** 31,106.
◔ **Michelin Map:** 585 A 9 and map this section.
🖺 **Info:** ✆888-221-1010. www.seemonterey.com.
◔ **Timing:** Plan to spend a minimum 2hrs in Historic Monterey; stop first at Stanton Center to get opening hours for each structure you wish to visit. Enjoy lunch in Cannery Row, then browse the shops and visit the Aquarium. Take 17-Mile Drive early in the morning before tourist traffic crowds the route.
👥 **Kids:** The Aquarium, Museum of Natural History.

In 1849 the state capital was moved to San Jose and gold fever swept California. By 1850 the old capital had fallen into obscurity.
In the late 19C, fishermen discovered the rich harvests of Monterey Bay. In the early 1900s a sardine-canning operation opened in town, and Monterey was soon the "Sardine Capital of the World." This lucrative industry lasted until the early 1950s, when the local fish supply sud-

PRACTICAL INFORMATION
Area Code: 831
GETTING THERE From San Francisco
(130mi): US-101 south to Rte. 156 west
to Hwy. 1 south. From Los Angeles
(347mi): US-101 north to Rte. 68 west.
Monterey Peninsula Airport (MRY):
domestic flights ☎648-7000 or *www.
montereyairport.com*; taxi service *($15 to
downtown)* and hotel courtesy shuttles.
Major **rental car** agencies. Amtrak **train**
station: 30 Railroad Ave., Salinas *(15mi
from Monterey)*; fare includes transfer;
☎800-872-7245. Greyhound bus depot:
19 W. Gabilan St., Salinas (connecting
service to Monterey, ☎800-231-2222.

**GETTING AROUND Monterey-
Salinas Transit** *(www.mst.org)* operates
a free trolley service to major attractions
throughout the city *(Memorial Day–
Labor Day daily)* ☎899-2555. Parking
garages & metered lots located
throughout city; parking regulations
strictly enforced.

VISITOR INFORMATION Monterey
County Convention & Visitors Bureau's
Monterey Visitors Center, Lake El
Estero at Franklin St. & Camino El Estero
☎831-657-6400 or 888-221-1010,
www.seemonterey.com.

ACCOMMODATIONS *Monterey Land &
See*, a visitors guide to Monterey County
available by mail or by download from
the visitor center *(above)*, includes a
lodging directory. Accommodations
range from elegant hotels & resorts
($250–$750/day), to moderate inns
($90–$250/day). Most bed & breakfasts
are located in residential sections of
the city *($120–$550/day)*. Reservation &
referral services: **Monterey Peninsula
Reservations** ☎655-3487 or 888-655-
3424; **Resort 2 Me** ☎646-9250;
www.resort2me.com. There are 40
campsites at Veterans Memorial Park
($25/night, first-come first-served);
☎646-3865.

denly gave out. Sea life has bounced
back since then, thanks to the formation
of the **Monterey Bay National Marine
Sanctuary**. Since 1958 the city has
hosted the acclaimed annual **Monterey
Jazz Festival**, drawing thousands to
hear jazz greats like Dave Brubeck, Mar-
ian McPartland and Branford Marsalis.

HISTORIC MONTEREY★★
Monterey's Spanish colonial past is visible in the two dozen mid-19C adobes
scattered downtown. Preservation of
these adobes began in the early 1900s;
today, more than 20 historic buildings
and gardens are maintained by city,
state and private owners. Historic adobes are designated by plaques.
Many of Monterey's historic adobes are
linked by the **Path of History Walking
Tour**, a route marked on the sidewalks
by gold buttons, with decorative tiles
and explanatory signs at each site. A
map of the route is available at the Monterey State Historic Park visitor center in
Stanton Center *(below)*.

Monterey State Historic Park
🕐*Open year-round daily 10am–4pm.*
🕐*Closed Jan 1, Thanksgiving Day & Dec
25.* ☎831-649-7118. www.parks.ca.gov.
The park operates many of the historic
adobes listed below; the City of Monterey maintains others. 🚶The Stevenson House, Casa Soberanes, Larkin
House and Cooper-Molera Adobe are
accessible by guided tour only *(free)*.
Visitors may take one of two historic
walking tours *(45min)* that leave daily
from Stanton Center, the park's visitor
information center on Custom House
Plaza *(below)*.
*Sights below follow the Path of History
route, from Custom House Plaza.*
📍*Opening hours for each building are
available at Stanton Center.*

Custom House Plaza★
Historic buildings cluster around the
waterfront near **Fisherman's Wharf**
(Wharf I). Beyond the boat harbor, where
barking sea lions play in the waves, the
Municipal Pier (Wharf II) still maintains
some commercial fishing facilities.

Larkin House

Before touring the adobes, stop at the **Stanton Center** to view a **film** *(17min)* on Monterey's exciting history. Exhibits at the adjoining **Monterey Maritime and History Museum**★ (**M**) *(open year-round Tue–Sun 10am–5pm; 831-372-2608; www.montereyhistory. org)* cover the nautical history of Monterey from the 17C to the 20C.

Considered the oldest government building in California, the adobe **Custom House**★ bears the designation of California Landmark No. 1. Its two-story north section was erected in 1827, and the building, with later additions, functioned as a custom house until 1868. The interior re-creates the building's appearance in the 1830s and 1840s. The flagpole at the north end of the building marks the site where the American flag was raised in 1846.

Pacific House, a two-story adobe built in 1847 to house US troops, now has a museum of Monterey history featuring interactive exhibits and displays. Upstairs you'll find the Monterey Museum of the American Indian, featuring intricately woven baskets and beautiful pottery.

At the far end of the nearby Heritage Harbor complex lies the **First Brick House**, begun in 1847 as the town's first home constructed of kiln-fired (rather than adobe) bricks. It now traces the lifestyles of past owners during the home's 100-year occupancy. Beside it rises the **Old Whaling Station** (1847), a two-story adobe modeled after its builder's ancestral home in Scotland.

A block south on Pacific Street, California's **First Theatre** (1848) mounts 19C melodramas in its adobe wing, adjacent to the original redwood tavern. One block east on Olivier Street, the two-story **Casa del Oro**, built by Thomas Larkin in the mid-1840s as a general store, has been restored and reopened as a gift shop.

Casa Soberanes★

336 Pacific St. Visit by guided tour (45min) only, year-round daily 11.30am & 3pm. Gardens open daily 9am–5pm. 831-649-7118.

Built in the 1840s, the adobe, with its 3ft-thick walls, is a charming example of Monterey Colonial architecture.

A cantilevered balcony runs along the two-story facade, while the rear of the house slants down to one story. Inside are 19C New England pieces, China trade pieces, Mexican folk art and other belongings of past owners.

Colton Hall★

Open year-round daily 10am–4pm. Closed Jan 1, Thanksgiving Day, Dec 25. 831-646-5648. www.monterey. org/museum.

This porticoed building, constructed in 1849 of Monterey shale, was conceived as a public meeting hall and school. In 1849 California's Constitutional Convention met here. The large meeting room

(2nd floor) is furnished as it was during the convention. On the south side of Colton Hall, the restored cells of the stone **Old Monterey Jail** trace the jail's history (1855–1959).

Monterey Museum of Art Pacific Street★

559 Pacific St. Open year-round Wed–Sat 11am–5pm, Sun 1pm–4pm. Closed Jan 1, Jul 4 & Dec 25. $5 (includes admission to La Mirada museum). 831-372-5477. www.montereyart.org.

Founded in 1959, this museum is devoted to folk, tribal, ethnic and contemporary art. Its permanent collection, concentrating on regional and California art plus arts of Asia and the Pacific Rim, includes works on paper by Henri Matisse, Wayne Thibaud and Pablo Picasso and photography by Ansel Adams.

Larkin House★★

Calle Principal and Jefferson St.; entrance through garden. Visit by guided tour (45min) only, year-round Fri–Wed 10am & noon. Gardens open daily 9am–5pm. 831-649-7118.

This substantial adobe was built in 1835 by Thomas O. Larkin, a prosperous merchant who served as US consul and secret agent before and during the American takeover of Alta California. He designed a two-story home that melded elements of New England architecture—including hipped roof and central hallway—with the adobe motif, giving rise to the style now known as Monterey Colonial. The walled garden encompasses a one-room stone structure that temporarily served as William Tecumseh Sherman's residence when he was stationed in Monterey as a young lieutenant in 1847.

Cooper-Molera Complex★★

Alvarado St. at Munras Ave. & Polk St. Visit by guided tour (45min) only, year-round Fri–Wed noon & 3pm. Museum store & grounds open year-round daily 10am–4pm. 831-649-7118.

The two-acre site includes a 20C garden of local plants, a 1902 carriage house, and a large adobe home built in 1823 by John Rogers Cooper. When Cooper's fortunes fell, he subdivided the property and moved his family into the east wing, selling the other half of the adobe but later adding a second story to his half of the structure.

The separate wings are now furnished in the respective manners of Anglo and California families of the mid-19C; Cooper's second floor is decorated with later Victorian antiques.

Across Polk Street stands **Casa Amesti** (**A**), another example of the Monterey Colonial style. The two-story adobe, (1830s), was home to interior decorator Francis Elkins from 1918–53 and still contains many of her furnishings.

Stevenson House★

530 Houston St. Open Sun–Wed 1.30 4pm, Sat 1pm–4pm. Guided tour Fri–Wed 2pm. 831-649-7118.

The original back wing of this adobe was built in the 1830s and served as the residence of the town's customs collector. After 1850, the building was expanded into an adobe boardinghouse. Scottish author Robert Louis Stevenson resided here in 1879 while courting Californian Fanny Osborne. The interior contains period furnishings along with Stevenson's furniture and memorabilia.

Royal Presidio Chapel

550 Church St. at Figueroa St. 831-373-4345. www.historicmonterey.org.

California's only extant presidio chapel, this stone-and-adobe structure (1795) claims direct descent from the original Monterey mission founded by Padre Serra in 1770. After Serra moved his mission in 1771 to its present location in Carmel, Monterey's presidio chapel continued to serve the military.

Monterey Museum of Art La Mirada★

720 Via Mirada. Open year-round Wed–Sat 11am–5pm, Sun 1pm–4pm. Closed Jan 1, Jul 4 & Dec 25. $5 (includes admission to Monterey

Museum of Art). 🅿️ 🖊️*831-372-3689. www.montereyart.org.*

This early-19C adobe, expanded in the early 20C, is furnished with antiques and surrounded by gardens. Galleries display the museum's collection of *netsuke* (Japanese carved toggles), early Chinese ceramics and bronzes, and works by San Francisco-born artist Armin Hansen, the "Winslow Homer of the West."

CANNERY ROW★

"A poem, a stink, a grating noise," author John Steinbeck called it in his literary classic *Cannery Row*, set in the raucous industrial area north of downtown. Sardine canneries first appeared here in the early 20C, but in 1950 the fish abruptly disappeared from the bay—either from overharvesting or oceanic changes—and most canneries shut down.

Today Cannery Row has been reborn as a tourist area, its old buildings, bars and brothels now housing shops, restaurants and an **IMAX theater** screening popular movies and ocean-themed 3-D shows *(640 Wave St.,* 🕐*open daily, call or check website for showtimes;* 💲*$10–13;* 🖊️*831-372-4629; www.bellacinema.com).*

Be sure to stroll by no. 800, the weather-beaten marine lab of "Doc" Ricketts, Steinbeck's friend and the main character in *Cannery Row.*

👥👤Monterey Bay Aquarium★★

886 Cannery Row (west end). 🕐*Open late May–early Sept daily 9.30am–6pm (8pm closing weekends Jul & Aug). Rest of the year daily 10am–6pm.* 🕐*Closed Dec 25.* 🎟️*$29.95, children $17.95.* ✖️♿🖊️*831-648-4888. www.monterey bayaquarium.org.*

This state-of-the-art aquarium, housed in a converted cannery, is devoted to presenting and conserving the rich marine life of Monterey Bay. The 322,000sq ft aquarium includes decks and open spaces that incorporate the sea into the architecture.

Highlights include the **Kelp Forest**★, a 335,000gal, 28ft-high tank with giant kelp that can grow to 6in a day; the monkeyface eels, sea urchins and barnacles of the **Rocky Shore**★; the **Sea Otter pool** *(interior)*, home to rescued animals no longer able to survive in the wild; **The Outer Bay**★★, with its **open ocean tank**★★ measuring 35ft deep and holding one million gallons of ocean water, where sharks, California barracudas and other denizens swim. Kids especially will like the **Great Tide Pool**★ with its sea stars, anemones and crabs; and the **Splash Zone**★, a special hands-on gallery. The **Giant Octopus**★ exhibit features several of these awe-inspiring denizens of the deep; other fearsome deep-reef predators like lingcod and wolf-eels are displayed nearby.

Bubble windows offer a unique perspective on sea life in the Monterey Bay Habitats exhibit

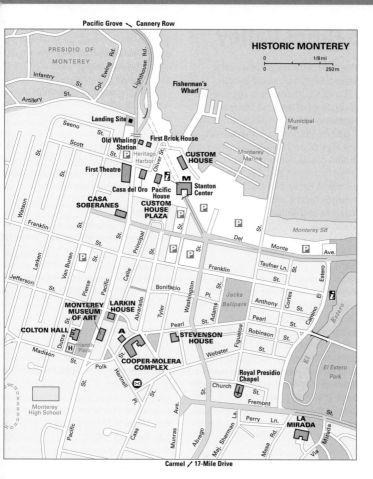

Pacific Grove ⌐ Cannery Row

HISTORIC MONTEREY

0   1/8mi
0   250m

EXCURSIONS
Pacific Grove

Visit this seaside resort's **Point Pinos** with its oldest continuously operating (1855) **lighthouse** (Asilomar Blvd.; ○ open Thu–Mon 1pm–4pm; ✆831-648-5716; ▨$2 contribution requested) in the western US. The **Museum of Natural History** (M) (165 Forest Ave.) has exhibits on butterflies, mammals and local Native American peoples (🚹🚺 ○ open year-round Tue–Sun 10am–5pm; ○ closed holidays; ♿🅿 ✆831-648-5716; www.pgmuseum.org).

17-Mile Drive★★

🚗 Map see Carmel. Accessible via Pacific Grove Gate, off Sunset Dr.; Country Club Gate, off Congress Ave; and Samuel B. Morse Gate, off Rte. 68, in Pacific Grove.

○ Open year-round daily dawn–dusk. ▨$9.25/vehicle. ✗♿🅿 ✆831-624-6669. www.pebblebeach.com.

Celebrated for exquisite views of the Pacific, this private toll road winds through the exclusive Pebble Beach enclave and into the Del Monte Forest with gnarled Monterey cypress trees. Much of the road follows the Paciic coastline.

Highlights include the turbulent surf off **Point Joe**; the sea lions and harbor seals at **Seal Rock** (picnic area); **Cypress Point Lookout** with its **views**★ of the sea stacks that stretch toward Point Sur, 20mi south; the classic landmark of the Monterey Peninsula, the **Lone Cypress**, clinging to its bald rock promontory above the Pacific; and the renowned Pebble Beach resort.

Salinas Valley

The Salinas Valley embraces the Salinas River as it snakes north 150mi from its source in the Sierra Madre east of San Luis Obispo to Monterey Bay. The Franciscan padres founded missions here to convert the area's Costanoan and Salinan Indians; later, Anglo farmers raised crops in the rich soil. The valley also yielded a harvest of characters and settings for the stories of Nobel laureate and Salinas native John Steinbeck.

SIGHTS
Salinas
111mi south of San Francisco via US-101.
In 1898 Claus Spreckels established a sugar refinery in the Salinas region, and farmers cultivated sugar beets, lettuce and other crops, earning Salinas the title "salad bowl of the nation." Today the city serves as the valley's commercial hub. Salinas was the birthplace and boyhood home of renowned author **John Steinbeck** (1902–68), who set many of his best-known works here and in Monterey County. The author's remains lie in the Garden of Memories (768 Abbott St.).

National Steinbeck Center★★
1 Main St. ◷Open year-round daily 10am–5pm. ◷Closed major holidays. ◑$10.95. ♿✕🅿 ℘831-796-3833. www.steinbeck.org.
This splendid archive and museum—a glass-walled atrium with brick-faced wings—rises in historic Old Town Salinas, itself a setting from Steinbeck's novel *East of Eden*. The 37,000sq ft museum (1998) illustrates the themes and settings of Steinbeck's writings with multimedia exhibits, written excerpts and film clips. A film *(12min)* previews the author's life. Highlights include "Growing Up East of Eden" featuring a 1917 Model T automobile and an old street map of Salinas to evoke the era of Steinbeck's childhood; "An' Live Off the Fatta the Lan'" exploring the rural lifestyle known to characters in *Of Mice and Men* and *The Red Pony*; "Grapes of Wrath" describing the migration of desperate Dust Bowl families; and "Cannery Row," evoking Doc Ricketts' laboratory and a fish-packing plant.

> ♿ **Michelin Map:** 585 A 9; also see Big Sur map.
> 🔲 **Info:** ℘831-758-9216. www.destination salinas.com.

Castroville
9mi north of Salinas via Rte. 183.
As the reputed "Artichoke Center of the World," the fields surrounding this town produce 90 percent of the nation's 'choke crop. Castroville's annual festival honoring the thistle delicacy occurs the fourth week in September.

Moss Landing
3mi north of Castroville on Rte. 1. ℘831-633-4501.
A quaint fishing village reborn as a shopping, dining and marine-recreation center, Moss Bay is located where Elkhorn Slough empties into Monterey Bay. **Elkhorn Slough National Estuarine Research Reserve★** *(1700 Elkhorn Rd.; ◷open year-round Wed–Sun 9am–5pm; ℘831-728-2822, www.elkhorn slough.org)*, an expansive tidal salt marsh, provides habitat for some 300 species of birds as well as marine animals and rare plants. A visitor center offers interactive exhibits and guided walks *(◑$2.50)*.

Pinnacles National Monument★
12mi east of Soledad (22mi south of Salinas). West entrance: exit US-101 at Rte. 146 east and follow signs to monument (12mi). East entrance: take US-101 south 19.5mi to King City (Broadway exit) and go 14.5mi east on Rte. G13. Turn left on Rte. 25 and continue 14mi north to Rte. 146 ; follow signs to monument. West entrance ◷open mid-Mar–Nov daily 7.30am–7pm; rest of the year daily 7.30am–dusk. East entrance open 24hrs. ◑$5/vehicle

(good for 7 days). 🅿️ ⛺ 📞*831-389-4485. www.nps.gov/pinn.*

Rising from the granite bedrock of the Gabilan Mountains east of Soledad, the park's distinctive ridgetop rock formations are the remnants of an unnamed volcano, formed 23 million years ago in an area now known as the San Andreas rift zone.

The 38sq mi park is accessible only by hiking trails. The west entrance accesses a small ranger station and vantage points offering stunning views of the Pinnacles. The east entrance leads to the campground and visitor center, with exhibits on natural and cultural history. Several trails, particularly the **Juniper Canyon Loop**★ *(4.3mi round-trip; trailhead at west entrance)* and the **High Peaks Trail** *(5.3mi loop; trailhead at east entrance),* climb steeply up to the Pinnacles themselves, leading to viewpoints with glorious vistas. You'll also find easy-to-moderate footpaths from Bear Gulch leading to caves and other features.

Nuestra Señora de la Soledad Mission

29 mi south of Salinas; exit US-101 at Arroyo Seco Rd.; drive 1mi west to Fort Romie Rd. and turn right; continue 1.5mi north to mission. 🕐*Open year-round daily 10am–4pm.* 🕐*Closed major holidays.* ♿🅿️ 📞*831-678-2586.*

Founded in 1791, the 13th mission was named for Our Lady of Solitude. An 1824 flood destroyed the original church; subsequent chapels were washed away. Restoration began in 1954.

Only the chapel and the seven-room convento have been rebuilt; the remainder of the quadrangle lies in ruins. The original bell hangs from a low beam outside the church, while the original stations of the cross adorn the interior.

San Antonio de Padua Mission★

26mi southwest of King City. Exit US-101 at Rte. G14 (Jolon Rd.) and go 18mi south to Jolon Store. Turn right to enter Fort Hunter Liggett (driver's license, vehicle registration & proof of insur-

ance required). Sentries direct visitors 5.1mi through the military base to the mission. 🚗*Posted speed limits are strictly enforced.* 🕐*Open year-round daily 10am–4pm.* 💲*$5 contribution requested.* ♿🅿️ 📞*831-385-4478. www.missionsanantonio.net.*

California's third mission was founded by Padre Junípero Serra in 1771. Following secularization in 1834, the mission lands were sold and San Antonio lay abandoned for decades. One wing of the renovated quadrangle and the church (1813) are open to the public; the remaining two wings house a Franciscan retreat center.

An elegant colonnade fronts the quadrangle; at the church entrance stands a red brick *campanario.* The front wing houses exhibits of mission life. In the music room, take a look at the wall markings showing how the padres taught the neophytes to sing. In the wine vat and cellar, grapes were crushed a half-floor above the convento; the juice drained into barrels in the cellar.

San Miguel Arcángel Mission★

775 Mission St., San Miguel, off US-101. 🕐*Open year-round daily 9.30am–4.30pm.* 🕐*Closed major holidays.* 💲*Contribution requested.* ♿📞*805-467-3256. The church is closed for retrofitting (planned reopening: late 2009); exhibits in the convento may be visited (enter through the gift shop).*

Named for St. Michael the Archangel, California's 16th mission was founded in 1797. In 1806, the mission succumbed to fire; a tile-roofed church was built to withstand disasters. After secularization, the structures housed stores and private residences, and priests who remained in residence kept the church in good repair. In 1859 the property was returned to the Catholic Church, and in 1928 it was granted to the Franciscan order, which operates it today as a monastery. Rooms in the *convento* display artifacts of the mission period.

The church's **interior**★★ features 19C frescoes by Native Americans; the murals are considered the California missions' finest examples of interior decoration.

San Juan Bautista★

Nestled in the foothills of the Gabilan Mountains, this historic mission village lies just southwest of the San Andreas Fault. With its simple adobe and board-and-batten architecture, San Juan Bautista retains the flavor of a 19C farming community.

A BIT OF HISTORY

In May 1797 Spanish soldiers arrived, and the mission was soon established. In the mid-18C the town served as a nexus for stagecoach routes, but the boom ended in 1876 when the Southern Pacific Railroad bypassed it enroute from San Francisco to San Diego.

The original plaza and surrounding historic buildings now form the San Juan Bautista State Historic Park, though the mission complex remains in church hands, functioning as a parish.

SIGHTS
San Juan Bautista Mission★★

Rte. 156, 3mi east of US-101. Open daily 9.30am–4.30pm. Closed major holidays. $2. ℘831-623-4528. www.oldmissionsjb.org.

California's 15th mission was named for St. John the Baptist. The site bordered the San Andreas Fault, and structural trauma due to seismic activity has marked the mission's history. A series of temblors in 1800 damaged the buildings, but construction began three years later on a grand new adobe church, completed in 1812. The great earthquake of 1906 then wreaked havoc on the complex; today restored, the church remains the largest on California's mission chain.

Arches grace the facade of the adobe **padres' quarters**, which house a museum of artifacts and re-created rooms (kitchen, library). The interior of the adobe **church** is distinctive for its three naves and frescoed arches. The ornate wall designs were executed in 1820 by American sailor, Thomas Doak, believed to be the first US citizen to settle in California.

⚅ **Michelin Map:** 585 A 9; also see Big Sur map.
🛈 **Info:** ℘831-623-2454; www.san-juan-bautista. ca.us.
◗ **Location:** The town lies north of the Salinas Valley, amid a rich agricultural region dotted with small towns.
🧒 **Kids:** Gilroy Gardens, a family-themed amusement park.

The steep slope behind the cemetery wall marks the San Andreas Fault line. A section of **El Camino Réal,** the late-18C thoroughfare that traversed this part of California, can be seen north of the cemetery.

San Juan Bautista State Historic Park★

Entrance tickets available at Plaza Hotel. Open daily 10am–4.30pm. Closed Jan 1, Thanksgiving Day & Dec 25. $2. ℘831-623-4526. www.parks.ca.gov.

The grassy **plaza** fronting the mission is bordered on the south and east by restored mid-19C buildings, today maintained as a state historic park. The large **Plaza Hotel**, originally a single-story adobe structure, was built in 1814 as a mission barracks. It was converted to a hotel (with a second story) by one Angelo Zanetta in the 1850s. Re-created period rooms include a **saloon** with the original carved-wood bar.

Castro Adobe retains its 1840s appearance on the exterior. The interior reflects the 1870s, when the adobe was home to the Breen family, survivors of the ill-fated Donner Party. **Plaza Hall** was expanded in 1868 by Zanetta, and later became his home.

EXCURSION
Gilroy

14mi north of San Juan Bautista via US-101. The self-proclaimed "Garlic Capital of the World," Gilroy anchors the southern end of the fertile Santa Clara Valley. Beyond its residential streets stretch vast fields that each year produce copious crops of the "stinking rose."

Each July, the **Gilroy Garlic Festival** draws thousands of garlic lovers.

👪 Gilroy Gardens

3050 Hecker Pass Hwy. (Rte. 152), 2mi west of downtown. 🕐*Open daily June–late Aug Mon–Thu 11am–5pm, Fri–Sun 10am–6pm; Apr–May and late Aug–Nov weekends only.* 🕐*Closed Dec–Feb.* 💵*$42.99, children $32.99.* ♿🅿 📞*408-840-7100. www.gilroy gardens.org.*

This one-of-a-kind amusement park, built around a horticultural and historical theme, combines five individual gardens and more than 40 rides and attractions on 28 acres.

San Luis Obispo

This pleasant city, home to California Polytechnic State University, grew up around the mission that Padre Junípero Serra founded in 1772.

SIGHTS

San Luis Obispo de Tolosa Mission

751 Palm St. 🕐*Open Jun–Oct daily 9am–5pm. Rest of the year daily 9am–4pm. Contribution requested.* ♿📞*805-543-6850. www.mission sanluisobispo.org.*

Padre Serra named the fifth mission for St. Louis, a 13C bishop of Toulouse, France. Ravaged by fire, earthquake and secularization, the mission was renovated in the popular Victorian style for its 1872 centennial, but was returned in the 20C to its original mission style.

The **church** (1793) features a vestibule-belfry with Peruvian bells.

The hand-hewn oak rafters are original. The **museum** exhibits religious and historical objects and **Chumash artifacts★** (pottery, stone tools and baskets).

Cuesta Ridge★

Take US-101 north 5mi; turn left on unmarked road at top of Cuesta Grade.

This one-lane, potholed road climbs 5mi along the ridge overlooking the Atascadero hills (north) and the Santa Lucia Wilderness (east).

A dirt turnout (1.6mi) along the road commands a stunning **view★★** of the 21-million-year-old "Nine Sisters" peaks (🕐*see Morro Bay*).

▶ **Population:** 42,928.
🕐 **Michelin Map:** 585 A9; also see Big Sur map.
ℹ **Info:** 📞805-781-2777; www.visitslo.com
▶ **Location:** The city lies in the southern foothills of the Santa Lucia mountains about halfway between Los Angeles and San Francisco on Hwy. 101.

EXCURSION

Morro Bay

13mi northwest of San Luis Obispo. Take Main St. exit off Hwy. 1.

This fishing port town centers on its Embarcadero. The bay's 576ft **Morro Rock★** *(take Main St. to right on Beach St. and follow signs)* is one of the "Nine Sisters," extinct volcanic peaks extending from San Luis Obispo to Morro Bay.

Morro Bay State Park Museum of Natural History★

Morro Bay State Park Rd. (follow Main St. extension). 🕐*Open year-round daily 10am–5pm.* 🕐*Closed Jan 1, Thanksgiving Day, Dec 25.* 💵*$2.* ♿🅿 📞*805-772-2694. www.parks.ca.gov.*

Here you'll find interactive exhibits on estuary and bay ecosystems, tidal forces and geology. The state park itself is a great spot for birders; along its western edge is a vast saltwater marsh and marine estuary, habitat for an astonishing variety of birds and a flyover spot for migratory species.

Santa Barbara★★

Red-tile roofs, whitewashed stucco buildings and palm-fringed beaches create a distinctly Mediterranean atmosphere in this chic yet easygoing Southern California city arrayed along a coastal ledge and extending up into the hills between the Pacific Ocean and Santa Ynez Mountains.

▶ **Population:** 92,325.
◔ **Michelin Map:** 585 B 10; and map this section.
🛈 **Info:** ℘805-966-9222. www.santabarbaraca.com.
◖ **Location:** The city sits on the coast, 90mi northwest of Los Angeles.

THE CITY TODAY

WIth its attractive buildings, welter of inviting shops and restaurants (especially around lower State Street), high-class cultural offerings and near-perfect climate, Santa Barbara feels upscale, yet laid-back. The city enjoys just-close-enough proximity to Los Angeles, and the bustling University of California–Santa Barbara (and four other higher-education institutions) brings an edgy academic dimension to the community's beach-resort atmosphere.

A BIT OF HISTORY

Sixty years after Juan Rodríguez Cabrillo entered the Santa Barbara Channel, King Philip III of Spain dispatched Sebastián Vizcaíno to find a good harbor off the California coast. Vizcaíno arrived here on the feast of St. Barbara in 1602 and named the channel for the 4C martyr from Asia Minor. In 1782 Padre Junípero Serra consecrated the site of the last Spanish fort on the coast, El Presidio de Santa Bárbara.

After California fell to the US in 1846, Yankee settlers looking for gold arrived. By the late 19C, Easterners came, attracted by the mild climate.

The city began its transformation to Spanish Colonial Revival in the 1920s. **El Paseo** (814 State St.), a shopping arcade, was the first major development built in the new style. After an earthquake in 1925, residents reconstructed the city in a style reminiscent of its Spanish roots.

WATERFRONT

Stearns Wharf and Santa Barbara Harbor embrace the mile-long waterfront, fringed by **East Beach★**, **West Beach** and **Leadbetter Beach**. **Chase Palm Park** boasts a carousel and open-air amphitheater. **Shoreline Park** provides a vantage point for whale-watching *(Nov–Apr)*.

Stearns Wharf★

Foot of State St. 🅿 *(at wharf).*
Built in 1872 this 2,640ft pier, lined with shops and restaurants, is the oldest working wooden wharf in the state. **Dolphin Fountain** graces the State Street entrance. The **Nature Conservancy Visitor Center** features displays on the Channel Islands.

👪 Sea Center

211 Stearns Wharf. ◷*Open year-round daily 10am–5pm.* ◷*Closed Jan 1, Thanksgiving Day & Dec 25.* ✆*$8, children $5.* ♿🅿 ℘*805-962-2526. www.sbnature.org/seacenter.*
This small aquarium, operated by Santa Barbara Museum of Natural History, draws kids to its outdoor touch tank. Interactive, kid-oriented exhibits draw budding oceanographers into the world of marine science.

👪 Santa Barbara Maritime Museum

113 Harbor Way. ◷*Open late May–Labor Day Thu–Tue 10am–6pm; rest of the year Thu–Tue 10am–5pm.* ◷*Closed major holidays.* ✆*$7, children $4 (free 3rd Thu).* ✕♿ ℘*805-962-8404. www.sbmm.org.*
This museum in Waterfront Center explores local maritime history. Visitors can join a high-speed virtual tour of the channel, check out ship models, peer through a 45ft US Navy periscope, or reel in a trophy marlin.

Area Code: 805

GETTING THERE

From Los Angeles *(92mi)* take US-101 north. From San Francisco *(316mi)* take US-101 south. **Santa Barbara Municipal Airport** (SBA): domestic flights *℘683-4011. www.flysba.com.* Taxi service *($25 to downtown area)* and hotel courtesy shuttles. Major **rental car** agencies. Amtrak **train** station: 209 State St. *℘800-872-7245.* Greyhound **bus** station: 34 W. Carrillo St. *℘800-231-2222.*

GETTING AROUND

Public parking lots are located throughout city; first 75min free. The **Downtown-Waterfront Shuttle** offers transport between the wharf and various attractions *(year-round daily 10am–6pm every 30min; 25¢; ℘683-3702).* **Santa Barbara Trolley** offers narrated rides to major sights as it loops around the city *(90min; year-round daily; $19/day; ℘965-0353; www.sbtrolley.com).* **Bicycle rentals:** Open

Air *℘962-7000;* Wheel Fun Rentals *℘966-2282.*

VISITOR INFORMATION

Santa Barbara Chamber of Commerce Visitor Information Center *(1 Garden St. ℘965-3021).* **Santa Barbara Conference & Visitors Bureau and Film Commission** *(1601 Anacapa St., Santa Barbara CA 93101 ℘966-9222 or 800-676-1266, www.santabarbaraca. com)* offers free information packets.

ACCOMMODATIONS

Reservation services: **Coastal Escapes** *℘692-9005 or 800-292-2222;* **Santa Barbara Hot Spots** *℘564-1637 or 800-793-7666; hotspotsusa.com.* Accommodations range from elegant hotels *($200–$400/day),* to moderate inns and chain hotels *($100–$200/day).* Most bed & breakfasts are in residential areas *($75–$200/day).* **Campsites** at Santa Barbara State Parks *℘800-444-7275.* Santa Barbara Sunrise RV Park *℘966-9954.*

Santa Barbara Yacht Harbor

West Cabrillo Blvd., .5mi west of wharf. Catering to the city's commercial fishing fleet, the harbor area contains bait shops, boat supply stores, gift shops and restaurants. Stroll out along the breakwater past the forest of masts for expansive views of Santa Barbara backdropped by mountains.

🚶🚶Santa Barbara Zoo★

500 Niños Dr., 1.5mi east of wharf. ⏰*Open year-round daily 10am–5pm.* ⏰*Closed Dec 25.* 🎟*$11, children $9.* ✕♿🅿$4. *℘805-962-5339. www.santabarbarazoo.org.*
Set amid 30 lush acres of cacti and palm gardens, the zoo, established in 1963, contains some 600 animals displayed in environments that approximate their native habitats.
Adjacent to the zoo, the 42-acre **Andree Clark Bird Refuge** surrounds a lagoon that harbors some 200 species of birds *(1400 E. Cabrillo Blvd.;* ⏰*open year-round*

daily 6am–10pm; 🅿 *).* Lovely views extend from the park's excellent bike/footpath.

DOWNTOWN

Past blends with present in downtown Santa Barbara. Today a house museum, **Casa de la Guerra** *(15 E. De la Guerra St.;* ⏰*open weekends noon–4pm; ℘805-965-0093),* built in 1827, exemplifies the early adobes that grew up around the presidio during the community's early days. Santa Barbara's business and shopping district beats along **State Street** bounded by Ortega and Victoria Streets.
The late 19C brought a wave of new construction in the style of New England; remants survive on **Brinkerhoff Avenue** *(2 blocks southwest of State St. between Cota & Haley Sts.).* The **Moreton Bay fig tree (1)** *(Chapala & Montecito Sts.),* with its intricate web of gnarled roots and a massive, 171ft branch spread, is reportedly the largest of its kind in the US.

Santa Barbara Museum of Art★

1130 State St. ⏱Open year-round Tue–Sun 11am–5pm. 💲$9 (free Sun).✕ ♿
📞805-963-4364. www.sbmuseart.org.
Housed in an elegant Italian Renaissance-style structure, the museum is one of the country's outstanding regional art museums.
The broad scope of the permanent holdings reflect the nature of the gifts to the museum, with particular strengths in Ancient art, Asian art, and turn of the 20C European and American art. Don't miss *Portrait of Mexico Today, 1932*, a rare US example of the work of muralist David Alfaro Siqueiros.

Karpeles Manuscript Library★

21 W. Anapamu St. ⏱Open Tue–Sat noon–4pm. ⏱Closed Dec 25. ♿ 🅿
📞805-962-5322. www.karpeles.com.
Original historical documents, including the Treaty of Ghent, are preserved in this gracefully designed house. The permanent collection of more than one million manuscripts rotates quarterly among the library's eight US locations.

Santa Barbara County Courthouse★★

1100 Anacapa St. ⏱Open year-round Mon–Fri 8am–5pm, weekends 10am–5pm. 🎧Guided tours (60min) Mon, Tue & Fri 10.30am & 2pm; Wed, Thu & Sat 2pm. ⏱Closed Dec 25.
📞805-962-6464. www.sbcourts.org.

The L-shaped Moorish courthouse (1929) surrounds a sunken courtyard; arched doorways, open-air galleries and curving staircases distinguish the interior. The Board of Supervisors' Assembly Room *(2nd floor)* features **murals** illustrating the area's history. Climb to the observation deck atop the 85ft clock tower for a **panorama**★★ of the city.

El Presidio de Santa Bárbara State Historic Park

123 E. Cañon Perdido St. ⏱Open year-round daily 10.30am–4.30pm. ⏱Closed Jan 1, Thanksgiving Day, Dec 25. ♿
📞805-965-0093. www.parks.ca.gov.
Completed by 1788, this Spanish fortress served as a military and government headquarters. Today the only original structures are the soldiers' residences (c.1788), known as **El Cuartel (A)** *(122 E. Cañon Perdido St.)* and Cañedo Adobe (c.1782); the **chapel (B)** was rebuilt according to existing records.

Santa Barbara Historical Museum

136 E. De la Guerra St. ⏱Open year-round Tue–Sat 10am–5pm, Sun noon–5pm. ⏱Closed Jan 1, Thanksgiving Day, Dec 25. ♿ 🅿 📞805-966-1601. www.santabarbaramuseum.com.
The museum features *The Story of Santa Barbara*, a permanent exhibit chronicling the region's colorful past. Highlights include Chumash artifacts, a Chinese joss house altar from the city's

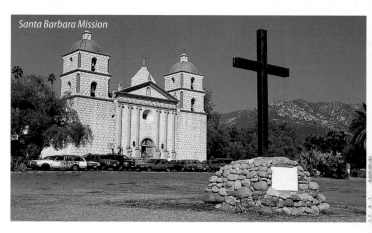

Santa Barbara Mission

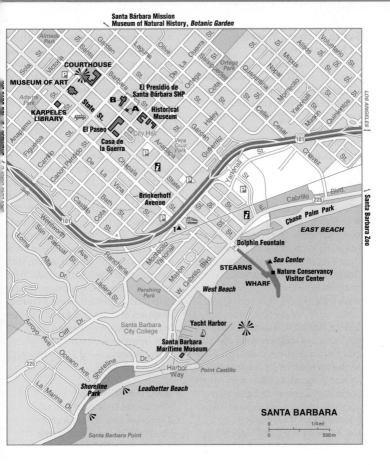

Santa Bárbara Mission
Museum of Natural History, *Botanic Garden*

SANTA BARBARA

0   1/4 mi

0   500m

19C Chinatown and saddles from the rancho period.

MISSION CANYON
Santa Barbara Mission★★★

2201 Laguna St. ◷*Open year-round daily 9am–4.30pm.* ◷*Closed Easter Sunday, Thanksgiving Day, Dec 25.* ⊜*$5.* ⓟ ✆*805-682-4713. www.santa barbaramission.org.*

Its twin towers rising against the foothills of Mission Canyon, the church of California's 10th mission, "Queen of the Missions," overlooks Santa Barbara from its lovely foothill site. The mission was dedicated in 1786; the first small church (1787) was replaced three times by larger structures.

The complex had to be entirely rebuilt after an earthquake in 1812, and the present church was completed in 1820.

Today the mission serves as an active parish center and a research library for the California mission chain.

The regal facade shows off a central pediment and six Ionic engaged columns crowned by twin pink-domed towers. The **interior** of the long, narrow church is adorned with the painted canvas reredos (1806); only fragments remain.

Thick-walled, heavily beamed rooms of the **padres' quarters** contain mission artifacts from the late 18C to early 19C. Behind the padres' quarters is the **sacred garden**.

A skull and crossbones over the side door of the church mark the shady **cemetery**, where neophytes lie buried.

Home to a community of Franciscan friars, the modern Mission has a retreat center with guest rooms, dining room, shop and museum.

Santa Barbara Museum of Natural History★

2559 Puesta del Sol. From the mission turn right on Los Olivos St.; follow signs. ◷*Open year-round daily 10am–5pm.* ◷*Closed Jan 1, Thanksgiving Day, Dec 25.* ◉*$10.* ♿🅿 ☎*805-682-4711. www.sbnature.org.*

Exhibits in this complex of Spanish-style stucco buildings display the flora, fauna, geology and ethnography of the West Coast. The **Chumash Indian Hall** contains one of the state's largest collections of artifacts from this tribe. In the Mineral & Gem Gallery, visitors can touch some of the glittering specimens and admire others, including a rare embedded ruby from Tanzania. Weekend shows in the Gladwin Planetarium present seasonal celestial phenomena (*call ahead for show times*).

Santa Barbara Botanic Garden

1212 Mission Canyon Rd. From the mission (above) turn right on Los Olivos St., right on Foothill Rd. and left onto Mission Canyon Rd.; follow signs to right at fork. ◷*Open Mar–Oct daily 9am– 6pm. Rest of the year daily 9am–5pm.* ◷*Closed Jan 1, Thanksgiving Day, Dec 24–25.* ◉*$8.* 🅿☎*805-682-4726. www.sbbg.org.*

Trails meander across 78 acres of wooded canyons, open meadows and high ridges. More than 1,000 species of native California plants grow here, including redwoods and cacti. In the north section is the original **Mission Dam**, built by Chumash neophytes in 1806 to provide water for the mission.

EXCURSIONS
Chumash Painted Cave State Historic Park

10mi northwest of Santa Barbara. Take Rte. 154 west to San Marcos Pass; turn right on Painted Cave Rd. (steep and narrow) and continue 2mi to cave on left. ◷*Open year-round daily dawn– dusk.* ◷*Closed Jan 1, Thanksgiving Day, Dec 25.* ♿🅿☎*805-733-3713. www.parks.ca.gov.*

This small cave allows a glimpse of rare **Chumash pictographs**. Primitive motifs representing the supernatural world, including a black disc that may depict a solar eclipse, were created using animal-tail brushes and red, black and white mineral pigments.

Solvang

34mi northwest of Santa Barbara via US-101N to Rte. 154, northwest to Rte. 246W. www.solvangca.com.

Groups of Danish settlers from the Midwest arrived here 1911 to start a colony in the Santa Ynez Valley, christening their farming village Solvang ("sunny field") and building Danish provincial-style dwellings and a folk school. Though its Danish population is less evident these days, Solvang still attracts visitors with its incongruous, yet charming windmills and half-timbered buildings. Danish culture is preserved in the **Elverhøj Museum of History & Art** (*1624 Elverhoy Way;* ◷*open year-round Wed & Thu 1pm–4pm; Fri–Sun noon–4pm;* ◷*closed major holidays;* ♿🅿☎*805-686-1211; www.elverhoj.org*).

Santa Inés Mission★

1760 Mission Dr., 1 block east of downtown Solvang, 4mi east of US-101. ◷*Open year-round daily 9am– 4.30pm.* ◷*Closed Jan 1, Easter Sun, Thanksgiving Day & Dec 25.* ◉*$3.* 🗣*Guided tours (2hrs;* ◉*$2) Wed 10am.* ♿🅿☎*805-688-4815. www.missionsantaines.org.*

The mission was founded in 1804 and named after Saint Agnes, an early Christian martyr (4C). Today the church, part of the convent and the gardens are all that remain of the original quadrangle. In the **museum** (*enter through the gift shop*), a recording (*30min*) summarizes the mission's history and describes the highlights of the museum's large collection of artifacts, including some noteworthy handmade **vestments**★ dating from the 15C.

In the **church**★, an engraving of a Roman theater stage may have inspired the trompe l'œil painting on the wall in back of the sanctuary. The Madonna Chapel contains a 17C painted wood carving of the Mother of Sorrows.

Ventura

This low-key coastal city grew up around San Buenaventura Mission. Today it's an easygoing beach town with attractive stretches of waterfront, abounding with recreational opportunities and a great base for whale-watching trips and excursions to Channel Islands National Park.

▶ **Population:** 98,366.
🖒 **Michelin Map:** 585 B 10.
🗎 **Info:** ✆805-648-2075; www.ventura-usa.com.
◐ **Location:** Ventura sits on the California coast about an hour's drive northwest of Los Angeles, between Santa Barbara and Oxnard.

A BIT OF HISTORY

This busy commercial town was originally incorporated as San Buenaventura in 1866. In the late 19C, brick structures replaced the modest adobe dwellings; **Ortega Adobe** (215 W. Main St.), built in 1857, is an example of the early adobe structures (🅿 ✆805-658-4726).

In the 1920s, oil fields were developed offshore and the population boomed. A mission and historic sites are preserved along Main Street, but the city's commercial area thrives around busy Ventura Harbor (access via Spinnaker Dr.).

SIGHTS

Olivas Adobe Historical Park★

4200 Olivas Park Dr. ◷Open year-round weekends 11am–4pm. ◷Closed major holidays. Contribution requested. ✆805-658-4728. www.olivasadobe.org.
This Monterey Colonial-style hacienda (1847) once occupied private land that formed part of the 4,692-acre Rancho San Miguel. Surrounded by a walled courtyard, the two-story house is furnished with period pieces. A visitor center contains artifacts and historical photographs.

San Buenaventura Mission

211 E. Main St. ◷Open Mon–Fri 10am–5pm, Sat 9am–5pm & Sun 10am–4pm. ◷Closed Easter Sunday, Thanksgiving Day, Dec 25. ◉$2. ✆805-643-4318. www.sanbuenaventuramission.org.
Padre Junípero Serra named the ninth mission for St. Bonaventure. The first church was replaced by a large stone structure (1809) that still serves as the parish church.
Now restored to a close approximation of its original appearance, the **church** is distinguished by its stone-and-brick construction, arched side entry and tiered bell tower. Inside, the Romanesque reredos, painted to resemble marble, was made in Mexico City. Vestiges of the original interior paintings can be seen in the Serra Chapel. A **museum** displays the only wooden bells used in any of the 21 missions.

EXCURSIONS

Oxnard

10mi south via Harbor Blvd. In 1898 the Oxnard brothers opened a sugar-beet factory south of the Santa Clara River. The fledgling factory spurred the growth of the city that reigns today as Ventura County's manufacturing center.
The region's heritage as a shipping center is recalled at the **Ventura County Maritime Museum** (2731 S. Victoria Ave.; ◷open year-round daily 11am–5pm; ◷closed Jan 1, Thanksgiving Day & Dec 25; ✆805-984-6260; www.vcmm.org). Models of tall ships dating from the mid-17C are on exhibit.

CEC and Seabee Museum

Naval Construction Battalion Center Bldg. 99, Port Hueneme. From Channel Islands Blvd., turn right on Ventura Rd. Enter Sunkist gate and obtain pass from guard. Visits restricted to groups fewer than six (Tue–Fri 8am–4pm, Sat 10am–3pm) and active military personnel. ◷Closed major holidays & Dec 25–Jan 1. ♿ 🅿 ✆805-982-5165. wwwseabeehf.org.
The museum honors members of the US Navy Construction Battalions (Seabees), who have served as military construction forces in combat zones since 1942.

CENTRAL VALLEY

Encompassing some of the richest agricultural real estate in the US, the Central Valley (also known as the Great Valley) produces an amazing variety and abundance of vegetables, fruits and other crops on huge farms, most of which today operate as corporations. Hot, dry summers and fertile soils watered by massive irrigation projects provide ideal growing conditions.

Highlights

1 A train ride behind a steam locomotive at **California Railroad Museum** (p112)

2 The strange sight of a fruit orchard flourishing underground at **Forestiere Underground Gardens** (p110)

Surrounded on the west by the Coast Ranges, on the east by the Sierra Nevada, on the south by the Peninsular Ranges and on the north by the Cascade and Klamath ranges, the Central Valley is in fact two separate valleys drained by the two rivers whose names they bear: the San Joaquin in the south and the Sacramento in the north. The streams join at the **Delta**, a 750sq mi expanse of natural marsh east of San Francisco Bay, where dikes have created waterways and low-lying islands. The 260mi-long **San Joaquin Valley** stretches from near Bakersfield to Stockton. The 180mi **Sacramento Valley** extends from near Redding, through Sacramento to the Delta. Game and waterfowl made the valley a hunters' paradise for the Native American tribes. Spanish military parties explored the valley and named the major rivers in the late 18C and early 19C.

Johann (**John**) **August Sutter** built a fort in 1839 at the confluence of the Sacramento and American rivers. In 1848 his foreman, **James Marshall**, discovered gold on the South Fork of the American River (*see Sacramento: A Bit of History*). That discovery ushered in the Gold Rush. Today, around 6.5 million people live in Central Valley, the fastest growing region in California.

San Joaquin Valley

© Matthew Clayson/Dreamstime.com

ADDRESSES

🏨 STAY

⊜⊜⊜⊜ *(all-inclusive)* **Quarter Circle U Rankin Ranch** – *11mi north of Caliente (41mi east of Bakersfield) via Rte. 58. Open late Mar–Sept.* ☎661-867-2511. www.rankinranch.com. *14 rooms (single or duplex cabins).* 🖵. Sequestered at 3,500ft elevation in remote Walker's Basin in the Tehachapi Mountains, this historic working cattle ranch is operated by the sixth generation of the family that founded it in 1863. There's no phone or TV here: guests fill their days riding, hiking, fishing, swimming and eating hearty meals.

⊜⊜⊜ **Sterling Hotel** – *1300 H. St., Sacramento.* ☎916-448-1300 or 800-365-7660. www.sterlinghotel.com. *17 rooms.* 🖵. An exquisitely restored 1890s Victorian mansion three blocks from the State Capitol, the Sterling presents designer furnishings, Italian marble and a Jacuzzi bath in every room. Within the dignified white estate is Chanterelle (⊜⊜⊜), a fine-dining restaurant serving California cuisine. Guests enjoy a complimentary continental breakfast.

⊜⊜ **Riverboat Delta King** – *1000 Front St., Sacramento.* ☎916-444-5464 or 800-825-5464. www.deltaking.com. *44 rooms.* During Prohibition, this "floating pleasure palace" ran from Sacramento to San Francisco. Today the red paddle-wheeler remains on the Sacramento River in Old Town. Guests can stroll on the promenade deck, listen to Dixieland jazz and dine in the **Pilothouse Restaurant** (⊜⊜). Cozy cabins are outfitted with solid oak and polished brass.

⊜⊜ **Johnson's Country Inn** – *3935 Morehead Ave., Chico.* ☎530-345-7829. www.accessnow.com/johnsonsinn. *4 rooms.* 🖵. Set amid almond orchards on the outskirts of a university town, this sprawling Victorian-style farmhouse features spacious rooms decorated in different styles, a broad, shady wraparound porch, and inviting guest areas replete with board games, books and other diversions; you can even play horseshoes or croquet in the garden. Breakfasts are copious and delicious.

⊜ **Springville Inn** – *Hwy. 190, Springville (40mi southeast of Visalia).* ☎559-539-7501 or 800-484-3466. www.springvilleinn.com. *10 rooms.* 🖵. Nestled in the Sierra foothills south of Sequoia National Park, an hour's drive from Bakersfield and Fresno, this lovingly restored 1912 inn boasts intimate rooms with pine furnishings, country quilts and ceiling fans. In the **Stagecoach Bar & Grill** (⊜⊜), diners can choose from a selection of steaks, ribs, seafood and other dishes.

🍽 EAT

⊜⊜⊜ **Slocum House** – *7992 California Ave., Fair Oaks (13mi east of Sacramento).* ☎916-961-7211. www.slocum-house.com. *Closed Mon. No lunch Sat.* **International**. This manse offers dining in a classical indoor setting or a large garden with free-roaming fowl. The creative menu choices range from Australian lamb to Sesame Wasabi Ahi to Moroccan chicken flavored with orange and served with couscous.

⊜⊜ **Benji's French Basque** – *4001 Rosedale Hwy., Bakersfield.* ☎661-328-0400. Closed Tue. **Basque**. With its large population of Basques, Bakersfield has, to no one's surprise, at least a half-dozen Basque restaurants. At Benji's, traditional cuisine is served family-style at large shared tables, and features excellent soups, lamb and pork dishes with paprika.

⊜⊜ **Red Tavern** – *1250 The Esplanade, Chico.* ☎530-894-3463. www.red-taverncom. Closed Sun. Dinner only.* **Mediterranean.** This restaurant's fresh sheet menu embraces simple foods with a Mediterranean-Asian flair. Try the marinated lamb with fava beans and curried rice, or the duck confit with roasted vegetables.

⊜ **S&S Produce and Barbecue** – *1924 Mangrove, Chico.* ☎530-343-1187. **Barbeque**. A small natural foods grocery, this Chico institution operates a thriving barbecue stand with large quantities for takeout *(closes 7pm).* The signature dine-in offering is a sandwich featuring a Northern California standard, flavorsome beef tri-tip; the thinly sliced roast is piled on fresh buns, without sauce (add your own).

Bakersfield

Sprawling Bakersfield was founded in the 1860s with the discovery of gold in the Kern River. The city boomed as an agricultural center (for vegetables and especially cotton) in the late 19C, and again with the discovery of oil here in the early 20C; machines continue to pump on the northern edge of the city. Nowadays the city is the nexus of California's country & western music scene, thanks to the enduring popularity of native son Buck Owens and the presence of several live music theater venues.

▶ **Population:** 328,692.
✦ **Michelin Map:** 585 B 10.
▤ **Info:** ℘661-852-7282. www.bakersfieldcvb.org.
● **Location:** Edged by the Kern River, the city lies inland southeast of San Luis Obispo and 110mi north of Los Angeles by I-5.
👪 **Kids:** Kern County Museum.

SIGHT
👪Kern County Museum★
3801 Chester Ave., 1mi north of downtown. ◷*Open year-round Mon–Sat 10am–5pm, Sun noon–5pm (ticket sales end 3pm).* ◷*Closed major holidays.* ♿$10, children $7. ♿ ▣ ℘661-852-5000. www.kcmuseum.org.
A 16-acre assemblage of historic structures offers an excellent depiction of life in Kern County from the 1860s to the 1930s. In the main museum building, view exhibits of old vehicles, county wildlife, pioneer history and Bakersfield's contributions to country & western music.

Outdoors are some 50 buildings either relocated here from their original sites in Kern County or rebuilt according to photographs. You'll find a sheepherder's cabin, a large assortment of oil-drilling equipment, a restored 1930s gas station and even a ranch chuck wagon.

EXCURSION
Colonel Allensworth State Historic Park★
Rte 43, 9mi west of Earlimart; 41mi northwest of Bakersfield. Take Rte. 99 north 2mi to Delano, turn west 5.6mi on Cecil Rd., then north 6.7mi on Rte. 43. ◷*Open 8am–6pm.* ♿$4/vehicle. ⚠♿▣ ℘661-849-3433. www.parks.ca.gov.
This reconstructed pioneer town commemorates its founder, **Col. Allen Allensworth** (1842-1914), a retired military

Colonel Allensworth State Historic Park, restored school, original built in 1916

officer who escaped from slavery and became an advocate of African American self-sufficiency. Along with several others he founded the town of Allensworth as an independent black American community in 1908.
The two-room Allensworth School served as the town hall and a church.

Col. Allensworth lived part-time in the Allensworth Home *(Dunbar Rd. and Sojourner Ave.)*, now furnished in period style. On the north end of the town stand Singleton's General Store (1910), a hotel and the Tulare County Free Library.

Chico

This farming hub and university town is home to California State University, Chico, which boasts strong programs in the research sciences and ranks among the most environmentally friendly college campuses in the US. **Bidwell Park**★ is graced with gardens and oak trees along Big Chico Creek.

▶ **Population:** 84,491.
✦ **Michelin Map:** 585 A 7.
🔲 **Info:** 530-891-5556. www.chicochamber.com.
▶ **Location:** Near the north end of the Sacramento Valley, Chico lies between Redding and Sacramento.

SIGHT
Bidwell Mansion State Historic Park
525 The Esplanade (north end of Main St.). Visit by guided tour only *(50min on the hour), year-round Tue–Fri noon–4pm, weekends 11am–4pm.* Visitor center open Tue–Fri noon–5pm, weekends 10am–5pm. Closed Jan 1, Thanksgiving Day, Dec 25. $4. 530-895-6144. www.parks.ca.gov.
This Italianate mansion at the edge of the university campus was built in 1868 by businessman **John Bidwell** (1819–1900). While employed by John Sutter, Bidwell discovered gold on the Feather River in mid-1848. Bidwell founded Chico in 1860 and was active in state politics before serving a term in the US House of Representatives.
Today refurbished in the style of the late 19C, the house offers glimpses into Bidwell's life and times.

EXCURSIONS
Oroville Chinese Temple
21mi southeast of Chico at 1500 Broderick St., Oroville. Open Feb–mid-Dec daily noon–4pm. Closed mid-Dec–Jan & major holidays. $2. 530-538-2496.

A reminder of the 10,000 Chinese gold miners who lived in the area in the late 19C, this compound (1863) comprises a Taoist temple, a Buddhist temple, a Confucian chapel, a hall of Chinese folk arts and a garden with plants of Chinese origin (bamboo, water lily).

Gray Lodge Wildlife Area
25mi south of Chico. Drive 17.5mi south on Rte. 99 to Gridley; 6.3mi west on Sycamore Rd. (which becomes Colusa Rd.); 3.2mi south on Pennington Rd. to entrance on west side; 2mi west to Parking Area 14. Open year-round. $2.50. 530-846-5176. www.dfg.ca.gov.
This 9,000-acre refuge is home to beaver, deer and coyote. Geese, ducks and other waterfowl winter here during migrations along the Pacific Flyway. The preserve is flanked on the south by the Sutter Buttes, 3-million-year-old volcanic peaks of 2,117ft. Levee trails are open to the public, except during hunting season *(mid-Oct–mid-Jan)*. Around Parking Area 14, birdwatchers may drive along a 3mi car route. The paved **Viewing Platform Trail** *(0.5mi)* leads to a deck overlooking the marshes. The **Wetlands Loop Trail** *(2mi)* follows the levee, with views south to Sutter Buttes.

Fresno

California's eighth-largest city is the seat of Fresno County, which leads the nation in agricultural output. Much of the world's grape harvest is produced here, along with oranges, figs, olives and livestock.

> ▶ **Population:** 490,487.
> ⊙ **Michelin Map:** 585 B 9.
> 🗐 **Info:** ℘559-445-8300. www.fresnocvb.org.
> ▶ **Location:** Fresno lies inland, 110mi north of Bakersfield and 120mi south of Stockton by Hwy. 99.
> ᎯᎯ **Kids:** Chaffee Zoo.

A BIT OF HISTORY

Fresno was founded after the Gold Rush. Its proximity to the region's agricultural abundance led to its growth as a center of the food-processing industry.

SIGHTS

ᎯᎯ Forestiere Underground Gardens★

5021 W. Shaw Ave., 2 blocks east of Rte. 99 in north Fresno. ⟿*Visit by guided tour (60min) only, Memorial Day–Labor Day daily 10am–2.30pm; May & Sept Wed–Sun 10am–3.30pm; Apr & Oct Thu–Sun 10am–2.30pm; Mar & Nov weekends 11am–2pm.* ⊛*$12, children $7. Reservations requested.* ✕ᎯᏢ *℘559-271-0734. www.underground gardens.info.*

Sicilian immigrant Baldasare Forestiere (1879–1946) sculpted this amazing underground garden and orchard, excavating more than 10 acres and using skylights to bring natural light belowground. The complex today preserves 40 rooms on five acres.

ᎯᎯ Chaffee Zoo

894 W. Belmont Ave. in Roeding Park, 2mi northwest of downtown. ⊙*Open year-round daily 9am–4pm.* ⊛*$7, children $3.50.* ✕ᎯᏢ *℘559-498-5910. www.chaffeezoo.org.*

This 18-acre zoo harbors is the only zoo in the country to display rare Northland green geckos. Successes from the zoo's breeding programs include Sumatran tigers and Galápagos tortoises.

Meux Home Museum

1007 R St. at Tulare St. ⟿*Visit by guided tour (1hr) only, Feb–Dec Fri–Sun noon–3pm.* ⊙*Closed major holidays.* ⊛*$5.* ✕ᎯᏢ *℘559-233-8007. www.meux.mus.ca.us.*

This elaborate Victorian mansion (1889) houses lovely period furnishings. Victorian-era plants and flowers festoon the gardens.

Kearney Mansion Museum

7160 W. Kearney Blvd., in Kearney Park. ⟿*Visit by guided tour (1hr) only,* ⊙*Fri–Sun 1pm, 2pm & 3pm.* ⊙*Closed major holidays.* ⊛*$5.* ᎯᏢ *℘559-441-0862. www.valleyhistory.org.*

This French Renaissance-style residence was built in 1903 by M. Theo Kearney, who used canal systems to cultivate orchards and vineyards. Today the mansion exhibits original furnishings.

ᎯᎯ Fresno Metropolitan Museum

1555 Van Ness Ave. ⊙*Open year-round Thu–Sun 11am–5pm (1st Thu 8pm).* ⊛*$9, children $5.* ᎯᏢ *℘559-441-1444. www.fresnomet.org.*

Don't miss the unique assortment of jigsaw puzzles at this kid-friendly art and science museum. The permanent collection ranges from American landscape photographs by Ansel Adams to Native American basketry.

Fresno Art Museum

2233 N. First St. (between Clinton & McKinley Aves.) in Radio Park. ⊙*Open year-round Tue–Sun 11am–5pm (Thu 8pm).* ⊙*Closed major holidays.* ⊛*$5 (Sunday free).* ᎯᏢ *℘559-441-4221. www.fresnoartmuseum.org.*

This modest art museum maintains a collection of French post-Impressionist prints and drawings; Mexican art from the pre-Columbian era to the present and California and Asian art.

Sacramento★★

California's capital possesses a rich heritage and an appealing all-American gentility. This flat site at the confluence of the Sacramento and American rivers was urbanized with a grid of straight, tree-lined streets that remind many visitors of the Midwest. Yet the city has an aura of a modern metropolis, with many contemporary cultural attractions to complement the vestiges of its pioneer past.

THE CITY TODAY

With the state government and several universities here, Sacramento exudes a stable, family-friendly air. Its culturally diverse residents seem indifferent to the fads of California's trendy hotspots, but the city boasts an active local music and theater scene. Sacramento's relatively low cost of living compared to California's other urban centers has brought a recent influx of new residents.

A BIT OF HISTORY

Sacramento began as Sutter's Fort, built in 1839 by German-Swiss adventurer **John Sutter**. Having persuaded the Mexican government at Monterey that it would benefit from the settlement of the Central Valley, he received a grant of 47,827 acres and began work on his "New Helvetia."

In 1848 Sutter's employee, **James Marshall**, discovered gold in the tailrace of a lumber mill that Sutter had commissioned him to build in Coloma. This discovery set in motion the California **Gold Rush**. The new American administration in California only partially recognized Sutter's land holdings and the town of Sacramento was founded about 2mi west along the Sacramento River. Ships from San Francisco Bay landed here, and other businesses found it advantageous to locate near the docks. After floods and fires in the early 1850s, a protective levee was constructed and new buildings were constructed mostly of brick. Sacramento remained an important inland port into the 1860s, when it

- ▶ **Population:** 460,242.
- 🚗 **Michelin Map:** 585 A 8; and map this section.
- 🛈 **Info:** ℘916-808-7777. www.sacramentocvb.org.
- ◗ **Location:** The capital of California lies inland at the head of the Central Valley some 90mi east of San Francisco by I-80.
- 🅿 **Parking:** Metered street parking is available. For Old Sacramento, parking garages are located on I St. under I-5 and on Front St. at L St. For State Capitol Area, garages are located at 10th St. between P and O Sts. and between L and K Sts., 11th St. between O and P Sts., and 14th and P Sts.
- 👪 **Kids:** Railroad museum; Sacramento History Museum

became the terminus of the first transcontinental railroad. Later it surrounded the intersection of important highways crossing the Sierra and those traversing the Central Valley lengthwise.

In 1854 Sacramento became the capital of California. State government was relatively small until the 1860s, but has grown rapidly in numbers of buildings and employees.

OLD SACRAMENTO★★

I to L Sts., the Sacramento River and I-5. The city's premier tourist attraction, Sacramento's original downtown constitutes the nation's largest ensemble of Gold Rush-era buildings.

An ambitious restoration project has transformed the original downtown into a 24.5-acre state historic park. Two- and three-story buildings lining **Second** and **Front Streets** evoke the ambience of a 19C frontier town despite the souvenir shops that occupy several storefronts today. *Self-guided walking tour brochure and audio tours are available at the visitor center (Second and K Sts.; ☎916-442-7644; www.oldsacramento.com).*

California State Capitol

▲▲ California State Railroad Museum★★

125 I St. at 2nd St. ⊙Open year-round daily 10am–5pm. ⊙Closed Jan 1, Thanksgiving Day, Dec 25. ⊜$8, children $3. ♿ ☏916-445-6645. www.csrmf.org.

This excellent museum (1981) celebrates railroading's role in the development of the American West.

A passage leading to the main floor documents the monumental challenge of building the Central Pacific Railroad over the Sierra Nevada in the 1860s. A train buff's dream, the large exhibit hall holds 21 impressively restored locomotives like Central Pacific's **Engine No. 1**. Railroad cars at the reconstructed1876 depot include a sleeping car and a luxurious private car. The second-floor galleries feature a collection of toy trains.

Adjacent to the museum, a row of brick storefronts includes a reconstruction of the 1850s **Huntington, Hopkins & Co. Hardware Store (A)**. The original store was the financial base of Collis Huntington and Mark Hopkins, two members of the "Big Four," who organized and directed the Central Pacific *(113 I St.)*.

Sacramento History Museum★

▲▲ *101 I St. ⊙Open Jul–Aug daily 10am–5pm; rest of the year Tue–Sun 10am–5pm. ⊙Closed major holidays. ⊜$5, chhildren $3. ♿☐ ☏916-264-7057. www.thediscovery.org.*

This museum presents the history of Sacramento by telling the colorful stories of the town's founders, the riv-

ers, and the Gold Rush, with artifacts from the Native American period to the present. One gallery documents Sacramento's agriculture and food-processing industries; another highlights Gold Rush-era mining methods.

Along Front Street extends a replica of the Central Pacific **passenger station (B)** as it existed in 1876; a "sound stick" provides sound effects to re-create the atmosphere of a working train station. At the **Central Pacific Freight Depot (C)**, steam trains offer 6mi excursions along the river (⊙*depart Apr–Sept weekends 11am–5pm; round-trip 40min; commentary; ⊜$8; California State Railroad Museum ☏916-445-6645; www.csrmf. org).*

The 1930s riverboat **Delta King**, permanently docked behind the depot, functions as a floating hotel *(see Address Book).* Across the street, the wooden-canvas **Eagle Theatre**—the first theater in California, when it opened in 1849—presents a historical slide show *(975 Front St.).*

B.F. Hastings and Co. Building (D)

2nd & J Sts.

In its late 19C heyday, this handsome building served as the terminus for the Pony Express and the transcontinental telegraph line. Nicely restored, it now contains the **Wells Fargo History Museum** (⊙ *open daily 10am–5pm; ☏916-440-4263; www.wellsfargohistory.*

com), featuring gold samples and other Gold Rush-era souvenirs.

Outside, a corner **monument** remembers the Pony Express riders who made the 1,966mi mail run between St. Joseph, Missouri, and Sacramento.

STATE CAPITOL AREA
California State Capitol★★
1315 10th St. between L & N Sts.
◷*Open Mon–Fri 8am–6pm, weekends 9am–5pm.* ☛*Guided tours on the hour daily 9am–4pm.* ◷*Closed Jan 1, Thanksgiving Day, Dec 25.* ✕&*916-324-0333. www.assembly.ca.gov/ museum.*

Topped by a massive dome, Sacramento's most prominent landmark embodies the Neoclassical style. The pediment over the main entrance *(west side)* shows Minerva, the central figure in the state seal, surrounded by Justice, Mining, Education and Industry.

Begun in 1860 and renovated to its original splendor, the building boasts mosaic floors and crystal chandeliers. A decorated dome 210ft overhead dominates the grand **rotunda**. The museum theater (basement) screens short films about the building and its restoration. The 40-acre grounds surrounding the building boast some 300 labeled species of tree.

California State Library
914 Capitol Mall. ◷*Closed for renovation; projected reopening early 2011.* &*916-654-0261. www.library.ca.gov.* This Neoclassical granite building (1926), boasts art deco motifs and allegorical murals. An archive and library of state history, the **California Room** *(library annex building, 900 N St., Room 200; &916-654-0176)* hosts changing exhibits.

Leland Stanford Mansion State Historic Park
8th & N Sts. ◷*Visitor center open year-round daily 9.30am–5pm.* ☛*Mansion visit by guided tour (1hr) only, daily 10am–5pm (last tour 4pm);* ☉*$8.* ◷*Closed Jan 1, Thanksgiving Day, Dec 25.* &*916-324-0575. www.parks.ca.gov.* Governor, railroad magnate and Stanford University founder Leland Stanford purchased this Italianate mansion in 1861; it served as his gubernatorial residence until 1863. Today it hosts state government events and meetings.

California Museum★
1020 O St. ◷*Open year-round Tue–Sat 10am–5pm (last admission 4.30pm), Sun noon–5pm.* ◷*Closed major holidays.* ☉*$7.50.* ✕&P *916-653-7524. www. californiamuseum.org.*

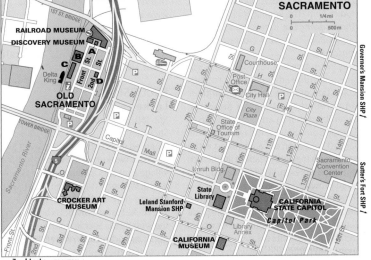

Zoo / Locke, STOCKTON

Occupying a corner of the California State Archives building, this museum presents engaging displays oriented around the state's leading personalities. The **Legacy Trails** gallery highlights the journeys taken by some of the state's outstanding women, including culinary innovator Alice Waters, astronaut Sally Ride, costume designer Edith Head, as well as furniture designer Ray Eames. The **Hall of Fame** showcases other remarkable California men and women.

Governor's Mansion State Historic Park

16th & H Sts. Visit by guided tour (45min) only, year-round daily on the hour 10am–4pm. Closed Jan 1, Thanksgiving Day, Dec 25. $4. 916-323-3047. www.parks.ca.gov.

This Second Empire Italianate mansion (1877) was acquired by the state in 1903 as the official residence for the state's chief executive. The interior contains furnishings and artifacts—including First Ladies' gowns—left by the families of 13 governors who set up household here, the last of whom was Ronald Reagan. Subsequent governors have resided in a modern home elsewhere in Sacramento.

ADDITIONAL SIGHTS
Crocker Art Museum★

216 O St. Open year-round Tue–Sun 10am–5pm (Thu 9pm). Closed Jan 1, Thanksgiving Day, Dec 25. $6. 916-808-7000. www.crockerart museum.org.

This institution was founded in 1885 to present Judge Edwin Bryant Crocker's collection of more than 700 paintings and around 1,344 master drawings, assembled during an extended trip to Europe from 1869-71. Today it boasts the largest collection of California art in the state, with pieces by leading lights such as Robert Arneson, Wayne Thiebaud and Joan Brown.

The mansion's splendidly restored **interior★★** spotlights 19C California landscape painters, among other works. Temporary exhibits are mounted in the adjoining contemporary wings.

Sutter's Fort State Historic Park★★

27th & L Sts. Open year-round daily 10am–5pm. Closed Jan 1, Thanksgiving Day, Dec 25. $4, children $2. 916-445-4422. www.parks.ca.gov.

Built in 1839, this landmark complex was John Sutter's "castle" as he sought to establish his commercial empire in California. The only structure that is mostly original is the administration building; the rest of the fort was in ruins in the 1890s, when restoration began.

Visitors explore the compound assisted by self-activated audio stations. The tools of daily life have been assembled in the buildings as exhibits and as material for **living-history reenactments** (*$6; inquire about schedule*).

Adjacent to the fort is the **State Indian Museum★**, where Native American dance regalia, baskets, a Yurok boat and other artifacts are showcased (*open year-round daily 10am–5pm; closed Jan 1, Thanksgiving Day, Dec 25; $2; 916-324-0971; www.parks.ca.gov*).

Sacramento Zoo

3mi south of downtown at 3930 W. Land Park Dr. Take I-5 south to Sutterville Rd. exit and follow signs. Open Feb–Oct daily 9am–4pm; rest of the year daily 10am–4pm. Closed Thanksgiving Day & Dec 25. $9.50, children $7. 916-808-5888. www.saczoo.com.

This small zoo is home to Siberian tigers, jaguars, margay cats and other animals. A children's theme park, **Fairytale Town**, sits opposite the zoo.

EXCURSION
Locke

Rte. 160, 27mi south of downtown Sacramento.

Founded in 1915 by Chinese levee and railroad workers, this once-thriving village presents a composite of dilapidated, Western-style architecture with Chinese signs and motifs.

The Locke Historic District is bounded to the west by the Sacramento River, to the north by Locke Rd., to the east by Alley St., and to the south by Levee St.

THE DESERTS

A journey into California's deserts is a trek through a vast land of sparse rainfall, torrid days and freezing nights, mountains shaped by water and the lack thereof. Mineral-rich rock struts varied colors like a peacock parading its tail feathers. Hidden, spring-fed wetlands seduce songbirds to palm-laced oases. Rare wildlife like desert tortoises and Salt Creek pupfish have adapted to conditions alien to most species, including man. Forests of cacti and ancient Joshua trees, their knotty arms reaching heavenward, find pockets of habitability.

The deserts extend south 350mi from Death Valley National Park to the Mexican border. There are two principal deserts.

The **Mojave Desert**, cooler and higher, descends to the hotter, drier **Colorado Desert** in Joshua Tree National Park; observers at Keys View can witness the botanical transition from Joshua trees to the thorny green-limbed paloverde and smoke trees. Farther south, the arid stretches of Anza-Borrego Desert State Park and the Imperial Valley run to **Baja California**.

No direct north-south thoroughfare links the deserts, although inventive four-wheel drivers can create their own itineraries from Death Valley, through Mojave National Preserve and Joshua Tree National Park to Palm Springs or the Salton Sea. Greater continuity is provided by the multiple mountain ranges that confounded overland immigrants, many of whom perished essaying a southern route to the ranchland and riches of coastal California in the mid-19C.

Highlights

1   Sunrise over Telescope Peak seen from **Dante's View** (p120)
2   Sunset on the Red Cathedral in **Golden Canyon** (p120)
3   The jaw-dropping ascent and descent on the **Palm Springs Aerial Tramway** (p126)
4   Vista from Keys View in **Joshua Tree National Park** (p122)

The US military uses the harsh conditions for survival training, weapons testing and jet maneuvers. Restricted-access bases dot the region.

Although Death Valley's name evokes the direst aspects of these deserts, the national park is a magnet for bicyclists and hikers braving the extreme conditions, even in summer. Simmering heat in one season is offset by the colorful blaze of wildflowers and cacti blossoming in February in desert valleys, a progressive bloom that can last into May in higher mountain elevations.

Sand Dunes, Death Valley National Park

©Robert Holmes/California Travel & Tourism Commission

ADDRESSES

⛺STAY

🛏🛏🛏🛏 **Furnace Creek Inn and Ranch Resort** – *Highway 190, Death Valley National Park.* ☎*760-786-2345 or 800-236-7916. www.furnacecreek resort.com. 290 rooms.* One of the few areas where services and supplies are available within the park, Furnace Creek offers 66 rooms in a luxurious Mission-style **inn** *(closed mid-May–mid-Oct)* or 224 rooms at its family-style ranch. The sprawling ranch offers such amenities as a general store, stables, steakhouse, tennis courts and a spring-fed pool. Dining options include a steakhouse and a cafe at the ranch, and more upscale offerings at the inn's dining room.

🛏🛏🛏🛏 **Miramonte Resort** – *45-000 Indian Wells Lane, Indian Wells.* ☎*760-341-2200 or 800-237-2926. www.miramonteresort.com. 215 rooms.* Guests at this Tuscan villa-style resort 30min east of Palm Springs enjoy elegant rooms and rose and herb gardens. Rooms are done in earth tones with Mediterranean-style furnishings. Poolside cabanas and hammocks invite relaxation. **The Grove Artisan Kitchen** (🛏🛏🛏) specializes in fine cuisine made with local, organic ingredients.

🛏🛏🛏🛏 **Orbit In** – *562 W. Arenas Rd., Palm Springs.* ☎*760-323-3585 or 877-996-7248. www.orbitin.com. 9 rooms.* Furnishings by the famed designers of the 1950s—Eames, Bertoia, Noguchi, Saarinen—still find a place amid the vintage modernism of this renovated motel. Perks include the poolside boomerang bar and individually designed studios, whose private patios, kitchens and other amenities lend themselves to discreet getaways.

🛏🛏🛏🛏🛏 **The Willows Historic Palm Springs Inn** – *412 W. Tahquitz Canyon Way, Palm Springs.* ☎*760-320-0771 or 800-966-9597. www.thewillow spalmsprings.com. 8 rooms.* 🍴. Set against a backdrop of Mount Jacinto, this striking Mediterranean villa has its own private hillside garden and waterfall. Rooms are individually decorated with antique furnishings, deluxe linens, fireplaces and hardwood floors. Partake of the full gourmet breakfast in the formal dining room, on the veranda, or on your private balcony.

🛏🛏 **(7-night rate) Palm Springs Rendez Vous** – *1420 N. Indian Canyon Dr., Palm Springs.* ☎*760-320-1178 or 800-485-2808. www.ballantineshotels. com. 10 rooms.* 🍴. Kitsch and glamour join hands at this colorful "retro boutique" hotel, authentic to the modernist architecture and interior design of the 1950s. Generous gourmet breakfasts might include stuffed French toast and fresh-squeezed juice; evenings bring complementary martinis and appetizers around the pool or the fire pit. Cruiser bikes are available for guests' use.

🍴EAT

🍴🍴🍴 **Le St. Germain** – *74-985 Hwy. 111, Indian Wells.* ☎*760-773-6511. www.lestgermain.com.* **French**. An elegant and spacious bistro toward the eastern end of the Coachella Valley, this popular restaurant with a garden patio claims to "bring Paris to the desert." The emphasis is on seafood (try the unforgettable mussels) but the wild mushroom soup with truffle oil is also a big hit.

🍴🍴🍴🍴 **Le Vallauris** – *385 W. Tahquitz Canyon Way, Palm Springs.* ☎*760-325-5059. www.levallauris.com.* **French**. Ficus trees overhang the tables on the pleasant outdoor patio at this popular (and pricey) restaurant, a fixture on the Palm Springs dining circuit for three decades. Regulars applaud the lobster ravioli, the champagne brunch and the Grand Marnier souffles for dessert.

🍴🍴 **Idle Spurs Steak House** – *690 Old Hwy. 58, Barstow.* ☎*760-256-8888. www. idlespurssteakhouse.com.* **American.** The tree rising through the center of the dining room is testimony to Idle Spurs' more than five decades in business. Built as a residence, the house boasts spacious gardens and a skylit fountain atrium. The menu, naturally, focuses on beef—aged steaks and slow-roasted prime rib—but also includes chicken, pork and seafood.

Barstow

Once a 19C stop for miners and pioneers on the Old Spanish Trail, Barstow is now a no-nonsense services town. In the 1940s and 1950s the town was a popular stop along on Route 66, the historic highway that ran from Chicago to Los Angeles.

▶ **Population:** 23,164.
◉ **Michelin Map:** 585 C 10.
▯ **Info:** ☏760-256-8617. www.barstow chamber.com.
◖ **Location:** Barstow is situated inland, about midway between Los Angeles and Las Vegas and 60mi west of Mojave National Preserve.

SIGHTS

♟♙Calico Ghost Town★

From Barstow, drive 8mi east on I-15 to Ghost Town Rd. exit; continue 3mi north to entrance gate. ◐*Open year-round daily 8am–dusk (most buildings open 9am–5pm).* ◐*Closed Dec 25.* ☞*$6, children $3.* ⚠✕♿☏*760-254-2122. www.calicotown.com.*

This amusement park was formed from the vestiges of a silver and borax boomtown that nearly passed into oblivion when the mineral deposits gave out. Walter Knott, creator of Knott's Berry Farm, acquired the town in 1951, and restored its Old West flavor before deeding it to San Bernardino County.

Ascend a long flight of steps (or take the incline railway) from the parking lot to Calico's main street. Lil's Saloon, the Town Office, Lucy Lane's Home (now a museum with living history displays and fascinating photos of Calico during its heyday), the R&D Store and the General Store are original structures; the others have been rebuilt. The railroad offers short rides *(10min)* that circumscribe the hill east of town.

Calico Early Man Site★

From Barstow drive 15mi east on I-15 to Minneola Rd. exit ; continue northeast to end of 2.4mi dirt road. ◐*Open Oct–Jun Wed 12.30pm–4.30pm, Thu–Sun 9am–4.30pm. Jul–Sept Thu–Sun 9am–1pm.* ➷*Guided tours Wed 1.30pm & 3.30pm, Thu–Sun 9.30am, 11.30am, 1.30pm & 3.30pm.* ◐*Closed major holidays.* ☞*$5.* ▣☏*760-254-2248. www.blm.gov.*

Excavations on this barren hillside have revealed what may be crude scrapers and choppers made by very ancient humans, lending credence to the theory that an early species of humans may have been present in California before the arrival of *Homo sapiens* (20,000 BC). Renowned archaeologist Louis S.B. Leakey directed excavations here from 1964 until his death in 1972. At the visitor center, several excavated artifacts are on view. Tours led by site archaeologists depart from the miner's shack that Leakey used as his field headquarters and continue to the excavation pits.

Calico Ghost Town
©James Feliciano/Dreamstime.com

Death Valley National Park★★★

This sun-blasted realm of stone, sand and wide-open spaces has the lowest elevations and highest temperatures in the Western Hemisphere. Here, the silent, stark grandeur of earth-forming processes is unobscured by vegetation or scars of human encroachment.

A BIT OF GEOLOGY

Death Valley is not a riverine valley, but rather a deep, 130mi-long **basin** with no outlet, formed about 3 million years ago, as a block of the earth's crust sank, leaving adjoining blocks standing high on either side to form the Panamint and Amargosa ranges. The mountains are flanked by **alluvial fans**, delta-like deposits built up as debris washes out of canyons during flash floods. Elevations within the park range from 11,049ft above sea level to 282ft below.

The average annual rainfall in the valley is just 2in because the Sierra Nevada mountain range blocks most incoming moisture from the Pacific Ocean. The sun shines relentlessly here, heating the basin floor to some of the highest average **temperatures** on earth. The basin's highest recorded temperature of 134° has been exceeded only in the Libyan Sahara Desert.

Cacti are not prominent in Death Valley; the creosote bush is the most common plant. In spots where groundwater is not too saline, thickets of mesquite trees thrive. Death Valley's large **animals**—bighorn sheep, deer, mountain lions, bobcats, coyotes and foxes—stay out of sight, but it's easy to spot jackrabbits, rodents and lizards.

For at least 10,000 years, **Shoshone** and **Paiute** Indians hunted here, but the Death Valley moniker was bestowed on the basin by a group of gold-seeking emigrants who were stranded here for several weeks in 1849. The only mineral of lasting economic importance was **borax**. In 1883 a 20-mule-team wagon route traced the 165mi from the Har-

- ⓒ **Michelin Map:** 585 C9 and map this section.
- 🅱 **Info:** ℘760-786-3200. www.nps.gov/deva.
- ⓓ **Location:** Lying northeast of Barstow, the park extends along California's eastern border with Nevada. Furnace Creek is the site of park headquarters and a center for food, lodging and other amenities.
- ⓒ **Don't Miss:** Dante's View and Zabriskie Point.

mony Borax Works here to the Southern Pacific railroad station at Mojave, but five years later, a borax strike at Calico, only 12mi from the railroad, eclipsed the Death Valley deposits.

To supplement the railroad's income, managers began to promote tourism at the Furnace Creek oasis in the late 1920s. Designated a national monument in 1933, Death Valley gained national park status in 1994.

At just under 3.4 million acres, it ranks as the largest national park in the US outside of Alaska.

SIGHTS
Jubilee Pass

This pass (1,290ft) offers the first view of Death Valley to visitors entering the park from the south on Rte. 178. Shoreline Butte exhibits terrace-like shorelines created by wave action in the lakes that filled Death Valley during the ice ages.

Badwater★

This shallow pool of alkali water, 279.8ft below sea level, is virtually the nadir of the Americas (the lowest points, measuring 282ft below sea level, lie 3.3mi and 4.6mi away on the salt flat and are unmarked). Glance up to see the sign marking sea level, high on the rocky east wall of the valley.

The **Devil's Golf Course** (6mi north of Badwater; 1.3mi west to end of dirt road), a jagged chaos of low salt pinnacles, is

Area Code: 760

GETTING THERE

There is no public transportation into or around Death Valley. To get there from Los Angeles *(252mi)* take I-10 east to I-15 north to Rte. 127 north to Rte. 178 west; from San Francisco *(476mi)* take I-80 east to I-580 east to I-205 east to Rte. 99 south to Rte. 178 east to Rte. 190 east. Las Vegas (LAS) is the closest **airport** with commercial flights (123mi east); to get to the park from there take US-95 north to Rte. 373/127 south to Rte. 190 west.

GETTING AROUND

Stay on marked roads in summer and keep your vehicle's gas tank at least half full. Notify a park ranger before exploring Titus Canyon and roads where high-clearance vehicles are recommended. Radiator water is available at the Rte. 190 and Rte. 374 entrances, as well as at Furnace Creek. Gas is available at Furnace Creek, Panamint Springs and Stovepipe Wells.

DESERT SAFETY

Notify someone of your daily itinerary when visiting Death Valley. Cell phone service can be spotty within the park. If your car breaks down, stay with it until help arrives. Always carry water with you and drink at least a gallon a day. It's best to wear sunscreen, a hat and loose, long-sleeved clothing.

GENERAL INFORMATION

Furnace Creek *(center of park on Rte. 190)* is the park center for amenities.

WHEN TO GO : A good time to visit is Oct–May when the weather is mild and dry. Temperatures can be unbearably hot in summer *(Jun–Sept)*.

VISITOR INFORMATION: Death Valley National Park, PO Box 579, Death Valley CA 92328 ℘786-3200. www.nps. gov/deva. Visitor information is available at **Furnace Creek Visitor Center** *(year-round daily 8am–5pm; ℘786-3200)*; **Beatty Information Center** *(Rte. 95,*

Beatty NV; Wed–Sun 9am–4pm; ℘775-553-2200); and **Scotty's Castle Visitor Center and Museum** *(Rte. 267; 8.30am–5pm; ℘786-2392).* **Eastern Sierra Interagency Visitor Center** *(Lone Pine; year-round daily 8am–5pm; ℘876-6222).* **Kelso Depot Visitor Center** *(Baker; year-round daily 9am–5pm; closed Dec 25; ℘733-4456).*

Hours and Fees – The park is open daily year-round. The $20/vehicle entrance fee is valid for seven days.

ACCOMMODATIONS:

Accommodations available in the park include **Furnace Creek Ranch** and **Furnace Creek Inn** *(see Address Book).* Motels include **Panamint Springs Resort** *($79–$149; ℘775-482-7680)* and **Stovepipe Wells** *($80–$120; ℘786-2387 or 888-786-2387).* Lodging is also available in Beatty NV *(10mi east),* Shoshone *(22mi east),* Trona *(27mi west)* and Lone Pine *(60mi west).*

Camping – Of the nine campgrounds within the park only Furnace Creek, Mesquite Spring, Emigrant and Wildrose are open year-round; the rest are open during the camping season (October 15–April 15). Reservations can be made for the Furnace Creek campground only (*℘877-444-6777 or online reservations: www.recreation. gov)* during the camping season. Direct other inquiries about camping to the National Park Service ℘786-2331. Free **backcountry camping** is allowed 2mi beyond developed areas or roads; register at the visitor center or ranger station before entering the backcountry.

AMENITIES

Facilities and services for visitors are available in the park at Furnace Creek and Stovepipe Wells, and in the nearby towns of Bishop, Tonopah, Lone Pine, Ridgecrest, Pahrump NV and Beatty NV.

RECREATION

Rangers conduct guided hikes in peak season *(Nov–Apr).* Horseback rides *(Oct–mid-May; $45–$65)* are available at Furnace Creek Ranch (*℘786-2345 ext. 339).*

continuously re-created as salty ground-water rises to the surface.

Artist's Drive★

This narrow and often steep one-way scenic drive winds 9mi across alluvial fans at the base of the Amargosa Range. The landscape is splashed with colors from volcanic ash and ancient lake deposits: one remarkable spot is **Artist's Palette★★**, about midway through the drive. The reds, pinks and yellows are produced by iron compounds, the greens by mica and copper, and the purples by manganese.

Just north of the exit juts **Mushroom Rock**, an outcrop of basalt.

Golden Canyon★★

A gently ascending trail *(2mi round-trip)* winds through a canyon created by flash floods. The rocky walls give way to softer lake sediments that have eroded less precipitously, forming gentle badlands. After a mile the trail divides, the right fork going 2mi through the badlands to Zabriskie Point and the left fork continuing a half-mile to the base of a cliff called the Red Cathedral.

Late afternoon visit recommended for best light effects.

Furnace Creek

Junction of Rtes. 178 & 190.

The hub of services in the park grew up around a pleasant oasis created by a naturally occurring spring. Stop in at the **Borax Museum★**, (open year-round daily 9am–5pm; 760-786-2345), housed in a former borax mine office. Today it houses a display of borax mining tools, and minerals gathered around Death Valley.

Death Valley Museum★

Just north of Furnace Creek Ranch, in same building as the National Park Service Furnace Creek Visitor Center. Open year-round daily 8am–5pm. 760-786-2331.

This small museum provides an introduction to Death Valley geology, natural history and mining history, and displays a remarkable relief map of the park.

Zabriskie Point★★

4.5mi southeast of Furnace Creek via Rte. 190 east.

This point overlooking Golden Canyon badlands from the east offers a splendid **view**. The toothlike prominence is **Manly Beacon**, named for William Manly, one of the gold seekers who stumbled into the basin in 1849.

About 1.2mi east on Rte. 190 is the entrance to a one-way 2.9mi scenic drive through **20-Mule Team Canyon (A)**.

Dante's View★★★

24mi southeast of Furnace Creek via Rte. 190 east and Dante's View Rd.

From its 5,475ft perch atop a peak of the Amargosa Range, Dante's View offers a renowned **view** of the enormous basin.

Across the basin to the west is the park's highest point, 11,049ft Telescope Peak. Below it is the alluvial fan of Hanaupah Canyon. *Early-morning: best visibility.*

Harmony Borax Works

The remains of a processing plant and a restored 20-mule-team borax wagon commemorate the boom of the 1880s.

Some 12mi north of the borax works, **Salt Creek★** and the surrounding marsh form a patch of life amid rock and sand. A boardwalk extends out into the marsh.

Stovepipe Wells Sand Dunes★

Accessible on foot from Rte. 190 (park on the shoulder within sight of the dunes and keep track of the location of your vehicle as you venture about the dune field).

The dunes are home to a variety of animals, including sidewinder rattlesnakes, kangaroo rats, jackrabbits, coyotes and kit foxes. *Early morning is best for viewing animal tracks.*

Mosaic Canyon

2mi round-trip trail; trailhead 2.3mi from Stovepipe Wells gravel access road.

This canyon is noteworthy for a layer of dolomite that metamorphosed into a rosy-ivory marble, then was smoothed and fluted by the passage of water.

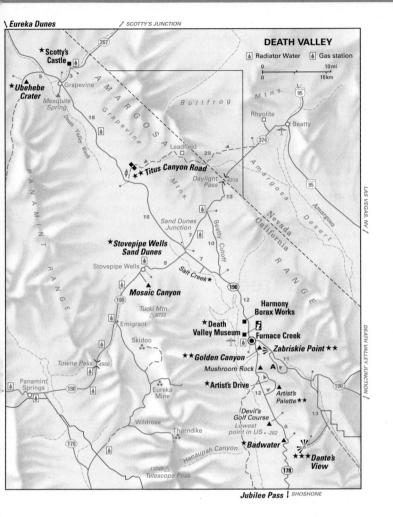

DEATH VALLEY

⊕ Radiator Water   ⊕ Gas station

Titus Canyon Road★★

Allow ½ day. 98mi round-trip from Furnace Creek. Drive north on Rte. 190; take the Beatty Cutoff to Daylight Pass & Nevada Rte. 374. 4-wheel-drive vehicle highly recommended.

One of the most spectacular drives in the park, this one-lane dirt road traverses a geologically complex landscape of layered cliffs, peaks of tilted and twisted sediments and remnants of volcanic eruptions. From a high point at 5,250ft, it squeezes through the narrow passages of Titus Canyon, where the mining ghost town of Leadfield lies.

Scotty's Castle★

53mi north of Furnace Creek. (No gasoline available.) Visit by guided tour (50min) only, Oct–May daily 9am–5pm. Rest of the year hours vary. $11; 2-tour combination ticket $20. Long waits during peak season. ☎760-786-2392.

Begun in 1924, this luxurious Spanish-Moorish retreat was commissioned by Chicago insurance magnate Albert Johnson as a healthful desert retreat. While here, Johnson became acquainted with Walter Scott, a former rodeo cowboy and gold prospector known as "Death Valley Scotty." Johnson allowed Scott to live permanently at the castle, charming visitors with his tall tales of a secret gold mine in the desert.

The cavernous **Great Hall** is appointed with heavy, stuffed leather furniture and a rock fountain. The **music room** boasts a 1,121-pipe theater organ.

Ubehebe Crater★

8mi west of Scotty's Castle.

This 600ft deep cauldron with orange-and-gray layered walls, was created only a few thousand years ago by a titanic steam explosion caused by groundwater heated and pressurized by magma below the earth's surface. Debris from the blast was scattered over 6sq mi.

Eureka Dunes

98mi north of Furnace Creek. 2.8mi after turnoff for Scotty's Castle, turn right on Death Valley Rd. (unpaved). Continue 21mi to Crankshaft Junction, bear left, proceed 12.3mi to South Eureka Rd.; drive 10mi to dunes. 4-wheel-drive vehicle recommended.

This impressive dune field looms at the southern end of the Eureka Valley. The tall, rounded golden dunes invite exploration; from the top, a view extends north over the valley and the colorful striations of the Last Chance range.

Joshua Tree National Park★★

 Michelin Map: 585 C 11.

Named for a tree-like member of the Yucca genus whose long, contorted branches made early Mormon travelers think of Joshua pointing to the promised land, this 1,240sq mi park preserves two very distinct deserts: the high (Mojave) and low (Colorado). The transition from one to the other can be experienced in a short drive. The park is known for its picturesque rounded hills and desert landscapes.

A BIT OF HISTORY

The quartz monzogranite boulders in the park were formed 135 million years ago when molten rock pushed up toward the surface, failed to break through and cooled underground. Erosion eventually removed the softer overlying rock, exposed the solidified masses, enlarged the cracks formed when the rock cooled, and rounded the remaining chunks into the smooth formations seen today.

The **Joshua tree** (*Yucca brevifolia*) is common in the high, cool **Mojave Desert** (above 3,000ft) and is distinguished from other yucca by its height (it can grow as tall as 40ft). The trees propagate and colonize broad areas to form sparse "forests."

The southern and eastern portion is made up of hotter, drier **Colorado Desert** (below 3,000ft), with ocotillo and cholla cacti. The road from the northwestern part down to the Cottonwood Springs entrance in its southeastern corner *(38mi)* crosses a transition zone where characteristics of both deserts mingle.

The Chemehuevi, Serrano and **Cahuilla** Indians who originally occupied this land knew how to survive in the desert, but could not withstand the diseases introduced by white settlers in the 18C. Gold discoveries in the 1870s and 1880s, and cattle ranching in the early 20C, attracted some white settlement, but cities promised better jobs. Designated a national monument in 1936, the area gained national park status in 1994.

VISIT

Joshua Tree National Park (*open daily year-round; $15/vehicle 7-day pass; (9 campgrounds); 760-367-5500; www. nps.gov/jotr*) is located about 140mi from Los Angeles via I-10 and Rte. 62 (Twentynine Palms Hwy.). Towns along Route 62 offer a full range of amenities. Passes and park brochures may be acquired at the entrances or at the visitor centers situated near the park's main gates. At the west entrance lies the **Joshua Tree Visitor Center** (*south of Rte. 62 on Park Blvd. in the town of Joshua Tree;* 🕐 *open daily 8am–5pm;* 📞 *760-366-1855*). Near the north entrance, the **Oasis Visitor Center** (*.5mi south of Rte. 62 in Twentynine Palms; follow signs;* 🕐 *open daily 8am–5pm*) has a small museum, bookstore and information desk. The south entrance and **Cottonwood Visitor Center** (🕐 *open year-round daily 9am–3pm*) are accessible from Palm Springs via I-10 *(50mi)* and Cottonwood Springs Road. Campsites are the only accommodations in the park; there are no services.

Joshua Tree National Park

© PhotoDisc

Geology Tour Road★

From Oasis Visitor Center drive 13.6mi south and west; follow signs.

This rugged dirt road *(18mi)* is marked with 16 stops that highlight evidence of the geological forces that shaped and continue to shape the landscape. Quartz monzogranite boulders display horizontal grooves that were formed by blowing sand. The black basalt of Malapai Hill, an ancient volcano, rises to the west. At Squaw Tank, grinding holes made by Native Americans are visible. The road descends an alluvial fan into Pleasant Valley, a sinking valley, formed by movement on the Blue Cut Fault.

Keys View★★

From Oasis Visitor Center, drive 19mi south and west on main park road, turn left at Ryan Campground and continue 6.2mi south. 📷 *Morning visit recommended for best light.*

This perch on the crest of the Little San Bernardino Mountains at 5,185ft offers a sweeping **view** of Coachella Valley, from the Palm Springs area to the Salton Sea. To the south and west loom Mt. San Jacinto (10,804ft) and San Gorgonio Peak (11,499ft), the highest point in Southern California. Both peaks are snow-covered for much of the year.

Cholla Cactus Garden★

18mi southeast of Oasis Visitor Center via main park road and Pinto Basin Rd.

Cholla *(Opuntia bigelovii)* grows here in great abundance thanks to favorable groundwater conditions. Although the plant appears soft and fuzzy, its spines penetrate the skin easily and are painful and difficult to remove. About 1.5mi farther east, the **Ocotillo Patch** harbors a splendid stand of this tall shrub *(Fouquieria splendens)*. The ocotillo looks like a bundle of thorny sticks most of the year, but it sports a fur of brilliant green leaves after rains, and bright orange flag-like flowers in spring.

Walks Among the Rocks★

Brochures available at Oasis Visitor Center.

These short nature trails, several with interpretive signs, provide easy access to mysterious quartz monzogranite formations.

Hidden Valley Nature Trail★

1mi loop. Trailhead 21.5mi southwest of Oasis Visitor Center on the main park road.

An easy trail winds through a natural enclosure formed by hills of monzogranite, said to have been used by cattle rustlers in the 1880s for hiding stolen cattle. Today the area is a mecca for rock climbers.

Skull Rock Nature Trail★

3mi round-trip. Trailhead 9mi south of Oasis Visitor Center on the main park road.

This moderate trail winds across open country to a rock that resembles a human skull, then crosses the road and ascends a dry wash. Formations here reveal remarkable dikes, light-colored bands formed when molten rock was forced into cracks in already existing monzogranite.

Indian Cove Nature Trail
0.5mi round-trip. From Twentynine Palms drive 5mi west on Rte. 62; turn left and proceed 2.7mi south. Trailhead at west edge of the camping area.

This easy trail passes the monzogranite formations and winds through a typical Mojave Desert wash, offering an expansive view of the desert to the north.

Cap Rock Nature Trail
4mi round-trip. Trailhead at intersection of main park loop road & spur road to Keys View.

This paved, level trail circumnavigates a monzogranite dome. Next to the parking lot, another dome sports a balanced boulder.

Mojave National Preserve★

This roughly pie-shaped area of 1.6 million acres is wedged near the Nevada state line between Interstates 15 and 40. The rugged landscape here, where elevations range from 900ft to 7,929ft, is home to some 700 species of plants and nearly 300 species of animals. A threadbare carpet of creosote bush covers the lowlands, while open forests of pine and juniper, and extensive stands of Joshua trees thrive in higher, cooler areas.

A BIT OF HISTORY
The eastern Mojave (Mow-HA-vay) Desert has long been crossed by important transportation routes. Native Americans followed the Mojave River, and Spanish travelers, including 18C Franciscan padre-explorer **Francisco Garcés**, followed in their footsteps. The Santa Fe Railroad from Chicago to Los Angeles crossed just south of the region in 1885, and the Union Pacific's line between Salt Lake City and Los Angeles came through in 1905. The only sustained economic activity was ranching. Today the preserve draws hikers, backpackers and campers seeking recreation amid the lovely desert landscapes.

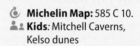

  Michelin Map: 585 C 10.
  Kids*: Mitchell Caverns, Kelso dunes*

VISIT
The park is always open. Visitor center hours below. Large sections of this sparsely populated region are accessible only by four-wheel-drive vehicle.
Visitor information is available at the **Hole-in-the-Wall Information Center** *(20mi north of I-40 on Essex & Black Canyon Rds.; open Oct–Apr Wed–Sun 9am–4pm; rest of the year Fri–Sun 9am–4pm; closed Jan 1 & Dec 25; ℘760-928-2572; www.nps.gov/moja)* and at the 1923 Spanish Mission Revival-style **Kelso Depot Visitor Center** *(34mi southeast of Baker on Kelbaker Rd.; open year-round daily 9am–5pm; closed Dec 25; ℘760-252-6108; www.nps.gov/moja).* There are two developed campgrounds and primitive campsites within the preserve but no public facilities. For lodging, restaurants and gas stations, visitors should head to he nearby towns of Barstow, Baker and Needles.
The volcanic cinder cone of **Amboy Crater** *(2mi west of Amboy off Rte. 66)* and the remnants of the **Cinder Cone Lava Beds** *(17mi east of Baker off Kelbaker Rd.)* are designated National Natural Landmarks.

Mitchell Caverns

In Providence Mountains State Recreation Area. From Barstow, drive 102mi east on I-40; take Essex Rd. exit and continue 16mi northwest to end of road. Visit by guided tour (1hr30min) only, Sept–May Mon–Fri 1.30pm, weekends 10am, 1.30pm & 3pm; rest of the year daily 1.30pm. No tours Jan 1, Thanksgiving Day, Dec. 25 $5, children $2. 760-928-2586. www.parks.ca.gov. Light jacket recommended.

Six limestone caverns reveal dripstone and flowstone formations including stalactites, stalagmites, cave columns, lily pads and coral pipes. The predominantly fossil formations were created by percolating groundwater millions of years ago.

Kelso Dunes

From Barstow drive 80mi east on I-40, then 14mi north on Kelbaker Rd. From Baker drive 47mi south on Kelbaker Rd. Access on foot from a 3mi dirt road that turns west off Kelbaker Rd., 7.4mi south of Kelso Depot. Evening or early-morning visit recommended for best light.

Sand dunes measuring 560ft have accumulated in this spot where mountains weaken the winds that blow sand in from the dry Mojave River. The dunes "boom," emitting an unusual sound described as like a tympanic drum.

Palm Springs★

Palm Springs is the largest and most famous of the resort and retirement communities that huddle in the desert between the San Jacinto and Little San Bernardino mountain ranges. Visitors and part-time residents, among them celebrities and politicians, come each year to play its extensive golf courses and browse its upscale galleries and boutiques.

A BIT OF HISTORY

The Cahuilla Indians were the area's first recorded residents, and much of present-day Palm Springs occupies land purchased or leased from them. The first white settler built an adobe house (the McCallum Adobe) here in 1884, and by 1893 the town's hotel owner had constructed his home. Now operated as museums, these historic buildings have been relocated to the **Village Green Heritage Center** (221 S. Palm Canyon Dr.; *open mid-Oct–May Thu–Sat 10am–4pm, Wed & Sun noon–3pm; closed major holidays; $1; 760-323-8297; www.palm-springshistoricalsociety.org).* Hollywood celebrities discovered desert-living in the 1930s and Palm Springs boomed.

> ▶ **Population:** 43,942.
> 🜨 **Michelin Map:** 585 C 11 and map this section.
> 🛈 **Info:** 800-967-3767. www.palmspringsusa.com.
> ◐ **Location:** The city sits east of Riverside and west of Joshua Tree National Park, in the western end of Coachella Valley. **North Palm Canyon Drive** is the shopping, dining and entertainment spine. Affluent communities Rancho Mirage and Indian Wells surround Palm Springs, and the neighboring town of Palm Desert is home to **El Paseo**, a 2mi boulevard lined with chic boutiques.
> **Kids:** Living Desert; Tramway; Air Museum

Strict zoning maintains the elegant character of the city. More than 80 golf courses dot the Coachella Valley, and the region annually hosts such major golf tournaments as the Bob Hope Classic, the Kraft Nabisco (formerly the Dinah Shore) LPGA Golf Championship and the Frank Sinatra Celebrity Invitational.

SIGHTS
Palm Springs Aerial Tramway★★★

Rte. 111 north to Tramway Rd., about 2mi from center of town, then 3.8mi to parking lot. Open year-round Mon–Fri 10am–9.45pm, weekends 8am–9.45pm. *$22.25, children $15.25.* 760-325-1391. *www. pstramway.com.*

Revolving, 80-passenger gondolas with picture windows ascend *(10min)* the vertiginous face of the San Jacinto range to a mountain station (8,516ft). En route, spectacular **views**★★ stretch across the Coachella Valley. The station houses a restaurant, souvenir shop and video on the tramway's construction, and serves as a base for exploring Mt. San Jacinto State Park. Activities include hiking to the 10,804ft summit, cross-country skiing *(Nov–Apr)* and guided mule rides.

Palm Springs Art Museum★★

101 Museum Dr., 2 blocks west of N. Palm Canyon Dr. at Tahquitz Way. Open year-round Tue,Wed, Fri–Sun 10am–5pm, Thu noon–8pm. Closed major holidays. *$12.50 (free Thu 4pm–8pm).* 760-322-4800. *www.psmuseum.org.*

Established in 1938, this museum offers an excellent overview of the art of the California deserts. The permanent collection ranges from pre-Columbian artifacts to Western American paintings and sculptures to contemporary works.
In the spotlight is 20C California art; pieces by Sam Francis, Ed Ruscha and Nathan Oliveira are likely to be on view. Native American basketry and works by glass artist Dale Chihuly are highlights.

Palm Springs Air Museum★

745 N. Gene Autry Trail. Open year-round daily 10am–5pm. Closed Thanksgiving Day & Dec 25. Guided tours available by appointment. *$12, children $5.* 760-778-6262. *www.air-museum.org.*

Military history of World War II is the focus of this museum, which showcases a rotating collection of restored aircraft. Accompanied by the swinging sounds of period music, visitors can move in for up-close examination of a Curtiss P-40 Warhawk, a P-51 Mustang and a Boeing B-17 Flying Fortress, a Supermarine Spitfire and other aircraft. Most of the craft in the collection are fully restored to flying condition.

Indian Canyons★

End of S. Palm Canyon Dr. about 4mi south of the town center. Open mid-Sept–mid-Jun daily 8am–5pm. *$8 (ranger-led hikes additional fee).* 760-325-3400.

The Agua Caliente Band of Cahuilla Indians owns three canyons containing groves of **fan palms**, California's only native species of palm. A trail through **Palm Canyon**★★ traverses the sandy area in the shade of the trees. The path leading to **Andreas Canyon**★ *(turn right 100yds past entrance gate and continue .8mi)* winds around boulders fallen from the wall above. The trail through more remote **Murray Canyon** *(1mi trail from parking lot at Andreas Canyon)* crosses low vegetation until it comes upon palms growing in a rocky stream bed.
From the **Tahquitz Canyon Visitors Center** *(500 W. Mesquite Dr.;* open Oct–Jun daily 7.30am–5pm, Jul–Sept Fri, Sat, Sun 7.30am–5pm; *$12.50;* 760-416-7044; www.tahquitzcanyon.com), rangers lead tours of a canyon notable for its rock art and waterfall.

Moorten Botanical Garden

1701 S. Palm Canyon Dr., about 2mi south of the town center. Open year-round Mon, Tue, Thu–Sat 9am–4pm, Sun 10am–4pm. *$3.* 760-327-6555.

Strange and curious plants from the world's deserts flourish here in a dense diversity usually associated with tropical rain forests—3,000 species in the garden's four acres.

The Living Desert Zoo and Gardens★★

47-900 Portola Ave., Palm Desert, 15mi east of Palm Springs & 1.3mi south of Rte. 111. Open Sept–mid-Jun daily 9am–5pm; rest of the year daily 8am–1.30pm. Closed Dec 25. *$12.50, chil-*

dren $7.50 (off-season ⊛$9.50, children $5.25). ✕ ♿ 🅿 ☎*760-346-5694. www. livingdesert.org.* ☺*Early morning, when temperatures are cool and the animals are active, is the best time to visit.*

This 1,200-acre complex, established in March 1970, offers a comprehensive view of North American desert plant communities, as well as animals from arid lands.

Walk the central path (or ride the tram) through gardens representing, among others, the Upper Colorado Desert, the Yuman Desert and the arid territory of the Baja Peninsula. You'll see birds, coyotes, desert tortoises and other denizens along the way. Bighorn sheep, Arabian oryx, gazelles and zebras graze within larger enclosures. Eagle Canyon holds endangered golden eagles, mountain lions and bobcats. Village WaTuTu, a 5-acre replica of a North Kenyan village,

Palm Springs Aerial Tramway

© California Travel & Tourism Commission

gathers East African species, including striped hyenas, dromedaries and Amur leopards.

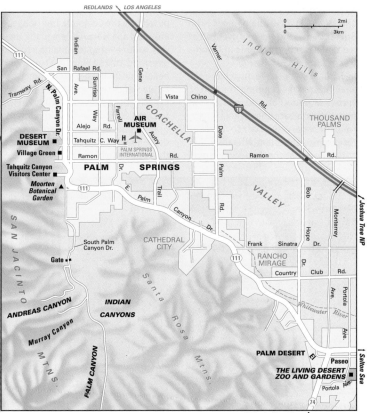

GOLD COUNTRY

These steeply rolling foothills, extending from the Central Valley plain to the forested mid-level belt of the Sierra Nevada, was the center of the California Gold Rush of 1849. The discovery of gold in the American River at Coloma brought waves of fortune hunters and immigrants seeking a better life in the western US. The rush placed California at the forefront of America's economic frontier for several decades. Nicknamed the "Mother Lode" after a large quartz vein, the region now forms a pastoral landscape of scenic vistas and residential communities, many of which retain the flavor of the 19C.

Highlights

1 An authentic train ride at **Railtown 1897 State Historic Park** (p136)
2 A stroll along charming Broad Street in **Nevada City** (p131)
3 The glittering Landmark Room at **Black Chasm Cavern** (p134)

During the Spanish and Mexican periods, the region remained unsettled, its grasslands and forests home to Native American peoples including the Miwok and Maidu. In 1839 the pioneer **John Sutter** began the chain of events that led to the discovery of gold at Coloma (see Sacramento: history).

In January 1848, while inspecting the sawmill he was building for Sutter, **James Marshall** discovered flakes of metal in the tailrace (the channel leading from the waterwheel back to the river). He informed Sutter and, after tests, they concluded that the flakes were pure gold. Though sworn to secrecy, Marshall was unable to stay silent; soon his crew began roaming the riverbanks, digging out gold nuggets with pocket knives.

By May 1848, many California towns were virtually deserted as residents headed for the Sierra foothills. Word of the discovery reached the eastern US by September. To justify US efforts to acquire the territory, President James K. Polk publicized its unmined riches in a December address to Congress and the rush began in earnest.

Throughout 1849, gold seekers ("Forty-niners," as they were called) traveled by land via the California Trail or by sea around Cape Horn. Others made their way south by ship to Panama, crossed overland to the Pacific Ocean and headed north by ship to California.

As placer gold (the type of ore available in riverbeds and near the earth's surface) became difficult to find, immigrants from Europe took jobs in the developing deep-mining industry. Within a decade, the rush was over.

Columbia State Historic Park

Northern Gold Country★★

Placerville, which makes a good hub for exploration of the mine-rich northern Gold Country, lies along US-50 just 35mi east of Sacramento, not far from the spot where John Marshall made his gold discovery in 1848.

🚗 DRIVING TOUR

113mi.

▷ *Begin on Rte. 49 at US-50 in Placerville.*

Placerville
www.visit-eldorado.com.
The placer mining camp founded here in 1848 developed as a transportation hub on the main route over the Sierra Nevada, linking California with the Nevada silver mines. Today the city is the bustling seat of El Dorado County. The 19C buildings retain their historical charm, among them the brick-and-fieldstone structure housing the **Placerville Historical Museum** *(524 Main St.; open year-round Wed–Sun 11am–4pm; contribution requested; ℘530-626-0773).* The **Apple Hill** district of orchards and farms east of town is lovely during the fall harvest season when visitors meander scenic back roads sampling local products from roadside stands, bakeries, restaurants and wineries.

El Dorado County Historical Museum
104 Placerville Dr., in county fairgrounds, 0.25mi east of US-50. Open year-round Wed–Sat 10am–4pm, Sun noon–4pm. Closed major holidays. ℘530-621-5865. www.co.el-dorado.ca.us/museum.
Among the exhibits detailing El Dorado County's colorful past are a Concord coach that crossed the Sierra Nevada via Placerville; a country store; and mining and railroad equipment, including a flywheel, a five-stamp mill, and an operable Shay locomotive (1907).

- **Michelin Map:** 585 B 7, 8 and map this section.
- **Location:** Most sights in the Gold Country lie along or near Route 49, which traverses eight counties on its winding route between Mariposa and Sierra City. Northern Gold Country encompasses Placerville and points north to Sierra City.
- **Don't Miss:** Marshall Gold Discovery State Historic Park, where you can pan for gold.

Hangtown's Gold Bug Park & Mine
2635 Gold Bug Ln., 1mi north of US-50 via Bedford Ave. Open year-round daily 8.30am–5pm (mine open Apr–Oct daily 10am–4pm; rest of the year weekends only noon–4pm). $5, (mine). ℘530-642-5207. www.goldbugpark.org.
This 61-acre municipal park preserves a hardrock mine that operated from 1888 to the beginning of World War I. A taped narration accompanies visitors through the 352ft mine tunnel to the quartz vein that lured gold seekers to sink some 250 shafts in the immediate vicinity. Nearby are an original stamp mill and an interpretive museum.

Marshall Gold Discovery State Historic Park★★
8mi north of Placerville, in Coloma. Park open year-round daily 8am–dusk. $5/vehicle. ℘530-622-3470. www.parks.ca.gov.
This 276-acre park, which encompasses most of the town of of Coloma, commemorates the site where James Marshall stumbled across nuggets of gold. Historic structures line the peaceful streets, and the rapids of the American River invite panners to try their luck. Begin in the **Gold Discovery Museum** *(open Apr–Jun daily 10am–4pm; rest of the year daily 10am–3pm; closed Jan 1, Thanksgiving Day, Dec 25, Mon Jul–Feb),* where exhibits and a video *(12min)* sum-

Buried Treasure

In the 19C, gold deposits existed in three forms: loosely mixed with the sand and gravel in rivers and streams; immobilized in buried riverbeds, and locked in quartz veins deep within the earth. The three principal methods of gold mining were: **placer** (*PLASS-er*) **mining**, the process of agitating stream gravels to separate gold ore from non-gold-bearing sand and rock (panning is the simplest form); **hydraulic mining**, washing away hillsides with huge water nozzles known as **monitors** (resulting floods led to forbidding the practice); and **hardrock mining**, tunneling deep into the earth to blast apart quartz veins. The **stamp mill** employed piston-like stampers to crush ore prior to gold extraction; the **Pelton wheel** operated by force of a high-pressure stream of water aimed into rounded, bisected cups.

marize the geology of gold and the history of the Gold Rush. Mining equipment is on display next to the center, and a small path leads to two restored **Chinese stores**, once owned by Coloma's Chinese immigrant population.

The wood-frame **sawmill**, reconstructed from Marshall's drawings, stands upstream from the original mill site. A narrow road passes the buildings of historic Coloma and up the hill to Marshall's restored cabin and his grave.

Auburn★

25mi northwest of Placerville.
www.auburn-ca.com.

Auburn was founded in 1848 as a tent camp that grew into a major transportation center, which helped Auburn to escape the post-Gold Rush decline common to other boomtowns.

Old Town

Auburn's nucleus of settlement is today an assortment of antique stores, specialty shops and restaurants, many located in buildings dating to the mid-19C. Particularly noteworthy are the **Old Firehouse** (1891) and the Placer County **courthouse** (1898), overlooking Old Town from an adjacent hill. The statue in the center of town commemorates town founder Claude Chana, a French immigrant who first found gold here.

Gold Country Museum

*1273 High St., in the county fairgrounds. From Old Town drive north on Sacramento St., cross Auburn-Folsom Rd. and continue .5mi east to fair-*grounds entrance. Open year-round Tue–Sun 11am–4pm. Closed major holidays. &P 530-889-6500. www.placer.ca.gov/museum.

This small museum invites visitors to explore a simulated mine tunnel and exhibits highlighting the mining, processing and uses of gold. Located within walking distance is the **Bernhard Museum**, a Victorian-era house museum and winery complex (291 Auburn-Folsom Rd.; visit by guided tour (1hr) only, year-round Tue–Sun 11–4pm; closed major holidays; &P 530-889-6500).

Grass Valley

24mi north of Auburn.
www.grassvalleychamber.com.

Grass Valley owed its prosperity to innovations in deep-mining technology. Laborers came from as far away as Cornwall, England, noted for its tin-mining tradition; Cornish "pasties" (meat pies) remain a local specialty.

In the historic area around Main and Mill streets, note the 1862 **Holbrooke Hotel** (W. Main St.), which welcomed US presidents in the late 19C.

Empire Mine State Historic Park★★

10791 E. Empire St. at Mill St., .5mi southeast of downtown. Open May–Aug daily 9am–6pm; rest of the year daily 10am–5pm. Closed Jan 1, Thanksgiving Day, Dec 25. $1.
P 530-273-8522. www.parks.ca.gov.

California's largest and richest deep mine boasted 367mi of tunnels. In the main shaft, visitors stand on a platform 50ft below the surface to gaze into the tunnel extending 10,000ft to a depth of nearly a mile. In the **visitor center** exhibits evoke the hard life of a miner. Within the park is the handsome, redwood house of William Bourn Jr., owner of the mine from 1879 to 1929.

North Star Mining Museum★

South of downtown at Allison Ranch & McCourtney Rds., just beyond the Rte. 20 viaduct. ◷*Open May–mid-Oct daily 10am–5pm.* ♿ 🅿 ✆*530-273-4255.*
The mine's historic stone powerhouse (1895) has been refurbished as one of the state's most comprehensive museums of mining technology. Especially noteworthy is a working Cornish water pump (coin-activated) and the world's largest Pelton wheel.

Nevada City★★

4mi north of Grass Valley.
www.nevadacitychamber.com.
This picturesque town is a haven of shops, restaurants and 19C architecture. Placer claims on Deer Creek led to the founding of the community, first incorporated in 1851 simply as Nevada; the "City" was added later to avoid confusion with the Nevada Territory, created in 1862.
Listed on the National Register of Historic Places, the well-preserved business district is highlighted by **Broad Street**, which slopes down from the square-towered Methodist church (1864) to the **National Hotel**★ (1856). The Art Deco Nevada County **courthouse** (1937) overlooks the downtown area, and the two-story Victorian firehouse *(214 Main St.),* built in 1861, holds artifacts such as the altar from a mid-19C Chinese joss house (temple or shrine).

Downieville

47mi northeast of Nevada City.
Downieville sits in a forested canyon at the confluence of the Yuba and Downie rivers. Its main street is lined with 19C structures. The town is one of the smallest county seats in the US, and the homes of its inhabitants perch on steep slopes rising from the riverbanks. The **Downieville Museum** *(330 Main St.),* occupying an old Chinese store (1852) houses artifacts from mining days (◷*open mid-May–mid-Oct daily 10am–4pm; rest of the year weekends only, weather permitting;* ◉*contribution requested).*

Sierra City

13mi east of Downieville.
www.sierracity.com.
The highest of the Gold Country towns enjoys a spectacular setting at the foot of the 8,590ft summits of the Sierra Buttes. The community survived several deadly avalanches of snow and ice. Today, Sierra City's homes overlook the business district from the surrounding slopes.

Empire Mine State Historic Park, tunnel interior

© California Travel & Tourism Commission

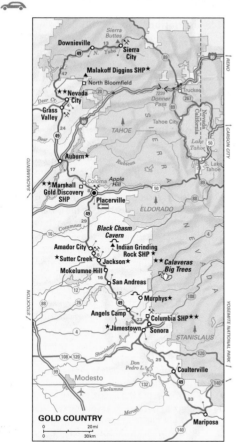

GOLD COUNTRY

0   20mi
0   30km

Last worked in 1953, the Kentucky Mine is a unique attraction—a hardrock gold mine with an operable ore-processing stamp mill. Guided tours depart from the mine's portal, cross an ore-cart trestle and proceed down through the levels of the mill, with stops to explain each step in the milling and extraction process.

EXCURSION FROM NEVADA CITY
Malakoff Diggins State Historic Park★

54mi round-trip from Nevada City at 23579 N. Bloomfield Rd. Take Rte. 49 north 11mi and turn right on Tyler Foote Crossing Rd.; bear left on Cruzon Grade Rd. and follow signs. ○*Open dawn–dusk.* ⊛*$6/vehicle.* ⚠ P ☎*530-265-2740. www.parks.ca.gov.*

In 1855 hydraulic operations began on this site that became California's largest hydraulic mine operation. Today, the **Malakoff Pit** remains bare of vegetation, the raw badland a testament to the environmental effects of hydraulic mining. Gold Rush-era buildings survive at the site of **North Bloomfield**, a village of 800 residents in the early 1880s. A film of a hydraulic monitor in action is shown in the museum (○*open Jun–Aug daily 9am–5pm; rest of the year weekends only 10am–4pm;* ♿ P), and a short drive *(2mi)* leads past the Hiller Tunnel (from which mine tailings drained into the Yuba River) to lookout points on the pit's south rim.

Kentucky Mine
Historical Park and Museum★
1mi north of Sierra City via Rte. 49. ○*Open Memorial Day–Sept Wed–Sun 10am–4pm.* 👄*Guided tours (⊛$7) available (11am & 2pm).* ⊛*$5 (museum).* ♿ P ✆*530-862-1310.*

Preserving the Past

Like many Gold Rush communities, Nevada City experienced a decline in the early 20C as hydraulic mines fell out of environmental favor and deep veins of ore petered out. Determined to keep their community from becoming a ghost town, city leaders hatched a plan to preserve and restore the welter of attractive buildings in the town center. A reputation as a 1960s nexus of rural counterculture also bolstered Nevada City's economy, as flower children opened herb shops and natural foods stores here. Today Nevada City is known as one of the best-preserved towns in the West, and boasts an unusual number of live-performance theaters and music stages, including the well-regarded Foothills Theater Company (www.foothilltheatre.org).

ADDRESSES

🏠 STAY

🛏️🛏️🛏️ **The Gate House Inn** – *1330 Jackson Gate Rd., Jackson.* 📞*209-223-3500 or 800-841-1072. www.gatehouseinn.com. 5 units.* 🅿️. A life-size mural of an angel greets guests at this National Register property, and each of the four Victorian-style bed-and-breakfast rooms and an outlying cottage has its own "protector." Italian marble fireplaces and landscaped grounds are earmarks of this gracious mid-19C Victorian mansion. Rates include a full breakfast with muffins, fruit, breakfast casseroles and the inn specialty, baked French toast.

🛏️🛏️ **City Hotel** – *22768 Main St., Columbia.* 📞*800-532-1479. www.cityhotel. com. 10 rooms.* Columbia State Historic Park is California's best-preserved Gold Rush town, so it's no surprise that this integral hotel—and its sister, the **Fallon Hotel** (🍴🍴)—offers a purely 1857 experience. Authentically restored, right down to wrought-iron railings, the Farallon holds simple rooms with shared showers. Some rooms have balconies overlooking the street. At the **City Hotel Restaurant** (🍴🍴) the creative regional menu changes seasonally.

🍴 EAT

🍴🍴🍴 **Sequoia at the Bee-Bennett House** – *643 Bee St., Placerville.* 📞*530-622-5222. www.sequoiaplacerville.com.* **Eclectic**. Although the space is traditional—an 1853 manor with tables clustered around a fireplace—the culinary theme is not. The chef fuses modern world cuisines (Continental, Asian, Latin) and pairs them with Gold Country wines. Shrimp bisque with a puff pastry lid is a favorite; entrées range from beef and lamb to seafood.

🍴 **Posh Nosh** – *318 Broad St., Nevada City.* 📞*530-265-6064. Lunch daily, dinner Wed–Sun.* **American.** Local vegetarians love this casual eatery with its extensive list of vegetarian options, but meat eaters are equally delighted with the sandwiches and pastas served indoors or on a garden patio. Try the open-face ratatouille sandwich with eggplant, zucchini, bell pepper and tomatoes, topped with feta cheese.

Southern Gold Country

Route 49 south of Placerville continues in the same vein as the northern portion, although you'll find here a greater concentration of historic towns with accommodations and dining establishments. You'll also find snippets of Native American heritage and rail history mixed in among the Gold Rush sights.

🚗 DRIVING TOUR

PLACERVILLE TO MARIPOSA
144mi.

▶ *Begin on Rte. 49 in Placerville.*

Placerville
🕐*See Northern Gold Country.*

🧭 **Michelin Map:** 585 B 8; also see N. Gold Country.

Amador City
29mi south of Placerville. www.amador-city.com.
Founded in 1848, California's smallest incorporated city nestles in a valley along Route 49. Amador City's elegant brick Imperial Hotel (1879) boasts an award-winning restaurant, and wineries dot the area as well.

Sutter Gold Mine
0.5mi south of Amador City. 🕐*Open mid-May–mid-Sept daily 9am–5pm; rest of the year Mon–Fri 10am–4pm, weekends 10am–5pm.* 🎫*Guided tours (1hr)* 🎟️*$17.50, children $11.50.* 🅿️ 📞*209-736-2708. www.caverntours.com.*

Acorn grinding rock, Indian Grinding Rock State Historic Park

© Jeff Foott/Getty Images

You'll get an excellent introduction to traditional and modern gold mining techniques at this hardrock mine. The tour includes a ride aboard an underground mine car and a chance to pan for gold, crack a geode or mine gemstones (☞additional fees apply).

Sutter Creek★
2mi south of Amador City.
www.suttercreek.org.
This community began in 1848 as a placer mining camp but thrived with the establishment of the Central Eureka hardrock mine south of town. The resulting prosperity can be seen along **Main Street**, where antique and specialty shops occupy original 19C storefronts.

Jackson★
4mi southeast of Sutter Creek.
www.ci.jackson.ca.us.
Seat of Amador County, this bustling town began in 1849 as a placer mining camp. By 1859 hardrock operations were chiseling out the ore in a rich quartz vein. Today you can admire the pleasing balance of old and new in the 19C architecture along Main Street. The **National Hotel** *(foot of Main St.)* claims to be the oldest continually operating hotel in California (1863). From a scenic overlook about a mile and a half north of town on Route 49, the **view** encompasses the defunct Kennedy and Argonaut mines.

Amador County Museum★
225 Church St. ⏱*Closed for structural renovation; check website for projected reopening.* 🅿 ☎*209-223-6386.*
www.co.amador.ca.us/depts/museum.
This brick home (1859) portrays life in Jackson from the Gold Rush to the 1920s. An adjacent building contains working models of the Kennedy Mine *(below)* headframe and tailing wheels.
Five blocks away on North Main Street is the **St. Sava Serbian Orthodox Church**, founded in 1894 to serve Jackson's immigrant Serbian population.

Kennedy Mine
Jackson Gate Rd., 2mi north of downtown via Main St. Information kiosk at edge of parking lot. ⏱*Open Mar–Oct weekends 10am–3pm.* ☞*Guided tours available (1hr).* ☞*$9.* ☎*209-223-9542. www.kennedygoldmine.com.*
The Kennedy Gold mine claimed to rank among the world's deepest gold mines (5,912ft below the surface). Tours cover the remaining structures of the mine, now under reclamation. Note especially the towering headframe and two of the original four 58ft **tailing wheels**, used to carry rubble along a series of inclined flumes over two ridges from the mine to a holding pond.

🧑‍🤝‍🧑 Black Chasm Cavern
15701 Pioneer-Volcano Rd., Volcano, 9mi east of Jackson via Rte. 88.
☞*Visit by guided tour only (45min) daily 10am–4pm.* ☞*$14.25, children $7.15.* 🅿 ☎*209-736-2708.*
www.caverntours.com.
This cave was designated a National Natural Landmark for its foot-long helictite crystal formations, deep lakes and huge underground rooms, particulary the **Landmark Room**, draped with sparkling crystals.

Indian Grinding Rock State Historic Park★
12mi east of Jackson via Rte. 88 and Pine Grove-Volcano Rd. ⏱*Open daily year-round dawn–dusk.* ☞*$6/car.* ⚠ ♿ 🅿
☎*209-296-7488. www.parks.ca.gov.*

Prior to the Gold Rush, Miwok Indians lived in this meadow, now a 135-acre park where you can experience Miwok culture firsthand. Be sure to see the lime-stone outcrop pitted with *chaw'se*, or mortar holes, used for grinding acorns into meal. Nearby are re-created Miwok bark dwellings and a ceremonial round-house. The **Chaw'se Regional Indian Museum** (*open year-round Mon–Fri 11am–3pm, weekends 10am–4pm; closed Jan 1, Thanksgiving Day, Dec 25, Dec–Jan Tue–Thu*) is dedicated to Sierra Nevada indigenous peoples.

Mokelumne Hill
8mi southeast of Jackson.

This village sits atop a mountainous ridge blessed with lovely views. In the early 1850s, "Moke Hill" boasted a popu-lation of 15,000 and served as the center of a rich placer gold district. A large con-centration of French immigrants settled here, and the historic **Hotel Leger** (1851) remains in operation today.

San Andreas
8mi south of Mokelumne Hill.
www.visitcalaveras.org.

Founded in 1848 by Mexican settlers, San Andreas was the scene of the 1883 trial of Charles E. Bolton, better known as **"Black Bart."** A prominent San Fran-cisco socialite, Bolton robbed 28 stage-coaches between 1875 and 1883.

Calaveras County Museum★
30 North Main St. Open year-round daily 10am–4pm. Closed Thanksgiv-ing Day, Dec 25. $3. 209-754-1058. www.calaverascohistorical.com.
Located in the Hall of Records *(2nd floor)*, this museum highlights the history of the Miwok people as well as lumber-ing, mining and agriculture in Calaveras County. A short stroll through the rear garden leads to a row of jail cells, where "Black Bart" was incarcerated during his trial. The courthouse where the robber was tried is also part of the complex.

Angels Camp
12mi southeast of San Andreas.
www.angelscamp.com.

The setting for Mark Twain's short story "The Celebrated Jumping Frog of Calav-eras County," this town commemorates the tale with an annual frog-jumping contest in May. The **Angels Camp Museum** presents buggies and other horse-drawn vehicles along with Gold Rush artifacts *(753 S. Main St.; open Mar–Dec Thu–Mon 10am–4pm; rest of the year weekends 10am–4pm; closed Easter Sunday, Thanksgiving Day, Dec 25; $3; 209-736-2963).*

Mercer Caverns
1.3mi from Main St. at 1665 Sheep Ranch Rd. Visit by guided tour (45min) only, Memorial Day–Labor Day 9am–5pm; rest of the year weekends 10am–4.30pm (call for weekday hours). Closed Dec 25. $12, children $7. 209-728-2101. www.mercercaverns.com.
Visitors descend 160ft through cham-bers containing limestone formations, including stalactites, stalagmites and calcite curtains awash in color.

Columbia State Historic Park★★
15mi southeast of Angels Camp.
Most businesses open year-round daily 10am–5pm. Closed Thanksgiv-ing Day, Dec 25. 209-588-9128. www.parks.ca.gov.
Founded in 1850, the boomtown of Columbia declined as nearby gold deposits were exhausted. In 1945 Main Street was acquired by the state and preserved as an historic park.
Some 12 square blocks of park-owned streets with costumed employees re-create daily life between 1850 and 1870 in a Gold Rush boomtown. The Wells Fargo depot and Masonic lodge are maintained as museums. Live per-formances are staged in the theater of the **Fallon Hotel**; and the restored **City Hotel** boasts a fine-dining restaurant. Housed in a former miner supply store (1854), the **Museum** *(State & Main Sts.; open daily 10am–4pm; 209-532-3184)* presents local history and large mineral specimens, with a slide show *(13min)* of historic Columbia.

Jamestown, along Main Street

The park stages regular special events such as bucket brigades, costumed re-enactments and dance workshops to help visitors experience life during Gold Rush days *(call the park for schedule)*.

Hidden Treasure Mine★

○*Open Mar–Sept daily 10.30am–5pm; rest of the year hours vary; call ahead.* ○*Closed Dec 25.* ℘*209-532-9693.*
The perfect place to try panning for gold, this hardrock mine penetrates a hillside overlooking a steep canyon.

Sonora

4mi south of Columbia.
www.thegreatunfenced.com.
Established in 1848 by miners from the Mexican state of Sonora, this vibrant commercial center and county seat boasts a variety of architectural styles along its hilly streets. Housed in the former county jail, the **Tuolumne County Museum and History Center**★ showcases historical photographs; and exhibits on mining, lumbering and immigrant wagon trails over the Sierra Nevada *(158 W. Bradford Ave.; ○open year-round daily 10am–4pm; ○closed Jan 1, Thanksgiving Day & Dec 25; ℘209-532-1317; www.tchistory.org).*

Jamestown★

4mi southwest of Sonora.
Founded in 1848, this town sports original false-front buildings and boardwalks along Main Street. "Jimtown," as it is nicknamed, is known for its numerous restaurants and 1860s-era saloons.

Railtown 1897 State Historic Park★

5th Ave. & Reservoir Rd., just east of Main St. ○*Open Apr–Oct daily 9.30am–4.30pm; rest of the year daily 10am–3pm.* ○*Closed Jan 1, Thanksgiving Day, Dec 25.* $2. *Narrated excursions (round-trip 6mi, 60min) depart Apr–Oct weekends hourly 11am–3pm;* $8, children $3. ℘209-984-3953. www.railtown1897.org.
This complex was a maintenance station for the Sierra Railway, which linked the gold mines with supply and financial centers. As the industry declined, the trains came into demand by Hollywood; some 200 films and television shows have been shot here.
Departing from the visitor center in the former freight house, guided tours *(50min;* $2) allow exploration of the working steam **roundhouse**★.

Coulterville

25mi southeast of Jamestown.
Coulterville was home to 1,000 Chinese immigrants during the Gold Rush. The **Hotel Jeffery** and other 19C buildings survive along Main Street. Local history exhibits are housed at the **Northern Mariposa County History Center** *(10301 Rte. 49 at Rte. 132; ○open Feb–Dec*

Wed–Sun 10am–4pm; closed major holidays; 209-878-3015).

Mariposa

33mi southeast of Coulterville. www.visitmariposa.net.

A Gold Rush boomtown, Mariposa ("butterfly" in Spanish) is now a county seat. Built in 1854, the Greek Revival courthouse *(Bullion St. between 9th & 10th Sts.)* is said to be the West's oldest continuously functioning county courthouse.

California Mining and Mineral Museum★★

1.8mi south of town, in the county fairgrounds. Open May–Sept daily 10am–6pm; rest of the year Wed–Mon 10am–4pm. Closed Jan 1, Thanksgiving Day, Dec 25. $3. 209-742-7625. www.parks.ca.gov.

Home of the state **mineral collection**, of some 13,000 specimens, including the 201oz "Fricot Nugget" of crystalline gold, the museum offers changing displays of mineral splendors and oddities. A simulated mine tunnel and working model of a 1904 Union Iron Works stamp mill highlight presentations on mining technology and California mining history.

Mariposa Museum and History Center

5119 Jesse St. Open daily 10am–4pm. Closed January, Thanksgiving Day, 2 wks in Dec, Dec 25. $3. 209-966-2924. www.mariposamuseum.com.

This small museum showcases the life of John C. Frémont; it's also packed with artifacts and memorabilia from daily life in 1850s Mariposa.

EXCURSIONS FROM ANGELS CAMP

Murphys★

18mi round-trip northeast from Angels Camp via Rte. 4. www.visitmurphys.com.

Among the mid-19C buildings lining Main Street of this charming community are the still-operating **Murphys Hotel**★ (1856), with an historic guest list including Mark Twain and other luminaries; and the **Old-Timers Museum**, presenting early California pioneer memorabilia and Indian baskets *(open year-round Fri–Sun 11am–4pm; 209-728-1160).* Guided walking tours of historic Murphys depart from here *(Sat 10.30am).*

Calaveras Big Trees State Park★★

48mi round-trip northeast from Angels Camp via Rte. 4 (15mi northeast of Murphys). Park open year-round daily dawn–dusk. Visitor Center open May–Oct daily 11am–3pm (summer 9am–5pm); rest of the year weekends 11am–3pm. Closed Jan 1, Thanksgiving Day, Dec 25. $7/car. 209-795-2334. www.parks.ca.gov.

This preserve harbors giant sequoia trees; the gargantuan wonders attracted worldwide attention to the **North Grove** in the early 1850s, when tourists arrived in droves. Today, a self-guided trail *(1mi)* leads to 150 giant sequoias. The more remote **South Grove** *(1mi from end of paved road at Beaver Creek; closed mid-Nov–mid-Apr)* remains in its natural state; a 3.5mi loop trail offers the opportunity to experience untouched primeval forest. The visitor center has exhibits on natural and human history and a theater with slide shows.

Calaveras Big Trees State Park

© Christopher Russell/Dreamstime.com

Nestled east of the Los Angeles Basin and west of Palm Springs, wedged between the Mojave Desert and the Peninsular Ranges, Southern California's Inland Empire has evolved a character of its own.

Highlights

1   A summer drive in the cool elevations around **Big Bear Lake** *(p139)*

2   The fabulous lobby of the **Mission Inn** *(p140)*

3   Whizzing down the slopes at **Big Bear Mountain** *(see Planning your Trip)*

4   For Civil War buffs a quiet stop at Riverside's **Lincoln Memorial Shrine** *(p140)*

Tired of being ignored after World War II had brought population and wealth to other parts of Southern California, San Bernardino and Riverside counties devised the "Inland Empire" name to promote their region. Public relations and civic boosterism aside, the moniker fits this realm of citrus. Oranges, lemons, grapefruit and other fruit had turned semi-arid acreage to green in the late 19C, and the agricultural lifestyle created millionaires and gracious mansions in Riverside, Redlands and San Bernardino. Apple orchards, vineyards and dairy farming added to the wealth of the region.

Today, the Inland Empire is one of California's fastest-growing areas. The two counties have a population exceeding three million. At its metropolitan core, citrus groves are increasingly sacrificed for residential subdivisions and service businesses. Mindful of this disappearing heritage, Riverside preserves an 11mi section of Victoria Avenue where citrus will be forever cultivated; the state main-

Kayakers at Big Bear Lake

tains **California Citrus State Historic Park** in Riverside to recall the industry's heyday.

The rugged **San Bernardino Mountains** dominate the landscape to the north of their namesake city. Snow-dusted in winter—rising to 11,499ft at San Gorgonio Mountain—the range harbors several beautiful, jewel-like lakes that invite four seasons of recreational use. Best known is man-made **Big Bear Lake**★, 6mi long with a crenelated 24mi shoreline; locals gather in its refreshing climate for winter skiing and summer hiking and water sports. The 40mi **Rim of the World Drive**★★ (Route 18) links Big Bear with other San Bernardino National Forest resort areas, including **Lake Arrowhead**.

The **Temecula Valley**, halfway from San Bernardino to San Diego on the southern side of the Inland Empire, has in recent years boomed as a wine region. San Diegans are the most frequent visitors here, drawn to the wineries and the

Rim of the World Drive
© Ron Chapple Stock/Corbis

antique shops of Old Town Temecula, on the west side of the wine country.

ADDRESSES

🛏 STAY

🍷🛏 **The Mission Inn** – *3649 Mission Inn Ave., Riverside.* 📞*951-784-0300 or 800-843-7755. www.missioninn.com. 239 units.* The region's most celebrated hotel is an architectural masterpiece built in 1876–1931 (🍷*see Riverside*). Re-opened in 1993 after a $55 million restoration, the hostelry now offers luxurious rooms and suites with modern amenities; spa services, and four restaurants. Unique rooms feature elements such as domed ceilings and stained-glass windows. Humphrey Bogart, Bette Davis and Richard Nixon all had weddings here.

🍷 **Hillcrest Lodge** – *40241 Big Bear Blvd. (Rte. 18), Big Bear Lake.* 📞*909-866-6040 or 800-843-4449. www.hillcrestlodge.com. 12 rooms.* Spacious suites, motel rooms and cabins—some with spas, fireplaces and kitchens—overlook Big Bear Lake just west of the main village. Nearby Pleasant Point Marina offers discount boat rentals to lodge guests.

🍽 EAT

🍷🍷🍷 **Le Rendez-Vous** – *4775 N. Sierra Way, San Bernardino.* 📞*909-883-1231. Dinner only. Closed Mon.* **French.** Inlanders' Gallic cravings are sated at this classic, family-owned French restaurant with white-tablecloth service. The menu focuses on traditional cuisine; baked Brie, vichyssoise, escargots to start; main courses include deliciously prepared fish dishes, plus coq au vin, filet mignon and veal sweetbreads. Chocolate mousse makes a fitting finish to the meal.

🍷🍷 **Caprice Café** – *104 E. State St., Redlands.* 📞*909-793-8787. www.caprice cafe.com. Closed Sun.* **Mediterranean.** Nestled on the ground floor of Redlands' historic JC Penney building, this restaurant delivers outstanding eastern Mediterranean cuisine—Greek, Lebanese, Middle Eastern—such as salads, pizzas, pastas, lamb kababs and vegetarian dishes like falafel and hummus. Steak, fish and chicken are also on the menu. Luscious house-made desserts run the gamut from tiramisu to pecan pie to chocolate soufflé cake.

Redlands

Today a university town, Redlands thrived as an agricultural center and winter resort. Built from the wealth of the orange industry, some 300 mansions survive today.

SIGHTS
San Bernardino County Museum
2024 Orange Tree Ln.; exit I-10 at California St. and drive 1mi north. ○Open year-round Tue–Sun & holiday Mon 9am–5pm. ○Closed Jan 1, Thanksgiving Day, Dec 25. ⚏$6. ♿ P ℘909-307-2669. www.sbcountymuseum.org.

This excellent regional museum, founded in 1952, celebrates local anthropology, agriculture and mining heritage. The **Hall of Anthropology** focuses on the prehistoric Indians of Southern California; you'll find items excavated from the Calico Early Man Site near Barstow *(p117)*. The upper floor is devoted to ornithological collections, including an assemblage of 30,000 bird eggs from all over the world. The museum has three floors of exhibits, an "Exploration Station", education center, native plant and cactus gardens and citrus groves.

> ▶ **Population:** 69,941.
> ⚏ **Michelin Map:** 585 B 10.
> ▤ **Info:** ℘909-335-4731. www.redlandstourism.org.
> ▶ **Location:** This city sits at the base of the San Bernardino Mountains, about 65mi east of Los Angeles.

Lincoln Memorial Shrine
125 W. Vine St. ○Open year-round Tue–Sun 1pm–5pm. ○Closed major holidays. ♿ P ℘909-798-7632. www.lincolnshrine.org.
This octagonal structure houses samples of an extensive collection of Lincoln memorabilia and Civil War weaponry.

Kimberly Crest House and Gardens★
1325 Prospect Dr. ⌇House visit by guided tour (1hr 30min) only, Sept–Jul Thu–Sun 1pm–4pm. ○Closed major holidays. ⚏$7. ♿ ℘909-792-2111. www.kimberlycrest.org.
Built in 1897, this residence was purchased in 1905 by the founder of Kimberly-Clark Corp. The interior showcases early 20C decoration.

Riverside

This city is heralded as the birthplace of California's citrus industry. In 1873, a resident received two seedling orange trees from trees propagated in Brazil; the seedlings thrived in Riverside's fertile soil and mild climate.

SIGHTS
Mission Inn★★
3649 Mission Inn Ave. ✕♿ P ℘951-784-0300. www.missioninn.com.
Riverside's most celebrated landmark looms like a Spanish palace above downtown. In 1876 Christopher Columbus Miller, a local engineer, constructed a two-story adobe home. His son, Frank Augustus Miller, began expanding the

> ▶ **Population:** 311,575.
> ⚏ **Michelin Map:** 585 B 10.
> ▤ **Info:** ℘951-683-7100. www.riverside-chamber.com.
> ▶ **Location:** Riverside lies on the banks of the Santa Ana River, some 55mi east of Los Angeles.

hotel in 1902, adding wings that eventually resulted in a 239-room pastiche of Oriental, Mission and Spanish Renaissance Revival styles. The small **museum** *(○open daily 9.30am–4pm)* highlights the various stages of development. The museum organizes guided tours of the inn *(⌇Mon–Fri 11am, 1pm,*

2pm, 3pm; weekends 10am–11.30am, 1pm–3pm; ⊜*$12; 75min).* The **St. Francis Chapel**★ highlights Frank Miller's prized possessions: an 18C Mexican altar and Tiffany windows.

Riverside Art Museum
3425 Mission Inn Ave. ◷*Open year-round Mon–Sat 10am–4pm.* ⊜*$5.* ℘*951-684-7111. www.riversideart museum.org.*
Hearst Castle architect Julia Morgan designed this 1929 building. Expertly curated temporary exhibits focus on American contemporary works by California and Inland Empire artists.

UCR/California Museum of Photography
3824 Main St., on the mall. ◷*Open year-round Tue–Sat noon–5pm.* ◷*Closed Jan 1, Jul 4, Thanksgiving Day, Dec 25.* ⊜*$3.* ℘*951-784-3686. www.cmp.ucr.edu.*
Founded in 1973, this museum of photographic art and technology showcases the Keystone-Mast Collection of 350,000 stereographic negatives dating from 1870–1940. You'll also find changing exhibits of photography, and—fun for kids—interactive exhibits demonstrating color, light and other aspects of vision.

UC Riverside Botanic Garden
On the University of California campus. ◷*Open year-round daily 8am–5pm.* ◷*Closed major holidays.* ⊜*$1.* ▣*(fee).* ℘*951-827-4650. www.gardens.ucr.edu.*
Collections feature species native to California, Australia and southern Africa; a geodesic lathhouse shades rare plants.

Heritage House★
8193 Magnolia St. ☛*Visit by guided tour (45min) only, Labor Day–Jun Fri noon–3pm, weekends noon–3.30pm.* ◷*Closed major holidays.* ⊜*$3.* ▣℘*951-826-5723. www.riversideca.gov/museum.*
This Victorian residence (1891) sports exceptional craftsmanship typical of the prosperous houses that lined Magnolia Avenue during the late 19C. Exterior embellishments reveal the Moorish, Palladian and Chinese influences so common to Queen Anne-style houses of the day. The interior features Victorian "hobby art," simple craft projects such as handmade picture frames.

EXCURSIONS
March Field Museum
11mi east of downtown Riverside at March Air Force Base (Van Buren exit from I-215). ◷*Open year-round Tue–Sun 9am–4pm.* ◷*Closed Jan 1, Easter, Thanksgiving Day, Dec 25.* ⊜*$8, children $5.* &▣℘*951-697-6600. www.rth.org/march.*
This 44-acre museum features a noteworthy collection of 70 restored aircraft including bombers, troop transports, and fighter jets. In the main hangar you'll see photos, uniforms and weapons used by US aviators in past wars.

Orange Empire Railway Museum
⚏*2201 South A St., Perris. 20mi south of Riverside via I-215.* ◷*Open year-round daily 9am–5pm.* ◷*Closed Thanksgiving Day, Dec 25. Train & trolley rides available weekends & holidays (11am–4.30pm;* ⊜*$12, children $8)* ▣℘*951-657-2605. www.oerm.org.*
This museum preserves relics of the era of steam and diesel trains. Highlights include "Big Red Cars" from Los Angeles' Pacific Electric Railway and a 1924 Santa Fe Railway post-office car.

Planes of Fame Air Museum
⚏*7000 Merrill Ave., Chino. 15mi west of Riverside via Rte. 60, exit Euclid Rd. (Rte. 83) and drive 3.4mi south; turn left on Merrill Ave. and continue 1mi to Chino Airport.* ◷*Open year-round daily 9am–5pm.* ◷*Closed Thanksgiving Day, Dec 25.* ⊜*$14, children $4.* &▣℘*909-597-3722. www.planesoffame.org.*
This museum celebrates aviation history in a collection of some 100 restored historical aircraft. Outside, a B-17 "Flying Fortress" is on display. Hangar 2 features a large collection of Japanese warplanes. A highlight of the adjacent Fighter Jets Museum, is an ME-109G developed in Germany.

Filling a vast coastal plain framed by towering mountains, this sprawling, sun-drenched megalopolis is the largest metropolitan area in the US, a collection of once-distinct cities and towns that have grown together through time and necessity. Its enviable climate, its role as an international entertainment center, and its remarkable ethnic and cultural diversity contribute to a heady mix of sights and experiences with an ambience so casual that locals refer to their home merely by initials: "L.A."

Highlights

1 A star-studded movie premiere at **Grauman's Chinese Theater** (p177)
2 Sunset from Palisades Park in **Santa Monica** (p198)
3 An evening performance at the **Hollywood Bowl** (p181)
4 The tram tour at **Universal Studios** (p180)
5 Window-shopping on **Rodeo Drive** (p182)
6 Visiting the Ice Age at **La Brea Tar Pits** (p172)
7 Saturday morning at the **Farmers' Market** (p173)

Greater Los Angeles spills beyond the Los Angeles Basin that runs inland from the Pacific Ocean to surrounding mountain ranges (Santa Monica to the northwest; San Gabriel to the north; San Bernardino to the east; and Santa Ana to the southeast). These mountains are reminders of geological stress which often manifested in **earthquakes**: They also form a natural barrier that retains **smog**—a layer of airborne sludge created by smoke and air pollutants.

Anthropologists estimate that 5,000 Gabrieleños lived in an area stretching from present-day Orange County to Malibu when, on August 2, 1769, a Spanish colonizing expedition led by Gaspar de Portolá arrived near the present site of City Hall. Having just observed the jubilee of Our Lady of Los Angeles de Porciúncula, the settlers named the river Porciúncula in her honor.

About 88 incorporated cities lie within the county, many of them completely surrounded by the city of L.A. The city itself covers more than 467sq mi. Almost ten times that area composes L.A. County, and the metropolitan area stretches beyond county boundaries to some 34,000sq mi.

Both city and county are governed from Los Angeles Civic Center. City population exceeds 3.8 million, the county 9.8 million (nearly a third of California residents) and the metropolitan area 17.8 million.

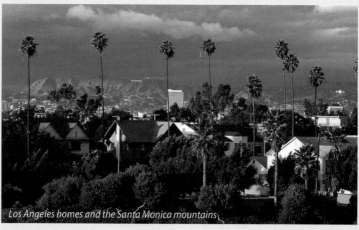

Los Angeles homes and the Santa Monica mountains

© PhotoDisc

ADDRESSES

For a more comprehensive selection of hotels and restaurants, see the red-cover **Michelin Guide Los Angeles.**

🍴 STAY

🛏️🛏️🛏️🛏️🛏️ **Casa del Mar** – *1910 Ocean Front Way, Santa Monica.* ☎*310-581-5533 or 800-898-6999. www.hotelcasa delmar.com. 129 rooms.* An opulent beach club for well-to-do Angelenos in the 1920s, Casa del Mar was neglected after use as a military hotel in World War II. A $60 million restoration in the 1990s returned the seven-story inn to its former stature. **Catch** (🛏️🛏️🛏️🛏️) restaurant, specializing in seafood, looks out on Santa Monica Bay.

🛏️🛏️🛏️🛏️🛏️ **Hotel Bel-Air** – *701 Stone Canyon Rd., Los Angeles.* ☎*310-472-1211 or 800-648-4097. www.hotelbelair.com. 92 rooms.* Long ranked among the world's finest hotels, these 12 acres of lush gardens and waterfalls resemble a private estate. Individually decorated rooms sit within pink Mission-style, tile-floored bungalows, each with a private entrance. Fireplaces and Italian linens are added touches. **The Restaurant** (🛏️🛏️🛏️🛏️) serves California-French cuisine; the bar boasts a large selection of port.

🛏️🛏️🛏️🛏️🛏️ **Mosaic Hotel** – *125 Spalding Dr., Beverly Hills.* ☎*310-278-0303 or 800-463-4466. www.mosaichotel.com. 49 rooms.* Situated on a quiet street, this boutique property offers a palm-shaded swimming pool and a cozy restaurant. Contemporary-style rooms are done in muted colors; deluxe rooms feature marble bathtubs, Bose stereo systems and luxurious, Fili'Doro linens.

🛏️🛏️🛏️🛏️🛏️ **Shutters** – *1 Pico Blvd., Santa Monica.* ☎*310-458-0030. www. shuttersonthebeach.com. 198 rooms.* A beachside-cottage feel undergirds this property set on the sands of Santa Monica Bay. Relax by the pool or have a massage at the spa. In the evening, sip an aperitif in the lobby's piano bar before sampling the New American cuisine at **One Pico** (🛏️🛏️🛏️) restaurant.

🛏️🛏️🛏️ **Artists' Inn and Cottage Bed and Breakfast** *1038 Magnolia St , South Pasadena.* ☎*626-799-5668 or 888-799-5668. www.artistsinns.com. 9 rooms.* 🛏️. Each guest room in this Victorian home reflects a different artist or period: the Gauguin suite takes guests to Tahiti with a bamboo bed, while bright colors in the Expressionist suite bring Matisse to mind. Gourmet breakfasts are served on the porch overlooking the garden.

🛏️🛏️🛏️ **Chamberlain** – *1000 Westmount Dr., West Hollywood.* ☎*310-657-7400 or 800-201-9652. www.chamberlainwest hollywood.com. 114 suites.* Secluded on a residential hillside, this upscale hidea-way offers its guests privacy, spacious quarters and a rooftop pool that oozes Hollywood glamor. All rooms have gas fireplaces, large desks and high-tech amenities including flat-panel TVs.

🛏️🛏️🛏️ **Hotel Queen Mary** – *1126 Queen's Hwy., Long Beach.* ☎*562-435-3511. www.queenmary.com. 314 rooms.* Permanently docked at Long Beach Harbor, this luxury liner boasts three decks of wood-paneled staterooms. Of the dining options onboard, the best are **Sir Winston's** (🛏️🛏️🛏️🛏️), for Continental cuisine, and **Chelsea** (🛏️🛏️🛏️), for seafood. A complimentary Shipwalk tour awaits guests.

🛏️🛏️🛏️ **Millennium Biltmore** – *506 S. Grand Ave., Los Angeles.* ☎*213-624-1011 or 866-866-8086. www.millennium-hotels.com. 683 rooms.* Home of the first (1927) Oscars ceremony and once a magnet for presidents, kings and celebs, the Italian Renaissance-style Biltmore has maintained its prestige through the decades. It remains a presence in the heart of downtown.

🛏️🛏️ **Hotel Figueroa** – *939 S. Figueroa St., Los Angeles.* ☎*213-627-8971 or 800-421-9092. www.figueroahotel.com. 285 rooms.* This downtown hotel, built in 1926, feels like an enclave of Morocco. The arched terracotta entrance leads to a lobby decked in stone columns, cacti and Mexican tiles, and the pool is surrounded by a lavish garden. Exotic in style, rooms feature wrought-iron bed frames and reflect a desert palette. Downstairs, Club Fes and Room Tangier frequently host parties for Hollywood's glitterati.

🛏️🛏️ **The Venice Beach House** – *15 30th Ave., Venice.* ☎*310-823-1966. www. venicebeachhouse.com. 9 rooms.* 🛏️.

Framed by a picket fence and charming garden, this bed-and-breakfast inn recalls the early 20C days of its beach community's founding as a Venetian-style artists' community. Some rooms have private entrances, others have cathedral ceilings.

¶/ EAT

Patina – *141 S. Grand Ave., Los Angeles. ☎213-972-3331. www.patina group.com. Dinner only; closed Mon.* **Contemporary**. Ensconced in downtown's Walt Disney Concert Hall, chef Joachim Splichal's signature restaurant stays on key with Frank Gehry's striking structure. A varied seasonal menu reinterprets the familiar in refreshing unusual ways, from a lobster sausage to an olive-oil poached breast of squab.

Campanile – *624 S. La Brea Ave., Los Angeles. ☎323-938-1447. www. campanilerestaurant.com. Brunch only Sun.* **Mediterranean**. Immaculate decor, impeccable table settings, fabulous cuisine and an extensive list of wines and spirits define chef Mark Peel's Beverly Hills stalwart. Since 1989, Angelenos have loved this airy place, where the breads come fresh from the ovens of Peel's La Brea Bakery next door. The menu highlights the likes of rustic rosemary-charred baby lamb, and seared pompano atop sliced cucumbers.

JiRaffe – *502 Santa Monica Blvd., Santa Monica. ☎310-917-6671. www. jirafferestaurant.com. Dinner only.* **Californian**. From the airy storefront of this chic bistro, chef/owner Raphael Lunetta prepares such dishes the likes of almond-crusted Pacific swordfish, roasted rabbit with herb polenta, and pancetta-wrapped tiger shrimp. Save room for the chocolate truffle cake.

Spago Beverly Hills – *176 N. Cañon Dr, Beverly Hills. ☎310-385-0880. www.wolfgangpuck.com. No lunch Sun.* **Contemporary**. Celebrity chef Wolfgang Puck draws the Hollywood glitterati to feast on his "designer" pizzas, risottos, fish and duck, or Austrian classics like Wiener Schnitzel. This super-chic establishment is painted in amethyst, green and amber and decorated with Italian marble. Regulars favor the outdoor brick courtyard on warm nights.

Water Grill – *544 S. Grand Ave., Los Angeles. ☎213-891-0900. www.watergrill.com. No lunch Sat–Sun.* **Seafood**. Located in downtown's vintage Pacific Mutual Center, this fine restaurant is hailed as the city's finest seafood restaurant. An ever-changing menu may include the likes of Alaskan day-boat halibut, line-caught wild John Dory, poached Columbia River sturgeon and Pacific big-eye tuna. Save room for the outstanding desserts.

Bistro 45 – *45 S. Mentor Ave., Pasadena. ☎626-795-2478. www. bistro45.com. Closed Mon. No lunch Sat–Sun.* **Californian**. Lavendar and herbs scent the garden in front of this downtown bistro. Inside, friendly servers deliver delectable plates of lightly battered wild-caught calamari, Niman Ranch bone-in pork loin, and citrus-marinated free-range chicken breast.

Tiapazola Grill – *11676 Gateway Blvd., Los Angeles. ☎310-477-1577. No lunch Sat–Mon.* **Mexican**. Ignore the tired strip-mall setting and the unassuming exterior of this little grill; step inside and experience the feel and flavors of Oaxca. Daily specials complement the wide selection of Mexican dishes, which pair fresh California products with south-of-the-border recipes.

Il Capriccio on Vermont – *1757 N. Vermont Ave., Los Angeles. ☎323-662-5900. www.ilcapriccioonvermont.com. No lunch Fri–Sun.* **Italian**. This charming trattoria in Los Feliz dishes up authentic Italian fare with fresh ingredients and in generous portions from an extensive menu. From pasta to *pollo*, Il Capriccio delivers a lot of flavorful bang for the buck. The best place for lunch is on the heated sidewalk patio.

Saladang Song – *383 S. Fair Oaks Ave., Pasadena. ☎626-793-5200.* **Thai**. The original Saladang was so successful that the owners opened a second location right next door. This restaurant one-ups its older sister by serving breakfast and adding an outdoor patio. Try flavorful noodle dishes, ground grilled shrimp or marinated pork.

Catalina Island★

👤 **Michelin Map:** 585 B 11.

Boating, fishing and the harbor town of Avalon, are the attractions of this mountainous island, 21mi off the coast south of Los Angeles. Chewing gum magnate William Wrigley, Jr., bought the island and used it for his Chicago Cubs' spring training site. The Catalina Island Conservancy now owns most of the island.

SIGHTS
Avalon
Catalina's only town is a mix of pastel-colored houses and bungalows, hotels, restaurants and souvenir shops. Cars are restricted on the island. From the **Green Pleasure Pier**, glass-bottomed boats depart to view undersea life or visit sea lion colonies. Buses to the island's wilderness interior, Catalina Airport and the Wrigley family's Arabian horse ranch depart from the town center (*Tour Plaza between Catalina & Sumner Aves.*).

The tall, circular, art deco **Casino Building**★★ was built as a tourist attraction by Wrigley (*1 Casino Way;* 🚶 *visit by 50min guided tour;* ⊜*$15.25; call for hrs and reservations;* ♿🅿️ 🕿*800-626-1496*). Despite its name, gambling was never permitted here.

Inside, the ornate **Avalon Ballroom** holds the world's largest circular dance floor. On the casino's lowest level, a small **museum** presents exhibits on Catalina's history, natural history and archaeology (🕐 *open Apr–Dec daily 10am–4pm; rest of the year Fri–Wed 10am–4pm;* 🕐*closed Thanksgiving Day & Dec 25* ⊜*$5;* ♿ 🕿*310-510-2414*).

Casino Point Marine Park
Offshore from the Casino Building. 🕐*Open daily year-round.* 🅿️ 🕿*310-510-0330. www.visitcatalinaisland.com.* Established in 1965, this marine preserve includes several wrecks and artificial reefs popular with scuba divers. The preserve is the only place within Avalon's limits where diving is permitted.

Wrigley Memorial & Botanical Garden
1400 Avalon Canyon Rd. 🕐*Open daily 8am–5pm.* ⊜*$5.* ♿🅿️ 🕿*310-510-2595. www.catalina.com/memorial.html.*
This 38-acre garden in Avalon Canyon highlights Catalina's native plants, along with cacti and succulents. The 130ft memorial honors William Wrigley, Jr. Below the garden, the **Santa Catalina Island Interpretive Center** (🕐*open year-round Fri–Wed 10am–5pm;* 🕿*310-510-0954*) has exhibits on the island's flora, fauna and marine ecology.

Catalina Island, Harbor
© Brigitta L. House/MICHELIN

Area Code: 310

GETTING THERE

Passenger ferries serve Avalon and Two Harbors daily year-round from Long Beach Downtown Landing *(I-710 S to Downtown Long Beach/Shoreline Dr.)*, Dana Point *(I-5, exit Pacific Coast Hwy)*, San Pedro *(I-110 South to Harbor Blvd.)* and Newport Beach *(Balboa Pavilion, off Pacific Coast Hwy.)*. Fares range from $26–$38 one-way, parking $8–14/day, crossing time 60–90min one-way.

Catalina Express *(✆519-7971 or 800-481-3470; www.catalinaexpress.com)* departs from San Pedro, Dana Point and Long Beach Downtown Landing.

Catalina Flyer departs from Newport Beach *(daily 9am, return from Avalon 4.30pm; schedules vary; $68 round-trip; ✆949-673-5245 or 800-830-7744; www.catalinainfo.com)*.

Catalina Ferries departs from Marina del Rey to Avalon and Two Harbors *(daily; $79 round-trip; ✆310-3305-7250; www.catalinaferries.com)*.

GETTING AROUND

Catalina Safari Bus *(✆510-2800 or 800-322-3434)* offers scheduled bus service between Avalon and Two Harbors year-round daily *($33 one-way; reservations required)*. To get around Avalon, rent a golf cart *($40/hr; Island Rentals ✆510-1456)* or bicycle *($12-$25/day; Brown's Bikes, ✆510-0986)*. Biking outside of Avalon's city limits requires a permit; check with the **Catalina Island Conservancy** *(125 Claressa St.; ✆510-2595; www.catalinaconservancy.org)*.

VISITOR INFORMATION

Catalina Island Chamber of Commerce *(1 Green Pleasure Pier, Avalon; ✆510-1520; www.catalina.com)*. **Two Harbors Visitor Services** *(✆510-0303)*, at the foot of the pier.

Long Beach★

Sprawling Long Beach is home to the Port of Long Beach; together with adjacent Worldport L.A., it is the largest waterborne shipping center in the US. The city balances large areas of heavy industry with charming residential streets and developed shoreline with beach areas.

SIGHTS
👤👤 Queen Mary★★★

1126 Queens Hwy., south end of I-710. ◷Open year-round daily 10am–5pm. General admission ⊚$24.95, children $12.95; additional fees for guided tour packages. ✕ℙ($12) ✆562-435-3511. www.queenmary.com.

This renowned passenger ship was permanently docked here in 1967 after 31 years of service in Great Britain's Cunard White Star line. Built in Scotland, the Queen Mary made her maiden voyage in May 1936, but was converted for mili-

▶ **Population:** 430,905.
⚙ **Michelin Map:** 585 B 10 and map this section.
ℹ **Info:** ✆562-436-3645. www.golongbeach.org.
◐ **Location:** Long Beach sits on the shore of San Pedro Bay, 30mi south of Los Angeles via I-710.
👤👤 **Kids:** Queen Mary, Sub, Aquariums, Maritime Mus.

tary use during World War II. The massive, 81,237-ton vessel measures 1,019ft long. As the world's largest and reputedly most luxurious passenger vessel, the ship was a favorite of international celebrities.

By the mid-20C, air travel had eclipsed the era of the great passenger ships, and the Queen Mary's traffic declined. The city of Long Beach now operates the ship as a hotel and tourist attraction. On board, visitors can explore the operational centers, officers' quarters, passenger suites, dining rooms, and the engine room. Guided tours penetrate the ship's luxuriously furnished staterooms. Restaurants and snack and souvenir shops are scattered throughout the ship, and a hotel occupies three of its 12 decks.

🏊🏊 Scorpion Submarine★

1126 Queens Hwy. Open year-round daily 10–5pm. 🎫 *$10.95, children $9.95.* 🅿 *($10)* ☏ *562-435-3511.* *www.queenmary.com.*

The 3,000-ton Scorpion—more officially, the Soviet Foxtrot-class submarine Povodnaya Lodka B-427—is moored next to the Queen Mary. Nearly all of this 1972 diesel-electric sub (decommissioned in 1994) is open for tours, including the forward and aft torpedo rooms.

🏊🏊 Aquarium of the Pacific★★ (A)

▥▥▥ *100 Aquarium Way (off Shoreline Dr. south of Ocean Blvd.).* 🕐 *Open year-round daily 9am–6pm.* 🕐 *Closed Apr 17–19 & Dec 25.* 🎫 *$23.95, children $11.95.* ✕🔖🅿 *($7)* ☏ *562-590-3100.* *www.aquariumofpacific.org.*

This $117 million shoreside aquarium (1998) contains one of the most comprehensive marine-themed exhibits in California. Three marine eco-zones are divided into 19 major indoor and outdoor habitats and 32 smaller exhibits with more than 500 species of marine creatures of the Pacific Ocean.

In **Southern California and Baja**, rehabilitated seals and sea lions highlight displays of local sea life. Child-oriented **Explorers Cove** has touch tanks, a shark lagoon and a lorikeet forest. **Northern Pacific** harbors sea otters, giant octopi, and other denizens. Coral reefs teem with colorful fish in **Tropical Pacific**.

Shoreline Park★ (B)

Shoreline Dr. south of Ocean Blvd.
Grassy knolls and pedestrian paths offer splendid **views**★ of the Queen Mary across Queensway Bay. To the north, downtown's office towers rise behind the massive **Long Beach Convention and Entertainment Center (C)**. The park's east end is fringed by **Shoreline**

Aquarium of the Pacific's Shark Lagoon

© Aquarium of the Pacific

Village★, an ersatz seaport village of shops, restaurants and a carousel. Adjacent is **The Pike at Rainbow Harbor**, a shopping and entertainment complex.

Museum of Latin American Art★ (D)

628 Alamitos Ave. 🕐 *Open Wed–Sun 11am–5pm.* 🕐 *Closed Jan 1, Thanksgiving Day & Dec 25.* 🎫 *$9.* ✕🔖🅿 ☏ *562-437-1689. www.molaa.com.*

The museum is dedicated exclusively to contemporary Latin American art. Selections from a permanent collection of post-World War II oil paintings and prints share wall space with traveling exhibits. In 2007 the museum completed work on a major expansion designed by Mexican architect Manuel Rosen, which increased the museum's exhibit space and added a new sculpture garden.

Rancho Los Cerritos Historic Site

4600 Virginia Rd., 1 block west of Long Beach Blvd. at San Antonio Dr. 🕐 *Open year-round Wed–Sun 1pm–5pm.* 🚶 *Guided tours (1hr) weekends.* 🕐 *Closed major holidays.* 🅿 ☏ *562-570-1755. www.rancholoscerritos.org.*

Focal point of one of the original ranches in Southern California, the two-story Monterey-style 1844 adobe building has been restored to reflect domestic life from the 1870s.

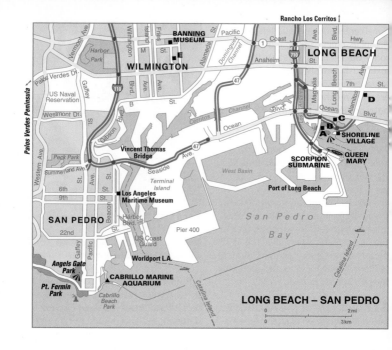

LONG BEACH – SAN PEDRO

Rancho Los Alamitos Historic Ranch and Gardens

6400 Bixby Hill Rd., off Palo Verde Ave. south of E. Anaheim Rd. ○*Open Wed–Sun 1pm–5pm.* ⟶*House and barns visit by guided tour (90min) only.* ○*Closed major holidays.* ⟶ ▣ ✆*562-431-3541. www.rancholosalamitos.com.* This historic house illustrates life on an early 20C ranch. The seven-acre property has a c.1800 adobe ranch house, several early 20C barns with resident livestock, and a blacksmith shop.

EXCURSIONS
San Pedro

Linked to Long Beach by the Vincent Thomas Bridge, San Pedro was Southern California's predominant harbor community until the 1920s. Its vast Worldport L.A. is one of the nation's busiest container ports and the West Coast's leading passenger terminal.

Angels Gate Park *(end of Gaffey St.).* atop the crest of the Palos Verdes Peninsula, affords sea **views**★★ that extend as far as Catalina Island on clear days. Below lies 37-acre **Point Fermin Park**.

Cabrillo Marine Aquarium★

⟶⟶*3720 Stephen White Dr. off Pacific Ave. Parking in Cabrillo Beach Park.* ○*Open year-round Tue–Fri noon–5pm, weekends 10am–5pm.* ○*Closed Thanksgiving Day & Dec 25.* ⟶*$5.* ▣*($1/hr)* ✆*310-548-7562. www.cabrilloaq.org.* This small aquarium and museum offers an introduction to Southern California's marine life. More than 500 species of fish are displayed in 35 aquariums.

Los Angeles Maritime Museum

⟶⟶*Berth 84, foot of 6th St.* ○*Open year-round Tue–Sat 10am–5pm, Sun noon–5pm.* ○*Closed holidays.* ⟶*$3, children $1.* ⟶ ▣ ✆*310-548-7618. www.lamaritimemuseum.org.* San Pedro Bay and its history and industry are the focus of this excellent museum housed in the historic art deco Municipal Ferry Building (1941). In among the vestiges of the building's ferry days are a collection of nautical memorabilia and a fascinating exhibit on commercial hardhat diving. The display of seamen's knots is impressive, and an active ham radio station permits eavesdropping on port traffic.

Los Angeles ★★★

Los Angeles enjoys the benefits and faces the challenges of a major metropolis, though both the pros and cons of life in the city are magnified by its enormous size and its near-mythic reputation.
Los Angeles' ethnic diversity endows it with rich cultural resources and can make a drive across town seem like a dizzying world tour. While its differences have produced clashes throughout the city's history, they also endow L.A. with a distinctive vitality and sense of possibilities.

LOS ANGELES TODAY

Diversity – Los Angeles is one of several American cities without a majority ethnic population. 47.3 percent of Angelenos are Hispanic, 29.2 percent are non-Hispanic Caucasian, 13.1 percent are Asian or Pacific Islander, 8.9 percent are African-American and 0.3 percent Native American and other. Although these ethnic groups are spread throughout the city, specific communities do exist, including Chinatown, Little Tokyo, the Mexican-American enclaves of East Los Angeles, the African-American neighborhoods of South Central Los Angeles, Koreatown (south of Wilshire Boulevard) and Little Saigon (Westminster in Orange County).

Such diversity can, particularly in the face of social and economic adversity, lead to civic strife: devastating riots occurred in Watts in August 1965, and again in April and May of 1992 in other neighborhoods of South Central Los Angeles and beyond.

Yet Los Angeles continues to preserve, heal and renew itself, largely through the efforts of individuals and local and federal organizations. Groups such as the **Los Angeles Conservancy** and **Project Restore** dedicate themselves to preserving the city's historic architecture. The city hosted the Summer Olympic Games in 1932 and 1984, and its unquenchable dynamism attracts international visitors and events. Los Angeles' coastal setting favors it

- ▶ **Population:** 3,849,738.
- **Michelin Map:** 585 B 10 and maps p151–151, 160, 161, 168, 169, 186, Metro Map p156.
- **Info:** ℘213-624-7300. www.discoverlos angeles.com.
- ▶ **Location:** Use the Los Angeles map herein to familiarize yourself with the major areas of L.A. (Downtown, Exposition Park, Hollywood and so on).
- **Don't Miss:** Griffith Park Observatory; a day at the beach.
- **Timing:** You'll need at least a week to truly experience L.A. Save a weekday for Downtown, and bear in mind that museums may be closed on Mondays. Griffith Park requires one day, as does Universal Studios. See Hollywood Blvd. at night when the neon lights are aglow. You must reserve timed entry tickets for The Getty Villa at Malibu.
- **Kids:** L.A. Zoo, Exposition Park museums, Universal Studios Hollywood, the beach and many more.

with perpetually fine weather and a beachy vibe that finds its way into the local culture. Given their city's role as an entertainment, commercial and fashion capital, locals habitually find themselves on the cutting edge of national trends. This is where fads are born: by the beach, at the shopping mall, in the kitchen, on camera. Angelenos take it in their stride, with a carefree readiness to embrace (and create) the new.

The Performing Arts – The Los Angeles County Museum of Art, the J. Paul Getty Museum, the Museum of Contemporary Art and other institutions house outstanding collections and mount exhibits that tour the nation. The Los

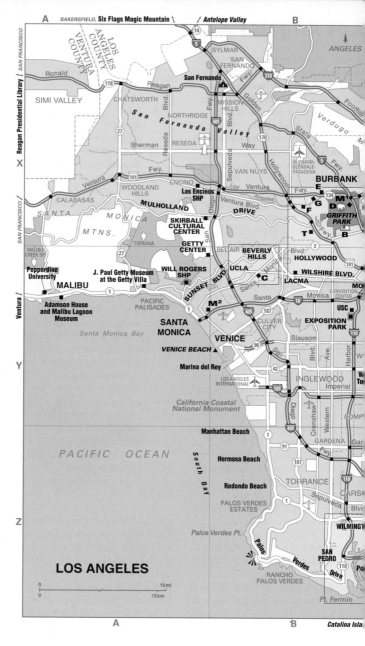

Angeles Philharmonic Orchestra, now under the baton of Gustavo Dudamel, rose to world-class status under conductors Zubin Mehta, André Previn and Esa-Pekka Salonen. The University of California, Los Angeles, and the University of Southern California enjoy international esteem as institutions of higher education. The theaters of the Music Center of Los Angeles County (including the Walt Disney Concert Hall), the Shubert Theatre and other local stages present a wide range of award-winning original and visiting produc-

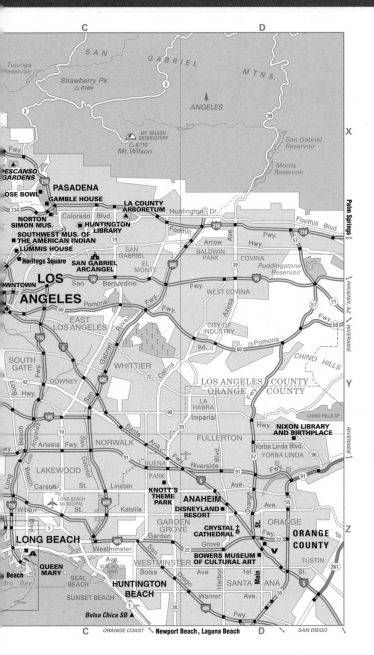

tions of drama, music, opera and dance.
Metro Rail – Los Angeles' public rapid-transit system of underground and sur-face light-rail cars was inaugurated in 1990 to combat air pollution and reduce freeway traffic. It is the indirect descend-ant of the Pacific Electric Red Car system and LA Railway Yellow Car lines (early to mid-20C). **Metrolink**, a network of high-speed commuter trains, connects Los Angeles with outlying cities in Los Ange-les, Ventura, San Bernardino, Riverside and Orange counties. *See Practical Information and the Metro map.*

LOS ANGELES – SITES INDEX

LOS ANGELES – STREET INDEX

SPECTATOR SPORTS

Tickets for major sporting events can be purchased at the venue or through
Ticketmaster ☎800-745-3000; www.ticketmaster.com.

Sport/Team	Season/Venue	Information
⚾ **MAJOR LEAGUE BASEBALL**	**April-October**	
Dodgers (NL)	Dodger Stadium	866-363-1507 www.dodgers.com
Anaheim Angels (AL)	Angel Stadium	888-796-4256 www.angelsbaseball.com
🏈 **COLLEGIATE FOOTBALL**	**September-December**	
USC Trojans	Memorial Coliseum	213-740-4672 www.usctrojans.com
UCLA Bruins	Rose Bowl, Pasadena	310-825-2101 www.uclabruins.com
🏀 **PROFESSIONAL BASKETBALL**	**November-April**	
Lakers	STAPLES Center	310-426-6000 www.nba.com/lakers
Clippers	STAPLES Center	888-895-8662 www.nba.com/clippers
Sparks (WNBA)	STAPLES Center	213-929-1300 www.wnba.com/sparks

GETTING THERE

By Air: Los Angeles International Airport (LAX): 17mi southwest of downtown serves major international and domestic airlines (*℘310-646-5252; www.lawa.org).* Travelers Aid booths located in all terminals (*℘310-646-2270).* **Airport Guides** Information booths (open daily 24hrs) in Tom Bradley International Terminal. **Car rental:** Agencies offer courtesy vans; check the information boards in the baggage claim areas. **Public transportation:** Bus lines leave from City Bus Center *(free shuttle service to Lot C);* Metro Green Line. Average taxi fares: to downtown *($45),* Hollywood *($35).* Commercial shuttles to Greater Los Angeles area *($15–$35).*
Other Airports: Bob Hope Airport (BUR), 13mi north of downtown Los Angeles (*℘818-840-8840; www.bobhopeairport.com).* **Long Beach Airport** (LGB), 22mi south of downtown (*℘562-570-2600; www.lgb. org).* **Orange County/John Wayne Airport** (SNA), Anaheim (*℘949-252-5200; www.ocair.com).*
By Bus and Train – Greyhound bus station: *(E. 7th & Alameda Sts.; ℘800-231-2222; www.greyhound.com).* **Amtrak** train station: Union Station *(800 N. Alameda St.; ℘800-872-7245; www.amtrak.com.)*
By Car – Several interstate highways pass through downtown Los Angeles. **I-5** is a major north-south artery. **I-10** comes in from the southeast, goes through downtown and ends at the beach. **I-15** connects Las Vegas and San Diego, through San Bernardino and Riverside *(see chart on following pages).*

GETTING AROUND
BY PUBLIC TRANSPORTATION:
Los Angeles County Metropolitan Transit Authority (MTA) provides express-bus service throughout L.A. and operates the Metro Rail network of **subways** and **light rails**: see Metro map *(p156)* for routes. The base one-way fare is $1.25; an

additional ticket must be purchased when changing lines; additional zone fares (.60/zone) may apply on some lines. Day passes ($5) and weekly passes ($17) are available. Tickets and reusable Transit Access Pass (TAP) cards can be purchased from vending machines located at each station, drivers (exact fare required) and some retail outlets. For route information *℘213-922-6000* or 800-266-6883, www.metro.net. **DASH** (Downtown Area Short Hop) shuttle operates throughout downtown L.A. and other neighborhoods *(daily, 25¢ with one free transfer; ℘213-808-2273; www.ladottransit.com).*
Metrolink provides **commuter train** service to suburban cities. *℘800-371-5465,* www.metrolinktrains.com.
By Car – When traveling via **freeway**, visitors are advised to review their routes before departing, making note of freeway on- and off-ramps and interchanges. Since most freeways have a name and number designation, note both when planning an itinerary. If possible, avoid traveling during the **rush hours** *(6am–10am and 4pm–7pm),* when traffic can be heavy.
Parking regulations: Red line on curb means no parking, green line indicates 20min parking and white line indicates passenger loading and unloading only. Fees for parking lots and garages: $1–$2/half-hour and $8-$30/day.
By Taxi – Checker Cab Co. (*℘213-481-2345);* **Independent Taxi Co.** (*℘800-521-8294);* **Yellow Cab** (*℘877-733-3305);* **Beverly Hills Cab Co.** (*℘800-273-6611).*

GENERAL INFORMATION
VISITOR INFORMATION
Contact the **Los Angeles Convention & Visitors Bureau** *(333 S. Hope St., Los Angeles CA 90071, ℘213-624-7300; www.discoverlosangeles.com).* Visitors can also stop at the **Downtown Visitor Information Center** *(685 S. Figueroa St., Los Angeles CA 90017;*

open Mon–Fri 8.30am–5pm; *213-689-8822)* and the **Hollywood Visitor Information Center** *(6801 Hollywood Blvd. at Hollywood Blvd. and Highland Ave.; open Mon–Sat 10am–10pm, Sun 10am–7pm; *323-467-6412).*

ACCOMMODATIONS

For a selection of hotels see the Address Book at the beginning of the Los Angeles Area section. The Convention & Visitors Bureau's vacation guide contains a lodging directory. Accommodations range from elegant hotels *($400+/day),* bed & breakfasts *($150–$350/day)* and budget motels *($100–$139/day).*
Youth Hostels: Hostelling International Santa Monica *(1436 2nd St., Santa Monica 90401 *310-393-9913).* **HI South Bay** (summer only), *(3601 South Gaffey St., Bldg. 613, San Pedro CA 90731 *310-831-8109. www.hiusa.org).*

RESERVATION SERVICES:
Accommodations Express
www.accommodationsexpress.com
*800-444-7666
Quikbook www.quikbook.com
*800-789-9887
Hotels.com www.hotels.com
*800-246-8357
Local Press – Daily news: The *Los Angeles Times (www.latimes.com).* Weekly entertainment information can be found in the "Calendar" entertainment section of the *Times* and in *LA Weekly (www.laweekly.com),* a free newspaper.
Currency Exchange Offices – LAX (Tom Bradley Terminal): **ICE Currency** *(open daily 7am–12.30am; *310-417-0364).* **American Express Travel** *(327 N. Beverly Dr., Beverly Hills; open Mon–Fri 10am–6pm; Sat 10am–3pm; *310-274-8277);* **Travelex offices** *(in US Bank, 8901 Santa Monica Blvd. West, W. Hollywood *310-659-6093; 9595 Wilshire Blvd., Beverly Hills *310-247-0892; 3243 Glendale Galleria, Glendale *818-242-6884).*

USEFUL NUMBERS
Police/Ambulance/Fire *(multilingual)* *911
Police *(non-emergency; multilingual)* *877-275-5273
Dental Referral Service *(5am–6pm)* *800-422-8338
Weather *213-744-1212
Safety Tips – This vast city includes a wide variety of neighborhoods. Be sure to have accurate directions; stick to major thoroughfares; and avoid deserted streets after dark.

SPORTS AND LEISURE
Sightseeing – City bus tours are provided by L.A. Tours (*323-937-0999; www.la-tours.com),* Starline Tours (*800-959-3131; www.starlinetours.com)* and Guideline Tours (*323-465-3004 or 800-604-8433; www.guidelinetours.com).* **Architectural and historical walking tours** are organized by the Los Angeles Conservancy, *(523 W. 6th St., Suite 826, Los Angeles; schedules and reservations *213-623-2489; www.laconservancy.org).* The City of Beverly Hills offers narrated **trolley tours** *(40min; depart from corner of Rodeo Dr. & Dayton Way; $5; call for schedule *310-285-2438).* For a customized tour of art and architecture, contact **Architours** (*323-294-5821; www.architours.com).* For reduced prices to several Hollywood attractions, buy the **CityPass** *($49.95; children $39.95 valid for nine days; tickets available online at www.citypass.net. *888-330-5008).*
Entertainment – Tickets for local events can be obtained from **Ticketmaster** (*213-365-3500; www.ticketmaster.com);* and **Musical Chairs** (*310-207-7070 or 800-659-1702; www.musicalchairstickets.com).*
Music Center of Los Angeles County *213-972-7211 www.musiccenter.org
Ahmanson Theater, Plays, musicals *213-972-7401
Mark Taper Forum, Contemporary stage plays *213-628-2772
Dorothy Chandler Pavilion, L.A.

Philharmonic, L.A. Opera, L.A. Master Chorale, plays, ballet ✆213-972-7211
Hollywood Bowl, Outdoor amphitheater for concerts, L.A. Philharmonic summer season ✆323-850-2000 www.hollywoodbowl.com
Hollywood Palladium, Concerts, special events ✆323-962-7600 www.livenation.com
Wiltern Theater, L.A. Opera, pop, rock and dance ✆213-380-5005 www.livenation.com
Shopping – Downtown: Macy's Plaza, 750 W. 7th St.; Fashion District, 110 E. 9th St.; Jewelry Mart, 650 S. Hill St. **Hollywood:** Melrose Avenue, Sunset Strip, Universal City Walk.
Beverly Hills: Rodeo Drive, Wilshire Blvd. **Westside:** Beverly Center, 8500 Beverly Blvd.; Century City Shopping Center, 10250 Santa Monica Blvd.; Westside Pavilion, 10800 W. Pico Blvd.
San Fernando Valley: Fashion Square Sherman Oaks, 14006 Riverside Dr., Sherman Oaks; Glendale Galleria, 2148 Glendale Galleria, Glendale. **San Gabriel Valley:** Ontario Mills Mall (outlet mall), One Mills Cir., Ontario.
Santa Monica & Venice: Santa Monica Place, 3rd Street Promenade, Santa Monica Antique Market, 1607 Lincoln Blvd.; Venice Boardwalk.
Recreation – Griffith Park has 53mi of **hiking** and **horseback riding** trails, **swimming**, **tennis** courts, pony and train rides for kids; for information contact the Visitor's Center (*✆323-913-4688 or 323-644-2050*) and the Equestrian Center (*✆818-840-9063*). For all outdoor activities check www.laparks.org. Four public golf courses are located within the park; call Wilson and Harding Municipal Golf Courses (*✆323-663-2555*) for fees and information on tee times. There are more than 100 public **golf** courses in the Los Angeles area.

Park rangers lead hikes in the Santa Monica Mountains National Recreation Area; contact the National Park Service (*✆805-370-2301; www.nps.gov/samo*).

Miles of coastline offer unlimited water-related activities including swimming, **boating**, ocean kayaking, **surfing**, fishing and **scuba diving**. For information on cruises, deep-sea fishing excursions and boat rentals contact the Marina del Ray Information Center (*✆310-305-9545*). **Roller-blading** and **biking** are especially popular along Venice Beach and Santa Monica's Ocean Front Walk. For organized bicycle and roller-blading tours (*1hr30min, $35*) contact Perry's Beach Café and Rentals (*✆310-939-0000*). At the Santa Monica PierBlazing Saddles Bicycle Rental & Touring Center rents bicycles (*$9/hour, $25/day; ✆310-393-9778*).

A BIT OF HISTORY

In 1781 the Spanish governor of California called for volunteers in Mexico to settle a new community on the Porciúncula River, named El Pueblo de Nuestra Señora la Reina de Los Angeles de Porciúncula, meaning "The Town of Our Lady the Queen of the Angels by the Porciúncula." The name was shortened by the mid-19C to Los Angeles, and by the time the city was designated capital of Mexican California in 1845, it had become the commercial center for a region of vast cattle ranches and vineyards controlled by wealthy families such as the Picos and Sepúlvedas.

Americanization – Settlers from the eastern US trickled into Los Angeles as early as 1826, and the city officially passed into American control with the end of the Mexican War in 1848. Inexorably, Los Angeles was Americanized, and an orderly rectangular street grid was laid out that is still evident today in older areas of downtown Los Angeles.

The Gold Rush of 1849 brought fortune seekers, and the combination of seemingly limitless money and a large transient population gave 1850s Los Angeles an unsavory reputation as a center of gambling, drinking, crime and violence.

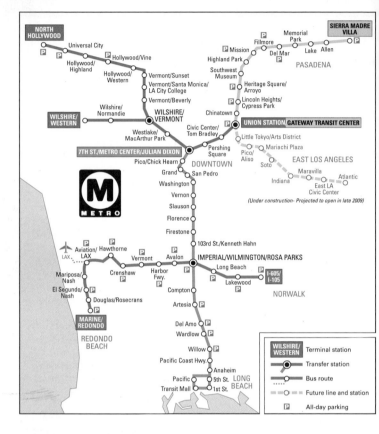

Meanwhile, commissions set up by the US Congress to examine and certify Spanish and Mexican land grants froze the assets of Los Angeles' ranch owners in a legal mire. A three-year drought in the early 1860s pushed many owners into bankruptcy; their lands eventually passed into American hands.

Late 19C: Growth – In 1876 rail links to the east via San Francisco were opened, and beginning in 1885, competition from the Santa Fe Railroad engendered fare reductions and a new influx of settlers.

Los Angeles' reputation as a latter-day Eden was further enhanced by the citrus industry. The arrival in Riverside of seedless navel oranges from Brazil in 1873, coupled with refrigerated railroad cars that could ship them east in perfect condition, led to the establishment of vast orange groves. With wine grapes,

wheat, and other fruits and vegetables also growing abundantly, agriculture became the new mainstay of Los Angeles' economy.

Located in a semi-desert region, Los Angeles' growth was severely limited by a lack of readily available water. But in 1904, county water superintendent William Mulholland initiated a $24.5 million project to bring water to Los Angeles from the Owens Valley 250mi north. The Los Angeles Aqueduct opened in 1913. Although the controversial project laid waste to the Owens Valley and led to protracted legal battles with the farmers whose livelihoods it ruined, it enabled unprecedented growth for Los Angeles. The city expanded its boundaries; by the 1920s it had incorporated the neighboring cities of Beverly Hills, Santa Monica, Long Beach and Pasadena, all of which lacked adequate groundwater.

Freeway Number	Freeway Name(s)
Rte. 2	Glendale Freeway
I-5	Golden State Freeway (north of downtown)
	Santa Ana Freeway (south of downtown)
I-10	Santa Monica Freeway (west of downtown)
	San Bernardino Freeway (east of downtown)
Rte. 22	Garden Grove Freeway
Rte. 57	Orange Freeway
Rte. 90	Marina Freeway
Rte. 91	Artesia Freeway-Gardena Freeway
US-101 (south of Rte. 134) and Rte. 170	Hollywood Freeway (north of downtown)
US-101 (west of Rte. 170) and Rte. 134	Ventura Freeway
Rte. 110	Pasadena Freeway
I-110	Harbor Freeway
Rte. 118	Simi Valley-San Fernando Freeway
I-210	Foothill Freeway
I-405	San Diego Freeway
I-605	San Gabriel River Freeway
I-710	Long Beach Freeway

Early 20C: Population Boom – The first decade of the 20C brought the fledgling motion-picture industry from New York City and Chicago to the Los Angeles area in search of spacious locations and the consistently gentle climate necessary for outdoor filming. Established largely in and around Hollywood, the studios soon made that community's and Los Angeles' names synonymous with movies.

In 1897, when the first automobile drove along the streets of Los Angeles, more than 500 oil wells were already pumping in the downtown area, contributing to California's ranking at that time as the third-largest oil-producing state in the nation after Pennsylvania and New York. Local oil speculators, among them G. Allan Hancock, become millionaires almost overnight.

By the start of World War II, Los Angeles had a population of some 1.5 million. Following the war, the city's population boomed again as servicemen who had passed through Southern California en route to or from the Pacific decided to settle here. Orange groves gave way to housing tracts as the city's boundaries expanded and its population grew. By 1960 the city's population was 2.5 million people; more than 6 million people lived in Los Angeles County.

1 DOWNTOWN★
EL PUEBLO DE LOS ANGELES HISTORIC MONUMENT★

Union Station. Map p160.
Historic sites are open year-round.
Museums closed Thanksgiving Day & Dec 25. ✕ & ✆ *213-628-1274.*
www.cityofla.org/ELP.

The city's historic heart is a 44-acre cluster of 27 buildings, many restored or undergoing restoration. Popularly known as Olvera Street after its main commercial spine, El Pueblo is a vibrant showcase of an early Spanish settlement, which was moved to its present location about 1825.

As Los Angeles grew, its centers of government and business gradually moved south to the current downtown. By the 1920s, Olvera Street was a dirty alleyway, with decaying buildings surrounding it. In 1926 city resident **Christine Sterling** launched a campaign that revitalized El Pueblo: Olvera Street reopened on April 20, 1930, as a colorful Mexican marketplace. The area was designated a state historic park in 1953.

Year-round, El Pueblo is the site of cultural celebrations, among them Cinco de Mayo, commemorating the Mexican rout of French troops at the Battle of Puebla in 1862 (May 5); the City's Birthday

157

El Pueblo de Los Angeles

Pierre Ethier/MICHELIN

Celebration; and Mexican Independence Day (both Sept).

▷ *Begin at the visitor center located in Sepulveda House.*

♣♣Olvera Street★

🕐 *Open daily 10am–8pm.*
The brick-paved pedestrian street, originally called "Wine" or "Vine" Street, was renamed in 1877 for Agustín Olvera, the first Los Angeles County judge. Shops and wooden stalls sell a jumble of crafts, clothing, souvenirs and food.

Sepulveda House

W-12 Olvera St. 🕐 *Open daily 9am–4pm.*
This two-story Victorian structure (1887) was built by Eloisa Martinez de Sepúlveda as a commercial space and boardinghouse. Exhibits include a period kitchen and bedroom. The Main Street facade is an example of the local Eastlake style. In the **visitor center**, a video *(18min; shown upon request)* presents the early history of Los Angeles.

Avila Adobe★

E-11 Olvera St. 🕐 *Open daily 9am–4pm.*
The oldest existing house in L. A., this one-story adobe (c.1818) was built by cattle rancher Don Francisco Avila. The state purchased it in 1953. Six rooms are furnished in the 1840s ranch style. Across the spacious courtyard, an annex features exhibits on the Los Angeles Aqueduct and the history of El Pueblo.

The Plaza

El Pueblo's central plaza has occupied this site since c. 1825. Moreton Bay fig trees flank a wrought-iron bandstand (1962). A plaque on the southern side lists the names of the first 44 *pobladores*. On the eastern side, a bronze **statue (1)** of Felipe de Neve, erected in 1932, commemorates the man who drew up the plans for the city's settlement.

Our Lady Queen of the Angels Catholic Church

535 N. Main St., west side of the plaza.
℘ *213-629-3101.*
Popularly known as Old Plaza Church, the city's oldest existing church (1822) has been restored and enlarged considerably over the years. On the exterior, facing the plaza is a mosaic of *The Annunciation* (1981, Isabel Piczek).

Pico House★

Southwest corner of the plaza.
Upon its completion in 1870, this three-story Italianate building was considered the finest hotel in Southern California. Behind the house are the 1870 **Merced Theatre (A)**, the city's first theater *(⊙ not open to the public)*; and the 1858 **Masonic Hall (B)**, meeting place of the city's first Masonic Lodge *(⊙ not open to the public)*.

Firehouse No. 1

Southeast corner of the plaza. 🕐 *Open year-round Tue–Sun 10am–3pm.*
The two-story brick building (1884) served as the city's first firehouse until 1897. It now houses a museum of firefighting memorabilia.
Behind it stands the **Garnier Building** (1890) built as a commercial and residential space for Chinese tenants. It now holds a **museum** of Chinese-American history *(🕐 open year-round Tue–Sun 10am–3pm; 🕐 closed major holidays; ⊛ $3; ℘ 213-485-8567; www. camla.org).*
East of El Pueblo rises **Union Station** (1939, Parkinson & Parkinson), a combined venture of the Southern Pacific, Union Pacific and Santa Fe railroads. Blending Mission Revival, Spanish

Colonial, Moorish and Art Deco styles, the building is considered the last of the grand train stations built during the heyday of rail travel. The **interior**★, featuring marble and tile floors, walnut-beamed ceilings and art deco seats, has appeared in several Hollywood films. It is an important hub in the city's Metro Rail system.

CHINATOWN

Union Station. 🚶*Guided walking tours available 1st Sat of the month.* 📞*213-680-0243. www.chinatownla.com.*
Comprising roughly 15 square blocks, Los Angeles' Chinatown is a small district compared to its San Francisco counterpart. Its chinoiserie-embellished buildings and modern shopping plazas serve as one of two main centers for the city's residents of Chinese descent. (The other center is Monterey Park, 7mi east.) Chinatown is also a noted dining destination, popular for its Chinese and other Asian cuisines.

The growing city's need for laborers drew more to settle here—despite racial tensions that, in 1871, led to the murder of 19 Chinese men and boys by a racist mob. By 1900, more than half of Los Angeles' Chinese-American residents, most of them independent vegetable farmers and peddlers, lived in cramped alleyways east of Olvera Street. Union Station's construction in the 1930s led to the area's demolition and the open-ing (in 1938) of the present-day China-town.

A pagoda-style **gateway** along the 900 block of North Broadway marks the entrance to Gin Ling Way, main street of Central Plaza. Beyond the gate is a **statue** of Sun Yat-sen, first president of the Chinese Republic. Chinatown's supermarkets, herbalists, curio and souvenir shops and discount stores attract locals and visitors, and the area is the setting for the annual **Chinese New Year Parade** *(late Jan or Feb).*

LITTLE TOKYO

Union Station. ♿*Map see p. 160.* *www.visitlittletokyo.com*
The cultural, social, business and spiritual center of North America's largest Japanese-American community occupies about seven square blocks southeast of El Pueblo. Although touches of traditional Japanese style can be seen in the buildings and signs around the area, Little Tokyo is a bustling, contemporary enclave of office buildings, shopping centers, apartments and cultural and religious institutions.

Restricted from owning businesses or homes among Caucasian citizens, early settlers congregated in the area today preserved as the **Little Tokyo Historic District** *(1st St. between San Pedro St. & Central Ave.).* During World War II, the neighborhood's entire population was forcibly removed to camps.

Chinatown Gateway

Pierre Ethier/MICHELIN

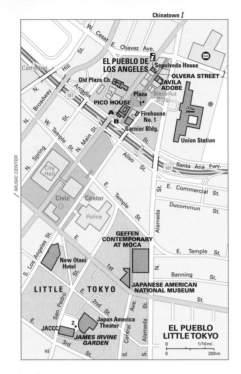

James Irvine Garden★

Adjacent to the JACCC,
244 S. San Pedro St.
⏱Open year-round daily
9am–5pm. ⏱Closed major
holidays. ☎213-628-2725.
www.jaccc.org.

Designed in the traditional Japanese style by Takeo Uesugi, the garden features a bamboo glen, a cascading stream and more than 30 species of Asian and local semitropical plants. City native and acclaimed artist **Isamu Noguchi** (1904–88), designed the adjacent brick JACCC plaza, anchored by a massive, pillarlike stone **sculpture** entitled *To the Issei.*

The Geffen Contemporary at MOCA★

152 N. Central Ave.
⏱Open year-round Thu–Mon
11am–5pm (Thu 8pm, week-
ends 6pm). ⏱Closed Jan 1,
July 4, Thanksgiving Day, Dec 25. ⌖$10
(free Thu 5pm–8pm). ♿ ☎213-626-
6222. www.moca-la.org.

The Museum of Contemporary Art's first shows were held in this former warehouse complex, with interiors redesigned by architect Frank Gehry. The structure remains a branch of the Museum of Contemporary Art (MOCA) and is used for large-scale exhibits as well as changing displays of works from the museum's permanent collection.

Today, Little Tokyo thrives as a self-contained community. The **New Otani Hotel** embodies the redevelopment of the area begun in the 1970s. The **Japanese American Cultural and Community Center (JACCC)** (*244 S. San Pedro St.; ☎213-628-2725*) and adjoining **Japan America Theatre** are focal points for community programs.

Japanese-American National Museum★

369 E. 1st St. ⏱Open year-round
Thu noon–8pm, Fri–Sun 11am–5pm.
⏱Closed major holidays. ⌖$9.
✕♿ ☎213-625-0414. www.janm.org.

America's first museum dedicated to Japanese-American history occupies the renovated former Nishi Hongwanji Buddhist Temple (1925) and a new Pavilion (1998), linked by a plaza. Changing exhibits draw from the permanent collection of over 60,000 Japanese-American photographs, documents and artifacts, the largest collection in the US.

CIVIC CENTER AREA

Civic Center. ♿Map see p. 161.

The largest center for municipal administration in the US, this group of buildings and plazas occupies 13 blocks. The structures range in style from the monumental 1925 **Hall of Justice Building** (*northeast corner of S. Broadway & W. Temple St.*), to the contemporary Music Center.

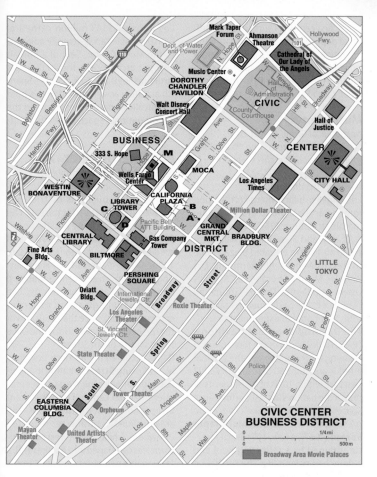

Los Angeles City Hall★★

200 N. Spring St. 🚶*Tours depart Mon–Thu 10am & 11am from 3rd floor, in front of the Mayor's Office.*
📞*213-978-1995.*

City Hall's 28-story, pyramid-topped tower (1928) is one of downtown Los Angeles' most widely recognized symbols. It reopened in 2002 after restoration of its art deco splendor and seismic retrofitting to protect against earthquakes.

The 135ft-wide **rotunda**★ reveals French limestone walls and a floor composed of inlays cut from 46 varieties of marble. The tiled dome depicts the eight primary duties of municipal government: Public Service, Health, Trust, Art, Protection, Education, Law and Government. On clear days the observation deck *(27th floor)* affords sweeping **panoramas**★★.

Los Angeles Times Building

202 W. 1st St. 🚶*Visit by guided tour (45min) only, year-round Mon–Fri 9.30am, 11am & 1.30pm; reservations req.* ♿🅿📞*213-237-5757.*
www.latimes.com.

A block long, this complex is the fourth home of Los Angeles' renowned newspaper, which enjoys one of the largest circulations in the nation (about 851,000 copies daily; 1.2 million Sunday).

The **lobby**★ features an original linotype machine, a large revolving world globe and a display tracing *The Los Angeles*

Times' first century. Tours cover the editorial departments and newsgathering operations. You can also take a separate tour of the *Times'* high-tech production facility, the **Olympic Printing Plant** *(2000 E. 8th St.)*.

Music Center
North side of Grand Ave. at 1st St. Self-guided audio tours and ⟨guided tours (1hr) available; check website for dates. ✕&🅿 ✆213-972-7211. www.musiccenter.org.

Los Angeles' hilltop mecca for the performing arts is a group of three white marble structures (1967, Welton Becket & Assocs.) and a new concert hall, occupying an 11-acre elevated plaza. Home to the Los Angeles Philharmonic, Los Angeles Master Chorale, Los Angeles Opera, and Center Theatre Group, the complex hosts performances ranging from traditional to experimental.

The **Dorothy Chandler Pavilion**★ (1964) is the largest of the three original buildings. Artworks grace the palatial interior, and some 90 percent of its 3,197 seats are within 105ft of the stage, itself one of the nation's largest performance spaces. Innovative dramatic works are presented at the 752-seat **Mark Taper Forum** (1967), a low, cylindrical structure framed by a reflecting pool and a detached colonnade. The rectilinear 2,000-seat **Ahmanson Theatre** (1967) hosts plays, musicals, dance concerts and individual performing artists.

The 2003 **Walt Disney Concert Hall** is the home of the L.A. Philharmonic and L.A. Master Chorale. Designed by Frank Gehry, the striking structure holds a 2,265-seat auditorium with hardwood walls and ceiling. A curved stainless-steel exterior of multiple facades wraps the entire building; two towering glass panels rise above its main entrance.

Cathedral of Our Lady of the Angels
Bounded by N. Hill St. & N. Grand Ave., W. Temple St. & the Hollywood Fwy. (US-101). ⟨Guided tours (1hr 15min) year-round Mon–Fri 1pm. ✆213-680-5200. ww.olacathedral.org.

Los Angeles' $163 million cathedral (2002) occupies a 5.6-acre site adjacent to the Music Center. Seat of a Roman Catholic archdiocese, the 48,000sq ft structure holds 2,500 worshipers. Spanish architect José Rafael Moneo's bold design allows natural light to flood the congregational space beneath a copper roof.

BUSINESS DISTRICT★★
🕭Map p161. Bounded roughly by Figueroa, 2nd, Spring & 9th Sts.

Los Angeles' business district has evolved into two distinct areas. The older one, anchored by Broadway and Spring Street, reveals Beaux-Arts and art deco buildings dating from the late 1800s to the 1920s; today it is the setting for a lively street scene dominated by the city's Latino community. The newer section's gleaming towers of commerce, built since the 1960s, cover the rise between Flower, Hope and Olive streets north of 6th Street.

Banks occupied the art deco buildings along **Spring Street**, creating its early-20C reputation as the West Coast's premier financial center. From the Great Depression through the 1950s, the area declined as businesses relocated elsewhere. A hilltop area west of downtown was developed into **Bunker Hill**, a fashionable neighborhood of Victorian mansions accessed by Angel's Flight, a two-car inclined railroad. Today, streets in the older section pulse with activity, though some buildings have taken on a seedy air.

Eastern Columbia Building★★
849 S. Broadway.

The extraordinary **exterior** of this striking 13-story art deco building (1930) is faced in a pattern of turquoise-and-gold glazed terracotta rising to a two-story clock tower.

Broadway
Beginning in 1910, nickelodeons and vaudeville houses sprang up along this thoroughfare, paving the way in 1918 for showman Sid Grauman to open the Million Dollar Theater. More theaters fol-

lowed, and by 1931 Broadway boasted the world's highest concentration of ornate movie palaces. Today, several of the original dozen are still operating but many are converted for other purposes. *Interiors accessible by guided walking tour (Sat 10am; $10; Los Angeles Conservancy; 213-623-2489; www.laconservancy.org).*

Bradbury Building★★

304 S. Broadway. Open year-round daily 9am–5pm. 213-626-1893.
Mining magnate Louis Bradbury commissioned this five-story building (1893). The extraordinary **atrium**, with wrought-iron railings, open-cage elevators, red-oak trim and stair treads of pink Belgian marble, is one of the finest interior spaces in Los Angeles.

Grand Central Market★

317 S. Broadway. Open year-round daily 9am–6pm. Closed Jan 1, Thanksgiving Day, Dec 25. 213-624-2378. www.grandcentralsquare.com.
A cavernous hall open to both Broadway and Hill Street, the building (1897) was converted in 1917 into a public market catering to local European immigrants. Since the 1960s it has mirrored the neighborhood's bustling downtown atmosphere, with a profusion of stalls selling everything from ready-to-eat Mexican food to fresh produce, meats and cheeses. Near the market's Hill Street entrance, the funicular cars of the restored **Angels Flight (A)** ascend and descend the slope of Bunker Hill (*daily 6.20am–10pm; 213-626-1901; www.angelsflight.com*).

California Plaza★

Grand Ave. between 3rd & 4th Sts.
This 11-acre complex comprises two curvilinear reflecting-glass office towers, an apartment building, a luxury hotel and the Museum of Contemporary Art. With fountains and outdoor stages, the Spiral Court and the **Watercourt (B)** are popular gathering places.

Museum of Contemporary Art (MOCA)★★

250 S. Grand Ave. Open year-round Mon & Fri 11am–5pm, Thu 11am–8pm, weekends 11am–6pm. $10 (free Thu 5–8pm; includes admission to The Geffen Contemporary). 213-626-6222. www.moca-la.org.
Commonly referred to as MOCA, this museum (1986) showcases visual art produced since the 1940s.
Prominent Japanese architect **Arata Isozaki** was commissioned in 1981 to design the structure, a low-lying **complex★**. Cubes, a cylinder and 11 pyramidal skylights define MOCA's two- and three-story office, library and bookstore buildings; these above-ground buildings flank a sun well leading to 25,000sq ft of underground galleries. Changing selections from the permanent collection of paintings, drawings, photographs, sculptures, videos, installations and works in other visual media are exhibited. Prominent artists represented in the collection include Louise Nevelson, Jackson Pollock, Mark Rothko, Frank Stella and Jonathan Borofsky. Most of the museum's display space is devoted to temporary shows.

Wells Fargo Center

Grand Ave. between 3rd & 4th Sts., across from California Plaza.
The trapezoidal twin towers of brown granite and tinted glass (1983, Skidmore, Owings & Merrill) sharply slice the Bunker Hill skyline. Between them, a three-story atrium court features casual dining amid **sculptures** by Joan Miró, Jean Dubuffet, Nancy Graves and others.

Wells Fargo History Museum (M)

333 S. Grand Ave. Open year-round Mon–Fri 9am–5pm. Closed bank holidays. 213-253-7166. www.wellsfargohistory.com.
The museum traces the Wells Fargo Company's role in California's history, from its founding in 1852 to its current position as a foremost financial institutions. Displays include the **Challenge Nugget**, a lump of gold weighing 26.4 troy ounces, found in 1975.

333 South Hope Street

Hope St. between 3rd & 4th Sts.
Set at a 45-degree angle to the streets, the 55-story building (1974) is distinguished by the red Alexander Calder **stabile**, *Four Arches*, at its entrance.

Westin Bonaventure Hotel★

404 S. Figueroa St. ✕ ♿ 🅿 ☎ *213-624-1000. www.westin.com.*
Composed of five mirrored-glass cylindrical towers, the 35-story hotel (1976, John Portman), reveals an interior atrium with several levels of shops and meeting spaces. The glass elevators scaling the building's exterior offer **panoramas**★ of downtown.

US Bank Tower★

633 W. 5th St.
Soaring 1,017ft, the 73-story Italian-granite building (1992, I.M. Pei & Partners) ranks as the nation's tallest office building west of Chicago. Flanking the building's west side, the **Bunker Hill Steps**★ **(C)**, inspired by the Spanish steps in Rome, descend from Hope to 5th Street, their four flights split by a cascade of water.
Adjacent to the tower on the east sits **One Bunker Hill (D)** (601 W. 5th St.), an art deco structure built in 1931 as the headquarters of the Southern California Edison Company. Some 17 varieties of marble adorn the lobby, which is graced by a mural by Hugo Ballin.

Los Angeles Central Library★

630 W. 5th St. between Flower St. and Grand Ave. ⊙*Open year-round Mon–Thu 10am–8pm, Fri–Sat 10am–6pm; Sun 1pm–5pm.* ⊙*Closed major holidays.* ♿ 🅿 ☎*213-228-7000. www.lapl.org.*
Its imposing tower crowned by a pyramid, this handsome building (1926, **Bertram Goodhue**) features a **rotunda** decorated with murals depicting eras in California history. The Children's Literature Room *(2nd level)* holds the California History Murals.
The 1993 Tom Bradley Wing's soaring **atrium** sports whimsical fiberglass and aluminum chandeliers.

On the Flower Street side, a 1.5-acre **garden** has a cascading pool.

Gas Company Tower

555 W. 5th St.
Crowned with a blue-glass ellipse, the 52-story tower (1991) features a water garden adjacent to the lobby. The lobby's glass wall showcases the lower portion of Frank Stella's *Dusk* (1992), a largest abstract mural painted on the adjacent Pacific Bell/AT&T building.

Biltmore Hotel★★

506 S. Grand Ave. ✕ ♿ 🅿 ☎*213-624-1011. www.millenniumhotels.com.*
Known as the Millennium Biltmore Hotel, this 11-story, 683-room hotel (1923, Schultze and Weaver) facing Pershing Square was built at a cost of $10 million. Extensively renovated since 1984, it still merits its reputation as one of Los Angeles' most distinguished hotels.
Although the main public entrance is now on Grand Avenue, the original Olive Street lobby, renamed the **Rendezvous Court**★, exemplifies the opulent detailing that won the hotel renown, with brickwork and terracotta in the 16C Italian style and hand-painted ceilings.

Pershing Square★

Bordered by S. Hill, S. Olive, W. 5th & W. 6th Sts.
The city's first public park in 1866 was named in 1918 for John J. Pershing, commander of the American Expeditionary Force during World War I. A 1993 renovation by Mexican architect Ricardo Legorreta bestowed a modern air on the square, adorning it with a 125ft campanile, a fountain, amphitheater, cafe and kiosks.

Oviatt Building

617 S. Olive St.
In 1925 clothing entrepreneur James Oviatt became enamored of the art deco style at the Paris Exposition Internationale des Arts Decoratifs. He commissioned this 13-story office building and men's haberdashery (1928, Walker and Eisen), incorporating French marble, glass and fittings—including René Lal-

ique's largest commercial commission of art deco etched and frosted glass (now largely replicated). The acclaimed restaurant Cicada, featuring Northern Italian cuisine, occupies the former ground floor quarters of Oviatt's men's store.

Fine Arts Building

811 W. 7th St.
A two-story Spanish Renaissance lobby of molded terracotta and colored tile sports an elaborately painted, beamed ceiling, sculpted figures and 17 bronze showcases. The building was originally meant to provide space for artisans to create and display their work.

ADDITIONAL SIGHTS

Map pp150–151.

Southwest Museum of the American Indian (M6)

234 Museum Dr. (Ave. 43 exit, Pasadena Fwy./Rte. 110). Open year-round Sat–Sun noon–5pm. Closed major holidays. 323-221-2164. www. southwestmuseum.org. The building is closed for extensive repair; projected completion late 2010. The museum shop is open.

This Mission Revival building (1914) housed Los Angeles' oldest museum dedicated to comprehensive collections on Native American cultures; the museum was founded by Charles Lummis (*see Lummis House*). Some of the collections may be temporarily on view in "open storage" while restoration work continues on both the building and the artifacts.

The museum shop sells authentic contemporary art of numerous Southwestern US Indian tribes.

Lummis House★

200 E. Ave. 43 (off Pasadena Fwy./Rte. 110), about 3mi northeast of downtown. Visit by guided tour only year-round Fri–Sun noon–4pm. 323-222-0546. www.socalhistory.org.

Hand-built of local stone by Southwest Museum founder **Charles Lummis** (1859–1928)—a noted local historian, preservationist and archaeologist—the

unique structure (nicknamed El Alisal) combines Mission, Pueblo and Craftsman styles. The house now is headquarters of the Historical Society of Southern California.

Though few original furnishings remain, the **interior** preserves some of Lummis' personal collection of Native American artifacts, including a window glazed with photographic plates of Indian dances.

Heritage Square Museum

3800 Homer St. (Ave. 43 exit, Pasadena Fwy./Rte. 110), about 3mi northeast of downtown. Open year-round Fri–Sun noon–5pm. Interiors accessible by guided tour (1hr) weekends only, noon–3pm. Closed Jan 1, Thanksgiving Day, Dec 25. $10. 6323-225-2700. www.heritagesquare.org.

Arrayed alongside the Pasadena Freeway is a rather forlorn collection of Victorian-era buildings. The structures were moved here from their original locations when they faced demolition. Today they offer an opportunity to view a variety of Victorian styles. The collection of eight structures in varying stages of restoration features the **Hale House**, a fully restored and furnished exemplar of the Queen Anne and Eastlake styles.

② EXPOSITION PARK AREA★★

Map pp150–151.
Bounded by Flower St., Vermont Ave. and Exposition & Martin Luther King Blvds.
Located near the Los Angeles Convention Center some 3mi southwest of downtown, 125-acre Exposition Park has long been one of the city's preeminent sports and cultural centers.

In 1872 a 160-acre agricultural park was established on the site for livestock shows, fairs and horse racing. In 1913 the park was renamed Exposition Park and rededicated as a setting for museums, athletic facilities and gardens, laid out in the grand Beaux-Arts tradition.

Today, the park is bordered on one side by the University of Southern California campus and on three others by the South Central Los Angeles area. The historic coliseum and several museums

'Dueling Dinosaurs'

draw a multitude of visitors, especially groups of school children.

SIGHTS
Los Angeles Memorial Coliseum★★

3911 S. Figueroa St. ◐Open to public for events only. Box office open Mon–Fri 10am–6pm. ♿ 🅿 (fee varies) ✆213-747-7111. www.lacoliseum.com.

Built at a cost of $1 million, the oval coliseum (1923, Parkinson & Parkinson) is the city's preeminent sports stadium, hosting college football games, international soccer competitions, rock concerts and other outdoor events.

Adjoining it, the 16,000-seat turquoise **Sports Arena**, built in 1958, hosts basketball games and other indoor events. With its original 75,000-seat capacity then boosted to 105,000, the Coliseum became the world's largest arena of its day and gained international prominence as the site of the 1932 Summer Olympic Games.

To mark its role as the principal venue of the 1984 Summer Games, an **Olympic Arch** was built just outside the coliseum's eastern peristyle. A large bronze structure by sculptor Robert Graham, the arch depicts headless male and female nude figures atop a gateway of two piers.

Natural History Museum of Los Angeles County★★

👤👥*900 Exposition Blvd. ◐Open year-round Mon–Fri 9.30am–5pm, weekends 10am–5pm. ◐Closed Jan 1, Jul 4, Thanksgiving Day, Dec 25. ⊙$9. ✕♿🅿 ($6) ✆213-763-3466. www.nhm.org. ♿ The Dinosaur Hall is closed for restoration; projected reopening 2011.*

This collection of more than 35 million specimens and artifacts is among the largest in the US. Opened in 1913, the institution is housed in a Beaux-Arts structure featuring an elaborate marble rotunda at its eastern end.

Main Level – In the main foyer, the skeletons of a tyrannosaur and a triceratops ("Dueling Dinosaurs") are poised for battle. The **Halls of African and North American Mammals** present lifelike dioramas of preserved animals in natural habitats. The museum boasts the largest natural gold collection in the US; more than 2,000 specimens of these and other minerals display in the **Hall of Gems and Minerals★**. The **Hall of American History** spotlights vehicles and machinery from 1865 to 1914. The **Insect Zoo** has terrariums with live scorpions, tarantulas and millipedes.

Upper Level – Exhibits in the **Hall of Birds★** include three walk-through habitats: a Canadian prairie marsh,

a tropical rain forest and the California condor's mountain home.
Lower Level – California History★★ traces the period from 1540 to 1940 with replica dwellings, dioramas, artifacts and vehicles, including a **scale model** of downtown Los Angeles.

Near the museum's original entrance, the 7-acre sunken **Rose Garden★**, showcases over 190 rose varieties.

California ScienCenter★

👤👥*700 Exposition Park Dr.* 🕐*Open year-round daily 10am–5pm.* 🕐*Closed Jan 1, Thanksgiving Day, Dec 25.* ✕🦽🅿*($8)* 📞*323-724-3623. www.californiasciencecenter.org.*

This museum of the sciences, the largest and oldest institution of its kind in the western US, opened in 1951. The Aerospace Museum, the Mark Taper Hall of Economics and a giant-screen IMAX Theater became part of the museum complex in 1984. On the west side, exhibit space for the new World of Ecology is under construction, with expected completion slated for 2010.

Two themed areas, **World of Life** and **Creative World**, focus on science and technology, as well as the role of science in everyday life as humans discover new ways to communicate, travel and understand the environment.

The adjoining **IMAX Theater** projects films on natural history, adventure, science and space flight onto a five-story screen (🎟*$8, children $4.75*).

At the adjacent Air and Space Gallery 👤👥, an F-104 Starfighter penetrates the wall of this stark building (1984, Frank Gehry). Inside, the three-story open space provides close-up glimpses of replica aircraft ranging from a 1902 Wright glider to satellites and space capsules. You'll also find star displays and telescopes.

Galleries in the Science Court host temporary exhibits on themes of science, space and ecology.

California African American Museum★

600 State Dr. 🕐*Open year-round Tue–Sat 10am–5pm, Sun 11am–5pm.*

🕐*Closed Jan 1 & Dec 25.* 🦽🅿*($8)* 📞*213-744-7432. www.caam.ca.gov.*

Opened in 1981, this museum is dedicated to the presentation of the art, history and culture of black people in the Americas. Changing exhibits of artworks and artifacts are displayed in three galleries around a central sculpture court, and a groundbreaking permanent exhibit documents the contributions of African-Americans to the settlement of the American West.

ADDITIONAL SIGHTS
University of Southern California

North of Exposition Park; main entrance on Exposition Blvd. 🚶*Student-led campus tours (45min) depart from Admissions Center Mon–Fri 10am–3pm on the hour. Self-guided tour maps available through the website.* ✕🦽🅿*($8)* 📞*213-740-6605. www.usc.edu.*

Founded in 1880, the university now consists of a 226-acre main campus, 100 major buildings and more than 28,000 students and 2,000 faculty members. The white clapboard **Widney Alumni House** dates from 1880. The **Fisher Museum of Art** features a permanent collection of European and American art (🕐*open Aug–May Tue–Sat noon–5pm;* 🕐*closed university holidays;* 🅿*($7)*☎*213-740-4561; www.uscfishermuseumofart.org*). USC's School of Cinema-Television was one of the first of its kind when it was established in 1929. Recently renamed **USC School of Cinematic Arts**, the school moved into a new state-of-the-art facility in late 2008, funded largely by famed director George Lucas.

Hancock Memorial Museum★

Childs Way at Trousdale Pkwy. 🕐*Visit by appointment only, year-round Mon–Fri.* 🦽🅿*($8)* 📞*213-740-5144.*

Located within the Hancock Foundation Building, this house museum consists of rooms preserved from the Hancock mansion, which was donated to USC in 1936 by oil tycoon G. Allan Hancock. The Moorish-style building opposite the northeast corner of the USC campus is the **Shrine Civic Auditorium** (665 W. Jefferson Blvd.), built in 1926 as a movie-set mosque. It once hosted the Oscars.

Automobile Club of Southern California★

2601 S. Figueroa St. ♿ 🅿️ 📞213-741-3686. www.aaa-calif.com.

With its octagonal tower, this 1923 building is an good example of the Spanish Colonial style. The rotunda features imported Mexican terrazzo tilework, and a collection of antique California road signs is displayed in the patio.

③ GRIFFITH PARK★★

♿Map p. 169.

One of the largest urban parks in the US, Griffith Park straddles some 4,100 acres of the Santa Monica Mountains, 5mi northwest of downtown Los Angeles.

In 1882 Col. Griffith J. Griffith, a Welsh immigrant who made his fortune quarrying granite, bought 4,071 acres of a Spanish land grant, and donated 3,015 of them to the City of Los Angeles for public use. The park reached its current size in the 1960s.

Griffith also donated money for an observatory within the park as well as the **Greek Theatre**, an open-air venue. The Los Angeles Zoo, a merry-go-round, children's pony rides and two museums have joined those attractions. Four golf courses, tennis courts, a baseball field, an equestrian center, picnic grounds and playgrounds are also available for public use.

Just north of Los Feliz Boulevard, near the park's southwestern corner, the cool glade known as **Ferndell** shelters tall pines shading a fern-fringed brook. The **Bird Sanctuary**, at the head of Vermont Canyon invites wandering along wooded pathways alive with birdsong. Hiking and bridle trails allow closer appreciation of the park.

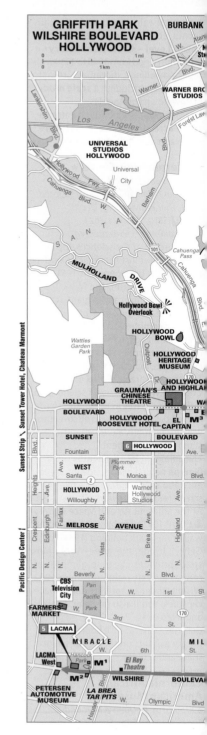

GRIFFITH PARK
WILSHIRE BOULEVARD
HOLLYWOOD

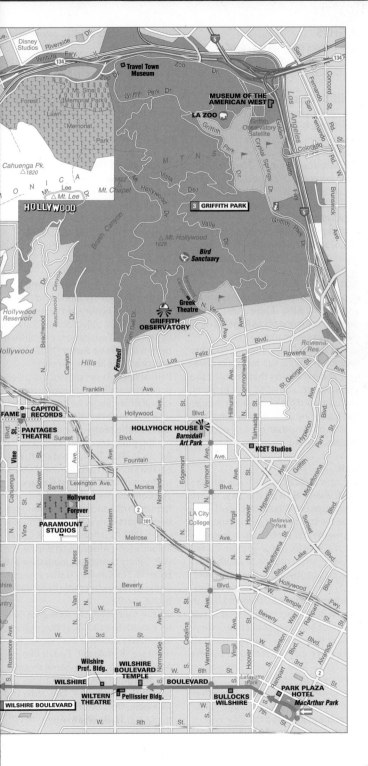

Disney Studios

Riverside Dr.

Ventura Fwy.

134

Travel Town Museum

MUSEUM OF THE AMERICAN WEST

Griffith Park Dr.

LA ZOO

Griffith Observatory Satellite

Crystal Springs Dr.

Golden State

San Fernando Rd.

Concord St.

Colorado

Los Angeles

Brunswick Ave.

Griffith Park Blvd.

Forest Lawn Memorial Park

Mt. Sinai Memorial Park

Memorial Park

Cahuenga Pk.
△1820

MONICA

Lee
Mt. Lee
△Mt. Lee Dr.

HOLLYWOOD

Mt. Chapel

1522

Vista Del

Valle

Del

3 GRIFFITH PARK

Brush Canyon

Beachwood Canyon

Hollywood Dr.

△ Mt. Hollywood
1625

Bird Sanctuary

N. Vermont Ave.

Greek Theatre

GRIFFITH OBSERVATORY

Hollywood Reservoir

Hollywood Hills

Canyon

Ferndell

Fern Dell Dr.

Los Feliz

Commonwealth Ave.

St. George St.

Rowena Res.

Rowena Ave.

Franklin

Ave.

FAME

CAPITOL RECORDS

PANTAGES THEATRE

Sunset

Hollywood Ave.

St.

Blvd.

HOLLYHOCK HOUSE

Barnsdall Art Park

Hillhurst

Talmadge St.

Hyperion

Griffith Park

Blvd.

KCET Studios

Vine

Gower St.

Lexington Ave.

Santa

Fountain

Monica

Normandie

Edgemont

Vermont Ave.

Blvd.

Micheltorena St.

Sunset

Blvd.

Cahuenga

Hollywood Forever

PARAMOUNT STUDIOS

Ness

Wilton

Western Ave.

2

101

Melrose

LA City College

Virgil

Hoover

Bellevue Park

Silver Lake Blvd.

Hollywood Blvd.

Beverly

1st St.

Catalina

Vermont

Virgil

Blvd.

Temple Fwy.

Beverly

Way

Benton

N. Rampart Blvd.

Alvarado

3rd St.

Rossmore

W.

3rd St.

Wilshire Prof. Bldg.

WILSHIRE BOULEVARD TEMPLE

Normandie

6th

Vermont St.

Hoover

Lafayette Park

2

WILSHIRE

BOULEVARD

PARK PLAZA HOTEL

MacArthur Park

WILSHIRE BOULEVARD

WILTERN THEATRE

Pellissier Bldg.

BULLOCKS WILSHIRE

9th St.

W.

7th

169

SIGHTS

Park entrances on Los Feliz Blvd., from the Ventura Fwy. (Rte. 134) and from the Golden State Fwy. (I-5).

Griffith Observatory★★★

👥 *2800 E. Observatory Rd.* 🕐*Open Tue–Fri noon–10pm, weekends 10am–10pm.* 🕐*Closed Thanksgiving Day, Dec 25.* ☞*$7 planetarium show.* 🅿*Limited parking available at the main lot, and on the roadway leading to the observatory (uphill walk required).* ✕ 🖉*213-473-0800. www.griffith observatory.org.*

From a promontory on the south slope of 1,625ft Mt. Hollywood, Griffith Park's highest peak, this art deco observatory (1935) was donated by Col. Griffith at a cost of $255,780. With its central 84ft copper planetarium dome and two smaller flanking domes, this public observatory is one of Los Angeles' most distinctive landmarks.

In November 2006, the observatory reopened after a $93 million renovation and expansion that doubled the public space, added 60 new exhibits, and upgraded the planetarium theater. You'll also find a 200-seat presentation theater, a cafe with an outdoor deck and a museum store.

Visit

The new West entrance leads into the main level's **Hall of the Sky**, where interactive exhibits focus on such topics as the sun, moon, tides, seasons and the elements. Three solar telescopes are available for use only on clear days. In the central rotunda, a 240lb brass Foucault pendulum is the focal point. Steps lead up to the revamped **planetarium** *(shows ☞$7, children $3)*, with its new Zeiss Universarium Mark IX star projector and laser projection system. East of the central rotunda, the **Hall of the Eye** exhibits include a camera obscura, a Tesla coil and a display on California's observatories.

The lower level holds the **Gunther Depth of Space**, which features exhibits on the planets and the solar system. The adjacent **Edge of Space** spotlights the moon and meteorites, among other topics.

Located in the roof-top dome of the building's east end is the observatory's original 12-inch **Zeiss refracting telescope**, which is open to the public for night viewing. Outside, the Promenade Walkway and the East and West terraces permit expansive **views★★★**.

Museum of the American West★★

👥 *4700 Western Heritage Way, off Zoo Dr.* 🕐*Open year-round Tue–Fri 10am–4pm, weekends 11am–5pm. (late May–Labor Day Thu 8pm).* 🕐*Closed major holidays.* ☞*$9, children $3.* ✕🅿 🖉*323-667-2000. www.autrynationalcenter.org.*

This museum, housed in a contemporary Mission Revival-style building (1988), presents the history of the American West. The initial collection was donated by the Autry Foundation, established by film star **Gene Autry** (1907–1998), known as "The Singing Cowboy."

Permanent galleries present the collection thematically and in roughly chronological order. Begin on the lower level with the **Opportunity Gallery**, which looks at the motives and challenges for 19C pioneers, who traveled to the American West. The railroad and the telegraph's roles in transforming the West is a focus of the **Conquest Gallery**.

The **Community Gallery★** depicts the formation of a social fabric among settlers. Wyatt Earp's drawing of the so-called 1881 "Gunfight at the OK Corral" in Tombstone, Arizona is on display. The Colt Gallery showcases more than 200 firearms. The **Cowboy Gallery** focuses on the working-class cattle hand exalted by 20C media.

On the main level, the **Romance Gallery** examines the West through art, advertising and Wild West shows. Featured are "Buffalo Bill" Cody's rifle and Annie Oakley's double-barrel shotgun. The **Imagination Gallery** traces the portrayal of the West in film, radio and TV media. Outside are environmental displays in **Trails West**.

Los Angeles Zoo★★

🚹🚻 *5333 Zoo Dr.* 🕐*Open year-round daily 10am–5pm.* 🕐*Closed Dec 25.* 💵*$12, children $7.* ✗♿🅿 ✆*323-644-4200. www.lazoo.org.*

The city's first zoological garden opened in the early 20C east of downtown. The zoo rented out its animals for use in motion pictures; with 700 species, it constituted one of the world's largest wild animal collections.

Financial difficulties led the owner to donate the zoo to the city in the early 1920s; in 1966 it was moved to its present location on 80 acres in Griffith Park. Today the zoo is home to more than 1,200 mammals, birds, amphibians and reptiles, representing some 400 species.

From the entrance, a walkway leads to the **Winnick Family Children's Zoo**, which features animal environments of the American Southwest. There are interactive exhibits, a 250-seat amphitheater for animal shows, and the zoo's nursery. Additional trails follow the hilly terrain, leading to areas devoted to aquatic animals, Australia, North America, Africa, hillside animals, Eurasia and South America. At the indoor Koala House, nocturnal animals enjoy a natural twilight setting. On the pathway below the aviary, a display is devoted to the California condor. Don't miss the Gorilla Reserve in the heart of the zoo, where these fascinating primates gambol and interact in a gorgeous setting. Plans call for the opening of the new exhibit on Asian elephants *(late 2009).*

Travel Town Museum

🚹🚻 *Zoo Dr. at Forest Lawn Dr.* 🕐*Open year-round Mon–Fri 10am–4pm (5pm in summer), weekends 10am–6pm.* 🕐*Closed Dec 25.* 🅿 ✆*323-662-5874. www.laparks.org.*

This open-air museum of railroad cars and steam locomotives, dating primarily from the 1880s to the 1930s, was founded in 1952. From the entrance, a quarter-scale four-cylinder propane locomotive takes visitors on a tour of the museum's perimeter *(💵$2),* and an indoor display includes antique firefighting equipment from the Los Angeles area.

④ WILSHIRE BOULEVARD★

Wilshire Boulevard is the city's grandest thoroughfare, reaching westward 16mi from downtown through Beverly Hills to Santa Monica. Its architecture, particularly the stretch between downtown and Fairfax Avenue, chronicles the growth of modern Los Angeles.

In the mid-19C, the boulevard was a dirt road leading from the El Pueblo toward the present site of the La Brea Tar Pits. For centuries, local Native Americans had followed the trail to collect asphalt from the pits for use as a sealant. In the late 1880s, publisher H. Gaylord Wilshire bought a tract of land between 6th and 7th Streets west of downtown. He subdivided the land and, in 1895, widened the dirt trail into a boulevard. Development followed and retail, office and theater buildings marched westward.

In recent decades, shifts in population and business have led to the neglect, and even demolition, of some of the boulevard's most historic buildings. However, the so-called "Miracle Mile" is slowly regaining its former glory. A number of museums, including the Los Angeles County Museum of Art, have chosen to locate along this strip, giving rise to the nickname "Museum Row on the Miracle Mile."

🚗 DRIVING TOUR

5mi. 🕐*Map pp168–169.*
Begin at MacArthur Park, 1.3mi west of downtown.

MacArthur Park

✆*213-368-0520. www.laparks.org.*
H. Gaylord Wilshire developed this property in the 1890s as a 32-acre park. In 1934 Wilshire Boulevard was rerouted through its heart, and in 1942 the park was renamed in honor of Gen. Douglas MacArthur. A lake with a boathouse and paddle boats for rent *($12/hr)* dominates the green space. Facing the northwest corner, the enormous art deco **Park Plaza Hotel**★ *(607 Park View St.)* was

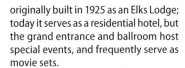

originally built in 1925 as an Elks Lodge; today it serves as a residential hotel, but the grand entrance and ballroom host special events, and frequently serve as movie sets.

Bullocks Wilshire★★

3050 Wilshire Blvd. Department-store owner John G. Bullock built a branch of his downtown retail store here, conceived for the driving shopper.
The 241ft tower calls attention to the terracotta-clad building (1929, Parkinson & Parkinson)—an art deco masterpiece—detailed in copper zigzag and snowflake patterns. Today a law school occupies the building.

Wilshire Boulevard Temple★

3663 Wilshire Blvd. ⏰*Open year-round Mon–Thu 8.30am–5pm, Fri 8.30am–4.45pm.* ⏰*Closed major and Jewish holidays.* ♿🅿️✆*213-388-2401. www.wilshireboulevardtemple.org.*
This imposing, Byzantine-inspired synagogue (1929) is home to the first Jewish congregation established in Los Angeles.Beneath a 125ft mosaic-inlaid dome, the **Edgar F. Magnin Sanctuary**★★ is an octagonal auditorium paneled in rare woods with marble and wood inlays. A bronze screen encloses the ark with Torah scrolls on the north wall. Depicting 3,000 years of Jewish history, the **Warner Memorial Murals** by Hugo Ballin form a frieze on the remaining seven walls, and a rose window faces the ark on the south wall.

Wiltern Theatre★

3790 Wilshire Blvd.
⏰*Open to the public for performances only. www.livenation.com.*
This theater is the centerpiece of the turquoise terra-cotta **Pellissier Building** (1931), a 12-story Art Deco tower. Designed by G. Albert Landsburgh, it features an elaborate sunburst on the ceiling beneath the corner marquee. Originally a Warner cinema, the theater now hosts live performances and is open only to ticket holders.
Fewer than two blocks west stands the **Wilshire Professional Building**

(3875 Wilshire Blvd.), a pale, terra-cotta-sheathed office tower (1929) revealing the chevrons and stylized ornamentation of the Art Deco substyle known as Zigzag Moderne.

Miracle Mile

Wilshire Blvd. roughly bounded by La Brea & Fairfax Aves.
In 1920 real-estate developer A.W. Ross paid $54,000 for 18 acres along Wilshire Boulevard between La Brea and Fairfax avenues, within a 4mi radius of L.A.'s wealthiest neighborhoods at the time. His ambitious plan to transform the strip into a grand suburban shopping center, geared to the driving shopper, led friend and investor Foster Stewart in 1928 to dub the area "The Miracle Mile."
Some of the city's most remarkable art deco buildings rose along the "mile" over the next three decades.

La Brea Tar Pits★

North side of Wilshire Blvd., west of Curson Ave.
Home to the Los Angeles County Museum of Art (LACMA), Hancock Park is also the setting for the world's largest cache of Ice Age fossils.
Some 38,000 years ago, now-extinct animals such as saber-toothed cats and imperial mammoths came to drink from pools here, and became trapped in the tarlike asphalt (*brea* in Spanish) lying on the surface. In 1900 **G. Allan Hancock** (1876–1965) established the Hancock fortune when he discovered oil on the property. In 1905 scientists from the University of California confirmed the site's fossilized bones' true age, and scientific excavations began that have unearthed more than 100 tons of specimens to date. Hancock donated 23-acre Hancock Park to Los Angeles County in 1916.
Today, asphalt still bubbles up through the water in the **lake pit** beside Wilshire Boulevard; near the pit's edges, life-size statues portray Ice Age mammals struggling for their lives. There's an observation area at Pit 91 behind the art museum. Currently, archaeologists are focusing their attention on the recent

excavation of 23 blocks of asphalt, which have yielded a wealth of new fossils, including that of a rare Colombian mammoth.

🚶🧒 Page Museum at the La Brea Tar Pits★★

5801 Wilshire Blvd. 🕐*Open year-round daily 9.30am–5pm.* 🕐*Closed major holidays.* ◎*$7, children $2 (free first Tue of the month).* ♿🅿*($8)* ✆*323-934-7243. www.tarpits.org.*

Designed to appear as if on a burial mound and topped by cast-fiberglass friezes of Ice Age animals, this square-sided, single-story museum was funded by George C. Page, a Nebraska native who made his fortune shipping gift baskets of dried California fruit nationwide. The collection, administered by the Natural History Museum of Los Angeles County, features skeletons reconstructed from the more-than-4.5 million bones of 390 animal species—including more than 3,000 dire wolves—found at the La Brea Tar Pits.

Two theaters present short computer-generated films on prehistoric life and the tar pits. Display cases create the illusion that skeletons of a **saber-tooth cat** and 9,000-year-old **La Brea Woman** transform into flesh and blood. In the glass-windowed "fishbowl" **paleontology laboratory**, scientists and volunteers clean and examine bones.

Los Angeles Craft and Folk Art Museum (M2)

5814 Wilshire Blvd. 🕐*Open year-round Tue–Fri 11am–5pm (Thu 7pm), weekends noon–6pm.* 🕐*Closed major holidays.* ◎*$5 (free 1st Wed of the month).* ♿ ✆*323-937-4230. www.cafam.org.*

This small museum, founded in the mid-1960s, seeks to foster appreciation of other cultures through the presentation of art created in social and cultural context, as well as objects used in everyday life. It features high-quality traveling exhibits, often from the realm of design. Hand-crafted ethnic and folk-art items are for sale in the museum shop.

Los Angeles County Museum of Art (LACMA)★★★

🕐*Description following page.*

Petersen
🚶🧒 Automotive Museum★★

6060 Wilshire Blvd. 🕐*Open year-round Tue–Sun 10am–6pm.* 🕐*Closed major holidays.* ◎*$10, children $3.* ♿🅿*($8)* ✆*323-930-2277. www.petersen.org.*

Opened in 1994, the Petersen presents a collection of some 200 rare, restored cars, trucks and motorcycles to show how developments in automotive transport, influenced the growth of Los Angeles, the quintessential "car town."

The permanent exhibit **Streetscape** *(1st floor)* sets classic vehicles into dioramas illustrating Los Angeles at various points in history; highlights include a 1911 American Underslung, as well as a 1915 Stutz White Squadron racer. A 1922 Willys-Knight, a 1932 Duesenberg Model J Roadster and a 1932 Harley Davidson motorcycle spotlight car-related innovations such as residential driveways, separate garages, tract homes, gas stations, car dealerships and strip malls.

Other displays detail civic decisions to build broad boulevards, parkways and eventually freeways in place of trolley and streetcar lines. Completing the exhibit are a sobering presentation on crashes and technological innovations to improve safety, and illustrations outlining design conception in the late 20C. Galleries on the second level feature rotating thematic exhibits. On the third floor is the **May Family Children's Discovery Center**, a hands-on learning facility that teaches the fundamental functions of a car.

Farmers' Market★

6333 W. 3rd St. at Fairfax Ave. 🕐*Open Mon–Fri 9am–9pm, Sat 9am–8pm, Sun 10am–7pm.* 🕐*Closed Jan 1, Dec 25.* ✕🅿 ✆*323-933-9211 or 866-993-9211. www.farmersmarketla.com.*

Though the farmers' stalls of 1937 have long since been replaced by more than 70 permanent businesses, the landmark open-air market retains a rustic charm. Greengrocers and butchers serve locals, while numerous international food and souvenir stands cater to visitors.

Behind the market on South Fairfax Avenue, the black-and-white **CBS Television City** (1952) is the national broadcasting network's local headquarters; a box office on the Fairfax side offers tickets for TV programs being taped here.

5 LOS ANGELES COUNTY MUSEUM OF ART★★★

Map pp168–169. 5905 Wilshire Blvd. Open year-round Mon–Tue & Thu noon–8pm, Fri noon–9pm, weekends 11am–8pm. Closed Thanksgiving Day & Dec 25. $12 (free after 5pm and 2nd Tue of the month). Additional fees for some special exhibitions; check the website. ($7) 323-857-6000. www.lacma.org.

Construction and reinstallation of some galleries is ongoing as part of the LACMA Transformation project. Check the website for updates, or contact the Registrar to determine if a particular work of art is on view: 323-857-6061.

This sprawling seven-building complex (soon to be eight), generally referred to by the acronym **LACMA**, is the nation's largest art museum west of Chicago. Housing a broad collection ranging from Egyptian and pre-Columbian art to contemporary works, LACMA is also the city's principal venue for major traveling exhibitions. On a regular basis, it offers programs of lectures, music and films.

The Complex

This prestigious institution began as part of the Museum of History, Science and Art, which opened in 1913 in Exposition Park. In 1961 the art collection was formally separated from the museum and reopened three years later in its present location as LACMA, occupying three imposing buildings by Pereira & Assocs. Continued growth of the collections led to the addition of the Robert O. Anderson Building (1986, Hardy Holzman Pfeiffer), a bold, four-level structure; its facade of limestone, glass blocks and green-glazed terracotta echoes the art deco traditions of the Miracle Mile, and

its grand entry now leads to the complex's partially covered Central Court. The opening of the Pavilion for Japanese Art (1988, Bruce Goff and Bart Prince), a curvilinear, Asian-inspired structure surrounded by Japanese gardens, underscored the city's close ties to Pacific Rim culture.

The former May Co. department store, a 1939 Streamline Moderne edifice one block away *(Wilshire Blvd. & Fairfax Ave.)*, became **LACMA West** in 1998. The refurbished building now hosts special exhibits and events; it also has an interactive children's gallery *(closed for renovation)* and a satellite gallery to the Southwest Museum.

In 2005 ground was broken for the first phase of the 10-year LACMA Transformation Project, designed by renowned architect Renzo Piano. Phase I brought the construction of the new 60,000sq ft Broad Contemporary Art museum next to LACMA West. A new entrance pavilion links this new building and the Ahmanson Building. In 2008 LACMA began construction of the new Resnick Pavilion directly north of the Broad Museum; this space will host the museum's frequent temporary exhibitions *(projected completion 2010)*.

The Collections

LACMA's holdings now comprise more than 100,000 works, their range evident in the museum's many curatorial divisions: American Art, Art of the Middle East, Costumes and Textiles, Decorative Arts and Design, European Painting and Sculpture, Chinese and Korean Art, South and Southeast Asian Art, Japanese Art, Photography, Prints and Drawings, and Modern Art, and Contemporary Art. Though such a far-reaching curatorial approach sometimes leads to greater breadth than depth in the works on view, the museum is justifiably renowned for its particular strengths in Asian art; Latin American art ranging from pre-Columbian artifacts to contemporary works; and the world's most important collection of Middle Eastern art. Other highlights include the Rifkind

Center for German Expressionist Studies, and Old Masters paintings.

VISIT
Ahmanson Building
One of the museum's original buildings, the four-level structure houses a large share of LACMA's permanent collections, displayed in galleries leading off a central atrium.

Plaza Level – Selections from the collection of **Modern** art may include works of Pablo Picasso's blue and Cubist periods, and works by Belgian Surrealist René Magritte, Joan Miró, Hans Hoffman, Isamu Noguchi, Mark Rothko, Frank Stella and Richard Diebenkorn.

You'll also find selections here from the museum's holdings in African art: body adornments, masks, sculptures and textile works. The plaza level also houses the Rifkind Gallery for German Expressionism.

Third Level – Rooms provide a survey of ancient Egyptian, Mesopotamian, Iranian, Greek and Roman art; highlights are stone relief panels from the palace of Assyrian King Ashurnasirpal II and a gallery of ancient glass.

European art from the Middle Ages to the 19C occupies most of this level. The **Renaissance** and **Mannerist collections** highlight works by Titian, Tintoretto, Vasari, Veronese and El Greco. Among 17C **Dutch** and **Flemish** works are canvases by Rembrandt van Rijn, Frans Hals and Peter Paul Rubens.

Fourth Level – The galleries highlight works from **Southeast Asian**, and **Middle Eastern** art. Composed of approximately 3,500 paintings, sculptures, ceramics, textiles and works in silver, jade and crystal, the collection is considered among the finest in the Western world.

You'll also find here selections from the museum's collections of **Costumes and Textiles** (closed for renovation; projected reopening late 2009).

Hammer Building
The Hammer Building displays the museum's outstanding holdings in **Chinese** and **Korean** art on the sec-

ond level (closed for construction; projected reopening 2009). You'll also find changing exhibits of photography on the third level.

Art of the Americas Building
Plaza Level – This level is devoted to special exhibitions.

Third Level – This level features an integrated installation of American painting and decorative arts. The **American Decorative Arts** collection reveals outstanding pieces from the Arts and Crafts movement, including works by Gustav Stickley, as well as a broad sweep of styles ranging from Queen Anne, William and Mary, Chippendale, rococo and Federal. **American Painting and Sculpture** from the 18C to the early 20C includes works by George Bellows, Thomas Moran, Thomas Eakins, Thomas Cole (founder of the Hudson River school). Mary Cassatt, John Singer Sargent and Thomas Hart Benton.

Fourth Level – Selections from the core collection of **Art of the Ancient Americas and Latin American Art** (Colonial-Contemporary) are displayed on this level. You'll see sculptures, pottery, textiles and gold from western Mexico and central Mesoamerica, ceramics from central Panama and ancient pottery. Also worth seeing are pieces from the museum's outstanding holdings of works by modern masters such as Diego Rivera, Frida Kahlo, Rufino Tamayo and Gabriel Orozco.

Pavilion for Japanese Art
In 1982 Joe D. Price and his Japanese-born wife, Etsuko, donated to LACMA their **Shin-enkan collection** of scroll paintings and screens created during Japan's Edo period (1615–1868), considered the outstanding collection of its kind in the Western world.

Off the lobby, a gallery presents **netsuke**—small, intricate carvings of wood, ivory or stag antler intended as toggles for attaching tobacco pouches or medicine boxes to the sashes of traditional Japanese kimonos.

A ramp spirals up past alcoves in which scrolls and screens from the collection are displayed. The structure's walls approximate the translucency of rice-paper screens, illuminating the artworks in soft natural light. In the west wing, Japanese textiles and Buddhist sculptures, ceramics and lacquerware from the permanent collection are on view. In the east wing, the selection changes regularly.

Broad Museum of Contemporary Art

Take the red escalator up to the third level to enter the airy, skylit galleries of this intriguing new structure, one of the largest column-free art spaces in the US. Opened in 2008 as the result of a cooperative agreement between the Broad Art Foundation and LACMA, the museum brings to view art from 1945 to the present through its changing exhibitions of works from LACMA's permanent collection and the Broad Foundation as well as pieces on loan from other institutions. Featured artists may include Jean-Michel Basquiat, Cindy Sherman, Jenny Holzer, Jasper Johns, Ed Ruscha, Richard Serra, Anselm Kiefer, Robert Rauschenberg, and Eric Fischl.

Sculpture Gardens

Two open-air displays of large sculptures flank the building on Wilshire Boulevard. The sculpture garden on the west side (access via the Central Court) is dominated by Rodin bronzes. On the eastern side (access immediately to the right of the main entrance) are nine contemporary works by such sculptors as Alexander Calder and Henry Moore.

6 HOLLYWOOD★★

Map pp168–169.

As much a state of mind as a location, Hollywood is the symbolic heart of the movie industry. The renowned district of business, entertainment and residential areas is situated about 8mi west of downtown and 12mi east of the Pacific coast, sweeping from the Santa Monica Mountains' Hollywood Hills south to the city below. Crossed east-west by major boulevards, "Tinseltown" is a bustling part of Los Angeles; its main thorough-

fares have an active street life, attracting a cross section of visitors and locals.

A BIT OF HISTORY

Kansas prohibitionist H.H. Wilcox founded the suburb in 1883. Named Hollywood by Mrs. Wilcox, the town was incorporated in 1903. Seven years later it was annexed by the city of Los Angeles in anticipation of the arrival of water from the Los Angeles Aqueduct and the growth that would ensue.

Hollywood's first movie studio opened in 1911, and by 1912, five large East Coast film companies had relocated to Hollywood, attracted by Southern California's year-round weather and varied geography.

A group of investors in the early 1920s developed "Hollywoodland," a tract of elegant Spanish Mediterranean homes in the hills of Beachwood Canyon. To publicize the development, in 1923 the financiers erected what has come to be known as the **Hollywood Sign**★. Composed of white-painted sheet metal letters 30ft wide and 50ft tall, the sign read "HOLLYWOODLAND." Since the 1950s, with its last syllable removed, the sign has been maintained as Hollywood's most visible landmark. *The sign is best viewed from the Griffith Observatory.*

Through the 1940s, Hollywood remained the center of the motion-picture industry, although many major studios had relocated: Warner Bros. to Burbank; Metro-Goldwyn-Mayer to Culver City; Twentieth-Century Fox to Century City; Universal Studios to Universal City. Since then, the town has experienced its share of urban woes, like deteriorating buildings and a significant population of penniless souls seeking fame and fortune. Since the 1980s, energetic efforts by private investors and local government have begun to remove some of the tarnish. Their efforts are visible in recently restored landmarks along Hollywood and Sunset boulevards.

HOLLYWOOD BOULEVARD★★

Hollywood's main thoroughfare is 4.5mi long. The 1mi stretch through the center, between Gower Street and

Sycamore Avenue, is easily navigable on foot. Here, along a sidewalk paved with embedded metal stars, stand some of old Hollywood's grandest movie palaces, rubbing shoulders with souvenir stands and gaudy theme museums. The intersection of **Hollywood and Vine** is immortalized as the hub of Hollywood in the 1930s and 40s. Sardi's and the Brown Derby restaurants were located along two blocks of Vine Street at Hollywood Boulevard.

Walk of Fame★

Hollywood Blvd. between Gower St. & La Brea Ave.; Vine St. between Sunset Blvd. & Yucca St. For location of individual stars, call the Hollywood Chamber of Commerce or access the online directory. ℘323-469-8311. www.hollywoodchamber.net.

Embedded in the sidewalks are more than 2,500 bronze-trimmed coral-terrazzo stars conceived in 1958 by the Hollywood Chamber of Commerce as a tribute to major entertainment personalities. Some 2,000 stars (assigned by the Chamber) have been dedicated, at the rate of about 12 per year; names are inset in bronze along with circular plaques bearing symbols that indicate each honoree's field of achievement.

Grauman's Chinese Theatre★★

6925 Hollywood Blvd. ◥◣Backstage tours daily; call for times. ℘323-463-9576. www.manntheatres.com.

An ornate fantasy of chinoiserie, the theater (1926, Meyer & Holler) was commissioned by showman **Sid Grauman**; it is now owned by the Mann Theatres chain. Opened in 1927 with a gala premiere for Cecil B. DeMille's *King of Kings*, the theater has hosted more premieres than any other Hollywood theater, a tradition that continues today.

A mansard-roofed pagoda topped by stylized flames and flanked by white-marble dogs dominates the exterior; the ornate interior took its inspiration from Chinese Chippendale furniture. The U-shaped cement **forecourt** features the footprints and signatures of more than 180 Hollywood celebrities, with new

Musso & Frank Grill

6667 Hollywood Blvd. ℘323-467-7788. www.mussoandfrankgrill.com. Movie-industry insiders (and outsiders trying to be insiders) set up shop in the high-walled booths of this venerable Hollywood hangout. Photos of the many, many stars who have frequented the grill grace the dark-paneled walls, and the daily specials (Tuesday, corned beef & cabbage; Thursday, chicken pot pie) haven't changed in decades.

ones added almost every year. Various accounts exist of how the tradition began, most involving either Grauman, Mary Pickford, Douglas Fairbanks or Norma Talmadge accidentally stepping in wet cement during the theater's construction. Pickford and Fairbanks were the first to officially leave their prints, on April 30, 1927.

Hollywood & Highland Center★

Hollywood Blvd. & Highland Ave. ✕♿🅿 *℘323-817-0200. www.hollywoodandhighland.com.*

Today, the hub of Hollywood is not a theater or "walk of fame," hotel or restaurant. It's a bit of all of those, with a shopping mall thrown in. The $615 million development (2001, Ehrenkrantz, Eckstut & Kuhn) is anchored by David Rockwell's 3,650-seat **Kodak Theatre**, home of the Academy Award ceremonies *(late Mar)* and even "American Idol" finals. The **Awards Walk**, a staircase from Hollywood Boulevard, cites every "best picture" honoree since the first Oscars were doled out in 1927. Retail shops surround **Babylon Court**, with 33ft-high elephant statues flanking a courtyard that echoes a 1916 D.W. Griffith movie set; winding into it is a granite path of anonymous "How I Got to Hollywood" quotes by everyone from actors to caterers.

The Los Angeles Convention & Visitors Bureau maintains a **visitor center** in the complex (*℘323-467-6412*).

Hollywood Roosevelt Hotel★

7000 Hollywood Blvd. ☎323-466-7000. www.hollywoodroosevelt.com.

Named in honor of Theodore Roosevelt, the 12-story hotel (1927) was a popular gathering spot for stars of the 1930s and 40s. The first Academy Awards ceremony was held here in 1929. Extensively renovated in 2005, the hotel, now a member of the Thompson Hotels group, features a two-story Spanish-Moorish lobby with a beamed ceiling. In 1987 the walls and bottom of the hotel's **swimming pool** *(behind main building)* were painted with blue swirls by artist David Hockney.

El Capitan Theatre★★

6838 Hollywood Blvd. Interior open during movie showings. ☎323-467-7674. www.disney.go.com.

Restored in 1991, the theater (1926, Morgan, Walls & Clements), now operated by The Walt Disney Company, features an ornate Churrigueresque facade. Originally presenting live shows, it was converted into a movie palace with the 1941 world premiere of Orson Welles' *Citizen Kane*. The East India-inspired interior, designed by G. Albert Lansburgh, sparkles with ornate grillwork and gold leaf.

♣♣ The Hollywood Museum (M3)

1660 Highland Ave. ☾Open Wed–Sun 10am–5pm. ✆$15, children $12. ☎323-464-7776; www.thehollywoodmuseum.com.

This fanciful museum, mecca for fans of Hollywood old and new, occupies the 1931 Max Factor Building just south of Hollywood Boulevard (note the original pink-and-white marble facade of the cosmetic king's palace). The museum gathers props, costumes, sets and other movie artifacts, seemingly as soon as they come off the lot. There's also a significant collection of memorabilia from movies of yesteryear. It all makes for a fun immersion into Hollywood kitsch.

Egyptian Theatre★ (B)

6712 Hollywood Blvd. ☛Guided tours (60min) Tue–Sun 10.30am & 4pm. ✆$5 (tour & movie combination ticket $10).

✆☎323-466-3456. www.americancinematheque.com.

Built in the wake of worldwide excitement over the discovery of King Tut's tomb, this faux-Egyptian movie palace (1922, Meyer and Holler) opened to tremendous fanfare when Sid Grauman chose it to stage the world's first Hollywood premiere. Fully restored with a period marquee, palm trees and Egyptian motifs in the entrance portico, and an ornate sunburst-pattern ceiling, it reopened in 1998 as home to the American Cinemathèque's independent film program. A 1hr **film** on the history of Hollywood is screened several times daily with an audio track available in multiple languages *(call for schedule).*

Capitol Records Tower★

1750 Vine St. ☞Closed to the public.

Touted as the world's first circular office building (1954, Welton Becket & Assocs.), this 150ft complex of offices and studios resembles a stack of vintage records topped by a phonograph needle. Hollywood legend says the design was suggested by recording stars Nat King Cole and Johnny Mercer. The rooftop beacon light blinks out H-O-L-L-Y-W-O-O-D in Morse code.

Pantages Theatre★

6233 Hollywood Blvd. Interior open only during shows. ☎800-745-3000 (Ticketmaster). www.broadwayla.org.

Vaudeville impresario Alexander Pantages opened the theater (1930, B. Marcus Priteca) as the first art deco movie palace in the US; from 1949 to 1959 it hosted the Academy Awards. In recent years, the theater has hosted touring stage musicals and dance companies. The concrete-and-black-marble exterior is relatively understated in contrast to the interior with its vaulted, detailed lobby and 2,812-seat auditorium.

The **MetroRail station** on Hollywood Boulevard just east of Vine Street is one of Hollywood's most extravagant tributes to itself. Opened in May 1999, it boasts a ceiling covered with film reels, walls rife with movie memorabilia, and a floor designed to resemble the Yellow Brick Road from *The Wizard of Oz*.

SUNSET BOULEVARD★

Stretching some 20mi from El Pueblo to the Pacific Ocean, Sunset Boulevard cuts through a cross section of life in Los Angeles; the Latino neighborhoods of Elysian Park; the street life of Hollywood; the mansions of Beverly Hills; and the upscale neighborhoods of Westwood, Bel Air, Brentwood and Pacific Palisades. The street's most famous stretch is the 1.5mi **Sunset Strip★★**. Hugging the Santa Monica Mountains between Crescent Heights Boulevard and Doheny Drive, the street passes through an area that was once an unincorporated strip (hence its nickname) between Angeles and Beverly Hills. It is now part of the city of **West Hollywood**, whose identity as one of L.A.'s largest gay enclaves is more evident south of the Strip on Santa Monica Boulevard.

The Strip's former civic status and resulting lack of regulations gave rise to fashionable nightclubs and restaurants that attracted the entertainment industry and still define the Strip's character. Giant **billboards** above the low buildings tout the latest Hollywood productions. Above the easternmost end of the Strip is the renowned **Château Marmont** (*8221 Sunset Blvd.; 𝄞323-656-1010; www.chateaumarmont.com*); the seven-story hotel—an amalgam of Norman and Moorish influences—has long been a hideaway for actors, directors, producers, writers and musicians.

Sunset Tower Hotel★

8358 Sunset Blvd. 𝄞323-654-7100. www.sunsettowerhotel.com.
Originally known as the Sunset Towers Apartments (1931), and subsequently as the St. James Club, then the Argyle Hotel, the 15-story building was home to such stars as Errol Flynn, Jean Harlow, Clark Gable, John Wayne and Marilyn Monroe. The art deco exterior and interiors were restored in 1985. The hotel received an extensive facelift in 2005.

MELROSE AVENUE★

Although it stretches 7mi from Hollywood's eastern edge to the Beverly Hills border, Melrose Avenue seems to distill the creativity and craziness for which Los Angeles is known into the 16 blocks between La Brea and Fairfax Avenues. Originally serving the surrounding, predominantly Orthodox Jewish neighborhoods, the shops in the low-lying buildings lining the avenue were taken over in the late 1970s and 80s by hip boutiques, galleries, restaurants and shops specializing in bizarre collectibles and gifts—and appealing to a swath of humanity that ranges from Versace-clad business people, to pierced-and-tattooed Generation Xers.

Paramount Studios

5555 Melrose Ave. ☞Visit by guided tour (2hr) only, Mon–Fri 10am–2pm; advance reservations required. ⊘No tours major holidays. ☜$35. ⓟ($4.50) 𝄞323-956-1777. www.paramount studios.com.
Approximately 1.3mi east of Melrose Avenue's boutiques and restaurants, this film and television production facility is the only major studio remaining within the boundaries of Hollywood. The wrought-iron Spanish Renaissance-style **studio gates**, surmounted by "Paramount Pictures" in script, endure as a well-known symbol just north of Melrose at Marathon Street.

Hollywood Forever

6000 Santa Monica Blvd., adjoining the Paramount Studios lot. ⊕Open year-round daily 8.30am–5pm. Free maps at cemetery office next to entrance. 𝄞323-469-1181. www.hollywoodforever.com.
The 65-acre cemetery (formerly Hollywood Memorial Park) shelters the grave sites and crypts of such Hollywood legends as Rudolph Valentino, Douglas Fairbanks, Tyrone Power, Peter Lorre, Jesse Lasky and Cecil B. DeMille.

Pacific Design Center★★

⊕Map p186. 8687 Melrose Ave. 𝄞310-657-0800. www.pacificdesign center.com.

Television Recordings

To attend a recording, contact the following three weeks in advance for free tickets. A ticket does not guarantee admittance, which is first-come, first-served.

Audiences Unlimited (all major networks), 100 Universal City Plaza, Bldg. 153, Universal City CA 91608; ℘818-753-3470; www.tvtickets.com.

CBS Television City, 7800 Beverly Blvd., Los Angeles CA 90036; ℘323-575-2458 or www.cbs.com. Check online first for each show's ticket-ordering procedure.

NBC Tickets, 3000 W. Alameda Ave., Burbank CA 91523; ℘818-840-353. For same-day tickets, go to the Guest Relations office, or send a written request six weeks in advance, and include a self-addressed stamped envelope. For *The Tonight Show with Conan O'Brien* (at Universal Studios), email requests to conantickets@nbc.com.

On Camera Audiences, 224 E. Olive Ave. #205, Burbank, CA 91502; ℘213-833-6469; www.ocatv.com.

Anchoring Melrose Avenue's western end, the massive, seven-story building (1975, Cesar Pelli) sheathed in cobalt-blue glass quickly acquired the local nickname "The Blue Whale." In 1988 its hexagonal green glass annex, known as "The Green Turtle," expanded the center to some 1.2 million sq ft of showrooms for the interior design trade, and in 2009, Pelli's 400,000sq ft Red Building completed the design center's campus.

UNIVERSAL STUDIOS HOLLYWOOD★★★

100 Universal City Plaza, Universal City. Take Highland Ave. north to Cahuenga Blvd. or US-101; continue north to Barham Blvd., Universal Center Dr. or Lankershim Blvd. and follow the signs. ⏱*Open daily year-round, 10am–6pm during summer, Thanksgiving and December holiday seasons; rest of the year hours vary, check the website for schedule.* ⊜*$67 ($57 children under*

On board the trams, Universal Studios Hollywood

Rachel Mills/MICHELIN

48in tall). ⊜*Check the website or entrance booths for front-of-the-line passes and other combination offers.* ✕&🅿 *($12)* ℘*800-864-8377. www.universalstudios.com.*

Part functioning film and television studio, part live-entertainment complex and amusement park, 420-acre Universal Studios Hollywood sprawls across and down a hillside overlooking the San Fernando Valley, 3mi northwest of Hollywood Boulevard.

Silent film producer Carl Laemmle bought the property (then a chicken ranch) in 1915 and quickly established a movie studio on it. He erected bleachers beside the sets and charged the public 25 cents to watch films being made. But the advent of motion-picture sound in the late 1920s, with the need for "quiet on the set," put an end to such visits.

In 1964 Universal began to offer tram rides to boost lunchtime revenues at the studio commissary; visitors were shown makeup techniques, costumes, a push-button monster and a stunt demonstration. The popularity of the Universal Tour, as it was then called, led to the addition of new attractions.

Today, Universal Studios Hollywood is among the largest purpose-built tourist attractions in the US, annually welcoming 5 million visitors. Adjoining the park are the Universal Amphitheatre, a live concert venue; the Universal Cineplex Odeon, an 18-screen movie theater; and several large restaurants. The **Universal CityWalk**, a shopping, dining and entertainment complex, designed as a compressed version of L.A., is popular with Angelenos and out-of-towners.

Entertainment Center

Live-performance stages in the upper lot section of the park present rides and live shows *(15–30min; schedule available at entrance),* some inspired by popular films and television programs. Among them, **WaterWorld** is a rough-and-tumble pyrotechnic thrill show. The **Animal Actors Stage** presents stunts performed by more than 60 trained animals. **Terminator 2: 3-D** combines three-dimensional movie effects with a live-action story line that picks up where the hit movie *Terminator 2: Judgment Day* left off. The movie **Shrek 4-D** delights children and adults, who don 3-D glasses and sit in a theater with seats that tilt; special effects make Shrek, Donkey and other characters 'jump' from the screen. In the **Curious George** play area, kids can join their favorite monkey in his adventurous quests to satisfy his curiosity. **The Simpsons** ride, based on the popular television show, features a harrowing visit to Krustyland theme park, courtesy of Krusty the clown.

Studio Center

Descend the **Universal Starway**, a 0.25mi covered escalator, to the park's lower lot. Situated around Universal's actual sound stages and backlot, the center includes the **Universal Experience**, a behind-the-scenes look at the art of filmmaking. **Jurassic Park** begins as a pleasant river journey past gentle herbivorous dinosaurs before something goes awry; a harrowing escape ensues. Visitors to **Backdraft** witness a warehouse full of chemicals burst into flames. **Revenge of the Mummy: The Ride** is a stomach-churning roller coaster ride that moves forward *and* backwards. At the **Special Effects Stages**, demonstrations are based on scenes from popular films like *The Scorpion King.*

Studio Tour★★

Visitors board trams at Entertainment Center for 45min of history and thrills, along with an up-close look at a working movie studio. Trams wind through sets portraying the Wild West, small-town America, Europe and other locales. En route, the tour is attacked by the shark from Steven Spielberg's *Jaws* (1975); passes the steam ship of a bellowing King Kong; witnesses robotic racers in fast-paced street races; and endures a collapsing bridge, a flash flood, and an earthquake, among other adventures.

ADDITIONAL SIGHTS

♿ *Map pp168–169.*
Hollywood Bowl★★
2301 N. Highland Ave. 🕐*Grounds open daily dawn–dusk.* ✕♿🅿 ✆*323-850-2000. www.hollywoodbowl.com.*
A broad hollow of the Santa Monica Mountains has been turned into the largest natural amphitheater in the world, the summer home of the Los Angeles Philharmonic and the Hollywood Bowl Orchestra.

The site was acquired in 1919 for community concerts. In 1926 a concrete stage was built and permanent seating was installed on the hillside. The band shell is a 100ft white quarter-sphere. Frank Sinatra, The Beatles, Igor Stravinsky and Luciano Pavarotti have performed here, among many others.

Mulholland Drive★

Begins at Cahuenga Blvd., less than 1mi north of the Hollywood Bowl, and ends in Calabasas, almost 20mi west.
Named for William Mulholland, engineer of the Los Angeles Aqueduct, this spectacular road curves along the crest of the Santa Monica Mountains. It offers abundant **vistas**★★ of the Los Angeles Basin and the San Fernando Valley, along with views of luxury homes dotting steep hillsides and ravines. From the **Hollywood Bowl Overlook**, views extend to the Bowl, the Hollywood Sign and the city. Laurel Canyon, Coldwater Canyon and Beverly Glen allow an easy return to the city below after a few miles' drive. Much of the road is unpaved (not open to vehicles) between I-405 and Topanga Canyon Road, toward Mulholland's western end.

7 BEVERLY HILLS★★

Map p186. www.beverlyhills.org.
Beverly Hills is an independent munici-
pality covering almost 6sq mi of commercial and residential developments.
The city's name is deservedly synonymous with wealth and elegance: its vil-
lage-like shopping streets are lined with
international boutiques, fashionable
restaurants and luxurious mansions.

A BIT OF HISTORY

Beverly Hills was originally part of a
Spanish land grant. During the 19C,
most of the land was given over to farming and cattle-raising. In 1907 Burton E.
Green and associates developed a new
community that Green named Beverly
Hills. Single-acre lots were offered for
as little as $400.
The 1912 opening of the Beverly Hills
Hotel attracted Hollywood stars to the
area. In 1920 Mary Pickford and Douglas
Fairbanks built the city's first celebrity
mansion, Pickfair, high on Summit Drive
north of Sunset Boulevard.
Today Beverly Hills ranks among the
nation's highest in average household
income, and is home to many motion-
picture and television actors and entertainment moguls. Wilshire Boulevard, its
main thoroughfare, is dotted with high-
rise office buildings, and the exclusive
shopping district bordered by Wilshire
and Santa Monica boulevards and
Cañon Drive merits its reputation as the
"Golden Triangle." But much of the area
maintains a privacy and exclusivity that
enhance the city's aura of privilege.

SIGHTS
Rodeo Drive★★

The city's world-renowned luxury shopping street and heart of the "Golden Triangle" is a three-block stretch of mostly
two- and three-story buildings between
Wilshire and Santa Monica boulevards.
Within that space are dozens of fashionable boutiques and clothiers, jewelers,
antique dealers and art galleries catering to a range of expensive tastes.
In the block between Dayton and
Brighton ways, **Anderton Court** *(328
N. Rodeo Dr.),* an angular, three-story
white shopping complex with an open
ramp winding around a central geometric spire, was built in 1954 from a design
by Frank Lloyd Wright. Occupying the
northeast corner of Wilshire Boulevard
and Rodeo Drive, Via Rodeo *(Two Rodeo
Dr.),* a four-story shopping complex
(1990) lined with trendy boutiques,
whimsically resembles the street of an
Italian hillside town.

Paley Center for Media★

465 N. Beverly Dr. ◷*Open year-round
Wed–Sun noon–5pm.* ◷*Closed major
holidays.* ⊚*$10 contribution requested.*
♿🅿 ℘*310-786-1000. www.paley
center.org.*

Rodeo Drive

Opened in 1996, the West Coast location of New York City's Museum of Television & Radio occupies a glass-and-marble structure designed by noted architect Richard Meier, with public galleries, education and listening rooms and a 150-seat theater.

Visitors use easy-to-access computer workstations to scan the collection of news broadcasts, documentaries, sports events, variety shows, dramatic and comedy productions and commercial advertising to select programs for viewing in the Console Center *(2nd floor)*. A listening room and studio for radio programs are located on the ground floor.

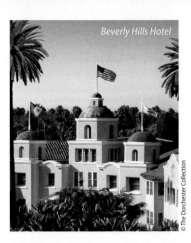

Beverly Hills Hotel

© The Dorchester Collection

Beverly Hills Civic Center

455 N. Rexford Dr. ◷*Open year-round Mon–Thu 7.30am–5.30pm, Fri 8am–5pm.* ◷*Closed major holidays.* ♿ 🅿 *☏310-285-1000. www.beverly-hills.org.*

An eight-story Spanish Baroque tower crowned with a dome finished in multicolored tiles, the City Hall (1932) sets the tone for a harmonious two-square-block contemporary addition (1990, Charles Moore/A.C. Martin & Assocs.) that arrays police and fire stations and a public library around landscaped courtyards.

Beverly Gardens

Lining the northern edge of Santa Monica Boulevard, this narrow strip of gardens forms a verdant buffer between the commercial and residential sections of Beverly Hills. Facing the gardens at 507 N. Rodeo Drive, the **O'Neill House** (1989) is a private residence with swirling white walls and a blue-tiled roof reminiscent of the fantastical art nouveau designs of Catalan architect Antonio Gaudi.

The Beverly Hills Hotel★

9641 Sunset Blvd. ✕♿🅿 *☏310-276-2251. www.thebeverlyhillshotel.com.*

The pink-stucco, Mission-style main building (1912) and its secluded bungalows are partly concealed by 12 acres of tropical gardens. The hotel has long served as a refuge for Hollywood celebrities. Charlie Chaplin and Marlene Dietrich are just a few of the star names

studding the hotel's list of former guests. The booths at the rose-and-green **Polo Lounge** attract movers and shakers who clinch deals over power breakfasts.

Virginia Robinson Gardens★

1008 Elden Way. From Beverly Hills Hotel take Crescent Dr. to Elden Way. ☞*Visit by guided tour (1hr 30min) only, year-round Tue–Fri 10am & 1pm.* ⊜*$10. Two-week advance reservation required.* 🅿 *☏310-276-5367. www.robinson-gardens.com.*

This lushly landscaped 6-acre estate was a grassland when local department store heir Harry Robinson and his wife, Virginia, purchased it in 1911. The Robinsons built a Mediterranean-style villa and pool house surrounded by formal English and terraced Mediterranean gardens, including 50 varieties of camellias. An additional 2-acre **palm forest** features the largest stand of king palms outside of Australia.

Greystone Park

905 Loma Vista Dr. at Doheny Rd. ◷*Open May–Oct daily 10am–6pm; rest of the year daily 10am–5pm.* 🅿*. ☏310-550-4796.*

Descending a terraced slope, this 18-acre formal garden of Italianate sensibility surrounds **Greystone Mansion**, a 55-room English Tudor and Jacobean mansion (1928, Gordon B. Kaufmann) of brown-gray stone built by oil millionaire Edward L. Doheny for his son, Ned. The house, popular as a movie *(Batman)* and television set, is open to the public only for musical performances. The garden affords panoramic views of the city.

Margaret Herrick Library

333 S. La Cienega Blvd. ◷*Open for research only, year-round Mon–Tue & Thu–Fri 10am–6pm (Tue 8pm).* ◷*Closed major holidays.* ♿ ☎*310-247-3020. www.oscars.org/library/.*

A slender tower and arches evoking the Spanish Colonial Revival style top the former La Cienega Water Treatment Plant (1928), which was restored in 1991 by the Academy for Motion Picture Arts and Sciences. Today the building is home to the Fairbanks Center for Motion Picture Study, which houses the Herrick Library, a non-circulating research collection of more than 32,000 books, 8 million photographs, 60,000 screenplays, clipping files and special collections of material relating to the film industry. The Academy Film Archive contains a research collection devoted to early cinema works, Academy Award nominees and winners, and the personal film collections of Academy members.

SCENIC DRIVES

An automobile drive can reveal lush scenery and occasional glimpses of mansions in a variety of architectural styles, including Tudor, Colonial, Mediterranean, Ranch and Mission.

Sunset Boulevard★

Four lanes wide and curving through the city's foothills, the boulevard offers some of the best views of large mansions surrounded by spacious grounds.

Beverly Drive

This street is broad, gently curving and lined with towering palm trees. North of Sunset Boulevard, it becomes **Coldwater Canyon Drive** and allows views of larger houses on the canyon's slopes.

Whittier Drive

In spring, jacaranda trees burst forth in blue blossoms along this scenic street.

Summit Drive★

Access via Benedict Canyon Dr. The narrow, curving drive winds uphill past gated mansions to **Pickfair** *(1143 Sum-mit Dr.),* a private residence originally built in 1920 by Mary Pickford and Douglas Fairbanks.

ADDITIONAL SIGHTS
Museum of Tolerance★★

9786 W. Pico Blvd. ◷*Open year-round Sun 11am–5pm, Mon–Fri 10am–5pm (Fri 3pm Nov–Mar).* ◷*Closed major and Jewish holidays.* ⊛*$15, children $11.* ✕♿🅿 ☎*310-772-2505. www.museumoftolerance.com.* ⊚*The Toloerancenter and the Holocaust Exhibit not recommended for children under 12.*

Dedicated in 1993, this museum has two main goals: raising awareness of racism and prejudice in American life; and exploring atrocities against humanity throughout history, with primary emphasis on the Holocaust.

A high-technology multimedia journey, the visit begins in the **Tolerancenter**, where a series of interactive exhibits are designed to provoke a powerful emotional response. This section includes *In Our Time*, a film chronicling contemporary examples of human rights violations. Visitors then enter the **Holocaust Exhibit**, a walk-through presentation of the events of the Holocaust *(1hr).* **Finding Our Families, Finding Ourselves** details diversity in the personal histories of several famous Americans. The second-floor Multimedia Learning Center offers access to historical data on the Holocaust and World War II. The **Archival Collections** feature concentration camp artifacts and some 10,000 documents, including original letters of Anne Frank.

Century City★

Bordered by Santa Monica & W. Pico Blvds., Century Park E. & Century Park W. The 180-acre complex (1961) of hotels, office buildings, apartments and townhouses, theaters, cinemas and shops occupies a former ranch owned by Western film star Tom Mix. The site served as the backlot of the adjoining Twentieth Century-Fox Studios. At its hub today is **Westfield Century City** shopping center *(10250 Santa Monica Blvd;* ✕♿🅿 ☎*310-277-3898; www.westfield.com).*

8 THE WESTSIDE
Map p186.

Although "the Westside" does not exist as an administrative entity, the term is used throughout Los Angeles to refer to those parts of the city west of Hollywood and the Miracle Mile: the residential neighborhoods of West Los Angeles, Westwood, Rancho Park, Cheviot Hills, Bel Air, Brentwood and Pacific Palisades, as well as the cities of Beverly Hills, Santa Monica and Culver City.

The area also incorporates a business corridor of high-rise buildings along Wilshire Boulevard, as well as Westwood Village adjoining the campus of the University of California, Los Angeles.

Westwood Village★
Bounded by Wilshire Blvd. and LeConte, Glendon & Gayley Aves.

Covering roughly nine square blocks immediately south of the UCLA campus, Westwood Village is the closest thing Los Angeles has to a student quarter. Pedestrians outnumber automobiles, and a compact assortment of mostly two-story Mediterranean-style buildings, largely developed by 1929, houses casual clothing boutiques, book and record stores, stationery and gift shops, cafes and restaurants. Several cinemas and a small playhouse offering live performances make the neighborhood a popular evening and weekend haunt.

UCLA Hammer Museum★
10899 Wilshire Blvd., Westwood.
⊙Open year-round Tue–Sat 11am–7pm (Thu til 9pm), Sun 11am–5pm. ⊙Closed Jan 1, Jul 4, Thanksgiving Day, Dec 25. ⊚$7 (free Thu). & ⯐ ($3) ℘310-443-7000. www.hammer.ucla.edu.

This university art museum presents historical and contemporary art exhibits, as well as a program of performing arts and selected works from the private collection of its billionaire founder, industrialist Armand Hammer (1898–1990). The permanent holdings include the **Grunwald Center for the Graphic Arts** *(⊙open by appointment only Mon–Fri 10am–4pm; ℘310-443-7078)*, one of the top collections in the US of works

on paper; and selections from the Hammer Collection: paintings and drawings by Old Masters and French Impressionists and post-Impressionists. Highlights are Rembrandt's *Juno* (c.1662).

Westwood Memorial Park★
1218 Glendon Ave., Westwood.
⊙Open year-round daily 8am–dusk. & ⯐ ℘310-474-1579.

The small, unassuming cemetery is the final resting place of many Hollywood stars, among them **Marilyn Monroe** *(left of the main entrance, in the Corridor of Memories)* and **Natalie Wood** *(near center of the lawn)*. Those who search a bit will also find the graves of Helen Hays, Dean Martin and Mel Tormé, among others.

University of California, Los Angeles (UCLA)★
Bounded by Le Conte, Hilgard & Veteran Aves. and Sunset Blvd. ⬮⬮ Student-led walking tours (90min) Mon–Fri 10.15am & 2.15pm, Sat 10.15am; reservations required ℘310-825-8764. ✕& ⯐ ($8). www.ucla.edu.

Lodged on a 419-acre campus, UCLA began in 1882 as a state normal school in downtown Los Angeles. In 1919 the school became a branch of the University of California. The site for the Westwood campus was selected in 1925. Campus planners designed 40 brick and stone buildings in the Lombard Romanesque style of northern Italy.

Today UCLA is the largest member of the University of California's nine-campus system, with an enrollment of more than 39,000 students and an academic staff of some 5,000. The university has achieved prominence in many areas; its enormous medical school, located in the Center for the Health Sciences, is among the best in the country.

Royce Quadrangle
This spacious plaza is bordered by the university's earliest structures. Inspired by a basilica in Milan, **Royce Hall★** (1929) houses classrooms and a theater. **Powell Library** (1929) sports an octagonal dome; the interior features terracotta-

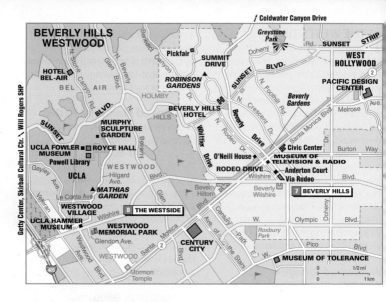

tiled staircases and ornate ceilings. From the quadrangle the **Janss Steps** sweep downhill to the student union and athletic facilities. Near its foot stands **Pauley Pavilion**, a 12,500-seat arena that is home court to UCLA's acclaimed basketball teams. In the heart of campus, on Westwood Plaza, stands the **Bruin Bear** (1984, Billy Fitzgerald), a 6ft-high bronze statue of a snarling grizzly, the campus symbol.

Fowler Museum at UCLA ★

Open year-round Wed–Sun noon–5pm (Thu til 8pm). Closed major holidays. &.℘310-825-4361. www.fowler.ucla.edu.
Downhill from Royce Hall, the three-story brick building (1992) houses one of the leading university-based museums of anthropology in the country. On permanent display is the **Fowler Family Silver Collection** of 400 silver objects from England, Europe and America. Other galleries exhibit changing displays of art and artifacts drawn from the museum's permanent collection, especially strong in African and Southeast Asian textiles and Latin American art.

Mildred Mathias Botanical Garden ★

777 Tiverton Ave., near intersection of LeConte & Hilgard Aves. Open year-round Mon–Fri 8am–5pm, weekends 8am–4pm. Closed university holidays. &.℘310-825-1260. www.botgard.ucla.edu.
Established in 1930, the seven-acre garden features some 5,000 species in 225 families, with an emphasis on tropical and subtropical plants.

Franklin D. Murphy Sculpture Garden ★★

Near intersection of Hilgard Ave. & Wyton Dr. Open daily year-round. &.
Named for a former UCLA chancellor who promoted the idea of art in a natural setting, this tree-shaded, 5-acre garden (1967) showcases works by such leading sculptors as Rodin, Matisse, Hepworth, Moore, Calder and Noguchi.

Hotel Bel-Air ★

701 Stone Canyon Rd., Bel Air. ✕&.▣ ℘310-472-1211. www.hotelbelair.com.
Hidden behind dense vegetation on a quiet residential street, this 92-room luxury hotel complex (1946) comprises one- and two-story pink Mission-style buildings. The 11-acre **gardens★★** surrounding the hotel are lushly landscaped with native sycamores and California live oaks, as well as floss silk trees, redwoods, Arizona cypresses, Japanese maples, apricots, figs, ferns, bougainvil-

lea, camellias and azaleas. Nearby Stone Canyon reservoir feeds a small stream, miniature falls and pond.

The Getty Center★★★

🎧 *Map p.188. 1200 Getty Center Dr., just off I-405; take the Getty Center Dr. exit from I-405 to the main gate at Sepulveda Blvd.* 🕐 *Open Tue–Fri Sun 10am–5.30pm, Sat 10am–9pm.* 🕐 *Closed Jan 1, July 4, Thanksgiving Day & Dec 25.* ✕ 👤 🅿 *($10). Museum access by tram from parking structure at bottom of hill.* 📞 *310-440-7300. www.getty.edu.*

Perched on a north-south ridge high above the San Diego Freeway, a cluster of low-lying buildings holds one of the nation's most extensive facilities for the study, conservation and presentation of visual art. The 110-acre campus was created to house the organizations of the J. Paul Getty Trust.

The only child of oil millionaire George F. Getty, **Jean Paul Getty** (1892–1976) by the age of 23 had become a millionaire himself in Oklahoma's oil fields. Getty began collecting paintings in 1931. After World War II, he started acquiring antiquities and other art holdings. He commissioned a museum in Malibu to display them, but the collections outgrew that original space. In 1989 work began on the Getty Center. American architect Richard Meier designed the gleaming, travertine-clad complex melding six buildings with courtyards, walkways, fountains. The various branches of the trust occupy several structures; the **J. Paul Getty Museum★★★** occupies the remainder of the complex, showcasing its founder's assemblages of French decorative arts; European paintings from the 17C to the 20C; and works on paper.

Stop at the information desk in the glass-walled Entrance Hall to pick up a museum floor plan and schedule of the day's activities. The audioguide desk distributes tape-recorded tours in English or Spanish. Also in the hall are two theaters showing orientation **films** *(10min; recommended)*, a bookstore and other guest services.

The museum occupies five pavilions of two to three stories around an open courtyard. The four main pavilions are arranged chronologically: North (pre-17C art), East (17C–18C), South (17C–19C) and West (19C–20C).

WIthin each pavilion, sculpture and decorative arts of the period occupy the lower level; paintings are displayed on the upper level.

The **Exhibitions Pavilion** houses temporary exhibits, as does the **Getty Research Institute for the History of Arts and the Humanities**.

North Pavilion – Courtyard-level exhibits cover 16C European bronzes, including works by Cellini and Campagna; 15C–16C European ceramics; German and Italian glasswork; and **illuminated manuscripts★★**. On the upper level are

J. Paul Getty Museum courtyard

© Brigitta L. House/MICHELIN

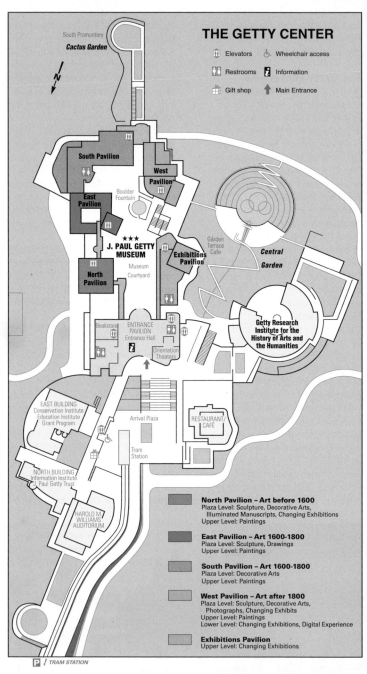

THE GETTY CENTER

- 🛗 Elevators
- ♿ Wheelchair access
- 🚻 Restrooms
- ℹ️ Information
- 🎁 Gift shop
- ⬆️ Main Entrance

South Promontory
Cactus Garden

South Pavilion

West Pavilion

Boulder Fountain

East Pavilion

Garden Terrace Cafe

Central Garden

★★★
J. PAUL GETTY MUSEUM

Exhibitions Pavilion

North Pavilion

Museum Courtyard

Getty Research Institute for the History of Arts and the Humanities

Bookstore

ENTRANCE PAVILION
Entrance Hall

Orientation Theaters

EAST BUILDING
Conservation Institute
Education Institute
Grant Program

Arrival Plaza

RESTAURANT/ CAFÉ

Tram Station

NORTH BUILDING
Information Institute
J. Paul Getty Trust

HAROLD M. WILLIAMS AUDITORIUM

North Pavilion – Art before 1600
Plaza Level: Sculpture, Decorative Arts, Illuminated Manuscripts, Changing Exhibitions
Upper Level: Paintings

East Pavilion – Art 1600-1800
Plaza Level: Sculpture, Drawings
Upper Level: Paintings

South Pavilion – Art 1600-1800
Plaza Level: Decorative Arts
Upper Level: Paintings

West Pavilion – Art after 1800
Plaza Level: Sculpture, Decorative Arts, Photographs, Changing Exhibits
Upper Level: Paintings
Lower Level: Changing Exhibitions, Digital Experience

Exhibitions Pavilion
Upper Level: Changing Exhibitions

🅿️ / TRAM STATION

Italian Renaissance paintings such as Fra Bartolommeo's *The Rest on the Flight into Egypt with St. John the Baptist* (1509). Also here are works by Titian and Veronese.

East Pavilion – On the courtyard level are European sculpture and drawings from the Renaissance to the rococo. Exhibits on the upper level include

Baroque paintings and Rembrandt works such as *St. Bartholomew* (1661).

South Pavilion – On view in the courtyard level are Getty's French tapestries from the period of Louis XIV. Paneled rooms showcase French decorative arts. The **Régence Paneled Room** (1670–1720) features a marquetry floor. The **Régence Room** (1710–30) shifts from the overwrought elegance of Louis XIV's court toward lighter lines of white, gold and red. The **Rococo Paneled Room** (1730–55) features trailing vines, flowers, shells and water as favored motifs. The **Neoclassical Paneled Room** (1765–95) originally was the salon in a Paris residence.

On the upper level are works by British portraitist Thomas Gainsborough, Frenchman Jean-Baptiste Siméon Chardin and other European artists.

West Pavilion – Changing displays of European sculpture and Italian decorative arts are presented on the courtyard level, along with rotating exhibits from the Getty's photography and drawings collection.

The upper level concentrates first on early 19C Romantics, such as Goya and Géricault. The Impressionist collection features works by Renoir (*La Promenade*, 1870), Pissarro, Monet, Manet, Van Gogh (*Irises*, 1889) and others.

Gardens – Robert Irwin's 110-acre **Central Garden** crosses a ravine between the main museum and the Research Institute, and includes a stream and a waterfall. On the South Promontory, behind the South and West Pavilions, the **Cactus Garden** offers a marvelous view across greater Los Angeles.

Skirball Cultural Center★★

2701 N. Sepulveda Blvd., just off I-405.
Open year-round Tue–Fri noon–5pm, weekends 10am–5pm. Closed major national and Jewish holidays. $10, children $5 (free Thu). ✕♿🅿 *310-440-4500. www.skirball.org.*

Designed by renowned architect Moshe Safdie, the West Coast's preeminent Jewish cultural center and museum uses selections from its repository of artifacts and art objects to interpret the beliefs of the Jewish religion and chronicle the history of the faith up to the present.

To the left of the main entrance lies the permanent exhibit **Visions and Values: Jewish Life from Antiquity to America.** Beginning with a 19C Torah scroll, the Journeys section tells of cultural influences affecting the Jewish people. Sacred Time spotlights holidays such as Passover and Hanukkah, as well as the weekly Sabbath.

The Life Cycle focuses on the stages of life—birth, mitzvah, marriage and death—while Sacred Space explains symbolism in temples. Passage to America tells of the arrival of Jews in this country.

Large galleries on the upper level host temporary exhibits. On the ground floor, the fascinating **Noah's Ark** exhibit immerses visitors in the Bible story through a fantastical reproduction of the Ark and its occupants, with surprise happenings and interactions as part of the experience (*advance tickets suggested on weekends; 877-722-4849, or through the website*).

Will Rogers State Historic Park★

1501 Will Rogers State Park Rd., off Sunset Blvd., Pacific Palisades.
Open year-round daily 8am–dusk.
$8/vehicle. 🅿 *310-454-8212. www.parks.ca.gov.*

Radio commentator, newspaper columnist, humorist and movie star **Will Rogers** (1879–1935) purchased this 186-acre ranch in 1922. Dubbed the "Cowboy Philosopher" by his admirers, Rogers moved here permanently with his family in 1928; the ranch became a state park after Mrs. Rogers' death in 1944.

The grounds include a visitor center focusing on Rogers' life; the 31-room **ranch house** (*guided tours year-round Tue–Fri 11am, 1pm & 2pm; weekends 10am–4pm on the hour*), with original furnishings and Western memorabilia; stables; and riding and roping rings. Hiking trails lead into the mountains. On weekends from April to October, polo matches are held on the field below the house.

LOS ANGELES ENVIRONS
Watts Towers of Simon Rodia State Historic Park
Map p150-151. 1727 E. 107th St. (Watts). From downtown take Harbor Fwy. (I-110) south to I-105 east; exit north at Wilmington Ave. and follow signs. 213-847-4646. www.parks. ca.gov. Open by public tour (30min) only, on the hr & half hr, Thu–Sat 10.30am–3pm, Sun 12.30pm–3pm, except on rainy days. $7. Watts is subject to crime and gang activity. Avoid exploring beyond the immediate vicinity of the towers.

In the largely African-American neighborhood of Watts is a celebrated work of folk art, a symbol of the human spirit. Sabato (Simon) Rodia, an Italian immigrant construction worker, erected the group of sculptures between 1921 and 1954. He covered a complex framework of discarded pipes, bed frames and steel rods with bits of tile, shards of glass and pottery, and seashells. The tallest of the three slender spires measures 100ft.

In the adjacent **Arts Center** (*open Tue–Sat 10am–4pm, Sun noon–4pm; closed major holidays; 213-847-4646*), folk instruments and works by African-American artists are on view.

BURBANK
Map p.150-151.
This city, located in the eastern end of suburban Los Angeles' San Fernando Valley, was named in 1887 for Dr. David Burbank, one of its developers. The city is known as the site of several major film and television studios.

Warner Bros. Studios★
4301 W. Olive Ave. at Warner Blvd. Exit Ventura Fwy. (Rte. 134) eastbound at Pass Ave. or westbound at Alameda Ave.; go to Hollywood Way, turning south across Olive Ave. Follow signs to Gate 6 parking area. Visit by guided tour (2hrs) only, year-round Mon–Fri 8.20am–4pm. $45. Reservations suggested in peak season by calling 866-777-8932 or at www.wbstudiotour. com. ($5) 818-972-8687. www.wbsf.warnerbros.com.

Warner Bros. Studios VIP Tour

© Warner Bros. Entertainment

Since 1928 the 110-acre complex has been the headquarters of Warner Bros., the motion-picture company founded in 1912 by Sam, Harry, Albert and Jack Warner. Today its sound stages, office buildings and bungalows are in constant use for the production of movies, television programs and commercials.

Guided tours of the backlot offer a no-frills walk through outdoor and indoor sets, prop rooms, construction shops, and the **Warner Bros. Museum**, featuring changing memorabilia exhibits.

NBC Studios
3000 W. Alameda Ave. Exit Ventura Fwy. (Rte. 134) eastbound at Pass Ave. or westbound at Alameda Ave., and go east on Alameda to studio entrance on south side of road. Visit by guided tour (1hr) only, Mon–Fri 9am–3pm. $8.50. 818-840-3537. www.nbc.com.

This expansive complex serves as the West Coast headquarters of the National Broadcasting Company and home of its network-owned and -operated local station, KNBC.

SAN FERNANDO VALLEY
Map p.150.
Circumscribed by the Sierra Madre, the Santa Monica and San Gabriel mountains, the 235sq mi suburb is L. A.'s largest residential enclave. Most of its

22 contiguous towns, notable for tract housing and commercial strip malls, are part of the city of Los Angeles, though Burbank, Glendale and San Fernando are independent municipalities.

Los Encinos State Historic Park

16756 Moorpark St., Encino, one block north of Ventura Blvd. east of Balboa Blvd. ⏰*Open Wed–Sun 10am–5pm.* ✆*818-784-4849. www.los-encinos.org.*
The remaining 5-acres of Rancho del Encino (Oak Ranch) marks the site where the expedition party of Spanish explorer Gaspar de Portolá camped in 1769. Most prominent among several 19C buildings on the grounds are the **De La Ossa Adobe** (👁*guided tours available Wed, Sat, Sun 2pm*), an eight-room ranch house built in 1850 and the **Garnier Building**, a two-story limestone Greek Revival farmhouse built in 1872, now restored to contain a visitor center and exhibits on local history.

San Fernando Rey de España Mission

15151 San Fernando Mission Blvd., Mission Hills. Exit San Diego Fwy. (I-405) east or Golden State Fwy. (I-5) west at San Fernando Mission Blvd. and go .6mi to mission on north side. ⏰*Open year-round daily 9am–4.30pm.* ⊕*$4.* ♿✆*818-361-0186.*
The 17th California mission was founded in 1797. After secularization in 1834, the mission's buildings fell into ruin. Restoration began in 1916.
The largest extant mission building in California, the restored **convento** holds original guest and missionary quarters (1822). The church is an exact replica of the original 1806 structure.

Ronald Reagan Presidential Library Museum

40 Presidential Dr., Simi Valley. Take San Diego Fwy. (I-405) or Golden State Fwy. (I-5) north, then Simi Valley-San Fernando Fwy. (Rte. 118) west; exit on Madera Dr. S. and turn right, continue 3mi to Presidential Dr. and proceed uphill. ⏰*Open year-round daily 10am–5pm.* ⏰*Closed Jan 1, Thanks-giving Day, Dec 25.* ⊕*$12, children $3.* ✖♿🅿 ✆*805-577-4000 or 800-410-8354. www.reaganlibrary.com.*
This 153,000sq ft facility (1991) houses the archives of the 40th US president. Mission-style elements are evident in its exterior; within, interactive exhibits highlight Reagan's life from boyhood through his two presidential terms (1981–89). You can visit a replica of the White House Oval Office and walk aboard the retired **Air Force One**, the specially outfitted jet that served seven presidents, housed it its own pavilion. A section of the Berlin Wall (colorfully painted on the former west side, gray on the east) is on permanent display here. The 29-acre hilltop perch affords gorgeous **views**★ of the Simi Valley the Tehachapi Mountains and the ocean.

EXCURSIONS
Six Flags Magic Mountain★

👥*30mi north of Los Angeles In Valencia. Take Golden State Fwy. (I-5) north to Magic Mountain Pkwy. exit.* ⏰*Open May–mid-Sept daily, hrs vary. Rest of the year weekends & school holidays only.* ⏰*Closed Dec 25.* ⊕*$59.99, children under 48in $29.99.* ✖🅿*($15)* ✆*661-255-4100. www.sixflags.com.*
This family-oriented amusement park in the western foothills of the Santa Clarita Valley features three dozen rides: most popular are thrill rides like the wood-framed roller coaster **Colossus**; and tubular-steel roller coasters like **Ninja**, **Viper**, **Revolution**, **The Riddler's Revenge** and the giant **Goliath**. Smaller children gravitate to **Bugs Bunny World**, with its gentler, fairground-style rides.

Six Flags Hurricane Harbor

👥 ⏰*Open Memorial Day–Labor Day daily, hrs vary; May & rest of Sept weekends only, hrs vary.* ⊕*$29.99, children under 48in $20.99.* ✖🅿*($15).* ✆*661-255-4111. www.sixflags.com.*
Adjoining Magic Mountain, this water park offers lagoons from an imaginary lost world. Water features carry such names as **Lizard Lagoon**, **Bamboo Racer** and **Black Snake Summit**.

ANTELOPE VALLEY

A vast expanse some 100mi north of downtown Los Angeles, the 3,400sq mi Antelope Valley lies in the southwest corner of the **Mojave Desert**.

The Shoshonean, Yokut, Chumash and Gabrieleño cultures shared this valley, where antelopes roamed, but probably not in great numbers. In the early 20C the **California Aqueduct** cut along its southern edge. Today a growing commuter suburb is centered in Lancaster and Palmdale. Yearly, the 1,745-acre **Antelope Valley California Poppy Reserve** presents mass displays of the official state flower *(visitor center ⊙open late Mar–early May Mon–Fri 9am–4pm, weekends 9am–5pm; ⊜ $5/vehicle; 🅿 ℘661-724-1180; www.parks.ca.gov).*

Malibu★

Stretching along 27mi of coastline where the Santa Monica Mountains meet the Pacific, Malibu attracts a casual crowd of beachgoers and resident glitterati to its restaurants and shops, arrayed mainly along the Pacific Coast Highway, the "PCH."

▸ **Population:** 13,041.
◔ **Michelin Map:** 585 B 10 and map p150–151.

A BIT OF HISTORY

The name Malibu is derived from the Chumash word *humaliwo*, thought to mean "the surf sounds loudly."

In 1892 businessman Frederick Hastings Rindge established a country retreat and cattle ranch here; the property was later developed as the exclusive residential **Malibu Colony**, today populated by Hollywood stars and their multimillion-dollar homes.

Public beaches abound, and coastline views are accessible from turnouts along Malibu Canyon, Latigo Canyon and Kanan Dume roads, which lead north from the PCH. Corral Canyon Road ends 6mi inland at Malibu Creek State Park, which offers a sweeping **view**★★ of Santa Monica Bay.

SIGHTS

J. Paul Getty Museum at the Getty Villa★★★

17985 Pacific Coast Hwy., between Sunset & Topanga Canyon Blvds. ⊙Visit by timed-entry reservation only, Thu–Mon 10am–5pm. ⊙Closed Jan 1, Jul 4, Thanksgiving Day, Dec 25. ✕&🅿($10 cash only). Call or go online for details & reservations ℘310-440-7300. www.getty.edu.

Sequestered in a lushly landscaped 64-acre canyon, this re-creation of a 1C BC Roman villa replicates one that was completely buried during the eruption of Mt. Vesuvius in AD 79. The building was erected in 1974 to house the art collections of **J. Paul Getty**, one of the 20C's wealthiest American businessmen. It serves as a center for the conservation and appreciation of antiquities, as well as a showcase for Getty 's outstanding collection of Greek, Roman and Etruscan art.

Visit

At the Entry Pavilion, pick up a site plan and a schedule of the day's tours and gallery talks. Getty Guide audio wands are also available for self-guided tours. An orientation film *(12min)* is shown in the museum theater every 15min. The permanent collection encompasses over 44,000 works, of which 1,200 are displayed in themed galleries on two floors within the Villa *(entrance opposite the outdoor theater)*. Highlights include the Lansdowne Herakles, a life-size statue found at Tivoli; the Marbury Hall Zeus; and the Elgin Throne theater chair. Jewelry, wall fragments, vessels and storage jars, busts and small sculptures round out the works on view. The **Timescape Room** provides a visual overview of the antiquities from the perspective of time, place and style. In the interactive **Family **Forum**, visitors can handle and draw ancient artifacts. The gardens, especially the **Outer Peristyle**★★★ with its long reflecting pool, enhance the magnificence of the villa.

Adamson House and Malibu Lagoon Museum

23200 Pacific Coast Hwy., 12mi west of Santa Monica. House accessible by ◄‿ *guided tour (1hr) only, year-round Wed–Sat 11am–3pm (last tour 2pm).* ◐*Closed Jul 4, Thanksgiving Day, Dec 25.* ◉*$5.* ℘*310-456-8432. www.adamsonhouse.org.*

Overlooking the Malibu Lagoon and the Pacific Ocean from a 13-acre garden setting, the two-story Spanish Colonial Revival house (1929, Stiles Clements) was built for the daughter and son-in-law of Frederick and May Rindge. Colorful **tilework**★★ from Malibu Pot-teries enlivens both the exterior and the furnished interior, and adorns a Moorish-style star fountain in the gardens. Adjoining the house is a small museum devoted to local history from the Native American period to the present.

Pepperdine University

24255 Pacific Coast Hwy., 13.5mi northwest of Santa Monica. ℘*310-506-4000. www.pepperdine.edu.*

From its perch in the Santa Monica foothills, Pepperdine commands a memorable view of the Pacific coastline.

Visitors are welcome to drive through the modern campus of this private Christian institution, built in the early 1970s. Of note is the **Weisman Museum of Art** (℘*310-506-4851;* ◐*open Tue–Sun 11am–5pm*), which presents rotating exhibits of 20C California artists.

Pasadena★★

Located less than 9mi from downtown Los Angeles, Pasadena seems a world away from the bustle and sprawl of its neighbor. Bordered to the west by the Arroyo Seco, a "dry gulch" of the San Gabriel Mountains, the city moves at a leisurely pace and boasts architecture, cultural attractions and civic events worthy of a much larger city.

A BIT OF HISTORY

Pasadena (derived from an Indian word meaning "crown of the valley") was born in 1874 when Indiana farmers were induced to grow citrus here by an orange grove association. Their efforts failed, but within decades, railroads connected Pasadena to Chicago and the East, and the community became a winter resort for the wealthy.

In 1889 Pasadena's elite Valley Hunt Club voted to mark New Year's Day with an annual parade of flower-decked coaches. Over the years the carriages evolved into elaborate floats covered with flowers, and in 1916 a college football match was

▶ **Population:** 133,936.
⊙ **Michelin Map:** 585 B 10 and map p150–151.
▯ **Info:** ℘626-795-9311. www.pasadenacal.com.
▷ **Location:** Pasadena lies just northeast of downtown via the 110 Freeway. The Huntington Library is located in neighboring San Marino.
◐ **Timing:** Visit the Huntington Library first (allow 4hrs), arriving at noon when it opens. The Norton Simon Museum remains open until 9pm on Friday. If you have 2 days, visit the Arboretum and the Huntington the first day, and the Norton Simon and Gamble House (open Thu–Sun) the second day.

held, pairing the winners of the Big Ten and (now) Pac-10 conferences. Today the **Rose Parade** and the **Rose Bowl Game** are televised across North America.

SIGHTS
Norton Simon Museum★★★
411 W. Colorado Blvd. ⏰Open year-round Wed–Mon noon–6pm (Fri 9pm). ⏰Closed Jan 1, Thanksgiving Day, Dec 25. ⬤$8 (free after 6pm first Fri/mth). ✕♿🅿 *✆626-449-6840. www.nortonsimon.org.*

Elegantly displayed in a contemporary building overlooking Pasadena's main thoroughfare are selections from one of the world's choicest private art collections spanning seven centuries of European art and 2,000 years of Asian sculpture.

Through the mid-20C, entrepreneur **Norton Simon** (1907–93) built a multinational corporation that included Hunt-Wesson Foods and Canada Dry Corp. He began collecting paintings in 1954, beginning with canvases by Gauguin, Bonnard and Pissarro. A visit to New Delhi in 1971 inspired him to collect Asian art. At his death, Simon had amassed more than 11,000 pieces with strengths in 14C–18C European art, French Impressionist paintings, the works of Edgar Degas and Southeast Asian sculpture.

In the late 1960s, Simon loaned works to major museums, including exhibits of 19C and 20C sculpture to the financially troubled Pasadena Art Museum. In 1974 Simon's foundations took over that museum, reestablishing it as a permanent home for his collections and renaming it for its benefactor.

Visit
14C–18C European Paintings – *To the right of the main entrance.* Outstanding among the collection's earliest works are *Madonna and Child with Book* (c.1503-04) by Raphael; *The Coronation of the Virgin* (1344), an altarpiece by Guariento di Arpo, who introduced the Gothic style into Venetian painting; and two life-size depictions of *Adam and Eve* (c.1530) by Lucas Cranach the Elder. Baroque canvases from the 17C include works by Jan Steen, Frans Hals, Francisco de Zurbarán and Peter Paul Rubens, as well as Rembrandt's *Self Portrait* (1636–38). Paintings in the Rococo style of the 18C include works by Jean-Honoré Fragonard. An additional gallery displays monumental paintings from that period, including Canaletto's *The Piazzetta, Venice, Looking North* (1730s); Tiepolo's *The Triumph of Virtue and Nobility Over Ignorance* (c.1740–50), originally a ceiling painting; and Goya's fervently spiritual *St. Jerome in Penitence* (1798).

19C–20C European paintings – *To the left of the main entrance.* Holdings are strong in works by French Impressionists: Renoir's *The Artist's Studio, rue Saint-Georges* (1876), Monet's *The Artist's Garden at Vétheuil* (1881), Van Gogh's *Portrait of the Artist's Mother* (1888) and *The Mulberry Tree* (1889), as well as Degas' best-known sculpture, *The Little Dancer* (1878–81). Also well represented here are Picasso (*Woman With a Book*, 1932), Daumier, Manet, Pissarro, Toulouse-Lautrec, Gauguin, Vuillard,

Norton Simon Museum's front entrance

Cézanne, Matisse, Modigliani, Braque, Klee and Kandinsky.

Southeast Asian Sculpture – *Stairwell rotunda and lower level galleries.* Selections from the museum's extensive holdings of Jain, Buddhist and Hindu sculptures from India are displayed on a rotating basis, along with Buddhist and Hindu sculptures from the Himalayas, Thailand, Cambodia and Vietnam, and Nepalese watercolors. A small Asian sculpture garden adjoins the galleries. In the museum's forecourt, throughout its galleries and in the **sculpture garden** are works by 19C and 20C sculptors, most notably Auguste Rodin (studies of the *Burghers of Calais*, 1884–95), Aristide Maillol and Henry Moore.

Gamble House★★

4 Westmoreland Pl., paralleling the 300 block of N. Orange Grove Blvd. Visit by guided tour (1hr) only, year-round Thu–Sun noon–3pm. Closed major holidays. $10. Ticket office in bookstore adjacent to house. 626-793-3334. www.gamblehouse.org.

Considered a masterpiece of the Arts and Crafts movement and the finest surviving home designed by famed Pasadena-based architects Charles and Henry Greene, this 8,100sq-ft house was built in 1907–09 as the winter family residence of David B. Gamble, heir of the Procter & Gamble soap company.

Covered in redwood shingles, the sprawling, two-story gabled "bungalow" and its contents exemplify the Greene brothers' dedication to fine craftsmanship and integrated design. Wide overhanging eaves shelter broad verandas, while 15 exterior doors and lots of windows ensure cross-ventilation. The **interior** abounds with decorative masterworks executed by John and Peter Hall, including furnishings and intricate woodwork incorporating some 20 types of wood. The stained-glass windows were created by Emile Lange.

Fans of Arts & Crafts-style architecture might like to drive along **Westmoreland Place** and nearby **Arroyo Terrace** and **Grand Avenue**, to see eight more examples of Greene & Greene bungalows in varying states of preservation.

Rose Bowl★

1001 Rose Bowl Dr. 626-577-3101. www.rosebowlstadium.com.

Set on the floor of the Arroyo Seco with views of the surrounding San Gabriel Mountains, this famed oval stadium (1922, Myron Hunt), measuring 880ft by 695ft, was originally horseshoe-shaped. Its south end was enclosed in 1932, and later modifications enlarged it to its current capacity of 92,542. Annual New Year's Day site of the Rose Bowl Game, it is also the home stadium for UCLA football and other events.

Tournament House and Wrigley Gardens

391 S. Orange Grove Blvd. Gardens open year-round daily dawn–dusk. House visit by guided tour (1hr) only, Feb–Aug Thu 2pm–4pm (last tour 3pm). 626-449-4100. www.tournamentofroses.com.

This Italian Renaissance mansion (1911) was owned by chewing-gum magnate William Wrigley, Jr. The house, now headquarters for the Tournament of Roses Association, is notable for its lavish, well-maintained grounds. Rose beds surround the terrace, pergola and gazebo fountain; lawns are planted with palms, coast redwood, Norfolk Island pine, Moreton Bay fig, eucalyptus and southern magnolias.

Pacific Asia Museum

46 N. Los Robles Ave. Open year-round Wed–Sun 10am–6pm. Closed Jan 1, Thanksgiving Day & Dec 25. $9 (free 4th Fri of the month). 626-449-2742. www.pacificasiamuseum.org.

This two-story building (1924) mimics the Chinese Imperial Palace style. The permanent collection of more than 14,000 works dating back 5,000 years includes Chinese, Japanese, Indian, Korean, Southeast Asian and Pacific Island artworks and cultural objects. Completed in 1979, the **courtyard garden★** is one of the few authentic Chinese gardens in the US.

Pasadena Museum of History

470 W. Walnut St. at N. Orange Grove Blvd. Mansion ☞ House visit by guided tour (1hr) only, Oct–Jul Wed–Fri 1pm, weekends 1.30 & 3pm; Aug–Sept by reservation only Thu–Sun. ☎$4. ⏰*Museum open year-round Wed–Sun noon–5pm. ☎$5. 🅿 ☏626-577-1660. www.pasadenahistory.org.*

The 18-room Fenyes Estate (1906) boasts original furnishings and paintings on its main floor. Archival photos are in the basement library, where historical exhibits also are presented. A Finnish folk-art collection is maintained in the adjacent former sauna house.

Pasadena Museum of California Art

490 E. Union St. ⏰*Open year-round Wed–Sun noon–5pm.* ⏰*Closed Jan 1, Jul 4, Thanksgiving Day, Dec 25. ☎$7 (free 1st Fri of the month). 🅿 ☏626-568-3665. www.pmcaonline.org.*

This three-story museum showcases changing exhibits of California art, architecture and design, from 1850 to the present. Enter the museum by way of a dramatic open-air staircase. A special highlight is a garage gallery spray-painted in whimsical cartoon designs by Pop artist Kenny Scharf.

AROUND PASADENA
Huntington Library, Art Collections and Botanical Gardens★★★

📍Map p197. 1151 Oxford Rd., San Marino. Take Allen Ave. south from E. Colorado or E. California Blvds. ⏰*Open late May–early Sept Wed–Mon 10.30am–4.30pm; rest of the year Mon & Wed–Fri noon–4.30, weekends 10.30am–4.30pm.* ⏰*Closed major holidays. ☎$15 (weekends & holiday Mon $20). ✕♿🅿 ☏626-405-2100. www.huntington.org.*

This distinguished cultural institution comprises one of the world's finest research libraries of rare books and manuscripts; a world-class collection of 18C and 19C British art, along with French and American works; and internationally renowned botanical gardens. Estab-lished in 1928 in the upscale Pasadena suburb of San Marino, the Huntington occupies 207 acres of the former ranch established by rail tycoon **Henry E. Huntington** (1850–1927) and his wife Arabella.

Huntington began his career in the employ of his uncle, railroad magnate Collis P. Huntington. After his uncle died, Henry settled in Los Angeles, where he made his fortune expanding the Pacific Electric Railway.

In 1902 he bought a working ranch, commissioning a Beaux-Arts style residence and a library, and hiring landscape gardener William Hertrich. At age 63, Huntington retired to devote his life to collecting books and art. One of America's more notable collectors, Arabella Duvall Huntington, his uncle's widow, became his second wife.

Library★★

The building (1920, Myron Hunt) houses some 6 million manuscripts, rare books and reference works, with an emphasis on British and American history, literature, art, science and technology from the 11C to the present. While most of the library's space is devoted to closed stacks and research facilities, the exhibition hall displays about 200 outstanding pieces from the collection. Highlights include the **Ellesmere Chaucer**, an illustrated manuscript (c.1410) of *The Canterbury Tales*; a **Gutenberg Bible** (c.1450); a **First Folio** of Shakespeare's plays; four volumes of *Birds of America* by **John James Audubon**; and handwritten letters by Benjamin Franklin, George Washington, Thomas Jefferson, Abraham Lincoln, Mark Twain and other famous Americans. The Dibner Hall of the History of Science offers a fascinating exploration of great scientific achievements in astronomy, natural history, medicine and light.

Huntington Art Gallery★★

Works focus on 18C–19C British art and 18C French art. The collection of **British art★★★** is considered among the finest outside London, particularly for its grouping of late-18C life-size, full-length portraits by Sir Joshua Reynolds, Thomas

Gainsborough, George Romney and Sir Thomas Lawrence. Most notable among these are Gainsborough's *Jonathan Buttall: "The Blue Boy"* (c.1770); Lawrence's *Sarah Barrett Moulton: "Pinkie"* (1794); and Reynolds' *Sarah Siddons as the Tragic Muse* (1784). Another highlight is a collection of English miniature portraits (late 16C to early 19C), along with early-16C English silver pieces.

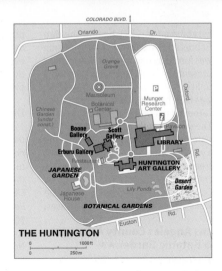

Orlando

COLORADO BLVD.

Dr.

Orange Grove

Mausoleum

Munger Research Center

Chinese Garden (under const.)

Botanical Center

Oxford

Boone Gallery

Scott Gallery

Pavilion

Erburu Gallery

LIBRARY

Restaurant

HUNTINGTON ART GALLERY

Rd.

JAPANESE GARDEN

Lily Ponds

Desert Garden

Japanese House

BOTANICAL GARDENS

Euston

Rd.

THE HUNTINGTON

0   1000ft
0   250m

Virginia Steele Scott Gallery –
This small gallery spotlights American art from the 18C to the early 20C, including works by Gilbert Stuart, John Singleton Copley, John Singer Sargent, Robert Henri, Thomas Moran, Mary Cassatt, John Sloan and Edward Hopper, among others. A separate room presents early-20C decorative pieces and room settings by Arts and Crafts architect-designers Charles and Henry Greene (&see Gamble House).

Adjacent to the Scott Gallery is the **Lois and Robert F. Erburu Gallery**, displaying selections from the Huntington's expanding collection of American works.

George and MaryLou Boone Gallery
Housed in a carriage house (1911) that once sheltered Henry Huntington's early automobiles, the Boone Gallery presents changing exhibits of American and English art, rare books and manuscripts.

Botanical Gardens★★
Covering 150 acres, the gardens include 14,000 species and cultivars, all labeled and presented in 15 thematic groupings. The 11-acre **desert garden** presents one of the world's largest outdoor collections of mature cacti and succulents, with more than 4,000 species. The terraced **Japanese garden**★ encompasses a koi pond and moon bridge, a traditional Japanese house, a Zen garden and bonsai trees. Both the rose and camellia gardens feature more than 1,400 cultivars of their species. Other gardens display lily ponds, Australian plants and subtropical species, and there's a sizable Chinese garden near the Boone Gallery.

San Gabriel Arcángel Mission★
428 S. Mission Dr., San Gabriel. From the Foothill Fwy. (I-210) in east Pasadena, take Sierra Madre Blvd. south, cross Huntington Dr. onto San Marino Ave.; turn right on Junipero Serra Dr. to Mission Dr. ◷*Open year-round daily 9am–4.30pm.* ◷*Closed major holidays.* ⊗*$5.* ♿ᴾ*626-457-3035. www.sangabrielmission.org.*

Sarah Barrett Moulton: "Pinkie" (1794) by Sir Thomas Lawrence, Huntington Art Gallery

© The Huntington

Established in 1771 beside the San Gabriel River, California's fourth mission was forced by flooding to relocate to its present site in 1775. By 1805, a church unlike any other in the mission chain was built here, inspired by the Moorish cathedral in Cordova, Spain.

The grounds hold remnants of a water cistern and an aqueduct; a kitchen and a winery share the courtyard with olive trees dating from 1860. The cemetery (1778) is the oldest in Los Angeles County. The church exterior has adobe walls supported by capped buttresses.

Los Angeles County Arboretum & Botanic Garden★★

301 N. Baldwin Ave. at I-210, Arcadia. ◷*Open year-round daily 9am–4.30pm.* ◷*Closed Dec 25.* ⌨*$7 (free 3rd Tue of the month).* ✕♿🅿 ℘*626-821-3222. www.arboretum.org.*

Set against the San Gabriel Mountains, the 127-acre arboretum features 30,000 plants, largely arranged by continent of origin. Highlights include 150 species of eucalyptus and one of the largest collections of orchids in the US. The centerpiece is the spring-fed lake.

Descanso Gardens★

1418 Descanso Dr., La Cañada-Flintridge. Take Foothill Fwy. (I-210) 3.7mi northwest from Pasadena; exit and turn left at Foothill Blvd. for 1.3mi, then left on Verdugo Blvd. and left on Descanso Dr. ◷*Open year-round daily 9am–4.30pm.* ◷*Closed Dec 25.* ⌨*$8.* ✕♿🅿 ℘*818-949-4200. www.descansogardens.org.*

Nestled in the San Rafael Hills, this 160-acre botanical haven features a five-acre rosarium boasting 5,000 roses; a **camellia forest**★ *(in bloom Jan–Mar)*; and a Japanese **tea house** with traditional gardens and a koi fish pond.

Santa Monica★

Santa Monica is a thriving urban center that hosts a wide array of cultural and commercial activities, yet maintains a seaside ambience and casual lifestyle.

A BIT OF HISTORY

Legend pins the city's name on 18C Spanish missionaries, who likened the trickling water of natural springs to the 40 tears of St. Monica as she mourned her heretical son, Augustine. Registered as a townsite in 1875, Santa Monica developed as a beachfront community, known for grand hotels, summer estates, beach clubs and amusement parks. Land values skyrocketed with the completion of the Santa Monica Freeway in 1966. Today the city is one of Southern California's leading arts and entertainment centers. Visitors and residents throng the **Third Street Promenade**★, an outdoor pedestrian mall (*3rd St. between Wilshire Blvd. & Broadway; www.downtownsm.com*), and **Santa Monica Place** (1979), an innovatively designed shopping center by architect Frank Gehry.

▷ **Population:** 89,552.
♿ **Michelin Map:** 585 B 10 and map pp150–151.
🛈 **Info:** ℘310-319-6263. www.downtownsm.com.
◖ **Location:** Santa Monica is situated on the Pacific coast and inland, 13mi west of downtown Los Angeles.
👪 **Kids:** The Pier and the broad, sandy beach.

SIGHTS

Santa Monica Pier★★

👪 *Western end of Colorado Ave. www.santamonicapier.org.*

Jutting 1,000ft out over the ocean, this wooden pier has been a landmark and gathering place since the early 1890s. It holds an antique **carousel**★, arcades, curio shops, food stands, fishing decks and an amusement park. The pier also affords **views**★ of the coastline of Malibu to the north, and the Palos Verdes Peninsula to the south. **Pacific Park** *(www.pacpark.com)*, a small collection of carnival rides, draws thrill-seekers to the large Ferris wheel. You can also ride a carousel, play games in the arcade, or visit the octopus and other sea creatures in the small aquarium located on the beach beneath the pier *(open Tue–Fri 2pm–6pm, weekends 12.30pm–6pm; closed holidays; $5; children free; 310-541-1500; www.healthebay.org).* Santa Monica's renowned sunset **views**★★ are best seen from **Palisades Park** *(adjacent to the pier)*, a stretch of green grass, palm trees and benches.

California Heritage Museum

2612 Main St. Open year-round Wed–Sun 11am–4pm. Guided tours available. Closed Jan 1, July 4, Thanksgiving Day, Dec 25. $5. 310-392-8537. www.california heritagemuseum.org.

This Queen Anne home (1894) was built for Roy Jones, son of city founder Senator John P. Jones. The structure was moved to its present site in 1977 and completely restored. Today it functions as a museum of life in California, with whimsically curated shows displayed throughout the building's three levels.

Bergamot Station Arts Center★

2525 Michigan Ave. at Olympic Blvd. Most galleries open Tue–Fri 10am–6pm, Sat 11am–5.30pm. 310-829-5854. www.bergamotstation.com.

This renovated trolley depot has been subdivided into 5.5 acres of contemporary art, architecture and design studios, as well as film-production facilities.
The largest of some 30 galleries is the **Santa Monica Museum of Art** *(open Tue–Sat 11am–6pm; $5 contribution requested; 310-586-6488; www.smmoa.org)*, with 10,000sq ft of space for temporary exhibits and performances.

Another highlight is the **Gallery of Functional Art** *(310-829-6990; www.galleryoffunctionalart.net)*, a living room-type installation displaying handcrafted home furnishings for sale.

EXCURSION
Venice and South Bay★

Map pp150–151.

A beachside community south of Santa Monica, Venice is one of the city's liveliest melting pots. Founded in 1904 as an artistic mecca modeled after Venice, Italy, it declined into a gaudy, bawdy seaside town that welcomed those who were down on their luck or embraced alternative lifestyles.

In the 1960s the community became a gathering place for local hippies, and today **Venice Beach**★★ is popular for its colorful street life, particularly along **Ocean Front Walk**, a beachside pedestrian thoroughfare.

On sunny days, the promenade is filled with folksingers and rappers, comic jugglers and swimsuit-clad skaters, muscle-bound weightlifters, vacationers and vagrants. In a recent return to its roots, Venice has also become a popular location for the studios of leading local artists.

South Bay – South along the coastline from Venice is the community of **Marina del Rey**, home to some 10,000 private sailboats and motor yachts. From **Fishermen's Village** *(13755 Fiji Way; 310-823-5411)* shopping complex you can hop aboard a harbor cruise.

The stretch of beach extending south from Marina del Rey is known as South Bay. Its three distinctive communities, well-known among the surf and volleyball set, are **Manhattan Beach**, **Hermosa Beach** and **Redondo Beach**. Manhattan is the most upscale of the three towns; Hermosa the most bohemian. Redondo's **Monstad Pier** is the biggest surfside boardwalk between Santa Monica and San Pedro.

North of San Francisco, and inland from the Pacific shore to the crest of the Coast Ranges, this swath of northern California embraces a dynamic medley of redwood forests, wild coastline, rugged mountains, charming towns and vineyards brimming over from the Wine Country. Western Marin County remains a favorite destination for day and weekend trippers from San Francisco, especially Sausalito, Muir Woods National Monument and Point Reyes National Seashore.

Highlights

1. Sighting a line of whales moving offshore at **Point Reyes National Seashore** (p205)
2. Tucking into a plate of flapjacks at the **Samoa Cookhouse** (p214)
3. Impulsively parking to walk among the trees along the **Avenue of the Giants** (p212)

Topography – The uplift of the Coast Ranges some 25 million years ago established a stern new coastline for California.

Today's many marine terraces, marking the shoreline of millennia past, are a visible legacy of this dramatic uplift that continues to raise the mountains. The ruggedness of these shores ensured their isolation for centuries after initial European exploration in the 16C.

Despite the claims of Sir Frances Drake for England in 1579, the Coast Miwok, Pomo, Yuki and other tribes lived vir-

tually untouched by the outside world until 1812, when the Russians established a colony at Fort Ross. Though Russian efforts were short-lived, they provoked greater interest in northern California from Mexican authorities, who parceled land grants in the Sonoma Valley in 1823.

Gold and Timber – While Sonoma prospered, the vast reaches to the north continued virtually unchanged until the discovery of gold on the Trinity and Klamath rivers sparked a rush of prospectors in 1850.

Thousands of outsiders established short-lived gold camps; more significantly, they discovered vast forests of huge coastal redwoods, a regional commodity more valuable than gold. The need for timber in California's burgeoning cities sparked the establishment not only of remote lumber camps throughout the northern mountains, but more importantly, of company milling towns like Scotia and coastal trading ports like Eureka, Arcata and Crescent City.

Marin Headlands

Preservation Efforts – As vast tracts of old-growth forest fell before loggers' saws, conservationists successfully lobbied the state government for the creation of parks to preserve the ancient trees. Only in 1968 did the federal government follow suit by establishing Redwood National Park. The increased strength of the environmental movement and reduction of old-growth tracts forced many lumber companies to close, though wood products still make up the preeminent industry throughout much of the Redwood Empire.

Tourism – Tourism continues to grow along California's northwestern coast, and is a mainstay of the regional economy in coastal towns along Highway 1.

Temperatures along the coast are moderate, with a year-round average high of 65°F. Most of the region's rain falls in winter; summer months bring frequent fog. The best times to visit are in spring, when the hillsides turn brilliant green and multicolored wildflowers festoon the meadows; and in fall, when the weather is apt to be dry and fine.

ADDRESSES

STAY

🍽️🛏️🛏️🛏️ **The Harbor House** – *5600 S. Hwy. 1, Elk.* 707-877-3203 *or* 800-720-7474. *www.theharborhouseinn.com. 10 rooms and cottages.* 🍴. This rural Craftsman-style house on the southern Mendocino coast, built atop rugged cliffs by lumber-company executives in 1916, offers luxurious lodgings and spectacular views. Rooms, with names like Redwood, Harbor and Meadowview, all sport a different decor. Four luxury cottages all have fireplaces and private ocean-view decks. Dinner-inclusive packages include nightly four-course prix-fixe menus in the **Seaside Dining Room** (🍽️🍽️🍽️), which complement California cuisine with an honored wine list.

🍽️🛏️🛏️🛏️ **Inn Above Tide** – *30 El Portal, Sausalito.* 415-332-9535 *or* 800-893-8433. *www.innabovetide.com. 29 rooms.* 🍴. Guest rooms at this inn, built over the water in tony Sausalito, boast large picture windows that frame spectacular views of San Francisco Bay (binoculars provided). Decorated in a seaside palette of soft blues and greens, rooms feature waterside decks; many have fireplaces. Rates include a continental breakfast delivered to your room and a sunset wine-and-cheese reception.

🍽️🛏️🛏️ **Joshua Grindle Inn** – *44800 Little Lake Rd., Mendocino. Two-night minimum stay on weekends and in Jul & Aug.* 707-937-4143 *or* 800-474-6353. *www.joshgrin.com. 12 rooms.* 🍴.

Two acres of colorful gardens surround this whitewashed 19C cottage overlooking the Pacific. A New England country feel pervades the guest rooms, furnished with Early American antiques, airy white lace curtains and handmade quilts. In addition to rooms in the main house, the inn offers lodgings in the historic wooden water tower and the saltbox cottage out back. Guests gather for breakfasts around the 1830 pine harvest table to compare sightseeing notes and feast on seasonal fruit, house-baked muffins and freshly prepared entrées like banana french toast and mushroom-crust quiche.

🍽️🛏️🛏️ **Mountain Home Inn** – *810 Panoramic Hwy., Mill Valley.* 415-381-9000. *www.mtnhomeinn.com. 10 rooms.* 🍴. High on the slopes of Mt. Tamalpais, this top-end bed-and-breakfast sits at a popular trailhead for hikers and mountain bikers. Most-requested rooms include the Canopy Room with a fireplace, Jacuzzi, vaulted ceilings and skylight; and the Mountain View Room, which offers sweeping vistas of Mt. Tamalpais and San Francisco Bay.

🍽️🛏️🛏️ **Mendocino Hotel & Garden Suites** – *45080 Main St., Mendocino.* 707-937-0511 *or* 800-548-0513. *www. mendocinohotel.com. 51 rooms.* Built in 1878, this restored structure is furnished with antiques and paintings. Victorian-style rooms sport porcelain sinks and brass beds, and some have bathrooms across the hall. Behind the house, modern garden suites have private bathrooms. **Dining room** (🍽️🍽️).

⊜⊜ **Gingerbread Mansion Inn** – *400 Berding St., Ferndale.* ☎*707-786-4000 or 800-952-4136. www.gingerbread-mansion.com. 11 rooms.* ⌣. Set in the National Historic Landmark village of Ferndale, this 1899 Victorian hotel is a wonder of turrets, spindles and gingerbread trim. Rooms are appointed with Victorian antiques and Battenburg lace comforters; some have fireplaces. Treat yourself to a stay in the regal, gold and black Empire Suite (⊜⊜⊜⊜), which boasts French doors with stained-glass insets, 12ft ceilings and a wet bar. The suite's spacious bath was made for luxuriating, with its two-person shower and claw-foot soaking tub. Rates include a full gourmet breakfast and afternoon tea.

⊻/ EAT

⊜⊜⊜ **Cafe Beaujolais** – *961 Ukiah St., Mendocino.* ☎*707-937-5614. www.cafebeaujolais.com.* **California French.** An 1893 farmhouse is the setting for this cafe, known for the purity and freshness of its ingredients. Locally grown organic produce, free-range meat and eggs, and locally caught seafood highlight the changing menu here. Artisanal breads are baked in wood-fired ovens at the restaurant's adjacent Brickery. A meal here might include roasted acorn squash and chipotle soup, oven-steamed Alaskan halibut, Niman Ranch top sirloin, or crimini mushroom polenta layered with greens and fontina cheese. Save room for the house-made fruit sorbets served with toasted almond cookies.

⊜⊜⊜ **Lark Creek Inn** – *234 Magnolia Ave., Larkspur.* ☎*415-924-7766. www.larkcreek.com. Dinner & Sun brunch only.* **American**. This charming Marin County restaurant occupies a spacious Victorian house surrounded by towering redwoods. Deft use of seasonal fresh produce yields elegant simplicity in dishes like Dungeness crab cakes, Sonoma duck breast, seared skate wing and roasted-chestnut ravioli. Weather permitting, Sunday brunch is served on the patio.

⊜⊜ **Mendo Bistro** – *301 N. Main St., Fort Bragg. Dinner only.* ☎*707-964-4974. www.mendobistro.com.* **American**. Located upstairs at the Company Store, Mendo Bistro serves a range of made-from-scratch dishes at affordable prices. Choose from the menu of house-made pastas, or pick your main ingredient (free-range chicken, pork tenderloin, local fish, portobello mushroom, tofu or steak), your preferred method of cooking (roasted, grilled, sautéed, fried or braised), and pair it with your choice of sauces. These main dishes are accompanied by mashed potatoes or polenta and seasonal vegetables.

⊜⊜ **Pelican Inn** – *10 Pacific Way at Rte. 1, Muir Beach.* ☎*415-383-6000. www.pelicaninn.com.* **Pub**. An authentic country inn and pub, the Pelican was established by a fourth-generation pub owner from Surrey, England. Pub fare and pints of British and Irish brews are served up in a low-beamed dining room and at a candlelit Tudor-style bar. Come mid-day Sunday for the traditional buffet of carved roast meats and salmon with plenteous vegetables and sides. The inn doubles as a bed-and-breakfast.

⊜⊜ **Fish** – *350 Harbor Dr., Sausalito.* ☎*415-331-3474. www.331fish.com.* **Seafood**. For the freshest catch of the day, this bayside, no-frills seafood shack on the harbor is hard to beat. Ask what's fresh, place your order at the counter, then find a picnic table or bench to enjoy your meal. The Marin specialty is barbequed local oysters. The fish parfait layers Dungeness crab with salsa fresca, tomatillo, lime crema and the house cocktail sauce. For kids, there's a variety of sandwiches.

⊜⊜ **Samoa Cookhouse** – *79 Cookhouse Rd., Eureka.* ☎*707-442-1659.* **American**. For more than a century, this "lumber camp-style" eatery has served three meals daily on platters and in big bowls, encouraging diners to help themselves and then pass the dishes around. What worked then for hungry lumberjacks still works for everyone today. After your meal, stop in at the on-site museum to see displays of antique logging equipment and 19C photographs from the timber industry.

Marin County★★

Marin County combines the sophisticated charm of Sausalito and the ancient redwoods of Muir Woods with the rugged seascapes of Point Reyes and the Marin Headlands. While some 240,000 suburbanites reside in this county, most settlement is on the eastern side of Mt. Tamalpais, leaving the coastal precincts in a largely natural state.

A BIT OF HISTORY

For thousands of years, the Marin area was home to the Coast Miwok Indians. Its first European visitor was purportedly Francis Drake, who set out from England in 1577 to reconnoiter Spanish defenses in the New World, but the British did not pursue their claim to the land and it became a Spanish colony. Mexicans grazed cattle here after they threw off the Spanish yoke in 1821; Americans logged the redwood forests nearly to depletion into the early 20C. During World War II, defenses were built along the Marin Headlands, and the Marinship naval shipyard employed thousands of workers. By the latter half of the 20C, upscale Marin County had become synonymous with the California lifestyle.

SIGHTS
Sausalito★

Map see SF. 4mi north of San Francisco. Take US-101 and exit at Alexander Ave.
This upscale residential community draws throngs of visitors to its winding streets and sophisticated boutiques, but the town has its bohemian element as well, in an eccentric community of houseboats, or **floating homes**.
Among its historic inns is the **Casa Madrona** *(801 Bridgeway; ☏415-332-0502; www.casamadrona.com)*, a much-enlarged and restored Victorian villa (1885) overlooking the Yacht Harbor.

Bridgeway Boulevard

Sausalito's main thoroughfare is the center of a commercial district that stretches several blocks in both directions from the ferry landing. Small,

 Michelin Map: 585 A 8; also see Mendocino and SF.

colorful, c.1900 buildings house restaurants, cafes, galleries and retail shops; the street affords **views★★** of San Francisco, and the bay islands. Stop in at the **Sausalito Visitor Center & Historical Exhibit** *(780 Bridgeway; ◷open year-round Tue–Sun 11.30am–4pm; ◷closed major holidays; ♿🅿 ☏415-332-0505; www.sausalito.org)*. Situated above the ferry landing is **Plaza Viña del Mar** *(Bridgeway & El Portal)*; its elephant-shaped light standards were designed for the 1915 Panama-Pacific International Exposition.
From Bridgeway, Princess Street *(south of Plaza Viña del Mar)* connects to winding Bulkley Avenue, where examples of Shingle-style architecture include **Sausalito Presbyterian Church** *(no. 112)*, completed in 1909 and designed by Ernest Coxhead.

Marinship
1mi north on Bridgeway to Marinship Way.
Ninety-three ships were built here during World War II in 1942–45. Artists and small manufacturers occupy part of the site today. The **Bay Model Visitor Center★** of the US Army Corps of Engineers *(2100 Bridgeway)* has a 1.5-acre hydraulic model of the San Francisco Bay, which simulates tidal flow through the estuary *(◷open Memorial Day–Labor Day Tue–Fri 9am–4pm, weekends 10am–5pm; rest of the year Tue–Sat 9am–4pm; ♿ ☏415-332-3871; www.spn. usace.army.mil/bmvc)*.

Marin Headlands★★
Take Alexander Ave. exit from northbound US-101; from ramp, turn left, then bear right onto Barry Rd.
This windswept landscape of coastal cliffs and hills at the north end of the Golden Gate Bridge is forms part of the Golden Gate National Recreation Area. **Conzelman Road** provides spectacular **views★★★** of San Francisco and the

bridge. The road terminates at **Point Bonita Lighthouse**★ (☉*open year-round Sat–Mon 12.30pm–3.30pm;* ⓟ *℘415-331-1540; www.nps.gov/goga/pobo.htm).*

The **Marin Headlands Visitor Center**★ (☉*open year-round daily 9.30am–4.30pm;* ☉*closed Thanksgiving Day, Dec 25;* ♿ ⓟ *℘415-331-1540; www.nps.gov/goga)* features displays on the headlands, and hiking trails thread the grassy slopes.

San Rafael Arcángel Mission

♿*Map see SF. 15mi north of San Francisco at 5th Ave. & A St., San Rafael. Take US-101 to Central San Rafael exit. Chapel* ☉*open daily 6am–4.30pm.* ☉*Closed holidays.* *℘415-456-3016.*

The 20th mission of the California chain was founded in 1817 as a branch, or *asistencia*, to Mission Dolores in San Francisco. It was also used as a sanitarium for San Franciscans in failing health. The buildings were razed in 1870; the current replica dates from 1949.

Mount Tamalpais State Park★★

20mi north of San Francisco. Take US-101 to Hwy. 1 (Shoreline Hwy.). Continue to Panoramic Hwy. and turn right, following signs to the park. ☉*Open year-round daily 7am–dusk.* ☉*Closed during high fire-risk days.* 🚌*$6/vehicle.* ⚠*(10-day advance reservations* *℘800-444-7275)* ⓟ *℘415-388-2070. www.parks.ca.gov.*

The serpentine ascent to the 2,572ft east peak of Mt. Tamalpais (tam-ul-PIE-us) is rewarded with **views**★★★ of San Francisco and the Pacific coastline.

Trails lace the mountain's flanks, drawing hikers and equestrians; the Pantoll ranger station *(junction of Pantoll Rd. and Panoramic Hwy.)* has maps and information on weather and trail conditions.

👥 Muir Woods National Monument★★★

▥*19mi north of San Francisco. Take US-101 to Hwy. 1 (Shoreline Hwy.). Continue to Panoramic Hwy. and turn right, then left on Muir Woods Rd.*

☉*Open year-round daily 8am–dusk.* 🚌*$5, children free.* ✕♿ⓟ *℘415-388-2595. www.nps.gov/muwo.*

This 560-acre plot of coast redwoods is one of the last virgin redwood forests in the Bay Area. Muir Woods became a national monument in 1908 after Congressman William Kent donated land to the US government, insisting the park be named for conservationist John Muir.

From the visitor center, the Main Trail *(1mi)* reaches **Cathedral Grove**, where trees as old as 1,000 years rise like spires. The return trail passes **Bohemian Grove**, site of the park's tallest tree, measuring 253ft *(tree is unmarked).*

A spur road from Hwy. 1, 3mi north of Panoramic Highway, leads to **Muir Beach Overlook**, where a platform affords **views**★★ of the coast.

Point Reyes National Seashore★★

♿*Map see Mendocino. 40mi N of SF. Take US-101 north to Green-brae Exit; turn west on Sir Francis Drake Blvd. for 10mi, then north on Hwy. 1 to 1st left at Bear Valley Rd.* ☉*Open year-round daily dawn–midnight.* ✕ⓟ *℘415-663-8522. www.nps.gov/pore.*

Spanish explorer Sebastián Vizcaíno in 1603 named the peninsula La Punta de los Reyes or "Point of the Kings."

An earthquake in 1906 thrust the peninsula—separated from the "mainland" by the San Andreas Fault—some 16ft to the northwest. In 1962 the 102sq mi park became a national seashore.

👥 Bear Valley Visitor Center★

Bear Valley Rd. west of Hwy. 1. ☉*Open year-round Mon–Fri 9am–5pm, weekends & holidays 8am–5pm.* ☉*Closed Dec 25.* ♿ⓟ *℘415-464-5100.*

This wood structure houses excellent exhibits on coastal wetlands, birdwatching and marine mammals. Near the visitor center, the **Earthquake Trail**★ *(0.6mi loop)* traces the San Andreas Fault. Another trail *(1mi round-trip)* leads to **Kule Loklo** 👥 (Miwok for "Bear Valley"), a re-created Miwok village with conical wooden structures and other artifacts to show how the Miwok lived.

Limantour Beach *(9mi from visitor center on Limantour Rd.)* is known for its **views** of the white cliffs of Point Reyes. This beach and Drakes Beach are open for swimming *(no lifeguards)*.

Point Reyes Peninsula

From the visitor center, turn left on Bear Valley Rd. and bear left on Sir Francis Drake Blvd.

Park Shuttles: *The Point Reyes Peninsula is an extremely popular place to visit during the winter whale-migration season when gray whales pass close to shore. To relieve traffic congestion on the peninsula, park shuttle buses make the loop from Drake's Beach to the Point Reyes Lighthouse parking lot and on to Chimney Rock during peak visit times (late Dec–mid-Apr weekends & holidays 9.30am–3pm; $5, children free). Purchase shuttle tickets at the Drake's Beach Visitor Center.*

Note that during shuttle operation periods, Sir Francis Drake Boulevard south of South Beach Junction is closed to private vehicles.

From Inverness Park, the road runs along Tomales Bay for 4.5mi, passing through **Inverness** with its quaint houses and gardens. The highway cuts west across treeless moors that terminate at Point Reyes. Mt. Vision Road *(turn left 1mi after Drake Blvd. turns west)* winds 2.3mi to an **overlook** that commands a **view**★★ across Drakes and Limantour beaches. The road continues 1.5mi to the summit of **Mount Vision** (1,282ft), where hikers may connect to several trails.

Point Reyes Beach

The 12mi strip comprising **North Beach** and **South Beach** *(follow Drake Blvd. southwest 4.7mi; turn right at sign)* faces northwest into the strongest winds and roughest ocean surf.

Nearby, **Drakes Beach** *(2mi east of South Beach)* is framed by high, chalk-white cliffs. A **visitor center** provides information and exhibits on the marine ecosystem *(open weekends & holidays only 10am–5pm; closed Dec25; ✗ ⚿ P 415-669-1250).*

Point Reyes Lighthouse

© John Anderson/MICHELIN

👥 Point Reyes Lighthouse★★

South end of Sir Francis Drake Blvd., 22mi from Bear Valley Visitor Center (0.5mi walk from parking lot to visitor center & lighthouse). Open year-round Thu–Mon 10am–4.30pm, weather permitting. Closed Dec 25. 415-669-1534. www.nps.gov/pore.

This beacon perches halfway down the 600ft precipice of Point Reyes. A flight of 308 steps *(closed in high winds)* descends to the lighthouse. The setting offers **views**★★★ southwest to the Farallon Islands. From the platform at nearby **Chimney Rock**, elephant seals may be spotted in season *(mid-Dec–Mar)*.

Tomales Point Area

From the Bear Valley visitor center, take Drake Blvd. 7.5mi north and turn right on Pierce Point Rd.

The spit of land extending north from Inverness borders Tomales Bay. At the end of Pierce Point Road lies **Pierce Point Ranch** 👥, a former dairy farm established in 1858 *(open year-round dawn–dusk; ⚿ P 415-464-5100)*.

At the south end of **McClure's Beach** *(turn left at end of Pierce Point Rd.; beach accessible by a steep .5mi dirt path)*, a narrow passageway through the rocks *(accessible only at low tide)* opens onto a pocket beach.

Mendocino-Sonoma Coast★★

Stretching 191mi from San Francisco to the intersection with US-101 at Leggett, Highway 1 snakes along the southern half of California's North Coast. Spectacular views abound of the roiling Pacific surf. Sleepy seaside towns and state parks dot the shoreline, which nurtures a variety of birds and marine animals.

A BIT OF HISTORY

As early as 10,000 BC, Coast Miwok, Pomo and Yuki tribes hunted and fished along this part of the coast. The Spanish claimed this region in the 16C, but left it unsettled, and so members of a Russian trading company met no resistance when they built Fort Ross here in 1812. As the 1850s gold rush dissipated, the "red gold" of the area's virgin redwood forests brought an influx of loggers. Residents still log, fish and farm here, but tourism is on the upswing as visitors discover the scenic vistas, pleasant beaches and pastoral peace of the coast.

🚗 DRIVING TOUR

116mi. ⊙Map this section.

Bodega

65mi north of San Francisco.
North of Point Reyes National Seashore, this hamlet is home to the building *(17110 Bodega Lane)* that served as the schoolhouse in Alfred Hitchcock's film *The Birds* (1962). Originally the Potter School (1873), the structure is now a private residence.

Bodega Bay

6mi west of Bodega. The largest protected small-boat anchorage between San Francisco and Noyo (south of Fort Bragg) bears the name of Spanish adventurer Juan Francisco de la Bodega y Cuadra, who explored here in 1775.

- **Michelin Map:** 585 A 7, 8 and map this section.
- **Info:** ℘866-466-3636. www.gomendo.com.
- **Location:** Amenities along this stretch of Highway 1 are limited. Bodega Bay, Gualala, Elk, Little River, Mendocino and Fort Bragg are good places to find lodging, restaurants and gas stations.
- **Timing:** Allow 2 days to enjoy this driving tour at a leisurely pace, overnighting in Menocino or Fort Bragg. Bear in mind that Point Arena Lighthouse closes at 3pm.
- **Kids:** The Skunk Train in Ft. Bragg.

On the far side of the bay rises **Bodega Head** *(turn left off Hwy. 1 on Eastshore Rd., north of Bodega Bay; 3mi to the park).* From the bluffs stretch **views**★ of the coast from Point Reyes to Fort Ross. Between January and May, the bluffs are a popular spot for whale watching.

Sonoma Coast State Beaches★

⊙*Open daily year-round. ☞$7/vehicle.* ⚠ *(reservations recommended ℘800-444-7275)* ♿🅿 ℘*707-875-3483.* www.parks.ca.gov.
Extending 16mi from Bodega Head to just north of Jenner, this strip of coast is great for fishing, hiking, camping and beachcombing. Some 15 sandy crescents punctuate the shoreline. **Duncan's Landing** *(5mi north of Bodega Dunes)* affords the most dramatic **views**★. Easily accessible is **Goat Rock Beach**★ *(8mi north of Bodega Dunes)*, at the mouth of the Russian River. Harbor seals vie with fishermen *(Nov–Mar)* to catch salmon that return to spawn.
North of Jenner, the road becomes a series of switchbacks winding high above the ocean *(average speed 25mph)*. Several miles north of Fort Ross, the road flattens out.

Fort Ross State Historic Park★★

22mi north of Bodega Bay. ⏰*Open year-round daily dawn–dusk. Fort & visitor center open daily 10am–4.30pm.* ⏰*Closed Thanksgiving Day, Dec 25.* ⚲*$7/vehicle.* ⚠♿🅿 ✆*707-847-3286. www.fortrossstatepark.org*

Established in 1812, Fort Ross reigned as Russia's easternmost outpost, from which colonists hunted sea otters. The fort has been partially restored to its early appearance. Costumed actors reenact scenes from fort history during Cultural Heritage Day *(last Sat in Jul).* The **visitor center** contains displays on fort history and on the Pomo tribes that first occupied the site. Most of the buildings are replicas; only the **Rotchev House** *(north wall)* is partially original. The **officials' quarters** *(southwest wall)* display artifacts. The small **chapel** was the first Russian Orthodox church in North America outside Alaska. In the stockade, two-story **blockhouses** were once armed with cannons against possible attack by the Spaniards.

Salt Point State Park

9mi. ⏰*Open year-round daily dawn–dusk. Visitor center open Apr–Oct weekends 10am–3pm.* ⚲*$7/vehicle.* ⏰*Closed during bad weather.* ⚠🅿 ✆*707-847-3221. www.parks.ca.gov.*

Named for the substance that Native Americans once collected from submarine crevices for preserving seafood, this 6,000-acre park encompasses an underwater sanctuary, the **Gerstle Cove Marine Reserve**, favored by divers. A short drive away at Fisk Mill Cove, a fern-lined path *(0.2mi)* winds uphill to a platform overlooking Sentinel Rock.

Kruse Rhododendron State Reserve

Entrance at right, 3mi north of Gerstle Cove. ⏰*Open year-round daily dawn–dusk.* 🅿 ✆*707-847-3221.*

Adjacent to Salt Point, the reserve protects 317 acres of coast rhododendron, which burst into bloom from April to June. Five miles of trails lead through the lush forest.

North of the reserve, Highway 1 skirts marine terraces where cattle graze. After some 7mi, the weathered-wood houses of **Sea Ranch**—a 5,000-acre, second-home community—appear tucked into meadows sloping down to the sea. The town of **Gualala** *(8mi north of Sea Ranch)* offers lodging and other amenities.

Point Arena Lighthouse★

15mi north of Gualala. Turn left on Lighthouse Rd. and continue 2.3mi to parking lot. ⏰*Open year-round daily 10am–3.30pm.* ⚲*$5.* ✆*707-882-2777. www.pointarenalighthouse.com.*

The approach to this lighthouse affords a **panorama**★ of high terraces carved by the Pacific. Built in 1870, the original brick lighthouse was damaged during the 1906 earthquake. Its replacement, made of steel-reinforced concrete, displays the original Fresnel lens, which

Fort Ross State Historic Park

© John Anderson/MICHELIN

flashed beams of light that could be seen 20mi from the coast. Next to the beacon, the former Fog Signal Building (1869) displays defunct compressed-steam foghorns and photographs of lighthouse history. Point Arena is a popular spot for whale watching during the migration season (Dec–Apr).

Van Damme State Park

28mi north of Point Arena, just past Little River. ◷*Open daily year-round.* *$6/vehicle.* ⚠ ♿ *707-937-5804. www.parks.ca.gov.*
The majority of the park's 2,160 acres falls on the inland side of the highway. Here, a short boardwalk loop *(10min)* threads a **pygmy forest**★, a phenomenon unique to the upper marine terraces in Mendocino County. These areas were once bogs; over centuries, acidic water leached nutrients from the soil, forming a hardpan layer just beneath the surface. The stunted plants that grow here, their roots unable to penetrate the hardpan to reach the water below, have adapted themselves to these conditions.

Big River State Park

2mi south of Mendocino. *707-962-0470. www.mendocinolandtrust.org.*
This 7,334-acre state park was created in 2002 when the Mendocino Land Trust purchased the Big River Estuary from a timber company, and transferred its title to the state park system. The park focuses on California's longest undeveloped estuary system. Laguna Marsh is among 1,500 acres of wetlands, a critical habitat for threatened species.

Mendocino★★

30mi north of Point Arena. www.mendocino.com.
Named for the first viceroy of New Spain, this Victorian village of quaint clapboard buildings appears little changed from its late 19C heyday as a lumber town.
Mendocino prospered until the 1920s, when loggers exhausted the timber supply. In 1959 the opening of the **Mendocino Art Center** brought an influx of artists who revived the sleepy village. Today shops and galleries cater to a sizable tourist trade, and the town's annual music and film festivals draw big crowds. Restaurants and wineries in the area also enjoy a growing reputation.
Main Street★ is home to the **Ford House Visitor Center and Museum** (◷*open year-round daily 11am–4pm;* *707-937-5397*), which has exhibits on area history, including a miniature model of the town in 1890.

Mendocino Headlands State Park★★

◷*Open daily year-round.* ⚠ *(reservations* *800-444-7275).* *$4/vehicle.* *707-937-5804. www.parks.ca.gov.*

Main Street, Mendocino

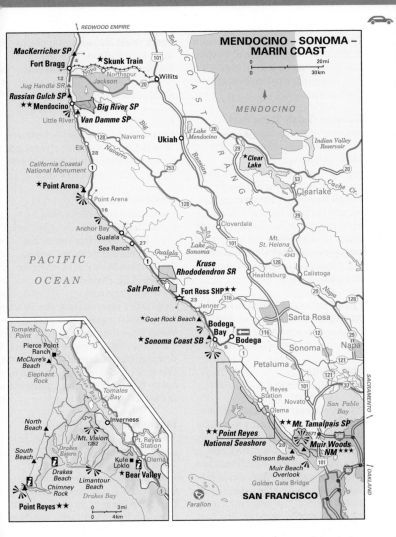

These headlands surrounding the town were saved from development by concerned residents. Paths reveal **views**★★ of the coast with its fissure-riddled rocks, sea caves and wildflowers in spring.

Kelley House Museum
45007 Albion St. ⏱*Open summer Thu–Mon 11am–3pm; rest of the year Fri–Mon 11am–3pm.* ᴗ*Guided tours (ᴗ$10) available weekends.* ⏱*Closed major holidays.* ᴗ*$2.* ☏*707-937-5791. www.kelleyhousemuseum.org*
Canadian entrepreneur William Kelley built this gabled redwood dwelling, one of the oldest in Mendocino, in 1861.

Today the headquarters of Mendocino Historical Research, Inc., the museum owns a collection of more than 4,000 historical photographs. Rooms are decorated with period furnishings.

Masonic Hall Building
10500 Lansing St.
This former Masonic temple (1872) is crowned with a sculpture carved from a single block of redwood.

Temple of Kwan Ti
45160 Albion St. Visit by appointment only. ☏*707-937-5123.*

The one-room joss house, or temple (c.1850), provided a place of worship for Chinese immigrants in the 1850s. Now preserved, the temple honors the Chinese god of war.

Russian Gulch State Park

2mi north of Mendocino. ○*Open daily year-round.* ☜*$6/vehicle.* ℘*707-937-5804. www.parks.ca.gov.*
Russian Gulch treats visitors to a close-up look at rock formations like **Devil's Punch Bowl**★, a collapsed sea cave located within a fenced area on the bluffs *(take first right after park gate).* In places the surf has carved a variety of **sea caves** and **blowholes** (eruptions in a cave's roof caused by water pressure) into the bedrock.

○ *North of the park, Highway 1 winds past Jug Handle State Reserve, which occupies marine terraces uplifted from the sea over the past 500,000 years.*

Fort Bragg

10mi north of Mendocino. ℘*707-961-2823. www.fortbragg.com.*
This workingman's town was established in 1857 as a US military post. Named for Mexican War hero Gen. Braxton Bragg, the town grew up around a mill built in 1885. When it closed in 2002, the town was devastated; apart from a small fishing industry, the lumber industry supported the local economy. Fortunately, tourism is rapidly growing. The **Fort Building** *(430 Franklin St.)* is the only remnant of the garrison.

Mendocino Coast Botanical Gardens★

18220 N. Hwy. 1. ○*Open Mar–Oct daily 9am–5pm; rest of the year daily 9am–4pm.* ○*Closed 2nd Sat in Sept, Thanksgiving Day, Dec 25.* ☜*$10.* ✕♿📶 ℘*707-964-4352. www.gardenbythesea.org.*
The 47-acre gardens' North and South trails weave through perennial beds and rhododendrons, pine-forests and a fern-blanketed **canyon** to a headland. Here the Coastal Bluff Trail offers good **views** of surf-washed cliffs.

Guest House Museum

343 N. Main St. ○*Open Apr–Oct Tue–Sun 11am–2pm; rest of the year Thu–Sun 11am–2pm.* ○*Closed major holidays and during inclement weather.* ☜*Contribution requested.* ℘*707-964-4251.*
A lumber baron once lived in this three-story Victorian (1892), built of redwood. Now it contains photographs and artifacts on the history of area logging.

♟♟**Skunk Train**★

Departs from Skunk Depot (Hwy. 1 & Laurel St.) ○*Open Mar–Dec.* ○*Closed Jan 1, Thanksgiving Day, Dec 25. 2wk advance reservations recommended. Fees & schedules vary; call or check the website.* ♿📶 ℘*866-457-5865. www.skunktrain.com.*
Originally a logging train, the Skunk Line snakes alongside the Noyo River to Willits. When the company began using gasoline-powered engines in 1925, residents accustomed to coal fumes claimed that they could smell the train coming before they could see it, thus giving rise to the sobriquet "skunk train."

MacKerricher State Park

3mi north of Fort Bragg. ○*Open daily year-round dawn–dusk.* ⚠📶 ℘*707-964-9112. www.parks.ca.gov.*
A popular area of this park, which spans 8mi of coast, is Laguna Point, where a boardwalk leads to an overlook that provides a fine view of harbor seals that reside on the rocks offshore.

○ *North of the park, the road becomes steep and tortuous (average speed 25mph) as it cuts east across the Coast Range to join US-101 at Leggett. Travelers to the Redwood Empire turn north (left) at this junction. The fastest way to return to San Francisco is via Highway 128 (junction 11mi south of Mendocino) to US-101 South.*

Redwood Empire★★

Majestic spires of coast redwoods tower along a 173mi swath of coast from Leggett (184mi north of San Francisco via US-101) to Crescent City, near the Oregon border. In this remote, rugged land, trees thrive in moderate temperatures and abundant rainfall. The greatest concentration of redwoods lies astride US-101, which traces a series of parks containing awe-inspiring groves.

A BIT OF HISTORY

A cool, dry climate caused by the southward movement of Ice Age glaciers caused the demise of all but three redwood species: *Sequoia sempervirens*, commonly known as the **coast redwood**; *Sequoiadendron giganteum*, found in California's Sierra Nevada; and *Metasequoia glyptostrobiodes*, unique to central China.

When Spanish explorers sighted them in 1769, these trees blanketed more than 2 million acres. By the early 1900s, however, loggers had stripped miles of virgin forest, causing alarmed environmentalists to take protective measures. Today 68,000 acres of virgin redwoods—some more than 2,000 years old—are preserved in California parks.

Now thriving only along a narrow, 500mi strip of the Pacific coast between Oregon and Big Sur, these trees can attain heights equal to that of a 36-story building.

🚗 DRIVING TOURS

FROM LEGGETT TO ORICK
133mi.

Chandelier Drive-Thru Tree Park

*Drive-Thru Tree Rd. in Leggett, just south of the junction of Hwy. 1 and US-101; follow signs.* 🕐*Open mid-Jun–Sept 8.30am–8.30pm; rest of the year hrs vary.* 🚗*$5/vehicle.* 📞*707-925-6363. www.drivethrutree.com.*

- 🚹 **Michelin Map:** 585 A 6, 7 and map this section.
- ℹ **Info:** 📞800-346-3482. www.redwoods.info
- ▶ **Location:** Amenities are scarce along this stretch of US-101 on the redwood coast. From south to north, principal service centers include the cities of Garberville, Ferndale, Eureka and Arcata.
- 🕐 **Timing:** The warmest months, September and October, are ideal times to visit; after October, some restaurants and shops close for the winter.

Commercial sites like this one, boasting a redwood carved so that a car can pass through its massive trunk, are considered popular tourist attractions in redwood country.

Smithe Redwoods State Reserve

4mi north of Leggett. 🕐*Open year-round daily dawn–dusk.* ♿ 📞*707-247-3318. www.parks.ca.gov.*
The highlight of this 620-acre park bordering the highway is the small Frank and Bess Smithe Grove, site of a private resort from the 1920s to the 1960s.

Richardson Grove State Park

15mi north of Leggett. 🕐*Open daily year-round dawn-dusk; visitor center open May–Sept.* 🚗*$6/vehicle.* ⚠ 🅿 📞*707-247-3318. www.parks.ca.gov.*
This stately stand of redwoods along the south fork of the Eel River honors William Friend Richardson, governor of California in the early 1920s.

North of Richardson Grove, US-101 passes through the commercial strip of Garberville (*8mi*). From Garberville, a detour (*25mi*) west on Shelter Cove Road crosses the King Range and emerges at the planned beach community of Shelter Cove. This is the only paved access to the isolated **Lost Coast**, which stretches for

23mi below the Mattole River through the King Range.

Avenue of the Giants★★★

Entrance off US-101, 6mi north of Garberville. Tour brochure free from box at south end of drive or from Humboldt Redwoods State Park visitor center.

Few experiences can equal the feeling of driving through the silent, breathtaking groves that line the scenic 32mi parkway running parallel to US-101. Along the way, numerous parking areas afford an opportunity to explore ancient forests.

Humboldt Redwoods State Park★★

South entrance 6mi north of Garberville. ⓄOpen year-round dawn–dusk. ⊜$6/vehicle for site visits (no charge for driving through). ⚠🅿 ☏707-946-2409. www.parks.ca.gov.

The first redwood park (1921) on the North Coast, this 51,000-acre park contains one of the world's finest reserves of coast redwoods. South of Weott on the Avenue of the Giants *(16mi from south entrance)*, the park **visitor center** *(Ⓞopen Apr–Oct daily 9am–5pm; rest of the year daily 10am–4pm; Ⓞclosed Thanksgiving Day, Dec 25 & during inclement weather; 🅿 ☏707-946-2263)* offers maps and exhibits—plus a vintage RV carved from a solid piece of redwood. A highlight is **Founder's Grove★★** *(3mi N of Weott)*, where a nature trail passes

Redwoods at State Park
© Damien/MICHELIN

the Founder's Tree—once considered the world's tallest (364ft before the top 17ft broke off)—and the **Dyerville Giant★** (362ft), which toppled in a 1991 storm.

Rockefeller Forest★★

Turn left on Mattole Rd., 2.5mi north of Weott. Comprising 10,000 acres, the world's largest remaining virgin redwood forest grows on the Bull Creek Flats. Parking areas and trails access the venerable groves. Superlatives include the **Giant Tree** and the **Tall Tree** *(access from Bull Creek Flats parking lot).*

From Rockefeller Forest, **Mattole Road** provides an alternate route *(62mi)* to Ferndale. This two-lane road climbs 2,000ft over the mountains and affords a **panorama★** of the King Range and Cape Mendocino. *(Gas station at Petrolia, 32mi from Rockefeller Forest.)*

▷ *Avenue of the Giants rejoins US-101 5mi north of Pepperwood.*

Scotia

7mi north of Pepperwood. Owned by the Pacific Lumber Co. since 1889, this mill town is home to the **Scotia Museum** *(Main St.; Ⓞ open Jun–Sept Mon–Fri 8am–4pm; Ⓞclosed major holidays; 🅿 ☏707-764-5063; www.palco.com)*, which contains local history exhibits.

Ferndale★

7mi north of Scotia. Turn left on Rte. 211 at Fernbridge. Danish and other European immigrants began a dairy industry here in 1852. The village became a State Historic Landmark in the early 1960s due to preservation efforts of residents who restored the Victorian architecture along **Main Street**. Built in 1899, the **Gingerbread Mansion★** *(400 Berding St.; ✆see Address Book)* is characteristic of the "butterfat palaces" constructed by prosperous citizens.

Eureka★

20mi north of Ferndale.

Pulp mills line the shores of the industrial and port city whose name (Greek

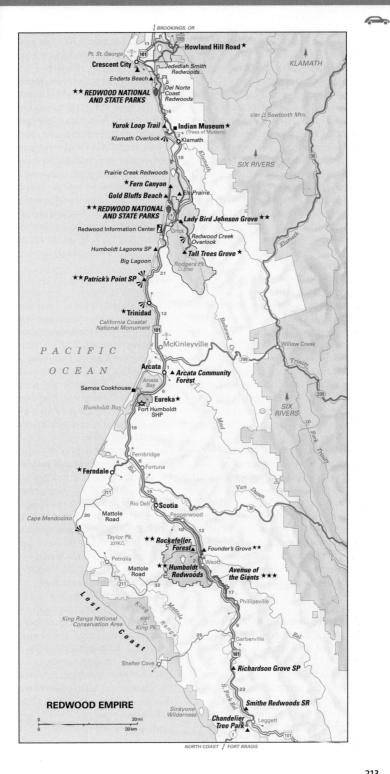

BROOKINGS, OR

Pt. St. George

11

101

Howland Hill Road ★

Crescent City ★

Jedediah Smith
Redwoods

Enders Beach ▲

**★★ REDWOOD NATIONAL
AND STATE PARKS**

Del Norte
Coast
Redwoods

KLAMATH

5781 △ Sawtooth Mtn.

16

Yurok Loop Trail ★   **Indian Museum ★**
(Trees of Mystery)

Klamath Overlook   Klamath

18

SIX RIVERS

96

Klamath

Prairie Creek Redwoods

★ Fern Canyon   Elk Prairie

Gold Bluffs Beach ▲

**★★ REDWOOD NATIONAL
AND STATE PARKS**   **Lady Bird Johnson Grove ★★**

Redwood Information Center   Orick

Redwood Creek
Overlook

Humboldt Lagoons SP ▲   **Tall Trees Grove ★**

Big Lagoon   Rodgers Pk.
2790

21

Klamath

★★ Patrick's Point SP

★ Trinidad   12

California Coastal
National Monument

101

McKinleyville   299   Willow Creek

Arcata   1   **Arcata Community
Forest ★**

P A C I F I C

O C E A N

Arcata
Bay

Samoa Cookhouse   6

Eureka ★
Fort Humboldt
SHP

Trinity

Humboldt Bay

16

Mad

SIX
RIVERS

299

S. Fork Trinity

Fernbridge

6   Fortuna

★ Ferndale   4

211   15   Van Duzen

Rio Dell   Pepperwood   36

Scotia

Cape Mendocino   30

Mattole
Road   10   12

Taylor Pk.
3374 △   **★★ Rockefeller
Forest ▲**   **Founder's Grove ★★**

Petrolia   2   Weott

Mattole
Road   **★ Humboldt
Redwoods**   **Avenue of
the Giants ★★★**

211   32   17   Phillipsville

L o s t   King Range National
Conservation Area   25   Garberville

King
Range   4087
△ King Pk.   101

C o a s t

Shelter Cove   **Richardson Grove SP ▲**

23   **Smithe Redwoods SR ★**

REDWOOD EMPIRE

0   20mi
0   30km

Sinkyone
Wilderness   **Chandelier
Tree Park ▲**   Leggett   101

NORTH COAST / FORT BRAGG

for "I have found it") is California's state motto. Established in 1850, Eureka became a shipping hub of the mining, and later lumber, industries.

Skirmishes between local Indians and settlers led to construction of a military post in 1853. **Fort Humboldt State Historic Park** now occupies the bluff on the southern edge of town where the original garrison stood *(3431 Fort Ave.;* ⏰*open year-round daily 8am–5pm;* 🅿 *𝒫707-445-6567; www.parks.ca.gov).* The Logging Museum has open-air displays of massive iron equipment that highlight the difficult and dangerous aspects of transforming forests into lumber.

Old Town★

2nd & 3rd Sts. between E & M Sts., adjacent to the waterfront.

At the western end of this 10-block historic district sits the Victorian **Carson Mansion★★** *(2nd and M Sts.;* ⛔ *not open to the public),* built in 1886. The redwood mansion reflects the prosperity that Eureka experienced in its heyday. Works by North Coast artists can be viewed at the **Wooden Sculpture Garden** *(317 2nd St.)* created by the late Eureka sculptor Romano Gabriel.

Clarke Historical Museum★

240 E St. ⏰*Open year-round Wed–Sat 11am–4pm.* ⏰*Closed major holidays.* ♿ *𝒫707-443-1947. www.clarke museum.org.*

Formerly a bank, this Classical Revival structure (1912) houses a collection of objects and photographs relating to the county's history. A separate wing displays a fine group of some 1,200 Hoopa, Yurok and Karuk artifacts, including baskets, stonework and a log canoe.

Blue Ox Millworks & Historic Park

👥1 X St. ⏰*Open year-round Mon–Fri 9am–5pm, Sat 9am–4pm.* 👓*$7.50, children $3.50.* ♿🅿 *𝒫707-444-3437. www.blueoxmill.com.*

At this active woodworking mill, visitors may watch construction of gingerbread trim for vintage house restorations, and demonstrations in blacksmithing, boat

building and other crafts. The historic park includes a reproduction logging camp and Victorian village.

Just off the coast of Old Town, **Woodley Island** *(take Rte. 255 from R St.)* maintains a rustic charm. Across the Samoa Bridge on the Samoa Peninsula is the **Samoa Cookhouse** *(left on Samoa Rd.; first left at sign),* founded in 1900 to feed hungry lumberjacks. The camp-style restaurant exhibits antique logging equipment and photographs that recount the early days of the timber industry *(*⏰*open Jun–Labor Day daily 7am–10pm; rest of the year daily 7am–9pm;* ⏰*closed Thanksgiving Day, Dec 25;* ♿🅿 *𝒫707-442-1659; www.samoacookhouse.net).*

Arcata

6mi north of Eureka.

This town was founded as a coastal supply center for mining operations nearby. The city maintains the **Arcata Community Forest** *(east end of 14th St., through Redwood Park;* ⏰*open year-round daily dawn–dusk; 𝒫707-822-8184; www.city-ofarcata.com),* more than 600 acres of second-growth redwoods. A nature trail threads the fern glade at the base of the lovely trees, and 10mi of trails crisscross the rest of the forest.

The only coastal access in Arcata is through the **Arcata Marsh and Wildlife Sanctuary** *(569 South G St.;* ⏰*open year-round daily dawn–dusk; interpretive center open Mon 1pm–5pm, Tue–Sun 9am–5pm,* ⏰*closed major holidays;* 🅿 *𝒫707-826-2359),* created in 1979 as part of a project to restore the bay's marshland using treated waste water.

Humboldt State University Natural History Museum★

👥1315 G St. ⏰*Open year-round Tue–Sat 10am–5pm.* ⏰*Closed Thanksgiving Day, Dec 5–Jan 1, Mar 31.* 👓*$3, children $2.* ♿🅿 *𝒫707-826-4479. www.humboldt.edu/~natmus.*

This small museum boasts a noteworthy international **fossil collection** with specimens ranging in age from 10,000 to 1.9 billion years.

Other exhibits depict Northern California's natural history, including a tidepool tank and live native animals.

Trinidad★

13mi north of Arcata.
This sleepy fishing town was first the site of Tsurai, the largest permanent Yurok village. Trinidad began as a coastal gateway for hopeful gold prospectors; today it's a hub for commercial and sport fishing.

Trinidad is also home to the **Humboldt State University Telonicher Marine Laboratory** *(570 Ewing St.)*, a marine research lab. Displays relating to coastal marine life are on view (⏰*open year-round Mon–Fri 9am–4.30pm, weekends noon–4pm during university semesters;* ⏰*closed major holidays;* ♿🅿 ☏*707-826-3671; www.humboldt. edu/~marinelb).*

Patrick's Point State Park★★

5mi north of Trinidad. ⏰*Open daily year-round.* ☞*$6/vehicle.* ⚠🅿 ☏*707-677-3570. www.parks.ca.gov.*
The park comprises 632 acres of dense forests and agate-strewn beaches. Overlooks at **Wedding Rock** and **Patrick's Point** provide **views★★** of wave-lashed shoreline. Rim Trail *(2mi)* links all the overlook points.

A re-created **Yurok Village** *(off Patrick's Point Dr., 0.3mi north of park entrance)*, including a dance pit and a sweat house, recalls the days when Yurok people built seasonal encampments in the area.

As US-101 continues north, notice **Big Lagoon** on the left *(4mi north of Patrick's Point State Park; entrance on Big Lagoon Park Rd.)*. Together, Big Lagoon, Stone Lagoon and Freshwater Lagoon *(also visible from the road traveling north)* form **Humboldt Lagoons State Park** *(*⏰*open daily dawn–dusk; visitor center open Jun–Sept daily 10am–3pm;* 🅿 ☏*707-488-2169)*, which preserves 1,036 acres of marshland used by birds traversing the Pacific Flyway.

⏵ *Continue north on US-101 to Orick.*

REDWOOD NATIONAL AND STATE PARKS★★
FROM ORICK TO CRESCENT CITY
61mi.

Redwood National and State Parks★★

The three state parks within the national park boundaries are open year-round dawn–dusk. There are five park visitor centers; most are open daily 9am–5pm. ☞*$6/vehicle day fee to visit sights within the parks. Day-use fee transferable to other state parks. Park headquarters located in Crescent City* ☏*707-464-6101.* ⚠🅿 *Campground reservations* ☏*800-444-7275. www.nps.gov or www.parks.ca.gov.*
This 106,000-acre site encompasses three state parks: **Prairie Creek Redwoods**, **Del Norte Coast Redwoods** and **Jedediah Smith Redwoods.** Harboring some of the world's tallest trees, the park has been designated a World Heritage Site and an International Biosphere Reserve.

Campsites abound within the park. Trinidad and Crescent City, at either end of the park, provide the widest selection of accommodations and other services.

Kuchel Visitor Center

1mi south of Orick on US-101. ⏰*Open Memorial Day–Labor Day daily 9am–6pm; rest of the year daily 9am–5pm.* ⏰*Closed Jan 1, Thanksgiving Day, Dec 25. Area state park camping and facility information available.* ♿🅿 ☏*707-465-7765.*
Park information and trail maps are available at this contemporary wooden structure near the beach. Exhibits detail the park's fascinating natural history.

Lady Bird Johnson Grove★★

5.7mi from visitor center via US-101 and Bald Hills Rd.
A level nature trail *(1mi)* loops around a stately old-growth forest named for the former First Lady. A brochure available onsite describes the flora encountered along the way.

▷ *Turn right on Bald Hills Rd.*

Coastal fog often settles in the forested valleys below **Redwood Creek Overlook** *(3mi from Lady Bird Johnson Grove)*, where the view spans acres of redwoods and firs to the ocean.

Tall Trees Grove★

Turn right on gravel Tall Trees Access Rd. (4mi from Lady Bird Johnson Grove; obtain permit at Kuchel Visitor Center above); follow 6.5mi to trailhead; loop trail (3.2mi; steep) to grove.
Set on fern-carpeted flats, the grove contains a 367.8ft-high **tree★** discovered in 1963; at the time, it ranked as the world's tallest known tree. The massive trunk on this 600-year-old giant measures 14ft in diameter.

▷ *Return to US-101 and continue 1.5mi north. Turn left on Davison Rd. (unpaved) and follow it 4mi to beach.*

Gold Bluffs Beach

When flakes of gold were found in its sands in 1851, this beach experienced a brief flurry of mining activity. A herd of Roosevelt elk now roams the sands.

Fern Canyon★

8mi from US-101 via Davison Rd.
Home Creek cleaves the bluffs here, creating a steep, canyon walled with a lush ferns, including five-fingered ferns, lady ferns and giant horsetails. A short loop trail *(0.7mi)* crisscrosses the creek.

▷ *Return to US-101 north.*

A short distance *(2.3mi)* past Davison Road, **Elk Prairie** appears on the left as the highway enters Prairie Creek Redwoods State Park via the Newton B. Drury Scenic Parkway. A herd of Roosevelt elk can often be seen. The parkway connects back to US-101.
As US-101 continues north, it crosses the Klamath River and passes through the fishing resort town of **Klamath**. Just north *(2mi)*, **Klamath Overlook** *(turn left on Requa Rd.)* commands a **view**★ of the river meeting the Pacific.

End of the Trail Indian Museum★

5mi north of Klamath. Located within the gift shop of the Trees of Mystery park (privately owned). ○*Open Jun–Aug daily 8.30am–5.30pm; rest of the year daily 9.30am–4.30pm.* ○*Closed Dec 25.* ⬤🅿 ☎*707-482-2251 or 800-638-3389. www.treesofmystery.net.*
This museum houses a remarkable collection of artifacts from Native American peoples west of Missouri. Six rooms, divided by geographic area, display clothing, jewelry, baskets and pottery.

Yurok Loop Trail

1mi. Turn left to Lagoon Creek parking lot.
This path leads over the bluffs past a driftwood-littered beach. A pamphlet *(available onsite)* explains the ways of the Yurok who inhabited the region.

North of Lagoon Creek, towering trees line the road as US-101 cuts through Del Norte Coast Redwoods State Park. The sandy stretch of **Enderts Beach** lies below steep bluffs *(3mi south of Crescent City, left on Enderts Beach Rd.; access to beach via a steep 0.5mi dirt trail)*.

Crescent City

☎*707-464-3174. www.northerncalifornia.net.*
Built around a crescent-shaped harbor, the largest city in Del Norte County was settled in 1852. In 1964 a tidal wave destroyed 29 blocks of the downtown. Lumbering, dairy farming, commercial fishing and the cultivation of lily bulbs are major industries.

Howland Hill Road★

Follow US-101 through Crescent City; turn right on Rte. 199. Turn right on South Fork Rd., then right again on Douglas Park Rd.
This one-lane, 5mi unpaved road enters **Jedediah Smith Redwoods State Park**, named for the first white man to travel overland to California in 1827 *(park* ○*open daily year-round;* 🚗*$6/vehicle;* ⚠ ☎*707-458-3018)*, and passes **Stout Grove★**, then parallels Mill Creek as it winds through redwood forests.

Sprawling east and south of Los Angeles, once-rural Orange County has grown into a metropolitan extension of neighboring Los Angeles. Its broad agricultural plain, once cloaked with its namesake orange groves, extends 22mi from the 5,687ft crest of the Santa Ana Mountains to the Pacific. Only seven of California's 68 counties are smaller in land area (785sq mi); only one, San Francisco, is more densely populated.

The hub of Orange County is the inland region surrounding Anaheim and Santa Ana. These once-sleepy farming centers now burst at their seams with suburban housing, retail developments and shopping malls. Most of the growth didn't begin until the mid-1950s, after a cartoonist from Missouri bought 180 acres of citrus groves for a theme park that he named Disneyland.

Orange County visitors who fail to venture beyond Disneyland will miss out on interesting attractions in neighboring Santa Ana, Garden Grove, Buena Park and Yorba Linda. Each Orange County beach community bears its particular stamp, but ritzy Newport Beach, artsy Laguna Beach and the old mission town of San Juan Capistrano all boast spectacular coastlines that draw sunworshipers by the hordes.

Today far more than just a suburb of L.A., Orange County supports its own

Highlights

1 Character meet-and-greets at **Disneyland** (p221)

2 Traveling exhibits at the **Bowers Museum of Cultural Art** (p220)

3 A date shake on the beach at **Crystal Cove State Park** (p231)

symphony orchestra and other cultural institutions, big-league baseball and ice-hockey teams.

Orange County has a reputation as a stronghold for white middle-class American conservatism, and statistics bear this out. The population here is 83 percent white, compared to Los Angeles County's 33 percent. About 61 percent of Orange County citizens go to the polls as Republicans.

Newport Beach

© FerrisPhotos.com/iStockphoto

ADDRESSES

🏨 STAY

◎◎🛏🛏🛏 **The Ritz-Carlton Laguna Niguel** – *1 Ritz-Carlton Dr., Dana Point. ℰ949-240-2000 or 800-241-3333. www.ritzcarlton.com. 393 rooms.* South of Laguna Beach, this grand Mediterranean-style hotel perches on a hilltop above a surfing beach. Inside, luxury abounds in crystal chandeliers, rich tapestry fabrics and Frette linens; oceanfront rooms enjoy cerulean Pacific views. At **Restaurant 162′** (◎◎🛏), fresh seafood dishes are served 162ft above sea level.

◎◎🛏🛏🛏 **The St. Regis Monarch Beach** – *1 Monarch Beach Rd., Dana Point. ℰ949-234-3200 or 800-722-1543. www.stregismb.com. 400 rooms.* A 172-acre luxury resort, the Tuscan-inspired hotel features a spa and fitness center, an 18-hole golf course, tennis courts, and nature trails. Spacious rooms feature contemporary decor with marble baths and private balconies. Restaurant choices (there are six) include **Stonehill Tavern ($$$$)** for a unique take on American tavern fare.

◎◎🛏🛏🛏 **Disney's Grand Californian Hotel** – *1600 S. Disneyland Dr., Anaheim. ℰ714-956-6425 or 800-225-2024. www.disney.com. 745 rooms.* Built in early 20C Craftsman style, this hotel is reminiscent of the great national-park lodges. Rooms feature bright decor. Together with the refurbished **Disneyland Hotel** (◎🛏🛏🛏)—which boasts Anaheim's only white-sand beach—and **Disney's Paradise Pier Hotel ($$$)**, the resort has 2,300 rooms. The **Napa Rose ($$$)** restaurant in the Grand Californian offers fine dining.

◎🛏 **Jolly Roger Inn** – *640 W. Katella Ave., Anaheim. ℰ714-782-7500 or 888-296-5986. www.jollyrogerhotel.com. 58 rooms.* This recently renovated family-oriented property, adjacent to Disneyland Resort, stands out from others clustered nearby. It offers tastefully decorated rooms done in light woods and pastel prints, a cafe, a lounge, and a large palm-shaded swimming pool. There's also an inexpensive shuttle to Disneyland across the street.

◎🛏🛏 **La Casa del Camino** – *1289 S. Coast Hwy. (Rte. 1), Laguna Beach. ℰ949-497-2446 or 888-367-5232. www.lacasadelcamino.com. 37 rooms.* A block from the ocean, this 1927 Spanish Colonial hostelry has smallish rooms and baths, but there's a welcoming lobby with a fireplace, and a rooftop lounge offering panoramic views. Room rate incudes a complimentary morning newspaper.

🍴 EAT

◎🛏 **Anaheim White House** – *887 S. Anaheim Blvd., Anaheim. ℰ714-772-1381. www.anaheimwhitehouse.com.* **Italian.** Located in a 1909 colonial-style home, the White House became a restaurant befitting a president in 1981. Today the eight elegant dining rooms (each is named for a US president) turned out in white-on-white decor with gold trimming, serve up classic Northern Italian fare like lobster ravioli and braised Sonoma rabbit created by Veronese owner-chef Bruno Serrato.

◎🛏 **Antonello Ristorante** – *3800 Plaza Dr., Santa Ana. ℰ714-751-7153. www.antonello.com.* **Italian.** With its faux-stucco walls, frescoes and dark woods, the warm dining room recalls a street scene in owner Antonio Cagnolo's native Piedmont region of Italy. The food is also Old World: richly sauced pastas, exquisite veal marsala.

◎🛏 **Bistango** – *19100 Von Karman Ave., Irvine. ℰ949-752-5222. www.bistango.com. Closed Sun.* **American.** Part restaurant, part art gallery, Bistango fills a stunning space in the Atrium shopping complex. Paintings, sculpture and mixed-media creations spark conversation as diners enjoy dishes like soy-glazed salmon and venison with shiitake mushrooms and spatzle. A three-course prix-fixe dinner is also on the menu.

◎🛏 **Bluewater Grill** – *630 Lido Park Dr., Newport Beach. ℰ949-675-3474. www.bluewatergrill.com.* **Seafood.** Set on the water on Lido Isle, this New England-style fish house serves up ample portions of fresh seafood in its light-filled dining room. Choose from Pacific snapper, Idaho trout, Hawaiian ahi, and California swordfish, all grilled to order over mesquite.

Anaheim Area★

Anaheim is the hub of a commercial district of motels, fast-food restaurants and shopping malls, most of it centered around Disneyland Resort. The Anaheim Convention Center is virtually across from the theme park, and the Anaheim major-league baseball stadium is barely a freeway exit away. Buena Park and Garden Grove are adjacent suburbs, while Santa Ana and Yorba Linda are but a few miles farther.

> ▶ **Population:** 295,153.
> ◉ **Michelin Map:** See LA.
> ▤ **Info:** ℘714-765-8888. www.anaheimoc.org.
> ◗ **Location:** Anaheim is located 30mi southeast of Los Angeles by the Santa Ana Freeway (I-5).
> ▲▲ **Kids:** Disneyland; Knott's Berry Farm; Kidseum. Discovery Science Centre.
> ◉ **Don't Miss:** Bowers Museum of Cultural Art and Laguna Beach.

A BIT OF HISTORY

Anaheim was founded in 1857 by German Jewish immigrants who formed a wine-growing cooperative that produced grapes on 20-acre plots along the Santa Ana River. They named their colony Anaheim, "home on the Ana." Other districts of inland Orange County had been contained within the Rancho Santiago de Santa Ana land grant; the county seat of Santa Ana was carved from the ranch in 1869. Today Anaheim ranks among the wealthiest metropolitan areas in the US.

SIGHTS

Disneyland Resort★★★
◉ See Entry Heading.

▲▲ Knott's Berry Farm Theme Park★

8039 Beach Blvd., Buena Park; exit I-5 at Beach Blvd. and follow signs.
◉*Open year-round daily 10am–6pm (5.30pm late Sept-Oct); extended hrs weekends & Jun-Aug.* ◉*Closed Dec 25.* ◎*$51.99, (children under 48in $22.99).* ✕& ₽($12) ℘714-220-5200.
www.knotts.com.

Situated on 160 acres, America's oldest independently owned theme park derives its flavor from old-fashioned charm and Old West atmosphere.

In the 1920s Walter Knott established a berry farm specializing in cherry, rhubarb and boysenberries—a new strain developed locally by grafting together loganberry, blackberry and raspberry plants. He established a tea room, where his wife sold chicken dinners. To amuse the lines of hungry patrons waiting to get in, Knott constructed a replica Old West town in 1940. Today Knott's comprises relocated or replicated historic structures, along with some 165 rides, shows and attractions.

Ride the Butterfield Stagecoach or the Denver & Rio Grande train to get your bearings. Among the newest rides is the **Sierra Sidewinder**, a roller coaster that rotates on its axis and drops 39ft. Other highlights include **Old West Ghost Town**, where you can pan for gold; **The Boardwalk**, with old-fashioned rides; Perilous Plunge, the world's "tallest, steepest and wettest" water ride; and Supreme Scream, a monumental free-fall. **Fiesta Village** features the "Incredible Waterworks Show." Especially for children are **Kingdom of the Dinosaurs**, **Indian Trails** and **Camp Snoopy**.

Knott's Berry Farm

© Robert Holmes/California Travel & Tourism Commission

Crystal Cathedral★

12141 Lewis St., Garden Grove; from I-5, take Harbor Blvd. south; turn east on Chapman Blvd. to Lewis St.
🕐*Open year-round daily 9am–4.30pm. ꙮGuided tours (45min) Mon–Sat 9am–3.30pm.* ✕👤🅿 ☎714-971-4000. *www.crystalcathedral.org.*

In 1961 evangelist Robert H. Schuller commissioned architect Richard Neutra, an Austrian-born practitioner of the International Style, to design the Garden Grove Community Church, a "drive-in church" with 1,400 parking spaces that enabled visitors to participate in the service from their cars. Phillip Johnson conceived the present glass sanctuary (1980), which seats nearly 3,000 and accommodates worshipers via a Jumbotron video screen.

Bowers Museum of Cultural Art★★

2002 N. Main St., Santa Ana; exit I-5 at Main St. and proceed .5mi south. 🕐*Open year-round Tue–Sun 10am–4pm.* 🕐*Closed Jan 1, Jul 4, Thanksgiving Day, Dec 25.* ☜*$12 ($19 weekends).* ✕👤🅿 ☎714-567-3600. *www.bowers.org.*

Housed in a classic Mission-style structure, Orange County's largest museum is dedicated to collecting and preserving the indigenous fine art of the Americas, Africa, the Pacific Rim and Oceania. Endowed by local rancher Charles Bowers (1842–1929), the museum opened in 1936 and was expanded in 2007 with a new wing that doubled exhibit space and added a new entrance, a 300-seat auditorium and a spacious court. Today the permanent collection comprises more than 130,000 artworks and artifacts dating from 1500 BC to the mid-20C, with strengths in Native American and Pre-Columbian art and artifacts. First-class international and temporary exhibits are mounted annually, such as the recent *Art of the Samurai* show featuring works from Japan's ancient culture.

Highlights of the permanent exhibits include relics of *ulama*, an ancient ball game played by Mayan, Aztec and Toltec cultures and dating from 1000 BC;

Native American baskets, beadwork and carved pipes dating from the 17C to the 1980s; religious and domestic artifacts from California's mission and rancho periods; Plein Air paintings (ꙮ*see Laguna Beach*) by California artists such as Frank Coburn and William Wendt; and art from ancient China, including ceramics, paintings and terracotta sculptures.

Adjacent to the Bowers is the **Kidseum** 👥👤 *(1802 N. Main St.;* ☎*714-480-1520;* 🕐*open Tue–Fri 10am–3pm; weekends 11am–3pm;* ☜*$5),* which brings kids in contact with the history and ceremony of world cultures.

Discovery Science Center

👥👤 *2500 N. Main St., Santa Ana, just off the Santa Ana Fwy. (I-5).* 🕐*Open year-round daily 10am–5pm.* 🕐*Closed Thanksgiving Day, Dec 25.* ☜*$12.95, children $9.95.* ✕👤🅿 ☎714-542-2823. *www.discoverycube.org.*

A 10-story tilted cube rises behind this 59,000sq ft interactive museum (1998), designed by Arquitectonica. Two floors of exhibit areas focus on human perception, earth geology, space exploration and more.

The Richard Nixon Library & Birthplace★

18001 Yorba Linda Blvd., Yorba Linda; exit Orange Fwy. (Rte. 57) at Yorba Linda Blvd. and continue 3.5mi east. 🕐*Open year-round Mon–Sat 10am–5pm, Sun 11am–5pm.* 🕐*Closed Jan 1, Thanksgiving Day, Dec 25.* ☜*$9.95.* 👤🅿 ☎714-993-5075. *www.nixonfoundation.org.*

Letters, papers, memorabilia and interactive exhibits commemorate the life of Richard Milhous Nixon (1913–94), 37th US President (1969–74).

The nine-acre complex incorporates the house where Nixon was born, his grave and that of his wife, Pat. Interactive galleries, video presentations and theaters enliven the displays of Nixon-era memorabilia and artifacts of US history. Nixon's 1960 campaign debates with John F. Kennedy are shown, and visitors can listen to tapes relating to the Watergate scandal.

Disneyland® Resort★★★

Though popular culture has changed dramatically since it opened more than 60 years ago, Disneyland retains its magic allure. Keeping pace with the times, the resort has added a second theme park, a shopping and entertainment district and new hotels. Yet California's Disneyland remains faithful to the vision of its creator, with attractions and cartoon characters embodying the fairy-tale enchantment symbolized by the name Disney.

A BIT OF HISTORY

Born in the Midwest, **Walter Elias Disney** (1901–66) headed for Hollywood at age 21 to make good on his talents as an artist and illustrator. By 1923 Walt and his brother Roy had established the Disney Brothers Studio and in 1928 scored their first success with the debut of *Steamboat Willie,* starring a character named **Mickey Mouse.** In 1932, production of the first Technicolor cartoon *Flowers and Trees* won Disney the first of 32 Oscars.

In the early 1950s Disney purchased a 180-acre tract of orange groves in then-rural Anaheim. He and a staff of "Imagineers"—engineers, architects and artists—set about designing a "Magic Kingdom." On July 17, 1955, the park opened to national fanfare. Today the Disneyland® Resort welcomes millions of visitors a year to what it calls "the happiest place on earth."

DISNEYLAND PARK★★★

Disneyland is organized into eight distinct sections that radiate out from a central plaza.

MAIN STREET, U.S.A.

This idyllic re-creation of an early-20C main street is complete with Victorian storefronts housing old-fashioned shops, while horse-drawn trolleys, fire engines and a double-decker omnibus ferry passengers up and down the

- **Michelin Map:** See park map in this section.
- **Info:** ℘714-781-7290. www.disney.com.
- **Location:** Disneyland park and Disney's California Adventure park face each other off the entrance plaza, which leads west into Downtown Disney. Three hotels form an arc opposite Downtown Disney: the Disneyland, Paradise Pier and Disney's Grand Californian hotels, the latter abutting Disney's California Adventure. Use the map in this chapter to locate the sections and attractions of Disneyland park.
- **Parking:** Nearest the parks are a multilevel garage off West Street, close to Ball Road, or lots just southeast of Disney's California Adventure. Both are served by trams running to and from the parks. The parking fee is $12/day for a car.
- **Timing:** A two- or three-day visit is recommended for families with young children. If you haven't acquired tickets in advance, arrive when ticket booths open, about an hour before the official opening time. At the entrance, you'll receive a brochure with a map of the park and show times. Lines get long at the roller coasters as the day progresses, so head for those first. Or, save them for the hour before closing, when crowds are thinner. Evening is the best time to enjoy Downtown Disney.

street. Evenings bring the **Remember… Dreams Come True** fireworks spectacular, featuring a Tinker Bell fly-by.

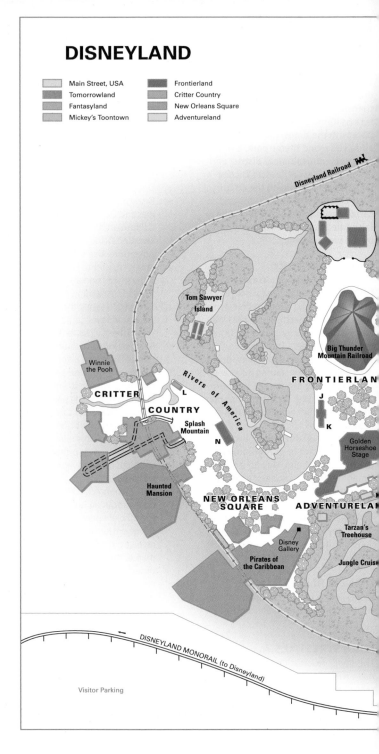

DISNEYLAND

- Main Street, USA
- Tomorrowland
- Fantasyland
- Mickey's Toontown
- Frontierland
- Critter Country
- New Orleans Square
- Adventureland

Disneyland Railroad

Tom Sawyer
Island

Big Thunder
Mountain Railroad

Winnie
the Pooh

CRITTER

FRONTIERLAND

COUNTRY

Rivers of America

Splash
Mountain

L

J

K

N

Golden
Horseshoe
Stage

Haunted
Mansion

NEW ORLEANS
SQUARE

ADVENTURELAND

Tarzan's
Treehouse

Disney
Gallery

Jungle Cruise

Pirates of
the Caribbean

DISNEYLAND MONORAIL (to Disneyland)

Visitor Parking

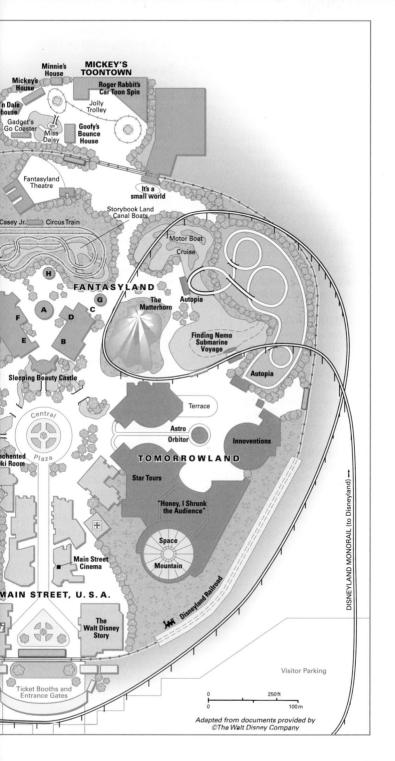

Minnie's House

MICKEY'S TOONTOWN

Mickey's House

Roger Rabbit's Car Toon Spin

'n Dale house

Jolly Trolley

Gadget's Go Coaster

Miss Daisy

Goofy's Bounce House

Fantasyland Theatre

It's a small world

Storybook Land Canal Boats

Casey Jr. Circus Train

Motor Boat Cruise

H

FANTASYLAND

G

A   C

F   D

The Matterhorn

Autopia

E   B

Finding Nemo Submarine Voyage

Sleeping Beauty Castle

Autopia

Central Plaza

Terrace

Astro Orbitor

Innoventions

nchanted ki Room

TOMORROWLAND

Star Tours

"Honey, I Shrunk the Audience"

Space Mountain

Main Street Cinema

MAIN STREET, U.S.A.

Disneyland Railroad

The Walt Disney Story

DISNEYLAND MONORAIL (to Disneyland)

Visitor Parking

Ticket Booths and Entrance Gates

0   250 ft
0   100 m

Adapted from documents provided by ©The Walt Disney Company

Disneyland Railroad

Passengers can board steam trains that circle the park, making stops at New Orleans Square, Mickey's Toontown and Tomorrowland. The railroad travels through a re-creation of the Grand Canyon and a Primeval World.

The Walt Disney Story

This combination museum/theater traces the construction of Disneyland and the Disney empire through photographs. The theater features Disney's crowning Audio-Animatronics success, **Great Moments with Mr. Lincoln**.

Main Street Cinema

Six small screens in an arcade-style room show Disney animated classics in black-and-white from the 1920 and 30s, including *Steamboat Willie*.

TOMORROWLAND

For decades Tomorrowland intrigued visitors with its 1960s-style vision of the atomic age, but in 1997–1998 it was refashioned as a "classic future environment." Overhead, the **Disneyland Monorail** whisks passengers between Tomorrowland, the Disneyland® hotels and Downtown Disney.

Finding Nemo Submarine Voyage

Voyage to the depths on a submarine ride through the undersea reefs and ruins of Tomorrowland's lagoon, where you'll encounter Nemo, Dory, Marlin and other characters from the popular Disney-Pixar film *Finding Nemo*.

Astro Orbitor

At the entrance to Tomorrowland, this 64ft-high kinetic sculpture is a 90-second spinning ride. A dozen rockets beneath the sculpture have individual controls that allow riders to move up and down as the "planets" revolve.

Astro Blaster

Climb aboard a star cruiser and join Buzz Lightyear in a laser shootout to save the galaxy from the evil Emperor Zurg. Each rider fires lightstreams from a laser canon against nefarious galactic creatures, winning points for a direct hit.

Space Mountain

Since it opened in 1977, this roller coaster, enclosed in a futuristic mountain, has been one of the park's most popular rides. Space Mountain is not for the faint-of-heart: thrill-seeking visitors are hurtled through space in near-darkness, plunging through sudden comet showers.

Star Tours

The adventure begins in the Tomorrowland Spaceport, where *Star Wars* droids C3PO and R2D2 are hard at work preparing for takeoff. Travelers then board a StarSpeeder 3000 for a voyage to the Moon of Endor. Excellent special effects result in the ride of a lifetime.

"Honey, I Shrunk the Audience"

This 3-D film presentation (viewers wear special glasses) is based upon the Disney hit film *Honey, I Shrunk the Kids*. Something goes awry, and the audience is shrunk to the size of a shoebox. Special physical effects built into the seats and floor add another dimension of reality.

Innoventions

Designed to showcase emerging technologies, Innoventions comprises two floors of electronic gadgets, video screens and computer applications introduced by Tom Morrow, a robot who bears a striking resemblance to comedian Robin Williams.

Autopia

Originally designed to teach young people how to drive safely, this updated attraction gives both novice and experienced drivers the chance to motor sports cars, coupes or off-road vehicles around a shaded roadway. Billboards and even traffic reports address the vehicles rather than their drivers.

FANTASYLAND

With the fairy-tale air of an old European village, the area appeals to adults with

Area Code: 714

GETTING THERE
By Car – From Los Angeles (25mi), take I-5 south, exit at Disneyland Dr.
By Air – Closest airports: **Orange County/John Wayne Airport** (SNA) 14mi south in Santa Ana (*☎949-252-5200; www.ocair.com*); **Los Angeles International Airport** (LAX) 35mi northwest (*☎310-646-5252; www.lawa.org*); **Long Beach Airport** (LGB) 20mi west (*☎562-570-2600; www.lgb.org*). Shuttles run to Disneyland-area hotels from LAX and SNA; average cost $15/one-way.
By Bus and Train – Greyhound terminal (*1mi from park*): 100 W. Winston Rd., Anaheim ☎800-231-2222. Amtrak station (*2mi from park*): 2150 E. Katella Blvd., Anaheim ☎800-872-7245.

GETTING AROUND
The Disneyland Monorail carries passengers between Downtown Disney and Tomorrowland (park entry ticket required). Many area hotels offer a shuttle service to the park (East Shuttle station on Harbor Blvd.), as does the Anaheim Resort Transit System. Within the park, visitors can move about via the Disneyland Railroad, which stops at Main Street, U.S.A., New Orleans Square; Mickey's Toontown; and Tomorrowland.

GENERAL INFORMATION
WHEN TO GO
The least crowded period falls between Thanksgiving and Christmas, followed by September and October, then January and February. Saturday is the busiest day of the week; midweek is less crowded. Some rides and facilities may be closed off-season.
VISITOR INFORMATION
For general information, contact Disneyland Guest Relations (*☎781-7290*), located in City Hall in Main Street, U.S.A.
HOURS AND FEES
The park is open at least 10am–8pm daily year-round, with extended

hours on weekends, in summer and on holidays. For hours, www.disney.com or call ☎781-4565. One-day one-park ticket (*$69/adult; $59/child 3–9*); "Park Hopper" tickets good for one day (*$94/adult; $84 child*) or three days (*$199/adult; $169/child, discounts available for online purchase*) allow entrance at both Disneyland and Disney's California Adventure. Tickets allow unlimited use of all attractions except arcades. Same-day **re-entry** to the park is permitted with a valid ticket and hand stamp (available at exits). Valid for selected attractions, **FASTPASS** assigns timed entry to avoid or reduce waiting in line; for details, www.disney.com.
ACCOMMODATIONS
Information is available from the **Anaheim/Orange County Visitor & Convention Bureau** ☎765-8888, www.anaheimoc.org. Reservations recommended six months in advance for hotel rooms and campsites, especially during high season. Accommodations within a 5mi radius of the park range from elegant hotels (*$225–$600/day*) to standard hotels (*$150–$300/day*) and budget motels (*$70–$125/day*). The Disneyland® Resort Hotels (*☎956-6400; $225–$5465/day*), are accessible from the park by the Disneyland Monorail; they include the long-established Disneyland Hotel, the recently renamed Paradise Pier Hotel and the newest, Disney's Grand Californian Hotel. Full service campgrounds are located nearby; call the Visitor & Convention Bureau (*above*) for information.
AMENITIES
Most visitor services (baby facilities, first aid, lost-and-found, storage lockers, ATMs) are located in Town Square and elsewhere in Main Street, U.S.A. Strollers, wheelchairs and kennel facilities are available for rent just outside the main entrance. Theme restaurants, cafeterias and shops abound throughout the park.

SIGHTSEEING

Guided tours include a 2hr30min "Welcome to Disneyland" tour *($25/person)*, and a 3hr30min "Walk in Walt's Footsteps" tour *($59/person, lunch included)*, offering a look at the park through the founder's eyes. Or try the 2hr30min "Discover the Magic" tour geared for visitors ages 3–9 *($59/person)*. Tour fees are in addition to park admission, while discounts are available to season passholders. Tours depart every morning; tickets are available at main entrance and City Hall *(℘781-4400 or www.disney.com)*.

SHOWTIME

Live-performance stage shows are presented throughout the day, with first-come, first-served seating.

WHEN TO EAT

Peak mealtimes are 11.30am–2pm and 5pm–8pm. Spend less time in line by planning to eat outside these hours, or exit the park and eat along Harbor Boulevard. Be sure to have your hand stamped at the park exit for re-entry.

DISNEY BY NIGHT

Nightly extravaganzas include Fantasmic! and "Remember... Dreams Come True" Fireworks. Most rides continue to run and lines are shorter.

---

a taste for whimsy, as well as to young fans of the Disney classics.

Sleeping Beauty Castle

Today a worldwide symbol of Disney, this small-scale castle, with its gold-leafed turrets and moat, serves as a majestic entrance to Fantasyland.

Matterhorn Bobsleds

Roller coaster-style sleds wind up and through the Matterhorn mountain, a Disney landmark. Once at the top, the sleds make a swirling downhill dash through ice caves and past an abominable snowman.

King Arthur Carrousel (A)

This merry-go-round with antique white horses is accompanied by Disney tunes pumped out of the calliope.

"it's a small world"

This international fantasy was conceived for the 1964 World's Fair. The facade is a pastiche of architectural images from many lands—the Taj Mahal, the Eiffel Tower, Big Ben and more. Inside, boats float visitors past 500 Audio-Animatronics children and animals representing nearly 100 nations, all singing the familiar theme song.

Disney Animated Classics

Carnival-style rides and enclosed, or "dark," rides are based on animated features, in which special vehicles trans-port visitors through the narrative as storybook images unfold before them. In **Peter Pan's Flight (B)**, pirate-ship gondolas fly riders out of the Darling children's bedroom and above a charming, fiber-optic version of London by night before plunging into a NeverLand adventure. The caterpillar cars of **Alice in Wonderland (C)** take passengers on a twisting trip through a fantasyland populated by the Queen of Hearts, the Mad Hatter and that elusive White Rabbit. In jaunty vintage sports cars, those who brave **Mr. Toad's Wild Ride (D)** hurtle through the English countryside and into London's foggy back streets. **Snow White's Scary Adventures (E)** takes visitors from the Dwarfs' cottage to an encounter with Snow White's evil stepmother. **In Pinocchio's Daring Journey (F)**, visitors are whisked from Geppetto's toy-making shop to accompany the puppet/boy on his misadventures, while Jiminy Cricket keeps an eye on everyone. In the **Mad Tea Party (G)**, a tilt-a-whirl of cups and saucers swirling about, riders control their spin by a wheel in the center of each cup.

For Little Dreamers

Several carnival-type rides are suited for the very young. On **Dumbo the Flying Elephant (H)**, small visitors can make their Dumbo soar up and down by manipulating a knob in front of the seat. The **Storybook Land Canal Boats** glide past a series of scale-model miniatures depicting such scenes as Mr. Toad's abode ("Toad Hall") and Alice's home; Storybook Land can also be toured aboard the **Casey Jr. Circus Train**.

MICKEY'S TOONTOWN

Toontown is an exclusive residential neighborhood for Disney cartoon characters. The **Jolly Trolley**, Toontown's public transportation, continuously huffs and chuffs its way through the village, and Toontown residents regularly stroll through to meet visitors.

Mickey's House

Walk through Mickey's modest, red-roofed home to investigate the lifestyle of a hardworking celebrity mouse. A quick screening of clips from his movies precedes meeting the star himself, a special highlight for kids of all ages.

Minnie's House

Bake a cake, wash dishes or try on Minnie's perfume in the residence of Mickey's loyal sweetheart, who occasionally drops in for handshakes and autographs.

Goofy's Playhouse

Small-size visitors can bounce off the walls and furniture of Goofy's inflatable dwelling. Then climb up to the bridge of Donald Duck's boat, the **Miss Daisy**, for a bird's-eye view of Toontown.

Chip 'n Dale Treehouse

A spiral staircase lets children explore the chipmunks' house, nestled in the branches of a Toonesque tree. Nearby, Gadget has recycled her toys into **Gadget's Go Coaster**, which offers pint-size thrills on its short ride.

Roger Rabbit's Car Toon Spin

Follow the skid marks to the Toontown Cab Co. building for an adventure in the darkened recesses of Toontown.

FRONTIERLAND

The Old West lives on in this frontier town, with its boardwalks, country stores and saloons. The town borders the Rivers of America, which circle Tom Sawyer Island. At night, river rides shut down and visitors crowd the shoreline to see **Fantasmic!**, a fiber-optic show *(22min)* that presents Disney animation at its pyrotechnic best. Several times daily, Frontierland's **Golden Horseshoe Stage** features Western-style music with Billy Hill & the Hillbillies and The Golden Horseshoe Variety Show.

Big Thunder Mountain Railroad

This reddish mountain's crags and caves are scaled by one of Disneyland's most thrilling roller coasters. Boarding a runaway train in an old mining town, passengers speed through caves and canyons down into a rickety old mine shaft.

Rivers of America

Those in search of riverine adventure have their pick of four different kinds of vessels plying the waters of Disneyland's "river." For a glimpse of Mississippi River history, board the **Mark Twain Riverboat (J)**, a reconstruction of an old paddle-wheeler. Navigating a similar route is the **Sailing Ship Columbia (K)**, giving a taste of life aboard an 18C merchant ship. Visitors paddle the river, accompanied by coonskin-capped guides, in **Davy Crockett's Explorer Canoes (L)** *(board in Critter Country)*. **Log Rafts (N)** offer transportation to Tom Sawyer Island, site of Injun Joe's cave, a swinging footbridge and more.

CRITTER COUNTRY

This small, bucolic corner of the park is home to a host of critters. The newest attraction here is based on the experiences of another beloved bear, the **Many Adventures of Winnie the Pooh**.

Splash Mountain

Riders board bark dugouts for a languid float through the swamps and bayous inside this mountain, as Brer Rabbit, Brer Fox and other characters from *Song of the South* (1946) serenade them. At the mountain's top awaits one of Disneyland's biggest thrills: a 52ft flume that hurtles the dugouts down a 47° slope to a monstrous splash at the bottom.

Meet-and-Greet

Popular Disney characters appear at various times throughout the park to shake hands, sign autographs and pose for pictures. It's a spine-tingling thrill for young fans. Look for TInkerbell and her fairy friends at Pixie Hollow in Fantasyland, Toy Story's Woody and Jessie in Frontierland, Goofy and his friends in Toontown, and Disney princesses at the Fantasy Faire in Fantasyland. Winnie the Pooh, Piglet and their friends appear in Critter Country.

NEW ORLEANS SQUARE

This squeaky-clean version of New Orleans' French Quarter features a narrow street of pastel shop facades and wrought-iron balustrades.

Pirates of the Caribbean

Considered among the most popular amusement park rides ever created (and the inspiration for a phenomenally successful movie series), this piratical adventure features excellent scenery, details and action. Boarding boats, visitors first weave through a swamp before entering a Caribbean village peopled by buccaneers, imperiled damsels, parrots, dogs and pigs.

Haunted Mansion

A host of ghosts and ghouls spooks this "deserted" mansion looming over New Orleans Square. From the stretch room, where heights and dimensions are not as they appear, visitors board small black "doom buggies" for an eerie trip among holographic images and haunting, if humorous, special effects.

ADVENTURELAND

The tropical motif of this area is obvious in the thatched roofs and massive tusk entrance gate. Stores here sell curios from "exotic" lands. **The Enchanted Tiki Room**, the first application of Audio-Animatronics, stars funny, fantastical tropical birds and flowers who inspire the audience to sing along.

Indiana Jones™ Adventure (P)

Rugged transport vehicles convey visitors on a harrowing journey—replete with spiders, snakes and skulls—to the Temple of the Forbidden Eye. Indy surfaces to help where he can, but even a hero can't stop the giant boulder.

Jungle Cruise

Visitors cruise aboard safari boats through an overgrown river forest populated by mechanized crocodiles, hippos, elephants and tigers. Walt Disney initially planned to use live animals in this attraction but was dissuaded by zoologists. That's been left to Disney's Animal Kingdom at Walt Disney World® Resort in Florida (see The Michelin Green Guide to Florida).

Tarzan's Treehouse™

Opened in 1999 to replace the long-standing Swiss Family Robinson Treehouse, this attraction invites visitors to climb through a sprawling, 80ft artificial banyan, which re-creates the legendary jungle dweller's arboreal home.

DISNEY'S CALIFORNIA ADVENTURE® PARK★★

California's historical, agricultural and recreational treasures are paid homage in this theme park. Each ride and attraction in its four districts is marked with the stamp of the Golden State.

THE GOLDEN STATE

Visitors enter beneath a replica of San Francisco's Golden Gate Bridge and make their way to view "Golden Dreams," a film about that city's Palace of Fine Arts. The **Condor Flats** area, designed as a 1940s high-desert airfield, features "Soarin' Over California" which simulates a flight around the state complete with salt breezes and the scent of orange blossoms.

There's hiking and whitewater rafting on **Grizzly Peak**; plus sourdough bread and tortillas on **Pacific Wharf**. You can even get a hint of Disney delights to come at the Blue Sky Cellar, showcasing the creative process of Disney's elite Imagineers.

A BUG'S LAND

This theme area is designed to appeal especially to younger kids . In the popular 3-D film *It's Tough to Be a Bug!* the audience, wearing 3-D glasses, experiences such special effects as termite sneezes (you'll get wet), stinkbug emissions and a cloud of "pesticide." At **Flik's Fun Fair**, everyday objects like a water spigot appear huge when seen from the perspective of a bug. **Bountiful Valley Farm** celebrates the spirit of California's agricultural industry.

HOLLYWOOD PICTURES BACKLOT

A tribute to the golden era of filmmaking, this two-block version of Hollywood Boulevard includes Disney's Animation studio and live-entertainment theater. Don't miss **Playhouse Disney—Live on Stage!**, a show that features characters seen on the Playhouse program on the Disney Channel. **Jim Henson's Muppet Vision 3D** places the audience in the midst of the lovable puppets. The newest attractions are the extremely popular **Twilight Zone Tower of Terror**, similar to the horrifying Walt Disney World 13-story elevator ride (yes, the cable breaks); and **Monsters, Inc: Mike and Sulley to the Rescue**, a top-favorite ride in the dark.

PARADISE PIER

This beachfront amusement zone, with roller coasters and other thrill rides, is not for the faint of heart. Among numerous rides is **California Screamin'**, a roller coaster that accelerates from 0 to 55mph in less than five seconds; **Maliboomer**, a hair-raising 180ft free fall; and **Jumpin' Jellyfish**, an underwater parachute ride. **Sun Wheel** is a giant Ferris wheel whose sunburst is a symbol of the new theme park. Budding coaster fanatics can hop on the **Mullholland Madness**, a pint-sized version of L.A.'s twisting roadway. **Toy Story Midway Mania** lets you hone your aim as you shoot light-beam darts at carnival attractions. Favorite spots for kids: the King Triton Carousel and the S.S. Rustworthy play zone.

DOWNTOWN DISNEY

Among the attractions at the resort's shopping, dining and entertainment district are performance venues for jazz, Latin, rock and blues music; a 12-screen cinema complex; and a 40,000sq-ft World of Disney store.

Orange Coast★

The oceanside communities of Huntington Beach, Newport Beach and Laguna Beach fringe the Pacific, each graced by a distinctive character and a charming waterfront where sun, sand and sea hold sway.

A BIT OF HISTORY

These seaside cities were born in the first decade of the 20C when the Pacific Electric Railway (the "Big Red Car") trolley line was extended from Los Angeles as far south as Newport Beach.

Today, coastal Orange County thrives from commerce and light industry, as witnessed by the glass-and-concrete

Info: ℘714-765-8888. www.anaheimoc.org.

Kids: Fun Zone, and a ride on the Balboa ferry.

Don't Miss: Laguna Beach.

office towers rising inland from the seashore. Residential housing developments blanket the inland areas. Sun enthusiasts flock to the northern part of the county between Huntington Beach and Newport Beach to loll on wide, sandy beaches; south of Newport Beach, the sandy stretches give way to the cliffs and promontories of the San Joaquin Hills.

SIGHTS

Huntington Beach

Pacific Coast Hwy. (Hwy. 1), 11mi southeast of downtown Long Beach. ℘714-969-3492. www.hbvisit.com.
Considered the birthplace of the surfing craze in California, Huntington Beach epitomizes the contemporary California beach town. Surf shops dot Main Street near Highway 1. The **International Surfing Museum** *(411 Olive Ave.; ⏰open year-round daily Mon–Fri noon–5pm, weekends 11am–6pm; ⬧$2; ℘714-960-3483; www.surfingmuseum. org)* profiles the sport and its personalities. Across from Main Street, a long concrete pier extends into the surf, marking the boundary between **Huntington State Beach** to the south and **Bolsa Chica State Beach** to the north.

Newport Beach★

Pacific Coast Hwy. (Hwy. 1), 6mi southeast of Huntington Beach. ℘800-942-6278. www.newportbeach-cvb.com.
The presence of the Pacific Electric Railway line boosted Newport Beach's development as a seaside playground; today it's an upscale residential community. **Fashion Island** *(Newport Center Dr., just off Hwy. 1)*, a mammoth open-air complex of department stores and boutiques, spreads over the slope overlooking the Balboa Peninsula.

Balboa Peninsula

Exit Pacific Coast Hwy. via Newport Blvd., which becomes Balboa Blvd. ℘949-722-1611.
This peninsula defines the boundaries of Newport Harbor, the largest small-boat harbor in the world. On its eastern portion is the resort community of **Balboa**, established in 1905; today it is a suburb of Newport Beach. The peninsula's ocean side invites swimmers and sunbathers to its broad, sandy beaches.
The **Newport Municipal Pier** (1888) is accessed by Ocean Front Street. Balboa Boulevard bisects the peninsula, leading to the **Harborside Restaurant and Grand Ballroom** a *(400 Main St.; www. harborside-pavilion.com)*, a Victorian pavilion (1904) popular in the 1940s big-band era. Extending along the bayfront next to the pavilion is the **Fun Zone** *(👤👶⏰open daily 11am–6pm, 9pm Fri & Sat; ⬧$2/ride; www.thebalboafunzone. com)*, a midway-style stretch of game arcades, restaurants, a Ferris wheel and a carousel. Several companies operate narrated **harbor cruises** from here.
A three-car **ferry** *(👤👶⬧$2 car and driver)* runs a short distance across the bay to **Balboa Island**, the largest of three islets created when the marshy harbor was dredged in the early 20C. Cottages of all styles crowd the island, and shops and cafes line Marine Avenue, which crosses a bridge to the mainland and the Pacific Coast Highway.

Orange County Museum of Art★

850 San Clemente Dr. ⏰Open year-round Wed–Sun 11am–5pm (Thu 8pm). ⏰Closed major holidays. ⬧$12 (free Thu). ✖️♿️🅿️ ℘949-759-1122. www.ocma.net.
This respected modern art museum features a permanent collection covering all the main movements in 20C California art, including Bay Area Figuration, Plein Air, Pop Art and Minimalism. You're likely to see works by Richard Diebenkorn, Ed Ruscha, Chris Burden and John Baldessari among others, in addition to a noteworthy schedule of temporary exhibits. A branch museum, the **Orange Lounge**, is located at South Coast Plaza *(3333 Bear St., Costa Mesa; ⏰open daily year-round Mon–Fri 10am–9pm, Sat 10am–8pm, Sun 11am–6.30pm; ℘949-759-1122).*

Sherman Library and Gardens

2647 East Coast Hwy., Corona del Mar; continue south from Newport Beach on Hwy. 1. ⏰Open year-round daily 10.30am–4pm. ⏰Closed Jan 1, Thanksgiving Day, Dec 25. ⬧$3. ✖️♿️🅿️ ℘949-673-2261. www.slgardens.org.
Specializing in tropical and subtropical plants and desert species, this two-acre garden was created in 1966 by the Sherman Foundation as a setting for its research library. The tiny adobe (1940) on the grounds displays old photographs from the library's Southwestern History collection.

Crystal Cove State Park★

8471 Pacific Coast Hwy., south of Corona del Mar. ⓞ*Open year-round daily 6am–dusk.* ⌨*$10/vehicle.* ✕⚠🅿 ✆*949-494-3539. www.parks.ca.gov.*
Orange County's longest expanse of undeveloped coastline is preserved in this state park. Recently restored, 13 beachfront cottages are open to the public for overnight stays. A full-service cafe is housed in a cottage and the Shake Shack serves milkshakes made from dates, a locally-grown treat.

Laguna Beach★

Pacific Coast Hwy. (Hwy. 1), 10mi southeast of Newport Beach. ✆*800-877-1115. www.lagunabeachinfo.org.*
Backdropped by rocky cliffs and pitted by deep canyons, Laguna Beach's natural **setting**★★ has long attracted artists, actors and poets. By the 1920s, some 40 painters had established studios here. The close proximity of these artists and their alliance as the **Laguna Beach Art Association** spawned several artistic movements, most notably "Plein Air," a variant of American Impressionism characterized by representations of the region's distinctive light and landscapes.

Although Laguna Beach's heyday as an art colony is past, the **Festival of the Arts** *(Jul–Aug)* is the most popular of Laguna Beach's three annual festivals, attracting 200,000 visitors each year. A festival highlight is the renowned "Pageant of the Masters," in which models pose in living representations of well-known paintings.

Laguna Art Museum★

307 Cliff Dr. at Pacific Coast Hwy. ⓞ*Open year-round daily 11am–5pm.* ⓞ*Closed Jan 1, Thanksgiving Day, Dec 25.* ⌨*$10.* ♿ ✆*949-494-8971. www.lagunaartmuseum.org.*
Founded in 1918, this museum is a recognized center for the study and exhibition of American art. The permanent collection features American Impressionist paintings, 20C photography and works of installation art. Changing exhibits focus on historical and contemporary trends, with particular emphasis on the development of modern art in California.

Heisler Park *(north of the museum)* offers views of Laguna Beach's gently curving coastline. A path leads from here to **Main Beach** *(foot of Broadway)*, the largest of the town's beach areas. On the northern edge of town, **Crescent Bay Point Park** *(west of North Coast Hwy. on Crescent Dr.)* offers a magnificent **view**★★ across the bay and cliffs to the center of town.

Laguna Beach

© Hilly Collective/iStockphoto

Mission San Juan Capistrano★★

California's seventh mission anchors the quiet town of San Juan Capistrano. Nicknamed the "Jewel of the Missions" for its beautiful site and impressive gardens, San Juan Capistrano ranked among the most prosperous of California's missions. Both town and mission are renowned for the swallows that arrive here each year on March 19 from their winter nesting grounds in Argentina; their annual return is celebrated with a popular annual festival.

- **Michelin Map:** 585 B 11.
- **Info:** ☎949-234-1300. www.missionsjc.com.
- **Location:** The town lies inland at the southern end of Orange County, southeast of Laguna Beach.

A BIT OF HISTORY

Founded by Padre Junípero Serra in 1775, San Juan Capistrano prospered, thanks to the thriving hide-and-tallow trade that furnished a market for mission-raised cattle. During its heyday the mission ranked as the most properous on the mission chain, with a resident population of 1,400 neophytes. Completed in 1806, the **Great Stone Church** stood for only six years before being toppled by an earthquake in 1812. Following secularization, the mission population declined, and in 1845 the buildings passed into private ownership. They were deeded back to the Church by President Abraham Lincoln in 1865. Work begun in 1920 is largely responsible for its present appearance. Today operated as an historic site, the mission is the focus of archaeological research—you'll see excavation pits here and there about the property.

VISIT

Ortega Hwy. at Camino Capistrano, 3 blocks west of I-5. ◑Open year-round daily 8.30am–5pm. ⛛Guided tours available weekends ◔Closed Good Friday afternoon, Thanksgiving Day, Dec 25. ⟴$9 (includes self-guided audio tour). ☎949-234-1300. www.missionsjc.com.

Dominating the mission's entrance courtyard, the ruins of the Great Stone Church reveal the size and splendor that made the cross-shaped edifice the grandest in the mission chain. Its 65ft-high roof was topped by seven domes and a bell tower that could be seen from 10mi away. The church's original four bells now hang in a low wall adjacent to the ruins, and the nearby garden shows remnants of original Romanesque arches, door frames and lintels.

Three rooms in the west wing of the central courtyard display items from San Juan Capistrano's Native American, mission and rancho periods. Behind the west wing lies the factory area where workers pressed olives and grapes, tanned leather, forged metal and made soap from tallow.

In the courtyard's east wing is the mission's original chapel (1776). Today known as the **Serra Church**, it is thought to be the only remaining building in California in which Serra offered Mass. The Baroque reredos from Barcelona, dating from the 17C, was added in 1924.

"The Miracle Return"

Each year around March 19, a flock of cliff swallows returns from winter nesting grounds in Argentina to occupy mud nests on the old mission church ruins. The number of returning birds has declined recently, probably due to habitat loss, but the event, which has been documented for more than a century, is celebrated with great fanfare by the town and the mission.

SAN DIEGO COUNTY

Beyond the city of San Diego, relaxed and well-defined residential communities are interspersed with pleasant beaches, scenic mountains and the beginnings of a vast desert that runs east into Arizona and south into Mexico. The county's 4,255sq mi encompass more than double the population of San Diego city. Inland, the county is a jumble of mountains and valleys that climax at Anza-Borrego Desert State Park. East of the park is the agriculturally rich Imperial Valley, with the Salton Sea at its north end. West of the mountains are the charming hamlet of Julian and the Palomar Observatory atop 6,126ft Palomar Mountain.

California began in San Diego. Hunter-gatherers of the Kumeyaay tribe probably watched Spanish ships under Juan Rodríguez Cabrillo enter San Diego Bay in 1542 during his early explorations, but some 200 years passed before Europeans came here to stay.

Jolted by English land claims in western Canada, Spain launched its own colonists, sending Gaspar de Portolá and Padre Junípero Serra to establish California's first mission and presidio (garrison) at San Diego in 1769. Following Mexican independence in 1821, a town grew below the presidio. It became a center for Californios, ranchers of Spanish and Mexican descent who owned parcels of California land.

An American corvette captured San Diego during the Mexican-American War in 1846, and Mexican Governor Pío Pico surrendered near San Diego the following year, completing the US conquest of California.

Today San Diego County is the second-most populous in California. Half of its residents live in the city of San Diego and its ever-spreading suburban com-

Highlights

1 Cinco de Mayo in **Old Town State Historic Park** (p241)

2 A night out in the **Gaslamp Quarter** (p255)

3 The Skyfari tram over Gorilla Tropics at the **San Diego Zoo** (p249)

3 The Journey into Africa at **San Diego Wild Animal Park** (p261)

munities. Residential communities dot the coastal areas all the way from the county's southern border (the international border with Mexico), to upscale suburbs like La Jolla to the north.

East of San Diego, the suburban sprawl gives way to vast and beautiful stretches of desert and mountain, popular for hikers, bikers, backpackers and hang-gliders.

Opportunities for outdoor recreation abound near the coastal areas, which enjoy near-perfect weather conditions year-round.

Anzo-Borrego Desert State Park

© California Travel & Tourism Commission

233

ADDRESSES

🛏 STAY

⊜⊜⊜⊜ **La Costa Resort and Spa** – *2100 Costa del Mar Rd., Carlsbad. ☎760-438-9111 or 800-854-5000. www.lacosta.com. 479 rooms.* This 400-acre coastal escape boasts two golf courses, 17 tennis courts and five heated pools, as well as spirulina wraps, shiatsu massage and a special activites club just for kids. Understated luxury prevails in the guest rooms, done in neutrals and earth tones. Spa cuisine is a menu option at the resort's restaurants, like **BlueFire Grill** (⊜⊜⊜) for fine dining.

⊜⊜⊜⊜⊜ **La Valencia** – *1132 Prospect St., La Jolla. ☎858-454-0771 or 800-451-0772. www.lavalencia.com. 115 rooms.* This 1926 landmark pastel-pink stucco palace is a statement of opulent beachside style. Palms surround the "Pink Lady of La Jolla," recognizable by its mosaic-tiled tower. All rooms, suites and villas sport light woods, seaside prints and windows that open to sea breezes. Of three restaurants, the 10th-floor **Sky Room** (⊜⊜⊜⊜), with its French cuisine and Pacific views, is most intimate.

⊜⊜⊜⊜ **Crystal Pier Hotel** – *4500 Ocean Blvd., San Diego. ☎858-483-6983 or 800-748-5894. www.crystalpier.com. 29 rooms.* On a dock that juts into the ocean at Pacific Beach, a series of comfortable, blue-and-white cottages provide unique over-the-water lodging. Ocean views abound in these 1927 bungalows, outfitted with fully equipped kitchenettes, wicker furnishings, and patios with umbrellas.

⊜⊜⊜⊜⊜ **Hotel del Coronado** – *1500 Orange Ave., Coronado. ☎619-435-6611 or 800-468-3533. www.hoteldel.com. 679 rooms plus 78 cottages.* A seaside Victorian castle of turrets and red-shingled roofs, "Hotel Del" has hosted 14 presidents and countless celebrities since it opened in 1888. Guests choose from small Victorian rooms in the original building to tropical-themed chambers in the Towers and Cabana buildings to oceanfront cottages at the Beach Village. In the stately **Crown Room** (⊜⊜⊜), whimsical crown-shaped chandeliers designed by Frank Baum (author of *Wizard of Oz*) hang from the wood-beamed ceiling.

⊜⊜⊜⊜ **Hotel Parisi** – *1111 Prospect St., La Jolla. ☎858-454-1511 or 877-472-7474. www.hotelparisi.com. 29 rooms.* This innovative property was designed using feng shui guidelines "to induce positive energy flow." Rooms reflect soothing earth tones and feature such thoughtful touches as ergonomic desks and tubs with contoured headrests. A full menu of holistic services—from accupressure to zen tone sound therapy—is available in your room.

⊜⊜⊜⊜ **Hotel Solamar** – *436 6th Ave., San Diego. ☎619-819-9500 or 877-230-0300. www.hotelsolamar.com. 235 rooms.* Conveniently located downtown, this 10-story Kimpton property is awash in eye-catching contemporary decor, from the floating-candle chandelier in the common room to the tented sofa in the lobby. Spacious bedrooms, done in deep brown and aqua blue, sport mahogany furniture; bathrooms combine shower and tub and have plenty of counter space. The rooftop terrace offers a lap pool, three fire pits, a bar and good views of the city.

⊜⊜⊜ **Horton Grand Hotel** – *311 Island Ave., San Diego. ☎619-544-1886 or 800-542-1886. www.hortongrand.com. 132 rooms.* This historic Victorian-era hotel has been restored to its 1886 heyday. Period decor—including the refurbished hand-carved oak grand staircase in the lobby bar—recaptures the glory of the Gaslamp District. Romantic rooms wrap guests in Victorian charm with antique beds, hand-carved armoires and gas fireplaces.

🍴 EAT

⊜⊜⊜ **Candela's** – *416 Third Ave., San Diego. Dinner only. ☎619-702-4455. www.candelas-sd.com.* **Mexican**. No tacos here... this East Village spot combines upscale Mexican cuisine (think Mexico City) with a dash of dark, European romantic decor. The menu presents new takes on fresh seafood and flavorful steaks; the ceviche is excellent, as is the ahi tuna carpaccio napped with a lemon-cilantro sauce.

Croce's – *802 5th Ave., San Diego.* ℘619-233-4355. www.croces.com. *No lunch Mon–Fri.* **American**.
This shrine to folk-rock singer Jim Croce was opened by his widow, Ingrid, and sparked the renaissance of the surrounding Gaslamp Quarter. The bar offers live music every night—often from Jim's son, A.J. Walls are decorated with photos, lyrics and guitars. Seafood specialties (like grilled sea bass with a wild-rice pepper crust) are consistently good choices.

George's at the Cove – *1250 Prospect St., La Jolla.* ℘858-454-4244. *www.georgesatthecove.com.* **Seafood**.
All three levels of this seaside showplace afford views of La Jolla Cove, whether inside the formal dining room or out on the rooftop terrace, under canvas market umbrellas. George's is famous for fish, such as Pacific swordfish wrapped in Serrano ham, or seared rare Ahi tuna, and for its soup of smoked chicken, broccoli and black beans.

Arrivederci – *3845 Fourth Ave., San Diego.* ℘619-299-6282. www.ristorante-arrivederci.com. **Italian**. An easygoing, Italian-family atmosphere rules this longstanding restaurant in the Hillcrest neighborhood. The menu is stocked with traditional Italian favorites; try the meltingly tender pork ossobuco, the lobster ravioli or any of the perfectly prepared risotti. Portions are generous, but try to save room for a cannoli or two.

Aqui es Texcoco – *1043 Broadway, Chula Vista.* ℘619-427-4045. http://aquies texcoco.com. **Mexican**. Barbacoa de borrego (barbecued lamb) takes center stage at this unassuming spot tucked away at the end of a strip mall in Chula Vista. The service and food here win raves, from the lamb-based flautas, tacos and soup to the menu centerpiece, an assortment of lamb head meats served with fresh condiments and sides. It doesn't get more authentic than this.

Anza-Borrego Desert State Park★★

Situated in the eastern region of San Diego County, this 600,000-acre state park encompasses rocky mountains, carved badlands, palm groves and relics of historic transportation routes. The park is named for the Spanish explorer who traversed the region in 1774, and for the elusive *borregos* or peninsular bighorn sheep that roam here.

A BIT OF HISTORY
The Peninsular Ranges to the west began uplifting about 5 million years ago, breaking and twisting the earth's surface into a beautiful, rugged landscape. As the mountains cut off moisture from the Pacific Ocean, subtropical savanna vegetation gave way to hardier desert plants. The water-loving California fan palms that once flourished here

- **Michelin Map:** 585 C 11.
- **Info:** ℘760-767-5311. www.parks.ca.gov.
- **Location:** The park is located about 80mi northeast of San Diego via I-15 and Route 78.
- **Don't Miss:** The panoramic views from Font's Point (Auto Tour).

are found only in canyons where runoff and groundwater reach their roots. Rock art and mortar holes in the park attest to the early presence of Kumeyaay tribes. Their way of life was disrupted in the late 18C when European settlers established migrant trails through the region. In 1776 Borrego Valley became part of the **Anza Trail**, the principal overland route connecting Spain's California settlements with Mexico. Pioneered by Juan Bautista de Anza in 1774, the trail was abandoned by the Spanish in 1781 for sea routes.

Borrego Palm Canyon

© Worldfall/Photoshot

In 1846, during the Mexican War, the Mormon Battalion laid out an east-west trail; gold seekers followed in their footsteps on this **Southern Emigrant Trail**, which traced a series of meadows and watering points through the mountains.

Originally named Borrego Palms Desert State Park, Anza-Borrego was created in 1933 and has since been expanded. Today it ranks as the largest US state park outside Alaska.

VISIT

Open daily year-round. $6/vehicle. Camping reservations 760-767-5311. Camping reservations 800-444-7275. www. parks.ca.gov. Although many of Anza-Borrego's main attractions can be visited by car, several areas are accessible only by four-wheel drive vehicle.

It's wise to begin a park visit at the **visitor center** *(200 Palm Canyon Dr., 1.5mi west of traffic circle in the town of Borrego Springs; open Oct–May daily 9am–5pm, rest of the year weekends & holidays 9am–5pm; 760-767-4205)*, which features a natural-history museum, bookstore and slide show *(15min)*. If you visit in spring, call the wildflower hotline (*760-767-4684)* for bloom updates.

Borrego Palm Canyon★

3mi round-trip. Trailhead in campground about 2mi north of visitor center.

The most popular of 25 palm groves is accessible by a moderately difficult trail that ascends to reveal fan palms in the mouth of the canyon ahead. Palm Canyon Creek creates a waterfall and pool.

Erosion Road Auto Tour★

Mileposts 22–36 of Rte. S22, east of Borrego Springs.

Ten marked points identify forces that shaped the landscape. The San Jacinto Fault, the most active in California, skirts the base of the Santa Rosa Mountains. At mile 32.6, hills on the north side of the road indicate fault movement. At mile 29.3, a sandy side road (*4-wheel drive strongly recommended)* leads 4mi to Font's Point, offering a **panorama**★★ over the Borrego Badlands.

Split Mountain Road

South of Rte. 78 at settlement of Ocotillo Wells, eastern edge of park.

South of Ocotillo Wells *(5.8mi)*, a gravel road leads to Elephant Trees Nature Trail. The trees were named for the skinlike appearance of their outer trunks. Continuing south *(.9mi)*, Split Mountain Road crosses the dry wash of Fish Creek. A right turn leads into the backcountry *(4-wheel drive required)*. About 3.6mi farther, an anticlinal fold structure can be seen in the canyon's west wall. A half mile beyond, a foot trail *(.5mi)* climbs uphill to Wind Caves, an outcrop of sandstone conglomerate eroded into a bizarre, miniature landscape.

Narrows Earth Trail

.5mi loop. Trailhead 12.2mi south of Borrego Springs on Rte. S3, then 4.7mi east on Rte. 78.

A short trail reveals types of rock formed by geologic processes. Numbered posts explain geologic forces that are present in the area.

Southern Portion

South on Rte. 78 from its intersection with Rte. S3; at Scissors Crossing, turn left onto Rte. S2.

This stretch follows the Southern Emigrant Trail; in places, ruts left by creaking wheels are still visible. A monument at **Box Canyon** (*mile 25.7*) points out the trails made by the Mormon Battalion and Butterfield Overland Mail; both trails are accessible on foot from this point.

Vallecito Stage Station

Mile 34.8.

A major stop on the Butterfield stage route, the station was an oasis for passengers, drivers and horses. The present building is a replica (1934).

In the southeast part of the park, the **Carrizo Badlands Overlook** (*mile 52.7*) offers a **panorama**★ of jagged ridges.

EXCURSION
Salton Sea

About 30mi east of Borrego Springs by Rte. S22.

This 525sq mi inland sea was created in 1905 when the Colorado River broke through levees into a desert depression 250ft below sea level. For almost two years the Colorado poured into the basin until engineers returned it to its channel. Drainage from irrigated agriculture prevents the lake from evaporating entirely, and the brownish-green water is now saltier than the Pacific Ocean. The **Salton Sea State Recreation Area** (*Rte. 111, 20mi north of Calipatria*) offers campgrounds, beaches and fishing (○ *open daily year-round;* ⊜ *$6/vehicle;* △ ♿ ℘ *760-393-3052; www.parks.ca.gov*).

South of the Salton Sea, agricultural crops thrive in the sub-sea level **Imperial Valley** (*107mi east of San Diego via I-8*). Its east side is part of the *Imperial* **Sand Dunes Recreation Area** (*Rte. 78;* ℘ *800-832-7664*), whose dunes crest up to 300ft. Most of these hills, once known as the Algodones Dunes, are open to off-highway vehicles (ORVs), but the Imperial Sand Dunes National Natural Landmark is a protected area. Hugh Osborne Overlook (*3mi east of Gecko Rd. off Rte. 78*) offers the best viewpoint.

La Jolla★★

Hugging the Southern California shore, wealthy La Jolla (la-HOY-ya) is famed for its boutiques, museums and glorious coastal setting. The city's name means "the jewel," from the identically pronounced Spanish words *la joya*.

A BIT OF HISTORY

La Jolla was laid out in the late 1880s. Among its earliest residents were members of the Scripps family of publishing tycoons. **Ellen Browning Scripps** in particular contributed greatly to La Jolla's character, commissioning architect **Irving Gill** to design her home and a phalanx of graceful buildings that con-

> 🖫 **Info:** ℘ 858-454-5718. www.lajollabythesea.com.
>
> ▶ **Location:** La Jolla overlooks the Pacific Ocean, 12mi northwest of downtown San Diego.
>
> 👫 **Kids:** The excellent Birch Aquarium, especially the giant kelp forest.

tinue to enhance the area's character. Today Mediterranean villas behold the Pacific from lush landscaped hillsides surrounding a shopping village that centers on **Prospect Street**. North of town are the University of California, San Diego; the Scripps Institute of Oceanography, and the Salk Institute. The La Jolla Playhouse stages acclaimed productions on the university campus.

SIGHTS
Museum of Contemporary Art, San Diego★★

700 Prospect St. ◐*Open year-round Thu–Tue 11am–5pm (Thu 8pm).* ☛*Guided tours available weekends 2pm.* ◐*Closed major holidays and during installation of exhibits.* ◉*$10 (valid for 7 days at both locations).* ✕♿*℘858-454-3541. www.mcasd.org.*
San Diego's premier venue for contemporary art occupies Ellen Browning Scripps' home (1916), remodeled in 1996 by Venturi, Scott Brown and Associates.

A pioneer in the exhibition of installation art, the museum creates temporary exhibitions drawn from its collection of 4,000 paintings, sculptures, photographs and works in video and mixed media, with strengths in Minimalist and Conceptual art, and art of Latin America. A **sculpture garden** at the rear of the building overlooks the ocean. Works are rotated between here and the museum's facility in downtown San Diego.

La Jolla Cove★★

This small, cliff-fringed cove sits off Prospect Street. Beside it, **Scripps Park** offers **views**★★ of ocean-facing bluffs. Stroll north along **Coast Walk** to see the seven **La Jolla Caves** carved by wave action against the rocks.

♟♟Birch Aquarium at Scripps★★

2300 Expedition Way, off Torrey Pines Rd. ◐*Open year-round daily 9am–5pm.* ◐*Closed Jan 1, Thanksgiving Day, Dec 25.* ◉*$11, children $7.50.* ✕♿▣ *℘858-534-3474. www.aquarium. ucsd.edu.*
Occupying a glorious site overlooking the coast, this excellent aquarium inspires interest in the marine sciences with its interactive displays and collections of sea creatures. The 49,400sq-ft **aquarium**★ (1992), named for the Stephen and Mary Birch Foundation,

overlooks the Scripps research campus, part of the University of California, San Diego. Ocean life from Southern California to the tropical seas is displayed in viewing tanks housing 3,700 fish of 390 species. A highlight is the **kelp forest**, a 70,000-gal tank containing a giant kelp environment.

Salk Institute★★

10010 N. Torrey Pines Rd. ☛ *Visit by guided tour (45min) only, year-round Mon–Fri noon. Reservations required.* ◐*Closed major holidays.* ✕♿▣ *℘858-453-4100. www.salk.edu.*
A leading world center for biological studies, the Salk Institute for Biological Studies was founded in 1960 by **Dr. Jonas Salk** (1914–95), who pioneered vaccines against influenza and polio. Today the institute conducts research in neuroscience, molecular-cellular biology and genetics. Designed by leading modernist Louis Kahn, the architecturally noteworty 26-acre complex is highlighted by two six-story buildings of reinforced concrete, teak and steel facing each other across a sleek plaza.

Torrey Pines State Reserve★

N. Torrey Pines Rd., 2mi north of Genesee Ave., 1mi south of Carmel Valley Rd. ◐*Open year-round daily 8am–dusk.* ◉*$8/vehicle.* ▣ *℘858-755-2063. www.parks.ca.gov.*
This 1,750-acre reserve is dedicated to the preservation of one of the world's rarest pine trees. Torrey pines *(Pinus torreyana)* occur naturally only here and on the Channel Island of Santa Rosa, and fewer than 6,000 survive.

The reserve occupies an isolated bluff overlooking Torrey Pines State Beach. In the early 1920s, Ellen Browning Scripps commissioned the Hopi-style adobe Torrey Pines Lodge, now home to a **visitor center** with a museum of local natural history.

From here, **Fleming Trail** *(.6mi)* passes several stands of Torrey pines. Other trails explore the blufftop, offering **views**★★ of the cliffs and the sea before leading down to the beach.

San Diego ★★★

With its gleaming high rises overlooking a vast, bustling bay, San Diego appears the very image of its ranking as the second-largest city in California (after Los Angeles) and the eighth-largest in the US.
The Balboa Park cultural institutions, which share the verdant mesas and canyons north of downtown with affluent neighborhoods of Spanish-style mansions, underscore the city's cosmopolitan nature.
Though its population is large, the 319.6sq-mi city feels as if it has room to spare. With such world-class tourist attractions as the San Diego Zoo and SeaWorld, San Diego merits its reputation as one of the most livable cities in the nation.

SAN DIEGO TODAY

San Diego is a sophisticated yet laid-back place to visit, easy to navigate and blessed with consistently fine weather (although a microclimatic peculiarity dubbed the "June gloom" brings fog to the immediate coastal areas in late spring).

With the Mexican border and the city of Tijuana just a short trolley ride south, you'll find Hispanic culture a lively force here, especially in the architecture, arts and cuisine. The business district occupies the flats along the water's edge, flanked to the east by the bustling Gaslamp Quarter. Atop the ridge to the north sits Balboa Park. The historic areas of Old Town and the Presidio rise to the northwest, at the head of San Diego Bay; from there, Friars Road leads east through heavily developed Mission Canyon to old Mission San Diego. SeaWorld, Mission Bay, and the northern coastal suburbs extend farther north.

A BIT OF HISTORY

Before the arrival of Europeans, the area was inhabited by the Kumeyaay tribe. In 1542 this peaceful tribe greeted the area's first visitors, as Spanish ships under Juan Rodríguez Cabrillo sailed into the bay. Sixty years later, in 1602, ships commanded by Sebastián Vizcaíno

> ▶ **Population:** 1,353,953.
> **Michelin Map:** Map 585 B 11 and maps pp240, 245, 248, 255.
> **Info:** ℰ619-236-1212. www.sandiego.org.
> ◗ **Location:** The city edges San Diego Bay, 124mi south of Los Angeles and 20mi north of the border with Mexico.
> **Don't Miss:** Balboa Park, Old Town.
> ◔ **Timing:** Take a trolley to Downtown, Old Town, Balboa Park (free tram within the park) and Seaport Village. Allow 4hrs to visit each, plus mealtime. Most Balboa Park museums are closed Mon, but free Tue on a rotating basis.
> ▲▴ **Kids:** San Diego Zoo, SeaWorld and many more.

arrived; he christened the harbor and environs San Diego, honoring the feast day of St. Didacus of Alcalá.
Spaniards returned in 1769 to colonize Alta California, led by Gaspar de Portolá and accompanied by Padre Junípero Serra, who was tasked with establishing a chain of Catholic missions. On July 16, 1769, Serra raised a cross beside a hastily built chapel on present-day Presidio Hill, thus establishing the first mission and first Spanish garrison in California. In 1774, the Spanish crown declared San Diego a Royal Presidio. But proximity of the garrison caused the mission to relocate inland from Presidio Hill to a new complex beside the San Diego River. Following Mexican independence in 1821, San Diego began to thrive. On land below the garrison, a *pueblo*, known today as Old Town, slowly developed.
In 1846, during the Mexican War, the 22-gun corvette USS *Cyane* sailed into San Diego and raised the US flag over the *pueblo*. But fierce fighting continued, most notably in the bloody Battle of San Pasqual.

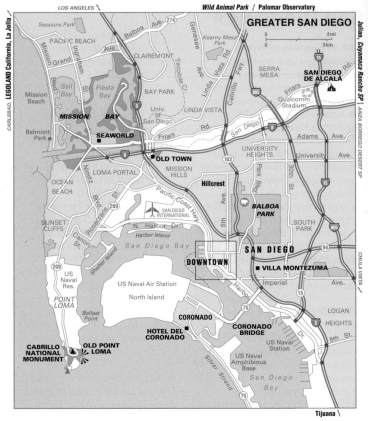

Visionaries – San Diego's potential for development as a seaport was limited by its distance from the harbor. With that in mind, citizens led by San Francisco financier **William Heath Davis** in 1850 bought 160 acres of bayfront land 5mi south of the town. But the few buildings they built soon stood deserted, ridiculed as "Davis' Folly."

That same vision struck **Alonzo Horton**, a San Francisco businessman, who bought 960 acres in 1867 and began to promote their sale. Just over a year later, buildings rose on almost every block of "New Town" San Diego.

Anticipation of the arrival of the Santa Fe Railroad in 1885 helped fuel a real-estate boom, and that same year, Elisha Babcock began developing Coronado and the Hotel del Coronado.

Military Presence – Stimulating both the population and the economy in 1900 was a growing military presence, as the US government came to recognize the strategic importance of San Diego Bay. Forts Rosecrans and Pico served during both World Wars as the headquarters of the Pacific Fleet. San Diego continues as an important naval center to this day.

In the years before World War I, naval aviators trained on the bay under the direction of **Glenn H. Curtiss**. In 1925 T. Claude Ryan began offering regularly scheduled flights between San Diego and Los Angeles; his service, known as Ryan Airlines, was the nation's first commercial passenger line. Two years later, that company was commissioned by Charles Lindbergh to modify a plane capable of making a solo transatlantic flight.

Two successful world expositions in 1915 and 1935 transformed Balboa Park into an enduring civic landmark and impressed thousands of visitors with the city's beauty. By the end of World

War II, San Diego County's population had reached half a million; that number again doubled before 1960.

The New Millennium – At the start of the 21C, San Diego is beset with political battles of development versus slow-growth or no-growth. Parts of downtown show signs of urban decay, and the need for water rationing occasionally looms in this desert region.

Yet San Diego has seen the revitalization of Old Town, the Gaslamp Quarter, and the **Hillcrest** neighborhood north of Balboa Park. New and ever-growing developments such as Mission Bay, Seaport Village, Horton Plaza and the San Diego Convention Center have increased tourism as an economic mainstay, while a recent surge in the number of biotech and pharmaceutical companies in the area has reinforced the sciences as an economic pillar.

San Diego enjoys a mild climate, with more than 300 sunny days most years. Temperatures average 70°F near the ocean, but east of the hills that block the daily sea breeze, they may soar into triple digits in summer.

In 2007 the first of seven new downtown parks opened (the last two are slated for the coming years) and the newly restored Balboa Theatre (1924) reopened.

OLD SAN DIEGO★★★
Map p245.

Sights preserving and commemorating the birth of San Diego and the beginnings of European presence in Alta California lie in the vicinity of Interstate 8 as it stretches east to west, roughly following the course of the San Diego River.

OLD TOWN SAN DIEGO STATE HISTORIC PARK★★
From downtown San Diego take I-5 north; exit at Old Town Ave. and follow signs. Begin at the visitor center in the Robinson-Rose House at the west end of the plaza (4002 Wallace St.). There's a diorama here of Old San Diego.
State park buildings open year-round

daily 10am–5pm; closed Jan 1, Thanksgiving Day, Dec 25;
619-220-5422; www.parks.ca.gov.
Shops and retail areas generally open 10am–7pm.

The original heart of San Diego, the restored historic buildings around a two-acre **plaza** are today joined by colorful shops and eateries to re-create the San Diego of the Mexican and early American periods.

Following Mexico's independence from Spain in 1821, the hub of settlement was little more than a cluster of single-story huts with dirt floors; only a few major land-owning families—most notably the Estudillos, Bandinis and Picos—built more substantial structures.

American forces occupied the town in the summer of 1846, during the Mexican War. The city was incorporated four years later, and Yankee influences became increasingly evident, particularly through the introduction of New England-style architecture. A major fire in 1872 destroyed many buildings.

In 1968 a 13-acre section of Old Town was designated a State Historic Park. Work began to restore the seven surviving buildings and reconstruct others according to archaeological and archival records. Today many visitors are drawn to this festive part of San Diego to shop, dine and enjoy the seasonal festivals and art shows that are staged in the plaza. Throughout the park, costumed

Covered Wagon, Old Town San Diego
© Ed Starr/Dreamstime.com

Area Code: 619

GETTING THERE

By Air – San Diego International Airport (SAN): 3mi northwest of downtown (*℘400-2400; www.san. org*). Taxi to downtown (*$15–$20*); commercial shuttles daily 24hrs (*$9*).

By Bus or Train – Greyhound **bus** station: 120 W. Broadway (*℘800-231-2222; www.greyhound.com*). Amtrak **train** station: Santa Fe Depot, 1050 Kettner Blvd. (*℘800-872-7245. www.amtrak.com*).

By Car – From Los Angeles (*122mi*), take the **I-5** into San Diego; from Las Vegas (*328mi*), take the **I-15**. **I-8** enters the city from the east.

GETTING AROUND

By Public Transportation – The **San Diego Trolley Blue Line** travels from Old Town through downtown south to the Mexican border; the **Orange Line** extends from the Convention Center through downtown then east and north; the **Green Line** goes from Old Town through Mission Valley. Trolleys operate daily 5am–midnight. Purchase tickets at automated ticket machines located at each stop before boarding. (*$2.50/one-way ticket good for 2hrs*). **Bus** routes serve the beaches, Balboa Park, San Diego Zoo and SeaWorld (*$1–$5 one-way; purchase on the bus; exact change required*). **Day Passes** offer unlimited rides on buses and trolleys, good for one (*$5*), two (*$9*), three (*$12*) and four (*$15*) consecutive days. Coastal **trains** travel from Oceanside in northern San Diego County to downtown with stops in many cities (*Mon–Sat; $5–$6.50 one-way*). Transit system route information ℘233-3004 or www.sdcommute.com.

By Car – Parking garages average $3hr or $12/day and sometimes offer free parking for shoppers with validation.

By Taxi – American Cab ℘858-234-1111; **Orange** ℘291-3333; **San Diego Cab** ℘226-8294.

GENERAL INFORMATION

VISITOR INFORMATION

San Diego Convention & Visitors' Bureau's **International Visitor Information Center**: 1040-1/3 W. Broadway, San Diego, CA 92101 (◐*open Jun–Sept daily 9am–5pm; rest of the year daily 9am–4pm ;* ◑*closed Jan 1, Thanksgiving Day, Dec 25;* ℘*236-1212; www.sandiego.org*). Disabled visitor information: Accessible San Diego (*PO Box 124526, San Diego CA 92112* ℘*858-279-0704; www.accesssandiego.com*).

ACCOMMODATIONS

Accommodations range from elegant hotels (*$300–$500/day*) to budget motels (*$100–$135/day*) and bed & breakfast inns (*$90–$150/day*).

Youth Hostels: Hostelling International offers low-cost lodging (*$19–$54/day*) downtown (*521 Market St.,* ℘*525-1531*) and near Point Loma (*3790 Udall St.,* ℘*223-4778; or www.sandiegohostels.org*).

RESERVATIONS SERVICES

Southwest Rooms (*www. southwestrooms.com*). San Diego Concierge (℘*800-979-9091; www. sandiegoconcierge.com*). Bed & Breakfast directory (℘*800-619-7666; www.bandbguildsandiego.org*).

FOREIGN CURRENCY EXCHANGE OFFICES

Travelex 177 Horton Plaza and Fashion Valley (℘*800-287-7362; www.travelex.com*). **Travelex** Air Terminal 1 (*open daily 7am–3.30pm*) and Terminal 2, upper level (*open daily 6am–2.30pm;* ℘*681-1941*).

USEFUL NUMBERS

Police/Ambulance/Fire (multilingual)	℘911
Police (non-emergency; Spanish & English)	℘531-2000
Dental Referral Service	℘800-336-8478
24hr pharmacy: Kaiser Permanente Medical Ctr., 4647 Zion Ave.	℘528-7770
Weather	℘289-1212

☆☆ SPORTS AND LEISURE

SIGHTSEEING

Gaslamp Quarter Historical Foundation walking tours of the historic Gaslamp Quarter (*Sat 11am; $10; ℘619-233-4692; www.gaslampquarter. org*). **Old Town Trolley Tours** city circuit with free reboarding at 8 attractions (*daily every 30min, 9am–5pm; $32; ℘298-8687; www.historictours.com*). **Gray Line Tours** city tours with commentary (*year-round daily, $35; ℘477-8687; www.sandiegograyline. com*). **Cinderella Carriages** horse-drawn carriage rides along the waterfront, downtown and Gaslamp Quarter (*daily noon–midnight, $75/half-hour to $110/hr; ℘239-8080; www. cinderella-carriage.com*). **Hornblower Cruises** harbor tours and fishing trips: (*daily $20–$25; ℘888-467-6256; www.hornblower.com*), H&M Landing (*reservations required; ℘222-1144; www. hmlanding.com*) and San Diego Harbor Excursion (*daily cruises; $17–$22; ℘234-4111; www.sdhe.com*).

SHOPPING

Downtown: Horton Plaza, Old Town, and Seaport Village. **Mission Valley**: Fashion Valley Center.

RECREATION

Water sports are popular at Mission Bay and the beaches and marinas near downtown. Public **golf courses** include Balboa Park Municipal Golf Course (*℘235-1184*), Coronado Municipal Golf Course (*☎435-3121*), and Torrey Pines Municipal Golf Course (*℘452-3226*).

Hiking and **biking** trails are located in Mission Trails Regional Park; **Camping** in Cleveland National Forest, San Elijo Beach State Park and Silver Strand State Beach.

Entertainment

Consult the Thursday arts and entertainment sections of the San Diego Union-Tribune and other publications (weekly *San Diego Reader*, bimonthly *San Diego This Week*) for a schedule of cultural events and addresses of principal theaters and concert halls, or access www.sandiego.org. Tickets may be purchased at theater box offices, from **Arts Tix** (*full-price advance-sale tickets and half-price tickets for selected events on day of performance; Horton Plaza booth at corner of 3rd Ave. and Broadway in downtown; ☎497-5000*), or from Ticketmaster (*℘800-745-3000; www.ticketmaster.com*).

Company	Performances	℘
Lamb's Players Theatre	Musicals, comedies, dramas	437-0600
Old Globe Theatre	Regional theater (Balboa Park)	234-5623
San Diego Opera	Opera (Jan–May)	533-7000
San Diego Symphony	Classical orchestra, holiday pops	235-0804
Starlight Musical Theatre	Broadway shows (Balboa Park)	544-7827
La Jolla Playhouse	Classical and contemporary theater	858-550-1010

Spectator Sports

Tickets for major sporting events can be purchased at venue or through ticket outlets (*above*).

Sport/Team	Season/Venue	℘
ⓘ **Major League Baseball**	Apr–Oct	795-5005
Padres (NL)	PETCO Park	www.padres.com
◉ **Professional Football**	Sept–Dec	280-2121
Chargers (NFL)	Qualcomm Stadium	www.chargers.com

interpreters in period attire regularly stage vignettes, answer questions, and provide interesting demonstrations of typesetting, blacksmithing, woodworking and compass-reading to illustrate life in times past.

Casa de Machado y Silvas (A)
San Diego Ave.
This modest, single-story adobe, built by José Nicasio Silvas between 1830 and 1843, was owned by the same family for more than a century; it then served as a boarding house, then a brothel, then a church. Today it is restored to resemble a period restaurant.

Colorado House
2733 San Diego Ave.
Now occupied by the **Wells Fargo History Museum** (○*open year-round daily 10am–5pm;* ○*closed Jan 1, Thanksgiving Day, Dec 25;* & ☎*619-238-3929; www. wellsfargohistory.com)*, this building is a reconstruction of the 1850 original. Wells Fargo became the principal gold-assay company in the American West during the 1849 California Gold Rush.

Mason Street School (B)
Mason & Congress Sts.
San Diego's first public schoolhouse, this one-room structure (1865) features artifacts representing the history of education in San Diego, and replicas of the 15 flags flown at various times over California.

Casa de Machado y Stewart★
Congress St.
An outstanding example of adobe restoration, this simple, single-story residence (1833) was still occupied by descendants of the Machado family when it was purchased by the state in 1966. Some 70 percent of the structure is original. The kitchen garden has been replanted with vegetables, herbs and spices used in the 19C.

San Diego Union Museum (C)
San Diego Ave. & Twiggs St.
Prefabricated on the East Coast and shipped around Cape Horn in 1851, this wood-frame structure served originally as a store. In 1868 it housed the offices of the *San Diego Union*, which as the *San Diego Union-Tribune*, remains the city's principal newspaper. Restored to its 1868 appearance, the interior replicates the newspaper's first offices; on view is a Washington handpress. Park interpreters regularly demonstrate typesetting on period equipment.

Seeley Stable★
Calhoun St.
Until the Southern Pacific Railroad was extended to San Diego in 1887, Albert Seeley's stagecoaches traversed the 130mi between San Diego and Los Angeles in as few as 24 hours. Seeley's reconstructed barns and stable now contain an extensive **collection** of horse-drawn vehicles, including covered wagons, carriages, buggies and coaches, plus intriguing new exhibits on overland transportation.

La Casa de Bandini★
Calhoun & Mason Sts. ⚬─ *Closed for restoration; projected reopening 2011.*
Peruvian-born Juan Bandini, one of Old Town's influential residents, built the first floor of this hacienda in 1829. Albert Seeley purchased the home in 1869, added an upper floor and converted it into the Cosmopolitan Hotel. In later years, it housed a store and apartments. Today the structure is under renovation, with plans to reopen as a bed-and-breakfast inn.

La Casa de Estudillo★★
Mason St.
The largest and most impressive of the park's original adobes was constructed in 1829 by presidio comandante José María Estudillo and offers an excellent glimpse of the lifestyle of an upper-class family during the pueblo's heyday. The elegant home, occupied by the Estudillo family for 60 years, was the social and political hub of Mexican and early American San Diego. Its 13 rooms, connected by an inner veranda, wrap around a central patio; a large garden flourishes in the rear. During the time of

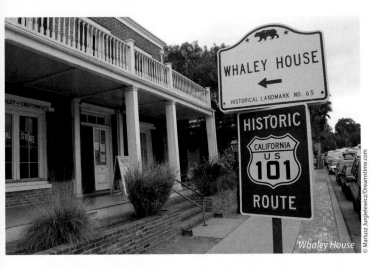

Whaley House
© Mariusz Jurgielewicz/Dreamstime.com

the family's residence, the main room, or **la sala**, was filled with the very best purchases from ships bringing goods from Europe, North and South America and Asia. The house was restored in 1910 and again in 1968.

Whaley House★

2476 San Diego Ave. ⏰*Open late May–Labor Day daily 10am–10pm; rest of the year Sun–Tue 10am–5pm, Thu–Sat 10am–10pm.* ⏰*Closed Thanksgiving Day & Dec 25.* 💲*$6 ($10 Thu–Sun 5pm–10pm).* 📞*619-297-7511. www.whaleyhouse.org.*

Considered to be the city's first two-story brick building (1856), this residence illustrates the influence of the East Coast on San Diego's architecture. The north room functioned as the county courthouse between 1869 and 1871, but forcible removal of county records by an armed mob marked the end of the pueblo's prospects as a city center. Now restored and appointed with local period furnishings, the house features one of six life masks of Abraham Lincoln. Whaley House is one of only two California houses certified (by the US Department of Commerce) as being haunted.

Heritage Park

Off Juan St. adjacent to Old Town.

Arrayed around a cobblestone cul-de-sac are seven Victorian buildings (1880s), all originally erected in Horton's elite neighborhood on the edge of downtown. Threatened with destruction in the 1960s, the buildings were relocated here, thanks to preservation efforts. Today the structures are leased to private organizations, but you can stroll among them to admire the several variants of Victorian architecture, including Queen Anne, Stick Eastlake and Colonial Revival.

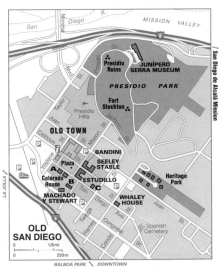

PRESIDIO PARK★

From Old Town, take Mason St. north to Jackson St.; turn left and follow signs.
🕐*Open year-round Tue–Sun.*

The foundations of Spanish colonial history in Alta California lie atop this prominent knoll. The beautifully landscaped park features an historical museum and archaeological remains of the first European settlement on the West Coast.

In 1769 Portolá and Serra designated this hill as the site for both mission and presidio. Soldiers built log stockades while Serra met Kumeyaay Indians at the nearby village of Cosoy. Although the mission was relocated in 1774, the Royal Presidio remained an active military installation into the Mexican period, and a small settlement was established in the area around the fortress. Upon Mexican independence in 1821, the fortress was abandoned as its occupants moved downhill to establish Old Town.

San Diego resident George White Marston acquired much of Presidio Hill, landscaping it with nearly 10,000 shrubs and trees, and commissioning the Junípero Serra Museum. Marston presented the park and the museum to the city of San Diego as a gift in 1929.

Serra Museum★

2727 Presidio Dr. ⌐*Not open to the public.* ☎*619-297-3258.*
www.sandiegohistory.org.

Looming over the western end of Mission Valley, this museum building (1929, William Templeton Johnson) is a San Diego landmark. Capped by a tower, the Mission Revival structure features Spanish Colonial elements, including red-tile roofs, arches and clerestory-type windows.

Presidio Ruins

Downhill from the museum.

A wall marks the perimeter of the original presidio complex, today a group of grass-covered mounds.

A flagpole at the summit of Presidio Hill indicates the site of **Fort Stockton**, built by Mexican soldiers in 1838 and commandeered by American forces during the Mexican War.

MISSION BASILICA SAN DIEGO DE ALCALÁ★★

♿*Map p240. From Old Town take I-8 east 6mi to Mission Gorge Rd. and follow signs. Enter through the gift shop.*
🕐*Open year-round daily 9am–4.45pm.*
☞*Guided tours available; reservation required.* 🕐*Closed Easter Sunday, Dec 25 (open for Mass only).* ☜*Contribution requested.* ♿🅿 ☎*619-281-8449. www. missionsandiego.com.*

California's first mission occupies a site on the north slope of the San Diego River valley, today known as **Mission Valley**, and marked by the urban sprawl of a 21C megalopolis. The mission was named for St. Didacus of Alcalá, a 15C Spanish Franciscan friar credited with miraculous healing power.

Art Students at Serra Museum

© John Anderson/MICHELIN

Balboa Park

© Brigitta L. House/MICHELIN

Originally established atop Presidio Hill in 1769 by Padre Junípero Serra, the mission was relocated here to be farther from the corrupting influences of presidio soldiers.

In 1775 the mission was burned in a Kumeyaay uprising. A larger complex, surrounded by high adobe walls, was completed in 1776. In 1813 a new, larger adobe church was completed with buttresses for earthquake stability.

Following secularization, the mission was abandoned and its buildings fell into disrepair. By the time ownership was returned to the Catholic Church in 1862, little from the original structures remained. The present restoration occurred between 1895 and 1931.

Visit – The original white stucco church featured a five-bell campanario. The sparsely furnished **casa del Padre Serra** is the only remaining fragment of the original monastery.

Restored to its 1813 appearance, the church **interior** measures 150ft by 35ft, its width kept narrow by the lack of tall trees to use for ceiling beams. In the sanctuary, note the 18C painting of St. Didacus and the hand-carved wooden statues that survive from the early mission period. In the **small garden** (adjacent to the church), crosses of adobe and burnt tile pay homage to Native Americans buried during the mission period. The mission **museum** (behind the church) displays artifacts of the Native American, mission, Mexican and American periods.

BALBOA PARK★★★
♿ Map p248.

San Diego's cultural focal point is a 1,200-acre park just north of downtown. Lawns, gardens and century-old shade trees harbor a world-renowned zoo, performance spaces and diverse museums housed in buildings cherished and restored from two world expositions.

A BIT OF HISTORY

A Slow Start – In 1868 San Diego's Board of Trustees, prodded by booster Alonzo Horton, designated a 1,400-acre tract on the outskirts as the future home for a city park. But the sandy expanse lay undeveloped and mostly unused for some 20 years.

In 1892 horticulturist **Kate Sessions** leased 30 acres for her nursery business. As her rent, she promised to plant 100 trees a year in the park. Over the next decade, she seeded lawns and flower beds, planted trees and laid out nature trails.

As the park took shape, the consulting architect for New York City was hired to oversee its development. Roads were graded and the soil was amended with street sweepings. John McLaren, the superintendent of San Francisco's Golden Gate Park sent plants as a gift. By 1910 the landscape resembled its present-day appearance and a contest was held to rename the park. The winning entry was Balboa Park, after Spanish explorer Vasco Nuñez de Balboa, who

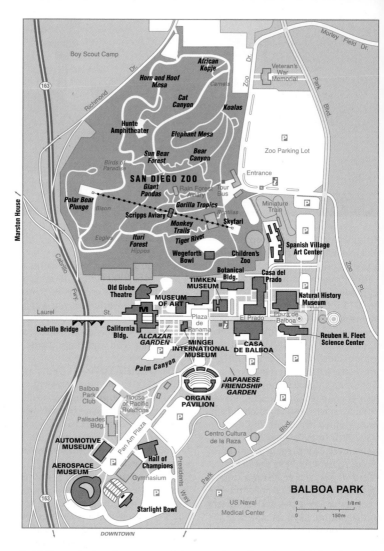

in 1513 was the first European to sight the Pacific Ocean.

Two Great Expositions – Balboa Park was chosen as the setting for the **1915 Panama-California International Exposition**, a yearlong world fair to promote San Diego as the US's first West Coast port of call from the newly opened Panama Canal. Architects led by Bertram Goodhue raised a stylized Spanish city of exhibit pavilions around two central plazas, Plaza de Balboa and Plaza de Panama, linked by El Prado, a broad pedestrian thoroughfare. The dominant style used was Spanish Colonial Revival, a hybrid of Moorish, Baroque and rococo ornamentation with colorful tiles and flat, unadorned walls.

Many of the buildings were later restored or rebuilt to house cultural institutions. As America wallowed in the Great Depression two decades later, San Diegans again looked to Balboa Park as they planned the **1935 California Pacific International Exposition**, to lift spirits and boost commerce.

Architect Richard Requa designed new pavilions in art deco, Mayan-Aztec and

American Southwestern styles; these too have survived to serve the city.

A Park for All – Today Balboa Park endures as a sylvan retreat and year-round cultural haven for people from all walks of life. Concert enthusiasts and theatergoers throng live performances at the **Starlight Bowl** (◷ open May–Sept; call for schedule & tickets; ✕☂ ☐ ✆ 619-232-7827; www.starlighttheatre.org) and a 1935 replica of Shakespearean London's **Old Globe Theatre** (◷ open year-round; ◷ closed major holidays; call for schedule & tickets; ✕☂ ☐ ✆ 619-234-5623; www.oldglobe.org). Construction began in 2008 on the **Prebys Theater Center**, a 4-story theater and education center on Copley Plaza near the Globe; the center will open in late 2009.

VISIT

The Balboa Park visitor center is located in the **House of Hospitality** *(1549 El Prado; ◷ open year-round daily 9.30am–4.30pm, extended summer hours; ◷ closed major holidays; ☂ ☐ ✆ 619-239-0512; www.balboapark.org). Admission to the park is free, but most museums and attractions charge admission fees. The* **Passport to Balboa Park** *(☒$39, children $21; good for 7 days) provides admission to 13 museums; the* **Passport/Zoo Combo** *ticket (☒$65, children $36) includes admission to the San Diego Zoo. Passports are available online (www.balboapark.org) or at the park visitor center in the House of Hospitality. Note that many museums are closed on Mondays. A free* **tram** *(every 8–10min; daily 8.30am–6pm) shuttles visitors to points throughout the park; the Tram Center stop is on Park Boulevard at Inspiration Point; you can leave your car in the parking lot there.*

⚲⚲ San Diego Zoo★★★

2920 Zoo Dr. (Park Blvd. & Zoo Pl.). ◷ Open year-round daily, late Apr–Jun 9am–6pm; rest of the year 9am–9pm. ☒$35, children $26 (includes Skyfari & Bus Tours); 2-day ticket $40, children $30. ✕☂ ☐ ✆ 619-231-1515. www.sandiegozoo.org.

One of the largest, most diverse and most celebrated zoological parks in the world, San Diego Zoo occupies 100 acres of landscaped hillsides and ravines at the north end of Balboa Park.

Some 4,000 animals represent 800 species in a setting shaded by plants representing more than 6,500 botanical species.

▶ **Location:** For an overview, purchase the Best Value Admission (☒$35), which includes the **Guided Bus Tour** *(departs just inside zoo entrance; 40min; ☂).* The double-decker buses cover about 80 percent of the zoo, including outer reaches less accessible on foot. Once oriented, you can wander the pathways in roughly clockwise order, aided by moving sidewalks that climb steep hills. **Skyfari**, an aerial tram that traverses the zoo's western end, allows easy access to Horn & Hoof Mesa along the zoo's northwestern edge.

😊 **Don't Miss:** The animal shows presented regularly in the **Wegeforth Bowl** in the zoo's southeastern corner and the **Hunte Amphitheater** on its northwestern side *(20–25min; check program for schedule).*

A Bit of History

During the Panama-California Exposition, a small menagerie of wild animals was assembled just northeast of the zoo's location. The roar of a caged lion there inspired local surgeon Dr. Harry Wegeforth to found the Zoological Society of San Diego. In 1922 the city granted the society its permanent home—a hilly, chaparral-covered tract of 100 acres.

Under Wegeforth's direction, the zoo increased its holdings, landscaping the enclosures to resemble the animals' natural environments. That spirit continues today, both in state-of-the-art walk-through habitats—part of a long-term plan to redesign the zoo into bioclimatic zones—and at the zoo's sister institution, the San Diego Wild Animal Park.

Western lowland gorillas, San Diego Zoo

© Ken Bohn/The Zoological Society of San Diego

San Diego Zoo has increasingly played a major role in conservation. In 1966 it hosted the first international conference on the role of zoos in conservation. Most notably, in 1975, it launched the Center for Reproduction of Endangered Species (now the center for Conservation and Research for Endangered Species, or CRES), dedicated to increasing animals' chances of reproduction and survival both in zoos and in the wild. In 2002, the zoo embarked on its largest construction project to date: a $26 million overhaul of the center of the park. Completed in 2005, Monkey Trails and Forest Tales is the new residence of some 30 species of African and Asian mammals, reptiles and birds. The zoo's newest exhibit, Elephant Odyssey, opened in 2009.

Visit

One of the zoo's newest exhibits, the **Monkey Trails and Forest Tales**, lies near the zoo entrance. Within this large exhibit area, you might spot colorful mandrill monkeys, bearded pigs, tinkerbirds and even pygmy hippos who call this habitat home.

In the **Children's Zoo** everything is small scale. Young visitors are drawn to a baby animal nursery, small walk-through aviaries and a petting paddock with barnyard animals.

In **Tiger River**, a winding trail descends through a tropical rain forest, passing crocodiles, Chinese water dragons, fishing cats, tapirs, pythons, mouse deer and a dozen species of birds. The walk concludes at three viewing stations overlooking an extensive habitat for Sumatran tigers.

Ituri Forest re-creates the Central African rain forest and displays okapi, forest buffalo, spotted-necked otters, monkeys and birds. Of special interest is the **hippopotamus** pond, where the massive "river horses" can be observed in unique behaviors above and below the water line.

The 2.5-acre **Gorilla Tropics**, a simulation of an African rain forest, includes an 8,000sq-ft enclosure for western lowland gorillas. Below the gorilla habitat are the **Scripps Aviary**, a walk-through multilevel enclosure housing more than 200 African bird species, surrounded by waterfalls and tropical foliage. You'll also find here the **Owens Rain Forest Aviary** and **Absolutely Apes**, populated by charming siamangs and orangutans and a 6,000sq-ft naturalistic environment for lively **pygmy chimps**.

Bear Canyon exemplifies the early zoo-without-cages philosophy, presenting various bear species in individual open-air enclosures. At the bottom of Bear Canyon is **Sun Bear Forest**, a 1.5-acre habitat featuring playful Malaysian sun bears in an environment of rocks, waterfalls and lush greenery. Farther along, in nearby Panda Canyon, the Giant Panda Research Station houses one of the zoo's premier exhibits: a group of **giant pandas** has grown from an initial pair loaned to the zoo from the People's Republic of China. The original two, Bai Yun and Shi Shi made world news when they became the parents of an infant daughter, Hua Mei, in August 1999.

Pronounced "copy," **African Kopje** is a volcanic-rock outcropping reflective of the terrain typical of the African plains; featured are soft-shelled pancake tortoises and klipspringers, a species of small antelope. Below lies **Cat Canyon**, showcasing habitats for cats and dogs of the wild.

The zoo's newest exhibit, the spectacular **Elephant Odyssey**, compares living animals of the present to the ancient counterparts that inhabited this area 12,000 years ago, represented by life-sized statues. You'll see the zoo's Asian and African elephants up close with a Columbian mammoth; a jaguar near a replica sabertooth cat; and an American lion next to his ancient ancestor. California condors, pronghorns and rattlesnakes share this exhbit area.

At the western end of the Elephant Odyssey lies the **Polar Bear Plunge,** where a group of the large carnivores cavort around and in their 14ft-deep pool.

San Diego Natural History Museum

🚹🧍1788 El Prado. 🕐Open year-round Sun–Thu 10am–7pm, Fri–Sat 10am–9.30pm. 🕐Closed Thanksgiving Day, Dec 25. ☜$13, children $7. ✖🚻🅿 𝄽619-232-3821. www.sdnhm.org.

Founded in 1874, the San Diego Society of Natural History opened its first museum in 1920 in Casa de Balboa. Ellen Browning Scripps funded the two-story building (1933, William Templeton Johnson). New construction (Bundy & Thompson), completed in 2001, incorporates a four-story, glass-ceilinged atrium and a giant-screen theater.

Much of the museum's collection of more than 7 million specimens is presented in a permanent exhibit that re-creates a walk across Baja California and San Diego County, from deep ocean through high mountains to low desert. State-of-the-art dioramas and computer stations add to the exhibit's interactive nature. Other displays highlight geology and paleontology, including a new permanent exhibit "Fossil Mysteries."

The adjacent **Casa del Prado** (1915, Carleton Winslow) was among the largest and most ornate structures of the first exposition. Completely rebuilt in 1971, it now holds a 1,500-seat civic theater and other cultural organizations.

Beyond a 145-year-old Moreton Bay fig tree lies the **Spanish Village Art Center** of studios and galleries and guilds for over 37 working California artists. The village was constructed for the California Pacific Exposition (🕐open year-round daily 11am–4pm; 🕐closed Jan 1, Thanksgiving, Dec 25; 🚻🅿 𝄽619-233-9050; www.spanishvillageart.com).

Reuben H. Fleet Science Center

🚹🧍1875 El Prado. 🕐Open year-round daily 9.30am, closing hours vary. Galleries only ☜$10, children $8.75; with 1 film $14.50, children $11.75; motion simulator $5. ✖🚻🅿 𝄽619-238-1233. www.rhfleet.org.

Changing interactive exhibit galleries, a dome-screen theater and a 23-rider motion simulator for "Escape From Dino Island" adventures share this Spanish Colonial structure, built in 1973 and doubled in size in 1998. The center is named for Reuben H. Fleet, founder of San Diego's Consolidated Aircraft Corp. The Space Theater features tiered seating facing a 75ft domed screen on which astronomy programs, laser shows and large-format IMAX films are projected.

Casa de Balboa★

1649 El Prado. ✖🅿.

This richly ornamented two-story structure was originally designed in 1914 by Bertram Goodhue after the Federal Government Palace in Queretaro, Mexico. In 1978 the building was destroyed by arson; a slightly larger reconstruction opened two years later and is now home to three museums.

Museum of San Diego History

🕐Open year-round Tue–Sun 10am–5pm. 🕐Closed Jan 1, Thanksgiving Day, Dec 25. ☜$5. 🚻 𝄽619-232-6203. www.sandiegohistory.org.

Permanent and changing exhibits on the city's history since the 1840s are presented here, including photos, decorative arts and children's items.

Museum of Photographic A3rts

🕐Open year-round Tue–Sun 10am–5pm (Thu 9pm). 🕐Closed Jul 4, Thanksgiving Day, Dec 25. ☜$6. 🚻 𝄽619-238-7559. www.mopa.org.

Expanded fourfold in 2000, this museum has reinvented itself with vast exhibition galleries, a 228-seat theater, and a learning center with a photo library. The permanent collection of 4,000 19C–20C works features Ansel Adams, Edward Weston, Margaret Bourke-White and many other notables.

San Diego Model Railroad Museum

👥👤🕐*Open year-round Tue–Fri 11am–4pm, weekends 11am–5pm.* 🕐*Closed Thanksgiving Day & Dec 25.* 👓*$6.* ♿🅿 📞*619-696-0199. www.sdmodelrailroadm.com.*

This museum houses one of the largest operating model railroad displays in North America. Actual former Southern California railroads are paid tribute with four working scale-model train exhibits and an interactive toy-train room.

Timken Museum of Art★★

1500 El Prado. 🕐*Open Oct–Aug Tue–Sat 10am–4.30pm, Sun 1.30pm–4.30pm.* 🕐*Closed major holidays.* ♿🅿 📞*619-239-5548. www.timken museum.org.*

Clad in Italian travertine marble, the compact, single-story museum (1965, Frank Hope) displays in its six galleries and rotunda a collection begun in 1951 by local art benefactors Anne and Amy Putnam. Funds for the building were largely provided by H.H. Timken Jr., brother of San Diego Museum of Art founder Amelia Bridges.

The Putnam sisters' passion for **European Masters** is evident in such works as *Portrait of a Gentleman* (1634) by Frans Hals, *Portrait of a Young Captain* (c.1625) by Rubens and Rembrandt's *Saint Bartholomew* (1657). Highlights of the **American Paintings** include *Cholooke, The Yosemite Fall* (1864) by Albert Bierstadt and *Mrs. Thomas Gage* (1771) by John Singleton Copley. Amy Putnam's private collection of **Russian icons**★★ (14C–19C) is displayed in a room on walls covered in velvet that was custom-woven in Florence. The museum also periodically hosts traveling exhibitions.

Behind the museum, a 257ft-long lily pond extends from El Prado to the **Botanical Building** (1915, Carleton Winslow), a Victorian-style pavilion built from 70,000 feet of redwood laths (🕐*open year-round Fri–Wed 10am–4pm*). A verdant collection of some 2,100 plants including ferns, orchids and palms thrives here.

San Diego Museum of Art★

1450 El Prado. 🕐*Open year-round Tue–Sat 10am–5pm, Sun noon–5pm.* 🕐*Closed Jan 1, Thanksgiving Day, Dec 25.* 👓*$10.* 🍴♿🅿 📞*619-232-7931. www.sdmart.org.*

After Balboa Park's first exposition, Amelia and Appleton S. Bridges donated $400,000 for construction of a municipal fine arts gallery, and hired William Templeton Johnson to design the structure on the site of the fair's fine arts building. The city's first art museum opened in 1926. Today the collection totals some 12,000 objects, with strengths in Renaissance, Baroque, Asian and American art.

American artists in the collection include Georgia O'Keeffe, George Inness, Eastman Johnson, Milton Avery and Jasper Johns. Works by Degas, Magritte, Matisse and Pissarro can be found in first-floor galleries. Temporary exhibits are mounted off in the East Wing.

Much of the European collection is on the second floor, including paintings by Luca Signorelli and Francisco de Zurbarán and 20C works by Braque and Vuillard, among others.

The **Asian Collections** include a sculpted pair of early-16C Shinto guardian deities and a suit of armor (1578) by Myochin Morisuke.

Adjoining the main building, the **sculpture court** displays works by Henry Moore, Alexander Calder and Joan Miró.

Japanese Friendship Garden★

2215 Pan American Rd. 🕐*Open Memorial Day–Labor Day Mon–Fri 10am–5pm, weekends 10am–4pm; rest of the year Tue–Sun 10am–4pm (last admission half hr before closing).* 👓*$4.* 🍴♿ 📞*619-232-2721. www.niwa.org.*

The garden was inspired by a magnificent tea house (1915) and garden created for the first exposition. After World War II, the deteriorating tea house was vandalized and in 1955, razed. The garden is currently undergoing an expansion in phases on 11 hillside acres. When finished, the garden will encompass a cultural center, two tea houses, a cherry grove, lotus pond, tea garden and waterfall. Currently open are an exhibit house within a garden, the koi pond, a bonsai collection and a tea pavilion serving light Japanese dishes and teas.

Facing the museum across Plaza de Panama is the 1914 **Spreckels Organ Pavilion**★ (*619-702-8138; www.sos organ.com*, housing a 72-rank, 4,445-pipe instrument, the largest outdoor pipe organ in the world. Concerts are held June through August.

Mingei International Museum★★

1439 El Prado. Open year-round Tue–Sun 10am–4pm. $7. 619-239-0003. www.mingei.org.
This excellent museum of craft and folk art relocated here from La Jolla in 1996. The exterior reconstruction of the 1915 Panama-California Exposition building, called the House of Charm since 1934, is historically faithful to the original building, which was condemned as an earthquake hazard.

The museum's outstanding collection of some 17,500 objects from 141 countries occupies six galleries on two levels. Its name, a coined term, combines the Japanese words for people *(min)* and art *(gei)*. Changing exhibits of historic, traditional and contemporary folk art, craft and design have run the gamut from dolls to dowry furniture, Haitian painting to Chinese jade. The Founder's Gallery presents functional elegance in American craft and Asian decorative art and furnishings. A quality museum shop is located near the front entrance.

California Building

1350 El Prado.
With its massive dome covered in Moorish tiles and its three-belfry, 180ft campanile, the Spanish Colonial structure (1915) was one of the few buildings intended to be preserved from

the Panama-California Exposition. The ornate facade is adorned with important figures from San Diego's early history. The campanile—called the **California Tower**—houses a 100-bell carillon that chimes the quarter-hour.

Diagonally across El Prado is the **Alcazar Garden**★, a Moorish courtyard inspired by those at Seville's Alcazar palace. Beyond lies **Palm Canyon**, a small trail-crossed ravine lushly planted with more than 50 palm species.

San Diego Museum of Man (M)★★

California Building. Open year-round daily 10am–4.30pm. Closed Thanksgiving Day, Dec 25. $10, children $5. 619-239-2001. www.museumofman.org.
Exhibits on human evolution, anthropology and ethnology were first gathered here by the Smithsonian Institution for exhibition at the Panama-California Exposition. The exhibits formed the core of the San Diego Museum, renamed the Museum of Man in 1942; the permanent collection numbers 70,000 objects.

Beneath the building's dome *(1st floor)*, the **Maya: Heart of Sky, Heart of Earth** exhibit displays life-size replicas of stelae and other massive stone monuments from the Mayan city of Quirigua in Guatemala, AD 780–805.

In the west wing, human evolution is the focus of **Footsteps Through Time**, chronicling 65 million years of human development with thought-provoking exhibits like the Time Tunnel, which explores technological achievements in anthropology; and the Human Lab, which looks at the future of human evolution.

Ancient Egypt presents, you guessed it, artifacts from ancient Egypt, including *ushabtis*, magical tomb figurines from 1250–300 BC. A separate display of **mummies** includes bodies unearthed in Peru, Mexico and Egypt.

Kumeyaay: Native Californians describes the lifestyle and arts of this indigenous tribe when first encountered by missionaries in the late 18C.

Cabrillo Bridge

Just west of the California Building, the 405ft-long, 125ft-high bridge (1914) was the first multiple-arched cantilever bridge built in California. The main entrance to the Panama-California Exposition, it was officially opened in April 1914 by then-Assistant Secretary of the Navy, Franklin D. Roosevelt.

San Diego Aerospace Museum★★

2001 Pan American Plaza. ⓘ*Open Memorial Day–Labor Day daily 10am– 5.30pm; rest of the year 10am–4.30pm.* ⓘ*Closed Jan 1, Thanksgiving Day, Dec 25.* *$15, children $6 (additional fees for flight simulator rides and special exhibitions).* *619-234-8291. www.aerospacemuseum.org.*

The white and blue ring-shaped Art Moderne structure (1935) housed a demonstration auto assembly line for the California Pacific Exposition. The Aerospace Museum, founded in 1963, opened here in 1980.

Chronicling the history of flight, the collection encompasses 66 full-size vintage aircraft, from biplanes to space capsules; 14,000 scale-model aircraft; and 10,000 aviation-related items. Just inside the entrance, in the **International Aerospace Hall of Fame**, oil portraits and plaques salute notable inventors, industrialists and pilots. Visitors can also climb aboard one of four **flight simulators** to experience the thrill of a controlling a flight over San Diego or a World War II-era dogfight. Encircling the interior wall is a mural (1935) by Juan Larinaga.

Adjacent to the Aerospace Museum is the **San Diego Automotive Museum★**, which presents changing displays of over 80 classic, exotic and special-interest automobiles and motorcycles *(2030 Pan American Plaza;* ⓘ*open year-round daily 10am–5pm;* ⓘ*closed Jan 1, Thanksgiving Day, Dec 25;* *$8;* *619-231-2886; www.sdautomuseum.org).*

The **San Diego Hall of Champions Sports Museum** in the restored Federal Building exhibits memorabilia, photographs and videos devoted to local amateur and professional athletes in some 40 sports. On its lower level is an interactive exhibit where visitors may test their strength, agility and reflexes *(2131 Pan American Plaza;* ⓘ*open year-round daily 10am–4.30pm;* ⓘ*closed Jan 1, Thanksgiving Day, Dec 25;* *$6, children $3;* *619-234-2544; www.sdhoc.com).*

Marston House★

3525 7th Ave., near NW corner of Balboa Park. *Closed to the public.* *619-298-3142. www.sandiegohistory.org.*

The 8,500sq-ft Arts and Crafts mansion (1905, Irving Gill) was built as the home of department-store owner George White Marston, benefactor of Presidio Park.

San Diego Aerospace Museum

DOWNTOWN

Map above.

Stretching between Balboa Park and San Diego Bay, downtown San Diego serves as the city's center for business, commerce and government.

In the mid-20C this urban center showed signs of decline as the city grew to the north, south and east, ignoring its historic heart. Civic leaders and developers began to stem that tide in the 1970s and 80s, restoring the Gaslamp Quarter, spurring new shops and offices along Broadway, and creating a waterfront renaissance with Seaport Village and the San Diego Convention Center. Across Harbor Drive from the convention center, **PETCO Park**, the $474 million, 42,445-seat Padres baseball stadium, was completed in 2004 (*tours available: 619-795-5000; www.padres.com*).

GASLAMP QUARTER★

The 16 square blocks bounded by Broadway, Harbor Drive and 4th and 5th avenues preserve the aura of late

19C and early 20C San Diego in a district now popular for its trendy restaurants and nightclubs, boutiques and offices. Nearly 100 historic buildings grace the Gaslamp Quarter today; a selection appears below. **Walking tours** *(2 hrs)* of the district, conducted by the Gaslamp Quarter Historic Foundation, depart from the William Heath Davis House (*year-round Sat 11am; $10; 619-233-4692; www.gaslampquarter.org*).

William Heath Davis House

410 Island Ave. Open year-round Tue–Sat 10am–6pm, Sun 9am–3pm. $5. 619-233-4692. www.gaslamp quarter.org

The district's oldest surviving structure, a two-story saltbox built from a Sears catalog on the East Coast in 1850 and shipped around Cape Horn, is an exact duplicate of one lived in briefly by Davis; Alonzo Horton occupied this house for a short period in 1867.

Rooms on both floors are decorated in period style. The house serves as a

Horton Plaza
Shopping Center

visitor center for the Gaslamp Quarter Foundation.

Horton Grand Hotel★

311 Island Ave. ✕♿🅿 *℘619-544-1886. www.hortongrand.com.*
Regal bay windows front San Diego's oldest Victorian-era hotel (1886). Restored in 1981, the structure combines two hotels that were dismantled from their original sites in the downtown area and relocated here. An atrium connects the two structures.

The narrow, three-story **Yuma Building** *(631 5th Ave.)* was one of downtown's first brick structures (1888); it variously housed offices, a Japanese bazaar and a brothel before restoration began in 1982. Twin gabled towers top the four-story, ornately embellished **Louis Bank of Commerce** *(835 5th Ave.),* San Diego's first granite building (1888). The interior of the 1907 **Ingle Building** *(801 4th Ave.)* reveals a 25ft stained-glass dome.

BROADWAY★
Horton Plaza★

Bordered by Broadway & G St., 1st & 4th Aves. 🕐*Open year-round Mon–Sat 10am–9pm, Sun 11am–6pm.* 🕐*Closed Easter Sunday, Thanksgiving Day, Dec 25.* ✕♿🅿 *℘619-239-8180. www.westfield.com.*
The open-air, multilevel, post-Modern shopping center (1985, Jon Jerde) is deliberately designed to disorient visitors, thus encouraging more browsing. The 11.5-acre complex encompasses

major department stores (including Nordstrom and Macy's), more than 180 specialty shops and restaurants, a 14-screen cinema and two live-performance theaters.

U.S. Grant Hotel★

326 Broadway. ✕♿🅿 *℘619-232-3121. www.usgrant.net.*
Downtown's stateliest hotel, this massive 11-story Italian Renaissance Revival structure (1910) faces Horton Plaza. In 1895 Fannie Grant, daughter-in-law of 18th US President Ulysses S. Grant, bought the Horton House Hotel that had occupied the site since 1870. The new hotel she and her husband built in its place, named to honor the former president, was considered one of the grandest of its day. Purchased by the Kumeyaay Indians in 2003, the hotel underwent a $50 million renovation and reopened in 2006 as a member of the Starwood hotel group. Its **interior** boasts lavish chandeliers; marble in more than two dozen colors; and woods that include mahogany, bird's-eye maple and American black walnut.

Spreckels Theatre

121 Broadway. Auditorium open for performances only. ♿ *℘619-235-0494.*
Sugar magnate John D. Spreckels commissioned the imposing Baroque theater (1912) to celebrate the opening of both the Panama Canal and San Diego's 1915 exposition. The lobby's walls and ceiling gleam with Predora onyx. Allegori-

cal paintings decorate the proscenium and ceiling of the 1,466-seat auditorium, considered acoustically perfect and still in use for music, theater and dance.

Emerald Plaza★

402 W. Broadway.
This 30-story cluster of eight hexagonal glass office towers (1990, C.W. Kim) lights the downtown skyline by night with the glow of emerald-green neon. The complex includes the Westin hotel, whose 100ft-high **atrium** is dominated by a hanging green glass sculpture (1990) by Richard Lippold.

America Plaza

1001 Kettner Blvd. at Broadway.
San Diego's tallest building, this tapered, 34-story office tower (1991, Helmut Jahn) rises to a star-shaped pinnacle above walls of glass and white granite. Adjoining, a glass-and-steel canopy shelters a trolley station and connects the tower to the 10,000sq-ft downtown branch of the **Museum of Contemporary Art San Diego** (◐*open year-round Thu–Tue 11am–5pm;* ◐*closed major holidays;* ◔*$10 (free 3rd Thu of the month);* ♿ ✆*858-454-3541; www.mcasd.org),* which mounts traveling shows and changing exhibits of works from the permanent collection of its La Jolla-based counterpart. In 2007 the renovated baggage building of the Santa Fe Depot and a new 3-story structure, both across the street, were added to the museum campus.

Santa Fe Depot

1050 Kettner Blvd. at Broadway.
♿🅿 ✆*619-465-7776 (weekdays); www.sdrm.org/sfd.html.*
Two towers distinguish this Spanish Colonial-style train station (1915, Bakewell & Brown Jr.), built to handle visitors arriving for the Panama-California Exposition. The depot houses offices of the remote **San Diego Railroad Museum**, which offers excursions into Mexico aboard vintage trains from its yard 57mi southeast of San Diego (*Rte. 94, Campo;* ◐*open year-round weekends 10am–5pm;* ✆*619-478-9937; www.sdrm. org).*

WATERFRONT★
San Diego Maritime Museum★

👥*1492 N. Harbor Dr.* ◐*Open Memorial Day–Labor Day daily 9am–9pm; rest of the year daily 9am–8pm.* ◔*$14, children $8 (additional $3 for harbor cruise).* ✆*619-234-9153. www.sdmaritime.com.*
Docked harborside opposite the Spanish Colonial **San Diego County Administration Building** (1938), three historic ships and their onboard exhibits form the core of a museum dedicated to the city's maritime history.
The **Berkeley** – Serving as museum headquarters, this historic steam ferry (1898) carried passengers between San

Star of India sailing ship, San Diego Maritime Museum

© Hemis/Photoshot

Francisco and Oakland. Moored alongside is the **Medea**. Built in 1904, the 140ft iron-hulled steam yacht saw military action during both world wars and served as a pleasure ship in the Mediterranean and Baltic seas. Launched as a British full-rigged ship in 1863, the **Star of India**★★ is the oldest iron merchant ship afloat; in 1871-97, she circumnavigated the globe 21 times. You can also climb aboard a faithful replica of the 18C frigate the H.M.S. Surprise, used in the 2003 film *Master and Commander: The Far Side of the World*, or cruise the harbor aboard the 1914 shuttle **Pilot** *(weekends 11am–3pm on the hour)*.

Seaport Village★
849 W. Harbor Dr. at Kettner Blvd.
🕐*Open year-round daily 10am–9pm; restaurants have extended hours.*
✕🕭🅿 🖉*619-235-4014.*
www.seaportvillage.com.
Hugging the harbor, this 14-acre complex of one- and two-story New England- and Mediterranean-style buildings connected by cobblestone pathways unites shops, restaurants and a waterside boardwalk. The 1890 **carousel** ♙♙ *(☜$2)* was moved here in 1980.

San Diego Convention Center★
111 W. Harbor Dr. 🕭🅿 🖉*619-525-5000. www.visitsandiego.com.*
With its open-air rooftop plaza surmounted by a giant white tent, this waterfront convention center resembles a futuristic sailing ship docked on its 11-acre site beside San Diego Bay. Inaugurated in 1990, the convention center now totals 1.7million sq ft.

The New Children's Museum★
♙♙*200 W. Island Ave.* 🕐*Open Mon–Tue & Thu–Sat 10am–4pm (Thu 6pm), Sun noon–4pm.* ☜*$10.* 🖉*619-233-8792. www.thinkplaycreate.org.*
Reopened in 2008 in a brand-new building in the heart of the downtown/waterfront area, this state-of-the-art facility entices and inspires young people ages toddler to teen to create, explore and (most important) play. The focus here is on the visual and performing arts and the environment, with artworks that visitors can handle and touch, studios for artmaking, and regular live performances.

MISSION BAY★★
🕭*See Greater San Diego map.*
This 4,600-acre seaside playground was first developed in the 1930s to stimulate San Diego's tourism industry. Today, with green lawns, concrete foot and bike paths and 44mi of sandy beach, Mission Bay is known as a recreational headquarters for both visitors and residents.

♙♙ SeaWorld San Diego★★
North from downtown San Diego on I-5; exit at Sea World Dr. & follow signs.
🕐*Open year-round Mon–Fri 10am, Sat–Sun 9am; closing times vary seasonally.* ☜*$65, children $55.* ✕🕭🅿*($12)* 🖉*619-226-3901 or 800-257-4268. www.seaworld.com.*
Opened in 1964, this adventure park has expanded to 189.5 acres with more than 25 marine-life exhibits and aquariums. The park pioneered breeding programs for orca whales, emperor penguins and other species, and operates a rescue-and-rehabilitation program for beached marine mammals. Below are highlights of the exhibits, tours and rides:
🐾**Guided Tour** – *60min. Tickets and schedules at park entrance; tours depart from tour booth.* This behind-the-scenes tour offers access to the park's animal rescue and rehabilitation facilities.
Animal shows – *Each show about 25min; schedule at park entrance.* The showpiece at Shamu Stadium is **Shamu Show: Believe**★, featuring the park's beloved orcas and their trainers in an aquatic ballet. A 300ft video screen displays live close-ups and underwater views. Pilot whales and dolphins take to the air in a display of skyward twists and leaps in **Dolphin Discovery**. 🐟*Spectators in the front 14 rows will get spashed.* Orcas and dolphins also take center stage seasonally after dark in the **Shamu Rocks** and **Ignight** nighttime shows. The park's sea lions cavort for fans in the **Sea Lions Live** show at Sea Lion & Otter stadium.

Palms on the beach of Mission Bay, San Diego

© Stas Volik/iStockphoto

Interactive Exhibits – Rocky Point Preserve★ invites visitors to touch and feed bottle-nosed dolphins in a sculpted habitat resembling a rocky shoreline. In the **California Tide Pool**, visitors can touch starfish, sea urchins and other examples of intertidal zone life, while bat rays swim close to the edge at the **Forbidden Reef** *(upper level)*.

Exhibits, Aquariums and Rides – The **Wild Arctic**★ begins with a ride in a simulated helicopter to a research station that shares its subpolar climate with polar bears, beluga whales, walruses and harbor seals.

At **Shark Encounter**★ visitors pass through a 57ft underwater viewing tube that offers good views of the bellies and mouths of Pacific blacktip and sandtiger sharks as they swim about in the company of rays and other fish. **Manatee Rescue** lets viewers observe the behavior of the endangered marine mammals through 800sq ft of windows. Youngest visitors can meet fishy friends up close in the Sesame Street **Bay of Play**, with its pint-sized rides and char-acer encounters.

Shipwreck Rapids – An inner tube-style rafting experience swishes through rapids, beneath waterfalls and through a dark tunnel to a near-collision with a ship's propeller. Expect to get soaked on the **Journey to Atlantis**, a roller-coaster splash ride that ends with a visit to a rare Commerson's dolphin.

Skytower – Bird's-eye **views**★★ of the park complex, the surrounding Mission Bay area and the San Diego skyline in the distance can be enjoyed from this revolving chamber as it ascends to its 265ft observation point.

ADDITIONAL SIGHTS
 See Greater San Diego map.
Villa Montezuma★
1925 K St. (between 19th & 20th Sts.). Closed indefinitely. www.sandiego-history.org. Due to street crime, it is advisable to arrive by car or taxi.
This elaborate mansion (1887) was commissioned by wealthy residents for Jesse Shepard, a musician, spiritualist and author. The villa's exterior exemplifies the Queen Anne style, with its towers and shingled walls.

Cabrillo National Monument★★
Cabrillo Memorial Dr., Point Loma. From downtown drive north 7mi on Harbor Dr., then left on Rosecrans St., right on Canon St., and left on Catalina Blvd. through Fort Rosecrans. Visitor center is 3mi from fort gate. Open year-round daily 9am–5pm. $5/ vehicle. & P 619-557-5450. www.nps.gov/cabr.
This park commemorates the European exploration of the US Pacific coast and preserves one of the oldest lighthouses on the West Coast.

259

Juan Rodríguez Cabrillo stepped ashore here in 1542, the first European to set foot on California soil. Activated in 1855, the light at Point Loma stood 462ft above sea level, making it the south-westernmost and highest lighthouse in the US. Coastal fog often obscured the beam, and in 1891 a new lighthouse was built at the southwest tip of the point. The old lighthouse was designated a national monument in 1913.

From the foot of a **statue** of Cabrillo, **views**★★★ extend over San Diego and its bay as far south as Mexico. The par-lor, kitchen and bedrooms of the **Old Point Loma Lighthouse**★ *(uphill from the visitor center)* have been restored to their 1880s appearance. Down a nearby pathway, exhibits in the old **Army Radio Building** highlight coastal defenses during World Wars I and II.

The scenic **Bayside Trail** *(2.5mi round-trip; brochure available at visitor center)* descends the point's eastern slope, and south of the lighthouse, the sheltered Whale Overlook is a vantage point for whale watching *(Dec–Feb)*. On Point Loma's western shore, a **tidepool area**★ offers exploration.

CORONADO★
See Greater San Diego map.
Take I-5 south to Rte. 75.
Situated on a peninsula across the bay from downtown San Diego, this pretty enclave seems sheltered from the urban center a half a mile away.

In 1884 ill health forced 36-year-old Indi-ana railroad executive Elisha Babcock Jr., to retire to San Diego. He and Hampton Story hunted on Coronado. In 1885 they bought the entire 4,100-acre peninsula. After streets were laid out and land-scaped, they welcomed potential inves-tors to a picnic and land auction. Having recouped the initial investment on that day's sales alone, they began planning the Hotel del Coronado.

For years, the town could be reached only by ferry or a spit connecting it to the bay's southern end. Coronado became more accessible in 1969 with the opening of the 11,179ft **San Diego-Coronado Bay Bridge**★.

Hotel del Coronado★★
1500 Orange Ave. ✕&🅿 *℘619-435-6611. www.hoteldel.com.*
&*See Addresses: Stay.*
Opened in 1887, this landmark struc-ture of white wood and red shingles is California's last surviving Victorian-era seaside resort; it preserves an aura of turn-of-the-19C grandeur.

The hotel has hosted US presidents and numerous celebrities. While staying here in 1920, Edward, Prince of Wales, report-edly first met Wallis Simpson, 16 years before he abdicated Britain's throne to marry her.

The English-style, two-story **grand lobby** is richly finished in Illinois oak. The vast main dining room, the **Crown Room**, boasts walls and ceiling of Oregon sugar pine; the crown-shaped chandeliers were designed by *Wizard of Oz* author L. Frank Baum. From the palm-shaded **Garden Patio**, the History Gallery, a hallway lined with exhibits, leads to ocean-view public terraces.

EXCURSIONS
Cuyamaca Rancho State Park
12551 Rte. 79, Descanso, 43mi northeast of San Diego via I-8 east and Rte. 79 north. ⏰*Open daily year-round.* ⬭*$6/ vehicle.* △&🅿 *℘760-765-3020. www.parks.ca.gov.*
This 25,000-acre park of oak trees and conifers preserves traces of Native American culture and a gold rush that brought renown to this remote region of San Diego County. It's an excellent spot for camping and hiking.

Julian★
57mi northeast of San Diego via I-8 east and Rte. 79 north. www.julianca.com.
This mountain village, situated at 4,200ft on the flank of Volcan Mountain, developed in the wake of the gold rush. Today its broad Main Street, lined with 19C-style storefronts, holds the **Julian Pioneer Museum** *(2811 Washington St.;* ⏰*open Apr–Dec Wed–Sun 10am–4pm; rest of the year weekends 10am–4pm;* ⏰*closed major holidays;* ⬭*$3;* ℘*760-765-0227)*, where artifacts dating from 1869 are on view.

Hotel del Coronado

© Paule858 Photography/iStockphoto

To the south, the 24mi **Sunrise National Scenic Byway** *(Rte. 51 between I-8 and Rte. 79)* traverses the Cleveland National Forest, offering views to the east of Anza-Borrego Desert State Park.

Santa Ysabel Asistencia Mission

8mi northwest of Julian via Rte. 79. ○*Open Memorial Day–Labor Day daily 8am–5pm; rest of the year daily 8am–3pm.* 🅿 ℘*760-765-0810.*
The surviving outpost of the San Diego de Alcalá Mission was founded in 1818. The stucco chapel (1924) serves as a parish church and houses a museum of mission photographs and Native American artifacts.

Palomar Observatory

55mi northeast of San Diego via Rte. 163, I-15 and Rte. 76 east. ○*Open year-round daily 9am–3pm (4pm closing during Daylight Savings Time).* ○*Closed Dec 24–25.* 🅿 ℘*760-742-2119. www.astro.caltech.edu/palomar.*
Located near the peak of Palomar Mountain (6,126ft), this observatory—owned and operated by the California Institute of Technology in Pasadena—boasts the largest optical telescope in the US. The celebrated **Hale Telescope**★, with its 200in Pyrex lens, has a range surpassing 1 billion light-years.

SAN DIEGO WILD ANIMAL PARK★★★

🕭*See Principal sights map.*
🚻*15500 San Pasqual Valley Rd., Escondido, 30mi northeast of San Diego; take I-15 to Via Rancho Parkway exit, turn right and follow signs.* ○*Open year-round daily 9am–4pm (patrons may stay until 5pm). Extended spring and summer hours. Best Value admission including Journey into Africa tour and carousel* ☜*$35, children $26 .*
△✕&🅿 (*$6*) ℘*760-747-8702 or 800-934-2267. www.sandiegozoo.org.*
Exotic and endangered animals from around the globe find safe haven in this 1,800-acre park managed by the Zoological Society of San Diego, which also operates the San Diego Zoo.
In 1953 zoo officials conceived of an open-air captive breeding center for endangered species as an adjunct facility of the zoo. The foothills of undeveloped San Pasqual Valley proved an ideal environment for many species.
Today as many as 600 creatures are born or hatched at the park each year, with five times the survival rate of newborns in the wild. The total collection of some 3,500 mammals and birds represents some 260 species, including 90 species of **ungulates** (hooved animals), the largest assemblage of these animals in captivity.

Elephants in San Diego Wild Animal Park

Nairobi Village
Inside the main entrance.
In this 17-acre area re-creating the atmosphere of a Congo fishing village, visitors pass through aviaries filled with exotic birds and vegetation, and view small-animal exhibits. Educational and entertaining **animal shows** feature birds of prey to Asian elephants. Experience life in the wild at the **Mombasa Lagoon**. A **petting Kraal** allows visitors to interact with hand-raised animals, and the **Hidden Jungle** features such unusual forest creatures as giant scorpions, poison-arrow frogs and tarantulas. Visitors can even interact with the colorful inhabitants of **Lorikeet Landing**.

Habitats★★
Habitats represent East and South African savannas, North African desert, Asian plains and waterholes, and Mongolian steppe, as well as North American ecosystems.
The 100-acre **Eastern Africa** enclosure houses Ugandan giraffes, white-bearded wildebeests and southern white rhinoceroses. Indian rhinoceroses share the **Asian Plain**. Hooved animals, including addra gazelles and African oryx, graze peacefully in **Northern Africa**, while **Southern Africa** features the park's prized collection of northern white rhinoceroses, the only group in the US. In the North American habitats, the **Condor Ridge** habitat is home to rare and endangered denizens of North American desert, prairie and woodland environ-

ments. Other, smaller habitats feature successes from the zoo's breeding programs, including Sumatran tigers, okapi and pygmy chimpanzees.
Thirty-two acres have been set aside for **Heart of Africa**, free of visible barriers in a savanna-like section of the San Pasqual Valley. In **Journey into Africa** *(30min; ☜$10)*, visitors seated in open-sided tour vehicles observe, at fairly close range, giraffes, cheetahs, rhinos, ostriches, Ruppell's vultures, Vaal rheboks (antelopes) and other animals.
African and Asian elephants, Sumatran tigers, and other large mammals can be seen in spacious enclosures along the 2mi **Kilimanjaro Safari Walk.** The trail passes Lion Camp, which features just-close-enough encounters with these big cats. The walk connects to a 1mi path through the lush **Kupanda Falls Botanical Center.**
The Wild Animal Park also is a fully accredited botanical garden, with some 4,000 species of plants native to every continent.

SAN PASQUAL BATTLEFIELD STATE HISTORIC PARK★
15808 San Pasqual Valley Rd., 30mi northeast of San Diego; 8mi east of Escondido on Rte. 78, and 1.5mi east of the San Diego Wild Animal Park. ○*Open year-round weekends 10am–5pm.* ○*Closed Jan 1, Dec 25.* ♿ 🅿 ✆*760-737-2201. www.parks.ca.gov.*
A highly informative visitor center tells the story of the bloodiest California bat-

tle of the Mexican War in which Brig. Gen. Stephen W. Kearny and a detachment of the Army of the West set out toward Los Angeles from Kansas. After hearing news that California was already in American hands, Kearny dispatched all but 100 of his troops to a garrison in Santa Fe and continued west. Near the San Pasqual Valley, they learned that the Mexican settlers, called "Californios," had taken back all of the southern part of the state except San Diego.

On the foggy morning of December 6, 1846, Kearny's troops engaged a Mexican troop commanded by Andrés Pico. After a series of battles, American reinforcements arrived from San Diego, enabling Kearny's troops at last to enter the city.

An observation area overlooks the scene of the battle, while interpretive displays and a video (10min) relate the history of the site and of the Mexican War.

SAN DIEGO COUNTY COAST

28mi. & See Principal Sights map.
Leave La Jolla by N. Torrey Pines Rd, which becomes Rte. 21.

North of La Jolla, the coast of San Diego County is lined with a string of residential towns and scenic beaches. North of Torrey Pines State Reserve, the road passes through **Del Mar**, an upper-class enclave famed for thoroughbred racing at the Del Mar Racetrack.

North of the town of Solana Beach, the road skirts Cardiff State Beach and San Elijo State Beach, both part of **Encinitas**, known for its production of poinsettias. The **Quail Botanical Gardens**★ are 30 acres of native, exotic and drought-resistant species (from Rte. 21 turn right on Encinitas Blvd., pass under I-5 and turn left on Quail Gardens Dr.; ◷open year-round daily 9am–5pm; ◷closed Jan 1, Dec 25; ◷$10 & 🅿($1) ℘760-436-3036. www.qbgardens.com).

Moonlight State Beach and Leucadia State Beach fringe the coastline east of Route 21 as it traverses northern Encinitas. Beyond the Batiquitos Lagoon ecological reserve lies **Carlsbad** (Visitor Information: 400 Carlsbad Village Dr.; ☎760-434-6093; www.carlsbadca.org),

named in 1887 when local mineral waters were found to be chemically identical to those of Karlsbad, the famed German spa.

LEGOLAND California★

👪1 Legoland Dr., off Cannon Rd. east of I-5. ◷Open summer daily 10am; closing hours vary. ◷Closed Tue–Wed in offseason. Check website for operating schedule. ◷$63, children $53. ✖& 🅿 ℘760-918-5346. www.legolandca.com. The first US theme park for the Danish-designed children's building blocks opened in 1999. In the LEGO Miniland, 30 million signature LEGO bricks are used in 5,000 separate models of animals, buildings and well-known places such as New England and Las Vegas. LEGO-themed roller coasters and other rides, both thrilling and tame, round out the offerings.

Next door is Legoland's sister park, the **California SeaLife Aquarium**, with emphasis on introducing youngsters to oceanic creatures in a fun and kid-friendly way (◷same hours as LEGOland; ◷$18.95, children $11.95).

North of Carlsbad, Route 21 passes through Oceanside, home to the popular **Oceanside Pier** and **San Luis Rey de Francia Mission**★★ (1798) (4050 Mission Ave.; ◷open year-round daily 10am–4pm; ◷closed Jan 1, Thanksgiving Day, Dec 25; ◷$6; & 🅿 ℘760-757-3651; www.sanluisrey.org). Named for 13C King Louis IX of France, the 18C mission was the largest of the California missions. Now run by Francisican friars, it serves an active parish community.

The **museum** holds one of the largest collections of old Spanish **vestments**★ in the US, and the only extant mission-era walking staff and padre's hat. The restored, cruciform **church**★★ measures 180ft long, 28ft wide and 30ft high. Inside you'll find the original baptismal font.

North of Oceanside, Route 21 joins Interstate 5, crossing vast Camp Pendleton Marine Corps Base, in the northwestern corner of San Diego County.

Globally recognized as a center of high technology and finance, the San Francisco Bay Area has always distinguished itself as a popular visitor destination. The artful elegance and sophisticated pulse of this fabled "City by the Bay," coupled with an agreeable climate and incomparable geographic setting, make it a most desirable place to live and an unparalleled destination for visitors.

Highlights

1 Riding the cable car as it crests **Nob Hill** (p290)
2 The garlic fragrance at about 5pm in **North Beach** (p292)
3 Watching the fog stretch its fingers across the **Golden Gate Bridge** (p302)
4 The chilling sight of the cell house at **Alcatraz** (p295)
5 Breathing the sweet perfume of roses at **Filoli** (p275)

The Bay of St. Francis – In 1579 English privateer Francis Drake sailed into a sheltered bay, probably near Point Reyes, and claimed the land for Queen Elizabeth I. The English did not pursue their claims, however, and it was 1769 before the Spanish colonial government in Mexico established mission colonies in Alta California. The Spanish mistook San Francisco Bay for Drake's haven and incorrectly but permanently renamed it for Saint (not Sir) Francis.

Boomtown – The mid-19C Gold Rush and Silver Bonanza established San Francisco as the leading metropolis of the Far West, launching a building frenzy of spectacular mansions, factories and transport systems—the most instrumental of which was Andrew Hallidie's cable car. Immigrants from all nations poured in, giving the young city an immediate international flair that persists today.

Precipitously perched on the San Andreas Fault, San Francisco was virtually destroyed by an earthquake and fire in 1906. But the city rebounded. Reconstruction led to growth on a grand scale: the Golden Gate and San Francisco-Oakland Bay bridges were completed in the late 1930s.

Hippies and Techies – In the last half century, San Francisco has established itself as a dynamic city that persists at the cutting edge of change while refusing to dismiss its colorful past. Young Americans who could venture no farther west by land became the North Beach beatniks of the 1950s, the Haight-Ashbury hippies of the late 1960s and early 70s, and the gay community that burgeoned in the Castro District in the later 1970s. The lasting impact of these various groups is evident in the city's cultural life: its visual and performing arts, its music and literature, its distinctive and innovative restaurants.

The dot-com boom of the 1990s inflated the region's economy, resulting in a relatively high cost of living in San Francisco and south along the peninsula, particularly in Silicon Valley and its capital, San Jose, nerve center of the high-tech industry. Academia reigns in Palo Alto and Berkeley, and a commuter lifestyle holds sway in modest suburban towns around the bay and inland. Though it's costly to live here, the area is blessed with consistently fine weather, innumerable recreational opportunities and myriad fresh-food farm markets, and Bay Area residents routinely rank among the nation's healthiest.

Lombard Street, San Francisco
©Kevin Connors/Dreamstime.com

ADDRESSES

For a more comprehensive selection of hotels and restaurants, see the red-cover **Michelin Guide San Francisco Bay Area and Wine Country**.

🛏 STAY

⊜⊜⊜⊜ **Campton Place** – *340 Stockton St., San Francisco. ✆415-781-5555 or 866-969-1825. www.campton place.com. 110 rooms.* An intimate hotel once popular with the white-gloved set, Campton Place is the epitome of elegance and fine service. Pear wood paneling and cozy window seats make up elements of the peaceful Asian-inspired room decor, while insulated glass filters out noise from nearby Union Square. Work off a rich but wonderful meal at **Campton Place Restaurant** (⊜⊜⊜) at the 9th-floor fitness center.

⊜⊜⊜⊜ **Claremont Resort & Spa** – *41 Tunnel Rd., Berkeley. ✆510-843-3000 or 800-551-7266. www.claremontresort. com. 279 rooms.* This striking white castle sprawls across the Berkeley/Oakland hills east of San Francisco. There's an expansive spa and fitness center, tennis club, pools, and kids' camp. Room decor reflects a casual West Coast elegance; rooms in the new wing boast spacious marble baths and custom-made furniture.

⊜⊜⊜⊜ **The Fairmont** – *950 Mason St., San Francisco. ✆415-772-5000 or 866-540-4491. www.fairmont.com. 591 rooms.* This famous grand hotel atop Nob Hill survived the 1906 quake and saw the 1945 creation of the United Nations. Choose from handsome rooms—appointed with refined fabrics and dark wood furnishings—in the original building or in a 1961 tower that offers broad views across the city. The hotel's restaurants include the domed **Laurel Court** (⊜⊜⊜) and the Tonga Room.

⊜⊜⊜⊜ **Westin St. Francis** – *335 Powell St., San Francisco. ✆415-397-7000 or 800-937-8461. www.westinstfrancis. com. 1,195 rooms.* Occupying a Renaissance- and Baroque-revival structure built in 1904, this landmark hotel facing Union Square is renowned for its legendary service. A historic charm still pervades the rooms in the main building; more contemporary rooms with dramatic city views occupy a 32-story tower built in 1972. **Michael Mina** (⊜⊜⊜⊜), the famed chef's eponymous fine-dining restaurant, offers an elegant pre-theater menu, and **Caruso's**, in the tower lobby, serves specialty coffees and light snacks.

⊜⊜⊜⊜ **Hotel Monaco** – *501 Geary St., San Francisco. ✆415-292-0100 or 866-622-5284. www.monaco-sf.com. 201 rooms.* This Theater District boutique hotel, a 1910 Beaux-Arts classic, offers high-style comfort. In the guest rooms, Provençale fabrics drape over canopy beds and Chinese-inspired furnishings lend an exotic look. Downstairs, the stunning **Grand Café** (⊜⊜⊜) offers bistro-style meals. Your four-legged friends are welcome here, but if you can't bring Fido, ask for a goldfish to keep you company.

⊜⊜⊜ **Hotel De Anza** – *233 W. Santa Clara St., San Jose. ✆408-286-1000 or 800-843-3700. www.hoteldeanza. com. 100 rooms.* Built in 1931 and fully renovated six decades later, the historic De Anza retains an art deco-era appeal. Rooms are spacious, and decor is contemporary with light woods and neutral colors. For a homey touch, guests are invited to "raid" the hotel's pantry for late-night sandwiches and cookies.

⊜⊜ **Hotel Bijou** – *111 Mason St., San Francisco. ✆415-771-1200. www.hotel bijou.com. 65 rooms.* 🖵. Located a block away from cable car stops, the Art Deco Bijou recalls a 1920s movie palace; on its walls hang photos of San Francisco's old movie houses. Bright, jewel-toned guest rooms are named for films shot in the city, many of which are screened nightly in the small lobby theater.

⊜⊜ **Washington Square Inn** – *1660 Stockton St. ✆415-981-4220 or 800-388-0220. www.wsisf.com. 16 rooms.* 🖵. A intimate European-style inn at the foot of Telegraph Hill in the heart of bohemian North Beach, this charming bed-and-breakfast offers antique furnishings and afternoon tea, plus evening wine and hors d'oeuvres. A continental breakfast is either delivered to your room or served downstairs at an antique table overlooking the square.

¶/EAT

◎◎◎◎ **Chez Panisse** – *1517 Shattuck Ave., Berkeley.* ☎*510-548-5525. www.chezpanisse.com. Dinner only. Closed Sun.* **Californian**. California cuisine was born in this casual dining room, under the watchful eye of culinary doyenne Alice Waters. Organic greens and baby vegetables pair with free-range poultry and meats to create stellar prix-fixe menus that change nightly (be sure to make reservations up to a month in advance). Upstairs, the **Café at Chez Panisse** (◎◎◎) serves simpler lunch and dinner fare.

◎◎◎◎ **Gary Danko** – *800 North Point St., San Francisco.* ☎*415-749-2060. www.garydanko.com. Dinner only.* **Contemporary**. Elegant but understated decor allows chef-owner Danko's culinary creations to take center stage at his Fisherman's Wharf restaurant. Five-course tasting menus may feature Dungeness crab cake with bell-pepper and wasabi sauces, seared filet of beef with Stilton cheese, or a passionfruit-and-mango Napoleon.

◎◎◎◎ **Jardinière** – *300 Grove St., San Francisco.* ☎*415-861-5555. www.jardiniere.com. Dinner only.* **Californian**. Hundreds of bubbles sparkle on the domed ceiling of the Champagne Rotunda in this elegant eatery, favored for pre- or post-theater dining. Chef-owner Traci Des Jardins may start diners with a chanterelle-and-asparagus tart or duck confit salad, then offer loin of lamb with potato gnocchi.

◎◎◎ **McCormick & Kuleto's** – *900 North Point St., San Francisco.* ☎*415-929-1730. www.mccormickandschmicks.com.* **Seafood**. Some of the best seafood in the Wharf area is served at this spacious and attractive restaurant with views toward Alcatraz. There's a full oyster bar and a wide-ranging menu of fresh fish, from Petrale sole to white sturgeon and mahi-mahi, prepared to order.

◎◎◎ **Terzo** – *3011 Steiner St., San Francisco.* ☎*415-441-3200. www.terzosf.com. Dinner only.* **Mediterranean**. Locals drop into this casual neighborhood spot with its zinc bar for upscale dining at reasonable prices. Look for the Mediterranean influences at play in dishes like roasted halibut with garbanzo beans and Meyer-lemon relish.

◎◎ **Café de la Presse** – *352 Grant Ave., San Francisco.* ☎*415-398-2680. www.cafedelapresse.com.* **French**. Casual brasserie meals are served at this cafe and international newsstand beside Chinatown Gate. Menus du jour may feature French onion soup, crab-and-mushroom cassoulet and grilled tournedos. A favorite of foreign residents and visitors is the espresso bar, with its tempting selection of pastries.

◎◎ **South Park Cafe** – *108 South Park Ave. Closed Sun; Mon lunch only.* ☎*415-495-7275. www.southparkcafesf.com.* **French**. Latin Quarter ambience pervades this casual sidewalk cafe facing a pretty park. A blackboard menu may feature a sautéed pear-and-roquefort salad, a chicken liver-and-cognac terrine, couscous with braised vegetables and coriander mint yogurt, or a housemade boudin noir.

◎◎ **Fior d'Italia** – *2237 Mason St., San Francisco.* ☎*415-986-1886. www.fior.com.* **Italian**. The city's oldest Italian restaurant, this institution opened in 1886 and faced Washington Square from 1954; but a recent fire forced its move. Today located in the San Remo Hotel, Fior d'Italia retains its old spirit with black-and-white photos and velvet curtains. The cuisine remains tradition-bound: calamari, gnocchi, osso buco and Caesar salad win raves.

◎◎ **The Slanted Door** – *1 Ferry Building, San Francisco.* ☎*415-861-8032. www.slanteddoor.com.* **Vietnamese**. This popular cafe, fomerly in the Mission District, became so popular, it had to relocate to a bigger space. Now in the Ferry Building, it continues to offer fresh, Vietnamese-inspired cuisine. Crowds arrive early for exotic dishes: green papaya salad, "shaking beef" with garlic, or grilled Muscovy duck with plum sauce.

◎ **Picante** – *1328 Sixth St., Berkeley.* ☎ *510-525-3121. www.picantecocina.ypguides.net.* **Mexican**. This upscale West Berkeley taqueria gets rave reviews from locals for its fresh ingredients, homemade chorizo tacos and tamales of braised pork, butternut squash and poblano chiles.

Berkeley★★

This dynamic university city has an unending appetite for political activism, energetic intellectualism and cultural diversity. Up in the Berkeley Hills, the city boasts beautiful neighborhoods with stunning views of San Francisco.

A BIT OF HISTORY
Berkeley remained a rural area with only one settlement until the establishment of an institution of higher learning in the 1860s. In 1866 the community at the edge of the undeveloped campus was named for English bishop and philosopher George Berkeley (1685–1753), and the town grew up steadily around "Cal," as the university is called.

Berkeley enjoys the reputation of a well-planned university town, home to academics and intellectuals. Gracious old residences surround the campus and climb into the Berkeley Hills. Commercial arteries radiating from the university, particularly **Telegraph Avenue★**, **College Avenue** and **University Avenue**, are lined with coffee- and curio shops, bookstores, cafes and restaurants. The variety of dining opportunities, including renowned Chez Panisse, has lent the moniker "Gourmet Ghetto" to upper Shattuck Avenue.

UNIVERSITY OF CALIFORNIA, BERKELEY★★
The first campus of the acclaimed University of California system, UC Berkeley is noteworthy for its varied architecture, outstanding museums and contributions to human knowledge, especially in the field of nuclear physics.

Clergymen scholars from the eastern US established the College of California in Oakland in 1854, but moved the college in 1861 to the banks of Strawberry Creek. The college merged with the Agricultural, Mining and Mechanical Arts College in 1867, and the following year, the new institution was dedicated as the University of California.

At the turn of the 19C, philanthropist and university regent **Phoebe Apper-son Hearst**, mother of William Randolph Hearst, helped finance a campus expansion. Architect John Galen Howard established Beaux-Arts as the hallmark architectural style. Additional buildings were designed by such noteworthy architects as Bernard Maybeck, Julia Morgan and George Kelham.

The 1960s anti-war and civil rights movements catapulted Berkeley into the national spotlight as a center of student activism. Today, an ethnically diverse student body now numbers some 30,000. Currently, there are 7 Nobel laureates among its 1,500-member faculty.

VISIT
*Map p. 269. Berkeley. Student-led guided tours (90min) year-round Mon–Sat 10am & Sun 1pm. Weekday tours depart from the **campus visitor center** (2200 University Ave.; open year-round Mon–Fri 8.30am–4.30pm; closed Dec 23–Jan 1; 510-642-5215; www.berkeley.edu);*

- **Population:** 107,268.
- **Michelin Map:** 585 A 8 and map p. 269.
- **Info:** 510-549-7040 or 800-847-4823. www.visitberkeley.com.
- **Parking:** Paid parking garages are located across the street from the visitor center. We recommend you take BART to Berkeley Station, then walk or take the campus shuttle (open Mon–Fri 7am–6pm; $1).
- **Timing:** Visit on a weekday, so you can begin at the Berkeley Convention & Visitors Bureau visitor center (2015 Center St., 1st floor; closed weekends). Allow at least four hours to visit the Berkeley campus and the town. A campus tour (daily; 90min) is recommended.

weekend and holiday tours depart from the Campanile in the center of campus. Though the campus totals 1,232 acres and stretches high into the Berkeley Hills, the developed core of the university lies in the 178 acres situated along Strawberry Creek. **Sather Gate** (1910), a filigreed wrought-iron and stone portal designed by John Galen Howard, fronts **Sproul Plaza★**, a main gathering area for students.

The Campanile (Sather Tower)★★

👥🕐*Open year-round Mon–Fri 10am–4pm, Sat 10am–5pm, Sun 10am–1.30pm & 3pm–5pm.* 🕐*Closed Dec 23–Jan 1.* ⊚*$2.*

Modeled on the bell tower in Venice's St. Mark's Square, this 307ft, granite-clad shaft (1917, J.G. Howard) supports a carillon of 61 bells. From its eighth-floor observation platform, arched windows frame **panoramas★★** of the Berkeley Hills, downtown Oakland and San Francisco Bay. When school is in session, carillonneurs play the bells (🕐*open Mon–Sat 7.50am, noon & 6pm; Sun 2pm).* Below the tower's southwest face stands the oldest building on campus, the red-brick **South Hall (E)** (1873), a stately Second Empire structure. Nearby, to the north, is **Doe Library★**, the university's central book repository, overseeing more than 8 million bound volumes.

A small hall in the **Bancroft Library (D)**, east of Doe Library, stores rare books and special collections, including the country's largest assemblage of papers belonging to Mark Twain.

Valley Life Sciences Building★

This massive pseudo-Egyptian "temple" to science is decorated with bas-relief tableaux, American bison skulls, griffins and other designs.

The renovated interior (1994) houses the **Museum of Paleontology★ (M1)** 👥 *(🕐open during academic session Mon–Thu 8am–10pm, Fri 8am–5pm, Sat 10am–5pm, Sun 1–10pm; extended hours in summer; ⚐ ☏510-642-1821; www.ucmp.berkeley.edu),* containing more than 5 million specimens, including the skeleton of a *Tyrannosaurus rex.*

Hearst Memorial Mining Building

Housing offices and classrooms, this granite-clad Beaux-Arts building (1907, J.G. Howard and Julia Morgan) boasts an interior lobby that soars three floors up to three domes in a vaulted ceiling.

Phoebe A. Hearst Museum of Anthropology(M²)

103 Kroeber Hall. 🕐*Open year-round Wed–Sat 10am–4:30pm, Sun noon–4pm.* 🕐*Closed major &*

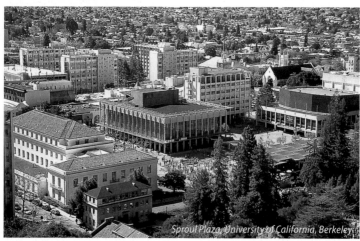
Sproul Plaza, University of California, Berkeley

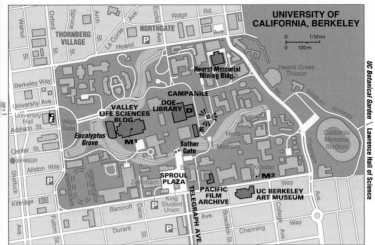

First Church of Christ Scientist, Claremont Resort \ Judah Magnes Museum

university holidays. ♿ ☎*510-643-7648.*
http://hearstmuseum.berkeley.edu.
This institution boasts a permanent
collection★ of 4 million artifacts, plac-
ing the Hearst among the country's most
significant anthropological research
museums. Changing exhibits draw
from prehistoric California, ancient Peru,
Classical Greece and Italy, ancient Egypt,
Central American textiles and ethnologi-
cal artifacts from West Africa, Oceania
and the Arctic and subarctic regions.

UC Berkeley Art Museum and Pacific Film Archive★

2626 Bancroft Way. ⏰*Open year-round
Wed–Sun 11am–5pm.* ⏰*Closed university holidays.* ☜*$8 (free first Thu of the
month).* ✗♿☎*510-642-0808.
www.bampfa.berkeley.edu. To meet
seismic standards, a new building is
under construction at Oxford and Center
sts.; expected completion is 2010.*
The museum was born in 1963 when
Abstract Expressionist painter and
professor **Hans Hofmann** (1880–1966)
donated 45 of his works and $250,000 to
the university to found an art museum.
The distinctive building (1970) unfolds
like a paper fan, with a vast interior space
featuring 10 cantilevered exhibition terraces linked by ramps and stairs.
The 9,000-piece permanent collection
is strong in 20C art, pre-20C European

painting, Asian ceramics and painting,
and contemporary art and sculpture.
Associated with the museum, the
renowned **Pacific Film Archive**★ *(2575
Bancroft Way;* ✗♿☎ ☎*510-642-1412)*
preserves 8,000 films, videos and prints
of classic movies, emphasizing Japanese,
Soviet and American art cinema *(screenings year-round nightly;* ☜*$9.50).*

UC Botanical Garden★

*Centennial Dr., first left off Stadium
Rimway.* ⏰*Open year-round daily
9am–5pm.* ⏰*Closed first Tue of each
month & major holidays.* ☜*$7 (free 1st
Thu/mth).* ♿☎*($1.50)* ☎*510-643-2755.
http://botanicalgarden.berkeley.edu.*
The 9,600 species of plants on this 34-
acre site, established in the 1920s, are
organized in sections representing the
flora of Asia, Africa, the Mediterranean
and Europe, New Zealand, Australia,
Mesoamerica, North America and California.

Lawrence Hall of Science

♿♿*Top of Centennial Dr.* ⏰*Open year-
round daily 10am–5pm.* ⏰*Closed Labor
Day, Thanksgiving Day, Dec 25.* ☜*$11,
children $6.* ✗☎☎*510-642-5132.
www.lawrencehallofscience.org.*
This futuristic museum (1968) is dedicated to teaching schoolchildren such
topics as physics, chemistry, navigation,

mathematics, computers and lasers through interactive exhibits, laboratories and classes. The planetarium adds to an active Saturday-night astronomy program. The **view**★★ from the patio overlooks much of the north Bay Area.

ADDITIONAL SIGHTS
First Church of Christ, Scientist★★

2619 Dwight Way. ⌕Visit by guided tour (45min) only, year-round 1st Sun/mth 12.15pm, or by reservation.
🅿 *ℰ510-845-7199. www.friendsof firstchurch.org.*
Bernard Maybeck harmonized a wealth of styles to create this Arts and Crafts-style structure of surpassing beauty. Dedicated in 1916, the church fuses multiple rooflines—typical of a Japanese temple—with Spanish tiles and rectangular, fluted columns. The sunken auditorium is naturally lit by side windows and diagonally spanned with arching beams, imparting a feeling of spaciousness. Note the exquisitely crafted, milled woodwork in the ceiling beams.

Judah L. Magnes Museum★

2911 Russell St. ◷Open year-round by appointment only Tue, Thu & Sun 2pm–4pm. ◷Closed major & Jewish holidays. 👝$6. ℰ510-549-6950. www.magnes.org.
This mansion (1908) houses the nation's third-largest museum of Jewish history and art and a renowned research institution, with particular focus on the history of Jews in the American West. Changing exhibits *(main level)* highlight Semitic history and the works of 19C–20C Jewish artists and photographers. Rotating exhibits of items from the museum's collections include Hanukkah lamps, amulets, Bibles, wedding robes and Torah cases.

Claremont Resort★

41 Tunnel Rd., Oakland. Take College Ave. to Ashby Ave. and turn left. ◷Open daily year-round. ✕⌖🅿 ℰ510-843-3000. www.claremontresort.com.
Looming like a massive white castle and visible from far across the bay, this

stately old hotel (1915) forms the centerpiece of an upscale resort and spa. The white Mediterranean-style structure is notable for its **views** of the bay.

EXCURSIONS
⌖*See San Francisco map.*
John Muir National Historic Site★

24mi northeast of Berkeley, in Martinez. Take I-80 north to Rte. 4 East. Exit at Alhambra Ave. in Martinez. ◷Open year-round Wed–Sun 10am–5pm. ⌕Guided tours available. ◷Closed Jan 1, Thanksgiving Day, Dec 25. 👝$3 (good for same-day entrance to Muir Woods NM). ⌖🅿 ℰ925-228-8860. www.nps.gov/jomu.
Part of Muir's 2,600-acre fruit ranch, this frame residence (1882) was home to legendary conservationist John Muir from 1890 until his death in 1914. Muir wrote many of his influential books in the second-floor "scribble den," which still contains his chair and desk. A film on Muir's life is shown in the visitor center.

Six Flags Discovery Kingdom★

*👥*1001 Fairgrounds Rd, Vallejo, 26mi north of Berkeley, by I-80 north; cross Carquinez Bridge and exit at Rte. 37. ◷Park open daily mid-May–Labor Day; weekends early Sept–Dec, Mar–mid-May. ◷Closed Jan–mid-May except school holidays. Hours vary seasonally; check the park's website. 👝$44.99, children under 48inches $29.99. ✕⌖🅿 ($15). ℰ707-643-6722. www.sixflags.com.*
This 160-acre park combines a zoo, an oceanarium and an amusement park. Plan your visit around the live animal performances *(20–30min shows; schedule at entrance),* such as the bottle-nosed acrobats of **Dolphin Harbor** or a tug-of-war with pachyderms at **Elephant Encounter**.
Popular rides include **V2: Vertical Velocity**, which spirals riders to speeds of up to 70mph in less than 4 seconds; **Tony Hawk's Big Spin**, a gravity-defying spinning coaster that's good for groups, and the splashing plunge of **Monsoon Falls**.

Oakland★

This East Bay city boasts gleaming waterfront and civic center districts, an exceptional museum, and ambitiously restored mid-19C to 20C residential and commercial buildings.

A BIT OF HISTORY

In 1868 Oakland became the western terminus of the Southern Pacific Railroad, ensuring the city decades of prosperity. Though the city suffered economic decline and social unrest in the mid-20C, the opening of eight BART stations here in 1974, the reestablishment of passenger ferry service to San Francisco in 1989, and a new Amtrak passenger station in 1995 have renewed Oakland's role as a Bay Area transportation center. The expanded, modernized **Port of Oakland** now ranks among the top 20 ports in the world.

SIGHTS
Downtown

Bounded by I-880, I-980, Grand Ave. & Lake Merritt. 🚇 *12th Street/City Center.* At the heart of downtown lies **Oakland City Center**★, a multi-block "office park" set amid fountained plazas. Across 14th Street rises **City Hall** (1914), a Beaux-Arts structure capped by a Baroque-style clock tower. The **Oakland Tribune Building** (1923), also with a clock tower *(13th and Franklin Sts.)*, formerly housed the offices of the *Oakland Tribune*. The monumental **Ronald Y. Dellums Federal Building**★ is a twin-towered pile linked by a 75ft glass rotunda.

Preservation Park

13th St. & Martin Luther King Jr. Way. These 16 Victorian homes were relocated to the site and restored as an office park. The Italianate **Pardee Home Museum**★ *(11th & Castro Sts;* ☎*visit by 90min guided tour only, year-round Mon–Sat 9am–4pm by reservation only;* 🕐*closed major holidays;* 💰*$5;* 📞*510-444-2187; www.pardeehome.org)* was once the family home of two Oakland mayors. Tours reveal a hodgepodge of furnishings and objets d'art.

Oakland info box

> ▶ **Population:** 397,067.
> ⊙ **Michelin Map:** 585 A 8 and map this section.
> ▣ **Info:** 📞510-839-9000. www.oaklandcvb.com.
> ◖ **Location:** The City of Oakland offers free walking tours May–Oct (90min) through Old Oakland, Chinatown, the waterfront, and other areas. 📞510-238-3234.
> ⊘ **Don't Miss:** The art deco Paramount Theatre, the Oakland Museum of California.

Old Oakland★

Bounded by Broadway, Washington, 7th & 10th Sts.

This restored historic district showcases an extraordinary grouping of 19C commercial buildings displaying Victorian craftsmanship.

Chinatown abuts Old Oakland east of Broadway *(between 7th, 10th & Harrison Sts.)*. Chinese immigrants gathered in the present nine-square-block quarter around the 1870s. Chinatown does not court tourists, but many visitors enjoy exploring its markets and restaurants.

Paramount Theatre★★

2025 Broadway. 🚇 *19th St.* ☎*Visit by guided tour (2hrs) only, year-round 1st & 3rd Sat 10am.* 🕐*Closed major holidays.* 💰*$5.* 📞*510-465-6400. www.paramounttheatre.com.*

This National Landmark structure is an fine example of art deco design. The theater (1931, Timothy Pflueger) boasts a towering exterior tile mosaic and an interior lavish with gilded and sculpted plaster walls, filigreed grillwork ceilings and murals. It is owned by the city as a cinema and performing-arts facility.

Lake Merritt

East of downtown. 🚇 *Lake Merritt.* At this man-made saltwater lake, an esplanade winds around the 3.5mi shoreline, broadening on the northern

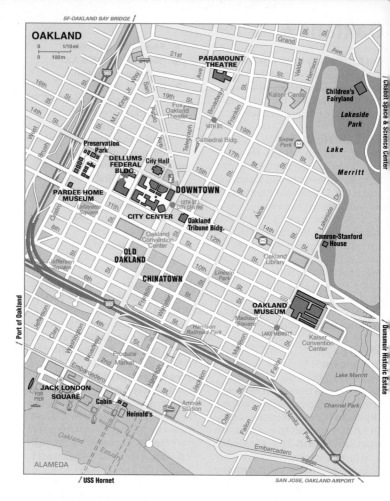

side into **Lakeside Park**, a lush oasis of 122 oak-shaded acres with show gardens and **Children's Fairyland** ♟♙ (○open Jun–Aug Mon–Fri 10am–4pm, weekends 10am–5pm; mid-Apr–May & Sept–Oct Wed–Sun 10am–4pm; Jan–mid-Apr Fri–Sun 10am–4pm; ∞$7; ℘510-238-6876; www.fairyland.org), a small amusement park for young children.

Camron-Stanford House

1418 Lakeside Dr. ☞Visit by guided tour (1hr) only, year-round 3rd Wed of the month 1–5pm.○Closed Jan 1 & Dec 25. ∞$5. 🅿 ℘510-444-1876. www.cshouse.org.

This Italianate residence (1876) on the shore of Lake Merritt was home to prominent personages such as Josiah Stanford, brother of railroad magnate Leland Stanford. The main floor showcases Victorian-era furnishings and interior decoration.

Oakland Museum of California★★

♟♙1000 Oak St. ○Open year-round Wed–Sat 10am–5pm (1st Fri 9pm), Sun noon–5pm. ∞$8, children $5 (free 2nd Sun). ╳⛄🅿 ℘510-238-2200. www. museumca.org. ☺The Art and History galleries are currently closed for renovation; scheduled reopening 2010. Check the museum's website for updates.

A city showpiece, this 5.9-acre cultural complex (1969) celebrates California's natural and cultural history and its art. Architect Kevin Roche, with assistance from architect John Dinkeloo, designed a series of tiered horizontal galleries overhung with roof gardens, fronting a central courtyard. The **Great Hall** features traveling exhibitions, art shows and temporary presentations drawn from the museum's own collections.

Natural Sciences Gallery★ – *1st level.* Specimens of native flora and fauna in dioramas re-create the eight distinct biotic zones across California.

Cowell Hall of California History★ – *2nd level.* The hall's permanent exhibit traces the state's human history through tableaux and more than one million artifacts.

Gallery of California Art★★ – *3rd level.* Devoted to artists who have lived, worked or studied in California, the collection contains works from the early 19C to the present. California landscapes (19C) include paintings of the Sierra Nevada by **Thomas Moran**, **Albert Bierstadt**, Thomas Hill and William Keith. The museum holds the largest collection of work from California Arts and Crafts practitioners Arthur and Lucia Kleinhans Mathews. California Impressionists represented include Guy Rose, Joseph Raphael and E. Charlton Fortune, as well as the Oakland-based "Society of Six" landscapists: William Clapp, August Gay, Selden Gile, Maurice Logan, Louis Siegriest and Bernard von Eichman. **Richard Diebenkorn**, Elmer Bischoff and other adherents of the Bay Area Figurative movement are well represented. Later 20C works by **Wayne Thiebaud** and others share space with contemporary sculpture by Manuel Neri and others. The museum owns the world's largest collection of **Dorothea Lange** photographs as well as photography by Eadweard Muybridge and group f/64 members Edward Weston, Ansel Adams and Imogen Cunningham.

Jack London Square★
Along the Embarcadero.
www.jacklondonsquare.com.
This once-gritty dock area has been developed into an attractive complex of shops, restaurants, hotels, cinemas, and a yacht harbor, all named for writer Jack London, who lived in Oakland as a boy and young man. The **Jack London Cabin** is a reconstruction of the one-room log cabin he occupied in 1897 while prospecting for gold in the Klondike. Nearby is one of his favorite watering holes, **Heinold's First and Last Chance Saloon** (℘510-839-6761; www.heinolds-firstandlastchance.com), still operating as a bar. On Sunday morning, a busy farmer's market attracts throngs of visitors (◷10am–2pm. ✕℘866-295-9853).

Chabot Space & Science Center★
10000 Skyline Blvd. Exit 1-580 at Park Blvd.; continue east across Rte. 13, then climb to ridgetop via Mountain & Ascot Blvds. ◷*Open year-round Wed–Thu 10am–5pm (early Jul–early Aug Tue–Thu), Fri & Sat 10am–10pm, Sun 11am–5pm. Museum (includes one planetarium show)* ◉*$14.95, children $10.95.* ✕&🅿 ℘510-336-7300. www.chabotspace.org.
This hilltop center features an acclaimed planetarium and theater, hands-on exhibits and science labs, and telescopes that invite public access and inspire interest in astronomy and science.

Dunsmuir Historic Estate★
2960 Peralta Oaks Ct., off 106th Ave. south of Knowland Park. ◷*Grounds open year-round Tue–Fri 10am–4pm.* ◗*Mansion open by 1hr guided tour Apr–Sept Wed 11am.* ◉*$5.* &🅿℘510-615-5555. www.dunsmuir.org.
Built in 1899 by Alexander Dunsmuir, son of a British Columbia coal baron, this 37-room mansion was built in Neoclassical Revival style. The 16,000sq ft, three-story house presents a Tiffany-style dome, 10 fireplaces and inlaid parquet floors.

USS Hornet★★
Pier 3, Alameda. ◷*Open year-round daily 10am–5pm.* ◷*Closed Jan 1, Thanksgiving Day, Dec 25.* ◉*$14, children $6.* ✕🅿 ℘510-521-8448. www.uss-hornet.org.

Commissioned in 1943, this 41,200-ton Essex-class aircraft carrier was designed to carry up to 3,400 servicemen and an attack force of F6F Hellcat fighters, TBM Avenger torpedo bombers and SB2C Helldiver dive bombers. Active in World War II and the Vietnam War, the ship was decommissioned in 1970.

Begin the visit with a short orientation program on the **Hangar Deck** before commencing self-guided tours of the **Flight Deck**, the Navigation Bridge, and the **Second Deck**. Here you can tour the officers' quarters, lounge and dining hall, the Marine Detachment quarters, the enlisted men's mess and the engine room.

Palo Alto

An affluent college town, Palo Alto derives its name from the coast redwood under which Gaspar de Portolá camped on his 1769 expedition. Now single-trunked and timeworn, El Palo Alto, "the tall tree," still stands in a small park off Alma Avenue. It remains the official symbol of Stanford University.

> ▶ **Population:** 57,809.
> ⚲ **Michelin Map:** 585 A 8 and see San Francisco map.
> ▯ **Info:** ℘650-324-3121. www.paloalto chamber.com.
> ⚑ **Don't Miss:** The Rodin sculptures at the Cantor Center on the Stanford campus.

STANFORD UNIVERSITY★★

Established by railroad magnate Leland Stanford, the campus of this renowned institution is graced with Spanish-flavored Richardsonian Romanesque buildings.

A lawyer by training, **Leland Stanford** (1824–1893) moved to California during the Gold Rush; served as the state's governor; then became president of the Central Pacific Railroad. In 1884 Stanford and his wife, Jane, lost their only child to typhoid fever. Declaring that "the children of California shall be our children," the bereft couple set out to establish a university on their ranch lands. Architect Charles Allerton Coolidge and landscape architect Frederick Law Olmsted conceived the campus plan for the university, which opened in 1891.

Stanford University has remained a leading academic and research center, with a current enrollment of some 14,000 students. Among its 1,878 faculty members are 17 Nobel laureates, 4 Pulitzer Prize winners, and 19 recipients of the National Medal of Science. The **Stanford Linear Accelerator Center**, devoted to research in particle physics, opened here in 1961.

VISIT

Visitor information at Memorial Auditorium. ↘ *Campus tours (1hr) depart from Memorial Auditorium year-round daily 11am & 3.15pm.* ◷*Closed midDec–1st weekend in Jan.* ✗⚲🅿 ℘650-723-2560. www.stanford.edu.

Main Quadrangle★

The historic heart of the campus, this tiled courtyard is bordered by the university's 12 original colonnaded buildings and anchored by the impressive **Memorial Church★★**. Built in 1903 by Jane Stanford to commemorate her husband, the church features elaborate Byzantine-style mosaics, stained glass and a renowned 7,777-pipe organ equipped to play Renaissance and Baroque music.

Hoover Tower★

Observation deck ◷*open year-round daily 10am–4.30pm.* ◷*Closed between academic quarters.* ◉*$2.* ♿ ℘650-723-2053.

The 285ft campanile houses part of the Hoover Institution on War, Revolution and Peace, a public-policy research center inspired by university alumnus Herbert Hoover. Two museum galleries are devoted to the accomplishments of Hoover and his wife, Lou Henry Hoover. The top of the tower features a 35-bell carillon and an observation deck offering a panorama of the campus, San Francisco and the Bay Area to the north.

Iris & B. Gerald Cantor Center for Visual Arts★

Lomita Dr. & Museum Way. ◷Open year-round Wed–Sun 11am–5pm (Thu 8pm). ◷Closed Thanksgiving Day & Dec 25. ✗♿🅿 ☎650-723-4177. www.museum.stanford.edu.

A premier university teaching museum, the Cantor Center houses a collection of 20,000 pieces of ancient to contemporary sculpture, paintings, crafts and ceremonial artworks from Africa, Oceania, Asia, Europe and the Americas. It is renowned for its Rodin sculptures.

Massive entry doors are encased in bronze panels depicting examples of ancient architecture. The two-story entry hall, clad in marble is presided over by a statue of Athena. Flanking the entrance, the two original wings exhibit the classical, historical and international collections in two floors of galleries, while the 1991 addition houses contemporary art and rotating exhibits, either on loan or drawn from the permanent collection.

A central gallery behind the entry lobbies acknowledges the museum's origin in the **Stanford Family Collection.**

Included are family portraits, curios from young Leland's collections and the **Golden Spike** from the ceremonial completion of the first transcontinental railroad.

The **Rodin Sculpture Garden**★ displays 20 large-scale bronze casts by French sculptor Auguste Rodin, including his famed *The Gates of Hell* (1900).

FILOLI★★

13mi north of Palo Alto in Woodside. Take Rte. G3 to I-280 north; exit west at Edgewood Road, turn right on Cañada Rd and continue 1.3mi to gate. ◷Open year-round Tue–Sat 10am–3.30pm (last admission 2.30pm), Sun 11am–3.30pm (last admission 2.30pm). ▸▸Guided tours (2hrs) available mid-Feb–Oct Tue–Sat 10am & 1pm (reservations required). ◷Closed major holidays. ◈$12. ✗♿🅿 ☎650-364-8300. www.filoli.org.

This 645-acre estate exemplifies a gracious, cultured, early-20C lifestyle made possible by fortunes derived from real-estate, mining and agriculture. The property's formal gardens and Georgian Revival mansion (1916, Willis Polk) were commissioned by William Bourn (1857–1936), owner of the vast Empire Gold Mine in Grass Valley.

The **mansion**★★ is appointed with family furniture and art, and pieces loaned from the Fine Arts Museums of San Francisco. A 16C Flemish tapestry hangs in the dining room, and the grand

Filoli Gardens

© John Anderson/MICHELIN

275

ballroom reveals French crystal chandeliers and murals of the Bourn estate in Ireland. Designed according to Italian and French styles, the 16-acre botanical **gardens**★★★ comprise several distinct areas. Some 30 species of flowering plants bloom here seasonally.

EXCURSION
Hiller Aviation Museum
🏛️601 Skyway Rd., San Carlos, just off US-101 north at Redwood Shores Pkwy. 🕐Open year-round daily 10am–5pm. 🕐Closed major holidays. ⬤$10, children $6. ♿ 🖉650-654-0200. www.hiller.org.

Exhibits proceed chronologically through more than a century of the history of manned flight, with special emphasis on the greater Bay Area. One of the earliest aircraft displayed is the 1883 Gull, a fully controllable glider. Exhibits progress from early fixed-wing aircraft to blended and oblique wing designs, and include such innovations as the Flying Platform (which resembles a magic flying carpet) and the high-altitude spyplane Boeing Condor.

San Francisco ★★★

Lying at the tip of a peninsula forming the western boundary of a 496sq mi bay, vibrant, sophisticated San Francisco attracts a huge number of visitors each year. The sea is a presence here, creating a climate of bracingly cool summers, brisk ocean breezes and sudden fog. San Francisco's natural setting lends it renown as a city of views: from hilltops, street corners, balconies and park benches. A broad mix of architectural styles graces both business and residential areas.

SAN FRANCISCO TODAY
San Franciscans enjoy life in their beautiful, cosmopolitan city, despite the high cost of living. From high-tech professionals to service-industry workers, residents take advantage of their city's attractions right along with the visitors, gathering produce at the Farmers' Market, hanging out in North Beach coffeeshops, shopping in Union Square, jogging in Golden Gate Park, biking along the waterfront, taking in a museum or two. The city is a center of West Coast fashion and a culinary mecca as well; San Franciscans dine out regularly and closely monitor the restaurant scene.
City by the Bay – About 43 named hills punctuate the cityscape, including Nob

▶ **Population:** 764,976.
◉ **Michelin Map:** 585 A 8 and maps pp277, 282, 287, 290–291, 300–301.
🔲 **Info:** 🖉415-391-2000. www.sfvisitor.org
◐ **Location:** There are 19 neighborhoods in San Francisco, plus the oceanfront, with their familiar names, like Nob Hill, Chinatown and North Beach.
◉ **Don't Miss:** Golden Gate Park, Lombard Street, Coit Tower, a ride on a cable car, sourdough bread at Fisherman's Wharf: the list is endless.
🕐 **Timing:** Allow at least a week to take in the best of the city. As always, let the stars guide you; start with the 3-star areas and then visit the 2-star areas.
🏛️ **Kids:** Ghirardelli Square, Pier 39, the Cable Car Museum, the Exploratorium and the zoo.

(376ft) and Telegraph (274ft) hills; Mt. Davidson, San Francisco's highest point, exceeds 929ft. San Francisco's remarkably equable climate is a boon to visitors

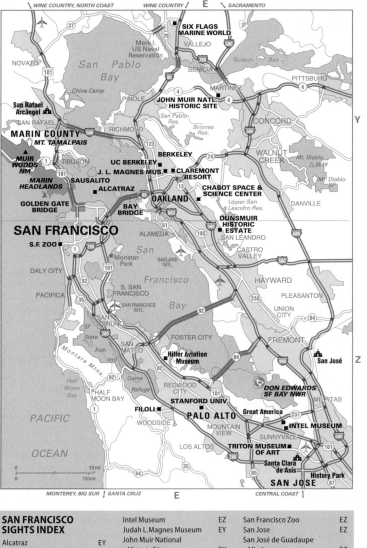

and residents. The California current, flowing south along the coast, moderates winter chill and affords San Francisco the lowest summer temperatures of any city in the continental US.

San Francisco is a Pacific Rim center of finance, trade and high technology. Waterfront warehouses and port structures have been transformed into offices, shopping centers, cafes and con-

Area Code: 415

GETTING THERE

BY AIR: San Francisco International Airport (SFO): 13mi south of downtown (*℘650-821-8211; www.flysfo. com*). **Oakland International Airport** (OAK): 17mi southeast of downtown (*℘510-563-3300; www.flyoakland. com*). From SFO, taxis to downtown average $45; from OAK, taxis average $75. Commercial shuttles range from $16–$37. Public transportation: from SFO, take the free AirTrain shuttle from the terminal to the airport BART station; from OAK, take the AirBart bus ($3) to the Coliseum/Oakland Airport BART station.

BY BUS AND TRAIN: Greyhound **bus** station (*425 Mission St.; ℘800-231-2222; www.greyhound.com*). Amtrak **train** station (*5885 Horton St.; ℘800-872-7245; www.amtrak.com*).
BY CAR: I-280 enters the city from the south. **US-101** runs along the coast, exiting the city north across the Golden Gate Bridge. **I-80** crosses the Bay Bridge from Berkeley and Oakland.

GETTING AROUND

BY PUBLIC TRANSPORTATION: For route and fare information on all Bay Area transportation systems contact **Bay Area Traveler Information System** (*℘511; within San Francisco 415-817-1717; www.511.org*). Most public transportation is operated by **San Francisco Municipal Railway (Muni).** All lines (except cable cars) operate daily 5.30am–12.30am; some routes operate 24hrs/day. Fare for **buses** and **streetcars** is $1.50; transfers are free, exact fare required. **Cable cars** operate daily 6am–12.30am; fare $5. Purchase tickets on-board, at selected hotels, or at the Visitor Information Center *(below)*. **Muni Passports** are good for one *($11)*, three *($18)* or seven *($24)* days ($1 surcharge for cable cars). Muni's **CultureBus** (74X line) serves stops convenient to San Francisco museums and cultural attractions *(daily 8.40am–5.50pm, every 20min; $7/day)*. Muni maps *($3)* are sold at retail outlets throughout the city. Riders with disabilities can call Muni Accessible Services *(℘701-4485)* for information. **BART (Bay Area Rapid Transit)** light-rail system accesses Berkeley and Oakland *(www.bart.gov)*.
BY CAR: Streets are often congested and street parking may be difficult. Drivers must yield to cable cars. When parking on a hill, drivers must block front wheels against the curb (facing downhill turn wheels *toward* the curb, facing uphill turn wheels *away* from the curb); use of parking brake is mandatory. Restricted parking indicated by color of the curb: red *(no standing or parking)*, yellow or black *(truck or car loading zone)*, white (limited to 5min), green *(limited to 10-30min)*, blue *(reserved for the disabled)*.
BY TAXI: Yellow Cab ℘282-3737; **Veterans** ℘648-4119.

GENERAL INFORMATION

VISITOR INFORMATION
San Francisco Convention & Visitors Bureau Visitor Information Center is on the lower level of Hallidie Plaza, 900 Market St at Powell St. *(open year-round Mon–Fri 9am–5pm, Sat–Sun 9am–3pm; ℘391-2000; www. onlyinsanfrancisco.com)*. Here you can purchase a San Francisco CityPass *($59, children $39)*, which offers discounted admission to various area attractions.
ACCOMMODATIONS
Accommodations range from elegant downtown hotels *($500–$500/day)* to budget motels *($90–$150/day)* and bed-and-breakfast inns *($150 and up/day)*. **San Francisco Reservations** (*℘800-677-1570; www.hotelres.com*).
Bed & Breakfast San Francisco (*℘899-0060; www.bbsf.com*). Quoted rates do not inlude 14% hotel tax.
Local Press – Daily news: *San Francisco Chronicle* (morning), *San Francisco Examiner.* Weekly entertainment information: *San Francisco Bay Guardian*, *SF Weekly* and *Where San Francisco.*

Currency Exchange – Travelex *(open Mon–Fri 8am–5pm, weekends 7am–3pm; ℘650-821-0900; www. travelex.com),* International Terminal main hall, San Francisco International Airport.

USEFUL NUMBERS

Police/Ambulance/Fire (*24hrs*) ℘911
Police
(*non-emergency, 24hrs*) ℘553-0123
Physician Referrals
(*Mon–Fri 9am-5pm*) ℘353-6566
Dental Referrals (*24hrs*) ℘421-1435
24hr Pharmacy, Walgreens, 3201 Divisadero St. ℘931-6415
Weather ℘831-656-1725

SPORTS AND LEISURE

Sightseeing – City tours include Gray Line Tours (℘434-8687; www. sanfranciscosightseeing.com) and Great Pacific Tour Co. (℘626-4499; www. greatpacifictour.com). **Specialized tours:** City Guides *(free walking tours of neighborhoods; daily; ℘557-4266; www.sfcityguides.org);* Wok Wiz Chinatown Tours (℘650-355-9657;

www.wokwiz.com); and Dashiell Hammett (literary) Tour (*℘510-287-9540; www.donherron.com)*. **Bay tours** through Blue & Gold Fleet (℘773-1188; www.blueandgoldfleet.com) and Red & White Fleet (℘673-2900; www. redandwhite.com).

Entertainment – Cultural Events Hotline: (℘391-2001; www. onlyinsanfrancisco.com). Tickets for local events from **Ticketmaster** (www.ticketmaster.com), **Tickets. com** (www.tickets.com) or **Tix Bay Area**, which offers half-price tickets for selected events on the day of the show; purchases must be made in person (cash or traveler's checks only) from the Union Square box office on Powell St. between Post and Geary Sts. (℘433-7827; www.tixbayarea.com).
Shopping – Downtown: Crocker Galleria, Maiden Lane, San Francisco Shopping Center, Union Square.
Financial District: Embarcadero Center. **Fisherman's Wharf:** Ghirardelli Square, Pier 39.
Cow Hollow: Union Street.

Spectator Sports

Tickets for major sporting events can be purchased at the venue or through ticket outlets *(above)*.

Sport/Team	Season/Venue	℘Information
⚾ **MAJOR LEAGUE BASEBALL**	Apr–Oct	℘415-972-2000
San Francisco Giants (NL)	AT&T Park	www.sfgiants.com
Oakland Athletics (AL)	Oakland-Alameda County Coliseum	℘510-568-5600 www.oaklandathletics.com
🏈 **PROFESSIONAL FOOTBALL**	Sept–Dec	℘415-464-9377
San Francisco 49ers (NFL)	Candlestick Park	www.49ers.com
Oakland Raiders (NFL)	Oakland-Alameda County Coliseum	℘800-724-3377 www.raiders.com
🏀 **PROFESSIONAL BASKETBALL**	Oct–Apr	℘510-986-2200
Golden State Warriors (NBA)	The Arena in Oakland	www.warriors.com
🏒 **PROFESSIONAL HOCKEY**	Oct–Apr	℘408-287-7070
San Jose Sharks (NHL)	HP Pavilion	www.sanjosesharks.com

dominiums. The prominence of professional and high-tech employment in

Size and Population – With a population of 764,976 (2007) inhabiting an area of only 46.38sq mi, San Francisco has the second-highest population density in the US after New York. It ranks as the fourth-largest city in California after Los Angeles, San Diego and San Jose. The **San Francisco Bay Area** encompasses a nine-county region with nearly 7 million people. About 28 percent of San Franciscans are foreign-born, from Latin America, China and the Pacific Rim. Japanese, Filipinos, Italians, Russians and African-Americans contribute to the rich ethnic mix.

Cultural Center – San Francisco's opera and ballet are internationally recognized, and a host of smaller performing-arts organizations mount productions each week. The city boasts an active theatrical community, four major art museums and a thriving experimental art scene in the South of Market area.

International Flavors – Dedicated food enthusiasts, San Franciscans throng the city's many restaurants to enjoy cuisine from around the globe. In North Beach, look for pasta, pizza and other Italian fare as well as the local specialty *cioppino*, a tomato-based seafood stew. Try Chinatown for *dim sum*, sweet or savory dumplings filled with meat, seafood or vegetables. Don't overlook the Mission District for Mexican and Central American fare, nor Clement Street in the Richmond District for Asian cuisine, including Burmese, Indonesian and Vietnamese. From November through April, Dungeness crab appears on menus. Other traditional San Francisco delicacies include Irish coffee and crusty sourdough bread.

A BIT OF HISTORY

Scouts from Gaspar de Portolá's party, led by **Sergeant José Ortega**, saw a large body of water in 1769, and incorrectly assumed it was the bay discovered in 1579 by Francis Drake. That bay had been renamed in honor of Saint Francis of Assisi in 1595 by Spanish explorers. The huge inlet discovered by Ortega

was thereafter referred to as Puerto de San Francisco—the Port of St. Francis.

Spanish and Mexican Rule – Growing realization of the strategic and economic importance of the bay led Spanish authorities in distant Mexico City to establish the Presidio and San Francisco de Asís Mission in 1776. When Mexico achieved independence from Spain in 1821, these remained small frontier settlements. In 1835 a third settlement was created by an Englishman and an American, and known as **Yerba Buena**, or "good herb," for the wild mint that grew in the area.

The primary economic activity during the first half of the 19C was the beef hide-and-tallow trade between local cattle ranchers and merchants. By the mid-1800s, that trade had brought greater awareness of California's economic riches to the colonizing forces of England, France and Russia, and the US Government moved quickly to wrest the territory from the weak grasp of Mexico. In 1846, during the Mexican War, **John Montgomery** sailed in on the USS *Portsmouth* and raised the Stars and Stripes over Yerba Buena's central plaza, renaming it Portsmouth Square. In 1847 Yerba Buena was renamed San Francisco by the village's first American mayor.

The Gold Rush – The little settlement of San Francisco was perfectly situated to benefit from the 1849 Gold Rush. Its port was a natural channel of transportation between inland California and the world. As ships unloaded men and equipment, Yerba Buena Cove sprouted warehouses, banks, offices, saloons and brothels. San Francisco boomed and grew.

Business Center of the West – California's geographic isolation worked to San Francisco's advantage during the first two decades after the Gold Rush. Cut off from the nation's major manufacturing centers, the city developed its own diversified economy including shipbuilding and the manufacture of farm implements and railroad equipment.

Gold from the Gold Country formed a tremendous pool of capital. Much of the late 19C economic development of the entire western half of the

US was financed from San Francisco. In 1872 Scottish immigrant **Andrew Hallidie** invented the **cable car**, which did much to mold the residential pattern of San Francisco through the 1870s and 80s. By the end of 19C, electric streetcars had largely replaced cable cars.

1906 Earthquake and Fire – In April 1906, an earthquake estimated at 8.3 on the (not-yet-devised) Richter scale shook the California coast, toppling structures from Fort Bragg to Monterey, and killing some 3,000 people. Small fires caused by broken gas mains and toppled chimneys soon coalesced into a blaze that raged unchecked for three days. By the time the fire burned itself out, flames had consumed 28,000 buildings, about 80 percent of the city's property value. Recovery and reconstruction efforts began almost immediately. By 1910 the downtown area had been largely completed. Spotting an opportunity to show off the rebuilt city, civic leaders won a bid to host the **Panama-Pacific International Exposition**, which attracted 19 million visitors in 1915.

Early 20C Growth – San Francisco prospered in the years after World War I. Larger buildings went up in the Financial District before the Great Depression halted skyscraper construction. Still, the 1930s saw completion of the San Francisco-Oakland Bay Bridge and the Golden Gate Bridge.

During World War II, the Bay Area became a major shipbuilding center and the main port of embarkation for the Pacific theater. The war also stimulated the high-technology sector when the nascent electronics and aircraft industries turned to military production.

DOWNTOWN

1 **CHINATOWN**★★★

🚋 *Powell-Hyde or Powell-Mason lines.* 🚌 *bus 30–Stockton.*

San Francisco's Chinatown constitutes one of the four largest Chinese settlements outside Asia. An estimated 30,000 people reside here, most of whom maintain their native culture.

🔲 **Info:** www.sanfrancis-cochinatown.com.

Chinatown's Religious Life

Chinatown's active spiritual life revolves around its numerous Taoist, Buddhist and Confucianist temples, commonly located on the upper floors of commercial buildings. Several welcome visitors to enter, view the elaborate altars and decorations, and absorb the atmosphere of prayer and tradition. (It is customary to leave a small donation.) Ongoing devotions often incorporate elements from all three religious traditions; prayers for specific personal requests, such as recovery from illness or success in business, are accompanied by offerings of money, food or incense. Temples mentioned in this guide include the Ching Chung Temple, Ma-Tsu Temple of USA, Tin How Temple and Kong Chow Temple.

▶ **Location:** Spreading along the lower slope of Nob Hill, Chinatown centers on a 24-block core bounded by Broadway, Montgomery, California and Powell streets. Portsmouth Square serves as the heart of Chinatown.

🕐 **Timing:** Allow 2hrs for the Walking Tour below. For an in-depth look, take an All About Chinatown walking tour, which includes a dim sum lunch (☎415-982-8839; *www.allaboutchinatown.com*).

A Bit of History

At the time of the 1849 Gold Rush, economic conditions in many areas of China were desperate. By 1852 some 10,000 Chinese had made their way to California in search of a better life.

From 1863 to 1869, thousands of Chinese worked on the construction of the Central Pacific Railroad. Upon its completion they turned to jobs in canneries, lumber mills, agriculture and construction, incurring the resentment of American and European immigrant workers forced to compete with their much-lower wage demands. Race riots in many Western

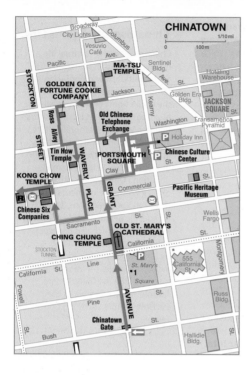

and dragons to symbolize auspicious fortunes. The eight blocks between Bush Street and Broadway bustle with shoppers in search of food, jewelry, electronics, T-shirts, Chinese art objects, and gifts. Visitors may wish to enter the **Ching Chung Temple**★ *(615 Grant Ave., 4th floor;* ◷ *open year-round daily 9am–5.30pm;* ✆*415-433-2623)* to view an authentic Taoist center of worship.

Old St. Mary's Cathedral★

660 California St., at Grant Ave. ◷*Open year-round Mon–Fri 7am–4.30pm, Sat 10am–6pm, Sun 8am–3.30pm.* ♿✆*415-288-3800. www.oldsaintmarys.org.* Predating the neighborhood, this brick edifice was dedicated in 1854 as San Francisco's first cathedral for a Roman Catholic diocese. The church was gutted by the great fire of 1906, though the stout walls survived. Photographs in the vestibule depict 19C Chinatown.

Across California Street lies St. Mary's Square, a patch of green amid tall buildings, anchored by a statue of **Sun Yatsen (1)** by sculptor Beniamino Bufano. Sun spent two years in Chinatown organizing revolutionary movements that eventually overthrew the Manchu Dynasty in China and established the Republic of China in 1911.

▶ *Return to Grant Ave. and continue north, turning right on Clay St.*

Portsmouth Square★

Formerly the central plaza of the Mexican settlement of Yerba Buena, this square is Chinatown's most important outdoor gathering point. From the square's east side, a pedestrian bridge leads across Kearny Street to the **Chinese Culture Center** *(Hilton Hotel, 750*

towns, including San Francisco, led to the **Federal Chinese Exclusion Act** of 1882, which barred Chinese laborers (though not merchants or their families) from entering the US.

In response to persecution, the Chinese congregated in the cities. With the 1943 repeal of the Exclusion Act and later immigration reforms, the door was opened to new waves of immigration. Chinese Americans began relocating from San Francisco's Chinatown to other city neighborhoods and suburbs. Despite this exodus, the neighborhood remains the soul of the now far-flung Chinese community. Importing, retailing, manufacturing and tourism are the mainstays of its economy.

🐾 WALKING TOUR

▶ *Begin at the intersection of Bush St. and Grant Ave. and walk north.*

Grant Avenue★★

Chinatown's principal tourist avenue is entered through the **Chinatown Gate** (1970), designed with ceramic carp

Kearny St., 3rd floor; ⏱open year-round Tue–Sat 10am–4pm; 📞415-986-1822; www.c-c-c.org), an active community center featuring exhibits of Chinese and Chinese-American art plus performances, cultural activities and walking tours. A block southeast of Portsmouth Square is the **Pacific Heritage Museum** (📖see Financial District).

▶ Leave the square and walk uphill on Washington St.

Old Chinese Telephone Exchange
743 Washington St.
The neighborhood's most exuberant example of chinoiserie rises in three pagoda-like tiers above a glossy, red-pillared pediment. Now a bank branch, the one-story building was opened as a telephone exchange in 1909 to serve the community's 800 telephones.

▶ Turn right on Grant Ave., walk one block and turn right on Jackson St. Walk half a block down the hill and turn left on Beckett St.

Ma-Tsu Temple of USA★
30 Beckett St., 1st floor. ⏱Open year-round daily 9am–5pm. ⌦Contribution requested. 📞415-986-8818.
This very accessible temple honors the Queen of Heaven. The central statue is guarded by figures of two ferocious warriors, Chien Li Yen and Shun Feng Er, noted respectively for their prodigious powers of seeing and hearing. Giant puppets of the pair can be seen striding the streets, arms swinging widely, in the annual Chinese New Year Parade.

▶ Return to Jackson St. Turn right up the hill, across Grant Ave., to Ross Alley; turn left and continue to Washington Street.

Jackson Street, Ross Alley and Washington Street traverse a densely populated enclave of herbalists, restaurants, grocery stores and bakeries. These side streets retain the dark, intriguing ambience of old Chinatown. Narrow **Ross Alley** is home to a number of clothing

Norras Temple
Brigitta L. House/MICHELIN

factories humming behind closed doors. Step inside the **Golden Gate Fortune Cookie Company**★ 🏃(56 Ross Alley; ⏱open year-round daily 9am–8pm; 📞415-781-3856) to see cookies being baked and stuffed with "fortunes" by workers seated at revolving machines.

▶ Cross Washington St., walk downhill and turn right on Waverly Pl.

Waverly Place★
This two-block alley is often dubbed "the Street of Painted Balconies" in reference to the chinoiserie that graces its otherwise plain three- and four-story Edwardian brick buildings. The colors are symbolic: red stands for happiness, green for longevity, black for money, and yellow for good fortune. The venerable **Tin How Temple** (125 Waverly Pl., 4th floor; ⏱open year-round daily 9am–4pm; 📞415-421-3628), devoted to the Queen of Heaven and protector of seafarers, accepts visitors to its smoky interior adorned with wooden statues. Farther along the street, in the welcoming **Norras Temple**★ (109 Waverly Pl., 3rd floor; ⏱open year-round daily 10am–4pm; 📞415-362-1993), a large, gilded statue of the Buddha surrounded by smaller, similar figures the hall of worship; this

was the first purely Buddhist temple in the mainland US when it opened in 1960.

▷ *Turn right on Sacramento St., walk uphill and turn right on Stockton St.*

Stockton Street★

Chinatown residents and Bay Area Chinese-Americans alike crowd the many food stores, tea shops and pharmacies of this busy commercial thoroughfare, especially on weekend mornings. The **Chinese Six Companies** *(no. 843; ⚷ not open to the public)*, a powerful benevolent association, still wields considerable influence over Chinatown business establishments; the building's eye-catching facade is one of the most elaborate in Chinatown. Well worth a stop is the **Kong Chow Temple**★ *(855 Stockton St., 4th floor; elevator entrance to the left of post office; ⏰ open year-round Mon–Sat 9am–4pm)*, containing excellent examples of Chinese wood carving.

▷ *Turn left on Clay St. for one block.*

Chinese Historical Society of America Museum (R)

965 Clay St. ⏰*Open Tue–Fri noon–5pm.* ☏*415-391-1188. www.chsa.org.*
This red-brick YMCA building (1932) was designed by famed architect Julia Morgan. Pagoda-like towers rise above a roofline crenellated with imported Chinese tiles, and a cast-stone arch with leaded glazing surmounts the double entrance doors. The main gallery tells the story of the Chinese in America through photographs and artifacts. Two other rooms display rotating exhibits.

② CIVIC CENTER★

Map pp. 290-291. 🚌 *bus 5–Fulton, 19–Polk, 47–Van Ness; all streetcars Civic Center station.* 🚇 *Civic Center station.*
Contained within the triangle of Market Street, Van Ness Avenue and Golden Gate Avenue, San Francisco's center of government occupies one of the finest groups of Beaux-Arts-style buildings in

the US. Though today the area suffers from its proximity to the downtrodden Tenderloin district, it was boosted with the opening of the Asian Art Museum in the refurbished old Main Library in 2003. The new, energy-efficient San Francisco Federal Building at Seventh and Mission streets (2007) is expected to foster development along the depressed Market Street corridor.

City Hall★★

1 Dr. B. Goodlett Pl. between McAllister & Grove Sts. ⏰*Open year-round Mon–Fri 8am–8pm.* 💬*Guided tours Mon–Fri 10am, noon & 2pm.* ⏰*Closed major holidays.* ♿📶 ☏*415-554-6139. www.sfgov.org/site/cityhall_index.asp.*
This massive Beaux-Arts edifice (1915, Arthur Brown, Jr.) houses city government offices, including the office of the mayor. Its splendid gold leaf-trimmed dome soars 307ft, about 13ft taller than that of the US Capitol Building in Washington, DC. The grand ceremonial staircase ascends to a 181ft open rotunda. To the east of City Hall lies **Civic Center Plaza**, scene of historic political demonstrations and rallies. Fronting its south side, the **Bill Graham Civic Auditorium** *(⚷ not open to the public)* was completed for the 1915 international exposition.

Asian Art Museum★★★

200 Larkin St. between McAllister and Fulton Sts. ⏰*Open year-round Tue–Sun 10am–5pm (Thu 9pm).* ⏰*Closed major holidays.* 👝*$12 (free 1st Sun of the month)* ✕♿📶 ☏*415-581-3500. www.asianart.org.*
Housed since 2003 in the greatly revamped old Main Library building, the Asian Art Museum owns what is considered the finest collection of Asian art in the nation. With particular strengths in Chinese art, including jades, ceramics, ritual bronzes and paintings from the Ming and Qing dynasties, the collection of some 17,000 works spanning 6,000 years also boasts the nation's most comprehensive assemblage of Japanese art; significant holdings of Indian and Southeast Asian religious statuary;

and Korean, Himalayan and Near Eastern artwork.

A Bit of History

Chicago engineering executive **Avery Brundage** (1887–1975), the museum's founder, traveled extensively in the 1920s as a member of the International Olympic Committee. His travels in Asia fostered a passion for collecting Japanese *netsuke* (carved bone toggles), Chinese bronzes and objects from Korea, Southeast Asia, India and its neighbors, and the Middle East.

In the 1950s, Brundage began to search for a permanent museum for his 5,000-piece collection. The city-owned Asian Art Museum opened in a wing of the de Young Museum in 1966, but with space to display only 15 percent of the collection, the museum outgrew its home. Structural damage to the building by the 1989 earthquake prompted a move, and the vacant library building seemed like an ideal place. Italian architect Gae Aulenti, who redesigned a c.1900 train station into Paris' Museé d'Orsay, drew up plans for the $160 million renovation. The design preserved the historic building's prominent elements, such as the marble staircase and great hall, while adding modern features.

Visit

The 2,500 works on display are arranged geographically, tracing the path of Buddhism as it spread through Asia. Works are rotated regularly.

Start on the third-floor South Asian gallery suite, then proceed through the exhibits down to the second-floor Japanese collection. Docent-led tours depart from the Information Desk; check at the desk for the day's tour schedule.

Third Floor – South Asian Art from India, Pakistan, Bangladesh and Sri Lanka boasts a wealth of religious statuary, carved ivories, jades and miniature paintings. A prize holding is the **silver elephant throne**★★★ made in india c. 1870-1920. In **Art of the Persian World and West Asia**, Luristani bronzes and other objects from present-day Iran,

Iraq, Afghanistan, Turkmenistan and Uzbekistan span 6,000 years. Sculptures in **Art of Southeast Asia**★ constitute much of the 500-piece collection, which includes textiles, rare Indonesian rod **puppets**★★, weapons and jewelry. The **Tibetan and Himalayan Art**★ gallery contains 300 items from Nepal, Tibet and Bhutan. The collection of *thangka*—brilliantly painted scrolls made of sized cotton—is one of the largest in America. Comprising over half the museum's holdings, the **Chinese Art**★★★ collection *(2nd and 3rd floors)*, embraces bronzes, sculptures, paintings, textiles and decorative artworks.

Second Floor – Korean Art★ consists of hanging scrolls, stoneware ceramics, gold jewelry, funerary pottery and celadon-glazed vessels. Two slate **daggers** (c. 500–600 BC) are the museum's oldest Korean artifacts. More than 4,200 objects make up the museum's collection of **Japanese Art**★★. Highlights are screens and scrolls, ceramics, bronzes, religious sculptures, **samurai swords**, decorative arts and a traditional **Japanese tea ceremony exhibit**.

San Francisco War Memorial and Performing Arts Center★★

401 Van Ness Ave., at Grove St. Visit by guided tour (30min) only, year-round Mon 10am–2pm; tours depart on the hour from Davies Symphony Hall. *Closed major holidays.* $5. 415-552-8338.

Flanking a formal courtyard designed by Thomas Church, these twin structures erected in memory of San Francisco's war dead have for decades been a center for the performing arts. The **War Memorial Opera House (E)** (1932, Arthur Brown, Jr.) hosted the meetings that established the United Nations in 1945. The acclaimed San Francisco Opera and San Francisco Ballet perform here in an elegant 3,176-seat auditorium.

To the north, the **Veterans Building (F)** houses city government offices and the 928-seat **Herbst Theatre**. The **San Francisco Art Commission Gallery** *(1st floor)*, showcases work by emerging Bay Area artists, and the **Museum**

of Performance and Design *(4th floor; ⏰open Wed–Sat noon–5pm; ⬤$5 donation; ✆415-255-4800; www.sfpalm.org)* presents exhibits related to the city's arts heritage.

Louise M. Davies Symphony Hall

Van Ness Ave. and Grove St. ✆415-864-6000 (tickets). www.sfsymphony.org. With its distinctive rounded facade, this contemporary structure (1980, Skidmore, Owings & Merrill), seating 2,743, is the home of the San Francisco Symphony Orchestra. The elegant bronze sculpture *Large Four Piece Reclining Figure* (1973) at the entrance is by Henry Moore.

San Francisco Public Library★

100 Larkin St. ⏰Open year-round Mon 10am–6pm, Tue–Thu 9am–8pm, Fri noon–6pm, Sat 10am–6pm & Sun noon–5pm. ⏰Closed major holidays. ✕♿🅿 ✆415-557-4400. *http://sfpl.lib.ca.us.*
San Francisco's Main Library (1996, James Ingo Freed & Cathy Simon) blends Civic Center's traditional architecture with modern elements. The main facade, facing City Hall, reveals an updated version of Civic Center's Beaux-Arts classicism, while the Hyde Street elevation presents an angular, contemporary face. The interior, replete with catwalk bridges, shelves of books, artworks and an asymmetrical skylit atrium, boasts the latest in high technology.
Ⓒ Visitors should resist the temptation to walk west from Civic Center to Alamo Square, Haight-Ashbury and Golden Gate Park. Distances are not great, but the intervening areas are subject to street crime. It's faster and safer to take public transportation.

③ FINANCIAL DISTRICT★★

Ⓖ Map p. 287. ▭ California St. 🚌 bus 1çCalifornia, 2–Clement, 3–Jackson, 4–Sutter, 5–Fulton, 6–Parnassus, 7–Haight, 12–Folsom, 41–Union. All streetcars Embarcadero or Montgomery St. stations. 🚇 Embarcadero or Montgomery St.

This dense forest of skyscraping steel, glass and stone, concentrated in a roughly triangular area north of Market Street along the city's eastern waterfront, represents the heart of San Francisco's financial community.
- ⏰ **Timing:** The district is practically deserted at night and on weekends. Visit on a weekday if you want to see it in full swing.
- Ⓒ **Don't Miss:** The Transamerica Pyramid: for a bird's-eye view of it, go to the Carnelian Room at the top of 555 California Street for a drink.
- 👥 **Kids:** Wells Fargo History Museum.

A Bit of History

In the 1850s the area experienced many construction booms. Banks and financial institutions set up shop along **Montgomery Street**, which became known as the "Wall Street of the West." The Financial District was extended out into the bay by landfill until it was eventually bounded in the 1880s by the **Embarcadero★**, a broad waterfront thoroughfare linking the city's piers. Another building boom from the early 1960s through the mid-1980s produced some of today's landmarks, including the Transamerica Pyramid. Preservationists lobbied for the protection of older buildings and for height limits, a movement that eventually resulted in the **Downtown Plan** of 1985, which put a cap on the square footage of new construction in the Financial District.

🚶 WALKING TOUR

▷ *Begin at the intersection of Post, Montgomery & Market Sts.*

One Montgomery Street

This grand building arose in the aftermath of the 1906 earthquake as the headquarters of First National Bank. A Wells Fargo branch bank now occupies the cavernous **banking hall★**.
From the corner, walk west on Post Street and enter the **Crocker Galleria★** (1983, Skidmore, Owings & Merrill), an elegant shopping center that cuts through the middle of the block, its three tiers of

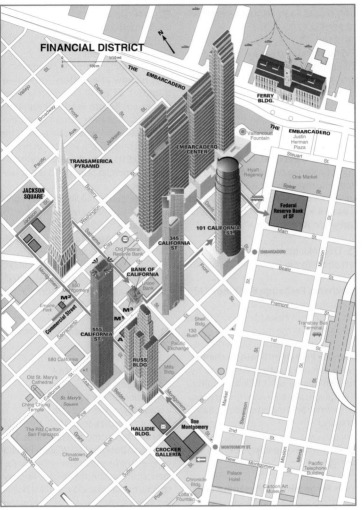

FINANCIAL DISTRICT

commercial spaces topped by a barrel-vaulted glass roof (○*open year-round Mon–Fri 10am–6pm, Sat 10am–5pm;* ✕ ♿ 🅿 ℘*415-393-1505; www.shopat-galleria.com*).

○ *Exit Crocker Galleria on Sutter St.*

Hallidie Building★★
130–150 Sutter St.
One of San Francisco's most noteworthy buildings, this seven-story office block (1917, Willis Polk) is widely considered to be the world's first glass-curtain-walled structure, a clear precursor of contem-

porary commercial architecture. It was named for Andrew Hallidie, the inventor of the cable car.

○ *Walk to corner of Sutter and Montgomery Sts. and turn left.*

Russ Building★
235 Montgomery St.
This 31-story Gothic Revival landmark (1927, George Kelham) stood as the tallest tower on the West Coast until the 1960s. The main entrance leads to a Gothic-style **lobby**★ that features stone vaulting over the cloister-like corridors,

inlaid mosaic floors and elaborate elevator panels.

555 California Street★★
555 California St.
San Francisco's largest building, this 52-story, dark-red behemoth (1971, Skidmore, Owings & Merrill) competes with the Transamerica Pyramid for dominance of San Francisco's downtown skyline. The central shaft rises 780ft from street level. The open plaza along California Street is anchored by *Transcendence* (1969, Masayuki Nagare), a dark, polished sculpture **(1)**. Panoramic **views**★★★ extend from the top-floor **Carnelian Room** lounge.

◉ *Cross Montgomery St. and continue east on California St.*

Merchants Exchange Building★ [A]
465 California St.
This 14-story office building (1903, Willis Polk) served as the focal point of commerce in turn-of-the-20C San Francisco. In the former **Grain Exchange Hall**★★ hang nautical paintings by the Irish marine artist William Coulter. *(☞Though currently closed to the public, the hall may be included on some historical tours.)*

◉ *Return to Montgomery St. and turn right.*

Wells Fargo History Museum★ (M1)
👥*420 Montgomery St.* ◐*Open year-round Mon–Fri 9am–5pm.* ◐*Closed major holidays.* ♿ ☎*415-396-2619. www.wellsfargohistory.com.*
Concord coaches of Wells Fargo & Co. began transporting freight and passengers in 1852. In this modern two-level gallery, photographs, gold nuggets, bank notes and coins are exhibited. Displays explore such topics as gold assaying, stagecoach robbery and telegraphing.
View a restored original **Concord coach**, and climb aboard a reconstructed one to hear a recorded description of a harrowing cross-country stagecoach journey in the 1850s.

◉ *Continue north on Montgomery St. and turn left onto Commercial St.*

Commercial Street
Between Montgomery and Kearny Sts.
This narrow alley offers intriguing glimpses of early commercial San Francisco. Before landfill extended the waterfront to its current line at the Embarcadero, this block formed the foot of Long Wharf, which ran across the mud flats along the line of present-day Commercial Street to deep water anchorage.
Housed in a bank building incorporating a carefully preserved remnant of the US Subtreasury building (1875), the small **Pacific Heritage Museum (M²)** *(608 Commercial St.;* ◐*open year-round Tue–Sat 10am–4pm;* ◐*closed major holidays;* ♿ ☎*415-399-1124; www.ibankunited. com/phm)* exhibits of art from Pacific Rim nations.

◉ *Continue on Montgomery St. and cross Clay St.*

Transamerica Pyramid★★
600 Montgomery St.
☞*Interior not open to the public. www.thepyramidcenter.com .*
Since its completion in 1972, this bold pyramid has come to symbolize San Francisco. Designed by William Pereira to house the headquarters of the Transamerica Corporation, the elegant 48-story structure is San Francisco's tallest building, rising 853ft from street level to the tip of its 212ft hollow lantern. Although the building is closed to the public, a lobby-level **Virtual Observation Deck** 👥 on the Washington Street side is wired to rooftop cameras that transmit bird's-eye views of the city.

◉ *Continue north on Montgomery St. to Jackson St. and turn right.*

Jackson Square★★
Jackson St. between Montgomery and Sansome Sts.
Not actually a square, San Francisco's oldest surviving commercial neighborhood encompasses five square blocks along

Jackson Street. The district formed the heart of the notorious **Barbary Coast**, the bawdy Gold Rush-era district of saloons, theaters and burlesque houses. The brick structures outlasted the great earthquake and fire of 1906, and since the 1960s many have been converted into upscale art galleries, design firms, law offices and antique stores.

◯ *Walk east on Jackson St. and turn right onto Sansome St. Continue south to the corner of California St.*

Bank of California★★
400 California St.
This stately Corinthian temple (1907, Bliss & Faville) is home to Union Bank of California. The interior boasts an opulent coffered ceiling and walls of pale marble. Stairs lead down to the **Museum of Money of the American West (M³)** (*open year-round Mon–Fri 9am– 4.30pm; closed major holidays*), which displays currency that circulated during the Gold Rush.

◯ *Walk east on California St.*

345 California Street★★
345 California St.
Two angular towers linked by a glass-enclosed "sky bridge" cap this futuristic skyscraper (1987, Skidmore, Owings & Merrill). To satisfy preservationists, the street frontages of existing historic structures were incorporated into the complex. The top 11 stories house the Mandarin Oriental Hotel.

◯ *Continue east on California St.*

101 California Street★
This stepped-back glass silo (1982, Johnson & Burgee) sports a three-story glass atrium that slices into the base of the building. A triangular plaza runs south to Market Street.

◯ *Turn left on Davis St. and cross Sacramento St.*

Cable Car and Transamerica Pyramid
PhotoDisc©

Embarcadero Center★
Enter from Davis St. between buildings Two and Three and take the spiral staircase to the Promenade (3rd) Level. 415-772-0700. www.embarcadero center.com.
The largest office and commercial complex in the city, this series of four slablike office towers (1967–82, John Portman and Assoc.) incorporates a three-level shopping center on its lower floors, running along historic Commercial Street.

◯ *Cross Market St.*

Federal Reserve Bank of San Francisco
101 Market St. Visit by guided tour (1hr) only; group tours available by reservation Mon–Thu 9.30am & 1.30pm; drop-in tours available Fri noon. Closed major holidays. 415-974-3252. www.frbsf.org.
Within this terraced bank building (1982, Skidmore, Owings & Merrill), **The Fed Center: Exploring Our Nation's Central Bank**★ exhibit offers entertaining but serious lessons in basic economics. Computer simulators enable visitors (pretending to be legislators, the US president or chairman of the Federal Reserve) to adjust the rate of money growth and set interest rates or taxes.

The newly designed **American Currency Exhibit** showcases paper money from colonial to modern times.

4 NOB HILL★★

🔎 *Map pp.290–291.*
🚌 *all lines.*

Nob Hill—like adjacent Russian Hill—served as a barrier to urban growth during San Francisco's early years: its sloping sides proved too steep for horse-drawn carriages. The advent of the cable car in the 1870s opened the hills for development, engendering Nob Hill's past and present reputation as a desirable residential address. Its name is a contraction of "nabob", a Hindu moniker for wealthy Europeans living in India.

The Central Pacific Railroad's wealthy "Big Four"—Collis Huntington, Mark Hopkins, Leland Stanford and Charles Crocker—built palatial residences here. All four mansions were destroyed in the 1906 earthquake and fire, but three live on in the names of structures crowning the hill today.

The **InterContinental Mark Hopkins** hotel (*southeast corner of Mason & California Sts.*) was the site of the Hopkins mansion; its swank, art deco-style rooftop bar, the **Top of the Mark**, features outstanding city **views**★★★.

The hotel stands just west of **The Stanford Court** hotel, site of Leland Stanford's mansion. **Huntington Park**, across Taylor Street from Grace Cathedral, marks the site of Collis Huntington's residence, and Charles Crocker's home occupied the present site of Grace Cathedral.

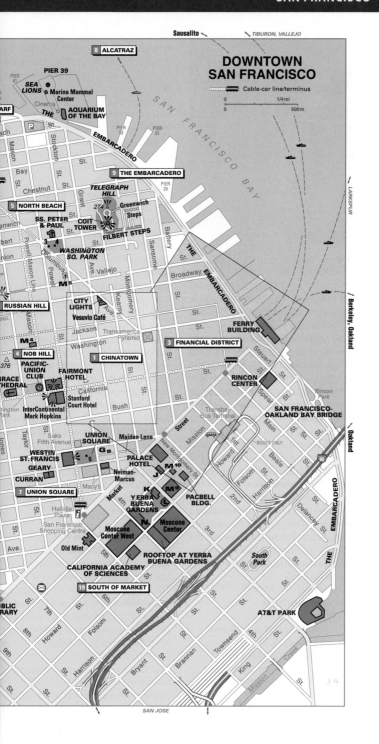

DOWNTOWN SAN FRANCISCO

▨▨▨▨ Cable-car line/terminus

| 0 | | 1/4 ml |
| 0 | | 500 m |

8 ALCATRAZ

PIER 39

PIER 41

SEA LIONS

Cinema

Marine Mammal Center

AQUARIUM OF THE BAY

WHARF

THE EMBARCADERO

PIER 33

PIER 31

SAN FRANCISCO BAY

9 THE EMBARCADERO

PIER 29

5 NORTH BEACH

TELEGRAPH HILL

274 △

Greenwich Steps

SS. PETER & PAUL

COIT TOWER

FILBERT STEPS

WASHINGTON SQ. PARK

FERRY BUILDING

RUSSIAN HILL

CITY LIGHTS

Vesuvio Café

Transamerica Pyramid

3 FINANCIAL DISTRICT

4 NOB HILL

1 CHINATOWN

RINCON CENTER

PACIFIC-UNION CLUB

FAIRMONT HOTEL

GRACE CATHEDRAL

Stanford Court Hotel

InterContinental Mark Hopkins

Transbay Bus Terminal

SAN FRANCISCO-OAKLAND BAY BRIDGE

Rincon Park

BUSES ONLY

UNION SQUARE

Maiden Lane

Saks Fifth Avenue

WESTIN ST. FRANCIS

GEARY

CURRAN

PALACE HOTEL

Neiman-Marcus

Macy's

7 UNION SQUARE

YERBA BUENA GARDENS

PACBELL BLDG.

Hallidie Plaza

San Francisco Shopping Centre

Moscone Center West

Moscone Center

Old Mint

ROOFTOP AT YERBA BUENA GARDENS

CALIFORNIA ACADEMY OF SCIENCES

South Park

19 SOUTH OF MARKET

PUBLIC LIBRARY

AT&T PARK

Sausalito

TIBURON, VALLEJO

LARKSPUR

Berkeley, Oakland

Oakland

THE EMBARCADERO

SAN JOSE

291

Murals, Coit Tower

Brigitta L. House/MICHELIN

Paradise replicate Lorenzo Ghiberti's doors to the baptistry of the Duomo in Florence, depicting 10 scenes from the Old Testament.
Inside are stained-glass windows and murals depicting 20C figures, an altar of California granite and redwood, and an oak reredos carved in Flanders about 1490. An Aeolian-Skinner organ resounds with 7,286 pipes.

Cable Car Museum★★ (M⁴)

1201 Mason St. at Washington St. Open Apr–Sept daily 10am–6pm; rest of the year daily 10am–5pm. Closed Jan 1, Easter Sun, Thanksgiving Day & Dec 25. 415-474-1887. www.cable carmuseum.com.
Sheltering the central powerhouse of the cable car system, this two-story brick structure houses a museum presenting the history of the cable car. From the mezzanine level overlooking the humming machinery, visitors get a close-up view of the giant wheels that loop the continuous cables from the Powell-Mason, Powell-Hyde and California Street lines. The mezzanine level has historical displays, memorabilia and several cable cars, among them **Car No. 8**, the only survivor of the Clay Street Hill Railroad, the city's first cable line, which began operation in 1873. Cable ports, through which the cables leave the barn to run under the street, are visible on the lower level.

5 NORTH BEACH★★

Map pp. 290–291. Powell-Mason. bus 30–Stockton, 45–Union-Stockton, or 39–Coit.
The longtime heart of San Francisco's Italian community and one of the city's oldest neighborhoods, this district was named for a sandy beach obliterated by landfill dredged from the bay. A refuge for San Francisco's Beat counterculture, this district retains, to some degree, the close-knit character of a village.
Italian immigrants (mostly from northern Italy) began settling here during the late 1870s. By the early 20C many immigrant residents had begun relocating to rich farmlands north of the city. Despite

The landmark **Fairmont Hotel★★** *(northeast corner of Mason & California Sts.)* memorializes **James Fair**, who made his fortune in the silver mines of the Comstock Lode. The Fairmont was nearly completed just before the 1906 fire, which gutted the interior, though the granite walls survived. The interior was restored and completed by renowned architect Julia Morgan. Its exterior elevator offers an expansive view of Chinatown, North Beach and much of the bay as it rises 24 stories to the **Crown Room** restaurant, famous for its panoramic **views★★★** of the entire city. Another partial survivor of the 1906 conflagration was the stone-walled mansion of Fair's partner James Flood *(across Mason St. from the Fairmont);* the building now houses San Francisco's exclusive **Pacific-Union Club★** *(not open to the public).*

Grace Cathedral★

1051 Taylor St. at California St. Open year-round Mon–Fri 7am–6pm, Sat 8am–6pm, Sun 8am–7pm. Guided tours (1hr) Mon–Fri 1pm–3pm, Sat 11.30am–1.30pm, Sun 12.30pm–2pm. 415-749-6300. www.gracecathedral.org.
Constructed in the French Gothic style, this landmark is the third-largest Episcopal cathedral in the US. Set in the Gothic eastern portal, the bronze **Gates of**

this trend, which continues today, and the encroaching spread of Chinatown, the neighborhood's traditional Italian flavor remains in evidence in its restaurants, cafes and shops.

As the Italian-American population began vacating North Beach, low-rent housing became available and was occupied by poor and disillusioned poets, artists and musicians.

This anarchic ("beaten") assortment, bent on rejecting established societal and artistic norms, became known as the **Beat Generation**. Poet Lawrence Ferlinghetti founded the **City Lights Bookstore**★ *(261 Columbus Ave;* ⏱*open year-round daily 10am–midnight;* ⏱*closed Thanksgiving Day & Dec 25;* ℘*415-362-8193; www.citylights.com),* where renowned literati Allen Ginsberg, Jack Kerouac and Gregory Corso also congregated, nurtured by the red-wine-and-espresso ambience of North Beach during the 1950s. Today the bookstore, along with the adjacent **Vesuvio Café** *(*℘*415-362-3370; www.vesuvio.com),* is one of the principal surviving landmarks of that period.

North Beach Museum (M⁵)

1435 Stockton St. (US Bank). ⏱*Open year-round Mon–Fri 8am–5pm, Sat 10am–2pm.* ⏱*Closed major holidays.* ℘*415-391-6210.*
This small bank-sponsored museum features photographs and artifacts to document the history of North Beach during the late 19C and early 20C.

Washington Square Park★

This grassy, open space, dotted with trees and benches, lies at the western foot of Telegraph Hill in the heart of North Beach. Elderly Asians gather each morning to practice t'ai chi, a graceful form of martial arts, and Italian retirees spend hours on the benches facing Union Street. A bronze monument to San Francisco's **Volunteer Firemen (3)** and a bronze figure of **Benjamin Franklin (4)** grace the park.

Saints Peter and Paul Church★

North side of the square. ⏱*Open year-round Mon–Fri 7am–4pm, weekends 6.30am–7pm.* ♿ ℘*415-421-0809. www. stspeterpaul.san-francisco.ca.us/church.*
The twin spires of San Francisco's "Italian Cathedral" (1924) loom over Washington Square. A verse from Dante's *Paradiso* adorns the facade, and impressive marble graces the interior. Reflecting North Beach's increasingly multi-ethnic character, the church offers Mass in Cantonese and English as well as Italian.

Telegraph Hill★

This 274ft hill was named for a semaphore constructed at the summit in 1849 to announce the approach of ships entering the Golden Gate. From the summit, presided over by a bronze statue of **Christopher Columbus**, some of the city's finest **views**★★ extend over the downtown area, the waterfront, East Bay and Marin County.

Descending Telegraph Hill's precipitous east slope, the lushly landscaped **Filbert Steps**★★ and the **Greenwich Steps** are staircased pedestrian paths *(access to Filbert St. indicated at uppermost curve leading to summit; to Greenwich St. at east side of summit parking lot).*

Coit Tower★★★

👤👤*Summit of Telegraph Hill. Access on foot from Washington Sq. by climbing Filbert St., following the "Stairs to Coit Tower" signs; or by taking the 39–Coit bus from Washington Square.* ⏱*Open May–Sept daily 10am–6pm; rest of the year same hours, weather permitting.* 🅿*(very limited)* ℘*415-362-0808.*
One of San Francisco's best-known landmarks, this 212ft fluted concrete shaft (1934) is an enduring gift to the city from **Lillie Hitchcock Coit** (1843-1929), an eccentric woman who spent part of her youth in San Francisco. At her death, Coit willed $125,000 to the city for beautification projects, one of which was Coit Tower.

The lobby in the tower's rectangular base features a trove of fresco **murals**★★ painted by 26 local artists as part of the Public Works of Art Project, an initiative of the New Deal whereby artists were hired as civil servants by the federal government to decorate public buildings. The murals, depicting vignettes of everyday life in California during the period of the Great Depression, incorporated both subtle and blatant expressions of social criticism that contradicted the conservative values of San Francisco's business elite; consequently, they sparked a heated political controversy between the artists and the San Francisco Art Commission.

Complicating matters was the concurrent Pacific maritime strike of West Coast longshoremen; the murals were viewed by the media and the public as sympathetic to the workers' position, and conservative groups threatened to alter or remove the offending images. In the heat of the debate, the Park Commission delayed opening Coit Tower for four months. When the doors finally opened to the public in October 1934, only the No. 4 mural, by Clifford Wight, had been altered.

From the tower's observation deck, sweeping **views**★★★ encompass the hills and streets of San Francisco.

6 RUSSIAN HILL★

See Downtown San Francisco map.
Powell-Mason or Powell-Hyde.

Best explored on foot or glimpsed from the Hyde Street cable car, Russian Hill harbors a number of pre-1906 architectural gems and a rich history of artistic activity. A small but active community of writers and artists thrived here in the late 19C and early 20C, including such literary lights as **Mark Twain**, **Robert Louis Stevenson** and **Bret Harte**.

Today several secluded pedestrian stairways and paths negotiate Russian Hill's two peaks, making for beautiful, if rigorous, walks. The Vallejo Street stairs ascend from Mason to Taylor streets, passing picturesque **Ina Coolbrith Park**; at the summit, a **view**★★ extends downtown and to the distant East Bay hills. Two blocks north lies **Macondray Lane**★, an unpaved, wooded pedestrian path lined with charming homes.

Lombard Street★★★

Between Hyde & Leavenworth Sts.

Affectionately dubbed "The World's Crookedest Street," the 1000 block of Lombard Street is undeniably one of San Francisco's most renowned (and most photographed) passageways. Originally an all-but-impassable grade of 27 percent, the hill was landscaped to a 16 percent grade in 1922, and a one-lane cobbled street of eight hairpin turns was built onto the slope. Nestled within the curves are terraces bedecked with flowers and shrubs; from the top of the hill, a **view**★★ extends north to Alcatraz and east to Coit Tower and beyond.

San Francisco Art Institute★

800 Chestnut St. Open year-round Mon–Fri 9am–5pm. 415-771-7020. www.sfai.edu.

This renowned school of fine arts is housed in a Spanish Colonial-style building (1926, Arthur Brown Jr.); its unadorned concrete annex was added in 1969. From the rooftop deck, grand **views**★★ encompass the northern waterfront and Telegraph Hill.

The **Diego Rivera Gallery** (*open year-round daily 9am–7.30pm; closed major holidays*), devoted to changing shows by institute students, features a two-story mural (1931) by the celebrated Mexican artist. rivera, a world-famous artists from Mexico, and husband of Frida Kahlo painted murals in San Francisco, Detroit and New york City in the 1930s.

7 UNION SQUARE

Map pp. 290–291. Powell-Hyde or Powell-Mason. bus 2-Clement, 3-Jackson, 4-Sutter, 30-Stockton, 38-Geary or 45-Union-Stockton; streetcars Powell St. Powell St. station.

Roughly bounded by Sutter, Taylor, Kearny and O'Farrell streets, the Union Square area bustles as San Francisco's most vibrant and prestigious urban shopping district. Some of the city's finest luxury department stores lie on, or within walking distance of, the square itself, including Saks Fifth Avenue, Macy's and Nordstrom. The post-Modern

Neiman-Marcus store (1982, Johnson & Burgee) features an interior **rotunda**★ topped by an elaborate art-glass dome removed from the City of Paris store that previously occupied the site.

Union Square Park★

This 2.6-acre parcel was named for the mass meetings held here by Union sympathizers to demonstrate their loyalty during the Civil War. At its center rises the 97ft **Dewey Monument (5)**, surmounted by *Victory*, a bronze sculpture commemorating Admiral Dewey's 1898 defeat of Spanish naval forces. A major restoration in 2002 spiffed up the square with new granite surfaces, steel benches and public art installations. Music and dance performances occur regularly on the stage along the park's north side. Street musicians avail themselves of the open spaces during the day, while adventurous skateboarders take over in the evenings.

Westin St. Francis Hotel★★

335 Powell St. Self-guided walking-tour maps are available at concierge desk. ☎*415-397-7000. www.westin.com.*
This elegant Renaissance and Baroque Revival pile (1904) was largely destroyed in the 1906 fire. Rebuilt and expanded by Bliss & Faville, it has since welcomed celebrities and dignitaries from around the world. Glass elevators zooming up the tower annex offer superb **views**★★ of the Financial District and the bay.

Maiden Lane

East of Union Square between Post and Geary Sts.
Previously flanked with Barbary Coast-style brothels, Maiden Lane was reincarnated after the 1906 fire as a quaint pedestrian street lined with maple trees, cafes, boutiques, salons and galleries. The **Frank Lloyd Wright Building**★**(G)** *(no. 140)* is the only San Francisco building designed by Wright (1948); home to the Xanadu Gallery for Asian fine art, it sports an interior reminiscent of the Guggenheim Museum in New York City.

Theater District

San Francisco's small but active theater district comprises over 10 venues. Grandest of the multibalconied palaces are the **Geary Theater**★ (1909, Bliss & Faville), adorned with fanciful columns of polychrome terracotta *(415 Geary St.)*, and the **Curran Theatre**★ (1922, Alfred Henry Jacobs), with a mansard roof and Romanesque arches *(445 Geary St.)*. The former is home to the American Conservatory Theater (ACT).

BAYSHORE

Relics of San Francisco's maritime past occupy the city's shoreline, particularly along the Northern Waterfront between Telegraph Hill and the Marina District. The view from the waterfront's splendid **setting**★ takes in passing freighters, the Golden Gate Bridge, Alcatraz and the rugged shoreline of Marin County.

8 ALCATRAZ★★★

♿*Map pp. 290–291.*
This infamous 12-acre island served variously as a fortress, military prison and US Federal Penitentiary until its conversion to a national park in 1972. A visit to "the Rock," as it is aptly nicknamed, provides a haunting journey into one of the harshest chapters of American judicial history.

- ℹ️ **Info:** National Park Service ☎415-561-4900. www.nps.gov/alca. Ferry company ☎415-981-7625. www.alcatrazcruises.com.
- ▶ **Location:** Alcatraz lies 1.5mi offshore from Fisherman's Wharf, and is accessible by ferry only. Alacatraz Cruises is the official ferry service for the national park; its ferries depart from Pier 33 at Fisherman's Wharf. To plan your visit, call or check both the park's and the cruise company's websites 3wks in advance. ♿*For ticket and schedules, see* Visit *below.* The island is steep, hilly and windy; wear sturdy walking shoes and dress in layers.
- 🅿️ **Parking:** Use one of the dozen commercial lots within a five-block radius of Pier 33.

Approaching Alcatraz

🕐 **Timing:** Reserve or purchase your ticket at least 2wks in advance. A visit is 3hrs from the time you step aboard the ferry *(15min passage each way, plus 2.5hrs on the island).* Food service is available onboard the ferry, but not on the island.

A Bit of History

As the story goes, the island was initially named Yerba Buena Island, and in 1775 the name Isla de los Alcatraces, meaning "gannet island" in Spanish, was given to the jut of land that today anchors the Bay Bridge's west pier. The names were reversed on an 1826 map, and the error was never corrected.

President Millard Fillmore designated Alcatraz a military reservation in 1850, and fortifications were constructed on there. Confederate sympathizers and Native Americans were incarcerated on the island in 1861, and for 30 years Alcatraz served simultaneously as a defense installation and military prison. In 1907 it became a US military prison.

In 1934 the island was acquired by the Federal Bureau of Prisons. Redesignated as a federal penitentiary, it served for 30 years as an isolated, maximum-security installation. With a strictly enforced "no talking" rule, one guard for every three prisoners, and infamous inmates like Al "Scarface" Capone and Robert "Birdman" Stroud, Alcatraz quickly gained a reputation as America's bleakest prison.

The high cost of maintenance, deteriorating facilities and a number of near-successful escape attempts led to the 1963 decision to close the prison. A group of Indians took over Alcatraz in 1969 in an unsuccessful attempt to establish a Native American Center there. In 1972 Alcatraz was incorporated into the Golden Gate National Recreation Area.

Visit

🕐*Alcatraz Cruises ferries depart from Pier 33 for Alcatraz Island about every 30–45min daily May–Sept 9am–3.55pm; rest of the year 9am–1.55pm. Evening tours available seasonally; check website for schedule.* 🕐*Closed Jan 1 & Dec 25.* 👁$26, children $16 (includes audiocassette cellhouse tour, orientation video by Discovery Channel, ranger and docent tours). An Alcatraz Night Tour is offered seasonally;* 👁*$33, children $19.50. Reservations should be made at least 2wks in advance by contacting Alcatraz Cruises* ✖👤 📞*415-981-7625 or www.alcatrazcruises.com.*

The ferry trip *(15min)* to and from the island offers splendid **views**★★ of the waterfront and the Golden Gate on fogless days. At the ferry dock, rangers provide an informative orientation near the landing, after which visitors are free to inspect the exhibit area on the lower floor of the Barracks Building (1867), view an **orientation video** *(12min)* in the theater, or climb the steep, switchback road past the ruins of the Post Exchange and Officers' Quarters to the cellhouse.

Cellhouse★★

Self-guided audiocassette tour available at prison entrance.
Now partially in ruins, the long, foreboding cellhouse structure (1911) of reinforced concrete offers a vivid, if chilling,

look at the daily life of Alcatraz inmates. Visitors may wander at will through the cavernous interiors, down the main cell block (nicknamed "Broadway"), past diminutive, steel-barred cells. The mess hall offers tantalizing views of San Francisco's skyline. Also worth inspecting are the inmates' library, to which access was rewarded for good behavior; and the solitary confinement cells, where prisoners were punished for infractions of the will-breaking rules.

9 THE EMBARCADERO★

See Downtown San Francisco map. bus 7–Haight, 14–Mission, 21–Hayes, 31–Balboa or 71–Haight-Noriega; all streetcars Embarcadero station. Embarcadero station.
This waterfront promenade *(3mi)* from Fisherman's Wharf to China Basin offers expansive bay views, public art and attractions. In Spanish, its name means "boarding place."

Ferry Building★★

Embarcadero at Market St. Open year-round Mon–Fri 10am–6pm, Sat 9am–6pm, Sun 11am–5pm; extended hrs in summer. Closed Jan 1, Thanksgiving Day & Dec 25. 415-983-8000. www.ferrybuildingmarketplace.com.
Before construction of the Bay Bridge, this three-story arcaded ferry terminal (1898), characterized by its 240ft clock tower, was the debarkation point for passengers arriving by ferry from the East Bay. A $100 million renovation completed in 2003 created 65,000 square feet of marketplace space along the first floor's central nave. Here you'll find artisan food shops, including Prather Ranch meats, Frog Hollow Farms organic produce and Cowgirl Creamery cheeses. The **Ferry Plaza Farmers' Market** takes place here twice a week (open Tue 10am–2pm, Sat 8am–2pm; 415-291-3276; www.cuesa.org).
Nearby, the two-acre Rincon Park *(along the waterfront at the foot of Folsom St.)* was dedicated in early 2003. Marked by a bayfront promenade with views of the bay and Bay Bridge, the park showcases a 60ft-tall fiberglass and steel bow and arrow by sculptors Claes Oldenburg and Coosje van Bruggen.

San Francisco-Oakland Bay Bridge★★

Open daily year-round. $4 toll westbound only from Oakland. Nonvehicular crossing of the bridge prohibited. 510-286-4444. www.dot.ca.gov.
Connecting San Francisco and Oakland, this two-tiered bridge, measuring a total length of 5.2mi, is one of the longest high-level steel bridges in the world. Engineered by Charles Purcell and completed in 1936, the Bay Bridge was conceived as two structures meeting at Yerba Buena Island, a rocky promontory midway across the bay.
The western section, comprising two 2,310ft suspension bridges, joins San Francisco and the island. The eastern section, joining Yerba Buena Island and Oakland, is a cantilever-truss design; due to earthquake damage, this section is currently being replaced over a lengthy period of time. Between the two sections, a tunnel pierces Yerba Buena Island; 76ft wide and 58ft high.
Westbound traffic on the entire bridgeway occupies the top tier, so that those approaching the city enjoy **views**★ of the bay and the San Francisco skyline.

Rincon Center★

101 Spear St. Open daily year-round. 415-777-4100.
The former Rincon Annex Post Office (1940) was transformed into this multistory shopping and residential complex (1989), a block south and west of the Ferry Building. The restoration preserved the original art deco exterior and lobby, which features **frescoes**★ depicting California's history.

AT&T Park★★

Kids *3rd & King Sts.* Tours year-round daily 10.30am & 12.30pm except when game conflicts. $12.50, children $7.50. Coca-Cola Fan Lot (free) open year-round Tue–Sun 11am–5pm on non-game days, 2hrs before scheduled first pitch on days of home games.

✕♿🅿 ⠿⠿ 🕿*415-972-2000.
www.sfgiants.com.

Baseball insiders consider this $319 million major-league stadium to be the finest in the world. Opened in 2000, it couples the mood of an early 20C urban ballpark with modern amenities.

The 40,800-seat stadium shields players and spectators from wind and fog; from upper-level tiers, views extend to the city skyline, the Bay Bridge and beyond. The **Coca-Cola Fan Lot**, above the left-field bleachers, features pop-bottle slides, a wiffleball field, speed-pitching and baserunning areas, and "the world's largest baseball glove," a huge sculpture of an old-fashioned three-finger mitt.

10 FISHERMAN'S WHARF★★★

♿*Map pp. 300–301.* ▭*Powell-Hyde or Powell-Mason.* *bus 19–Polk, 30–Stockton, 39–Coit or 47–Van Ness.*

One of San Francisco's most popular tourist attractions, Fisherman's Wharf—which extends along the waterfront between Hyde and Taylor streets—draws throngs to its colorful array of piers, docks, carnival amusements and seafood eateries. The number of working fishing boats here has declined, but early in the morning, fishermen can still be seen returning with the day's catch.

🛈 **Info:** California Welcome Center on the second level of Pier 39 *(Beach St. at Embarcadero).* *🕿415-981-1280. www.fishermanswharf.org.*

🅿 **Parking:** Take the F-Market streetcar or one of the Powell Street

cable car. There are large parking garages under Ghirardelli Square and across from Pier 39, but they are expensive and often full.

👥 **Kids:** Pier 39's carousel; an Earthquake sundae at the Ghirardelli Chocolate Shop.

Pier 39★

👥*Beach St. at Embarcadero.* 🕘*Shops and attractions open year-round daily 10.30am–7pm. Extended hrs on weekends and in summer.* ✕♿🅿*($7/hr)* *🕿415-981-7437. www.pier39.com.*

This festive, bi-level marketplace of shops and amusements was built in 1978 atop a c.1900 fishing pier.

A two-tiered 👥**carousel** anchors the far end of the complex, while a pod of wild California **sea lions★** occupies the docks of its west side. Interpretive talks on the creatures are offered by the **Marine Mammal Center**, which operates a gift shop in the marketplace (*🕿415-289-7373; www.marinemammalcenter.org*).

At the newly renovated **Aquarium of the Bay★** (👥🕘*open Memorial Day–Labor Day daily 9am–8pm; rest of the year Mon–Thu 10am–6pm, Fri–Sat 10am–7pm;* 🕘*closed Dec 25;* ⊜*$15.95, children $8;* ♿ *🕿415-623-5300; www.aquariumofthebay.com*), visitors view the undersea world up close while strolling through exhibits and two clear 300ft-long tunnels that burrow through tanks containing 23,000 creatures such as Pacific octopus, jellyfish, sharks and eels.

Fisherman's Wharf

©John Anderson/MICHELIN

Hyde Street Pier★★

👥*Foot of Hyde St; visitor center at 499 Jefferson St.*🕐*Visitor center open daily 9.30am–5pm; pier and ships open Memorial Day–Sept daily 9.30am–5.30pm (6.30pm mid-Jun–mid-Aug); rest of the year daily 9.30am–5pm.*🕐*Closed Jan 1, Thanksgiving Day & Dec 25.*🎫*$5 to board vessels, children under 16 free.* 📞*415-447-5000. www.nps.gov/safr.*

Before the Golden Gate and Bay bridges were erected, this historic wooden pier served car ferries to Sausalito and Berkeley. The pier is now part of the **San Francisco Maritime National Historical Park**, which maintains what may be the largest historic fleet afloat and serves as the mooring for six historic ships—all but one of which can be boarded. On the pier itself stand a turn-of-the-20C "ark" (a flat-bottomed houseboat that served as a summer retreat on the bay) and a small boat shop, offering lessons in boatbuilding. At the entrance to the pier lies the **Maritime Store (H)**, which provides park information and specializes in books on maritime subjects.

Eureka★

Right side of the pier.

This steam-powered passenger and car ferry, built in 1890 and still among the world's largest wooden floating structures, plied the waters between San Francisco and Sausalito from 1922 to 1939 and remained in service between Oakland and San Francisco until 1957.

C.A. Thayer★

Across from the Eureka.

This historic timber schooner (1895) was designed to carry lumber to San Francisco from North Coast "doghole ports," wave-pounded coves where the crew had to hold the ship steady as logs were loaded from the bluffs above. In the forecastle, a video *(11min)* recounts the story of the ship's last voyage.

Balclutha★★

End of pier on the left.

Looming majestically over the pier, this three-masted, steel-hulled square-rig-

---

Cruising on the Bay

A scenic cruise on San Francisco Bay offers an opportunity to view the Golden Gate Bridge, Alcatraz, the wharf areas and the city's celebrated skyline. Cruises generally last one hour, and prices average $22.

Blue & Gold Fleet (Bay Cruise) – departs from Pier 41 (📞*415-773-1188; www.blueandgoldfleet.com*).

Red & White Fleet (Golden Gate Bridge Cruise) – departs from Pier 43 at the foot of Taylor Street (📞*415-673-2900; www.redandwhite.com*).

---

ger, launched in 1886, made 17 trips around Cape Horn between Europe and California.

From 1903 to 1930 the *Balclutha* worked the salmon trade between Alaska and California. Today visitors board to inspect the wood-paneled captain's quarters in the stern, and try to imagine life in the cramped forecastle, where the crew slept.

In addition to these three ships, the steel-hulled steam tug *Hercules* (1907) and scow schooner *Alma* (1891) are open for public viewing on a limited schedule, subject to weather. Moored for dockside viewing *(o—not open for visits)* is the paddle-wheel steam tug *Eppleton Hall* (1914), which operated on the River Wear near Newcastle upon Tyne, England.

USS Pampanito★★

👥*Pier 45, near the foot of Taylor St.*🕐*Open Memorial Day–early Oct daily 9am–8pm (Wed 6pm); rest of the year daily 9am–6pm (Fri & Sat 8pm).*🎫*$9, children $4.* 📞*415-775-1943. www.maritime.org.*

Built in 1943, this World War II, Balao-class submarine made six patrols in the Pacific and sank six enemy ships. In 1944 the *Pampanito* and two Allied subs executed a mission to attack a convoy of Japanese ships carrying war supplies, ignorant of the fact that the ships also carried British and Austra-

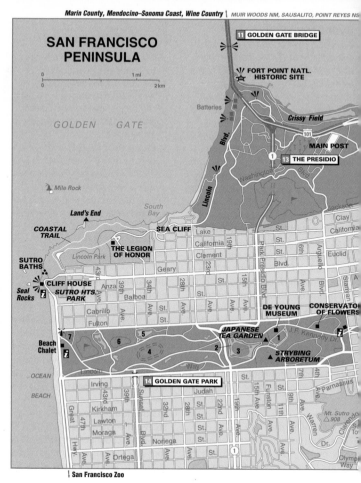

Marin County, Mendocino–Sonoma Coast, Wine Country | MUIR WOODS NM, SAUSALITO, POINT REYES NS

SAN FRANCISCO PENINSULA

11 GOLDEN GATE BRIDGE

FORT POINT NATL. HISTORIC SITE

Batteries

Crissy Field

101

MAIN POST

13 THE PRESIDIO

Mile Rock

Land's End

South Bay

COASTAL TRAIL

SEA CLIFF

THE LEGION OF HONOR

SUTRO BATHS

CLIFF HOUSE

SUTRO HTS. PARK

Seal Rocks

Lincoln Park

Geary

Anza

Balboa

Cabrillo

Fulton

DE YOUNG MUSEUM

CONSERVATO OF FLOWERS

Beach Chalet

7

6

5

4

JAPANESE TEA GARDEN

2

3

STRYBING ARBORETUM

1

OCEAN

BEACH

14 GOLDEN GATE PARK

Irving

Judah

Kirkham

Lawton

Moraga

Noriega

Ortega

Mt. Sutro

| San Francisco Zoo

lian prisoners of war. Returning to the scene three days later, the *Pampanito* discovered survivors clinging to pieces of wreckage, and rescued 73 Allied POWs. A self-guided audio tour begins on the upper deck and moves from the rear torpedo room through the engine rooms, crew's quarters, command centers and the fully functional galley before ending at the forward torpedo room.

SS Jeremiah O'Brien★
Pier 45. Open year-round daily 9am–4pm. Closed Jan 1, Thanksgiving, Dec 25. $8. 415-544-0100. www.ssjeremiahobrien.org.
This last remaining unaltered World War II Liberty Ship is one of 2,751 cargo ves-

sels hurriedly constructed between 1941 and 1945 to ferry supplies to battles in Europe and the Pacific. The *O'Brien* formed part of the 5,000-ship armada that stormed Normandy Beach on D-Day in 1944. Self-guided tours cover all areas of the ship, from the wheel house and crew's quarters on the bridge down to the bowels of the engine room. Liberty shi9ps were cargo ship invented during World War II orignally designed by the British.

The Cannery at Del Monte Square★★
2801 Leavenworth St., at Jefferson St. Shops open summer Mon–Sat 10am–8pm, Sun 11am–8pm; winter Mon–Sat 10am–6pm, Sun 11am–6pm. Restau-

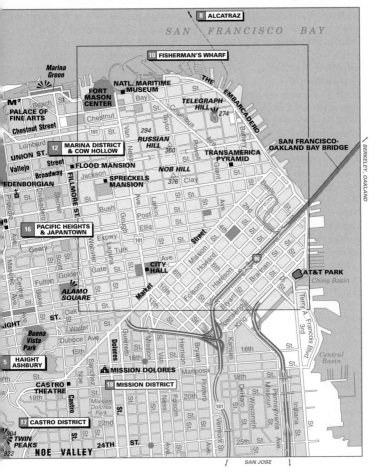

rants' hours vary. ✕占 ☎415-771-3112.
www.delmontesquare.com.

Built in 1907 as a packing plant for the
California Fruit Canners Assn., this brick
structure housed the most productive
peach-canning operation in the world
from 1916 to 1937. Saved from demolition and renovated in the mid-1960s, the
building is today one of San Francisco's
most attractive and well-known shopping complexes.

The interior reveals a seamless modern
design of open stairwells, bridges, walkways and passages within the original
external walls and set over three levels
around an inviting courtyard with several outdoor cafes.

Ghirardelli Square★

*Bounded by Polk, Larkin, Beach & North
Point Sts.* ☻*Open year-round daily
10am–6pm (Fri & Sat 9pm).* ✕ ☎415-
775-5500. www.ghirardellisq.com.

This famed group of industrial brick
buildings was renovated and landscaped in 1968 to form a multi-level
complex of upscale shops and restaurants. Domingo Ghirardelli purchased
the oldest building in 1893 to house a
chocolate factory. Ghirardelli added
more buildings, culminating in 1916
with the **clock tower**. Chocolate production continued here until 1962, when
the company transferred operations to
a new factory across the bay.

The old factory was renovated, and
today it houses condominiums, a hand-

ful of shops, a luxury hotel and the ever-popular Ghirardelli Ice Cream and Chocolate Shop. (⟲see sidebar).

National Maritime Museum★ (M[6])

Beach St. at Polk St. ⟲ *Closed for renovation until summer 2009.* ℘415-447-5000. www.nps.gov/safr.

A fine example of the Streamline Moderne style of art deco, the museum building (1939) resembles a luxury ocean liner, complete with decks, railings and portholes. A project of the WPA, the structure originally served as the Aquatic Park Casino restaurant; it now forms part of the San Francisco Maritime National Historical Park.

The museum features 37 interior murals by Hilaire Hiler and intaglios on slate by Sargent Johnson around the front door. The museum—focusing on the city's early years as a sea and inland port—houses model ships, figurines, historic photographs, whaling tools and other artifacts of ocean and inland water transport.

Coast Walk

⟲*Under renovation until early 2010.*

A paved pedestrian path leads west from **Aquatic Park Beach** to Fort Mason Center and the Marina District. Lined with Monterey cypress, the path overlooks the city's last remnant of undeveloped, natural bay shoreline and offers views of the bay and of Angel Island.

⊡⊡ GOLDEN GATE BRIDGE★★★

⟲*See San Francisco Peninsula map.*
🚌*bus 28–19th Ave., 29–Sunset or 76–Marin Headlands.*

The narrow, windy and fog-haunted Golden Gate passage connecting San Francisco Bay to the open ocean is the only sea-level entryway to California's interior. This art deco suspension bridge, San Francisco's most widely recognized symbol, spans the Golden Gate via twin 746ft towers and an intricate tracery of cables supporting a roadway (1.7mi excluding approaches). Painted in vibrant "international orange," the bridge attracts the eye from any point along the city's northern shore.

🛈 **Info:** ℘415-921-5858. www.goldengatebridge.org.

🅿 **Parking:** There are two parking lots on the San Francisco side, one on either side of the roadbed. The east lot is metered, the west lot is $5/day weekends only (reserved for employees weekdays). The spaces fill up quickly, especially during fine weather.

A BIT OF HISTORY

The idea of a bridge was taken seriously in 1916, when auto transportation was fast becoming a way of life. Feasibility studies were commissioned, and renowned bridge engineer Joseph Strauss of Chicago won with a bid of $27 million. By the time bonds to finance the bridge were issued, the Depression had begun and funding was in short supply. The majority of the bonds were ultimately purchased by the Bank of America, and construction began in January 1933. Work on the bridge was difficult and often treacherous. Divers anchoring the immense concrete pier for the south tower in bedrock 100ft underwater could operate only during the brief periods between tidal flows surging swiftly in and out of the bay. Those erecting the steel towers faced winds sweeping through the Golden Gate at 40mph and bone-chilling fog alternating rapidly with blinding sunlight. Tragedy struck just three months before the bridge's completion when a scaffold broke loose and tore through the safety net beneath the bridge, carrying 12 men into the outgoing tide; only two survived.

On opening day, May 27, 1937, some 200,000 people surged across the bridge on foot. Vehicular traffic was introduced the following day by a formal motorcade, and inaugural celebrations lasted a full week.

Viewing area

👥*Access from US-101 northbound, or take Lincoln Blvd. through the Presidio.* 👓*$6 toll, southbound only. Pedestrian*

Golden Gate Bridge

Rick Dole/MICHELIN

& bicycle access to the bridge (east side-walk only) *Mar–Oct daily 5am–9pm; rest of the year daily 6am–6pm.*

Today the bridge is crossed daily by some 130,000 vehicles (both directions) while pedestrians take to its sidewalks to admire its soaring towers, graceful cables and wondrous **views**★★. From this viewing area on the San Francisco side, visitors can inspect historical displays, drink in the sight of the bridge's massive towers and cables, or head across the bridge via the east sidewalk *(about 2mi round trip; warm clothing advisable).*

From the Vista Point on the Marin County side, more lovely **views**★★ extend over the bridge, backdropped by the forested hills within the Presidio.

1 2 MARINA DISTRICT AND COW HOLLOW★

⌖*See San Francisco Peninsula map.*
🚌 *bus 22–Fillmore, 28–19th Ave., 30–Stockton, 41–Union, 45–Union-Stockton, 47–Van Ness.*

In the mid-19C the sloped valley between Russian Hill and the hills of the Presidio was a grassland of dairy farms, popularly known as Cow Hollow. By the 1960s Cow Hollow had become a fashionable neighborhood, home to trendy galleries, boutiques, antique stores, upscale restaurants and cafes. Today **Union Street**★ between Van Ness Avenue and Fillmore Street is the district's busiest commercial thoroughfare.

After the 1906 earthquake the shallow flats off the shore of Cow Hollow were extended with landfill to create new land for the buildings of the 1915 Panama-Pacific International Exposition. When the fair closed, the structures (except the Palace of Fine Arts) were demolished, to be replaced by a middle-class residential housing area that became known as the Marina District.

Disaster struck with the 1989 Loma Prieta earthquake, when the landfill beneath some buildings liquefied, causing them to collapse. The neighborhood survived, however, and continues to be regarded as one of the city's more desirable residential locations. **Chestnut Street** *(parallel to Union St., four blocks north)* is pleasant for strolling in the blocks between Divisadero and Fillmore. Marina Green, a 10-acre shoreline greensward maintained by the Golden Gate National Recreation Area, is popular with joggers and bikers. **Views**★★ from the green extend across the bay to the Golden Gate Bridge.

Fort Mason Center★

⌖*See Downtown San Francisco map.*
📞*415-441-3400. www.fortmason.org.*
This bayside complex of barracks, warehouses and docks was the embarkation point for G.I.s bound for the Pacific in World War II.

A 1901 struction *(Bldg. 201, MacArthur St.)* now serves as headquarters of the **Golden Gate National Recreation Area** (GGNRA), a 26,000-acre system of national parks encompassing historic landmarks, military sites, beaches and redwood forests.

A leading example of adaptive resuse, the fort also houses nonprofit and cultural organizations, performance spaces and galleries, together hosting some 15,000 public activities each year. Some highlights are the **Museo ItaloAmericano** *(Bldg. C, 1st fl; ℘415-673-2200; www.museoitaloamericano.org),* which displays modern Italian art; and the **San Francisco Museum of Modern Art Artists Gallery** *(Bldg. A; ℘415-441-4777; www.sfmoma.org),* which exhibits contemporary art of Northern California artists. You'll also find theaters, a coffeeshop, a bookshop and a gourmet vegetarian restaurant here.

In the older section, a vast lawn known as the Great Meadow is graced by a representation of the **Madonna (1),** by Italian sculptor Beniamino Bufano (1898–1970), and a statue of the late Bay Area congressman **Phillip Burton (2),** who championed conversion of unused military land to parks.

Palace of Fine Arts★★
Baker & Beach Sts.

This grandiose rotunda and peristyle were replicated from structures designed by renowned architect Bernard Maybeck for the 1915 Panama-Pacific International Exposition.

The original wood and plaster structure, was to have been torn down at the end of the Exposition, but its popularity saved it from the wrecking ball. By the early 1960s, the elements were taking their toll and the Palace was replicated in concrete. Note the draped maidens along the colonnade; facing in rather than out, they pose in lamentation of the decline of culture.

Exploratorium★★ (M⁷)
👫3601 Lyon St. ⏰Open year-round Tue–Sun 10am–5pm & Mon holidays. ⏰Closed Thanksgiving Day & Dec 25. 💲$14, children $9 (free 1st Wed). ✕♿📶 ℘415-561-0360. www.exploratorium.edu. Tactile Dome $3 additional admission; reservations recommended; ℘415-561-0362.

Located in the annex structure of the Palace of Fine Arts, this innovative museum of science, art and human perception boasts more than 650 exhibits organized around the areas of sound, vision, the mind and the life sciences. Most of the exhibits require active participation like electrocuting a pickle or dissecting a cow's eye. Among the most popular exhibits are the miniature tornado demonstration; the photosensitive **Shadow Box,** where people's shadows are temporarily recorded on a wall; and the distorted room, where visitors can enter an optical illusion. The soundproof, pitch-black **Tactile Dome** is a multi-level crawl chamber through which visitors *(7 years or older)* must find their way only by sense of touch.

1️⃣3️⃣ THE PRESIDIO★★
♿See San Francisco Peninsula map. 🚌bus 28–19th Ave., 29–Sunset or 43–Masonic.

This 1,480-acre former military reservation boasts a lovely **setting,** a mix of architectural styles and great views of the Golden Gate and San Francisco Bay.

▶ **Location:** Use the free PresidioGo shuttle bus, which makes 40 stops around the park *(year-round Mon–Fri every 30min, weekends hourly)* to get oriented and visit the attractions.

🅿 **Parking:** There is ample free parking; follow signs.

A BIT OF HISTORY
The Presidio was established by the government of New Spain in 1776 as the third and northernmost of California's four garrisons. After Mexico gained independence from Spain in 1821, the Presidio was largely abandoned. But upon California statehood in 1850, the US Army restored and enlarged the garrison, especially with the outbreak of Civil War in 1861. The military base closed in 1994, and today the Presidio is maintained by the National Park Service.

Visit
Visitors can enter from the south via Presidio Avenue or Arguello Boulevard, or from the east via Lombard Street.

Lincoln Boulevard, tracing the perimeter of the complex, offers views of the Golden Gate Bridge, and glimpses of architecture in styles revealing Mission Revival, Spanish Colonial, Georgian and Victorian influences.

The **Main Post**★★ features historic barracks, from the Spanish Colonial period. The ranger- and docent-staffed **Presidio Visitor Center** (in the Presidio Officer's Club, Bldg. 50, Moraga Ave. at Arguello St.; ◷open year-round daily 9am–5pm; ◷closed Jan 1, Thanksgiving Day & Dec 25; ♿🅿 ℘415-561-4323; www.nps.gov/prsf) at the Main Post offers maps, books and walking-tour brochures.

Crissy Field, once a bayshore airfield, has been restored to tidal marsh, beach and dunes. ♣♣ **Crissy Field Center** (Mason St., west of Halleck St.; ◷open year-round daily 9am–5pm; ◷closed major holidays; ℘415-561-7690; www.crissyfield.org) houses a cafe and bookstore along with family-oriented interactive programs on the convergence of urban and natural environments.

The ♣♣**Gulf of the Farallones National Marine Sanctuary Visitors Center** (993 Marine Dr.; ◷open year-round Wed–Sun 10am–4pm; ◷closed Jan 1, Thanksgiving Day & Dec 25; ✕♿ ℘415-561-6625; www.farallones.org) presents exhibits on life in the 948sq mi sanctuary, extending 26mi west to the rocky Farallon Islands.

A row of crumbling coastal defense batteries along the Presidio's western edge offers spectacular **views**★★★ of the sea, the Marin Headlands and the Golden Gate Bridge. The Presidio shelters a trove of horticultural treasures as well as several rare and endangered plant species.

Fort Point National Historic Site★

♣♣North end of Marine Dr.; take Lincoln Blvd. to Long Ave. ◷Open year-round Fri–Sun 10am–5pm. ◷Closed Jan 1, Thanksgiving Day & Dec 25. 🅿 ℘415-556-1693. www.nps.gov/fopo.

Nestled beneath a giant arch of the Golden Gate Bridge, this imposing bastion (1861) guarded the Golden Gate during the Civil War against the threat of Confederate raids. Fort Point never saw combat, however, and shortly after its construction the invention of more powerful armaments made its brick ramparts obsolete.

The abandoned fort would have been demolished in the early 20C to make way for the Golden Gate Bridge but for the intervention of Joseph Strauss, the bridge's architect. Establishing his construction headquarters there, he designed an arch to carry the bridge over Fort Point.

Today the fort is administered by the GGNRA. The terrace reveals an astounding **view**★★ of the bridge's pier and underbelly.

OCEANFRONT
Legion of Honor★★★

100 34th Ave., Lincoln Park. ◷Open year-round Tue–Sun 9.30am–5.15pm. ◷Closed major holidays. ⊜$10 (includes same-day admission to the deYoung Museum). ✕♿🅿 ℘415-750-3600. www.famsf.org.

From its commanding hilltop site, this elegant museum houses a formidable collection of sculptures by Auguste Rodin, plus a treasury of European art spanning 4,000 years—a gift to San Francisco from **Alma de Bretteville Spreckels**, wife of sugar magnate Adolph Spreckels. The building was modeled after the Pan-Pacific Exposition's French Pavilion, itself a version of an 18C Parisian residence designated by Napoleon as the Palais de la Légion d'Honneur.

The museum opened in 1924 with a core collection of dance-related art and European decorative arts, along with one of the finest amassings of Rodin sculptures (now totaling 106) outside the Rodin museum in Paris.

In 1950 the Legion received the **Achenbach Foundation for Graphic Arts,** some 80,000 works on paper; selections from this immensely important collection are displayed on a rotating basis in galleries on the lower level, along with Greek, Roman and Etruscan antiquities, and temporary exhibits.

Visit

Self-guided audio tours (👓$6) available at the main lobby desk.

The 19 main-floor galleries arrayed around the central rotunda present works from the collection as a survey of medieval to modern European art, with sculptures and decorative arts displayed alongside paintings of the same period. Highlights of **Medieval**, **Mannerist** and **Baroque** and **rococo** art *(galleries 1-7)* include works by El Greco, Georges de la Tour, Watteau and Fragonard. Many of the casts by **Auguste Rodin** *(galleries 8, 10 & 12)* were acquired during the artist's lifetime, and include large-scale works like *The Burghers of Calais* (1889), *The Kiss* (1887) and *The Three Shades* (1880).

The **18C–19C British** Art collection *(gallery 13)* boasts masterpieces by Sir Joshua Reynolds and Thomas Gainsborough, and you'll find Dutch masters Rembrandt, van Dyck and Rubens represented in the **Dutch and Flemish** galleries *(nos. 14 & 15)*. Fine paintings by Corot and Géricault illustrate developments in **19C European** painting *(galleries 17 & 18)*, and the new visual vocabulary of **Impressionism and post-Impressionism** *(gallery 19)* appears in the works of Renoir, Seurat, Cézanne, Monet, Picasso and Matisse.

Cliff House★★

1090 Point Lobos Ave. ✕♿🅿 ℘415-386-3330. www.cliffhouse.com.

Renovated in 2000, this historic house offers both casual and upscale drinking and dining with panoramic views from its perch overlooking the Pacific. The building is the third incarnation of a roadhouse erected in 1863 to spark development in the area.

The modest roadhouse was replaced in 1896 by a flamboyant, eight-story castle-like building that perished in a fire in 1907.

In a cove just north of Cliff House lie the ghostly ruins of **Sutro Baths**★, a public baths that mining magnate Adolph Sutro constructed on his oceanfront property. Sutro's elegant mansion occupied the grassy bluff above Cliff House; the site now serves as **Sutro Heights Park**★,

and offers lovely views of the beach and the Pacific.

🧑‍🤝‍🧑 San Francisco Zoo★

Sloat Blvd. at 45th Ave. 🕐Open year-round daily 10am–5pm. 👓$15, children $9. ✕🅿 ℘415-753-7080. www.sfzoo.org.

Set on 125 acres south of Golden Gate Park, the zoo focuses on naturalistic habitats for its 1,000 denizens. Highlights include the Lemur Forest, harboring five species of this primate from Madagascar and the African savanna exhibit with giraffes, zebras, kudus and ostriches, among other animals.

CENTRAL NEIGHBORHOODS
1 4 GOLDEN GATE PARK★★★

♿See San Francisco Peninsula map.. Park entrances: 🚌bus 5–Fulton (north perimeter); or streetcar N–Judah (1 block south of south perimeter). Museums: 🚌bus 74X–CultureBus, 38–Geary to 6th Ave., transfer to 44–O'Shaughnessy (south).

Stretching 3mi inland from Ocean Beach to Stanyan Street, this 1,017-acre rectangular greensward is home to a complex of art and science museums in addition to a wealth of recreational opportunities. An enchantingly natural yet entirely purpose-built urban oasis of meadows, gardens, lakes and woodlands, the park is the result of careful planning by two inspired landscape architects and the labor of an army of gardeners.

🛈 **Info:** ℘415-751-2766. www.parks.sfgov.org.

▶ **Location:** The park is 3.5mi long and .5mi wide, with curving drives that connect with the city's street grid at some 20 points along the park perimeter. Museums and principal attractions are situated in the park's eastern half; sports and recreation areas spread toward the west. The visitor center at the **Beach Chalet** *(on Great Hwy. on the park's western edge)* offers schedule information and park maps. Information is also available at McLaren Lodge *(Fell*

& Stanyan Sts., just inside park's east entrance; 📞831-2700).

🅿 **Parking:** On Sundays, holidays and summer Saturdays, John F. Kennedy Dr. between Tea Garden Dr. and Transverse Dr. is closed to vehicular traffic. The Music Concourse Garage (10th Ave. & Fulton St.) is open 7.30am 10pm daily ($2.50/hr on weekdays; $3/hr weekends). To avoid parking altogether, take the Muni CultureBus (🛈see Practical Information).

🕐 **Timing:** To avoid large crowds, visit in the morning. In summer, a shuttle (free) runs from 10am– 5pm from McLaren Lodge to Ocean Beach, with stops at 9 locations within the park.

👪 **Kids:** Bison paddock, a boat ride on Stow Lake.

A BIT OF HISTORY

After the park's boundaries were drawn in 1870, superintendent William Hammond Hall created the basic landscaping plan and road pattern. In 1890 **John McLaren**, a Scottish estate gardener, became superintendent. During his 53-year tenure, he experimented with sand-holding grasses and plants and transformed the acreage into one of the nation's loveliest urban parks.

Golden Gate Park was permanently transformed when it hosted San Francisco's Midwinter Fair of 1894, conceived by Michael H. de Young partly to jolt the city into economic recovery following

a nationwide depression in 1893. That year some 2.5 million people came to peruse pavilions representing 20 nations. Crowds thronged the Japanese Tea Garden built especially for the fair, and the Conservatory of Flowers.

Refugees set up temporary homes in the park after the 1906 earthquake. Thousands flocked here during the "Summer of Love" in 1967; hippies hung out and crowds gathered for mass concerts at Speedway Meadow. Today the park is a favored recreation spot, with facilities for tennis, fly casting, horseback riding, football, polo, golf, skating, archery, rowing, lawn bowling and other activities.

San Francisco's principal museums of the arts and sciences are situated around a formal **Music Concourse (1)** created for the Midwinter Fair of 1894; the band shell at its western end was erected in 1899.

de Young Museum★★★

50 Hagiwara Tea Garden Dr. 🕐Open year-round Tue–Sun 9.30am–5.15pm (Fri 8.45pm). 💰$10 (free 1st Tue/mth); good for same-day admission to the Palace of the Legion of Honor. ✗♿🅿 📞415-863-3330. www.famsf.org.

Badly damaged in the 1989 Loma Prieta earthquake, the original museum has been replaced by a daring building by by Herzog & de Meuron, a Swiss architectural firm whose designs include London's Tate Gallery of Modern Art. Opened in the new building in 2005, the de Young is a major force on the West

de Young Museum

© Fine Arts Museums of San Francisco

Coast museum scene. It specializes in American fine and decorative arts from the pre-Columbian era to the present. It also has significant holdings in textiles, and African and Oceanic art.

Established by **Michael H. de Young**, cofounder and publisher of the *San Francisco Chronicle*, the museum began as the Fine Arts Building for an 1895 world's fair. When the fair closed, de Young persuaded the city to preserve the building, where he housed his personal eclectic assemblage of arts and curiosities. In 1972 the de Young organization was merged with that of the California Palace of the Legion of Honor into a single administrative entity known as the **Fine Arts Museums of San Francisco**.

Visit

Presented chronologically in 18 galleries, the extensive **American Art**★★ *(concourse and upper levels)* collection encompasses portrait, landscape and genre painting, decorative arts and sculpture. Paintings by John Singer Sargent, Thomas Hart Benton and John Singleton Copley; furniture by Chippendale and Greene & Greene; decorative ware by Louis Comfort Tiffany and postwar paintings by Willem de Kooning and Mark Rothko are examples of artworks from the colonial era through the Arts and Crafts movement to contemporary works in new media by emerging artists. Selected sculptures by Isamu Noguchi, Louise Nevelson and other artists are on display in the Barbro Osher Sculpture Garden. **Arts of the Americas**★ *(concourse level)* feature ceremonial and funerary objects from Mesoamerica and Central and South America before 16C European intrusion. Indigenous art from the West Coast of North America includes basketry and rare 19C totem poles. Objects from Mexico include Teotihuacan murals and a five-tone Olmec stone head.

The museum's holdings of **Textile Art**★ *(upper level)* from around the world include Turkish carpets and costumes. The **African Art**★ exhibit *(upper level)* contains pieces from a cross section of agricultural sub-Saharan cultures,

mostly West African from 1200 AD to the present. The **Oceanic Art**★ collection *(upper level)* comes from Indonesia, Polynesia, Melanesia, Micronesia and the Maori peoples of New Zealand. Wood carvings predominate here. The museum regularly presents temporary exhibits in its lower-level galleries. Recent crowd-pleasers included *Warhol Live*, a retrospective of Andy Warhol's works featuring famous faces in the music industry.

California Academy of Sciences★★

👤👣 ▓▓▓▓55 Music Concourse Dr. ◷Open year-round Mon–Sat 9.30am–5pm, Sun 11am–5pm. ◷Closed Thanksgiving Day & Dec 25. ⊛$24.95, children $14.95. ✕♿ℰ415-379-8000. www.calacademy.org. ⌨You can avoid long lines at the entrance by purchasing advance tickets through the museum's website.

After years of being shuttered and relocated, San Francisco's venerable museum of natural history and science reopened in 2008 in a brand-new structure in the heart of Golden Gate Park. Groundbreaking in more than one sense, the structure by prizewinning architect Renzo Piano has garnered raves for its "green" design which features natural light and ventilation and a 2.5-acre **living roof** of trees, plants and grasses planted on undulating hills. The roof , which absorbs rainwater runoff and also incorporates photovoltaic cells to help power the building, offers lovely park views from its observation area. The academy encompasses three main divisions: the Kimball Natural History Museum, the Morrison Planetarium and the Steinhardt Aquarium.

Visit

⌨It's best to acquire tickets for planetarium and theater shows (included with general admission) as soon as possible after entering; tickets are distributed first-come first-served, and shows routinely reach capacity.

Climb the spiraling path through the dome-enclosed 4-story **Rainforests of the World** *(entrance on main level)*, which shelters frogs, bats, birds and free-fluttering butterflies as well as tropical plants from around the world in its warm, humid environment. A glass elevator runs from the treetop reaches to the lower level where tunnels allow exploration below the water's surface on the flooded floor of an Amazon rainforest. In the **African Hall** *(main level)*, dioramas faithfully represent animals and plants from diverse African ecosystems; you'll see model zebras, lions and giraffes here as well as live penguins and tortoises.

Housed mostly on the lower level, **aquarium** tanks and exhibits represent a Phillipine coral reef and the Northern California coast; there's also a touchpool for interacting with starfish and other live creatures. Don't miss the **Swamp** exhibit with its rare albino alligator. The state-of-the-art projection system in the domed **planetarium** sends visitors on a journey beyond the edge of the solar system using real-time data from NASA. The Herbst Theater screens large-scale 3-D movies on topics of natural history and science.

Japanese Tea Garden★★

Northwest corner of Music Concourse. *Open Mar–Oct daily 9am–5pm; rest of the year daily 9am–4.45pm.* *Guided tours Wed & Sun 1pm.* *$5.* *415-752-4227.*
One of the park's most beloved attractions, the five-acre garden unites Japanese-style landscaping and architecture to create an atmosphere of serenity and tranquillity. Points of special interest include a pagoda, a Zen gravel garden, a hillside of bonsai trees with a miniature waterfall, a bronze Buddha dating from 1790 and an open-air Japanese **teahouse** offering cookies and green tea.

San Francisco Botanical Garden at Strybing Arboretum ★★

Main gate near park entrance at 9th Ave. & Lincoln Way.
Open year-round Mon–Fri 8am–4.30pm, weekends & holidays 10am–5pm. *Guided tours daily 1.30pm.* *Contribution requested.* *415-661-1316. www.strybing.org.*

Covering some 70 acres of rolling terrain, this outstanding botanical collection comprises 6,000 species of plants from all over the world. The primary emphasis is on regions of Mediterranean climate, with significant collections from California (coast redwoods), the Cape Province of South Africa, southwestern Australia and Chile.

Among other attractions are the Garden of Fragrances, where plants are labeled in Braille; a garden of succulents; and the New World Cloud Forest, where special mist-emitters supplement the fog.

Conservatory of Flowers★

North side of JFK Dr., .5mi west of Stanyan St. *Open year-round Tue–Sun 9am–4.30pm.* *Closed holidays.* *$5.* *415-666-7001. www.conservatoryofflowers.org.*
This ornate Victorian glass greenhouse composed of two wings flanking an octagonal rotunda is Golden Gate Park's oldest structure. Originally purchased by James Lick for installation on his estate in San Jose, the greenhouse was shipped in prefabricated parts from Dublin but arrived after Lick's death in 1876.
San Francisco businessmen purchased the building and donated it to the park. Seasonal blooms in formal geometric designs grace the parterres in front.

Stow Lake★ (2)

West of Strybing Arboretum. *Boathouse open year-round daily 10am–4pm, weather permitting.* *$24/hr pedal boat; $19/hr row boat.* *415-752-0347.*
Serving as the park's main irrigation reservoir, this moat surrounding **Strawberry Hill (3)** is the largest of the 15 man-made lakes and ponds that dot Golden Gate Park. The 428ft summit of Strawberry Hill, reached by footpath, is the highest point in the park and was famed for its panoramas of the city before trees grew to block the view. From the summit, water is released from an outlet to cascade down a purpose-built **waterfall** donated in the 1890s by railroad magnate Collis P. Huntington.

Halfway to the ocean from Stow Lake lies the immense **Polo Field (4)**, often active with simultaneous football, soccer and softball games, and surrounded by three concentric tracks used by runners, bicyclists, roller skaters and horseback riders. At **Spreckels Lake (5)**, model-boat enthusiasts launch their radio-controlled vessels. A bit farther west along JFK Drive is the **Bison Paddock ♣♣ (6)**, where a small herd of the shaggy beasts grazes under the eucalyptus trees. In the northwest corner of the park, the **Queen Wilhelmina Tulip Garden (7)**, a small, but beautifully cultivated formal garden provides a setting for the **Dutch Windmill★ ♣♣**, which pumped irrigation water for the park.

Golden Gate Park's western boundary is delineated by **Ocean Beach★**, now administered by the Golden Gate National Recreational Area.

1 5 HAIGHT-ASHBURY

See San Francisco Peninsula map.
bus 6–Parnassus, 7–Haight, 33 Stanyan, 37–Corbett, 43–Masonic or 71–Haight-Noriega; streetcar N-Judah.
Named for the two streets intersecting at its heart, "the Haight" gained renown in the late 1960s as a center of "counter-culture"—a mishmash of music, mysticism, drugs and alternative lifestyles. Today on **Haight Street★** between Stanyan Street and Central Avenue shoppers browse for secondhand records, books and clothing. Victorian-era residences are being rehabilitated. Just east, **Buena Vista Park** offers shaded strolls on hilly paths, and pleasing views.

Alamo Square★

Bounded by Fulton, Scott, Hayes & Steiner Streets.
This green-lawned square is famous for its **"Postcard Row" view★★★** of Financial District skyscrapers rising above the virtually identical, restored Victorians at 710–720 Steiner Street. The square, located four blocks north of the 600 block of Haight Street, forms the core of the Alamo Square Historic District.

Twin Peaks★★★

♣♣ bus 37–Corbett. From Haight St. drive south on Clayton St. to Carmel St.; cross and continue up Twin Peaks Blvd. to Christmas Tree Point on the left.
These two high points dominate the western skyline as seen from downtown. Most visitors content themselves with the grand **panorama★★★** of the northern and eastern sides of the city from the parking lot at Christmas Tree Point, though it is possible to climb up the grassy slopes of the north peak (904ft) or the south (922ft) for the panorama to the west as well. On clear days you can even see the peaks of Mt. Diablo to the east and Mt. Tamalpais to the north.

1 6 PACIFIC HEIGHTS AND JAPANTOWN★★

See Dowtown San Francisco map.
Pacific Heights: bus 3–Jackson, 22–Fillmore, 24–Divisadero, 41–Union, 45–Union-Stockton. Japantown: bus 2–Clement, 3–Jackson, 4–Sutter or 38-Geary.
Pacific Heights has been San Francisco's most fashionable residential district for more than a century. The elegant neighborhood lies atop the ridge running east-west along Broadway, Pacific and Washington streets between Van Ness Avenue and the Presidio.

The grandest Pacific Heights residences line **Broadway** and **Vallejo Street** west of Steiner Street. Highlights include the **Spreckels Mansion★★** (2080 Washington), commissioned in 1913 by Adolph and Alma Spreckels; and the former **Flood Mansion★** (2222 Broadway), built in 1916 for James Leary Flood.

Pacific Heights' only commercial district lies along lively **Fillmore Street★** between Jackson and Bush. Its art cinema, boutiques and cafes are good places to take a break while walking around the neighborhood.

South of Pacific Heights in the vicinity of Post and Buchanan streets is **Japantown**. Few Japanese Americans returned here after exile to internment camps during World War II, and in the 1960s whole blocks of Victorians were destroyed in urban renewal.

Japan Center, a contemporary shopping, office and hotel complex extending along Geary Boulevard is the focal point of the neighborhood today; it featues a striking **Peace Pagoda** on its central outdoor plaza. To the north, a block of Buchanan Street has become a pedestrian mall.

Haas-Lilienthal House★★

2007 Franklin St., Pacific Heights.
See Downtown San Francisco map.
Visit by guided tour (1hr) only, year-round Wed & Sat noon–3pm & Sun 11am–4pm. Closed major holidays. $8.
415-441-3004. www.sfheritage.org.
One of the few Victorian-era residences open to the public, this imposing edifice (1886) typifies the architectural aspirations of San Francisco's upper-middle class in the 19C.

Constructed for William Haas, a prominent San Francisco retailer, the house was donated in 1974 to the Foundation for San Francisco's Architectural Heritage, which maintains it as a house museum and headquarters.

The exterior is a fine example of the Queen Anne style, complete with a corner tower. Rooms on the first and second floors feature rich wainscoting, embossed wallpaper and a sitting-room hearth faced with red Numidian marble.

Cathedral of St. Mary of the Assumption ★★

1111 Gough St. at Geary Blvd., near Japantown. Open year-round daily 6.45am–4.30pm. Docents available Apr–Oct Mon–Sat 9am–noon, Sun after noon Mass. Organ and choir recitals Sun 3.30pm. 415-567-2020.
www.stmarycathedralsf.org.
Sheathed in white travertine and visible for miles from around the city, the enormous edifice (1971, Pietro Belluschi and Pier Luigi Nervi) is square rather than cruciform in floor plan, its four gently curved walls converging to a 190ft peak. Executed by artist Richard Lippold, a contemporary **baldachin** of shimmering anodized aluminum highlights the breathtaking sanctuary, and ribbons

of stained-glass windows traverse the walls to form a cross.

Swedenborgian Church★★

2107 Lyon St., Presidio Heights.
Open year-round Mon–Fri 9am–5pm, Sun service 11am. 415-346-6466.
www.sfswedenborgian.org.
This rustic church (1895) is one of the earliest examples of the Arts and Crafts movement in the West, sporting brick walls, wooden wainscoting and roof supports of bark-covered madrone trunks. The church was conceived in 1895 by the congregation's architect-founder, the Rev. Joseph Worcester, and designed with assistance from Bruce Porter, A. Page Brown, Bernard Maybeck and Willis Polk. Works by American landscape painter William Keith adorn the walls.

San Francisco Fire Department Museum (M[8])

655 Presidio Ave., Richmond District. Open year-round Thu–Sun 1pm–4pm. 415-563-4630.
www.sffiremuseum.org.
This converted firehouse garage (adjacent to present-day Firehouse no. 10) houses a collection of historic fire engines, including early hand-drawn pump carts and memorabilia.

SOUTHERN NEIGHBORHOODS
[1][7] CASTRO DISTRICT★

See San Francisco Peninsula map.
bus 24–Divisadero; streetcars F–Market, K–Ingleside, L–Taraval or M–Oceanview to Castro St. station.
Centered on the first two blocks of Castro Street south of Market Street, this lively neighborhood forms the heart of the city's gay community. Bars, restaurants, trendy stores and boutiques crowd along Castro, Market and 18th streets, while the residential side streets are lined with refurbished Victorians.

In the early 1970s, gay San Franciscans began buying neglected Victorian homes and restoring them to their former grandeur. By 1977 the gay residents here were instrumental in electing gay candidate **Harvey Milk** to the Board of

Supervisors. Milk's life and career (featured in the 2008 film *Milk*) were cut short a year later when he and then-mayor **George Moscone** were gunned down by City Supervisor Dan White. The 2008 film of his life won Sean Penn an Oscar for Best Actor.

Along the two blocks of **Castro Street** south of Harvey Milk Plaza *(intersection of Castro & Market Sts.)*, the Spanish Renaissance Revival **Castro Theatre**★ (1922, Timothy Pflueger) at no. 429 is a neighborhood institution that hosts several film festivals.

Harvey Milk's camera store was located at **575 Castro Street**. An upstairs mural shows him clad in a T-shirt adorned with a rainbow flag. Castro Street continues south into prosperous **Noe Valley**, with Victorians and shops along 24th Street between Dolores and Diamond streets.

1 8 MISSION DISTRICT★★

See San Francisco Peninsula map. bus 14–Mission, 22–Fillmore, 33–Stanyan. 16th St. or 24th St. stations.
This teeming Latino enclave began as a village surrounding the Mission Dolores. In the late 19C European immigrants, mostly German and Irish, settled in the neighborhood. After World War II, however, Mexicans and Mexican Americans returned to the area. Today an influx of immigrants from Central and South America continues to fuel the energetic Latino ambience.

Mission Dolores
Brigitta L. House/MICHELIN

Colorful murals adorn many a wall and door, and tiny shops and markets on **Twenty-Fourth Street**★ carry fresh produce, meats, cheeses and baked goods. Shaded by towering palms, **Dolores Street** is one of the city's most attractive thoroughfares.

Mission Dolores (Mission San Francisco de Asís)★

16th & Dolores Sts. Open May–Oct 9am–4.30pm; rest of the year 9am–4pm. Closed Jan 1, Thanksgiving Day & Dec 25. $5 contribution requested. 415-621-8203. www.missiondolores.org.
San Francisco's oldest extant structure was dedicated in 1776, marking the official founding of the city. A nearby lake named for Our Lady of Sorrows (Nuestra Señora de los Dolores) gave the mission its nickname. In 1791 a new chapel was built; it was renovated and reconsecrated as a parish church in 1859.
Restored in 1995, the **chapel**★★ retains the original tile roof and bells, but the interior was re-created in 1859. The ornate altar and statues are of late-18C Mexican origin. Adjacent is a larger basilica (1918), which serves as the parish church. A small passage north of the chapel contains a **diorama** of the mission as it appeared in 1799. The **museum** includes shards of artifacts discovered during restorations. A **cemetery**★ holds the remains of, among others, the first Mexican *alcalde* (mayor) of Yerba Buena.

1 9 SOUTH OF MARKET

See Downtown San Francisco map. bus 10–Townsend, 12–Fulsom, 30–Stockton, 45–Union-Stockton; streetcar N-Judah. Embarcadero, Montgomery St. or Powell St. stations.
Nicknamed "SoMa" (for South of Market), this area—largely dominated by warehouses and factory buildings—is fast becoming the city's prime niglife and cultural center, thanks to the redevelopment known as **Yerba Buena Gardens** and an influx of bars, nightclubs and galleries occupying former warehouse spaces.

Yerba Buena Centre for the Arts

© Rafael Ramirez Lee/Dreamstime.com

Tranquil, tree-shaded **South Park** was created in 1852 in imitation of a London square. A plaque marks novelist Jack London's nearby birthplace at 601 3rd St. In the early 1870s, financier William Ralston erected his grand **Palace Hotel**★★ *(639 Market St.)*. Gutted by fire in 1906, it was rebuilt in 1909 with a glass-roofed **Garden Court**★★. Ralston's dreams for SoMa failed to take root, and the terra-cotta-clad **PacBell Building**★ (1925, Timothy Pflueger) remained an isolated landmark at 140 New Montgomery Street for years. Construction of the **Moscone Convention Center** (1981, Hellmuth, Obata & Kassabaum) and the 1991 demolition of the Embarcadero Freeway inspired development.

San Francisco Museum of Modern Art (M⁹)★★

151 Third St. ⊙*Open Memorial Day–Labor Day Thu–Tue 10am–5.45pm (Thu 8.45pm). Rest of the year Thu–Tue 11am–5.45pm (Thu 8.45pm).* ⊙*Closed major holidays.* ☞*$12.50.* ✕&. ℘*415-357-4000. www.sfmoma.org.*
☞*We recommend taking the interactive SFMOMA Collection Highlights audio tour (☞$3), recorded by museum curators and directors.*
San Francisco's premier showcase for modern art occupies an innovative contemporary building (1995, Mario Botta) adjacent to Yerba Buena Gardens. Popularly known as SFMOMA, the museum was founded in 1935, and was the first in the state to showcase works from the 20C.

From the street, the building appears as a symmetrical pile of giant, brick-clad blocks rising in setbacks. A huge cylinder, slanted at the top, rises periscope-like from the center of the mass, filtering natural light to the interior spaces below. From the immense **atrium**★★ a grand staircase rises through the center of the building, culminating in a narrow steel **catwalk**★ across the rotunda, five stories above the floor.

Now numbering more than 20,000 paintings, sculptures, photographs and works on paper, the permanent **collection** was initiated with a gift of 36 works by local insurance magnate Albert M. Bender. The painting and sculpture represent all major movements of modern art in Europe, North America and Latin America, with strengths in early Modernism and works by California and Bay Area artists. Noteworthy artists include Henri Matisse (*Femme au Chapeau*) and Jackson Pollock (*Guardians of the Secret*), as well as Picasso, Braque, Miró, Kahlo, Kandinsky, Warhol, Rauschenberg, Stella, Johns and Clyfford Still.

Yerba Buena Gardens★★

750 Howard St.; entrances on Mission, Howard & Third Sts. ⊙*Open year-round daily 6am–10pm.* ℘*415-820-3550. www.yerbabuenagardens.com.*
Sitting atop the Moscone Center, the Yerba Buena Gardens unites a spacious children's center, a high-tech shopping and entertainment complex, museums, and a serene park area. The **Yerba Buena Center for the Arts**★ **(K)** (⊙*open year-round Tue–Sun noon–5pm,*

313

Thu 8pm; ⏱*closed major holidays;* 🎫*$7;* ✕&♿ 📞*415-978-2700; www.ybca.org)* specializes in exhibits and performances that reflect Northern California's diverse populations. The **Yerba Buena Center for the Arts Theater (L)** hosts presentations by local and touring performance groups. The **Esplanade** melds landscaped beds, paths and outdoor sculptures; its south side is dominated by a memorial to Dr. Martin Luther King Jr. A children's complex, **Rooftop at Yerba Buena Gardens**★★ ▲▲ *(750 Folsom St.; 📞415-820-3532. www.skatebowl.com),* includes an ice-skating rink, a bowling center and a carousel. The cornerstone is **Zeum**★ *(221 Fourth St.;* ⏱*open Sept–mid-Jun Wed–Fri 1pm–5pm, weekends 11am–5pm;* ⏱*call for holiday closures;* 🎫*$10, children $8;* ♿ 📞*415-820-3320; www.zeum.org),* a high-tech studio and theater for visual and performing arts. At 101 Howard Street, **Metréon(N)** offers a 15-screen cineplex and IMAX theater, restaurants and stores *(*⏱*open year-round Sun–Thu 10am–9pm, Fri–Sat 10am–10pm;* 📞*415-369-6000).*

Contemporary Jewish Museum (M¹¹)

736 Mission St. between 3rd and 4th Sts. ⏱*Fri–Tue 11am–5pm, Thu 1pm–8pm.* ⏱*Closed major and Jewish holidays.* ✕&♿🎫*$10.* 📞*415-655-7800. www.thecjm.org.*

This award-winning museum mounts dynamic exhibitions in a variety of media to explore and promote understanding of Jewish culture through contemporary art. The $50 million renovation of its new home (opened in June 2008), the Jessie Street Power Substation (1907, Willis Polk), was overseen by renowned architect Daniel Libeskind.

California Historical Society (J)

678 Mission St. ⏱*Open year-round Wed–Sat noon–4.30pm.* 🎫*$3 (free 1st Tue/mth).* 📞*415-357-1848. www.californiahistoricalsociety.org.* The state's official historical society invites visitors to peruse manuscripts, documents, journals, maps and photographs, some dating from the 17C. A regular exhibition program invites visitors to explore California's colorful, rambunctious past.

Cartoon Art Museum (M10)

▲▲*655 Mission St., between Third and New Montgomery Sts.* ⏱*Open year-round Tue–Sun 11am–5pm.* ⏱*Closed major holidays.* 🎫*$6.* ♿ 📞*415-227-8666. www.cartoonart.org.* Step into this unique museum to peruse a vast collection of cartoon drawings. Exhibitions here make the point that cartoons, comic strips and animation art provide a commentary on our social and cultural history.

ADDRESSES

🍴 **EAT**

The Tonga Room *950 Mason St., in the Fairmont Hotel (Nob Hill).* 📞*415-772-5278. www.fairmont.com.* Order anything with an umbrella at the Fairmont Hotel's Polynesian-style Tonga Room and Hurricane Bar. Thatched umbrellas hover over rustic tables, and every half-hour a sprinkler system simulates a tropical rainstorm above the indoor lagoon.

Ghirardelli Ice Cream and Chocolate Shop *In Ghirardelli Square (Fisherman's Wharf).* ▲▲*Open Sun–Thu 9am–11pm, Fri–Sat 9am–midnight.* 📞*415-474-3938.*

www.ghirardellisq.com. Break into the chocolate shell of the Alcatraz Rock, Strike it Rich with butterscotch and almonds, or experience your first Earthquake: a gargantuan sundae made of eight scoops, eight toppings, bananas, nuts and cherries.

Tadich Grill *240 California St., (Financial District).* 📞*415-391-1849.* Fresh fish is the fare, bulls and bears the topic of choice at this San Francisco institution, which began during the Gold Rush as a coffee stand. Go for the charcoal-grilled sole, the cold seafood salad, and for the no-nonsense service by white-jacketed waiters.

San Jose★

Now California's third-largest city, the capital of Silicon Valley bustles with high-tech prosperity. San Jose's downtown boasts stately old buildings, modern high-rises and a number of good museums.

> ▶ **Population:** 1,006,892.
> **Michelin Map:** 585 A 8.
> **Info:** ℘408-295-9600. www.sanjose.org.
> ▷ **Location:** The downtown heart of San Jose focuses on Plaza de Cesar Chavez *(Market St. & Park Ave.)*, site of civic festivals.

A BIT OF HISTORY

Spaniards chose this site in the fertile Santa Clara Valley in 1777 for Alta California's first civilian settlement, and a mission was founded nearby. Agriculture was San Jose's chief industry until the mid-20C technology boom. By the late 1960s IBM, Hewlett-Packard, Apple and other computer giants developed facilities here.

SIGHTS
Tech Museum of Innovation★★

201 S. Market St. at Park Ave. Open daily 10am–5pm. Closed Dec 25. $8 (includes one IMAX). ℘408-294-8324. www.thetech.org.
This state-of-the-art, interactive exhibit hall is designed to encourage the spirit of innovative curiosity characteristic of the original techno-tinkerers of Silicon Valley. The museum features participatory displays in microelectronics, space exploration, robotics and biotechnology. The **Hackworth IMAX Dome Theater** shows documentary films on a hemispherical screen.

Children's Discovery Museum of San Jose★

180 Woz Way off W. San Carlos St. Open year-round Tue–Sat 10am–5pm, Sun noon–5pm (and Mon mid-Jun–Labor Day). Closed Jan 1, Thanksgiving Day, Dec 25. $8. ℘408-298-5437. www.cdm.org.
Housed in a structure that resembles building blocks, this hands-on museum opened in 1990 in Guadalupe River Park. You'll find a plethora of kid-centric exhibits inside, including **Streets**, which demonstrates the workings of urban infrastructure; and **Current Connections**, explaining electricity.

History San José: Peralta Adobe and Fallon House★

175 W. St. John St. at San Pedro St. Visit by guided tour (90min) only, by appointment. Closed major holidays. ℘408-287-2290. www.historysanjose.org.
An early 19C adobe and an Italianate mansion (1855) recall San Jose's Spanish Colonial beginnings, and a small museum details development.

History Park at Kelley Park★

1650 Senter Rd. in Kelley Park, 3mi southeast of downtown. Open year-round Tue–Sun noon–5pm. Closed Jan 1, Thanksgiving Day, Dec 25. $4 weekends. ℘408-287-2290.
This 14-acre complex evokes life in San Jose in the late 1800s. Notable are a 115ft reproduction of the **San Jose Electric Tower**, a metal-beamed pyramid of street lights; the **H.H. Warburton Doctor's Office**; and a reproduction of the city's **Chinese Temple**.

Japanese Friendship Garden★

Adjacent to History Park in Kelley Park. Open year-round daily 10am–dusk. ℘408-277-5254.
The meticulously landscaped 6.5 acres are modeled after the Korakuen Garden in Okayama, Japan, San Jose's sister city. A large pool populated by brightly colored koi is spanned by a Moon Bridge.

Winchester Mystery House

525 S. Winchester Blvd. Visit by guided tour only; call or check website for schedule. Closed Dec 25. Three tours are offered: Mansion (1hr, $26);

Behind the Scenes (50min, ⌬$23); combination Grand Estate (⌬$31). ✗⌖ ☎408-247-2101. www.winchester mysteryhouse.com. ⊙Children under age 9 not permitted on Mansion tour. This rambling 160-room Victorian hodgepodge was the creation of the widow of rifle magnate William Wirt Winchester. Now largely unfurnished, the house has a collection of Tiffany and European **art glass**. The **Historic Firearms Museum** on the grounds displays a collection of pistols and rifles.

Rosicrucian Egyptian Museum★

1664 Park Ave. ⊙Open year-round Mon–Fri 9am–5pm, weekends 11am–6pm. ⊙Closed major holidays. ⌬$9. ☎408-947-3635. www.roscrucian.org. Modeled after the Temple of Amon at Karnak, the exterior sports gold-paneled doors incised with hieroglyphs. Inside there's an extensive display of Egyptian and Mesopotamian artifacts. Note in particular the display on mummification *(gallery A)*, with painted coffins; **sarcophagi**; and a full-scale reproduction of a Middle Kingdom **Rock Tomb** *(visited by guided tour only)*. Admission includes shows in the museum's planetarium *(⊙daily 2pm)*.

The museum is in **Rosicrucian Park**, headquarters for the English Grand Lodge of the Rosicrucian Order.

EXCURSIONS
San José de Guadalupe Mission

13mi northeast of San Jose in Fremont. Take I-680 to second Mission Blvd. exit and turn right. ⊙Open year-round daily 10am–5pm. ⊙Closed major holidays. ⌬Contribution requested. ⌖☎510-657-1797.

Named for St. Joseph, the 14th mission in California was founded in 1797. Its first adobe church was completed in 1809. In the early 1980s work began on the faithful reconstruction of the original adobe church that occupies the site today.

The interior features a historic **statuary**. Note the statue of St. Joseph (c.1600) from Spain and that of the Virgin (18C) from Mexico. A small garden separates the church from the original adobe **padres' quarters**, which now house a museum of mission history.

Santa Clara de Asís Mission

2.5mi northwest of San Jose, on Santa Clara University campus. Follow The Alameda (which becomes El Camino Real) to campus entrance. ⊙Open year-round daily 8am–6pm. ⌖☎408-554-4023. www.scu.edu/missionchurch.

Established on the banks of the Guadalupe River in 1777, the eighth mission was moved in 1781 to its present site on higher ground. An earthquake destroyed the complex in 1812. Offset by a campanile, the church features a roof covered in clay tiles gleaned from earlier mission structures. The **St. Francis Chapel** contains an original wall, ceiling and floor, and a relic of Padre Junipero Serra, founder of the mission chain.

Triton Museum of Art★

1505 Warburton Ave. at Lincoln St., Santa Clara, 2 blocks north of El Camino Real. ⊙Open year-round daily 11am–5pm (Thu 9pm). ⌖P ☎408-247-3754. www.tritonmuseum.org.

This modern museum displays the **Austen D. Warburton Collection of American Indian Art and Artifacts**★, which spans several centuries of basketry, pottery and other artifacts from California, Southwest and Pacific Northwest tribal traditions.

Intel Museum★★

2200 Mission College Blvd., Santa Clara. ⊙Open year-round Mon–Fri 9am–6pm, Sat 10am–5pm. ⊙Closed major holidays. ⌖P ☎408-765-0503. www.intel.com/go/museum.

As the world's largest semiconductor company, the Intel Corporation invented the technology—in 1968—that put computer memory on tiny silicon chips rather than in magnetic fields. Interactive exhibits here in the company headquarters walk visitors through the principles of transistor technology, from identification of conductors to chip design and production.

Great America

▦▦ ♟♟ *4701 Great America Pkwy., Santa Clara, off US-101, 6mi north of San Jose.* ◷*Mar–Oct: opening and closing hrs vary; call or check online.* ⬭*$53.99, under 48inches $35.99.* ✕♿🅿 ✆*408-988-1776. www.2cedarfair.com/greatamerica.*

This 100-acre amusement park is a favorite of roller-coaster fanatics. Its nine coasters include the new **Survivor–The Ride**, which whisks through tropical landscapes with 40ft-tall fiery torches. Other thrill rides include the inverted **Flight Deck** jet-coaster and the 210ft **Drop Zone Stunt Tower**.

Don Edwards San Francisco Bay National Wildlife Refuge★

Marshlands Rd., Fremont; from I-880 or Rte. 84 at east end of Dumbarton Bridge, take Thornton Ave. exit south to refuge road. Visitor center ◷*open year-round Tue–Sun 10am–5pm.* ◷*Closed major holidays.* ♿🅿 ✆*510-745-8695. www.fws.gov/desfbay.*

Named for a former congressman, the largest urban wildlife refuge in the US sprawls across 20,000 acres of salt marsh, tidal sloughs, mudflats and rolling hills at the southern end of San Francisco Bay. Some 200 species of waterfowl, shorebirds and migratory birds live and/or feed in the refuge. From the bluff-top **visitor center**, trails follow boardwalks and bridges across tidal flats.

Santa Cruz★

Curving around the northern end of Monterey Bay, this archetypal California beach community is widely known for its early 20C amusement park, its surfing beaches, arts community and casual atmosphere.

▸ **Population:** 54,778.
⏲ **Michelin Map:** 585 A 8.
🯄 **Info:** ✆831-425-1234. www.santacruzca.org.
🜄 **Don't Miss:** the Beach Boardwalk.

A BIT OF HISTORY

In the late 19C, the Southern Pacific Railroad came to town and Santa Cruz became a thriving seaside resort. The founding of a University of California campus in the mid-1960s overlaid the resort milieu with a college atmosphere that attracted artists and craftspeople. Today Santa Cruz has a lively cafe scene, several live-music venues and a number of book, art and curio shops.

SIGHTS

Santa Cruz Beach Boardwalk★★

♟♟ ◷*Open Memorial Day–Labor Day daily 11am; Sept–Apr weekends & holidays noon.* ◷*Closing hours vary.* ✕♿🅿 ✆*831-426-7433. www.beachboardwalk.com.*

California's oldest amusement park has a charming early 20C feel; its boardwalk features turreted buildings and rides fronting a wide beach (🜄*dangerous currents*). Since 1924 the **Giant Dipper** roller coaster has been the boardwalk's most distinctive attraction. The **Looff carousel** (1911) was carved by Danish woodcarver Charles I.D. Looff.

Nearby, the **Cocoanut Grove Banquet and Conference Center** (1907) is famous for its now-renovated Grand Ballroom. A few blocks west, the **municipal wharf** is lined with tackle shops and eateries.

Farther along the coast, the **Santa Cruz Surfing Museum** (◷*open Jul 4–Labor Day Wed–Mon 10am–5pm; rest of the year Thu–Mon noon–4pm;* ◷*closed Jan 1, Dec 25;* ♿ ✆*831-420-6289; www.santacruzsurfingmuseum.org*), housed in a lighthouse *(West Cliff Dr.)*, includes an exhibit on surfing history in the area.

The **Santa Cruz City Museum of Natural History** *(1305 E. Cliff Dr.)* displays artifacts and fossils detailing the Ohlone

Indians' way of life (⏱open year-round Tue–Sun 10am–5pm; ⏱ closed major holidays; ⌐$2.50; ♿🅿 ✆831-420-6115; www.santacruzmuseums.org).

Santa Cruz Mission and State Historic Park

Off Mission Plaza on School St. ⏱Open year-round Thu–Sun 10am–4pm.
♿ ✆831-425-5849. www.santacruz stateparks.org.

Founded in 1791, the 12th mission never really thrived, and its structures were destroyed by natural disasters. In 1931 a small replica of the adobe church was built 200ft from the original site. The original seven-room **barracks** (1824) was preserved by being encased within a Victorian-style house, which kept the adobe walls intact.

University of California, Santa Cruz★

Follow Bay St. northwest to campus main entrance. Campus and Cowell Ranch maps are available at main entrance kiosk. ✆831-459-0111. www.ucsc.edu.

Renowned for its architecture and **setting**★★ amid groves of redwood trees, the university comprises a loop of eight campuses. In 1965 the state purchased 2,000 acres of ranchland and integrated the ranch structures into the new campus, including 14 structures from the 1860s **Cowell Ranch**.

The **Mary Porter-Sesnon Art Gallery** (♿✆831-459-3606) and the **Eloise Pickard Smith Gallery** (✆831-459-2953) mount changing exhibits. The **arboretum** is devoted to exotic flora, particularly from South Africa, Australia and New Zealand *(Empire Grade, .3mi west of main entrance; ⏱open year-round daily 9am–5pm; ⏱closed Thanksgiving Day & Dec 25; ⌐$5; 🅿 ✆831-427-2998; www2.ucsc.edu/arboretum).*

EXCURSIONS

Año Nuevo State Reserve★

👥22mi north of Santa Cruz on Hwy. 1. ⏱Open year-round daily 8am–sunset. Elephant seal rookery open Apr–Aug 8.30am–3.30pm; Sept–Nov 8.30am–
3pm (visitor permit required; issued at reserve). ⏱Closed 1st 2 weeks in Dec. 🅿⌐$7/vehicle. ➤Access by guided tour (2hr 30min) only Dec 15–Mar 31 Mon–Fri 9am–5pm, Sat–Sun 9am–3pm; reservations recommended 8 weeks in advance ✆650-879-0227 or 800-444-4445. www.parks.ca.gov.*

This 4,000-acre coastal reserve encompasses an offshore island and a beautiful Pacific promontory, the only mainland rookery between Baja and Northern California for **northern elephant seals**. Guided walks (the only way to visit during the gathering season) allow you to spy on the seals as they come ashore.

Henry Cowell Redwoods State Park★

6mi north of Santa Cruz on Rte. 9. ⏱Open year-round daily 6am–dusk. ⌐$7/vehicle. ⚠♿✆831-438-2396. www.parks.ca.gov.

Trails weave through the woodlands of this biotically diverse 1,760-acre tract, bisected by the San Lorenzo River. The **Redwood Grove Trail** *(.8mi; begins south of parking lot)* loops past the park's largest redwoods.

Roaring Camp & Big Trees Narrow-Gauge Railroad

👥From Santa Cruz go north on Hwy. 17; take Mt. Hermon exit; continue in direction of Felton for 3.5mi; turn left on Graham Hill Rd and continue for 1mi. Ticket office east of parking lot. ⏱Apr–Nov daily; rest of the year weekends only. Call or visit website for schedule. ⌐Steam train $19.50, children $13.50; beach train $21.50, children $16.50. ✗♿🅿✆831-335-4484. www.roaringcamprr.com.

Departing from the site of a former logging camp, this old-time railroad offers two excursions. The steam train tour *(75min)* penetrates deep into the forest of ancient redwoods before arriving near the summit of Bear Mountain. The beach train (3hrs) crosses forests, trestles, gorges and a tunnel enroute to the Santa Cruz Boardwalk.

The arc of mountains around the northern end of the Central Valley embraces and defines a region of extraordinary beauty, with the agricultural center of Redding at its hub.

Glaciers and Volcanoes – Ice Age glaciers carved the spectacular peaks and lakes in the Trinity Alps, which rise to nearly 9,000ft. Gold flakes surfaced in the rivers and streams on these mountains' lower slopes, bringing miners and fortune-hunters to the area in the 1840s and 1850s. The placers of Trinity, Shasta and Siskiyou counties played out in the late 19C—leaving behind ghost towns, such as Whiskeytown and Shasta City, and lasting settlements like Weaverville. Trinity Dam today constrains the Klamath River; to the east, above Redding, Shasta Dam has created the largest reservoir on the Sacramento River.

The Cascades are a range of volcanoes extending from Washington and Oregon and culminating in northern California with Mount Shasta (14,162ft) and Lassen Peak, two of the largest volcanoes in the US. Lassen erupted between 1914 and 1917. Boiling mud pots and fumaroles still steam upon its slopes, now preserved within Lassen Volcanic National Park. Dormant for 200 years, Mount Shasta shows occasional signs of life.

Northeast of the Cascades, a high plateau of volcanic lava covers 26,000sq mi. The Modoc Lava Plateau, an upland desert of basaltic lava, comprises only about one-twentieth of a much larger volcanic region known as the Columbia Plateau. Near Tule Lake, Lava Beds National Monument preserves the scene of one of the last and most dramatic Indian wars in American history.

A Recreational Treasure – For the visitor, this remote corner of Californa bears little resemblance to the state's bustling, cosmopolitan cities. Towns and communities here cherish a slower pace of life less subject to the vagaries of fad and fashion. Campers, hikers, fishermen and other fans of outdoor adventuring benefit from an abundance of sparkling lakes and rivers, and mountainous, ruggedly beautiful landscapes.

Highlights

1 Ancient petroglyphs on the rock face at **Lava Beds National Monument** *(p323)*

2 Pure mountain water from a fountain in **Dunsmuir** *(p324)*

3 Houseboating on **Shasta Lake** *(p326)* or **Trinity Lake** *(p320)*

Lassen Peak

National Park Service / www.nps.gov

ADDRESSES

🛏 STAY

😊😊😊😊😊 **(3nights) Houseboats on Trinity Lake**– *Forever Resorts, Trinity Lake Marina.* 📞*800-255-5561. www. foreverhouseboats.com.* Rent a 44ft houseboat *(3-day minimum)* complete with living area, fully equipped kitchen and dinette, a private bedroom, queen sofa sleeper and a bath with a shower. Moor in a quiet cove, take a dip in the lake, and sleep to the lapping of water.

😊😊😊😊*(meals included)* **Coffee Creek Ranch** – *Coffee Creek Rd., Coffee Creek (72mi northwest of Redding). Closed late Nov-Mar.* 📞*530-266-3343. www.coffee creekranch.com. 15 cabins.* This 367-acre dude ranch near a creek offers every recreation imaginable, from horse riding and trout fishing to gold panning and square dancing. The ranch even has its own band. Rustic, cozy cabins have ceiling fans; most have wood-burning stoves.

😊😊 **J.K. Metzker House** – *520 Main St., Cedarville.* 📞*530-279-2650. 4 rooms.* 🍴. Set back from the street by a verdant expanse of lawn, this two-story clapboard-and-brick manor was built by Cedarville founder William Cressler in 1860. Rooms feature period antiques, quilt-clad queen-size beds and claw-foot tubs. You'll start your morning here with a sumptuous country breakfast.

🍴 EAT

😊😊 **Café Maddalena** – *5801 Sacramento Ave., Dunsmuir. Dinner only, Thu-Sun. Closed Jan.* 📞*530-235-2725. www. cafemaddalena.com.* **Mediterranean**. Maddalena Serra, a native of Sardinia, designed and built this intimate spot herself. The cuisine is as authentic as the old rail depot down the block: try the tagine of chicken in North African curry sauce with couscous.

😊😊 **Nipa's California Cuisine** – *1001 N. Main St., Alturas.* 📞*530-233-2520.* **Asian.** One of the most remote gourmet restaurants in the West, Nipa's melds Thai, California and Great Basin influences. Where else will you find a tri-tip steak with Thai spices? The curries are dependably rich and hot, and the pad Thai is made with hearty noodles.

Lassen Volcanic National Park★★

Ragged craters, barren lava dunes and steaming thermal areas contrast with placid lakes and evergreen forests in this 106,000-acre national park, dominated by Lassen Peak, a 10,457ft plug dome volcano renowned for devastating eruptions that occurred between 1914 and 1917.

♿ **Michelin Map:** 585 B 7.
ℹ **Info:** 📞530-595-4480. www.nps.gov/lavo.
☺ **Don't Miss:** The panorama from Lassen Peak.

A BIT OF HISTORY

Roughly 600,000 years ago, a volcano now called Mt. Tehama arose in the park's southwest corner, eventually topping 11,500ft and measuring 11mi in diameter.

As volcanic activity at Tehama declined, its summit wore away and domes formed on its flanks. The largest of these was Lassen Peak, which took shape about 25,000 years ago.

In 1914 Lassen Peak, long thought to be dead, spewed steam and rocks in the first of 298 eruptions over several years. The most destructive was in 1915, when hot lava melted accumulated snow, causing an enormous mudflow down the peak's eastern slopes. Three days later, a blast of pyroclastic gas laid waste to everything in its path.

In 1916 this phenomenal volcanic terrain was declared a national park. Though no eruption has been recorded for some 80 years, the peak, one of the largest dome

Area Code: 530

GETTING THERE

Southwest entrance *(Rte. 89):* from San Francisco (237mi) take I-80 east to I-505 north to I-5 north to Rte. 36 west to Rte. 89 north; from Los Angeles *(569mi)* take I-5 north to Rte. 36 east to Rte. 89 north. **Manzanita Lake entrance** *(Rte. 44):* from San Francisco *(269mi)* take I-80 east to I-505 north to I-5 north to Rte. 44 east. Closest **airport** *(47mi)* is Redding Municipal Airport (RDD) ☎224-4320.

GETTING AROUND

Lassen National Park is best visited by car. Southwest entrance to Lassen winter sports area open year-round; Lassen Park Road and other routes within the park are generally closed due to snow late Oct–mid-Jun.

VISITOR INFORMATION

Park entrance fee $10/vehicle (good for 7 days). Pick up a free Lassen Park Guide and wilderness permits at the **Kohm Yah-mah-nee Visitor Center** *(open Jun–Oct daily 9am–6pm; rest of year daily 9am–5pm)*; or the **Loomis Museum Visitor Center** *(at Manzanita Lake; open mid-May–mid-Oct daily 9am–5pm (mid–Jun–Sept 6pm); rest of year weekends & holidays 10am–4pm).* Additional information: **Lassen Park Headquarters** *(PO Box 100, Mineral CA 96063, ☎595-4444; www.nps.gov/lavo).* Information for the surrounding area: Chester/Lake Almanor Chamber of Commerce *(PO Box 1198, Chester CA 96020, ☎258-2426 or 800-350-4838; www.chester-lakealmanor.com).* Information about camping and recreation in **Lassen National Forest**: Hat Creek Ranger District, PO Box 220, Fall River Mills CA 96028, ☎336-5521 or Almanor Ranger District, PO Box 767, Chester CA 96020, ☎258-2141, or www.fs.fed.us/r5/lassen/contact.

ACCOMMODATIONS

At the southern end of the park is the rustic **Drakesbad Guest Ranch** *(Chester-Warner Valley Rd, Chester CA 96020; open Jun–Oct; reservations required; ☎529-1512; www.drakesbad.com).* Accommodations are also available in Mill Creek, Mineral and Chester. **Campsites** are abundant in the park and surrounding areas; fees range $10–$16. Limited winter camping. **Backcountry camping** requires a permit *(free)* obtainable in advance from park headquarters, at entrance stations and at visitor centers.

volcanoes in the world, still contains an active magma chamber and is considered very much alive.

LASSEN PARK ROAD★

30mi.

◗ *Park entrance fee ⌖$10. Begin at Manzanita Lake entrance (Rte. 44). For safety on foot, stay on marked trails or boardwalks.*

Manzanita Lake★

This sparkling lake was created about 1,000 years ago when an avalanche of rock from the collapse of one of the Chaos Crags *(below)* formed a natural dam across Manzanita Creek. A **trail** *(1.7mi loop)* circles the manzanita- and chaparral-covered shores of the lake. Beyond Manzanita Lake, Route 89 passes **Chaos Crags**, steep, 1,100-year-old dome volcanoes rising to the south. Landslides from the crags created the surrounding rock-strewn terrain known as **Chaos Jumbles**. Another 6mi farther, the road enters the **Devastated Area**, a bleak terrain once was covered by evergreens. The forest was obliterated in the 1915 mudflow and gas blast. Aspen and pine trees are reclaiming the area. After skirting the forested shore of **Summit Lake**, the road opens to vistas of the park's eastern expanse. Lake Almanor is visible 20mi to the southeast.

Bumpass Hell
©John Anderson/MICHELIN

Kings Creek Falls Trail★

Trail 3mi round-trip; trailhead across the road from the Kings Creek parking area.
This trail leads through forests and meadowland to a series of cascades formed as Kings Creek plunges over polished stone ledges. Beyond the falls, the trail continues another 6.1mi southeast into the Warner Valley.

Lassen Peak★

Trailhead at Lassen Peak Trail parking area. Trail 5mi round-trip; strenuous, with 2,000ft elevation gain. ☺Note: High altitude can cause altitude sickness. Check weather conditions before starting, as thunderstorms are frequent.
The park's centerpiece, this barren, gray volcanic dome, with its jagged pinnacles of dacite lava, towers over the central part of the park. From the summit, a **panorama**★ encompasses the volcanic features that characterize the terrain.

Bumpass Hell★★

Trail 3mi round-trip; interpretive brochure available at trailhead.
This bed of hydrothermal activity was discovered in the mid-19C by Kendall Vanhook Bumpass, an early tourism promoter and guide. The trail winds along the eroded remains of Mt. Tehama, offering views to the southwest of **Diamond Peak** (7,968ft) and **Brokeoff Mountain** (9,235ft) before descending into the steaming thermal area. A boardwalk leads past surface cracks that billow with sulfuric fumaroles (holes in the ground that emit steam and gas), boiling springs and thick, bubbling mudpots fueled by a chamber of magma (molten rock) far underground.

Sulphur Works★

Clouds of steam are emitted from this roadside hydrothermal area, believed to be part of the vent system that created Mt. Tehama.

SOUTHERN SECTION

Accessible from the town of Chester (31mi southeast of the park's southwest entrance via Rtes. 89 & 36).

Warner Valley★

17mi northwest of Chester; follow signs into valley.
This beautiful valley marks the site of ancient Mount Dittmar, which appeared some 2 million years ago as the first center of volcanic activity within the park's present-day boundaries. Located here is **Drakesbad Guest Ranch**, a Western-style cabin resort established in the 1880s as a cattle ranch.

Boiling Springs Lake Trail★

3mi round-trip.
Arcing south from Hot Springs Creek, this popular trail ascends through fir, pine and cedar forests to a steaming lake. Underground vents warm the water to about 125 degrees.

Juniper Lake★

12mi north of Chester; follow signs; last 7mi on rough, unpaved road.
Filling a glacial depression, this dark-blue lake is the largest and deepest in the park. Juniper trees grow near its eastern shore. A moderate trail *(1.6mi round-trip)* climbs to **Inspiration Point**★, from which extend views of Lassen Peak, Juniper Lake and Snag Lake.

Lava Beds National Monument★★

This eerie volcanic landscape occupies the heart of California's Modoc Plateau, a vast, volcanic tableland in the northeast corner of the state. Formed over the past 500,000 years by spewing lava and rocks, the rugged terrain was the scene, in 1873, of a brief but bloody war between displaced Modoc Indians and US Army forces.

A BIT OF HISTORY

The park lies on the northern flank of Medicine Lake Volcano, which last erupted about 1,000 years ago. More than 300 **lava tube caves** penetrate the earth's surface, some as far as 150ft; others extend horizontally for thousands of feet. Lava tube caves are formed when the outer surface of a lava flow cools and hardens, insulating an interior molten mass. This liquid rock continues to flow, leaving long tubular passages underground. When lava flows this way, it commonly spreads over a large area far from the eruption site, which explains the relatively flat profile of Medicine Lake Volcano.

This region was the site of the Modoc War, a standoff in 1873 between US Army troops and a band of Native Modoc resisting the occupation of their traditional homeland by settlers from the Eastern US. The Modoc, secure in a natural stronghold of lava formations, held out against a much larger military and civilian force for nearly five months before they were overwhelmed, captured and removed to a reservation.

SIGHTS

Park open daily year-round. ☜*$10/ vehicle (valid 7 days).* ◷*Visitor center* ◷ *open late May–Labor Day daily 8am– 6pm; rest of the year daily 8.30am–5pm.* ◷*Closed Dec 25.* ⚠ *($10)* ⛺ 🅿 ✆*530- 667-8100. www.nps.gov/labe.*

Michelin Map: 585 B 6.

Borrow a flashlight at the **visitor center**, where rangers and displays interpret the lava beds' natural and human history.

Mushpot Cave★

Entrance near visitor center.
Improved with lights and interpretive panels, this cave is a good place to begin exploring the park's lava tubes.

Cave Loop Road★

2mi. Begin at the visitor center.
The road loops atop an area of hardened lava that flowed from Mammoth Crater, located just inside the monument's southern boundary. Winding beneath the lava carapace is the park's densest concentration of lava tubes, many accessible by parking areas and stairways. Not part of Cave Loop but well worth a visit are **Valentine Cave**, discovered on Valentine's Day in 1933, and **Skull Cave**, cold enough to maintain a pool of ice at its bottom.

Schonchin Butte

2.2mi from visitor center via main park road. Trail (1.5mi round-trip; moderate to difficult) from parking area.
The fire tower atop this 500ft cinder cone offers a **panorama**★★ of the surrounding landscape.

Modoc War Battle Sites

9mi from the visitor center.
The main park road leads north, past sites where Modoc warriors (led by Kientpoos, called "Captain Jack by the US settlers) clashed with Army forces and armed settlers. **Canby's Cross** marks the place where Gen. Canby and the Rev. Eleasar Thomas, a negotiator, were killed by Captain Jack and his followers. At **Captain Jack's Stronghold**★, a self-guided trail *(interpretive pamphlet available at trailhead)* wanders through the caves that enabled the Modoc leader, his warriors and their families to keep the US Army forces at bay.

Mount Shasta★★

This 14,162ft mountain is the second-highest volcano (after Mount Rainier) in the **Cascade Range**, the majestic column of volcanic mountains traversing Washington, Oregon and northern California. Though not as high as Mount Whitney in the Sierra Nevada, Mount Shasta boasts a 17mi base and thus ranks as California's largest mountain mass.

A BIT OF GEOGRAPHY

Mt. Shasta began to take its present shape roughly 10,000 years ago; its peak is composed of several volcanic masses. Research indicates that for the past few millennia, the mountain has erupted an average of every 500 years, and the most recent activity appears to have occurred some 200 years ago. Mt. Shasta is now considered an active, though quiescent, volcano.

The Whitney Glacier, largest in California, sprawls between the main summit and Shastina, the mountain's lower western peak (12,433ft). Owing to its porous composition, the mountain is water-permeable; street-corner drinking fountains abound in nearby towns, offering a chance to sample the pure, sweet spring waters that seep from Shasta's base.

SIGHTS
Mount Shasta

The small city of 3,862, located below the mountain's southwestern flank, serves as a gateway to Mt. Shasta and to the ski slopes at Mt. Shasta Ski Park *(10mi east of Mount Shasta on Rte. 89; ℰ530-926-8610; www.skipark.com).* Hotels, campgrounds, restaurants, ski shops and other facilities cater to outdoor enthusiasts.

The Sacramento River's northernmost source is located here at **Big Spring** *(in City Park, off N. Mt. Shasta Blvd.).* The US Forest Service **ranger station** *(204 W. Alma St.; ⏲open Jun–Oct daily 8am–4.30pm; rest of the year Mon–Fri 8am–4.30pm; ℙ ℰ530-926-4511)* offers

⏳ **Michelin Map:** 585 B 6.
ℹ **Info:** ℰ530-926-4865. www.mtshastachamber.com.

information on recreational opportunities on the mountain, including hiking trails and fishing in Lake McCloud, Lake Siskiyou and other small alpine lakes on the mountain's lower elevations.

Sisson Museum and Mount Shasta Fish Hatchery

1 N. Old Stage Rd. at W. Lake St. ⏲Open Jun–Sept daily 10am–4pm; Oct–Dec Fri–Sun 1pm–4pm. ⏲Closed Jan–Mar, Thanksgiving Day, Dec 25. ⏳ℙ ℰ530-926-5508. www.mountshasta sissonmuseum.org.

This small museum has exhibits on mountaineering, geology and Native American crafts. It is adjacent to the hatching and rearing ponds of California's oldest trout hatchery; visitors can view fish in various stages of growth.

Everitt Memorial Highway

Begin at the east end of Alma St. in Mount Shasta.

This 12mi scenic highway affords extensive views of the surrounding terrain, including Lake Siskiyou. Some 2mi north of Mount Shasta, the highway passes Black Butte, a 6,325ft conical plug dome composed of dark andesite lava.

Bunny Flat Scenic Trail

10.8mi north of Mount Shasta. Trailhead at Bunny Flat parking area.

This trail climbs through meadows and forests of Shasta red-fir trees to Horse Camp, a base for hikers planning to ascend the slopes. The stone **Sierra Club Lodge** *(open to the public)* sits below the southern summit, allowing **views**★★ of the mountain. The stone Olberman's Causeway, a traditional route for climbers continuing to the summit, ascends above the tree line behind the lodge.

EXCURSIONS
Dunsmuir
6mi south of Mount Shasta via I-5.
This town, situated on the Sacramento River, was an important railroad division point from the late 19C to mid-20C. In 1886 a young Canadian named Alexander Dunsmuir offered to build a water fountain if city fathers would rename the town for him. The fountain, burbling with pure Shasta drinking water, still stands in City Park. At the northern edge of town, on Frontage Road, a short trail leads to **Hedge Creek Falls**, a 30ft waterfall.

Castle Crags★
14mi south of Mount Shasta at the Castella exit.

These polished granite spires rise to heights of more than 6,000ft like sudden, unexpected sentinels along the northwest side of Interstate 5. They are ancient, having formed between 170 and 225 million years ago. The formations are protected within the National Forest Service's 11,000-acre Castle Crags Wilderness Area, but are best seen from **Castle Crags State Park** to the south and east (*open daily year-round; $6/vehicle; 530-235-2684*). A narrow paved road winds 2mi through the park and up Kettelbelly Ridge to **Vista Point**, which affords a **view**★ of the crags and the asymmetrical rise of Mt. Shasta. The **Indian Creek Trail** (*1mi loop; trailhead across from park headquarters*) interprets regional flora, fauna and history.

Redding

The seat of Shasta County, this sprawling city serves as a convenient base for exploring interior Northern California's natural wonders, including Mt. Shasta, Lassen Volcanic National Park and Lava Beds National Monument. The city boasts several noteworthy attractions of its own.

SIGHTS
♣♣ Turtle Bay Exploration Park★★
840 Auditorium Dr. Take Exit 1 from Rte. 44E. Open Apr–Oct daily 9am–5pm. Rest of the year Wed–Mon 9am–5pm. $13, children $9. 530-243-8850. www.turtlebay.org.
On an oak-shaded bend along the Sacramento River, this 300-acre space seeks to explain the relationships between people and nature in the valley. A museum presents exhibits on logging, wildlife, Native Americans and the river itself. Children flock to the forest camp, with its playground and hands-on activities. But the star attraction is the **Sundial Bridge**★★, a pedestrian, cable-stayed span across the Sacramento, which leads to the arboretum and gardens.

> ▶ **Population:** 89,780.
> **Michelin Map:** 585 A 7.
> **Info:** 530-225-4100. www.visitredding.org.
> **Don't Miss:** Burney Falls.
> **Kids:** Lake Shasta Caverns, McArthur-Burney Falls Memorial State Park, Turtle Bay Exploration Park.

A stark white "arm" rises 217ft at one end, casting a shadow, like the gnomon on a sundial. Designed by Santiago Calatrava, it is the Spanish architect's first free-standing bridge in the US.

Shasta State Historic Park★
6mi west of Redding via Rte. 299. Open year-round daily 10am–5pm. 530-243-8194. www.parks.ca.gov.
Roofless brick walls and black iron shutters are all that remain of once-booming Shasta City, founded in 1848 as the mining camp of Reading Springs. Fires consumed most of the town in 1852 and 1853, but the wooden buildings were replaced by structures of brick and iron. The Central Pacific Railroad's decision to locate its terminus 5mi east sounded the town's death knell. Residents and busi-

nesses slowly relocated to Redding, and by 1900 Shasta City had been virtually abandoned.

Restoration and preservation began in the 1920s. The former **courthouse** has been refurbished as a museum with artifacts, photos and California artwork. (*open Wed–Sun 10am–5pm; closed Jan 1, Thanksgiving Day & Dec 25; $2; 530-243-8194*).

Shasta Dam★

14mi north of Redding via I-5; exit Shasta Dam Blvd. 530-275-4463. www.shastalake.com/shastadam.
Measuring 602ft high and 3,460ft long, this massive concrete barrier (1945) is the keystone of the **Central Valley Project**, a network of dams, canals and pumping stations for flood control and water supply for Sacramento and San Joaquin valleys farmland.

The Sacramento, McCloud and Pit rivers and Squaw Creek are impounded behind the dam to create **Shasta Lake**★, the state's largest reservoir and a popular spot for houseboating and outdoor recreation.

A vista point on the road approaching the dam allows a stunning **view**★ of the dam and lake. Displays in the visitor center tell the story of the dam's construction (*open daily 8am–4.30pm (5pm in summer); closed major holidays; 530-275-4463*).

Lake Shasta Caverns★

20mi north of Redding via I-5; exit Shasta Caverns Rd. Visit by guided tour (2hrs) only, Memorial Day–Labor Day daily every 30min 9am–4pm; rest of the year call for schedule. Closed Thanksgiving Day; Dec 25. $22, children $13. 530-238-2341. www.lakeshastacaverns.com.
Within the eastern bank of Shasta Lake's McCloud River arm are subterranean chambers created by dissolution of water-soluble limestone beneath the earth's surface. Beginning with a boat ride across the lake and a bus ride to the cavern entrance, tours introduce visitors to mineral features, such as flowstone, draperies and fluted columns.

EXCURSIONS
Weaverville

48mi west of Redding via Rte. 299. Tourist office 530-623-6101. www.weavervilleinfo.com.
Set between the summits of Weaver Bally, Oregon and Browns mountains, Weaverville was once a mining camp. Storefronts line sloping Main Street, and structures survive from the late 1800s. The **Jake Jackson Museum** showcases antique firearms, Native American jewelry and historic artifacts from Weaverville's Chinese residents. A two-stamp mill sits on the grounds (*open May–Oct daily 10am–5pm; Apr & Nov–Dec noon–4pm; Jan–Mar Tue & Sat only noon–4pm; closed major holidays; donation requested; 530-623-5211*).

Weaverville Joss House State Historic Park★

Adjacent to Jake Jackson Museum. Visit by guided tour (30min) only, year-round Wed–Sun 10am–5pm. Closed Jan 1, Thanksgiving, Dec 25. $3. 530-623-5284. www.parks.ca.gov.
This well-preserved Taoist temple (1874) is California's only authentic mid-19C joss house in its original location. Elaborate canopies and figures of Chinese deities enliven the dark interior.
Displays in the adjacent **visitor center** focus on the Chinese in California.

McArthur-Burney Falls Memorial State Park

65mi northeast of Redding via Rtes. 229 and 89. Open year-round daily dawn–dusk. $6/vehicle. 530-335-2777. www.parks.ca.gov.
Perhaps the loveliest phenomenon in a region endowed with an abundance of natural phenomena is 129ft **Burney Falls**★★. Though not exceptionally tall, the falls owe their uniqueness to an underground stream beneath Burney Creek, which cascades over a basalt cliff in a thundering shower. Water from the underground stream emerges from the fern-covered face of the cliff in myriad wispy falls, creating aquatic effects.

Stretching 400mi from the Cascade Range near Lassen Peak to Tehachapi Pass east of Bakersfield, the Sierra Nevada is the longest unbroken mountain range in the continental US. It contains the highest US summit outside of Alaska, one of the deepest canyons and highest waterfalls as well as the largest national parks.

Forces of Nature– Rising from over 7,000ft in the north to Mount Whitney (14,494ft) in the south, the gigantic Sierra Nevada range began uplifting 10 million years ago, when the Pacific and North American continental plates collided. During the ice ages between 3 million and 200,000 years ago, glaciers carved remarkable features of the Sierra, shaping hanging valleys, monumental rocks, waterfalls and lakes.

With winters too severe for year-round residence, the High Sierra served as a buffer between the Paiute and Shoshone Indians on the east, and the Maidu, Miwok, Monache and Foothill Yokuts of the west. Spanish explorers named the range from a distance but never probed beyond the Central Valley. American fur traders and explorers led difficult crossings of the Sierra, but systematic exploration by non-natives did not take place until the discovery of gold in 1848.

Reckless exploitation of the meadows and rivers spurred legislation banning hydraulic mining in 1884, and mass harvesting of the forests led conservation efforts by John Muir and others to preserve sections of the range. Their efforts sparked a national environmental movement that culminated in the establishment of national parks and forests.

A Fragile Balance – Sierra Nevada communities run the gamut from isolated Owens Valley towns offering basic visitor services to bustling Lake Tahoe cities replete with restaurants and luxury hotels (and casinos on the other side of the Nevada state line). The region is a paradise for skiers, backpackers and hikers venturing into the remote forests and mountains.

Highlights

1. Pretending you're a Lilliputian at **Grant Grove** (p341)
2. Drinking a cocktail while drinking in the view at **Heavenly** (p332)
3. A summer picnic at the edge of sparkling **Convict Lake** (p335)
4. Learning Native crafts at the **Yosemite Museum** (p345)
5. View east over Yosemite Valley at sunset from **Tunnel View** (p348)

The national parks draw more visitors every year, increasing the challenge of preserving the Sierra Nevada's fragile ecological balance and pristine beauty while keeping the natural wonders open and accessible to all.

Yosemite Falls, Yosemite National Park

Brigitta L. House/MICHELIN

Lake Tahoe★★

A serene expanse of deep blue water enclosed in a valley amid the snow-shrouded Sierra Nevada, Lake Tahoe straddles the California-Nevada border at an altitude of 6,229ft. The lake is world-renowned for its winter and summer sporting opportunities, glitzy casinos and live performances by celebrities.

A BIT OF HISTORY

Formed in a basin created by tectonic faulting some 24 million years ago, Lake Tahoe measures 22mi long and 12mi wide. Its maximum depth of 1,639ft makes it the second deepest lake in the country, after Oregon's Crater Lake. Its waters are so clear that visibility is often possible to depths of 75ft, and so cold (averaging 68°F in summer) that wetsuits are sometimes necessary.

Signs of human occupation date back 8,000 years. Washoe Indians summered here in more recent centuries and called the area *Da ow a ga* (thought to mean "water in a high place"), which was corrupted by later settlers to "Tahoe." **John C. Frémont** led the first party of Yankee explorers here in 1844. Following the 1859 silver rush on Nevada's nearby Comstock Lode, trees on the lakeshore were targeted as lumber for the mines and their boomtowns. In the ensuing two decades, scattered resorts grew up around the lake.

In 1915 the first major road linked Tahoe to more populous centers, and the area gradually became a summer playground for affluent Californians. In 1931 casinos were established along Nevada's side. The 1960 Winter Olympic Games, held at **Squaw Valley**, spotlighted the prime ski conditions of the region and increased the region's popularity as a winter vacation destination

🚗 DRIVING TOUR

70mi. Map on following pages.

▶ *Begin in Tahoe City, at the intersection of Rtes. 89 and 28.*

◔ **Michelin Map:** 585 B 8.
ℹ **Info:** ℘775-588-4591. www.visitinglake tahoe.com.
◷ **Timing:** The population often triples in summer, and traffic congestion is commonplace. Retreat to the state parks and stay away from the bigger towns, or visit at a less-crowded time of year.
👫 **Kids:** The Gondola at Heavenly.

Tahoe City
Visitor center at 560 N. Lake Tahoe Blvd.
One of the oldest settlements on the lake, this town serves as a northern gateway to the area's many attractions.

Watson Cabin Curios
0.5mi east of visitor center. ◷*Open Memorial Day–Jun weekends noon–4pm; Jul–Labor Day Wed–Mon noon–4pm.* 🅿 ℘*530-583-1762. www.northtahoemuseums.org.*
Nestled among the shops and restaurants lining North Lake Tahoe Boulevard (Route 28), this log cabin (1909) is one of the oldest structures in Tahoe City. It was home to a local family for 40 years and operates today as satellite shop to the Gatekeeper's Cabin Museum *(below)*.

Gatekeeper's Cabin Museum/Basket Museum
Follow Rte. 89 south to William B. Layton Park. ◷*Open mid-Jun–Aug daily 11am–5pm; May–mid-Jun & Sept Wed–Sun 11am–5pm.* 👁$3. 🅿 ℘*530-583-1762. www.northtahoemuseums.org.*
This building is a reproduction of the log cabin that served as home to the various "gatekeepers" who regulated the adjacent Lake Tahoe dam between 1910 and 1968. Built on the site of the original cabin, which burned in 1978, the museum displays Native American and early pioneer artifacts along with exhibits on the area's natural history.

The spillway of the simple concrete dam remains the lake's only outlet.

In the adjacent annex, the museum maintains a collection of some 800 Native American baskets, artifacts and dolls.

▷ *From Tahoe City, drive south on Rte. 89.*

Ed Z'berg-Sugar Pine Point State Park★

10mi. Western park entrance on right; access to Hellman-Ehrman Mansion .7mi farther, at eastern entrance. ⏰Open daily year-round. ☜$7/vehicle. ⛺ 🅿 ☎530-525-7232. www.parks.ca.gov.

This park encompasses part of the General Creek watershed west of the lake. One of the first settlers on the lake, Kentuckian "General" **William Phipps** chose this promontory to homestead in 1860. San Francisco financier **Isaias W. Hellman** began acquiring lakeshore land In 1897 and hired San Francisco architect Walter Danforth Bliss to design the rustically elegant Pine Lodge for his summer residence. Hellman's youngest child, Florence Hellman Ehrman, inherited the estate. Heirs sold the property to the state.

Hellman-Ehrman Mansion★

☞Visit by guided tour (45min) only, Memorial Day–Labor Day daily 10am–3pm. ☜$2. 🅿 ☎530-525-7982. www.parks.ca.gov.

Built of dark wood and stone quarried nearby, the eight-bedroom mansion (1903) features a wide veranda and twin cupolas. The living room sports a granite fireplace and a ceiling paneled in oak. The turreted tank house outside serves as a park nature center, with exhibits on the natural history of the lake environs. Phipps Cabin sits below the mansion. The interpretive **Dolder Trail** *(2mi round-trip)* winds through the forested Z'Berg Natural Preserve north of the mansion, leading ultimately to the small wooden Sugar Pine Point Lighthouse.

D.L. Bliss State Park★

6mi. ⏰Open Memorial Day–Labor Day daily dawn–dusk. ☜$7/vehicle. ⛺ ☎530-525-7277. www.parks.ca.gov.

While visiting this scenic park along the lake's southwestern shore, be sure to take the Balancing Rock Nature Trail (.5mi loop; easy), a self-guided loop that leads past **Balancing Rock**, a 130-ton granite boulder perched on a granite base.

The **Rubicon Trail** *(4.5mi; moderate)* hugs the cliffs above the lake, offering **views**★ along most of its length. Beginning at Rubicon Point, the trail reaches a turnoff *(.4mi)* for a small wooden lighthouse that functioned here from 1916 to 1919. Continuing south, the trail eventually descends to Emerald Point, continues into adjacent Emerald Bay State Park and terminates at Eagle Falls.

Emerald Bay State Park★★

2mi. ⏰Open daily year-round. ☜$7/vehicle. ⛺☎530-541-3030. www.parks.ca.gov.

Majestic alpine views, hiking trails and a Scandinavian-style mansion highlight a visit to this popular state park surrounding scenic **Emerald Bay**★★, a small, glacially sculpted inlet named for its deep blue-green color.

Vikingsholm★★

Access by Vikingsholm Trail (2mi round-trip), which gradually descends from parking area. ☞Interior by guided tour (1hr) only, late May–Sept daily 10am–4pm. ☜$5. ☎530-541-6498.

This imposing mansion (1929) resembles a 9C AD Nordic castle. The structure was commissioned by philanthropist Lora J. Knight, who hired Swedish-born architect Lennart Palme to create a 1920s version of a Viking residence as her summer home. After her death, the property was purchased by the state in 1953.

Built of locally quarried granite, the 48-room mansion incorporates such Scandinavian elements as dragons' heads, intricately hand-carved beams, sod roofing and hand-wrought door latches.

Mrs. Knight's stone tea house is visible offshore on Fannette Island. A visitor center just south of the mansion details the construction of Vikingsholm.

▷ *Continue south on Rte. 89.*

Ascending into open bluffs above the lake, the road passes Eagle Falls, visible as it courses beneath the road. Just beyond, ☀**Inspiration Viewpoint** offers a striking **view**★ of Emerald Bay. From here the road crosses a high narrow ridge with views of Emerald Bay to the left and Cascade Lake to the right. At the National Forest Service's **Lake Tahoe Basin Visitor Center** (🕐*open mid-Jun–Labor Day daily 8am–5.30pm, rest of the year hours vary;* ♿ ✆*530-543-2674; www.fs.fed.us),* exhibits detail the natural and human history of the area. A nature trail (♿ *0.5mi)* leads from the visitor center to a **stream chamber** where visitors may observe fish in a mountain creek from an underwater window. In mid-autumn, thousands of bright red kokanee salmon spawn upstream from Lake Tahoe.

Tallac Historic Site★★
5mi. Buildings 🕐*open mid-May–mid-June weekends 10.30am–4.30pm; mid-Jun–Sept daily 10.30am–4.30pm. Grounds open year-round daily dawn–dusk.* 🅿 ✆*530-541-5227. www.tahoeheritage.org.*

One of the earliest resort areas on the lake, this site on the south shore recalls Tahoe's late-19C era of opulence. Stagecoach entrepreneur **"Yank" Clement** established Tallac Point House, a rustic hostelry, here in 1873. In 1880 San Francisco mining and real-estate speculator **E.J. "Lucky" Baldwin** acquired the property and added a casino. His daughter Anita, who inherited the property, had all Tallac buildings removed from the lakefront in 1927 and the area returned to a more natural state.

Other mansions built to the east, along with the Tallac grounds, are maintained by the US Forest Service.

A short trail leads west along the lakefront, past the foundations of the Tallac casino and the sites of the old Point House and hotel, then across the remains of a paved promenade that once connected the two.

Baldwin Estate★
This U-shaped, pitch-roofed log home was built in 1921 by Dextra Baldwin McGonagle, Lucky Baldwin's granddaughter. Today, the open-beamed living room is furnished in the rustic style popular among Lake Tahoe's early 20C summer residents; adjoining rooms contain **photographs**★ of the life and history of the Washoe Indians.

Additional displays recount early resort life at Lake Tahoe.

Inspiration Viewpoint, Emerald Bay

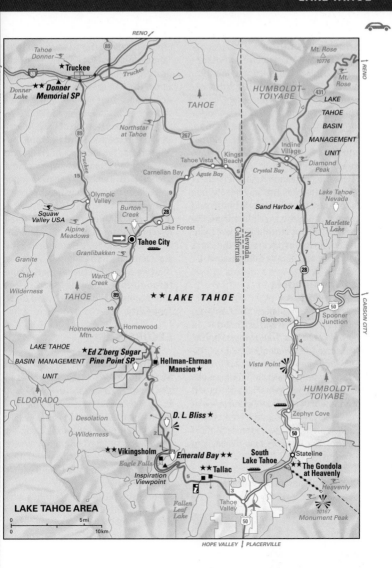

LAKE TAHOE AREA

The **Washoe Demonstration Garden** beside the house cultivates plants important to this tribe of hunter-gatherers. Also on display are examples of their traditional shelters.

Pope Estate

This five-bedroom mansion (1899) was built by the Tevis family. It was eventually acquired by George S. Pope, a Bay Area lumber and shipping executive. From 1923 to 1965, the Popes' lavish lifestyle at the estate became legendary.

The extravagant interior boasts coffered ceilings and wall paneling of California cedar and redwood.

A small **arboretum** includes giant sequoias and western red cedar.

A short walk to the east is **Valhalla**. (1924), a shingle-sided mansion with wide verandas, which was the summer home of San Francisco financier Walter Heller. Today it is open only for performances.

South Lake Tahoe

3mi. Chamber of Commerce and visitor center 2.5mi east of junction of Rte. 89 and Lake Tahoe Blvd. (US-50). Seasonal visitor center on US-50 just east of Rte. 89.

The lake's largest town offers lodging, dining, shopping and recreation. Commercial paddle wheeler, sailboat and glass-bottom boat lake excursions depart from the south shore, and the El Dorado Recreation Area offers direct access to the lakefront. Stateline Avenue marks the California-Nevada border and separates South Lake Tahoe from the Nevada town of **Stateline**, where high-rise hotel-casinos offer round-the-clock gambling and nightly entertainment.

👥 The Gondola at Heavenly★★

From US-50 turn south on Ski Run Blvd.; follow signs to Heavenly Ski Resort.
🕐*Open year-round daily, hours vary by season.* 💺*$30, children $20.* ✕♿ ✆*775-586-7000. www.skiheavenly.com.*

The 8-passenger enclosed cabins make the 2.4mi ascent up the flank of 10,167ft Monument Peak, affording **views**★★ of the lake and the surrounding mountains. The 9,123ft high observation deck offers a panoramic view of Carson Valley and environs.

▶ *Continue east and north on US-50.*

Donner Monument in Donner Memorial State Park

© Myopia/Corbis

From Stateline, the road skirts Lake Tahoe's less developed eastern shore; from Vista Point *(7mi)*, **views**★ extend across the lake to the western side.

At Spooner Junction *(4mi)*, the lakeshore road becomes Nevada Route 28 and traverses a portion of Lake Tahoe-Nevada State Park. **Sand Harbor** *(7mi)* offers picnic facilities, rounded granite outcrops and a sandy beach fringing a sheltered cove where the shallow water tends to be warmer than in other parts of the lake.

Route 28 continues through the small residential communities of Incline Village and Crystal Bay before crossing the state line back into California. The road then weaves along the northern shore through the well-developed resort community of Kings Beach, and on to Tahoe City.

EXCURSIONS

Donner Memorial State Park★★

13mi north of Tahoe City via Rte. 89 to Donner Pass Rd., or exit off I-80, 2.3mi west of Truckee. $7/vehicle. ⛺ 🅿
✆*530-582-7892. www.parks.ca.gov.*

This park is situated on the site where members of the westward-emigrating Donner Party spent the fateful winter of 1846–47.

Among the pioneering families who joined the Great Westward Migration of the mid-1840s were three prosperous Illinois families headed by George and Jacob Donner and James Reed. In late July, the party of 87 people set out on an untried new route, a shortcut they thought would save 350mi, but it proved treacherously difficult. When they began the trek over the Sierras, early snows trapped them.

As the torturous winter wore on, starvation took its toll and several members of the party died. Desperate with hunger, survivors were forced to cannibalize the dead to stay alive. It was not until mid-February that a relief expedition reached them. Only 47 survived the ordeal.

Pioneer Monument

Dedicated in 1918, this impressive, cast-bronze monument, sculpted by John McQuarrie, immortalizes the hardships and courage of early pioneer families.

Emigrant Trail Museum★★

🕐Open daily 9am–4pm. 🕐Closed Jan 1, Thanksgiving Day, Dec 25. 🎫$3. ♿ Displays and a film *(25min)* recount the history of the **Donner Party**. Dioramas and artifacts detail the area's natural and human history.

A nature trail *(.5mi loop)* leads along Donner Creek and past a large granite boulder now inset with a plaque listing the names of the survivors and of those who perished in the Donner Party.

Truckee★

15mi north of Tahoe City via Rte. 89.
This robust little railroad town of 10,213, named for a 19C Paiute chief, cultivates its Old West atmosphere. Formerly a way station on the first transcontinental train route, it is today a key stop on transcontinental Interstate 80. Its main street, **Commercial Row**, features quaint brick buildings dating from the 1870s and 1880s, today refurbished as restaurants and shops. A **visitor center** *(🕐open daily 9am-6pm; 📞530-587-2757; www.truckee.com)* is located within the

---

Cruising Lake Tahoe

Several commercial operators offer boat excursions on Lake Tahoe lasting 1.5 to 3.5 hours; prices average $19–$49, depending on the season.
Zephyr Cove Cruises – The M.S. Dixie II and the Tahoe Queen, historic paddle wheelers, depart from Zephyr Cove *(📞888-896-3830; www.zephyrcove.com)*.
North Tahoe Cruises – Departs from Lighthouse Shopping Center in Tahoe City *(📞800-218-2464; www.tahoegal.com)*.

1896 Southern Pacific Depot, which still serves bus and rail passengers.

Old Truckee Jail

Spring and Jibboom Sts. 🕐*Open mid-May–Sept weekends 11am–4pm.* 📞*530-582-0893. www.truckeehistory.org.*
This old-time jail was constructed in 1875, when the town's rowdy population and red-light district necessitated a local lock-up. The jail was modified in the early 1900s; downstairs rooms were lined with steel plates, and an upper floor of brick, now used to display local history exhibits, was added to house female and juvenile offenders. The jail remained in use until 1964.

ADDRESSES

🛏 STAY

◔◔◔◔◔ **The Ahwahnee Hotel** – *Yosemite Village, Yosemite National Park.* 📞*209-372-1000 or 559-253-5635. www.yosemitepark.com. 123 rooms.*
This towering timber-and-granite landmark has hosted luminaries from Winston Churchill to Charlie Chaplin. Treat yourself to the luxurious Sunday brunch at the **Ahwahnee Dining Room** (◔◔◔), with its 34ft pine-trestled ceiling. Other lodging options in the park include the **Yosemite Lodge ($$)**, **Curry Village ($$)**, the **Wawona Hotel ($$)** and the **High Sierra Camps ($$)**.

◔◔◔◔◔ **Château du Sureau** – *48688 Victoria Lane (Rte. 41), Oakhurst.* 📞*559-683-6860. www.elderberryhouse.com.*

10 rooms. Just 20min south of Yosemite Park lies this Provençal chateau in the Sierra Nevada forest. Opened by chef Erna Kubin-Clanin to complement her restaurant, **Erna's Elderberry House** (◔◔◔◔), the chateau boasts sumptuous rooms, and the luxurious 2,000sq ft Villa Sureau.

◔◔◔◔ **The Shore House** – *7170 North Lake Blvd., Tahoe Vista.* 📞*530-546-7270 or 800-207-5160. www.shorehouselaketahoe.com. 9 rooms.* 🚭. Each room at this B&B has a gas-log fireplace and a private entrance overlooking a sandy beach on Lake Tahoe's north shore. A kayak is available for guests' use, and there's even an outdoor hot tub.

◔◔◔ **Sorensen's Resort** – *14255 Hwy. 88, Hope Valley.* 📞*530-694-2203 or 800-423-9949. www.sorensensresort.com.*

33 rooms. This resort dating from 1926 offers classes in fly-fishing, water-color painting or astronomy. Lodgings range from log cabins with wood-burning fireplaces to a farmhouse for six.

⊜⊜⊜ **Wuksachi Village and Lodge** – *Rte. 198, Sequoia National Park.* ℘801-559-4930 or 866-807-3598. www.visitse-quoia.com. *102 rooms*. At the heart of the park village, the lodge occupies three beautiful cedar-and-stone buildings; rooms feature oak and hickory furnishings. The **dining room** (⊜⊜⊜) offers Southwestern and Asian-fusion cuisines.

⫙ EAT

⊜⊜⊜ **The Restaurant at Convict Lake** – *Convict Lake Rd. (2mi west of US-395), Mammoth Lakes.* ℘760-934-3803. www.convictlake.com. **American**. The menu at this fine restaurant boasts local ingredients like Sierra

trout, quail and prime rib of elk. The resort (℘800-992-2260) comprises **29 cabins** (⊜⊜-⊜⊜⊜⊜).

⊜⊜ **Sunnyside Resort** – *1850 West Lake Blvd., Tahoe City.* ℘530-583-7200 www.sunnysideresort.com. **American**. Patrons moor their boats at the Sunnyside Marina before heading to the Lakeside Dining Room or the more-casual Mountain Grill for dinners of steaks and chops, barbecued pork ribs with Western "giddy-up" sauce and crispy zucchini.

⊜ **Bodie Mike's** – *US-395, Lee Vining.* ℘760-647-6432. Closed Nov–early May. **American**. This homey roadhouse serves up tasty barbecue ribs and other down-home fare. Sides include fries and beer-battered onion rings, soups and the salad bar. The outdoor patio overlooks Mono Lake.

Mammoth Region★

Situated 40mi south of the Tioga Pass entrance to Yosemite National Park, and 318mi from Los Angeles, the region surrounding Mammoth Mountain offers year-round recreation among lovely alpine lakes.

VISIT

Founded in 1878, the town of **Mammoth Lakes** flourished as a ski resort in the mid-1950s. Today it's center of amenities for nearby Mammoth Mountain and June Mountain ski resorts. The Mammoth Ranger Station **visitor center**, offers interpretive programs and information (*Rte. 203, 3mi west of US-395;* ⊙*open daily 8am–5pm;* ⊙*closed Jan 1, Thanksgiving Day, Dec 25;* ⫶ 🅿 ℘760-924-5500; www.fs.fed.us/r5/inyo). Stretching to the south is the **Mammoth Lakes Basin★** (*3mi west of Mammoth Lakes via Lake Mary Rd.*), graced by six alpine lakes. The basin offers abundant opportunities for hiking and seasonal cross-country skiing on trails that wind through lush forests of evergreens.

⫶ **Michelin Map:** 585 B 8; and Yosemite Valley map.

🄸 **Info:** ℘760-934-2712. www.visitmammoth.com.

🄰 **Don't Miss:** Convict Lake.

SIGHTS

⫶*Map; see Sierra Nevada, Yosemite.*

Mammoth Mountain★

Storms drop an average of 335in of snow annually on this massive mountain's flanks, boasting one of California's most popular winter resorts. During summer, summit access roads open for biking. From the Mammoth Mountain Ski Center's Main Lodge (*4mi west of Mammoth Lakes via Minaret Rd.;* ℘760-934-2571; www.mammothmountain.com), a gondola ascends to the summit, from where **views★★** extend as far as Mono Lake (*call or check online for schedule;* ⊜*$18, children $9;* ⫶ ℘800-626-6684).

Minaret Summit

5mi west of Mammoth Lakes via Rte. 203 (Minaret Rd.). Situated on a granite outcropping at 9,265ft, this overlook offers a **panorama★★** of the rugged peaks of the Ritter Range and the crenelated tops of a thin, jagged ridge.

Devils Postpile National Monument★

14mi west of Mammoth Lakes via Rte. 203. Open late May–Oct daily 7am–7pm. 760-934-2289. www.nps. gov/depo. From early Jun–early Sept day visit by shuttle bus only (7am–7pm; $7, good for 3 days). Tickets available at Adventure Center in the Mammoth Mountain Ski Area Gondola Building.

Rising above the Middle Fork of the San Joaquin River is a 60ft gray wall of basalt columns formed 100,000 years ago when a river of molten lava was extruded from a nearby volcanic vent. A trail *(.4mi)* to the postpile passes **Soda Springs**, cold mineral springs situated on a gravel bar in the river. From the base of the postpile's basalt wall, a second trail leads to its top. The main trail continues south to **Rainbow Falls** *(2mi)*, where the river drops 101ft over a volcanic ledge. *A shorter trail to Rainbow Falls is accessible from the Reds Meadow area, and by shuttle bus from Mammoth Mountain Ski Areas during summer.*

Convict Lake★

4.5mi south of Mammoth Lakes via US-395, then 2mi west on Convict Lake Rd.

This sparkling alpine lake received its name in 1871, when posses pursued six escaped convicts into a nearby canyon and a fierce shootout ensued. Mt. Morrison (12,268ft) offers a backdrop to the south of Convict Lake, today a hiking, picnicking and fishing destination.

Hot Creek Geothermal Area★

3mi south of Mammoth Lakes via US-395, then 3.3mi east on Airport/Hot Creek Fish Hatchery Rd.

Traversing a volcanic basin, this creek is one of numerous manifestations of geothermal activity present in the region. Hot springs and fumaroles feed into the creek, and roiling springs and mudpots steam beside it. *Swimming here is hazardous. The town of Mammoth Lakes maintains a public pool fed by natural hot springs at Whitmore, 3mi farther south off US-395.*

June Lake Loop★

17mi north of Mammoth Lakes off US-395. Loop rejoins US-395.

Lying in the shadow of 10,909ft Carson Peak, this loop drive *(15mi)* leads past four mountain lakes, offering spectacular high desert and alpine scenery. Mountains rise above horseshoe-shaped valleys traversed by streams, and stands of aspen border the lakeshores.

Mono Lake★

Cupped in a broad basin below Yosemite National Park, this pale blue body of water and the small islands at its center offer a surreal spectacle of white, mineral-encrusted shores and eerie tufa towers.

Michelin Map:	585 B 8 and Yosemite Valley map.
Info:	760-647-3044. www.fs.fed.us/r5/inyo. www.monolake.org.
Location:	Off Hwy. 395 13mi E. of Yosemite National Park, near Lee Vining.

A BIT OF HISTORY

An Old Salt – One of the oldest lakes in North America, Mono Lake appeared 700,000 years ago when runoff from melting glaciers filled an extensive basin-like depression. Once five times larger than its present 60sq mi, the lake, which has no outlet, has slowly evaporated since the end of the last Ice Age, leaving behind a residue of minerals. Its milky water is three times saltier than ocean water and 80 times more alkaline. The distinctive tufa towers on the lakeshore were formed underwater when calcium deposits

Tufa on Mono Lake at wintertime

from submerged springs combined with lake-water carbonates, creating gnarled limestone spires that were gradually exposed as the water level decreased. Mono Lake's shores were inhabited by Native Americans as long as 5,500 years ago. Northern **Paiutes** harvested the alkali flies as food and traded them across the Sierra Nevada to the Yokuts people, whose word mono, meaning "fly-eaters," was attached to the lake itself.

A Conservation Battleground – In recent decades, Mono Lake has been the focus of a major legislative dispute that arose when four of its tributary streams were diverted into the **Los Angeles Aqueduct**, causing the lake level to drop some 45ft between 1941 and 1981. By the 1970s, conservationists had launched a campaign to preserve the lake, and in 1984 Congress designated a 116,000-acre region within Inyo National Forest as the Mono Basin National Forest Scenic Area. The Mono Lake Tufa State Reserve, established in 1981, encompasses 17,000 acres encircling the lake. In 1991 the El Dorado County superior court issued a preliminary injunction directing that the lake level be maintained at above 6,377ft, and in 1994 the California State Water Board facilitated an agreement to maintain the water level at 6,392ft. Since the Board's decision, the lake has risen 10ft *(www.monolake.org/live/level.html)*.

VISIT
15mi east of Yosemite National Park (Tioga Pass entrance) by Rte. 120.

Visitor Center★
North end of Lee Vining, off US-395.
◷*Open mid-Jun–Sept daily 8am–5pm. Apr–mid-Jun & Oct–Nov Thu–Mon 9am–4.30pm.* ☛*Guided walks available; call for schedule.* ⊜*$3 (South Tufa Area).* ♿ 🅿 ☏*760-647-3044. www.fs.fed.us/r5/inyo.*
Overlooking the lake, the Forest Service facility serves as a museum of the region's natural and human history. Exhibits and a film *(20min)* detail the lake's formation, the unusual food chain that it supports, its ecological status, and the Native American presence here.

South Tufa Area★★
6mi south of Lee Vining via US-395, then 4.5mi east on Rte. 120 to access road.
This area of the lakeshore is ornamented with towering tufa formations that range from 200 to 900 years old. An interpretive trail *(1mi)* leading through the tufa "forest" is edged with markers that trace the drop in the lake level over the past 50 years. ⌂**Navy Beach**, on the east side, is a good place to stop for a swim, to experience the buoyancy that results from the water's high salt content.

Panum Crater
Access via turnoff from Rte. 120, 1.5mi east of South Tufa turnoff.

This rimmed crater, formed 640 years ago, is the northernmost of a range of 21 volcanic cones extending south from Mono Lake. The Mono Craters began building 35,000 years ago through volcanic activity. A short trail leads up to the crater's rim; the obsidian dome in its center formed in a later eruption.

Situated on the west shore above the current water level, the Old Marina Site *(1mi north of visitor center on US-395; open daily year-round; 760-647-6331)* offers access to the lake. At Mono Lake County Park *(4.2mi north of visitor center, then .3mi east on Cemetery Rd.; open daily year-round; for interpretive activities 760-647-6331; www.parks.ca.gov)*, a boardwalk trail winds from the park area to more tufa formations along the lake; the platform at the end of the boardwalk is an excellent spot for birdwatching.

EXCURSION

Bodie State Historic Park★★

Map see Yosemite NP. 18mi N of Lee Vining on US-395, then 13mi E on Rte. 270. The last 3mi are unpaved. Road may be closed by snow in winter. Open late May–Labor Day daily 8am–7pm; rest of the year daily 9am–4pm; call for road conditions. $5, children $3. Self-guided tour booklet ($1) available at entrance booth or Miners Union Hall. 760-647-6445. www.parks.ca.gov.

An authentic, unrestored ghost town, Bodie today is virtually deserted, though torn curtains still hang in windows and glasses gather dust in saloons.

In 1859 Waterman S. Bodey discovered placer deposits in these hills. By 1880 some 30 mines were operating here, and the town boasted 10,000 people, 2,000 buildings and a very bad reputation. A fire in 1932 consumed 90 percent of the town structures.

The state acquired it as a historic park in 1962, and now maintains the site in a condition of "arrested decay," meaning that the buildings are protected from further deterioration.

Some 150 buildings, most of them weathered clapboard structures, still stand along the streets. Only the **Miller House** *(Green St.)*, with its threadbare furnishings, is open to visitors, while the simple interior of the **Old Methodist Church** *(Green and Fuller Sts.)* may be viewed through open doors. The **Miners Union Hall** functions as a park museum and visitor center, displaying photographs and other memorabilia.

Owens Valley★

Grand in its arid austerity, the Owens Valley sits at the geologic and climatic intersection of the Sierra Nevada, the Mojave Desert and the Great Basin. Flanked by two of the country's highest mountain ranges—the Sierra Nevada on the west and the White-Inyo Range on the east—the valley extends from the southern end of the Owens Dry Lake bed, south of Lone Pine, to the northern outskirts of Bishop.

- **Michelin Map:** 585 B, C 9.
- **Info:** 760-873-8405. www.bishopvisitor.com.
- **Don't Miss:** Mount Whitney.
- **Kids:** Laws Railroad.

A BIT OF HISTORY

The valley is named for Richard Owens, who never came here but did accompany John Frémont on an 1845 expedition to map overland routes into the area.

By the 1860s the area was a thriving farming, ranching and mining region, claiming one of California's most productive silver mines. But the valley's ecology and economy were forever altered by the 1913 completion of the **Los Angeles Aqueduct**, which diverted water from the Owens River southwest to the city, effectively ending the valley's lucrative ranching operatings.

Owens Lake, which covered 100sq mi in the 1860s, gradually dried up, as did the valley's population.

Today a smattering of small towns punctuates US-395, which traverses the valley from south to north, offering vistas of the majestic eastern Sierra Nevada.

🚗 DRIVING TOUR

80mi (not including excursions).

▷ *Leave Olancha by US-395 north.*

From the small crossroads community of **Olancha**, US-395 skirts the west edge of Owens Lake, now a vast, arid playa fringed with the pinkish glow of halobacteria organisms that thrive in its alkaline environment. The **Eastern Sierra InterAgency Visitor Center** *(north end of the lake at the junction of US-395 and Rte. 136;* ◷*open year-round daily 8am–5pm, extended summer hrs;* ✆*760-876-6222; www.r5.fs.fed.us/inyo)* offers information on the eastern Sierra corridor. While you're here, pick up a map of Movie Road film locations (⟳*see below)*. The peak of Mt. Whitney is visible from the visitor center grounds.

Lone Pine
23mi north of Olancha.
The primary tourist hub for the southern end of the valley, this little town serves as a gateway for climbers challenging Mt. Whitney. Hollywood stars come to shoot films in the **Alabama Hills**★, an area of fabulous granitic boulder formations. Errol Flynn, John Wayne, Gregory Peck and Gene Autry are among the celebrities who have starred in 200-plus films made here. **Movie Road** *(2.7mi west of Lone Pine on Whitney Portal Rd., then turn right)* winds for several miles among the rocks backdropped by the Sierras; you can immerse yourself in this aspect of Owens Valley culture at the **Museum of Lone Pine Film History** (◷*open year-round Mon–Wed 10am–6pm, Thu–Sat 10am–7pm, Sun 10am–4pm;* 👛*$5;* ✆*760-876-9909; www.lonepinefilmhis-torymuseum.org)*, which has displays and a small theater.

Mount Whitney★★
▷ *Excursion: 26mi round-trip from Lone Pine via Whitney Portal Rd.*
The highest peak (14,494ft) in the contiguous 48 states, Mt. Whitney was formed primarily by fault blocking and shaped by glaciation. Members of the California State Geological Survey named the mountain for Josiah Whitney, California's first state geologist. The first recorded ascent of the peak was made in 1873.

Views of the massif's stern visage can be seen from **Whitney Portal Road**, which ascends the eastern flank of the Sierra, allowing **views**★ down into the Owens Valley. The road ends at the **Whitney Portal**★, a mountain canyon (8,360ft) shaded by tall conifers and centered on a trout pond *(license required for fishing)*. The rugged **Mount Whitney Trail** *(21.4mi round-trip; permit required)* ascends steeply into the backcountry, crossing into Sequoia National Park and leading to the mountain's summit.

Horseshoe Meadow Road
▷ *Excursion: 48mi round-trip from Lone Pine. Take Whitney Portal Rd. west 3.2mi and turn left.*
Ascending from the valley floor to a meadowland lying at 10,000ft and laced with trails, this road offers **views**★ of the Owens Dry Lake Bed, the Inyo Mountains and the Owens Valley floor.

▷ *Continue north on US-395.*

On the northern outskirts of Lone Pine, US-395 passes the Tule *(TOO-lee)* Elk Refuge. Smallest of the elk subspecies, these mammals may be spotted anywhere between Lone Pine and Bishop.

Manzanar★
8mi north of Lone Pine. ◷*Open year-round daily dawn–dusk.* ◷*Closed Dec 25.* ✆*760-878-2932. www.nps.gov/manz.*
Site of the first of 10 Japanese-American relocation camps during World War II, this bleak square mile of scrub desert bears silent witness to the fear and ethnophobia that can arise in times of

international conflict. Manzanar was created in 1942 by executive order, which permitted the internment of Japanese Americans, many of them American citizens. Some 10,000 people resided here—amid high winds, dust-filled air and other harsh desert conditions—under surveillance until the war's end in 1945. The property was designated a national historic site in 1992.

Today all that remains are two pagoda-style gatehouses, a cemetery, stone garden walls and unpaved streets. An intrepive center exhibits documents, photographs and audiovisual presentations (◷ open Apr–Oct 9am–5.30pm; rest of the year 9am–4.30pm).

Independence
7mi north of Manzanar.

The seat of government for Inyo County, the town boasts a Classical Revival courthouse (1923) and the white clapboard **Commander's House** *(Main St. & US-395)*. Built in 1872 on the grounds of a nearby military outpost called Camp Independence, it was moved to town in 1887.

Eastern California Museum
155 N. Grant St. ◷ *Open year-round daily 10am–5pm.* ◷ *Closed major holidays.* &♿🅿✆760-878-0364. *www.inyocounty.us/ecmuseum.*

Notable for its documentation and photographs depicting life at Manzanar, this regional history museum also displays basketry, artifacts and stone tools of the Owens Valley Paiute and Panamint Shoshone of the Death Valley region. The museum grounds feature 1880s wooden buildings, mining equipment and farming implements relocated here to resemble a pioneer settlement.

▶ *Continue north on US-395 to Big Pine (28mi).*

Palisade Glacier
▶ *Excursion: 22mi round-trip from Big Pine via Glacier Lodge Rd.*

Glacier Lodge Road climbs the precipitous eastern face of the Sierra Nevada, terminating at the site of Glacier Lodge, which burned in 1998. From here, the southernmost of the Palisade glaciers can be seen tucked in the mountains. A steeply ascending trail *(21mi round-trip)* leads to the foot of the glaciers.

Ancient Bristlecone Pine Forest★
▶ *Excursion: 46mi round-trip from Big Pine. 13mi E of US-395 via Rte. 168 to Cedar Flat, then 10mi north on White Mountain Rd.*

Pride of the Inyo National Forest, this 28,000-acre designated botanical area protects the oldest living things on earth—the ancient bristlecone pine trees *(Pinus longaeva)*. Some of them have survived for more than 4,000 years. Knobbly and gnarled from enduring years of wind and ice, these small trees, which grow very slowly, attain heights averaging just 25ft and add less than an inch a century to their diameter.

Visit
◷ *Open late May–Oct daily, hours vary.* 🚍$3. ⚠♿🅿 ✆760-873-2500. *www.r5.fs.fed.us/inyo.* 🅐*The Schulman Grove visitor center was destroyed by fire in 2008; plans are underway to rebuild it. Note high elevations may cause altitude sickness.*

From Cedar Flat the road climbs through a mixed forest of piñon and juniper before reaching a turnout at **Sierra View Point** *(8mi)*. Here **views**★★ extend over the snow-capped Sierra Nevada. The paved road ends at **Schulman Grove** (10,100ft), where a visitor center is located. The Methuselah Trail *(4.25mi)* leads through the **Methuselah Grove**, which includes the world's oldest tree, the 4,600-year-old Methuselah Tree *(tree is unmarked)*.

Beyond Schulman Grove an unpaved road climbs to **Patriarch Grove**★ *(11mi)*, where the Patriarch, whose circumference measures nearly 37ft, ranks as the largest known bristlecone.

Bishop
16mi north of Big Pine.

The largest town in the Owens Valley, Bishop lies at the valley's northern end, serving as its commercial hub and an outfitting center. The town traces its origins to Samuel Bishop, a rancher who settled in the valley in 1861.

Owens Valley Paiute Shoshone Cultural Center★
2300 W. Line St.
⌖The museum is currently closed. For information, contact Bishop Chamber of Commerce ℘760-873-8405.
Located on the grounds of one of four Indian reservations in the Owens Valley, this museum interprets the history of the **Paiute** and **Shoshone** hunter-gatherers who occupied this region for 1,000 years.
Their stone tools, basketry, beadwork and other artifacts are exhibited, as are re-created traditional structures.

Laws Railroad Museum and Historical Site★
👥👤4.5mi northeast of Bishop via US-6.
🕐Open year-round daily 10am–4pm.
🕐Closed Jan 1, Easter Sunday, Thanksgiving Day, Dec 25. ☜Contribution requested. ♿P℘760-873-5950. www.lawsmuseum.org.
This small village depicts life in late 19C and early 20C Laws. The narrow-gauge Carson & Colorado Railway arrived in Laws in 1883, connecting the valley to the outside world. In 1900 the railroad was sold to the Southern Pacific, which continued to operate the line south from Laws to Keeler until 1960.
The site consists of some 20 structures, most of them moved here from various parts of the Owens Valley. Among the original structures are the Laws Depot and the Agent's House. On a portion of the original track stand boxcars and Old Engine No. 9.

Sequoia and Kings Canyon National Parks ★★

These two adjacent and jointly administered parks encompass the mighty granitic peaks of the southern Sierra Nevada, including 14,494ft Mt. Whitney, the highest point in the US south of Alaska. They also harbor the planet's finest stands of giant sequoias, the largest living trees on earth. Less developed and far less crowded than Yosemite National Park, Sequoia and Kings Canyon contain vast acres of wilderness accessible only on foot.

A BIT OF HISTORY
In the late 1880s, logging concerns were laying plans to fell giant sequoias (botanical name: *Sequoiadendron giganteum*) in western Sierra Nevada. The US Congress acted to protect the area: in

> ♿ **Michelin Map:** 585 B 9.
> 👥👤 **Kids:** Crystal Cave.

1890 a small parcel encompassing giant sequoia groves and watersheds that provided moisture to the San Joaquin Valley was designated as Sequoia National Park. In 1926 the park was doubled in size to include Mt. Whitney, and in 1940 Kings Canyon National Park was formed, encompassing General Grant National Park and a massive area of backcountry wilderness. Spectacular Kings Canyon itself, excluded from preservation because of its hydroelectric potential, was not incorporated into the park until 1965.

SEQUOIA NATIONAL PARK★★
Giant Forest★★★
30mi SE of Big Stump entrance, 16mi NE of Ash Mountain entrance.
Four of the largest known giant sequoias are found in this grove at the heart of Sequoia National Park. Trails allow serene acquaintance with the more

than 8,000 sequoias that flourish here. While here, stop in to the **Giant Forest Museum** (🕐 *open year-round daily, hours vary;* ☎*559-565-4880*) to see displays on the natural history of the grove and of giant sequoias. Across from the museum is the kid-friendly **Beetle Rock Nature Center** (🕐*open summer only*), with hands-on displays. Nearby Lodge-pole Village offers traveler facilities and amenities.

General Sherman Tree★

1.5mi north of Giant Forest Museum on Rte. 198 (Generals Hwy.).
Largest sequoia on earth, this behemoth rises 274.9ft, measures 102.6ft in circumference and is approximately 2,100 years old. Its lowest major branch hangs 130ft above the ground.

Congress Trail

500ft north of the General Sherman Tree on Rte. 198 (Generals Hwy.).
This paved loop trail (2mi) winds through a majestic forest of sequoias. Many of the park's most impressive trees stand at the far end of the trail, including the **President**, fourth largest tree in the world; and **Chief Sequoyah**, named for the 19C Cherokee who created a phonetic alphabet for his people. The botanical designation for the genus *Sequoiadendron* is thought to derive from the chief's name.

Crescent Meadow Road

South from Giant Forest Museum.
This scenic road accesses the Giant Forest's southern portion. The **Auto Log** (*1mi*) is a felled sequoia trunk large enough for cars to drive over it (*vehicles not permitted to drive over the log*). A short trail from a parking area (*.3mi*) leads to **Moro Rock★**; from its summit, the granite dome offers views the Great Western Divide to the east and the Kaweah River canyon to the west. A 400-step stairway ascends to the rock. The road loops past the **Triple Tree**, a three-trunked sequoia, then continues east to **Crescent Meadow** (*1.5mi*) where an easy loop trail offers views of the green bog's beauty.

Crystal Cave

🧍🧍*8mi south of Giant Forest Museum; 2mi on Generals Hwy. to turnoff on twisting access road.* 🔊*Visit by guided tour (45min) only, mid-May–Oct, call for hrs.* 💰*$11, children $6 (tickets sold at Lodgepole or Foothills visitor centers, not at cave's entrance, which is a 1.5hr drive from the visitor centers).* ☎*559-565-3759. www.sequoiahistory.org.*
One of 200 caves within the park, this subterranean wonderland reveals marble formations, including stalactites, stalagmites, draperies and flowstone.

KINGS CANYON NATIONAL PARK★

Big Stump Basin Trail

Access: 0.5mi from Big Stump Entrance.
The trail (*1mi loop*) leading through this basin reveals reminders of late 19C logging. The Mark Twain Stump, 24ft across, is all that remains of a giant sequoia felled in 1891 so that a section of it could be exhibited at the American Museum of Natural History in New York City.

Grant Grove★★

1mi west of Grant Grove Village.
A short loop trail (*.5mi*) passes among several noteworthy giants, among them the **General Grant Tree**, ranked as the world's third-largest sequoia. Towering 267ft with a circumference of 107ft, the tree was officially designated a living shrine to all American war dead in 1956. The **Gamlin Cabin** (*behind Grant Tree*), a reconstruction of an 1872 log cabin, contains some of the original structure's hand-hewn sugar-pine timbers.

Panoramic Point★

2.5mi northeast of Grant Grove Village; follow road to cabins, then turn right.
A trail (*.5mi round-trip*) leads up to this overlook, offering **views** of the austere, 14,000ft Sierra peaks to the east. Lake Hume is visible below the point to the north. From the overlook, the **Park Ridge Trail** (*4.7mi round-trip*) offers vistas of the high country to the east and to the west into the Central Valley.

Area Code: 559

GETTING THERE

To Sequoia National Park **Ash Mountain entrance** *(Rte. 198)*: from **Los Angeles** *(225mi)* I-5 north to Rte. 99 north to Rte. 198 east; from **San Francisco** *(275mi)* I-80 east to I-580 east to I-5 south to Rte. 198 east. To Kings Canyon National Park **Big Stump entrance** *(Rte. 180)*: from Los Angeles *(265mi)* I-5 north to Rte. 99 north to Rte. 180 east; from San Francisco *(240mi)* I-80 east to I-580 east to I-205 *(toward Manteca)* to Rte. 120 east to Rte. 99 south to Rte. 180 east. **Cedar Grove area** *(closed Nov–mid-Apr)*: 32mi past Big Stump entrance on Rte. 180. Closest **airport** *(84mi northwest)*: Fresno Yosemite International Airport (FYI) *(𝓅621-4500; www.flyfresno.org)*. Closest Greyhound **bus** *(𝓅800-231-2222; www.greyhound.com)* and Amtrak **train** *(𝓅800-872-7245; www.amtrak.com)* stations: Fresno, or Visalia *(51mi west)*.

GETTING AROUND

From late May–Aug, free shuttles ply two routes within the park; both stop at the Giant Forest Museum. In addition, the Sequoia Shuttle offers service from the city of Visalia to the Giant Forest Museum *($15 round-trip, park entrance included; 𝓅877-287-4453; www.sequoiashuttle.com)*. No gasoline is available within park.

WHEN TO GO

For seasonal road closures, check at visitor centers *(below)* or 𝓅565-3341; www.nps.gov/seki.

VISITOR INFORMATION

Sequoia and Kings Canyon National Parks *(𝓅565-3341; www.nps.gov/seki)*. Entry fee: $20/vehicle, valid for 7 days. Visitor centers: **Foothills**, **Giant Forest Museum** and **Grant Grove** *(open year-round daily)*; **Lodgepole** *(open Apr–Oct daily; rest of the year weekends only)*; **Cedar Grove** *(open late Jun–early Sept)*, and **Mineral King** *(open late May–early Sept)*.

ACCOMMODATIONS

Accommodations include rustic tent cabins, deluxe cabins, and modern lodges *($100–$350/day; meals-included packages available)*. For reservations for Wuksachi Village, contact **Delaware North Parks Services** *(𝓅866-807-3598; www.visitsequoia.com)*. For Kings Canyon, contact the **Kings Canyon Park Services** *(𝓅335-5500 or 866-522-6966; www.sequoia-kingscanyon.com)*. Rooms are also available in Three Rivers *(5mi west)*, Fresno and Visalia. **Camping** is by self-registration; Lodgepole campground accepts reservations *(𝓅800-365-2267; www.recreation.gov)*. **Backcountry camping** by permit only *(free, available at nearest ranger station)*.

Kings Canyon★★

North and east of Grant Grove Village.
Route 180 winds 30mi to Cedar Grove, hugging the walls of the canyon of the South Fork of the Kings River en route. From rim to base, the gorge measures 4,000ft to 8,000ft deep, making it one of the deepest canyons on the continent. Secreted within the lower canyon lies **Boyden Cavern**, a commercially managed marble cavern hung with luminous cave formations, including stalactites and stalagmites *(visit by 45min guided tour only, mid-May–mid-Sept daily ⏱Open 10am–5pm; Apr–mid-May & mid-Sept–Nov daily 11am–4pm; ⬕$11; 🅿 𝓅559-338-0959; www.kingscanyoneering.com)*.
From Boyden Cavern, Route 180 follows the South Fork to **Cedar Grove Village**, a cluster of park facilities and a small visitor center nestled below peaks that loom more than 3,000ft above.
At Roads End *(5mi beyond Cedar Grove Village)*, several trails lead into the backcountry; the Mist Falls Trail *(8mi)* follows the Kings River in a moderate ascent to **Mist Falls**★, where the river washes down a sheer granite face.

Yosemite National Park ★★★

A crowning jewel of America's national park system, this 1,170sq mi parcel in the Sierra Nevada encompasses alpine lakes and meadowlands, awe-inspiring granitic peaks, waterfalls and groves of giant sequoia trees. The rare natural beauty of Yosemite Valley attracts more than four million visitors annually.

A BIT OF HISTORY

Human History – In recent centuries, the area has been home to **Miwok**-speaking Native Americans. In 1851 a band of Caucasian volunteers, the **Mariposa Battalion**, set out to apprehend a Native chieftain accused of raiding nearby trading posts. Descending into the valley, the battalion named it Yosem-i-ty, apparently a corruption of the Miwok word for "grizzly bear."

Yosemite's beauty came to widespread attention through works of artists and journalists. Fearing commercial development, concerned citizens prompted Congress to pass the Yosemite Park Act in 1864, putting 39,200 acres and the Mariposa Grove of Big Trees under the stewardship of the state of California.

- **Michelin Map:** 585 B 8 and maps pp344, 349.
- **Info:** 209-372-0200. www.nps.gov/yose.
- **Location:** Most facilities are concentrated in Yosemite Village, which houses the valley's main visitor center, museums, shops and food concessions. Curry Village is the supply center for the eastern end. The premiere attraction is Yosemite Valley, a 7mi-long, half-mile-wide depression lying at 3,950ft. Granite peaks towering 2,000–3,000ft higher rim the valley, which is traced by the Merced River.

A Voice in the Wilderness – In 1868 a wanderer named **John Muir** (1838–1914) settled as a sawyer in Yosemite. In 1875 he wrote articles proposing that Yosemite be declared a national park. His efforts on Yosemite's behalf were the first in a long career as the nation's foremost spokesman for conservation. He is credited with the 1892 founding of the **Sierra Club**, a preeminent organization dedicated to preservation and expansion of wildlife and wilderness areas.

In 1890 Congress passed the Yosemite National Park bill, which set aside the

Hiking in the wilderness of Kings Canyon National Park offers spectacular views

National Park Service/www.nps.gov

wilderness around Yosemite Valley and Mariposa Grove. Not until 1905, after lobbying by Muir and others, did California cede the valley and Mariposa Grove back to the federal government to be incorporated in the park. Yosemite today encompasses 1,170sq mi. In 1984 it was named a UNESCO World Heritage Site.

Rock-Solid Testimony – The granite that characterizes Yosemite's landscape began as underground magma, forming from 200 million to 50 million years ago. Through the collision of continental tectonic plates, these granite masses, called batholiths, were forced upward. River courses became steeper, cutting into the granite and forming canyons. With the coming of the Ice Age, glaciers began to flow through the river courses, gouging out large U-shaped valleys.

Flora and Fauna – With elevations ranging from 2,000ft to 13,000ft, Yosemite offers an appealing diversity of both flora and fauna. Its lower elevations are covered in ponderosa and incense cedar, California black oak, willows, alders and cottonwoods; lodgepole pine, whitebark pine and red firs grow on higher slopes; white firs and quaking aspen grow at many elevations.

Park animals include mountain lions, black bears, badgers, weasels and deer mice. Visitors may encounter mule deer, California ground squirrels and coyotes. Common birds include Stellar's jays, Brewer's blackbirds, juncos and robins. The park also contains nesting grounds of endangered **peregrine falcons**.

YOSEMITE VALLEY★★★
Enter the valley at the intersection of Rte. 120 (from Big Oak Flat Entrance) and Rte. 140 (from Arch Rock entrance); .8mi after this junction the road splits into a pair of one-way thoroughfares separated by the Merced River. Note: Sights below are generally organized to reflect the shuttle route.

Curry Village
Shuttle stop 13b. Nestled directly beneath Glacier Point, this group of shops, eateries and lodgings is the center of visitor facilities in the eastern end of the valley. The village was established by David and Jennie Curry in 1899 as Camp Curry, offering inexpensive tent accommodations.

Half Dome★★★
This unique geologic landmark rises 4,800ft above the northeast end of the valley. Scientists believe glacial action cracked what was once a full granite dome along a vertical weakness, leaving only half of the formation in place. Relatively rare, domes such as those found throughout Yosemite are formed as surface rock exfoliates (or falls away) in concentric scales like an onion skin.

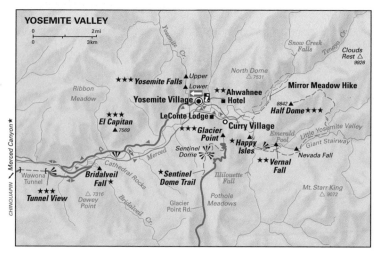

Half Dome, Yosemite National Park

© Robert Holmes/California Travel & Tourism Commission

Yosemite Village

Shuttle stops 2 & 10. At **Yosemite Valley Visitor Center**, geologic and natural history displays and slide presentations tell the story of the area. The **Yosemite Theater** *(rear of the visitor center)* features live dramas, musicals and films, and is renowned for one-man dramatizations depicting John Muir *(most summer nights)*. The film *Spirit of Yosemite* introduces the park.

Yosemite Museum

◷*Open year-round daily 9am–5pm; extended summer hrs.* ♿ ℘*209-372-0200. www.nps.gov/yose.*
This museum displays Miwok artifacts and changing exhibits. **People of the Ahwahnee** *(behind the museum)* interprets the Native American lifestyle in 1872, some 20 years after contact with Europeans; the re-created Miwok village features reproductions of Ahwahneechee bark structures.

Ansel Adams Gallery

◷*Open year-round daily 9am–5pm. Extended summer hrs.* ♿ ℘*209-372-4413. www.anseladams.com.*
This photography gallery features the work of **Ansel Adams** (1900–84), America's preeminent landscape photographer. Adams' photos of Yosemite are considered classics, and prints from his original plates are offered for sale.

Ahwahnee Hotel★★

0.8mi east of Yosemite Village center.
This massive granite-and-concrete hotel (1927) is Yosemite's largest, most elegant structure. The interior features Native American rugs and motifs echoing the geometric patterns of the art deco style. Floor-to-ceiling windows and wrought-iron chandeliers enhance the majestic proportions of the cavernous **dining room** *(130ft long by 34ft high).*

Yosemite Falls★★★

Trailhead 0.5mi west of Yosemite Village.
A paved trail *(0.5mi round-trip)* provides a stunning approach to the foot of these falls, formed as the waters of Yosemite Creek plunge 2,425ft in three stages. From the trailhead, both the **lower fall** (320ft) and the wispy **upper fall** (1,430ft) can be seen above, though the middle cascade (675ft) is only partially visible. A steep trail leads up the west side of the falls to a vantage point above the upper fall *(7mi round-trip; trailhead accessible from Yosemite Lodge shuttle stop).*

LeConte Memorial Lodge

This granite, Tudor Revival structure (1903) sports a floor-to-ceiling fireplace. The lodge serves as a Sierra Club reading room and public information center.

Area Code: 209

GETTING THERE

BY CAR: Yosemite's five principal entrances are **Big Oak Flat** (Rte. 120), **Hetch Hetchy** (Rte. 120), **Arch Rock** (Rte. 140), **South** (Rte. 41) and Tioga Pass (Rte. 120; summer only). From **San Francisco** *(193mi):* I-580 east to I-205 east to Rte. 120 east to Big Oak Flat entrance. From **Los Angeles** *(313mi):* I-5 north to I-99 north; at Fresno take Rte. 41 north to South entrance. From other points via **Merced:** Rte. 140 east to Arch Rock entrance.

BY AIR: Closest airport: Fresno Yosemite International Airport (FYI) 95mi; (℘559-621-4500; www.flyfresno. org); bus service connects to Yosemite.

BY BUS AND TRAIN: YARTS (Yosemite Area Regional Transportation System; ℘388-9589 or 877-989-2787; www. yarts.com) offers daily shuttle service to from Merced and Mariposa *(year-round)* and from Mammoth Lakes, and Lee Vining *(seasonal service).* Stops are convenient to parking, lodging and connecting transportation. VIA Adventures (℘384-1315; www.via-adventures.com) provides bus service from Merced *(84mi).* The closest Amtrak train station (℘800-872-7245; www.amtrak.com) is at Merced (fare includes bus transfer).

GETTING AROUND

Roads in Yosemite Valley become extremely congested during the summer, and sights in the valley's eastern portion are inaccessible by private vehicle. Visitors are encouraged to park in lots at Curry Village or Yosemite Village and take the free **Yosemite Shuttle** *(daily year-round; departures every 10–20min)* to points of interest. Free **shuttles** also run in summer between the Wawona area and Mariposa Grove, and between Tuolumne Meadows and Olmsted Point. There is limited short-term public parking at Yosemite Village, Lower Yosemite Falls and Merced River picnic areas. **Biking** on designated paths is a great way

to get around the eastern portion of the valley; rentals are available at Curry Village and Yosemite Lodge. Obey posted speed limits; wildlife often appear unexpectedly on the roadways. Chains may be required on some park roads in winter.

GENERAL INFORMATION

WHEN TO GO: Waterfalls slow in late summer, and dry up by fall. In fall, color in the park is lovely, but be prepared for cold nights. Several roads (Tioga Pass Rd., Glacier Point Rd. and Mariposa Grove Rd.) are closed to vehicles in winter. Wildflowers abound in spring and the waterfalls are at their most stupendous.

VISITOR INFORMATION: For information on seasonal hours, check the park's website *(www.nps. gov/yose).* The National Park Service (℘209-372-0200) publishes the free periodical *Yosemite Guide,* with up-to-date schedules and news about seasonal closures; view it online at the website above or order a copy by mail. **Yosemite Valley Visitor Center** *(Yosemite Village, shuttle stops 6 and 9)* is open year-round daily 9am–5pm. **Tuolumne Meadows Visitor Center** *(south of Tioga Rd.)* is open late May–mid-October daily 9am–5pm. **Big Oak Flat Information Station** (open May–Sept) and **Wawona Information Station** have limited hours.

HOURS AND FEES: The park is open daily year-round; $20/car, valid for 7 days; pay at entrance.

ACCOMMODATIONS: Reservations are strongly recommended; contact **Yosemite Reservations** (℘801-559-4884 for lodging; ℘877-444-6777 for camping; www.yosemitepark.com). The Ahwahnee Hotel and High Sierra Camps should be reserved a year in advance.

The Ahwahnee offers hotel rooms and cottages *($429–$543).* **Wawona Hotel** *($150–$230)* and **Yosemite Lodge** *($109–$220)* provide standard and upgraded hotel rooms. Tent cabins, wooden cabins and motel rooms can be found at Curry Village *($94–$179)*, Tuolumne Meadows Lodge *($94)*, and White Wolf Lodge *($83–$129)*. **High Sierra Camps** *(Jul–early Sept, reservations by lottery; applications available Sept–Oct annually)* offer dormitory-style cabins in conjunction with 4- to 7-day guided hikes or saddle trips *(☏559-253-5674)*. Lodging is also available in nearby Oakhurst, Fish Camp, Lee Vining and Bass Lake.

Campsites in the park can be reserved up to five months in advance through the **National Park Service Reservation Center** *(☏877-444-6777; http://www.recreation.gov.* Housekeeping Camp (campsites with shelters and cots) are also available spring–fall *($79; contact Yosemite Reservations: ☏559-253-5635; www.yosemitepark.com)*. Permits *(available 24 wks to 2 days in advance from Wilderness Permit Stations, ☏372-0200)* are required for **backcountry camping**.

AMENITIES: Shops and restaurants are located at Yosemite Valley, Tuolumne Meadows and Wawona. Gas is available at Crane Flat, Tuolumne Meadows (closed in winter), Wawona and El Portal.

USEFUL NUMBERS

Road and Weather Info	☏372-0200
Road Service	☏372-8320
(repair and towing)	
Ski Conditions	☏372-8430
(Badger Pass)	

RECREATION
SUMMER

More than 800mi of trails provide excellent **hiking** and **backpacking**. Trailhead quotas necessitate reservations for summer hikes *(mid-May–Sept; $5 plus $5/person)* through Wilderness Permits *(☏372-0740; www.nps.gov/yose/wilderness)*. Guided backpacking trips *(late Jun–early Sept)* and **rock climbing classes** *(mid-Apr–mid-Oct daily)* are available through the Yosemite Mountaineering School & Guide Service *(☏372-8344)*. Guided horseback rides *(☏372-8427; www.yosemiteparks.com)* depart from the stables in Wawona, Yosemite Valley and Tuolumne Meadows. **Bicycles** can be rented at Yosemite Lodge and Curry Village. A California license is required for **fishing** *(available at Yosemite Village and Wawona store)*. Rental rafts for **rafting** on the Merced River are available at Curry Village *(daily Jun–mid-July conditions permitting, life vests provided, ☏372-4386)*.

WINTER

Downhill and **cross-country skiing** instruction, rentals and tours are available at Badger Pass. **Snowboarding** lessons & rentals are also offered. A free ski shuttle departs twice daily from Curry Village, the Ahwahnee Hotel and Yosemite Lodge.

TOURS: Narrated **tram/bus tours** *(2–8hrs)* depart from Yosemite Lodge; one week advance reservations suggested *(☏372-4386)*.

Happy Isles★

As the Merced River tumbles into the valley here, it encircles these two small islands, accessible by footbridge. A **nature center** beside the river displays life-size dioramas of woodland scenes. Behind the nature center, an interpretive boardwalk trail leads through a pleasant fen, or marsh.

Vernal Fall Trail

3mi round-trip; trailhead at Happy Isles bridge.

This paved trail ascends the steep canyon of the Merced River before crossing a bridge *(.8mi)* which offers a view of 317ft **Vernal Fall★★**. Beyond the bridge, the often-slippery Mist Trail climbs above the river, soon reaching a man-made stairway of 500 steps that leads to the brink of the fall, with lovely Emerald Pool upstream.

The 594ft **Nevada Fall** lies a strenuous climb farther up *(7mi round-trip from Happy Isles)*. From there, vigorous hikers may continue to the top of Half Dome *(above; 16.8mi round-trip from Happy Isles),* scaling the final stretch of precipitous rock by a cable stairway.

Mirror Meadow Hike

2mi round-trip; trailhead at post V26.
A paved trail follows the west side of Tenaya Creek to this small meadow.

EXCURSION TO GLACIER POINT★★★

60mi round-trip
This scenic drive leads to Glacier Point, a sheer rock cliff towering above Curry Village. From the valley floor, an arduous trail *(4.8mi)* climbs 3,200ft to the point's summit.

▶ *From Yosemite Village, follow signs to Rte. 41 east, also called Wawona or Fresno Rd.*

El Capitan★★★

An open meadowland north of the road affords a superb view of this Yosemite landmark. The tallest unbroken cliff in the world, "the Chief" measures 3,593ft from base to summit. Composed of an extremely hard granite that resists weathering, its polished, yellow-hued surface attracts rock climbers, who often can be spotted high upon its face.

Bridalveil Fall★

A short paved path leads to the base of this filmy fall, formed as Bridalveil Creek plunges 620ft.

Tunnel View★★★

From the turnout at the north side of the Wawona Tunnel extends a classic view into Yosemite Valley. El Capitan dominates the northwest end, and on the south side rise humped Cathedral Rocks, Bridalveil Fall, Sentinel Rock and, in the distance, the distinctive shapes of Half Dome and Clouds Rest.
Beyond the Wawona Tunnel, Route 41 hugs the forested eastern slopes above the Merced River Canyon.

▶ *At the Chinquapin crossroads (post W5), turn east onto Glacier Point Rd. (may be closed Nov–May) and continue 1.9mi to turnout (post G1).*

This **view** overlooks the **Merced Canyon**★. The canyon's dry north side is sere, while the wetter south side is made up of green, lightly forested hills.

Tunnel View

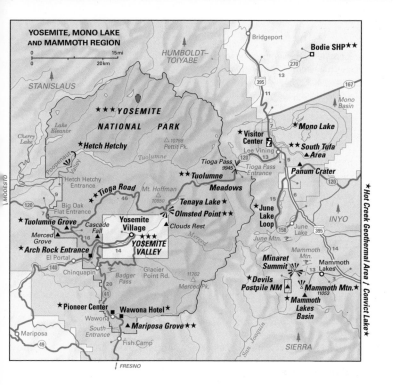

YOSEMITE, MONO LAKE AND MAMMOTH REGION

Sentinel Dome Trail★

Trailhead .1mi beyond post G8; 2.2mi round-trip.

A generally level trail leads through upland meadows to a paved fire road at the base of **Sentinel Dome**. *Follow the road to the right around the side of the dome and ascend its gently sloping north side.* The top of the dome affords a **panorama**★★★ that includes Yosemite Valley from El Capitan to Half Dome, and above it, Little Yosemite Valley and Clouds Rest. To the east rise the peaks of the Clark Range.

Glacier Point★★★

One of the nation's most spectacular viewpoints, this rocky peak hovers 3,000ft above the valley floor.

From here, Vernal and Nevada Falls and Little Yosemite Valley are visible to the east behind looming Half Dome, while Yosemite Falls pours down a cliff face to the northwest.

SOUTH YOSEMITE★

Map above.

Wawona Area

Since the mid-19C, the Wawona area has attracted travelers to its Mariposa Grove of Big Trees.

Galen Clark, a homesteader who settled here in 1856, fought to preserve the giant sequoias, and established Wawona's first lodging house. This portion of Yosemite was not incorporated into the park until 1932; a number of private cabins still stand along the Merced River.

Pioneer Yosemite History Center★

From the parking lot off Rte. 41 adjacent to the Wawona Hotel grounds, walk away from the road toward the old gray barn. ○*Open Jun–Sept daily 9am–5pm; rest of the year hours vary.* ℗ ☏*209-372-0200.*

Most of these historic structures depicting life in late 19C Yosemite were moved to this location from various parts of the park. The gray barn, built in the late 1880s to service stages traveling the

The Big Trees

Considered the largest things on earth, California's giant sequoias grow naturally only in scattered pockets along the western flanks of the Sierra Nevada mountain range, at elevations of 5,000–7,000ft. The giant trees sprout from tiny seeds lodged in cones the size of a chicken's egg (only one seed in a billion grows to gianthood), and it takes centuries for a tree to reach maturity. The high tannin content of the bark thwarts insect damage and heartrot, and the bark itself grows up to 18in thick, serving as a shield against fire. Giant sequoias grow extremely fast, adding as much as 500 board feet annually, but their roots penetrate a mere 3–5ft beneath the soil's surface, making them vulnerable to toppling from high winds or heavy snow. Excessive foot or auto traffic around their bases can further weaken the root systems of the venerable monarchs.

Sequoia 270ft   *Statue of Liberty 305ft*   *Coast Redwood 365ft*

Michelin

Wawona Road, is now used as a horse stable. The covered bridge across the Merced River (1875) served as the main thoroughfare across the river until 1931. The cluster of 19C structures on the west side of the river includes three private cabins, a blacksmith shop, a cavalry office, a ranger building and a Wells Fargo office. *Pamphlet available in the kiosk beside the covered bridge.*

Wawona Hotel★

Built in the 1870s, the two-story white frame hotel is fronted by a comfortable veranda; behind it and to the east lie clapboard cottages. To the west is a small, 19C Victorian cottage once used by Thomas Hill, the respected landscape artist. ○*Open periodically for art exhibits; check* Yosemite Guide *for schedule.* ℘209-375-9531.

Mariposa Grove of Big Trees★★

2mi east of South Entrance. Vehicles not permitted; parking available at post S2. Narrated tram tour departs May–Oct daily 9:30am–5pm, every 20min. 1hr 15min. ∞*$25.50. Reservations advised* ℘209-372-4386.

Spread over 250 acres, this grove encompasses roughly 400 mature giant sequoias. The narrated tram ride stops at major attractions. Alternatively, a hiking trail loops and branches through Mariposa's upper and lower groves.

Fallen Monarch – This tree fell to the ground several hundred years ago, but the amazingly resistant sequoia heartwood of its trunk has not decayed. Fallen sequoias can exist on the ground for 2,000 years or more.

Bachelor and Three Graces – These four trees demonstrate how sequoias, though enormous (the Three Graces each measure over 200ft), can grow in dense stands.

Grizzly Giant – Leaning at a 17-degree angle, this 2,700-year-old tree is one of the largest and oldest in the park, measuring 209ft tall and 96ft around at its base. The California Tunnel Tree *(150ft downhill)* is an example of the late 19C fashion of boring tunnels through the bases of these enormous trees.

Fallen Wawona Tunnel Tree – *Upper grove; about 2mi.* This famed giant had a 10ft-by-26ft tunnel cut through it in 1881. The impact of so much disturbance to the tree's shallow root system by spectators took its toll, and the tree toppled in the winter of 1968–69.

Mariposa Grove Museum
Upper grove, about 1.8mi. ◷Open mid-May–Labor Day daily 9.30am–5pm. ☏209-372-0200.
Housed in a replica of the original log cabin that Galen Clark built here in 1864, the museum features an exhibit on the natural history of the giant sequoias.

TIOGA ROAD★★
46mi one-way. Map p349.
◷Closed Nov–May.
One of the most scenic wilderness drives on the continent, this west-east road across the Yosemite high country passes through coniferous forests, granitic terrain and rolling alpine meadowland.

▷ *Begin at intersection of Tioga Rd. & Big Oak Flat Rd., just east of Crane Flat.*

After about 14mi, the forests become sparser and the vista opens onto the stone-clad landscape of the High Sierra, with 10,850ft Mt. Hoffman towering to the east and the Clark Range visible on the southeastern horizon.
A roadside turnout (T18) identifies five of the park's common coniferous trees. A short distance farther, **Clouds Rest** (9,926ft) looms into view to the east.

Olmsted Point★★
This renowned viewpoint is named for landscape architect Frederick Law Olmsted. Panels explain geologic processes and identify visible peaks. A trail *(.25mi)* leads to a dome overlooking Tenaya Canyon, from Half Dome to Tenaya Lake.

Tenaya Lake★
This large, alpine lake is skirted by white-sand beaches and shaded picnic spots. Named for an Ahwahneechee chief, the lake formed in a depression gouged by the Tuolumne Glacier.

Tuolumne Meadows★★
✕This famed alpine meadowland lies at 8,600ft, braided by the Tuolumne River. Tuolumne offers a visitor center *(◷open summer only, 9am–5pm)*, lodging, restaurants and numerous backcountry trails. Both the 211mi **John Muir Trail** and the 2,350mi **Pacific Crest Trail** pass through here.
Just east of the visitor center, the road runs below sharply angled Lembert Dome to the north and follows the Dana Fork of the Tuolumne River to Dana Meadows. Here it exits the park at 9,945ft **Tioga Pass**, the highest roadway pass in the state.
After leaving the park, Route 120 descends sharply along the north face of Lee Vining Canyon and continues on to its junction with US-395 *(13mi)*.

ADDITIONAL SIGHTS
Arch Rock Entrance★
Yosemite's picturesque entrance is named for the two boulders under which Route 140 (the Merced Road) passes as it enters the park. **Cascade Fall** *(2mi north of entrance)* tumbles off the canyon walls beside the river.

Tuolumne Grove of Big Trees★
More intimate and less developed than the Mariposa Grove, this stand contains 25 mature giant sequoias. Nearby **Merced Grove** is the smallest in the park *(accessible via a 2mi hike down a fire road off the new Big Oak Flat Rd.)*.

Hetch Hetchy★
From Yosemite Valley, exit park via Rte. 120 (Big Oak Flat entrance), turn right on Evergreen Rd. and right on Hetch Hetchy Rd.
The Tuolumne River was dammed in 1923, creating this reservoir to provide water and power for San Francisco. At the reservoir, a bridge *(foot traffic only)* crosses O'Shaughnessy Dam and provides access to the northern side, where trails follow the water's edge.

Lying inland within a two-hour drive north of San Francisco, Napa Valley and Sonoma County thrive on the sunshine and fertile soil that produce grapes for some of North America's finest wines. Though vineyards flourish along California's inland coastal areas from Eureka to San Diego County, and even as far east as the foothills of the Sierra Nevada, these two areas have garnered a reputation as the state's preeminent winemaking regions. Visitors and locals flock here, drawn by the temperate climate, varied natural beauty and acclaimed wineries.

Highlights

1 Breathing the winey draft of cool air as you enter almost any wine cave, but especially at **Buena Vista** (p368)

2 The tasting vineyard at **St.-Supéry** (p359)

3 A soak in a mineral pool in **Calistoga** (p361)

4 Picking perfect produce on the plaza at the weekly farmers market in **Sonoma** (p366)

5 A dawn balloon flight over **Napa Valley** (p356)

In the late 17C, cuttings of Criolla grapevines traveled north with the Franciscan padres as they established the Alta California mission chain. In the early 1830s, a French immigrant, Jean-Louis Vignes established a vineyard near Los Angeles using cuttings of European grapevines, and by the mid-19C winemaking had become one of Southern California's principal industries.

In 1857 **Agoston Haraszthy** (1812–69), a Hungarian immigrant and an experienced winemaker, purchased an estate in Sonoma County and cultivated Tokay vine cuttings imported from his homeland. Haraszthy distributed some 100,000 cuttings and trained area grape growers to the extent that the quality of California wines steadily improved, and areas around San Francisco began to supersede Southern California as the state's principal viticultural region.

Boom and Bust – Among the wineries established in the late 19C were **Gundlach-Bundschu (1)** (1858), founded by Bavarian immigrant Jacob Gundlach, and **Charles Krug (2)** (1861), the Napa Valley's first winery, established on land acquired by Krug, a native of Prussia. **Beringer**, **Beaulieu** and **Inglenook** were also established around this time.

In the late 19C, California grapevines fell prey to phylloxera, a root louse that decimated entire vineyards and severely hampered wine production. Somewhat recovered by the early 20C, the wine

Napa Valley Vineyards

Ballooning in Napa Valley

industry faced Prohibition when the US Congress ratified the 18th Amendment outlawing the manufacture, sale, importation and transportation of intoxicating liquors in the US.

Prohibition to the Present – Prohibition brought California's winemaking industry to a near-standstill. When it was repealed by the 21st Amendment in 1933, grape growers and winemakers were confronted with rebuilding the industry, a process slowed by the Great Depression. Not until the early 1970s did the demand for fine table wines increase and California's wine industry become fully re-established. In recent decades the Wine Country has experienced tremendous development. Besides significant increases in vineyard acreage, the late 20C witnessed an explosion of small-scale operations.

Wine Growing – The Wine Country is organized into **Approved Viticultural Areas**, each suitable for the cultivation of certain types of grapes. Growing conditions vary among these areas, depending upon soil type and climate. **Weather** is considered the most important factor in the cultivation of wine grapes, which require a long growing season of hot days and cool nights. The average annual rainfall of 33in occurs mostly between November and May. Differences in elevation, proximity to the sea and exposure to sun, fog and wind create numerous microclimates.

Best adapted to Wine Country growing conditions is the Cabernet Sauvignon, a small, blue-black grape from the Médoc district of France's Bordeaux region, which produces a rich, full red wine. Some of California's finest white wines are made from Chardonnay, the premier white grape of France's Chablis and Burgundy regions. Other popular reds include Pinot Noir and Zinfandel; Sauvignon Blanc is a white grape that grows well in cooler areas.

The Region Today – Most visitors come here for the wineries, of course, but even if your interest in wines and winemaking is limited, the Wine Country is an inspiring, even fun place to be. Picnicking is one of the joys of spending time here, especially if you stock your basket at one of the area's many excellent food shops. In addition to winery visits you can hike one of the invigorating trails crisscrossing the state parks; float over the vineyards in a hot-air balloon; admire historic old or innovative new architecture; dine out in a world-renowned restaurant; or have a relaxing soak at one of Calistoga's mineral-spring spas.

Area Code: 707

GENERAL INFORMATION

VISITOR INFORMATION

Maps and information on recreation, accommodations and seasonal events are available from: **Napa Valley Tourist Bureau** (6488 Washington St., Yountville CA 94599; ℘944-1558; www.napavalleytouristbureau.com); **Napa Valley Vintners Association** (899 Adams St., Ste. H, St. Helena ℘963-3388; www.napavintners.com); **Sonoma Valley Visitors Bureau**, (453 1st St. E., Sonoma ☏996-1090; www.sonomavalley.com); **Sonoma County Tourism Bureau** (420 Aviation Blvd., Ste. 106, Santa Rosa ℘522-5800; www.sonomacounty.com); **Sonoma County Vintners** (420 Aviation Blvd., Ste. 106, Santa Rosa ℘522-5840; www.sonomawine.com); **Santa Rosa Convention & Visitors Bureau** (9 Fourth St., Santa Rosa ℘577-8674 or 800-404-7673; www.visitsantarosa.com); **Russian River Wine Road** (Healdsburg; ℘433-4335 or 800-723-6336; www.wineroad.com). For the **Napa Valley Guidebook** and the **Sonoma County Guidebook** ($5.95 each plus $4.45 tax & shipping), contact Vintage Publications (℘800-651-8953, www.napavalleyguidebook.com).

ACCOMMODATIONS

Bed-and-breakfast inns are located throughout the Wine Country. Larger **hotels** are located in Napa, Sonoma and Santa Rosa. Reservation services: **Napa Valley Reservations Unlimited** (℘252-1985 or 800-251-6272; www.napavalleyreservations.com), **Wine Country Concierge** (℘252-4472; www.winetrip.com); and **Bed and Breakfast Association of Sonoma Valley** (℘800-969-4667; www.sonomabb.com). Reserve well in advance during summer and fall. **Camping** is available at Lake Sonoma (℘431-4533). For Bothe-Napa Valley State Park and Sugarloaf Ridge State Park, contact Reserve America (℘800-444-7275; www.reserveamerica.com).

RECREATION

Ballooning – Balloon tours (1–4hrs) depart at sunrise year-round. Prices average $220/person and may include a champagne brunch after the flight. Prices may vary with number of passengers; inquire when booking (advance reservations required). Napa Valley companies include **Adventures Aloft** (℘800-944-4408; www.napavalleyaloft.com); **Bonaventura Balloon Company** (℘800-359-6272; www.bonaventuraballoons.com); and **Napa Valley Balloons Inc**. (℘944-0228 or 800-253-2224; www.napavalleyballoons.com). In Sonoma County: **Above the Wine Country Balloons and Tours** (℘829-9850).

Biking – You'll find rental shops offering trail information in Napa, Sonoma and Calistoga. Weekend and day **bicycle tours** ($149/day including rental) as well as hiking, canoeing and kayaking trips (all-inclusive, prices vary according to length of trip) offered by **Getaway Adventures** (℘800-499-2453; www.getawayadventures.com).

Farmers' Markets – St. Helena (Crane Park, St. Helena; May–Oct Fri 7.30am–noon; ℘486-2662), **Santa Rosa** (4th & B Sts., Santa Rosa; mid-May–Aug Wed 5pm–8.30pm; ℘524-2123), **Sonoma** (Sonoma Plaza, early Apr–Oct Tue 5.30pm–dusk; Depot Park, year-round Fri 9am–noon; ℘538-7023); **Healdsburg** (Healdsburg Plaza at North & Vine Sts.; late May–late Nov Sat 9am–noon & at Town Plaza at Matheson & Healdsburg Ave. Jun–Oct Tue 4pm–6.30pm; ℘431-1956).

Sightseeing – California Wine Country Tours by motor coach through Marin County to the Sonoma Valley (9hrs; depart San Francisco Fisherman's Wharf year-round daily 9.15am; $68; Red & White Fleet; ℘415-673-2900; www.redandwhite.com). **Napa Valley Wine Train** departs from downtown Napa; dining and wine tasting on a 3hr excursion (lunch and dinner; $49–$149; ℘253-2111 or 800-427-4124; www.winetrain.com).

ADDRESSES

For a more complete selection of hotels and restaurants, see the red-cover **Michelin Guide San Francisco, Bay Area and the Wine Country.**

STAY

Meadowood – *900 Meadowood Lane, St. Helena. 707-963-3646 or 800-458-8080. www.meadowood.com. 85 rooms.* A private estate built in the early 1960s, this world-class resort off Napa's Silverado Trail offers heavenly service. Rustic cottages are set in a wooded grove; rooms have private terraces and stone fireplaces. A full-service spa and a superb restaurant are at hand.

La Résidence – *4066 St. Helena Hwy., Napa. 707-253-0337. www.laresidence.com. 26 rooms.* A gracious bed-and-breakfast complex in a rural setting near the town of Napa, La Résidence sprawls across two acres of gardens framed by towering oak and pine trees. Handsome antique decor and personalized hospitality make this a good Wine Country choice.

Villagio Inn & Spa – *6481 Washington St., Yountville. 707-944-8877. www.villagio.com. 112 rooms.* Two-story villas surround lush gardens and vineyards, fountains, swimming pools and tennis courts at this resort and spa, reminiscent of a Tuscan village. Rates include a welcome bottle of wine, afternoon tea and a champagne continental breakfast.

Beasley House – *1910 First St., Napa. 707-257-1649. www beazleyhouse.com. 11 rooms.* Napa's first bed-and-breakfast when it opened in 1981, this brown 1902 Colonial Revival mansion still ranks among the valley's best. Five rooms occupy a replicated carriage house; all lie within walking distance of downtown.

Camellia Inn – *211 North St., Healdsburg. 707-433-8182. www.camellia inn.com. 9 rooms.* A home-like hideaway just steps off the charming plaza in Russian River Valley town of Healdsburg, this Italianate-style Victorian hotel offers nightly wine tastings and eclectic antique decor.

Sonoma Hotel – *110 W. Spain St., Sonoma. 707-996-2996. www. sonomahotel.com. 16 rooms.* From the stone fireplace in the lobby to the claw-foot tubs in the guest rooms, this hotel exudes an old-west feel. The hotel is perfectly located right on the plaza in Sonoma, within walking distance of excellent restaurants and tourist sites.

EAT

La Toque – *1314 McKinstry St., in the Westin Hotel, Napa. Dinner only. Closed Mon & Tue. 707-257-5157. www. latoque.com.* **Contemporary French**. Straightforward French-inspired cuisine utilizing the best of local ingredients appears on the the nightly changing prix-fixe menus (cheese course is optional). You may find delicacies like Sonoma foie gras, diver scallops, and Niman Ranch beef and pork. Coffee and mignardises follow dessert.

John Ash & Co. – *4330 Barnes Rd., Santa Rosa. 707-527-7687. www.vintners inn.com.* **Californian**. In a secluded restaurant surrounded by vineyards at the Vintners Inn, 4mi north of Santa Rosa, chef Jeffrey Madura blends fresh seasonal ingredients with his own enthusiasm in dishes like pesto-crusted Alaskan halibut over mushroom ravioli.

Tra Vigne – *1050 Charter Oak Ave., St. Helena. 707-963-4444. www. travignerestaurant.com.* **Italian**. Italian for "among the vines," Tra Vigne reflects founder Michael Chiarello's success in bringing southern Italy to northern California. He has since moved on, but the kitchen continues his tradition in such dishes as pork tenderloin wrapped in grape leaves with fig and apple tart.

Mustards Grill – *7399 St. Helena Hwy. (Rte. 29), Yountville. 709-944-2424. www.mustardsgrill.com.* **Contemporary**. A long-standing Napa Valley favorite, this casual ranch-style restaurant draws winemakers and industry VIPs for its fresh cuisine and top-notch wine list. The menu ranges across American regional dishes with nods to Continental and Asian, from seared ahi tuna to barbecued baby back ribs. Try the sublimely thin and crispy onion rings with house-made ketchup.

Napa Valley★★

Cradled between two elongated mountain ranges, this renowned valley extends about 35mi from San Pablo Bay northwest to Mount St. Helena. Many of California's most prestigious wineries are clustered along Route 29 as it passes through Napa, Yountville, Oakville, Rutherford, St. Helena and Calistoga. Others dot the more tranquil Silverado Trail to the east and the intervening crossroads.

SIGHTS
Sights in the Napa Valley are described from south to north.

Napa
Originally settled in 1832, this sprawling city on the banks of the Napa River experienced its first significant population boom during the post-Gold Rush period. Banking and riverboat traffic transformed Napa into a mid-19C shipping and administrative center.

Downtown
1st & 2nd Sts. between Main & Randolph Sts.
At the heart of downtown Napa, the **Goodman Building** (1901), with its gray stone facade *(1219 First St.)*, is now home to the research library and museum of the Napa County Historical Society. Other noteworthy buildings include the Italianate 1879 **Napa Opera House** *(1018 Main St.)* recently renovated as a performance space; and the ornate **Winship-Smernes Building** *(948 Main St.)*. The Oxbow District, near the banks of the Napa River, has blossomed in recent years with the arrival of chic shops, tasting rooms, an elegant Westin resort hotel and the enticing **Oxbow Public Market** *(644 First St.; ○open year-round Mon–Sat 10am–6pm, Sun 10am–5pm; ○closed major holidays; ☎707-226-6529; www.oxbowpublicmarket.com)*, selling local, sustainably grown produce and gourmet foods.

Victorian Neighborhoods
South and west of downtown.

◔ **Michelin Map:** 585 A 8 and map opposite.
▯ **Info:** ☎707-226-7459. www.napavalley.com
◔ **Timing:** It's best to select no more than four wineries per day for tasting and to limit guided tours to one or two a day.

Napa's residential neighborhoods hold elegant houses from the late 19C and early 20C. A stroll or a slow drive in the vicinity of **Jefferson**, **1st, 3rd or Randolph Streets** reveals well-restored homes built in the Italianate, Queen Anne, Eastlake and Shingle styles.

The di Rosa Preserve: Art & Nature★★
5200 Carneros Hwy. (Rte. 121), Napa (2.5mi west of Rte. 12). ☎Visit by guided tour (2hr 30min) only, year-round Wed–Sat; call for times. ◔$15 (1hr introductory tour, $10). ○Closed major holidays. Reservations recommended. ℗ ☎707-226-5991. www.dirosapreserve.org.
René di Rosa came to San Francisco in the 1950s as a young newspaper reporter and began purchasing the work of undiscovered artists. In 1960 he bought an abandoned vineyard in Napa Valley, converting an 1886 winery into his home and eventually amassed a collection of more than 1,500 works by 650-plus artists including Robert Arneson, Joan Brown, Bruce Conner, Manuel Neri and William T. Wiley. In 1997 di Rosa opened the preserve to visitors, who are shuttled past a 35-acre lake to the historic residence and galleries.

Artesa Vineyards & Winery
1345 Henry Rd. From downtown Napa take Rte. 29 south to Rte. 121. Turn right and drive west 4mi, turning right on Old Sonoma Rd. Turn left on Dealy Lane, then veer left on Henry Rd. Continue .3mi to driveway. ○Visitor center ○open year-round daily 10am–5pm. ○Closed Jan 1, Thanksgiving Day, Dec

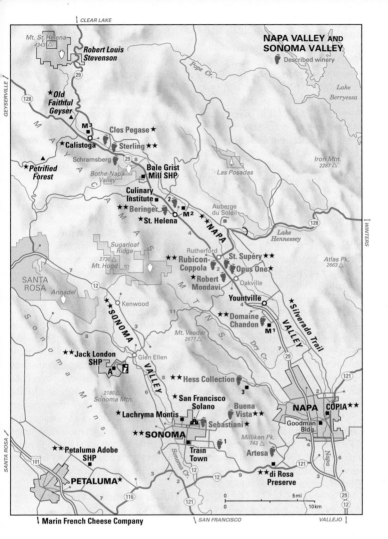

24–25.   ♿ 🅿 ℘707-224-1668.
www.artesawinery.com.
In 1872 the Codorniu family of Barcelona became Spain's first producers of sparkling wine made in the méthode champenoise tradition. Their Napa Valley operation is housed in this unusual contemporary structure (1991, Domingo Triay) at the foot of Milliken Peak. Sloping, grass-covered earth berms cover the winery walls, maintaining consistently cool temperatures in the storage and production areas. Galleries around a central courtyard house European winemaking equipment.

The Hess Collection Winery★★
4411 Redwood Rd. From Rte. 29 in Napa, take the Redwood Rd./Trancas exit and drive west on Redwood Rd. 6mi to winery entrance. ⏱*Open year-round daily 10am–5.30pm (museum closes 5.15pm).* ⏱*Closed major holidays.* ☞*$10 tasting fee.* ♿🅿 ℘707-255-1144. www.hesscollection.com.
Nestled on the slope of Mt. Veeder, this renovated structure contains one of the nation's largest and finest private collections of contemporary art open to the public, as well as a state-of-the-art winemaking facility and an audiovisual

program *(12min)*. The original stone structures (1903) were leased in 1983 by Swiss mineral-water magnate Donald Hess, who transformed it into a winery and gallery to house his collection of European and American art.

The property adjacent to The Hess Collection Winery is graced by the **Christian Brothers Retreat and Conference Center (3)** *(4401 Redwood Rd.; ℘707-252-3810; www.christianbrosretreat.com)*, a Mission Revival-style complex (1932).

Yountville

9mi north of Napa on Rte. 29. Note that Route 29 is alternately known as the St. Helena Highway.

This small community began in 1836 as a tract of land granted to George C. Yount (1794–1865), who planted extensive vineyards here. Yountville's inns and restaurants are popular with visitors to the southern Napa Valley. Of note is the historic brick Groezinger winery, restored as **V Marketplace** *(6525 Washington St.; ℘707-944-2451; www. vmarketplace.com)*, a festival marketplace for specialty shops, restaurants and winetasting.

Napa Valley Museum★

55 Presidents Circle. From Rte. 29/ Yountville Exit, drive west .3mi toward Veterans Home. Museum is on right. ⓞ*Open year-round Wed–Mon 10am– 5pm.* ⓞ*Closed holidays.* ⊛*$4.50.* ♿ⓟ *℘707-944-0500. www.napavalley museum.org.*

The highlight of this innovative museum (1998, Fernau and Hartman) is a multimedia display entitled **California Wine: The Science of an Art★★**, tracing a full year in Napa Valley winemaking.

Domaine Chandon★★

1 California Dr. From Rte. 29/Yountville Exit, drive west .2mi toward Veterans Home. Entrance is on right. ⓞ*Open daily 10am–6pm.* ⓞ*Closed Jan 1, Thanksgiving Day, Dec 25.* ⊛*$10-$30 tour and tasting fee.* ✕♿ⓟ *℘707-944- 2280. www.chandon.com.*

Commissioned by Moët-Hennessy, owners of France's famed Moët et Chandon,

these modern structures harmonize with the surrounding terrain; the arched ceilings are reminiscent of traditional wine caves in France's Champagne region. In the entrance hall, a gallery highlights skills related to winemaking; a guided tour explains the principal stages of sparkling wine production according to the traditional *méthode champenoise*. An upscale restaurant is located within the visitor center.

Opus One★

7900 St. Helena Hwy (Rte. 29). ⓞ*Tasting room open daily 10am–4pm by appointment.* ☞*Guided tour (1hr) available 10:30am; reservations required.* ⓞ*Closed major holidays.* ⊛*$35 tour (tasting included), $30 tasting fee.* ♿ⓟ *℘707-944-9442. www.opusonewinery.com.*

This innovative structure (1991, Johnson Fain & Pereira), with French-style limestone walls and California redwood pergola, is the result of a joint venture between Baron Philippe de Rothschild of France and Napa Valley vintner Robert Mondavi. Guided tours emphasize the distinctions between premium and ultra-premium winemaking. Descending a grand staircase shaped like the inside of a barrel, visitors enter a tasting room and the semicircular Grand Chai, containing row upon row of oak barrels.

Robert Mondavi Winery★

7801 St. Helena Hwy. (Rte. 29), Oakville. ⓞ*Open year-round daily 10am–5pm.* ⓞ*Closed Jan 1, Easter Sunday, Thanksgiving Day, Dec 25.* ☞*Guided tours available (45min–4hrs, $15–$110); reservations recommended.* ♿ⓟ *℘888-766- 6328. www.robertmondaviwinery.com.*

This striking building (1966) heralded a new generation of wineries designed to showcase art and architecture as well as wine. Sculptor Beniamino Bufano's figure of St. Francis greets visitors beneath the arched entry. A wide variety of tours is offered; some include gourmet lunch or dinner to illuminate the mysteries of pairing food and wine. The winery hosts a popular Summer Music Festival and a winter concert series.

St. Supéry★★

8440 St. Helena Hwy. (Rte. 29), Rutherford. ⏰*Open year-round daily 10.00am–5pm.* 🚶*Guided tours (1hr) available.* 🎟*$5 tasting fee.* ♿🅿 ☎*707-963-4507. www.stsupery.com.*

The modern winery structure houses a **Wine Discovery Center★** *(2nd floor)*, featuring in-depth displays on seasonal viticulture and the winemaking process. At the Smell-a-Vision exhibit, visitors can sniff and identify aromas.

Adjacent is a model vineyard with detailed panels and exhibits. The Victorian house *(🚶visit by 3hr guided tour only)* built by the first vintner to own the property has been restored to reflect the lifestyle of an 1880s winemaker.

Rubicon Estate Winery★★

1991 St. Helena Hwy., Rutherford. ⏰*Open year-round daily 10am–5pm.* 🎟*$25 tasting fee and guided tour.* ♿🅿☎*707-968-1161. www.rubicon-estate.com.*

The imposing stone winery (1882) was built for Gustave Niebaum, a Finnish sea captain who founded Inglenook Wines (1879). Most of Niebaum's property was purchased in 1975 by filmmaker Francis Ford Coppola *(The Godfather)*. In 2002 the estate was renamed in honor of its flagship wine.

A tree-lined courtyard surrounds a reflecting pool in front of the Inglenook Chateau, which is thought to have been the first gravity-flow winery in the valley. Upon entering the building, visitors can peek into the **Captain's Room** (1889) on the right, a replica of Niebaum's ship quarters that includes a 400-year-old lamp. The **Centennial Museum**, a monument to winemaking and film reflects the careers of both charismatic owners, Niebaum and Coppola.

St. Helena★

A picturesque main street distinguishes this town at the heart of the Napa Valley. Plentiful and widely varied accommodations, restaurants and a central location close to a number of popular wineries make St. Helena an excellent base for exploring the entire valley.

Robert Louis Stevenson Silverado Museum★

1490 Library Lane. From Main St. northbound, turn right on Adams St., cross the railroad tracks and turn left. ⏰*Open year-round Wed–Sun noon–4pm.* ⏰*Closed major holidays.* 🎟*Contribution requested.* ♿🅿 ☎*707-963-3757. www.silveradomuseum.org.*

Housed in a pleasant gallery within the town library building, this small, memorabilia-packed museum is devoted to the life and works of beloved author **Robert Louis Stevenson** (1850–1894), who honeymooned in a cabin on Mount St. Helena in 1880. The museum displays photographs, books, manuscripts and the author's personal belongings.

Beringer Vineyards★★

2000 Main St. (Hwy. 29), north of downtown St. Helena. ⏰*Open June–late Oct daily 10am–6pm; rest of the year daily 10am–5pm.* 🚶*Guided tours available (30min–1hr; 🎟$15–$35).* ⏰*Closed Jan 1, Thanksgiving Day, Dec 25.* ♿🅿 ☎*707-963-8989. www.beringer.com.*

Napa Valley's oldest continuously operating winery (1876) was established in 1876 by German immigrant brothers Jacob and Frederick Beringer. Extending into the sloping hillside at the rear of the complex are 1,000ft of tunnels where the temperature remains a constant 58°F, ideal for aging wine.

The centerpiece is **Rhine House** (1883), modeled after the Beringer ancestral home in Germany. The 17-room mansion features woodwork, inlaid floors and **stained-glass windows★**.

The Culinary Institute of America at Greystone

2555 Main St. (Rte. 29), north of downtown St. Helena. ⏰*Open year-round daily 10am–6pm. Cooking demonstrations year-round Fri–Mon 1.30pm & 3.30pm (also weekends 10.30am); reservations recommended (☎707-956-2320);* 🎟*$15.* ⏰*Closed Thanksgiving & Dec 25.* 🍴♿🅿 *www.ciachef.edu.*

The massive stone **building★** was built in 1889 as Greystone Cellars, a coopera-

Sterling Vineyards

© Coleong/Dreamstime.com

tive of Napa Valley winemakers in need of aging and storage facilities.

Today the **building**★ houses the West Coast campus of the renowned Culinary Institute of America, a preeminent training ground for chefs and other professionals in the food, wine and hospitality industries. Visitors are welcome to explore the delightful herb gardens or browse through the **Spice Islands Marketplace** *(open year-round daily 10am–6pm)*, a lively culinary retail outlet with a pastry café. In the Wine Spectator Greystone Restaurant (◷*open year-round Sun–Thu 11.30am–9pm; Fri–Sat 11:30am–10pm;* ◷*closed Thanksgiving and Dec 25; reservations* ℘*707-967-1010)*, professional chefs expertly prepare meals in an open kitchen.

A **corkscrew collection** of more than 1,800 wine openers, some dating from the 18C, was assembled over a period of 40 years by Brother Timothy, cellarmaster of the Christian Brothers.

🚹 Bale Grist Mill State Historic Park

3369 St. Helena Hwy. (Rte. 29), 3mi north of downtown St. Helena. Park ◷*open year-round daily 10am–5pm; grist mill weekends only.* ◷*Closed major holidays.* ⊜*$2/vehicle.* ♿🅿 ℘*707-942-4575. www.parks.ca.gov.*

From the parking area, a sylvan path leads to this historic **grist mill**★, powered by a 36ft waterwheel.

Established in 1846, the mill ground into flour the grain harvested by area farmers. The wooden mill building and waterwheel, which was replaced by a turbine in 1879, have been restored.

Sterling Vineyards★★

1111 Dunaweal Lane, 6.8mi north of downtown St. Helena via Rte. 29. ◷*Open year-round daily 10.30am–4.30pm.* 👣*Self-guided tour and tasting 11am daily (*⊜*$20).* ◷*Closed Jan 1, Easter Sunday, Thanksgiving Day, Dec 25.* ⊜*$20 includes tramway, wine tasting & self-guided tour.* ♿🅿 ℘*707-942-3344. www.sterlingvineyards.com.*

Perched like a monastery atop a 300ft knoll, this complex of white buildings (1969, Martin Waterfield) is one of the Wine Country's architectural grace notes. Visitors ascend to the winery by an **aerial tramway**, offering views of the surroundings. At the summit, informative panels enhance a self-guided tour across terraces with **views**★ of the northern Napa Valley. A collection of eight bells dating from the early 18C was acquired from London's church of St. Dunstan-in-the-East.

Clos Pegase★

1060 Dunaweal Lane, 6.8mi north of downtown St. Helena via Rte. 29. ◷*Open year-round daily 10.30am–5pm.* 👣*Guided tours (30min) daily 11.30am & 2pm.* ◷*Closed Jan 1, Easter*

Sunday, Thanksgiving Day & Dec 25.
$5–$7.50 (tasting fee). & P *707-942-4981. www.clospegase.com.*

Housed in terracotta and earth-toned structures, Clos Pegase (1987, Michael Graves) was founded by publishing magnate Jan Shrem. The winery is named for Pegasus, the famed winged horse of Greek mythology.

The complex reveals themes from classical antiquity, reflected in oversize columns and triangular pediments. Selections from the owner's private art collection appear throughout the winery, even in the storage caves hewn into the backdrop knoll of volcanic tufa *(open by guided tour only).*

Calistoga★

Founded in 1859, this resort town situated in the shadow of Mount St. Helena (4,343ft), serves as the northern commercial hub of the Napa Valley. The area's natural geysers and hot springs fueled Calistoga's development as a resort.

Town founder **Sam Brannan** (1819–88) spotted unlimited opportunities for resort development in Calistoga, where local Native Americans had long known of the hot springs' medicinal properties. Still renowned for its hot-spring spas, Calistoga today blends the flavor of the late 19C frontier era with 20C modernity.

Sharpsteen Museum★

1311 Washington St., 2 blocks N of year-round daily 11am–4pm. $3 suggested donation. & P *707-942-5911. www.sharpsteen-museum.org.*

Miniature **dioramas** in this small museum founded by one of Walt Disney's original animators re-create scenes of Calistoga's past. Adjoining the museum is a **cottage** from Sam Brannan's resort, relocated from its original site and fully refurbished to its heyday appearance.

Old Faithful Geyser★

From Calistoga drive east on Lincoln Ave.; bear left on Grant St. and continue 1mi. Turn left on Tubbs Ln. ○*Open Apr–Oct daily 9am–6pm; rest of the year daily 9am–5pm.* *$8, children $3.* & P *707-942-6463. www.oldfaithfulgeyser.com.*

Located at the foot of Mt. St. Helena, this privately owned geyser is one of the world's three known "faithful" geysers, so named for their regular eruptions. Approximately every 30min the geyser spews a column of superheated water some 60ft into the air, creating a shower of droplets and steam.

Petrified Forest★

6mi west of Calistoga. Drive north on Rte. 128 and turn left on Petrified Forest Rd. ○*Open Jun–Sept daily 9am–*

Mud Baths and Mineral Springs

Volcanic activity in the northern Napa Valley has produced numerous geysers and hot springs, many of which have been harnessed to fuel Calistoga's famed spas. A basic mud bath package, including mud bath, herbal wrap and mineral whirlpool bath, lasts about an hour, and costs $60–$200. Other options include massages, facials and mineral pool soaks.

Calistoga Spa Hot Springs – 1006 Washington St.		707-942-6269
Dr. Wilkinson's Hot Springs Resort – 1507 Lincoln Ave.		707-942-4102
Golden Haven Hot Springs – 1713 Lake St.		707-942-6793
Indian Springs – 1712 Lincoln Ave.		707-942-4913
Mount View Spa – 1457 Lincoln Ave.		707-942-5789
Eurospa – 1202 Pine St.		707-942-6829
The Baths – 1300 Washington St.		707-942-2122
Lincoln Avenue Spa – 1339 Lincoln Ave.		707-942-2950

7pm; rest of the year daily 9am–5pm.
$7, children $3. ♿ P 🕿 707-942-6667.
www.petrifiedforest.org.
A circuit trail through this small, privately owned forest winds past the stone remnants of fallen giant redwoods petrified more than 3 million years ago when Mt. St. Helena erupted, covering the surrounding area with ash and molten lava. The Giant measures 60ft long and 6ft in diameter.

Robert Louis Stevenson State Park

7mi north of Calistoga. Take Lincoln Ave. east and turn left on Rte. 29. Parking area on the left. 🕘Open year-round daily dawn–dusk. P 🕿 707-942-4575. www.parks.ca.gov.

This undeveloped park lies on the rugged slopes of Mt. St. Helena. A 5mi trail passes the site of the cabin where author Robert Louis Stevenson honeymooned in 1880. The trail joins an unpaved access road to the summit, with sweeping **views**★★ over the northern part of Napa Valley.

Silverado Trail★

This scenic road runs parallel to the east of Route 29 between Napa and Calistoga. Several crossroads link the pastoral Silverado Trail with the often traffic-choked Route 29. The road's many dips and curves accommodate the rolling terrain, and acres of serene vineyards separate numerous wineries.

Russian River Region★

This region of northern Sonoma County comprises three principal viticultural areas: the Russian River Valley, the Dry Creek Valley and the Alexander Valley. Other smaller areas in the region include Knights Valley, Green Valley, Northern Sonoma and Chalk Hill.

THE REGION TODAY

The **Russian River Valley** follows the curving path of the Russian River as it meanders south through Healdsburg and veers west toward the coast, passing wineries, vineyards and stands of redwood trees. Boating is popular on the river where it passes through the resort communities of Forestville, **Guerneville**, Monte Rio and Duncans Mills. Surrounding forests offer opportunities for hiking and camping.

Hemmed by majestic mountain ridges, the **Alexander Valley** extends along the Russian River east and north of Healdsburg. Small wineries dot the curves and corners of Route 128 as it wanders across a pastoral landscape of vineyard-covered foothills.

> ⚙ **Michelin Map:** 585 A 7, 8 and map opposite.
> ℹ **Info:** 🕿 707-869-9000. www.russianriver.com.
> 👪 **Kids:** The ice arena and the Warm Puppy Cafe.

Dry Creek Valley★ extends from the Warm Springs Dam on Lake Sonoma to just south of Healdsburg. About 12mi long, the narrow valley is laced with small, winding roads that meander among vineyards and across the valley floor. Zinfandel grapes have been grown here, and in the Alexander Valley, for more than a century.

The city of Santa Rosa, at the southern end, serves as its principal commercial hub and center of government.

SIGHTS
Santa Rosa

This sprawling city is the commercial hub and seat of Sonoma County. Santa Rosa was the home of botanist Luther Burbank (1849–1926), cartoonist Charles Schulz (1922–2000), and **Robert Ripley** (1893–1949) of *Believe It or Not!* fame. US-101 bisects the old and new sections of town. **Railroad Square** (*bounded*

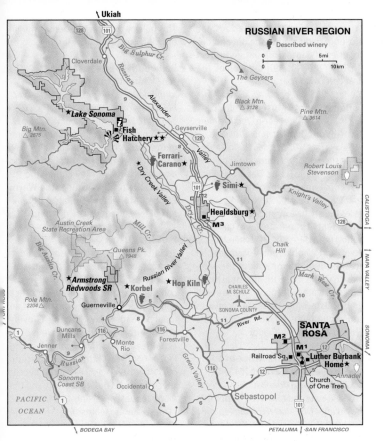

by 3rd, Davis & 6th Sts. and the railroad tracks), the city's historic district, has been transformed into offices, shops, boutiques, restaurants and inns, including the historic Hotel La Rose; a visitor center occupies the former train depot *(9 Fourth St.; ℘707-577-8674; www.visit santarosa.com)*.

East of US-101 is the downtown, centered on **Courthouse Square** *(Mendocino & Santa Rosa Aves. at 3rd & 4th Sts.)*.

Luther Burbank Home and Gardens★

Sonoma & Santa Rosa Aves.
House visit by guided tour (30min) only, ⊙*Apr–Oct Tue–Sun 10am–3.30pm.* *$3.* ⊙*Gardens and Carriage House Museum open year-round daily 8am–dusk.* ℘*707-524-5445.*
www.lutherburbank.org.

The modest, Greek Revival home of the renowned botanist, who moved to Santa Rosa from Massachusetts in 1875 is simply furnished. The gardens feature many of **Burbank**'s experimental hybrids, including 100 varieties of rose. In the renovated carriage house, displays highlight Burbank's life and work. Burbank's experiments in plant hybridization—resulting in such now-commonplace strains as the Russet Burbank potato, the Shasta daisy and the Santa Rosa plum—produced some 800 new varieties of fruit, nut and vegetable.

Church of One Tree

In Juilliard Park, across Santa Rosa Ave. from Luther Burbank Home.
Closed to the public. ℘*707-524-3282.*
Constructed of boards from a single 275ft redwood tree, this now-dilapidated Gothic Revival church *(under*

restoration) formerly housed a small museum dedicated to the life and discoveries of Santa Rosa native **Robert Ripley** (1893–1949), creator of the *Believe It Or Not!* cartoons.

Sonoma County Museum★ (M[1])

425 7th St. ⏲*Open year-round Tue–Sun 11am–5pm.* ⏲*Closed major holidays.* ⏲*$5.* ♿🅿 ☎*707-579-1500. www.sonomacountymuseum.com.*

Housed in Santa Rosa's Classical Revival style post office (1909), the museum's collection of nearly 25,000 works showcases the art, history and culture of Sonoma County. Historical exhibits cover the period from the early 18C, when Miwok, Pomo and Wapo peoples occupied the area, through the growth of the wine industry. The museum also boasts the largest private collection of works (more than 100 drawings, sculpture, collages and photographs) by site-specific artists Christo and Jeanne-Claude.

Charles M. Schulz Museum and Research Center (M[2])

👪*2301 Hardies Lane. Exit US-101 north at Steele Lane and turn left.* ⏲*Open late May–Labor Day Mon–Fri 11am–5pm, weekends 10am–5pm; rest of the year Mon, Wed–Fri noon–5pm, weekends 10am–5pm.* ⏲*Closed major holidays.* ⏲*$8, children $5.* ♿🅿 ☎*707-579-4452. www.schulzmuseum.org.*

For nearly 50 years, until his death in 2000, Santa Rosa resident **Charles Schulz** wrote and illustrated the popular comic strip, *Peanuts*. Underachiever Charlie Brown and his overachieving dog, Snoopy, appeared in 3,000 newspapers in 75 countries and 40 languages. The museum tells the story of Schulz's life and career, and celebrates the *Peanuts* characters through rotating exhibits of 6,000 original comic strips. A 100-seat auditorium presents daily screenings of the *Peanuts* animated shows.

Snoopy's Gallery and Gift Shop

👪*1665 W. Steele Ln.* ⏲*Open year-round daily 10am–6pm.* ⏲*Closed major holidays.* ♿🅿 ☎*707-546-3385. www.snoopygift.com.*

This gallery displays cartoons, original drawings and other memorabilia.

Redwood Empire Ice Arena

1667 W. Steele Lane. ⏲*Open year-round daily 9am–9pm.* ⏲*Closed major holidays. Call for hours.* 🍴♿🅿 ☎*707-546-7147. www.snoopyshomeice.com.*

Schulz himself directed the construction of this Swiss chalet-style arena in 1969. Today it is open for **public skating** and hosts concerts, hockey games and ice shows. The facility includes the **Warm Puppy Café**, where Schulz had a breakfast of jelly donuts every morning.

Healdsburg★

Founded in 1857 by Harmon Heald, a migrant farmer-turned-merchant, tranquil Healdsburg *(HEELDS-burg)* sits at the confluence of the Alexander, Dry Creek and Russian River valleys, making it an ideal base for forays into these lovely areas. At the heart of this town is one-acre **Plaza Park** *(Healdsburg Ave. and Plaza, Center & Matheson Sts.),* scene of civic festivals and events. Different species of trees grow in and around the plaza; request a walking-tour brochure, "Tree Walk of Healdsburg," from the Healdsburg Area Chamber of Commerce *(217 Healdsburg Ave.;* ☎*707-433-6935; www.healdsburg.com).*

Healdsburg Museum (M[3])

221 Matheson St., 2 blocks east of the plaza. ⏲*Open year-round Tue–Sun 11am–4pm.* ⏲*Closed major holidays.* ♿🅿 ☎*707-431-3325.*

Housed in the former Carnegie Library building, this small museum contains artifacts from indigenous peoples and from California's Mexican period. Highlights include photographs, Pomo Indian baskets, grinding rocks and weapons.

Simi Winery★

16275 Healdsburg Ave., Healdsburg. ⏲*Open year-round daily 10am–5pm.* ⏲*Closed Jan 1, Easter Sunday, Thanksgiving Day & Dec 25.* ☞*Winery visit by guided tour (1hr) only, daily 11am & 2pm.* ♿🅿 ☎*707-433-6981. www.simiwinery.com.*

Founded in 1883 by Italian immigrants Giuseppe and Pietro Simi, this winery today boasts some of the oldest vines and stone cellars in California alongside an ultra-modern winemaking facility. Legend has it that after Prohibition, with the winery all but bankrupt, Isabel Simi rolled a barrel onto the old highway and offered free sips of wine, thereby establishing California's first tasting room. The tour takes in the historic cellars and a high-tech fermentation center considered one of the finest in the state.

Hop Kiln Winery★

6050 Westside Rd., 5mi southwest of Healdsburg. From Healdsburg Ave. drive west on Mill Ave. and bear left on Westside Rd. ⏰*Open year-round daily 10am–5pm.* ⏰*Closed major holidays.* 🅿 ✆*707-433-6491. www.hopkiln winery.com.*

This historic **hop barn**★ (1905), one of the finest existing examples of its type, functioned as part of California's North Coast hop-growing industry. Hops were dried in the three huge wooden kilns resembling giant inverted funnels before being pressed and baled for shipment to area breweries. The kiln was renovated as a winery in 1975.

Korbel Champagne Cellars★

13250 River Rd., 2.5mi northeast of Guerneville. 👣*Visit by guided tour (50min) only, May–Sept daily 10am–3.45pm every 45min; rest of the year daily 10am–3pm on the hr.* ⏰*Closed major holidays.* ✗ ♿ 🅿 ✆*707-824-7000. www.korbel.com.*

In the early 1870s, Anton, Francis and Joseph Korbel, recent immigrants from Bohemia, acquired a lumber mill at this site. By the late 1870s the surrounding hillsides had been denuded of their redwoods, and the Korbels planted grapevines among the stumps. A large, handmade-brick winery building was completed in 1886 for the production of brandy and sparkling wine.

A guided tour covers both historical and contemporary versions of *méthode champenoise* sparkling-wine production. The **rose garden** on the slope below

the Korbel mansion (👣*guided tours mid-Apr–mid-Oct Tue–Sun 11am, 1pm & 3pm)* features 250 varieties. The old train depot was the terminus of a branch of the Northwest Pacific Railroad.

Armstrong Redwoods State Reserve★

👫*2mi north of Guerneville on Armstrong Woods Rd.* ⏰*Open year-round daily 8am–dusk.* ⏴*$7/vehicle.* ⛺ *(in adjacent Austin Creek State Recreation Area)* 🅿 ✆*707-869-2015. www.parks. sonoma.net.*

Dense forests of varied species of trees surround a 500-acre grove of ancient redwoods that survived 19C logging operations through the efforts of Col. James Armstrong. Today the grove forms the heart of an 800-acre state park that boasts some of Sonoma County's loveliest redwood trees. A nature trail *(.5mi)* passes through fern-laced glades.

Ferrari-Carano Winery★

9mi north of Healdsburg at 8761 Dry Creek Rd. ⏰*Open year-round daily 10am–5pm.* 👣*Guided tours Mon–Sat 10am by reservation.* ⏴*$5 tasting fee.* ✆*707-433-6700. www.ferraricarano.com.*

Five acres of parterre gardens surround an Italianate villa that is the focus of this estate. Garden paths meander past a rippling stream flanked by exotic shrubs and flower beds. An Italian courtyard provides the formal entrance to the Renaissance-style **Villa Fiore** (1997), its stone columns and arches rising above the Dry Creek Valley. From the tasting room and wine shop, a stone staircase descends to a vaulted, cobblestone-floored viewing area, revealing 1,100 French oak barrels aging red wines.

Lake Sonoma★

11mi north of Healdsburg via Dry Creek Rd. ⛺ 🅿 ✆*707-433-9483. www.parks.sonoma.net.*

This reservoir in the coastal foothills of northern Sonoma County was created in 1983 when the Warm Springs Dam was constructed at the confluence of Dry and Warm Springs creeks. It's now a popular recreation area.

Visitor Center and Fish Hatchery★★
3333 Skaggs Springs Rd. ○*Open year-round Wed–Sun 8.30am–5.30pm.* △P *707-431-4533. www.parks. sonoma.net.*

Displays of craftwork and artifacts highlight the traditions and beliefs of the region's indigenous **Pomo** peoples.

The adjacent state-of-the-art hatchery building *(○ open Wed–Sun 8.30am– 3.45pm)*, created by the Army Corps of Engineers to reduce environmental disruption caused by the dam, offers an opportunity to observe steelhead trout *(Jan–Mar)* and coho (silver) and chinook salmon *(early Oct–Dec)*.

Fish climb an inclined channel or "ladder" into the hatchery where they are held, sorted and spawned—activities visible from a mezzanine-level interpretive center.

Lake Sonoma Overlook
2.5mi from visitor center; follow signs. This wood-timbered overlook offers soaring **views**★★ of the lake, dam and surrounding mountains, including Mt. St. Helena in neighboring Napa Valley.

EXCURSION
Ukiah
45mi north of Healdsburg on US-101. Mendocino-Sonoma-Marin Coast map. Ukiah was first settled by farmers in 1856. Today lumber is the leading industry here, followed by agriculture and tourism. Nearby Lake Mendocino *(4mi north via N. State St. to Lake Mendocino Dr.)* and **Clear Lake**★ *(24mi southeast on Rte. 20)*, California's largest natural lake, provide recreation.

Grace Hudson Museum and Sun House★
431 S. Main St. ○*Open year-round Wed–Sat 10am–4.30pm, Sun noon– 4.30pm.* ○*Closed major holidays. Contribution requested.* &P *707-467 -2836. www.gracehudsonmuseum.org.*

Portraits of Pomo Indians by famed Ukiah artist **Grace Carpenter Hudson** (1865–1937) and the collections of her husband, ethnologist John Hudson (1857–1936), form the core of the art, history and anthropology exhibits here. The six-room Craftsman-style bungalow (1911) contains pieces from the couple's eclectic collection of furnishings.

Sonoma Valley★★

The Sonoma Valley is agriculturally and topographically more diverse than the Napa Valley. Anchored by the historic town of Sonoma, the valley dominates the southern portion of Sonoma County, where vineyards and wineries rub shoulders with orchards and fields. The region enjoys a reputation for excellent produce and other farm products, as well as for wines.

SIGHTS
Sonoma★★
Site of California's northernmost and final mission, this community was born as the site of the San Francisco Solano Mission, established in 1823 as part of

○ **Michelin Map:** 585 A 8 and Napa Valley map.

Info: *707-996-1090. www.sonomavalley.com.*

Location: Many wineries lie in the vicinity of Sonoma, and along or near Route 12 as it leads through Santa Rosa and northern Sonoma County's Russian River region.

an outpost to guard against the threat of Russian invasion from Fort Ross, 45mi northwest. After secularization in 1834, a young Californio general named Mariano Vallejo was assigned to establish a pueblo and presidio at Sonoma. Sonoma's central plaza was the scene, on June 14, 1846, of the **Bear Flag Revolt**, an uprising of American settlers trying to secure (unofficial) US control of California. Hoisting a white flag emblazoned with a brown-bear and a star, the group proclaimed California an independent republic. The following month, American forces captured Monterey, declared California a US possession, and effectively ended the short-lived republic. Incorporated in 1850, Sonoma served as a supply center for the area's nascent winemaking industry. The town retains the flavor of that period. Charming shops, restaurants and inns occupy its historic adobe buildings.

The **Sonoma State Historic Park**★★, headquartered near the Toscano Hotel, operates key historic sites, including the mission, the Sonoma Barracks and the Vallejo Home (*open year-round daily 10am–5pm; closed Jan 1, Thanksgiving Day, Dec 25; $2 for all sights; guided tours available; 707-938-9560; www.parks.ca.gov).*

Plaza★

Bounded by Spain St., Napa St. & 1st Sts. W. & E.

Laid out by Mariano Vallejo in 1835, Sonoma's eight-acre public square is the largest Mexican-era plaza in California. **City Hall** (1908), a Mission Revival structure of roughly hewn basalt stone, anchors the plaza. The **Sonoma Valley Visitor Center** *(453 1st St. E. 707-996-1090)* is lodged in a restored Carnegie Library building (1913). Near the north-east corner, a bronze **statue** of a soldier raising the Bear Flag commemorates the 1846 revolt.

At the **Sonoma Cheese Factory** *(2 Spain St.; 707-996-1931; www.sonomajack.com)*, the area's version of Monterey Jack cheese is produced.

San Francisco Solano Mission★

E. Spain St. & 1st St. E. 707-938-9560.
California's 21st mission was founded in 1823. All that remain of the mission complex today are the chapel (1834) and part of the priests' quarters, restored around 1913.

On view are period furnishings, artifacts and a collection of watercolor paintings of the California missions by Norwegian artist Chris Jorgensen (1859–1935). In the restored chapel, the stations of the cross and framed paintings are authentic to the mission period.

Across Spain Street at no. 217 stands the **Blue Wing Inn** (1840), a symmetrical adobe structure that formerly housed a saloon and hotel.

Sonoma Barracks★

Spain St. & 1st St. E. 707-939-9420.
This two-story adobe structure (1841) housed Mexican troops who guarded the new pueblo against possible attack. Following US occupation of California, they served American regiments in the Mexican War. Now a museum of the Sonoma State Historic Park, the barracks contain displays on Sonoma's history.

Sonoma Valley

© Captured Nuance/iStockphoto

Adjacent to the barracks sits the **Toscano Hotel** (☞docent tours Sat–Mon 1pm–4pm), built as a general store in the 1850s and converted to a boardinghouse in the 1880s for Italian immigrants working in nearby quarries. Today the wood frame building's Victorian furnishings belie its rough-and-tumble origins. Visitors can peek into cramped upstairs sleeping rooms, and explore the restored kitchen and dining room behind the main building.

Lachryma Montis (Vallejo Home)★

0.5mi from Plaza. Take W. Spain St. and turn right to north end of 3rd St. W. ☞Guided tours weekends 1pm–3pm. ☎707-938-9559.

The Gothic Victorian house was the final home of General **Mariano Vallejo** (1807–90). Born in Monterey, he was called by the Mexican governor to establish a pueblo and defense outpost. In return, Vallejo received 44,000 acres of land near Petaluma, which he developed as a private ranch. Appointed commander of all Mexican troops in California in 1835, Vallejo increased his land holdings. Jailed briefly during the Bear Flag Revolt, Vallejo accepted American rule. He was elected to California's first state senate in 1850 and served as mayor of Sonoma (1852–60).

The home's spacious interior is furnished to reflect the period when Vallejo lived here. Also on the property is a brick storehouse containing a small interpretive center and 19C artifacts.

Buena Vista Winery★★

18000 Old Winery Rd. Take Napa St. east from downtown Sonoma, turn left on 7th St. and right on Lovall Valley Rd., then left on Old Winery Rd. for .5mi to the winery. ◷Open year-round daily 10am–5pm. ◷Closed Jan 1, Thanksgiving Day, Dec 25. ◉$5–50 tasting fee; self-guided tour free. ⊡☎707-938-1266. www.buenavistacarneros.com.

Sonoma County's first premium winery was founded in 1857 by Agoston Haraszthy. Today, Buena Vista wines are made at another facility 5mi southeast of Sonoma.

Visitors may peer through an iron gate into Haraszthy's **wine cellars,** dug into the limestone hill behind the winery by Chinese laborers in 1863. The lovely stone **Press House** (1862), reputed to be California's oldest remaining winery structure, today reveals a refurbished interior; the wooden beams are original. The second-floor gallery hosts an artist-in-residence program featuring works by local artists and craftspeople.

Sebastiani Vineyards★

Take Spain St. east from downtown Sonoma and turn left on 4th St. E. ◷Open year-round daily 10am–5pm. ☞Winery visit by guided tour (30min) only, daily 10am–5pm. ◷Closed Jan 1, Dec 25. ⊹⊡ ☎707-938-3230. www.sebastiani.com.

This winery incorporates sections of a 1903 livery stable purchased by Italian immigrant Samuele Sebastiani in 1904. The reception room displays casks, crushers and early 20C other equipment. Sebastiani's two 60,000gal oak fermentation tanks are reputedly the largest in the world outside of Heidelberg, Germany.

Some 300 wooden cask heads and doors embellished with whimsical **carvings** were executed from 1967 to 1984 by local artist Earle Brown.

Train Town

⚐⚐ 20264 Broadway, 1mi south of Plaza on Rte. 12. ◷Open Jun–Sept daily 10am–5pm; rest of the year Fri–Sun & holidays 10am–5pm. ◷Closed Thanksgiving Day, Dec 25. ◉$4.75. ⊹⊡ ☎707-938-3912. www.traintown.com.

An old-fashioned carousel and working scale-model railroad make Train Town a fun place for families with small children. Passengers sit in low, open-top train cars for a 20min ride through 10 acres of countryside with bridges, tunnels, waterfalls and miniature buildings. The train stops midway at a petting zoo where anyone so inclined can make friends with goats and ponies. Fairground snacks and souvenirs add to the old-time carnival atmosphere.

EXCURSIONS

Jack London State Historic Park★★

10mi northwest of Sonoma at 2400 London Ranch Rd., Glen Ellen. From Sonoma, drive 5mi north on Rte. 12, turn left on Madrone Rd. and right on Arnold Dr. Continue into Glen Ellen and turn left on London Ranch Rd. ⏱*Open May–Nov daily 10am–5pm; rest of the year daily 9.30am–7pm.* ⏱*Guided tours available weekends; call for schedule.* ⏱*Museum closed Jan 1, Thanksgiving Day, Dec 25.* 🚗*$6/car.* 🅿 *☎707-938-5216. www.parks.ca.gov.*

Sprawling in the shadow of Sonoma Mountain is the 800-acre "Beauty Ranch," home of **Jack London** (1876-1916), author of such classic stories as *The Call of the Wild* and *White Fang*. Raised among the factories of Oakland, he set off at age 17 on a seven-month sealing expedition to Siberia. In the late 1890s, London joined the Klondike Gold Rush, roamed North America, and served as a foreign correspondent.

In 1905 he and his second wife, Charmian, settled on a 130-acre ranch near Glen Ellen. In 1911 they began construction of a four-story mansion of hand-hewn lava boulders and redwood logs. Days before the couple was to move in, a fire reduced the house to a stone shell. Devastated, the Londons never rebuilt but continued to live in a cottage on the ranch. Jack London died there, of uremic poisoning, at age 40.

Built by Charmian London in 1919 as her residence, with the intention of making it a museum to honor her husband, the rustic stone **House of Happy Walls**★ **(A)** today serves as the park visitor center. The massive building contains artifacts from Jack's life and work, letters, photographs, clothing and objects. A trail *(1.2mi round-trip; trailhead at House of Happy Walls)* winds through meadows and forests to the ruins of **Wolf House**★. A short detour from the Wolf House trail leads to the **gravesite** where the Londons' remains lie atop a peaceful hill. The **Beauty Ranch Trail**★ *(0.5mi loop; accessible from the upper parking lot)* wanders past stables, silos, a piggery and the modest cottage where the author lived and worked *(*⏱*open weekends).*

Petaluma Adobe State Historic Park★★

10mi west of Sonoma at 3325 Adobe Rd. Leave Sonoma by Rte. 12 south; turn right on Leveroni Rd. & left on Arnold Dr. Turn right on Rte. 116, continue 3mi and bear right on Adobe Rd. Continue 3.25mi to fork in road; turn sharply right and proceed .25mi to park entrance on right. ⏱*Open 10am–5pm.* 🚗*$2.* 🅿 *☎707-762-4871. www.parks.ca.gov.*

Mariano Vallejo established a 100sq mi ranch here on his Mexican government land grant. It thrived, yielding cattle, horses, sheep and crops of grain until Vallejo leased the property in September 1850. The state took it over in 1951. Today the restored two-story structure, half its initial size, contains authentic period pieces in Vallejo's personal chambers; ground-floor rooms are outfitted with looms, kitchen tools and candle-making equipment. In the courtyard stand hive-shaped ovens once used to prepare meals for adobe residents.

Petaluma★

12mi west of Sonoma via Rte. 116 West from Rte. 12. Tourist information: ☎707-769-0429. www.visitpetaluma.com.

This agricultural town grew to a grain-shipping port in 1852. The **Great Petaluma Mill** *(Petaluma Blvd. & B St.; restored as a shopping complex)* was once the region's largest feed mill.

In **Old Petaluma** historic district *(north of B St. along Petaluma Blvd. N. & Kentucky St.)*, rows of ironfront architecture *(Western Ave. between Kentucky St. & Petaluma Blvd.)* showcase the **Mutual Relief Building** (1885), the **Masonic Hall** (1882), and the **McNear Building** *(15-23 Petaluma Blvd.)*, and the **Old Opera House**★ *(149 Kentucky St.)*, (1870).

Walking tours of historic downtown depart *(May–Oct Sat & 1st & 3rd Sun 10.30am)* from the **Petaluma Historical Library & Museum** *(20 4th St.; ☎707-778-4398; www.petalumamuseum.com).*

INDEX

INDEX

INDEX

INDEX

INDEX

🏨 STAY

🍷 EAT

MAPS AND PLANS

★★★ **Highly recommended**
★★ **Recommended**
★ **Interesting**

Sight symbols

Recommended itineraries with departure point

Church, chapel – Synagogue	Building described
Town described	Other building
Sight letter reference	Small building, statue
Other points of interest	Fountain – Ruins
Mine – Cave	Visitor information
Windmill – Lighthouse	Ship – Shipwreck
Fort – Mission	Panorama – View

Other symbols

Interstate highway (USA)   US highway   Other route
Trans-Canada highway   Canadian highway   Mexican federal highway

Highway, bridge	Major city thoroughfare
Toll highway, interchange	City street with median
Divided highway	One-way street
Major, minor route	Pedestrian Street
Distance in miles	Tunnel
Pass, elevation (feet)	Steps – Gate
Mtn. peak, elevation (feet)	Parking
Airport – Airfield	Main post office
Ferry: Cars and passengers	Hospital
Ferry: Passengers only	Train station – Bus station
Waterfall – Lock – Dam	Subway station
International boundary	Observatory
State boundary, provincial boundary	Cemetery
Winery	Swamp

Recreation

Gondola, chairlift	Stadium – Golf course
Tourist or steam railway	Park, garden
Harbor, lake cruise – Marina	Wildlife reserve
Surfing – Windsurfing	Wildlife/Safari park, zoo
Diving – Kayaking	Walking path, trail
Ski area – Cross-country skiing	Hiking trail

Abbreviations and special symbols

NP	National Park	SP	State Park	SR	State Reserve
NM	National Monument	SHP	State Historic Park	SB	State Beach

Dry lake – Intermittent river

Cable car terminus, line   □ Ghost town

National Park   State Park   National Forest   State Forest

All maps are oriented north, unless otherwise indicated by a directional arrow.

NORTH AMERICA ROAD ATLAS

A geographically organized atlas with extensive detailed coverage of the USA, Canada and Mexico. Includes 246 city maps, distance chart, state and provincial driving requirements and a climate chart.

* Comprehensive city and town index
* Easy to follow "Go-to" pointers

MAP 585 WESTERN USA/ WESTERN CANADA

Large-format map providing detailed road systems; includes driving distances, interstate rest stops, border crossings and interchanges.

* Comprehensive city and town index
* Scale: 1:2,400,000
  (1 inch = approx. 38 miles)

MAP 761 USA ROAD MAP

Covers principal US road network while also presenting shaded relief detail of overall physiography of the land.

* State flags with statistical data and state tourism office telephone numbers
* Scale: 1:3,450,000
  (1 inch = approx. 55 miles)

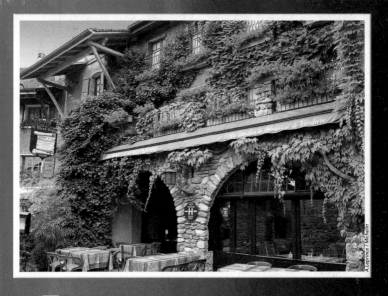 

Michelin Apa Publications Ltd

A joint venture between Michelin and Langenscheidt

58 Borough High Street, London SE1 1XF, United Kingdom

No part of this publication may be reproduced in any form
without the prior permission of the publisher.

© 2010 Michelin Apa Publications Ltd
ISBN 978-1-906261-74-0
Printed: November 2009
Printed and bound in Germany

Although the information in this guide was believed by the authors and publisher to be accurate
and current at the time of publication, they cannot accept responsibility for any inconvenience,
loss, or injury sustained by any person relying on information or advice contained in this guide.
Things change over time and travellers should take steps to verify and confirm information,
especially time-sensitive information related to prices, hours of operation, and availability.